P9-DTV-240

THE
LISTENING
PROCESS

THE
LISTENING
PROCESS

Robert Langs, M.D.

NEW YORK • JASON ARONSON • LONDON

to Joan,
still and continuing

Classical Psychoanalysis and Its Applications

A SERIES OF BOOKS
EDITED BY ROBERT LANGS, M.D.

Robert Langs
THE TECHNIQUE OF
PSYCHOANALYTIC
PSYCHOTHERAPY, VOLS. I AND II

THE THERAPEUTIC INTERACTION,
TWO-VOLUME SET

THE BIPERSONAL FIELD

THE THERAPEUTIC INTERACTION:
A SYNTHESIS

Judith Kestenberg
CHILDREN AND PARENTS:
PSYCHOANALYTIC STUDIES IN
DEVELOPMENT

Melitta Sperling
THE MAJOR NEUROSES AND
BEHAVIOR DISORDERS IN
CHILDREN

Peter L. Giovacchini
PSYCHOANALYSIS OF CHARACTER
DISORDERS

PSYCHOTHERAPY OF PRIMITIVE
MENTAL STATES

Otto Kernberg
BORDERLINE CONDITIONS AND
PATHOLOGICAL NARCISSISM

OBJECT-RELATIONS THEORY AND
CLINICAL PSYCHOANALYSIS

William A. Console
Richard D. Simons
Mark Rubinstein
THE FIRST ENCOUNTER

Humberto Nagera
FEMALE SEXUALITY AND THE
OEDIPUS COMPLEX

OBSESSIONAL NEUROSES:
DEVELOPMENTAL
PSYCHOPATHOLOGY

Willi Hoffer
THE EARLY DEVELOPMENT AND
EDUCATION OF THE CHILD

William Meissner
THE PARANOID PROCESS

Mardi Horowitz
STRESS RESPONSE SYNDROMES

HYSTERICAL PERSONALITY

Victor Rosen
STYLE, CHARACTER AND LANGUAGE

Charles Sarnoff
LATENCY

Heinz Lichtenstein
THE DILEMMA OF HUMAN IDENTITY

Simon Grolnick,
Leonard Barkin, Editors
in collaboration with
Werner Muensterberger,
BETWEEN FANTASY AND REALITY:
TRANSITIONAL OBJECTS AND
PHENOMENA

ARONSON

CONTENTS

Relating to Two Adaptive Contexts • The
Me–Not-Me Interface • Listening and the
Frame • The Embedded Derivative • The
Not-Me Part of the Interface, and
Introjection of Qualities from the
Therapist • Manifest References to the
Therapist as Derivatives of Unconscious
Fantasies and Perceptions

The Therapeutic Context • The Functional
Properties of the Patient's Associations
and the Therapist's Interventions • The
Therapist's Subjective Reactions •
Reformulating • The Patient's Responses
to Interventions • Further Considerations
of the Type C Field • An Evident
Countertransference Problem and the
Listening Process

Identifying Possible Adaptive Contexts •
Confidentiality and the Listening Process
• Listening in the Cognitive, Object
Relational, and Interactional Mechanism
Spheres • Levels of Listening and Levels of
Intervening • Factors in Therapists Who
Listen on a Manifest Level • Listening to
the Therapist's Projective Identifications

The Function of Premature Interventions
in Evoking Images and as Projective

PREFACE

I envision this book as a new beginning—for both the reader and myself. The novice or relatively inexperienced therapist or analyst will, I trust, find in these pages an important means of initiating his therapeutic pursuits. The more experienced clinician, I hope, will find new perspectives—an expansion of his capacity to listen, and the revisions in technique and self-understanding that inevitably will follow. As for me, I would like to think of this book as if it were my first contribution to the field; in retrospect, it is certainly, in many ways, the point at which I would have wished to begin.

Still, it is also true that I could not have written this book earlier. The reasons for this are, I think, relevant to understanding the efforts recorded herein.

I began my study of the therapeutic relationship and interaction with a clinical paper (Langs, 1971) that explored the interaction between day residues (meaningful external realities) and dreams (meaningful intrapsychic responses), and that provided me a basic model of mental functioning. I have always been very strongly committed to an empirical approach to basic questions of technique, a stance reflected in

my second paper (Langs, 1972); there I attempted to explore
the resources in material from patients in psychotherapy, and
generated the concept of the *primary adaptive task*, which I
later termed, as I do in this book, the *adaptive context*. In
attempting to evaluate the communicative function of various
types of material from patients—e.g., descriptions of recent
events, early memories, conscious fantasies, dreams—I was
forced to conclude that such an assessment was not feasible
without an awareness of the precipitant for the material under
study, the day residue or adaptive context which evoked a
particular sequence of associations and which proved to be the
key to their understanding, especially in terms of unconscious
fantasies and memories (perceptions and introjects).

And yet, while I was enormously stimulated by the fruits of
that study, I only now realize that my increasingly firm grasp
of the idea of the adaptive context was fundamental to every
other discovery—or rediscovery—that it has been my privilege to make. I was at first hardly aware of the implications of
this dimension of the *listening process*—a term that is used
throughout this volume in its broadest and most far-reaching
psychoanalytic sense. Only when I had completed the initial
version of my book, *The Technique of Psychoanalytic
Psychotherapy* (Langs, 1973a, 1974), did I recognize that the
assumption is unfounded that there is among analysts and
therapists a consensus on listening to patients and formulat-
its implications in the years that have followed and at the time
led me to add a chapter to the technique book on the
framework for understanding the communications from
patients in psychotherapy. There I elaborated upon the tools
with which we detect the derivatives of the unconscious
fantasies and memories crucial to the patient's "neurosis" (a
term that I use throughout this book to refer to all types of
psychopathology). Essential to this first effort, I found, was a
further elaboration of the important role of the primary
adaptive task in the listening process. As a result, the
technique books were written under the influence of a
burgeoning adaptive viewpoint that I termed the *adaptive-
interactional* approach. I believe that virtually all that was
original in that work derived from that particular vantage
point.

In tne years that followed, I became deeply involved in the investigation of a host of relatively unrecognized and unexplored phenomena within the therapeutic and analytic interactions, which I was able to identify and investigate using the adaptational-interactional approach. These efforts soon led me to the concept of the bipersonal field, which, I believe, provides the analyst or therapist with unique insights. For me, these were exciting years, filled with a sense of discovery that involved many dimensions of the therapeutic interaction. Throughout these explorations, which generated two early chapters, on responses to interventions and on the problems of confirmation and nonconfirmation (Langs, 1974), that I believe are virtually unprecedented, I continued to focus steadily on the issue of validation, defining the ways in which psychoanalytic tenets and interventions could be, in the true psychoanalytic sense, verified (Langs, 1976b, 1978a).

Through the idea of the adaptive context, as it related especially to the therapeutic interaction, and by investigating the full implications of every conceivable intervention by the therapist (verbal, nonverbal, and those connected with both interpretive work and the explication of the ground rules), I began to explore the framework of psychotherapy and analysis, and further unconscious aspects of the therapeutic interaction. An extensive review of the literature (Langs, 1976b) helped me identify the functions and meanings of the ground rules—the *frame,* as I termed it—and the implications of the therapist's or analyst's establishment and management of these basic tenets. My understanding of the communicative qualities of the bipersonal field established and maintained by this framework began to develop, and along with it came new insights into the unconscious communication and interaction between patient and therapist, including a conception of the patient's capacity for unconscious perception and introjective identification, and his curative efforts on behalf of the therapist—and himself; an understanding of interactional mechanisms and of the many influences of countertransference-based interventions; and an appreciation for the roles of reality and fantasy.

Repeatedly, I found myself in disagreement with the

prevailing clinical psychoanalytic theory and viewpoint, sometimes classical, sometimes Kleinian, and impinging upon collective blind spots, bastions of the psychoanalytic field, and upon the countertransference-based defenses and fantasies they appeared to be founded on. I also soon discovered that I was in the midst of strongly divergent reactions to my work: on the one hand, those who applauded, who were convinced that I was engaged in the pursuit of important and previonsly unrecognized truths; and, on the other, those who expressed intense opposition and made efforts to disrupt my endeavors.

It was in this climate that I began to reconsider the basics of the listening process. The experience of direct attacks upon the formulations that I had labored to develop empirically, and to validate in ways that actually were without precedent in the psychoanalytic literature, led me to seek ways to reaffirm (or, if necessary, modify) my findings in terms of what I now call *Type Two derivatives*—that is, through indirect, validating communications from the patient after a particular intervention, whether interpretation or management of the framework. I made every effort to divorce myself from all theoretical bias, except for the adaptational-interactional approach (the repeated use of sequential adaptive contexts from patient and therapist); yet, consistently, the same basic findings reasserted themselves.

It was this steady and consistent confirmation, and the nurturance derived from such indirect validation—gratifications achieved through the listening process—that enabled me to continue to pursue truths that for many reasons have been hard-won. Not one of my public or private critics had seriously considered the extensive clinical material I had presented; nor did they attempt to refute my theoretical derivations and clinical techniques through either different interpretations of my own data or the presentation of contradictory data of their own. I was quickly learning, as had many others before me (see Langs, 1978c), that there is an intense resistance among psychoanalysts and psychothera- pists to new ideas and concepts, especially those affecting psychoanalytic and psychotherapeutic technique. I soon realized, too, that there is a myth among experienced psychotherapists and psychoanalysts, often maintained unconsciously though readily denied consciously, that they know well the essentials of technique and that there is little more to be learned—especially concerning fundamentals. Once this is stated, I am sure that most would agree that this is a psychoanalytic cliché, a barrier against chaotic, underlying truths (Bion, 1977; Langs, 1978b); so envisioned, the pressing need to maintain this silent assumption becomes understandable.

Despite the strongly negative reaction in some quarters, I continued my investigation of the validating process (Langs, 1976b, 1978a), which I soon recognized to be a fundamental dimension of the listening process itself. It was the need to justify or validate my investigations of psychoanalytic methodology in the face of what seemed marked distortions, prejudice, and neglect of the data, that eventually strongly motivated me to understand in depth the essentials of the process.

Encouraged by my psychoanalyst publisher, Jason Aronson, who saw a need to return to—rather, to initiate—a thorough investigation of the details of listening, I began to crystallize some basic concepts that led me to perceive that there are many unrecognized, distinctive features of the listening process. Much of the misunderstanding of my own work—I say this with all humility—is derived, I believe, from a basic failure among therapists and analysts to develop a comprehensive capacity for listening and validating in the true psychoanalytic sense.

In this frame of mind I approached the seminars I was to offer on the technique of psychoanalytic psychotherapy; this book represents the first ten meetings. It was now absolutely clear to me that such a course must, of necessity, begin with a full delineation of the listening process. Still, I began these seminars with only the briefest outline of some basic elements of listening. Just before these meetings, I had developed the concept of Type One and Type Two derivatives (Langs, 1976b, 1978a), which I soon recognized to be a fundamental envision three types of communicative bipersonal field

(Langs, 1978b)—a *selected fact* (Bion, 1962) through which I was able to reformulate a wide range of previously perplexing problems related to the therapeutic interaction. I knew, then, that there are many enriching consequences to a clarification of the listening process, and anticipated substantial developments in the seminar that I was about to undertake—a hope that was fulfilled in many ways.

The sequence that unfolds in these chapters reflects a search ultimately designed to identify every meaningful component of the listening process, to the best of our clinical capacities. Each of the ten meetings unfolded around the presentation of process notes drawn from the psychotherapy situation. As we went along, I found that I myself learned and grew—repeating, clarifying, and evolving; revealing something of myself as I talked; and experiencing the tension of teaching new ideas to young therapists who suffered with the necessary pain and periods of confusion essential to growth.

This anguish is not a matter for apology, but is actually inevitable to the type of learning reflected here: it entails the destruction of myths and falsifications, of countertransference-based defenses, and of protective but pathological barriers; and it involves intrusion into awareness of painful, unconscious fantasies, memories, introjects and perceptions—and more—which must then be understood and mastered. It is quite evident that this is a remarkably hurtful and difficult task for any professional, and especially for the young therapist who discovers his pathological, protective shield shattered, his own therapeutic work in question, and the efforts of his other supervisors and even his own therapist or analyst called into doubt; the young therapist lacks the fundamental tools, insights, and adaptive resources which would allow him to quickly reconstitute himself as a more effective and pathology-free therapist. I am therefore deeply indebted to these therapists for their candid presentations, their searching and often difficult questions, and their endurance of this process so that they were able ultimately to grow and to reach at least a first juncture of reintegration and peace—a new beginning. One of the more difficult realities of psychoanalysis and analytic therapy is that crucial segments of learning must entail momentary chaos before reconstitution at a new and more effective adaptive level.

It was thus that I returned here to the listening process and attempted clinically to explore its basic dimensions. It is my hope—perhaps I still tend to overidealize analysts and therapists—that everyone will agree, at least, that we must be open to all avenues of communication from the patient, regardless of the techniques we then choose to practice. It seems inconceivable to me that anyone would deliberately state a wish not to listen, although unconsciously many in this field may function in just that way. It is remarkable that there are few papers on the listening process in general in the psychoanalytic literature; there are virtually none on many of its most important dimensions, including the validating process—this despite our recognition that listening is our basic tool, and the listener our basic instrument. Astonishingly, we have managed to avoid a careful dissection of the processes involved.

Still, this is no coincidence, since restricted or biased listening opens the way to the use of virtually any technical measure, no matter how countertransference-based it may be—one needs only listen "with a tin ear," as it were, to what follows in order to maintain false clinical premises and essentially invalid techniques. "Nonlistening" contributes to virtually impenetrable barriers against awareness of expressions of unresolved countertransferences, and against the difficult process of growth vital to every therapist and analyst.

In fact, I very much suspect that once we truly learn how to listen, and resolve to the greatest extent we can the countertransference-based impediments involved, once we truly listen to our patients and ourselves, we will discover that there is indeed only one basic psychoanalytic and psychotherapeutic technique, in the true sense of those terms, and that it can be applied with full sensitivity to the needs of every patient and the individuality of each therapist.

Any scientific work, however, can only represent the truth at a given moment. It is in the nature of science in general, and of psychoanalysis particularly, that we must constantly attempt to uncover and validate, as far as we can, new insights; and yet we must be prepared, in time, to learn that such formulations are not now—and can never be—a set of postulates devoid of unconscious influence and, therefore, of flaws and unrecognized untruths. Any lasting, creative work embodies essentially sound new discoveries, and yet it also paves the way for the revelation of its own limitations. In continuous cycles, these imperfections eventually must be detected and rectified for a science to advance.

I very much hope that it will be this way with the present volume. Inevitably, I know, I must someday look back upon this work as a flawed form of truth; but only at that moment will I genuinely know that I am still functioning as an innovative psychoanalyst and that I previously was, as well. Both humility and vitality derive essentially from the listening process itself.

In the end, it is all in the listening. The rest will follow in more directions than you and I can imagine.

Robert Langs, M.D.
New York, N.Y.
April, 1978

Helpful comments about the *The Bipersonal Field* (Langs, 1976a), which was written in the same format as this volume, have led me to develop several aids for easier reading of this book. In Appendix A, I have reprinted the paper "Some Communicative Properties of the Bipersonal Field." It offers an historical and systematic treatment of many subjects relevant to the main themes of this book. In Appendix B I have given, basically, a blueprint of the listening process, the details of which unfold only gradually in the course of these seminars. Appendix C provides a glossary, with brief and relatively loose definitions, mainly of the terms and concepts that are somewhat unique to my own writings, though I have also included rough definitions of some of the more important clinical psychoanalytic concepts to show how they are used in this volume; this is done with the full understanding that such definitions could be considerably discussed and elaborated (see Langs, 1976b). Finally, I have included a fairly comprehensive bibliography of writings pertinent to the listening process.

As always, I am deeply appreciative of the support and assistance that it is my privilege to receive in writing. Jason Aronson has been steadfast in his belief in my work, and helpful in countless ways. His staff labored long and hard with this volume, and in particular Michael Farrin has overseen the editorial and production efforts, while Laura Lamorte pursued the many details. Once again, Jan Blakeslee proved invaluable as an editor and Sheila Gardner tireless in transcribing these tapes and the necessary revisions.

Every effort has been made to present these seminars as they actually occurred. Each presentation has been heavily disguised, though the main drift of the material has been left intact. Other revisions have been largely in the direction of clarifying and elaborating upon comments made more briefly in the seminar; virtually no effort has been made to alter the human qualities or sequences of this teaching interaction. I am especially grateful to the therapists who participated in this course and for all that they helped me learn.

R.L.

"When I set myself the task of bringing to light what human beings keep hidden within them, not by the compelling power of hypnosis, but by observing what they say and what they show, I thought that the task was a harder one than it really is. He that has eyes to see and ears to hear may convince himself that no mortal can keep a secret. If his lips are silent, he chatters with his finger-tips; betrayal oozes out of him at every pore. And thus the task of making conscious the most hidden recesses of the mind is one which it is quite possible to accomplish."

Freud (1905, pp. 77-78)

Chapter One

A FIRST FORAY
INTO LISTENING

The framework of the book ● A basic methodology ● A briefly summarized session ● Some basic aspects of the listening process ● Its application to an intervention from the therapist ● The testing of some initial hypotheses ● Listening and the therapeutic interaction

Langs: This is a course on the technique of psychoanalytic psychotherapy, and I want to begin with an effort to define and clarify one of the absolute basics of this technique: the listening process. Before we delve into that important dimension, however, I would like briefly to establish a few ground rules for this seminar.

First, the entire course will be derived from your own case presentations, and I ask that each of you maintain total confidentiality about the material to be presented here in respect to both the patient and the therapist. Despite that request, I am asking for the permission of each of you to record these sessions, and to use them as a basis for a book on the listening process. Thus, in lieu of my guarantee that I too will maintain total confidentiality, I wish to assure you that the only use that I will make of these presentations will be to develop such a volume, within which both the patient and therapist will be fully and appropriately disguised. Beyond that, the total confidentiality of every aspect of these meetings will be maintained.

Within the modifications imposed by my need to teach analysts and therapists in the wider field of our profession, and by what I believe to be the important professional needs of others, I hope that you will join me in establishing as secure a frame as possible for this seminar. After all, we are going to try to discover the truth, and to speak the truth, with discretion, tact, and sensitivity, but also with an openness that is essential to sound pschotherapy and to its teaching. As you may already know, in psychotherapy and in all that is related to it, the truth rather consistently has to do with something very personal inside each of us—something that is often very painful as well—and there must be a sense of safety and protection here, so that I can properly teach and you can adequately learn. Total confidentiality, whenever possible, is essential to both therapeutic work and effective teaching and supervision.

In your presentations here, I ask that you present process notes, in strict sequence, and written as soon as possible after the session. Only because this is a seminar where you will be, as a rule, presenting single sessions, I ask that you begin with a brief description of the patient and his problems, and a condensation of the previous hour. I want to mention, however, that if this were a continuous case seminar, we would listen to each presentation without such reminders, developing an approach that is comparable to Bion's (1970) wise advice to therapists and analysts that they enter each session without desire, memory, or understanding.

Our focus here will be on the therapeutic process, the therapeutic interaction, and the field within which it takes place.

Discussant: You don't want a brief history?

Langs: It should be very brief. Because the main purpose of this course will be to develop general principles of technique, and to study the details of the therapeutic interaction, we will require only a minimum of historical information—though, certainly, the more we know of a patient's past life, the more our comprehension of that interaction will acquire a genetic perspective and a sense of depth. I simply ask that the basic introduction of the patient be brief, and that you add pertinent historical data as the presentation requires it.

Discussant: Is there a particular phase of treatment from which we should select these sessions?

Langs: For the moment, I leave it to you to select any hour. Since initially we are studying the listening process, any session will be pertinent. It happens that we will next be studying the ground rules and framework of the therapeutic situation, and then it might be helpful to present hours where relevant issues have come up, though even there, issues related to the framework may emerge in the absence of an obvious deviation.

In any case, I ask that the sessions be presented in strict sequence, since we do not want an advance look or a random temporal sequence. We want to share what the therapist and patient experienced, and to develop a valid methodology for psychotherapy. Hearing the sessions in sequence will enable us to study the material as representing an interaction with cause and effect aspects, so that we can make formulations, generate predictions, offer hypothetical interventions, and the like. We want to develop a valid predictive methodology as well, so we must work with the sequence. Predictions are easy to generate if you know what happened afterwards! I want us to risk the more difficult kind of prediction that has to be made without at all knowing what lies ahead and, in addition, I want you to learn to appreciate the crucial role played by interactional processes within the therapeutic situation.

Basically, we're going to attempt to validate every clinical formulation that we make. For my part, I will take the material that you present to me and will test various ways of structuring the therapeutic situation to determine its most valid form. I will also attempt to verify a series of formulations regarding the nature of the therapeutic interaction, of your interventions, of the patient's responses, and actually, of every aspect of what I call the *bipersonal field* (Langs, 1976a, b).

So I will not develop this course as dicta, but through validated hypotheses. I will attempt to define each hypothesis as our learning and teaching needs and the material permit, and I will then allow the interaction between your interventions and the patient's associations to serve as the proving ground, searching especially for what I call *indirect valida-tion*, through *Type Two derivatives* (Langs, 1978a,b). In brief, this means that what we are seeking in response to our interventions is not direct agreement, but some type of indirect, derivative, confirmatory communication, either in the form of important new material prompted by an actual intervention in the session at hand, or in the form of a derivative and somewhat disguised statement from the patient that corresponds to the very hypothesis that we develop here—a phenomenon that I term a *silent hypothesis* echoed indirectly in the patient's associations. And I must add that validation through Type Two derivatives should be the ultimate criterion for every clinical thesis in psychother-apy and psychoanalysis, though, as you may know, this is a criterion that has seldom been met. Still, I will establish it as essential to the methodology of this course, and state it as vital to the methodology of the therapeutic process itself.

I am sure that questions regarding the basic structure of this course will arise as we proceed, and much will be clarified as soon as we begin our work, but for now, I will allow this to suffice as the definition of the basic framework for this seminar. While I will be quite active, I want to encourage questions, comments, hypotheses, and challenges—I hope we will have an active interaction.

I am reminded of Winnicott's (1969) marvelous statement that he intervenes in order to let a patient know where his ignorance begins. In part, then, when you speak here you will be exposing both what you know and what you don't know. But I'm going to encourage that, because that is how you will learn. You know too what Freud (1900) said—and it's been restated in many different ways—there's no learning without unpleasure. Some people may think that that's an excuse for sadism on my part, but I think that you have to tolerate considerable disequilibrium in order to really learn.

Discussant: Oh, then you are going to be sadistic...

Langs: Well, I just read Greenson's (1969) paper on "The Origin and Fate of New Ideas in Psychoanalysis" and he suggested that creative individuals do not have well-sublimated sexuality and aggression. Others (Greenacre, 1954, 1959) have made similar suggestions; I don't know how one can develop valid comparative studies, but I do know that I will be offering new and I hope creative ideas in this seminar, and to the extent that the theory contains any degree of truth, I do expect that you will experience more of the aggression than the sexuality. But I can assure you that I will try to be tactful and sensitive, though I feel that some type of, perhaps "sublimated aggression"— a therapeutic or, more precisely, teaching form of "neutralized aggression"—is inevitable in this kind of learning experience.

After all, in this field, what you do not know and what you tend to do wrong with your patients are almost always related to some dimension of countertransference, especially now that you are advanced students. To the extent that this seminar will have valid, original concepts to offer, they will constitute an impingement upon an already established equilibrium, a threat to countertransference-based defenses and to the arousal of the disturbing underlying contents against which they defend.

Well, we are actually way ahead of ourselves, but I think that it is important that you sense early on the complexity of everything connected with the learning and practice of insight-oriented therapy. I suggest now that we get started with our first clinical presentation.

Therapist: I'm going to summarize some things about this woman briefly. I'm not presenting a first session, for a lot of reasons. This is a thirty-one-year-old, white woman, biochemistry graduate student, who made a suicide attempt several months ago—a highly lethal suicide attempt. She's been in therapy for about a month and a half, and she's been very unproductive: she just hasn't talked for most of the sessions, though she has recently. That is why I'm beginning later rather than earlier.

Langs: And that reminds me of something else, something I haven't said. You'll find that happens often: forethought and planning really don't serve very well in a course like this. As soon as I hear clinical material, I will begin to convey what I feel has to be said. Obviously, in respect to listening, almost any patient will teach us a great deal, though of course there will be variations.

But you should understand that I'm using the term *listening* as it appears in the title of this part of the course, in the psychoanalytic sense, which, as you know, applies to all of the data that we take in from the patient. Now, can you see what this comment by the therapist reminded me of, in terms of the listening process?

Discussant: He wasn't able to get her to talk.

Langs: Yes—so it is not just verbalizations to which we attend—what we're taking in is not just words to be heard. We call it *the listening process*—any other name for this effort becomes very cumbersome—but if we call it "the listening process in the psychoanalytic sense," we know that it involves more than word—what else?

Discussant: Nonverbal communication, silences.

Langs: Yes, and the other things—the way the patient dresses, moves, sits, comes and goes. Let me remind you—because you're going to be doing this within a bipersonal field—that everything that we're saying now about the patient is also true about whom? (Pause.) It's also true about the therapist, about ourselves. We too communicate in ways that are nonverbal, and not all therapists are meaningfully aware of that. Much of this applies to analysts and therapists alike, but since this is a course in psychotherapy, I'll speak almost always of therapists, and perhaps we'll get into the distinctions and similarities between therapy and analysis at some later point.

So—many therapists think of this situation in terms of words, especially when they consider their own contribution. In particular, they tend to see themselves as someone who is consciously and verbally interacting with the patient. We will soon see that even as the therapist speaks, he communicates many other implications, and he constantly makes use of the nonverbal mode as well. We will, therefore, have to learn a great deal about the various levels of unconscious communication between the patient and the therapist as they are initiated on either side of the therapeutic interaction.

You'll notice several implications in what I just said; first, both the patient and therapist are engaged in the listening process—later, I will contrast the two. Second, I am suggesting that on the surface, the listening process involves all of the intaking efforts of the therapist—to stick with him for the moment; that on a sensory level, it relies on sight as well as hearing—and sometimes it may extend to other senses, such as touch; but that it also has many nonsensory—or nonsensuous (Bion, 1977)—qualities, and it may be rational or irrational, conscious or unconscious. Thirdly, I am implying that we do not simply apply the listening process to the surface of the patient's communications, and that this initial, incorporative process which is, of course, quite open to distortion, quickly blends into a second phase, in which efforts are made at formulation and comprehension, again, on both a conscious and an unconscious level.

So, quite early in our work, we are faced with many complexities. We are not only developing and attempting to conceptualize the stages of the listening process, we must, since this is psychotherapy, immediately become aware as well of possible disruptive, countertransference-based influences at both levels—the directly experiential and the formulatory.

Without pursuing that further for the moment, it now occurs to me to clarify my decision to begin this course with the study of the listening process. I have, as you may know, taught a number of courses on the technique of psychoanalytic psychotherapy and until now, it's always been a moot point where to begin. The relationship is crucial; should I begin there? But listening is crucial, and so is the establishment of the framework; so should I begin there?

Bion (1977), a Kleinian analyst, describes this in some of his work. You know, Kleinians do not sit well with classical analysts, but my own growing interest in interaction led me to the Kleinian literature, because it is interactional. I have found it a very creative literature that can be managed and used quite constructively. Bion is probably the leading Kleinian theoretician; he has rather recently produced a series of very difficult, esoteric, remarkably creative and important books (Bion, 1977), in the first of which he says that the chapters are laid out in sequence, but that you will not understand the first chapter until you have read the last; you almost have to go through it again.

That's really what we're going to do. You won't understand the conception of the bipersonal field until we've identified and worked over *in extensio* all of its major components. And of those major elements, I finally realized that the listening process in its fullest sense is basic to the comprehension of everything else. I realized some of this very personally, in that I don't think anybody can evaluate what I myself have written until they have learned to listen as I have and do. Now that sounds grandiose —Freud, you may recall said, If you haven't been analyzed, you won't know what I'm talking about—but I do believe that if you haven't learned to listen properly, you won't know what I'm talking about.

If you learn how to listen, everything else will follow—you'll be able to create and understand the rest yourself. I'm not going to ignore the other elements—I'll be touching on them as we go along, and we'll be developing them specifically later on. But if you know the basics of listening, then you'll know about the relationship, because you'll learn the necessary details from the patient yourself, and you'll know about the functions of the frame and of interventions—and about what is valid technique and what is not—the patient will teach you.

In other words, in this course the patient is going to teach us how to do psychotherapy. The patient is really your best supervisor; indeed, he is always your supervisor, even though most of his efforts are unconscious. But in order to have the patient do that, we have to know how to appreciate what the patient is communicating. So, listening has to do with various sources of information, and listening, in analytic psychotherapy, ultimately implies organization—being open to chaos and uncertainty, being unconsciously receptive and sensitive, but it also means knowing how to organize the material, and how to understand it.

You can identify a series of steps if you want: unencumbered listening, understanding, new fragmenting, synthesizing, formulating, interpreting, and validating—and then starting the whole or part of the process over again. And where would you draw the line for the basic listening process? Maybe it includes everything up to the very point where you are about to interpret everything; until then everything can be considered as part of listening, while indications for interpretations—matters of timing—are somewhat separate. But if the listening process determines your interpretation and its timing, then really, the listening process covers everything that the therapist does, or is, at least, essential to all he does. I don't think we can divide this process into little separate sections and essentially what I will be talking about here, in terms of the listening process, will culminate in the formulation of an interpretation.

So we're covering first in this course a dimension of therapy that is absolutely basic to all the rest. Let's get back to the material now, though.

Therapist: Let me just say one or two other things. The patient disclaims any knowledge of why she made the suicide attempt. She'd been involved in a difficult relationship, she's very sensitive, and she always seems to get herself rejected. I think it's important for the session to know that she's susceptible to lesbian acting out.

Langs: Anything you knew before this session, we'll accept as data—whatever you think is relevant.

Therapist: It turns out—but I didn't know this for a while—that she's susceptible to homosexual acting out once she's rejected. Her father has been dead for a number of years; he kicked her out of the house when she was nineteen and she became pregnant. I'll stop there, and fill this in with anything that is pertinent later.

Langs: Yes, I do want us to concentrate on the immediate interaction, rather than on detailed case histories. This focus is not intended, as I said earlier, to suggest that genetic factors are anything but extremely important in understanding the therapeutic interaction. It is entirely an attempt to avoid many detours that are essentially irrelevant to the teaching purposes of this seminar, and to provide us with a concentrated view of the therapeutic process that we want to investigate. We will bring in important genetic links when they are necessary for our understanding of a particular session. In practice, one must maintain a balanced perspective between the here and now, and the relevant past. Countertransference-based errors are possible in either direction, though, as you will see, they tend to lean toward negating the here and now. We will make use of the *validating process* (Langs, 1976b, 1978a) as a means of maintaining a necessary balance.

Therapist: In the session before the session I'm going to give you, the patient is very much consumed with her sexual feelings toward both men and women, and with sadistic feelings. She verbalizes about actuality and fantasy, and for a change, she's quite negative about therapy and what it will achieve. She's been in therapy twice before.

Langs: Your summary is actually rather generalized, and conveys to me at least, in trying to listen, a sense of how difficult it is to formulate material without specific process notes. In addition, even though this is an extremely abbreviated condensation, you do something that is characteristic of many therapists-in-training, and of many experienced therapists as well, you summarize the hour in terms of the patient's material and omit your own interventions.

Therapist: No. My interventions are here.

Langs: Then we are to take it that you were totally silent in the session you just summarized.

Therapist: No. You told me to give the material from the previous hour, and I thought that implied a summary of what the patient had said.

Langs: Yes, and this is based on your assumption that the important material in the previous hour was the patient's associations, and not your interventions. This, I think reflects a very common conception of treatment: that a therapist can describe a session without alluding to his interventions and feel that he is providing a valid and functional description.

Such an approach lacks a sense of interaction, and is, in addition, divorced from a conception of psychotherapy as taking place within a bipersonal field within which both patient and therapist generate vectors that are relevant to every intrapsychic and interactional experience and occurrence. It is actually a static conception of therapy, one that excludes many important levels of meaning in delineating a particular therapeutic hour. In this seminar, we will find that both field and interactional concepts are absolutely vital, and this applies to the listening process, as well as to all other dimensions of therapy. In fact, we will soon discover that it will be impossible to listen appropriately to the patient without knowing the therapist's interventions, and of course, it would be impossible to understand the therapist's interventions without knowing the communications from the patient.

Listening itself is an interactional process. For the therapist, it is generated by both his own openness to attend and receive, as well as organize, and by the patient's efforts, often unconscious, to have him experience certain types of contents and processes as well. Listening is a precipitant of the bipersonal field, in the truest sense. The patient can actually facilitate or interfere with the therapist's capacity to listen, just as the therapist himself may have certain gifts or may suffer from specific countertransference-based difficulties that impair his listening capacity as it is defined here. Much of this takes me a bit ahead of this material, however, so let's reserve that as a tentative hypothesis in need of later validation.

I must, by the way, comment that some critics believe that the concepts and metaphors which I use, and which have expanded my understanding of the therapeutic interaction, are simply unnecessary and idiosyncratic terms for aspects of the therapeutic experience described long ago by Freud and others. As you can gather, I do not believe that this is the case, and I think that this presentation already points to some of the reasons for that belief. The concept of the bipersonal field insists that every session be considered as the interactional product of both participants. Had you been so taught, it would have been impossible for you to have presented this session without including your interventions, in an ordered sequence of patient's material, your intervention, and the patient's responses.

What, then, had you actually said in this session?

Therapist: Well, mostly I had asked for clarifications.

Langs: Okay, so you had asked some questions?

Therapist: I'd asked a few questions, and I had challenged her a little bit about her skepticism about therapy, since she had been working so actively outside to figure things out.

Langs: When you describe your interventions here, I would like you to simply state them as best as you can, much as you actually said them to the patient. So what had you said? You say you had challenged her? Roughly, what was your intervention?

Therapist: She had talked about the pain that she was in, and how she felt she couldn't do anything about it, and nobody could do anything about it. And I said something to the extent that I understand that your problems have been very painful; that only makes it the more important that we work together exploring them. I said, also, I find it interesting that you voice so much skepticism about therapy helping your pain, and yet you seem to be so actively involved in working these things out outside of sessions.

Langs: You know, it amazes me how often significant material emerges when one pursues the actual intervention of the therapist. It seems essential to me that we now pause and apply the listening process to what we have heard. Many critics have suggested that I overemphasize the contributions of the therapist, and tend to neglect those of the patient; this is far from the truth, and *The Therapeutic Interaction* (Langs, 1976b), I believe, clearly indicates a balanced appreciation for the contributions of both. But largely because the therapists-in-training who presented to me in the seminars that I used for *The Bipersonal Field* (Langs, 1976a) tended at times, actively to put so much more pathology into the field than did their patients, it became necessary rather often to explore their contributions to the therapeutic interaction, to a degree that outweighed our study of what their patients contributed. I hope that I have made it clear, both in that book and here, that I will concentrate on those areas that the presentations direct me to investigate, whether the focus is on the patient or the therapist.

It seems to me that for the moment, the material from the patient is ill-defined, almost too general to even discuss, or to apply the listening process in any meaningful way. If you disagree, I welcome your comments, and as we go along, we will certainly apply the listening process to the material from each patient. But for the moment, can anyone develop some ideas about this patient's associations? (Pause.) I would agree: there's little to go on, though some tentative effort could be made.

But the therapist's intervention almost asks to be understood. You can see, first, that as long as the therapist says that his interventions were largely in the form of asking for clarifications, we would as members of this seminar have had little to listen to and still less to formulate. However, once we hear the details of this intervention, once we have a part of the therapeutic interaction described in detail, in a form that approaches specific process notes, we have a communication to which we can apply the listening process, which requires specific material from *both* patient and therapist.

After all, as I said earlier, the patient is involved in a listening process of her own, though much of it, usually, is in terms of unconscious processes, while most of our own listening should eventually be registered on a conscious level.

Further, in developing our own ability, as therapists, to listen, we want to be aware of how the patient himself takes things in, and what it is that he is experiencing from us, on both a conscious and unconscious level. As you will soon see, such understanding provides us with an important means of organizing the material from our patients.

So—I really didn't plan it this way—we have just heard our first piece of specific material and even though it happens to be a communication from the therapist, I suggest that we attempt to apply the listening process to this intervention.

Perhaps it will help if I offer you a guiding hypothesis that we can attempt to validate later and that will enable us, in addition, to develop a conception of the validating process itself: Whatever else went on in this session, this intervention will be among the significant *adaptive contexts* for the session that we're about to hear. Proper listening and explorations will prepare us to test that particular hypothesis and its more general formulation: that the adaptive context for each session is always determined in part by the specific nature of the interaction of the prior session, to which may be added secondary, external precipitants.

I am well aware that this hypothesis has many extremely important implications, some of which are quite in dispute. The term *adaptive context* is, for instance, crucial to the listening process and I will soon define it. More broadly, the hypothesis deals with the main determinants and unconscious implications of the patient's communications. It involves many basic technical issues: for instance, do we, in psychotherapy, work primarily with the patient's relationship to the therapist? In this seminar, I will not call that relaticnship "transference" or "the transference," but, will term it "the patient's relationship with the therapist"—the patient's side of the therapeutic relationship, influenced by factors within himself and the therapist. This is an all-inclusive term, from which we can then sort out the true *transference component*—the distortions, pathological interactional mechanisms, and efforts to repeat the past with the therapist and to have him behave as those in the patient's past actually behaved or were imagined to behave—and the *nontransference component*, the realm of the patient's valid functioning and perceiving, his nondistorted introjections of the therapist, the nonpathological aspects of his interaction with the therapist, and some of the realistic dimensions of his relationship to the therapist that may be either unique and curative, or, to the contrary, actual repetitions on some level of past pathogenic experiences, and that may therefore serve as actual reinforcements to the patient's psychopathology.

Now all of that is some weeks ahead of us, but I will offer you a rather general orientation. Do we work with the therapeutic relationship in psychotherapy, or do we work with the patient's outside problems? In terms of the listening process, I can give a relatively simple answer: we deal with what the patient is dealing with; we work with the adaptive focus of his conscious, and especially unconscious, communications.

In this context, let me offer you another fundamental hypothesis to be validated over the weeks to come, one that comes from my own experience: the patient in psychotherapy is consciously or unconsciously concerned with, and reacting to, the therapist all the time—without exception. His outside relationships, which may at times generate significant traumas and evoke important unconscious communications, to the point where they should and must be interpreted, will tend, by and large, to be secondary; when they are central, they will always have a significant link to the therapeutic relationship.

As for the term *adaptive context*: I will wait for other meetings to permit you to identify, without prejudicial influence from myself, the essential adaptive context for the session that we will be hearing, but I am, nonetheless, asking you to develop the communicative implications of the intervention we have just heard, and to see if we will be able to use those formulations as an adaptive context for the hour that we are to hear in detail. Of course, this should have been done the other way around: I should have waited for material that would force us to identify an adaptive context, and to recognize how crucial these precipitants are to the patient's behaviors and associations, and to our listening process. But this is how it's actually unfolding in the seminar, and so this is how we will develop it.

I will briefly and generally clarify the concept of "adaptive context," however, to orient you a little. I am suggesting that the communications from the patient are adaptively determined and organized, that important experiences that impinge intrapsychically on the patient are worked over consciously and unconsciously, and that the proper understanding of this working-over process, as it is reflected in the patient's behaviors and associations, will require the identification of the adaptive context.

As some of you may have realized, this concept is a version of the relationship between the day residue and the dream—the reality precipitant for the significant intrapsychic response (Freud, 1900; Langs, 1971, 1972, 1973, 1976a, b)—and, just as the key to the dream, and its organizer, is the day residue which gives dynamic meaning to its manifest and latent contents, so the key to, and organizer of, the patient's associations and behaviors is the adaptive context.

Now, as we apply the listening process to the material from the patient, or as we will do now to the therapist's intervention, we will be taking an adaptive approach, a sequential and interactional approach, in which we will listen to a segment of material—on as many levels and in as many ways as we can—and then attempt to validate the silent hypothesis that we form. I have, earlier, attempted to define the components of the therapist's validating process (Langs, 1976a, b, 1978a) and in *The Therapeutic Interaction* (1976b) in particular, I also endeavored to describe the validating process within the patient; much of that, once again, occurs on an unconscious level, and we will, I hope, be able to delineate it from the material that we will be hearing as the course progresses.

Well, let's return to the intervention. In considering an intervention from the therapist, it is standard practice first to define its formal characteristics: is it a silence, question, clarification, confrontation, interpretation, or reconstruction—or is it noninterpretive (support and the like)? The lexicon of terms was provided us primarily through a basic paper by Bibring (1954), and I myself have attempted to refine and clarify it (Langs, 1973).

In a later work, much of which considerably extends and departs significantly from many of my earlier ideas (see

Langs, 1976a), I have stressed two new concepts: first, that we must specifically consider management of the framework as an intervention, and therefore as an adaptive context and meaningful communication to the patient; and second, that the unconscious reflections and communications of all the therapist's interventions, verbal and nonverbal, must be identified in terms of their form, nature, meaning, and functions. This level is often quite crucial for the therapeutic interaction.

Well, I have said a great deal, and perhaps you will want to hear the intervention again, before we evaluate it. By and large though, we must use the model of the functioning therapist in this seminar. In principle, it is inappropriate to ask a patient to repeat something because we have not heard or remembered it. It is the responsibility of the therapist to listen to the patient's associations, and to not permit subjective intrusions to disturb this listening process to the point that he does not hear the patient, hears only part of the associations, or suffers from an altered state of consciousness that interferes with his listening, remembering, and formulating.

Certainly, these interferences do occur, and they are an indication of a countertransference difficulty that requires self-analysis and rectification—efforts that must be undertaken privately by the therapist and not directly stated to the patient, who would then be inappropriately burdened with his therapist's pathology. By and large, the patient will repeat in some form his important communications, but we should not abuse or misuse this principle.

However, since I interrupted you and we want to learn, I will ask you to repeat your intervention, so we may once again apply the listening process to it.

Therapist: I said: I understand that your problems have been very difficult and painful. That only makes it more important that we work together exploring them. Also, I find it interesting that you continue to denigrate the therapy, while seeming to work so hard outside to work these problems out.

Discussant: "Outside?" I'm not sure what that means.

Therapist: Outside of the session.

Langs: What do you hear?

Discussant: I just was not clear about what he meant. Do you mean, trying to solve the problem?

Langs: I suggest that we take interventions as they are given, and that we not, as a rule, ask for clarification. For one thing, your question itself reflects an aspect of what you heard, but your efforts at clarification suggest that rather than utilizing your subjective experience of confusion, you are attempting to modify it. You seem to be suggesting that there is some ambiguity to the therapist's intervention—at the very least, this is how you experience it. When you attempt to get rid of that ambiguity, you are not using your subjective reaction to understand the therapist's communication, but instead are attempting to generate what would amount to a different intervention, one that would, of course, no longer be pertinent to this discussion and to the listening process, except that it would constitute an effort to modify what is heard without attempting to understand it.

You might, for instance, have suggested that there was some ambiguity to what the therapist had said, and you could then postulate that the patient would react to this quality of the intervention. You can all, I trust, readily recognize that the listening process is at all times a mixture of so-called objective or definitive sensory perceptions and a variety of unconscious or vague impressions, and an immediate subjective working over of this raw data. As I said earlier, the very process of listening to one's own words may be under the influence of the therapist's countertransference, or in this case, the intervention may be subjected to immediate distortions by the patient, who may directly misconstrue or mishear the therapist's comment, or who may validly or invalidly unconsciously sense certain implicit meanings, messages, or functions to his remarks, and respond accordingly.

Of course, the next step in the listening process is also open to transference or countertransference distortions, using both terms in the narrow sense, to allude to pathological elements in the therapeutic relationship. Your impression of ambiguity has to be recognized as an interactional product of vectors from the intervention itself and from your own subjective, inner way of perceiving, organizing, and understanding. If we apply this principle to the therapist who is listening to his patient, it means that everything that he hears is a product of the bipersonal field, and that he must recognize that his impressions, derived from the initial phase of the listening process, have contributions from both the patient and himself. In each evaluation the therapist makes, he must clarify their respective contributions and, further, recognize which of his subjective responses are empathic, intuitive, and understanding, and which are essentially pathological and distorting.

Don't be alarmed by the sense of confusion that all of this is generating; as we go along, we will be able to organize and clarify the listening process to the point where it becomes a sensible entity.

I am asking you to respond to these interventions as they are presented because I believe that both the therapist and the supervisor or observer should hear exactly what it is that the patient is hearing. Temporarily, in a controlled way, they must try to identify with the patient, empathize with him, and imagine how he will process what has been communicated to him or interactionally placed into him as well. Of course, the same principle applies to listening to the material from the patient. I prefer to work without extraneous explanations on the part of a presenter, and without the use of clarifying questions.

There are some supervisors who find it helpful to hear in some detail the therapist's subjective reactions, and when it comes to understanding interactional processes and counter-transferences, I am quite sure that this can be quite useful. This is probably best done by each individual therapist in his own direct work with his patients, and in the course of his personal analysis. I believe it is still an uncertain question whether this constitutes a valid methodology in the supervisory bipersonal field. I really don't want to get into these issues with you, but I do think that it is valuable for you to be acquainted with them.

Our basic approach, then, will be to hear the therapeutic interchange, and to respond with our own listening process; from there, we will formulate our conception of the details of the listening process as it occurs in both the patient and therapist. Let's work with the data as each experienced it in the therapeutic interaction, and we can go beyond that, when we feel the need to do so. What else did you hear in this intervention?

Discussant: Two things: first, he gives an empathic response: I understand your pain, that you're having difficulty. But then he does something that seems contradictory, at least to me; he says, I don't accept the fact that you feel that the therapy is not of value; whether you know it or not, you're working to help yourself here, in therapy.

Langs: Your comment has some fascinating implications, both general and specific to this situation. While you are bypassing the formal nature of this intervention, I hope that it is becoming evident that we could classify it in a number of ways. You have selected a continuum from empathic to nonempathic, and it is your impression that the first half of the intervention is empathic, while the second half is not. You are also implying that in the first half of his intervention, the therapist is accepting the reality of the patient's experiences, while in the second half, he is not doing so, and in a sense, he is attempting to negate her communicated experience.

Before we proceed further, who will identify the formal classification of this intervention?

Discussant: It has some qualities of a confrontation, but it also seems to involve a suggestion from the therapist.

Langs: Yes. Many communications from the therapist largely defy standard classification. At first, the therapist attempts to respond empathically, in a form that suggests a direct playback, and lacks the essential properties of either a confrontation or a clarification. We have, you see, already generated a new category for the therapist's interventions: direct or modified playbacks—though I must add that some would consider this a form of clarification or confrontation. It is, indeed, then followed by a suggestion—a somewhat complex aspect of the intervention that we will consider a bit later on. The final part of the intervention appears very much to be a kind of confrontation.

Perhaps you can already sense that the formal classification of an intervention is only a small part of our understanding of its nature, and that there is a great deal more to what the therapist has to say than is conveyed through its formal categorization.

Discussant: I don't believe that the second part of his intervention was nonempathic; it seemed to me that it was more like challenging the patient.

Langs: Challenging, to me, implies nonempathy, unless it's done in a very special way. I think it is fair to say that at first, the therapist identified with her and was both sympathetic and empathic. And then he was challenging, and no longer identified with her. What else do you hear in this intervention? How else could you formulate it?

Discussant: I felt that the second part of the intervention was a step above challenging—almost a reprimand...

Langs: A reprimand, a criticism, all right. What else?

Discussant: I heard her say that I'm in pain and you can't help me, and then he said, I understand you're in pain, but don't work outside therapy, work in therapy.

Langs: Yes, you heard some implication there about the outside. Now we're learning about the listening process. What's the point, now that we've heard some comments?

Discussant: We all hear something different.

Langs: Right. We are all exposed to the same material, from therapist or patient, but we immediately begin to color it, even as we experience it, and certainly, as it reverberates within us. This coloring, the influence of both our valid functioning and sensitivity, as well as our countertransferences, is always present. In psychotherapy, every experience and phenomenon is an interactional product—every word heard or sensed, and every formulation generated—and that is something to remember in all of your work. In virtually every sphere, the classical conception has leaned toward thinking in terms of isolated and unilateral phenomena and mechanisms—for example, that resistances are based on intrapsychic defenses within the patient, that they are defensive formations that can be observed by everyone, that exist per se, like sensory phenomena that can readily be consensually validated. In contrast, the concept of the bipersonal field states that resistances are, first, interactional products that are postulated to express themselves primarily within the patient, and secondly, that the very assessment of a state of resistance is in itself an interactional act, and that it depends as much on the state of the patient as it does on the state of the therapist.

But to come back to the listening process: we can be sure that subtle—sometimes gross—distortions are inevitable. We have seen, however, that as soon as we begin to deal with impressions, feelings, unconscious sensitivities, with formulations, with nonverbal qualities and unconscious communications, personal influences loom quite large. As I said, they can range from special, constructive sensitivities to intense, countertransference-based refractoriness and distortions. One goal in learning how to do psychotherapy is to develop a capacity to listen that enables you to maintain the psychotherapeutic process within a consensually validatable realm, in which your inevitable personal coloring does not distort the material. Of course, there will always be a degree of personal coloring, but the essential meaning should be preserved. I really believe that there is one basic way of formulating this, or any, intervention, and of formulating the patient's material, and as a result, that there is one basic way of intervening. I do believe that there is a correct and incorrect way of listening, formulating, and interpreting, and that this determination rests on the validating process, and ultimately on an understanding of the patient's reactions. Both principles hold: we must accept an individual style of listening, interacting, and interpreting, and allow for personal variations, but we must also establish valid and invalid techniques that require of each therapist that he work in a manner that can be validated. Within the framework of any individual style, there are appropriate and inappropriate approaches.

Are there any other comments to this point? I do want to delve a little deeper into this material

Therapist: Can I just make this one comment—not in defense, but just as a comment?

Langs: By all means, though I suggest that you not expect me to accept your negation of the function of what you are about to say. I certainly would not do so from a patient, and the same principle seems to apply here.

Therapist: I have read Haley's book (1963) on therapeutic interaction. He's not an analyst, but he has an interesting notion that all therapy is basically painful whether the statement is made empathically or not. He poses the idea that the process of therapy is inherently paradoxical: patient and therapist get together in a benevolent fashion, so that the therapist can help the patient, but the process itself is painful. The patient has to parade the difficulties of his life in front of a virtual stranger, and that in itself is a paradox, you know— pain under the aegis of pleasure. The whole therapeutic process, he thinks, is a process of the patient's correcting that paradox, and through that, getting better.

Langs: I won't address your remarks directly because it's not immediately pertinent to the listening process. At the end of this course, when we have all the pieces together, we'll get into the nature of therapy. I understand that you're implying that it influenced your intervention—in terms of acknowledging the pain of therapy or something of that kind.

Therapist: Yes, I had something like that in mind.

Langs: You see, the patient doesn't know that you read that book. She knows just what she hears. That's why I like to let interventions stand by themselves, and to allow her responses to serve as a commentary on your technique.

Therapist: Okay. I didn't make the intervention entirely on that basis, but I thought it might offer a perspective on my view of the therapeutic process.

Langs: For the moment, we must recognize that you are paraphrasing Haley; I will leave it to each of you, as this course unfolds, to decide on its utility and to determine the degree to which it is more a cliché than a meaningful insight into the nature of the therapeutic interaction or a concept from which you can derive sound and appropriate techniques.

It's common in seminars or supervision for students-in-training to have difficulty in maintaining a focus on the subject at hand—sometimes this is true of the supervisor or instructor as well. This is a very human tendency that can often serve an important defensive function. We are now having some difficulty in generating new conceptualizations of the unconscious implications of this intervention. And it is well to recognize the human tendency in such frustrating circumstances either to divert the focus or to restate what is already known in a seemingly different form.

Now, let's examine this intervention a bit more carefully. I would appreciate your repeating it again.

Therapist: I said, I understand that your problems have been difficult and painful. That only makes it more important that we work together.

Langs: Let's stop there. That only makes it more important that we work together: comments of this type have been termed by some, "an appeal to the therapeutic alliance." Such a notion implies that it is not so much a valid interpretation, but rather, a direct appeal for the patient's cooperation that fosters the development of the alliance sector or, at the very least, suggests a need for such comments beyond interpretive interventions. My own clinical experience, however, much of it based on supervisory work, has indicated that remarks of this kind, largely because of the detrimental unconscious qualities and communications reflected in them (I will soon attempt to identify these) are generally disruptive to the development of a sound therapetic alliance, rather than helpful.

After all, let's look at this segment of his intervention. It is by no means neutral, it is certainly not interpretive, and it begins with an effort at empathy and quickly shifts to an appeal or directive to the patient—something like, Look, something is prompting you to want to disrupt things here, but please don't. Let's work together, even if it is painful for you.

Perhaps you can begin to sense the unconscious message: I really can't tolerate such disruptive influences. Please try to control them; let's not have them. The message is manipulative and seductive, and reflects a sense of helplessness in the therapist. It's a rather naive appeal to the patient to be a good patient, to work with the theapist, and not to give him a hard time. I believe that unconsciously the patient will hear this message and its influence will be reflected in her communications in the following hour.

In principle, this intervention is an effort to bypass a resistance and a defense, rather than to analyze its unconscious basis within the patient and the therapeutic interaction. As a communication that directs the patient away from the pursuit of insight, it will have another impact upon her. In terms that I will develop a bit later on, this intervention seems to disturb the openness of communication, to ask for falsification, and barriers against a particular set of perceptions, feelings and fantasies within the patient. It could even become an invitation by the therapist to avoid this entire area, to create what the Barangers (1966) have called a *bastion*—a sector of the bipersonal field that is sealed off by both the patient and therapist from the rest of the communicative field. I would term it a defensive sector of misalliance (Langs, 1976a, b).

When you intervene noninterpretively, it's for your sake, rather than the patient's sake. I hope to be able to prove that point in the session we're about to hear. The appropriate intervention for the patient's sake would be some interpretation—intrapsychic and interactional—of her disruptive needs, behaviors, or whatever she's doing, and of the interference with the working relationship, whatever it's all about. An appeal of this kind, I would hypothesize, is more for the therapist's needs than for those of the patient.

Some other concepts emerge from this exchange. I will mention them now, largely because I want to show you that this intervention has important interactional implications. On another level, we could conceptualize this aspect of the therapist's intervention as an indication of his refractoriness to containing the patient's disruptive projective identifications. All of that is really way ahead of ourselves, but let me briefly indicate to you that projective identification is a term for what I call *interactional projection*—for interactional pressures—a mechanism through which the subject places into the object disturbing and other types of inner contents and functions.

The word *identification* is used in an unusual manner in the term *projective identification*. Rather than referring to an incorporative process through which the subject changes by taking in some dimension of the object, it refers to an externalizing or projecting process, in which the subject remains identified with the projected contents and, in addition, attempts to evoke an identification within the object.

I know that this is all rather confusing, but we will clarify these concepts in the course of this seminar. The therapist has in some sense an obligation to contain, metabolize, and interpret the projective identifications that the patient feels impelled to make. An intervention like this indicates that the therapist is refractory to containing such disruptive, resistance-prone feelings, and thus, to metabolizing and interpreting these interactional pressures from the patient. These are all unconscious communications that the patient will experience in the course of her own listening process which, as you can see, takes place within both the cognitive and interactional, verbal and nonverbal, conscious and unconscious realms.

There are, then, many potentially detrimental consequences to even the most seemingly innocuous intervention, especially when it is noninterpretive. As you become aware of the enormity of the unconscious communications embodied in your silences and interventions and your efforts to manage the frame, you will undoubtedly experience a sense of threat, of helplessness. But I want to assure you that, in time, it is possible to comprehend and master the greatest part of this unconscious network and to do really effective therapeutic work. Now, let's continue.

Discussant: On the surface, the way it's phrased, this is very painful for you, but the only way it's going to get less painful is if we work together.

Langs: Right. Consciously, this part of the intervention is intended as encouragement; unconsciously, it constitutes a threat to the patient, a discouragement to her communicative efforts, an effort at seduction, and an endeavor to set aside her defenses. Perhaps now you can see why it is essential that we apply the listening process not only to the patient's material, but to the therapist's interventions as well. It enables you, first, to identify the unconscious communications that the patient will experience, and secondly, to understand yourself and what, in retrospect, you have communicated on every level.

In applying the listening process to this intervention we have attempted first to formulate aspects of the surface implications, and second, in a sense, to decode its unconscious messages. We are always faced with interactional amalgams. This patient will not only validly incorporate the manifest content and evident latent communications but will, herself, also color it, distort it, generate certain reactions, and the like. In addition, the listening process is not restricted to the cognitive level, consciously and unconsciously. The therapist's verbal communications may serve as an important means of generating projective identifications which lead to introjects of his image of aspects of the therapeutic and interactional processes, of his inner mental contents and psychic functions, and of the cognitive, manifest and latent content. And as a rule, the patient's responses can be understood on both the cognitive and interactional (projective and introjective) levels.

Let's specifically apply these concepts, even though we are getting into unavoidable complexities, to the therapist's listening. We tend to think of the listening process largely in cognitive terms—and this is especially true of classical psychoanalysts—but it also includes another aspect in the interactional sphere, one studied primarily by the Kleinians: the experience of projective identifications, of introjects, and of other interactional pressures and processes.

The entire sequence of projective identification and response that I described to you earlier entails evaluating the extent to which the therapist's intervention constitutes a symbolic understanding of the nature and function of the patient's projective identification, or a pathological projective identification in itself—a projective counteridentification (Grinberg, 1962)—that the patient will either receive and contain, or be refractory to, and which the patient will, as a rule, tend to introject, metabolize on some level, and reproject back into the therapist. Much of this, I know, is new and strange. For now, I want merely to stress interactional mechanisms along with more cognitive considerations, so that you can appreciate the complex dimensions of the therapeutic relationship. Please continue.

Therapist: The other part of my intervention was, But I'm surprised that you continue to denigrate the therapy, though you seem to be working on the outside to solve these problems.

Discussant: One question has occurred to me. We are now hearing a summary of what the therapist said, and, based on your own formulations, this very report is subject to all types of distortions. I'm wondering: how can we examine such data in the detail that is being done here?

Langs: That's a bit of a side issue, but let me say this: of course, this report is open to distortion, but these are the very types of distortions that are also influencing the therapeutic interaction. In practice, I have found that these summaries do permit extensive and insightful predictions of the unfolding therapeutic interaction, and are sufficient for both the basic teaching of psychotherapy and for the supervision of a particular case. As you may know, I have objections to the tape recording of sessions because taping alters the framework and the communicative properties of the bipersonal field, as well as the introjections of the therapist. We will consider that factor when we take up the framework.

So, any further thoughts about this part of the therapist's intervention? (Pause.) Well, let's identify some of its unconscious communicative qualities. Your comment that you are surprised that the patient denigrates therapy tends to confirm one of my initial hypotheses. Thus we pursue a tactic of making a silent formulation, then seeking validation of each silent hypothesis that we make through our own subjective reactions as therapists and especially through the patient's continuing associations. In a seminar of this kind, the hypotheses that we generate will often be confirmed by a later intervention from the therapist, as well as by the patient's subsequent material. I cannot too strongly stress the overriding importance of validation from the patient, preferably in response to an offered interpretation or an effort to manage the frame.

Now, your surprise at her denigration of therapy is another appeal; it implies your wish that she desist, and it also conveys a kind of reprimand: she's working hard on the outside to solve her problems, but is not doing the same in therapy. You have responded with a kind of confrontation that lacks a sense of neutrality, and perhaps expresses your surprise or criticism. There is too, a sense of helplessness, of your not being able adequately to contain the implied devaluation of yourself and the therapy, as well as her resistances.

How, then, should we seek to validate such silent hypotheses, which are, so to speak, the precipitants of the listening process? We turn to the subsequent session, to your further interventions, and primarily to the communications from the patient.

Note, too, one aspect of what we have done. We have taken the therapist's intervention without seriously attempting to relate it to the patient's material. What we heard was that the patient was preoccupied with sexual feelings toward both men and women, and with sadistic feelings of some sort, and that she had negative feelings toward treatment. In taking the intervention in isolation, we have treated it as manifest content, and have attempted, on the basis of our own hunches and sensitivities, to derive a series of unconscious communications or latent contents. We have made no use of any adaptive context.

On the other hand, if we had made use of this general adaptive context, as we should have, to allow for the full use of the listening process, we would have been able to organize the unconscious meanings of this therapist's interventions around the adaptive stimuli generated by the patient's associations. For example, even given the little material that we have, I could suggest that the intervention was designed to avoid much of the sexual and aggressive material from the patient, and many of the possible unconscious implications that are related to feelings and perceptions that involve the therapist. Further, it was a response to the patient's discouragement with a treatment in which noninterpretive, manipulative measures are being utilized instead of interpretations.

In a sense, then, the dynamic and interactional qualities of the therapist's intervention could be appreciated far more specifically if we knew the details of the patient's associations and could treat them as the adaptive context for this intervention.

Again, we are moving a little ahead. All of this may be considered an initial exercise that will soon be shaped into a specific mode of the listening process.

For the moment, let me summarize my hypothesis. I would say that the therapist's remarks express a certain seductiveness; an appeal for unity and peace, as opposed to disharmony, aggression, and hostility; an exhortation to the patient to be less hostile and denigrating; and both helplessness and a

problem in managing on the part of the therapist. Interactionally, he seems to have difficulty containing the patient's
sexual and aggressive fantasies and perceptions, especially
because of their latent allusions to the therapist. The therapist
himself may have projectively identified into the patient his
own sense of helplessness, some degree of resentment, and his
wish for the defensive avoidance of certain aspects of the
patient's unconscious perceptions, introjects, and fantasies.

Perhaps now you begin to understand that these efforts to
pursue the truth with sensitivity, and to comprehend the
complexities of the therapeutic interaction, place a tremendous burden on the therapist and student. Long before I can
help you, in these seminars, to develop the therapeutic
armamentarium that you need for coping, I will be making
you aware of aspects of your countertransference difficulties
and of problems in undertaking therapeutic work that
undoubtedly will generate a great deal of anxiety and even a
sense of helplessness. These you must endure, and try to
master. I promise to help you by offering again and again the
cognitive and other tools that you will need, and by working
over with you any really pressing issues that arise. All of us
tend to deny the unconscious implications, whether beneficial
or traumatic, of our interventions. There is some immediate
sense of safety to be found in such barriers, but patients, as a
rule, will not share these defenses with you for very long and
they will respond rather extensively to your countertransferences and their influence. If we adopt from the beginning a
bipersonal field or interactional approach, it will very quickly
place us in touch with the unconscious processes and
communications from both patients and therapists. While
this creates a considerable conscious burden, you'll find that
any failure to accept and contain that burden, or to metabolize
it toward effective therapeutic work, will actually make it
impossible for you to be a truly helpful therapist.

I have not created these responsibilities and anxieties; they
lie within the complex nature of your chosen profession. My
main role will be to identify these factors, to assist you in
tolerating the anxiety that they evoke, and to teach you the
basic technical skills that you will need to deal appropriately

with your patient and your interaction with him. Throughout this course, we will remain keenly aware of the patient's pathology and pathological interactional mechanisms, but we will be equally sensitive to the pathology of the therapist, and we will not accept defenses in that area since they can only be disruptive to the therapeutic work.

All right, let's get into the session.

Therapist: Okay. She starts off the session by saying that she doesn't feel well. Do you want me to do this in the third person or the first person? Do you care?

Langs: That's your choice.

Therapist: She feels poorly. She can't get over being rejected by Leslie. Leslie's a male. Even though Leslie's making some advances again toward her, she feels terrible.

Langs: All right; stop. What did you hear?

Discussant: Looking at her reactions in the context of the last session: she can't get over the therapist's "rejection" of her feelings—in terms of not allowing her to express how dissatisfied she is with the treatment.

Langs: Does anybody want to add anything?

Discussant: I don't think that was necessarily implied in what the therapist said in the last session. Although this may refer to something about her relationship with him, it needn't be how he was treating her, but how she was responding to it. You're again saying he was unempathic toward her, but I don't think that was necessarily her perception of how he was; it may have been mainly how she experienced him.

Langs: Thank you for raising an extremely important issue. You are actually applying several important aspects of the listening process in arriving at these formulations, and also touching upon the issue of how this material may or may not confirm the formulations that I developed on the basis of the therapist's summary of the previous hour. In essence, you're suggesting a possible unconscious meaning for these initial associations. To some extent, you're making use of an adaptive context—the therapist's intervention—and we will get back to that point.

Your statement is a bit ambiguous, but it suggests a formulation that would stress transference in the narrow sense. You could be suggesting that these initial communications reflect not a valid, unconscious perception of the therapist, but a distorted one; that they derive primarily from the patient's unconscious fantasies and introjects, rather than from the actual qualities of his intervention. For the moment, then, we will both agree that we could meaningfully organize these initial associations around the specific adaptive context of the therapist's intervention in the prior hour, and that, in a more general way, this material takes on special unconscious meaning—fantasy in your terms, primarily valid perception in mine—when related to the therapeutic relationship.

All of this suggests that a very meaningful hypothesis about the listening process may be unfolding: namely, that all of the material from the patient in some way pertains to the therapeutic relationship, and can, at least on one level, be considered as conveying either unconscious fantasies or unconscious perceptions related to that relationship—probably, as a rule, mixtures of each. I hope I'm not stacking the deck by indicating that my own clinical experience suggests that we can validate this principle.

You know, it is vital to allow yourself genuinely to experience the rediscovery of every basic clinical concept in your therapeutic interaction with each patient, rather than forcing the qualities of each individual interaction into your preconceived concepts and ideas. Such biases often serve countertransference-based ends: the therapist perceives only that which he already knows, and will be refractory to that which is truly unknown and unanticipated (Bion, 1970). It is inevitable that any theory we generate will have an effect on our application of the listening process, but it is important, as

I said, to derive that theory anew from each therapeutic experience, to be open to communications that do not fit into present theory, and to be willing to modify the theory. Thus we widen our capacity to listen and afford it additional precision.

Discussant: The point that I was actually trying to make was that I felt that the patient and therapist were congruent with each other about what they mean—I think you are referring to congruence of that kind when you talk about the therapeutic interaction.

Langs: You think that one goal of what we're trying as therapists to do—I think I see what you're saying—is to be empathic, to have feelings that are congruent with what the patient is feeling?

Discussant: So that you understand exactly what the patient is saying. She's saying she's dissatisfied with the relationship, but she isn't saying why, or hasn't yet. Is the therapist showing some interest in her, but not enough interest? I mean, that may be what we're going to interpret— we might interpret what she said within the context of the transference.

Langs: You just said, "within the context of the transference." In this course, I propose that we not say "the transference" in referring to the patient's total relationship to the therapist, and that we say "the therapeutic relationship" instead. For the moment, let me just comment that this is largely because the term *transference* implies distortion; you are thereby implying that the relationship is essentially a distorted and pathological one. You actually leave no room for the patient's valid and nondistorted functioning and perceptions. This frequent use of the term *transference* reflects a common unconscious bias in therapists and analysts—one that is also evident in the fact that, historically speaking, one of the latest discoveries about the therapeutic interaction is that of the patient's valid functioning, his sound, unconscious perceptions of the therapist, and his curative efforts on the therapist's behalf (Searles, 1975; Langs, 1975a, 1976a, b).

Returning to the point that you are making: I hear you suggesting that these initial associations could reflect some kind of resonance between the patient and therapist, but I do believe that you are confusing this type of resonance with empathy, and that the latter implies a feeling of oneness that is almost entirely mental and emotional, and not enacted.

On another level, you may be suggesting that the therapist's hurtfulness merely brings out the patient's masochism—her tendency to feel hurt and rejected—and that he is not entirely responsible for these initial associations. I would say that this may well be the case, but so long as the therapist is actually hurtful, it is impossible to know whether the patient has a need to be hurt or the hurt has been traumatically imposed upon her.

The therapist's utilization of empathy is quite different from his behaving in a manner similar to the patient's introjects and to her past pathogenic and traumatic figures. To understand the patient's inner world and to empathize with it does not imply that you behave in a way that confirms that inner world. In fact, a valid understanding of that inner world, especially of its pathological components, requires that you— quite naturally, I might add—behave in a manner that is distinctly different from the pathological aspects of that inner world and from past, pathogenic figures.

Discussant: I know that you didn't want to get into it for the moment, but it would be helpful if you could just briefly clarify your definition of transference.

Langs: Transference is the inappropriate aspect of the patient's relationship with the therapist. It is the pathological component, based on unconscious fantasies, memories, and introjects that are distorting, and it also includes distorting defenses and interactional mechanisms. So the relationship isn't transference; the relationship is a total relationship, with distortion and nondistortion. I promise to amaze you with repeated demonstrations of how nondistorted so much of the patient's functioning in the therapeutic relation is. The patient as a constructive, unconsciously functioning person is the greatest potential that we've overlooked in the therapeutic relationship.

To focus on the listening process: you can see that, in principle, I am suggesting that the first step is to identify the adaptive context, to establish its realistic components, and its manifest and latent contents, and that to evaluate and organize any set of associations, we must take cognizance of this basic reality. Then, and only then, can we develop the next step of sorting out that which is realistic and valid in the patient's associations from that which is fantasy-based and distorted, or to put it another way: sort out the nonpathological from the pathological elements. More broadly, it is only on that basis that we can understand the patient's conscious and unconscious communications. Actually, that fundamental task is a good deal more complicated than I am indicating for now, but we can acknowledge its importance, and let the rest unfold as we go along.

This of course is an investigation of the adaptive context, and it shows us right off that the listening process must address both reality and fantasy, actuality and interaction, that it is not, as some believe, simply a matter of investigating fantasied contents and deriving underlying unconscious fantasies and memories. We listen for reality, not in the sense of simple manifest content, or of the patient's realistic problems, but largely as the precipitants of intrapsychic reactions, and as a set of events with manifest and latent meaning whose nature must be derived through the listening process itself. Since I am on this subject, allow me to also point out that we do, of course, attend to reality in other ways as well: we listen to its surface implications; we listen to the description of reality events and other adaptive contexts, and derive unconscious perceptions and fantasies from such efforts; and we especially attend to the realities of our own inner mental life and our behaviors with, and communications to, our patients.

We do not listen to material with the assumption that, essentially, it reflects the patient's fantasies, inner propensities and needs, and distortions of experiences. Our basic attitude in listening is essentially neutral, in that it will permit formulations of both reality and fantasy, and their interplay.

Much of this will be developed in bits and pieces initially, but eventually we should be able to integrate all of this into a basic conception of the listening process.

Inherent to the listening process is the therapist's capacity to relate to reality, to appreciate its meanings and implications, and to test it out in some sense. I trust that it is also clear that all of this ultimately relies on the therapist's capacity for self-knowledge, on an awareness, first, of his personal standards and guides to reality, and a need to resolve as far as possible any propensities toward distortions. It also relies on the therapist's ability fully to appreciate the nature of his unconscious and conscious communications, both to the patient and within himself. It all comes back to knowing your own personal equation, and recognizing the main issues that affect the listening process.

Discussant: Is the important thing how the therapist behaves, or is the important thing that she perceived that he has behaved in a particular way?

Langs: Well, what difference is implied in your question?

Discussant: Perhaps in what is communicated, as distinct from how it is perceived.

Langs: Is it important how he behaved, or how she perceived it? Which do you favor as important?

Discussant: It seems to me how she perceived his behavior is more important than how he actually behaved. He is responsible for how he actually behaved, but with her own use of distortion, she may hear what he says in her own idiosyncratic way. She's responding to the actual statement, the statement that he makes, but it will be on her own terms.

Langs: Allow me to restate what you're trying to spell out. Both are important: the reality of the therapist's intervention and how it is perceived by the patient. These are excellent questions, related to ideas that I want to crystallize about listening. You see, the very fact that you would ask that question shows how much you've been influenced by analysts who say that the patient's fantasies are far more important than reality. Some would even say that the reality isn't even especially relevant, when the fact of the matter is that what's important is the reality *and* the patient's perception of it.

So we have to know reality in order to conceptualize the patient's perception of it, and to evaluate and understand it. Evaluating what we're hearing from the patient, then, is knowing the realities of the adaptive context in depth—what it truly is that the patient is responding to. As I said, that means we have to know ourselves. It means, too, that implicitly the therapist is going to help the patient with these very crucial functions of reality testing, functioning in reality, appraising reality, and differentiating reality from fantasy— all of which have to do with neurotic and other kinds of emotional disturbances. The therapist must not only fully understand the implications of external reality, but also, his greatest responsibility is knowing inner reality. He cannot know one without the other—we come to that very quickly.

I've been accused of saying that every therapist has to be analyzed. If you're so sure you are healthy, and you know your own inner reality well, skip it; after all, it's a very painful process. But otherwise, if you want really to know the truth about your patients, you have to know the truth about yourself. Isakower (1963) called it the "listening instrument"—he saw basic self-knowledge as a determinant of all other types of knowledge.

Discussant: It seems to me that you are able to stress the importance of the therapist's contributions because of the fact that you focused on his interventions far more than on the material from the patient, in discussing the previous hour. It seems a bit prejudicial to me.

Langs: It certainly is, and I fully acknowledged that, soon after taking that approach. But this happened to be the way the material unfolded. We could have started our investigation of the listening process by having the therapist present this particular session without any reference to the prior hour. At some point later on, we will do just that in order to see whether it facilitates or hinders the listening process, and to define what I believe to be the limitations of such an approach.

I would also have wished to begin with a session that would have forced you to search out the adaptive context, and to acknowledge the lack of definitive meaning when we listen in its absence. But the presentation did not go that way, and I have very much biased your listening process by suggesting an adaptive context. Nonetheless, I am attempting to show you that the adaptive context does indeed serve as a meaningful organizer of the patient's material, if we are interested, as we should be, in its unconscious contents and perceptions.

If we think about this material without that adaptive context, it would be impossible to know just what's going on for the moment. The patient is talking about some fellow rejecting her and yet being seductive. Some might take this on a manifest level and suggest that she has a conflict with her boyfriend that may be evoking some conflict about sexuality and sexual identity, or whatever—even something related to rejection and her suicidal impulses. Many therapists would adopt these very formulations, focusing on the patient's outside life and conflicts, and directly reading into the material possible related, unconscious meanings, almost all involving the patient and her psychopathology. Now that I define it, at what level would this therapist be listening?

Discussant: Well, it's certainly not at the level of the therapeutic relationship—there is no sense of displacement.

Discussant: He would also be listening in terms of psycho-dynamics, rather than the therapeutic interaction.

Langs: Yes, that is all true, but I want to stress one major quality of such a listening process: the focus is on the manifest content. This is a listening process on the manifest level: the material about the boyfriend has to do with the boyfriend; the seductiveness has to do with sexuality. And therapists tend to

deceive themselves by suggesting that they are dealing with
latent content when they consider these associations as
involving some type of sexual conflict within the patient, or
some issue related to her femininity. Such an approach to
listening, however, is almost entirely tied to the manifest
themes, and at most, permits the development of a few rather
obvious inferences from that manifest content, entirely vis-à-
vis the boyfriend, the outside relationship.

Discussant: Does it make a difference what the reality is:
whether the patient actually saw the boyfriend in the time
since the last session?

Langs: Would it make a difference in regard to what?

Discussant: In other words, if she hadn't seen the boyfriend,
hadn't had anything to do with him since the last session and,
yet, this is what comes to her mind, that would seem to
corroborate the idea that it's got something to do with the
therapist. On the other hand, let's say, the night before the
session she got a call from her boyfriend, who again was
wishy-washy, somewhat rejecting, somewhat making
overtures—that would seem to lessen the possibility that it
relates to the therapist, and it would seem to pertain more to
the reality situation.

Langs: That's an excellent question, and it very much
reflects a common way of thinking among therapists,
especially those who, as I said, would deal with this material
in terms of the relationship with the boyfriend. As you might
suspect by now, I do not believe that it is the case that the
recency or actuality of an experience influences our listening
to it as a derivative of an unconscious fantasy or perception.
In fact, I hope to teach you that patients select for unconscious
communicative purposes all kinds of realities, recent and past,
outside the therapeutic interaction, or even, often, within that
relationship, so long as it alludes to something in the past
rather than the present or to one issue in that relationship as a
cover for, and expression of, another more disturbing and

pressing issue. It will be very important for us to document that thesis; it is a source of considerable confusion.

Now there certainly are differences when the patient utilizes a realistic experience—instead of a dream, for example, or even a conscious fantasy—to convey in derivative form some unconscious fantasy or perception. And we will consider the implications of different vehicles of communication throughout this course. Still, we must also recognize that in terms of the patient's neurosis, it is the unconscious communication and meaning that is crucial, and it is on that level that most effective analytic work must take place.

Discussant: Can you indicate how you see the meaning of different forms of communication?

Langs: For example, one important implication of the vehicle of communication relates to the extent to which the patient may be living out with an outside figure—or even the therapist—unconscious fantasies and perceptions related to the therapeutic relationship. The use of references to actual, recent outside events leads us to consider that possibility— here, the relationship with the boyfriend—while the report of a fantasy does not of course, readily imply enactment. I'm sure that you realize that a conscious fantasy or dream about the boyfriend may also point to possibilities of living out, but I will not pursue these complexities further.

Instead, I want to answer the earlier question in still another way. I believe that I have already offered some data that would contradict your hypothesis—after all, I do want to stick with the principle that every hypothesis offered in this seminar will be tested out against the clinical material. Now, while the true test will come from the patient's subsequent associations, let me point out that having established the therapist's intervention as an adaptive context and having identified some of its unconscious meanings, I was able to predict that the patient's material in this session would deal with her introjection of that communication. I would therefore suggest to you that it is not a coincidence of reality but a process of unconscious selectivity that has prompted the patient to begin the session with this particular set of associations, and that they were selected for their capacity to convey latent meanings—largely, her unconscious perceptions of the therapist, whatever her own further distortions might be. There is a valid unconscious perception of the therapist's inadvertent seductiveness here, and it would be impossible to ascertain the extent to which the patient, too, is seductive or sexualizes until that contaminant has been removed from the bipersonal field.

I am trying to show you that the patient's inner mind and unconscious faculties are astonishing to behold. Some have said that I overestimate these capacities, but I really don't think that this is so. Actually, I think that most therapists and analysts have underestimated the perceptiveness, creativity, and curative abilities of their patients.

So, I am proposing that my ability to predict the latent content of these initial associations—and as you can see now, it might have been possible to predict aspects of their manifest contents as well—may be taken as initial confirmation that these associations primarily were unconsciously determined, rather than reality determined.

Discussant: You're saying that the main concern of the patient, unconsciously at least, is the relationship with the therapist; that it is the primary vehicle of therapy. The other stuff is just a vehicle for communicating aspects of what the patient is reacting to in the relationship?

Langs: Right, the relationship is central. Look, I've stacked the cards for the moment, and we'll accrue validating evidence as we go on, but so far, in one session, one hypothesis has been validated. Every time you try to make predictions based entirely on outside relationships, they'll be wrong; every time you intervene solely in respect to outside relationships, you'll be wrong, and your intervention will not be validated, until you connect it to the ongoing therapeutic interaction. In listening you will not be able to organize the material properly if that is your guiding concept. That's sort of way ahead of us, but that's what this little piece has confirmed in a very tentative way.

Discussant: Do you think that's true in once-a-week therapy?

Langs: Yes. With schizophrenics? Yes. Children? Yes. With human beings. It is how they function, and it applies to any two human beings who get together in a therapeutic situation. I'm going to show you how crucial that relationship is, how it develops around what Searles (1965, 1970, 1971, 1973) has called *the therapeutic symbiosis*. I think that is a beautiful way of phrasing it, because it gives you all of the primitive qualities involved—the symbiotic, the dual, interactive, intimate qualities of such a relationship.

To return again to the listening process: I want to emphasize that I have been alluding, actually, to two basic levels of listening. The first relates to manifest content—here, something about her boyfriend, about rejection, seduction. We attend to the manifest content alone on this level, to the patient's conscious concerns, perceptions, and reactions. In a paper that I wrote recently (Langs, 1978a), I suggested that therapists who confine themselves to this level of the listening process cannot consider themselves to be psychoanalytically oriented. It denies unconscious processes and contents, and implies that neuroses are based on conscious disputes or conflicts, and that they can be modified through the exploration of conscious functioning. I think that you would be surprised how many therapists, who believe that they are doing psychoanalytically oriented psychotherapy, seldom get beyond that level of endeavor.

The same is even more true of the next level of therapeutic work, which I will state here, in terms of the listening process, as attending to and formulating *Type One derivatives*. The therapist listens to the manifest content from the patient and, entirely without an adaptive context, attempts to formulate possible unconscious meanings and implications, often confining himself to rather obvious inferences, though occasionally deriving seemingly deep formulations of unconscious fantasies and defenses. Here, I have already mentioned possible implications for the patient's sexual anxieties, sexual identity, vulnerability to hurt, and even her own seductiveness—the latter expressed, for the moment, through a projection onto the boyfriend.

A more sophisticated therapist of this kind will monitor all of the patient's material for indirect, derivative allusions to himself, so that in addition to formulating self-representations, he will generate latent contents related to object-representations, especially as they pertain to himself. These too will be based entirely on inferences from the manifest material, and I must stress to you that they will almost always involve the realm of fantasy and distortion. Seldom has such a therapist generated Type One derivatives related to unconscious perceptions, especially as they relate to himself. Actually, it is possible to do this, and in supervising as well as in working with my own patients, my own inclination, in the absence of an identifiable adaptive context, is to listen to the patient's material in terms of Type One derivatives related to the therapeutic relationship, and first to translate them into unconscious perceptions, before considering them as possible unconscious fantasies, memories, and introjects.

Now, as you can sense, a great deal of therapy is done in exactly this way, and there are many problems when the therapist confines his listening process to this level and derives his interventions almost entirely on this basis. I have already mentioned that it tends to divorce the treatment from realities and unconscious communications, but it also can be used to deny the therapist's countertransference-based interventions and their influence, and it can be used, more broadly, as a means of avoiding the realtionship between Type One derivatives and the therapeutic interaction. In addition, it will promote the use of psychoanalytic clichés which serve a variety of defensive functions, and may lead to a therapy characterized by general interpretations and by an avoidance of specific dynamics and genetics.

I would like to have a chance to hear a bit more material before we finish today, but I do wish to complete my classification of levels of listening, which actually relate to levels on which the patient communicates and, as I will later show you, to types of communicative fields. The third level involves what I call *Type Two derivatives*, and it consists of organizing the material from the patient around a specific adaptive context—most often, as I said, one that is ultimately related to the therapeutic interaction. In this way, the material from the patient is immediately considered in terms of unconscious fantasy and perception, and it also immediately acquires a sense of dynamic meaning and specificity. Quite often we can develop a sensitive initial formulation, a silent hypothesis, from Type One derivatives that is confirmed when the adaptive context emerges. Type One and Type Two derivatives may well overlap. In that type of situation, you are dealing with a coalescence of derivatives and unconscious meaning, strengthening and validating your formulation, so that often, with the identification of the adaptive context, you acquire a means of specifically interpreting the relevant material to the patient.

Therapist: I understand what you're saying, but I don't know how this differs from the way someone more traditional might comment upon the situation. For example, this patient has ambivalent relationships all the time on the outside, and yet she has in fact created one with me. That is part of the latent content of this material at the beginning of this session. How does your approach differ?

Langs: That too is an important question, but you have already provided me with part of the answer, because I am not suggesting to you that everything I teach you will be different from the teachings of traditional psychoanalysts. If I had to characterize what I will be teaching, I would say that it is founded entirely on classical psychoanalytic theory to which has been added certain selected concepts from Kleinian theory. I must say that the Kleinians consider themselves true classical analysts, and what I will be teaching extends basic, known concepts primarily into the interactional sphere—an effort not unlike that of many psychoanalysts who are attempting to integrate object-relations theory with the classical psychoanalytic theory that is focused on the intrapsychic realm.

I might add that these interactional considerations, in turn, shed new light on that very intrapsychic sphere. In contrast to some object-relations theorists and interactionalists, I will be teaching you a conception of the psychoanalytic situation that takes into full account intrapsychic processes along with those that are interactional. In fact, as time permits, I will be able to show you the historical roots of every one of the concepts that I offer to you. I have not done so in this initial seminar because we are focusing on the listening process, and as I said earlier, remarkably enough, there is, to my knowledge, virtually no psychoanlaytic literature on most aspects of the subject. My conception of the listening process is founded on that theoretical position, but I must emphasize again that I truly believe that I have derived this conception not from psychoanalytic theory, but from empirical clinical observation—in fact, the theoretical position that I just outlined developed in exactly that way.

To answer your question specifically, I would suggest first that it is not *she* who established this ambivalent relationship, but *you* and *she*. So far as I know for the moment you contributed as much, if not more, to her ambivalence as she did. Rather than seeing these initial associations as a manifestation of a segment of her intrapsychic pathology, I see it first as an unconscious perception of aspects of your inner pathology as communicated to the patient—your ambivalence, if you will, though there is more—a dimension that may well be consonant with her own ambivalence. We will not be able to determine that, however, until your provocations, which have produced an apparent sense of ambivalence, have been rectified. Then, and only then, would we be in a position to see what the patient brings to the therapeutic relationship when she is a prime mover.

Therapist: Okay; I begin to see what you mean.

Langs: The initial difference between myself and the usual classical analyst would be in my stress on the patient's valid, unconscious perceptions along with a readiness to identify and work with the patient's subsequent distortions and fantasies.

Returning to the concept of Type Two derivatives: I can illustrate this type of communication in the patient's material by pointing out again that it can be organized through the adaptive context related to the unconscious communications from the therapist, and that it therefore contains as Type Two derivatives, the patient's unconscious perceptions of his rejecting attitude and his seductiveness. The latter is a dimension of this material that those of you who have offered formulations have tended to leave out. After all, in my original thesis I stressed both a sense of rejection and of seductiveness. In her opening words, the patient beautifully puts together her version of exactly what I had developed as a silent hypothesis.

By the way, I would not at first invoke the concept of ambivalence here. I do not see two contradictory sets of feelings, or a mixture of love and hate, but a valid, unconscious perception. I should remind you that all of this will very much influence your intervention to the patient. If you tell her that she has a distorted or inappropriately ambivalent feeling toward you as her therapist, that she believes that you have been rejecting and seductive, because of her own mixed feelings toward you, and if you were later to add that this is based on her ambivalent relationship with her father, for example, and that it is also reflected in her ambivalence with her boyfriend, you would actually be quite insensitive and incorrect. In fact, it is well to remember, as Margaret Little (1951) so nicely stated, that when you interpret contents and reactions as transference, you deny their reality; you deny that you have actually behaved in the way that the patient is representing, and you can, when in error, greatly disturb the patient's capacities for reality testing—and sometimes even drive the patient crazy (Searles, 1959). In addition, you will be placing into her—projectively identifying into her, if you will—an intense sense of denial, lack of insight, blame. I think that these are important implications of the outcome of the listening process, and of the consequences of sound, validated listening as compared to unsound, erroneous, and distorted listening.

Therapist: Wait—wait one second. I think the argument has to be addressed, that you yourself said that I had made a clarification or an interpretation. I made a statement describing her behavior toward me—I didn't create her behavior toward me.

Langs: That may or may not be true; up to a point, both she and you may have some responsibility there.

Therapist: But, if I say, as I did, that she's in pain, which was fairly obvious, and also that she denigrates the therapy, but is working on the outside, which is also true, I don't know that that necessarily means I created her reaction in this session.

Langs: Let me try to help you to develop a perspective here. I said that confrontations of this kind may be very painful for the presenting therapist, but this can help you to understand why therapists are so defensive about their unconscious communications to their patients and the influence of the countertransferences on the therapeutic interaction.

This issue of responsibility is a difficult one. Both you and the patient have some measure of responsibility for her reactions, or to be specific for these initial communications. Certainly, the patient is always responsible for her own responses and behaviors, but at the same time, it is important that you acknowledge your own contributions to her reactions. It is quite easy to become overly defensive, and to deny all or some aspects of your responsibility, just as it is quite easy, for certain therapists, to masochistically overstate the other position, and to feel responsible for everything that the patient does. There is a more realistic and balanced approach, and I am trying to establish it, but it does mean an honest confrontation with your contributions.

Your response to my formulation is characteristic of many therapists. You shift here to the manifest content of your communication, or to its formal nature, as if to deny its unconscious communicative meanings. Now I am sure you can realize that that is a rather defensive position, and maintaining it would have a detrimental influence on your therapeutic work with this patient. On the other hand, my emphasis on the patient's unconscious perceptions of your latent meanings should not be taken to imply that the patient has made no contribution to this reaction. Each patient will respond to the therapist's conscious and unconscious communications in keeping with the actual nature of the intervention and out of his own inner needs, pathological and nonpathological. It's a rather undemocratic characteristic of psychotherapy to suggest that the patient speaks on a manifest level, but the real meaning is in the latent content, the unconscious realm, while the therapist talks manifestly, and that is where it should end—his unconscious and latent messages do not exist. Or to put this another way, that the therapist is the healthy one and only rarely pathological, while the patient is the sick one, and only rarely, if ever, well.

The truly fair and honest view acknowledges and attempts to sort out the conscious and unconscious communcations from the therapist and the patient, addresses them both without prejudice, and listens impartially to both.

Discussant: I just have to share this: it happened that in a session I said something and was aware right after I said it that it was critical and I really didn't think I intended to be that way. The patient got extremely upset, and I said to the patient something to the effect that I didn't mean it to be critical, and then went on. She spent the last part of the session saying exactly that: This is so unfair; I sit here and say all of this stuff and you can hide so much.

Langs: And she's speaking the truth. But to come back to the therapist's defense here—if I may call it that—you see, you're alluding to your manifest intentions and I'm trying to teach you that underneath that you're going to find the whole world of your unconscious intentions and effects, most of which, I agree with you, is unpleasant to be confronted with. But you will have to know about such things if you're going to be able to appreciate just what your patient is feeling and perceiving, and understand the real factors in her psychopathology—in a nutshell, if you're going to be able to do truly valid psychotherapy.

Discussant: It's just that all of this raises a different technical issue. After all, you're not in therapy in order to explore your own unconscious with the patient, and your approach raises an important technical issue about how you do this in reality.

Langs: You are quite right. The presence of such realities and my discussion of them certainly does not imply that psychotherapy is designed for the treatment of the therapist, or for the exploration of his unconscious fantasies, memories, introjects, and the like. It is designed for the resolution of the patient's psychopathology, and the exploration of his inner mental world. On the other hand, it turns out that in the real world there are always some countertransference-based contribution from the therapist. We cannot therefore take the position that, since the treatment is designed for the therapy of the patient, there is nothing that we can do about the pathology of the therapist or, to extend that, we cannot deny that the patient would unconsciously perceive and experience the influence of that pathology—that she might, in fact, not only attempt to exploit it, but might become involved in unconscious curative efforts on the therapist's behalf.

I am attempting to identify the actualities of the therapeutic interaction, and to put them into perspective, so that we can all be more effective therapists aware of the intricacies of the situation. There is little doubt that in a well-run psychotherapeutic experience, the therapist will from time to time experience countertransference-based disruptions, unconsciously communicate them to the patient, find the patient involved in unconscious curative efforts, and if he is capable of detecting the difficulty, he will not only benefit silently and implicitly from these therapeutic efforts, but he will also undertake self-analytic efforts to modify the underlying basis of his countertransference problems and rectify their influence in the therapeutic interaction, analyzing the patient's responses as the material permits and restoring the focus of the treatment on the patient's psychopathology.

Much of this lies ahead of us, though it all, quite obviously, relates to the listening process. But you seem be asking for some immediate principles, and I am attempting to out-line them. Actually, they begin with various indicators of a countertransference difficulty: the very search for countertransference-based expressions, that aspect of the listening process that is directed toward your subjective feelings, interventions, and management of the framework. Once you have identified a countertransference-based inter-vention, you utilize it as an adaptive context for the patient's ongoing material. You then make use of these associations, both their unconscious perceptiveness and subsequent distor-tions, to *implicitly* acknowledge to the patient the validity of her responses to your erroneous intervention, and to interpret her unconscious reactions, distorted and not. It is important to do this, by and large, implicitly rather than explicitly, since the explicit acknowledgment of a mistake is often, in itself, a self-revelation that alters the framework and burdens the patient with an unneeded confession. Implicit acceptance of the patient's perceptions, the adoption of a position in which you do not interpret them as transference-based and distorted, is more than sufficient for the patient's needs: reality testing, experiencing you as an honest person, and the like.

Discussant: How might you have handled this situation?

Langs: It is difficult to be specific as yet. We have just begun to get into this material, though I promise to offer very definitive illustrations as we continue. Here, my framework would be to plan to indicate to the patient that she had perceived my intervention as critical and seductive, implying acceptance of her perception and not suggesting that it was distorted or crazy.

Discussant: Don't you think that the patient might feel that when you said that she had perceived you as critical you were implying that there could, indeed, be some distortion in that perception?

Langs: This will not occur when you take her perception as your premise, and base the rest of your intervention on it, clearly accepting the perception and helping her to understand the consequences. This also does not occur when you contrast this kind of intervention with those that you use when the patient has indeed misperceived and distorted. For example, when you say to the patient that her feeling that you have been critical is derived from the way in which her father, in her past, had been critical and insensitive, you are suggesting that it was not based on the actualities of your behavior or communication, but on a displacement from her father, which led to a misperception. But notice again, to return to our basic theme, how so much of your intervention is shaped by the listening process—your conception of the patient's associations and your knowledge of yourself.

Discussant: When I make an intervention that's obviously going to seem critical, I don't take the approach that the patient will feel criticized because of some past relationship. It seems to me that she will feel criticized because there is, implicit to the intervention, some degree of criticism.

Langs: Here, you are touching upon another issue—the extent to which valid interpretations may well contain some degree of criticism of the patient, exercised in a constructive fashion. This is a very tricky issue that can be misused for countertransference-based aggressive needs, but one that we cannot address without specific material. For the moment, I am trying to address those unconscious qualities in an intervention of which a therapist may be quite unaware.

Discussant: Sometimes the mantle of responsibility in being a therapist seems to weigh very heavily.

Langs: Yes, there is little doubt about that. It is awesome to recognize just how much responsibility you have in your relationship with your patients, even when you do not overstate that responsibility. It is indeed a very special burden to become aware of these responsibilities, of the intricacies of the unconscious interaction between yourself and the patient, of the power of her unconscious perceptiveness and sensitivities, and as yet to lack a fully developed set of therapeutic tools, a sufficient sense of self-awareness and degree of resolution of your countertransference problems, to feel some sense of security in handling the weight of that mantle. On that note, we will stop for today.

Chapter Two

THREE LEVELS OF LISTENING

Subjective factors in listening • Manifest content, and Type One and Type Two derivatives • Associations as commentaries • Listening for derivatives, for the state of the framework, and for the conditions of the communicative field • Appending the listening process to the therapeutic interaction • The validating process • Interactional influences on the listening process • Unconscious fantasy

Langs: Under normal conditions, I would ask our present-ing therapist to simply begin his presentation where he had left off last time. We could then develop an exercise in beginning each session without desire, memory or understanding—the approach suggested by Bion (1970)—as means of fostering the quest for the unknown, and of counteracting the natural tendency among therapists to rediscover that which they already know, and to shy away from that which is unrecognized and often anxiety-provoking for them. Such an attitude is based on the need to create conditions under which listening, remembering, recalling, and the like unfold as open-ended, interactional products, without special and active efforts by the therapist, but in an essentially relaxed and passive manner that permits the patient to shape your listening and formulating processes as far as possible.

For the moment, however, I believe that such an exercise is premature until we have identified and worked over the basic dimensions of the listening process itself. So I will ask the therapist, especially since he had just started to describe the hour that we will be studying, to begin again with the patient's initial communications in that session. We will proceed in the seminar in a fashion modeled upon Bion's recommendation, allowing it to be an interactional product that directs us toward the basic elements of the listening process that we must rework again today, and that also guides us toward the discovery of aspects of that process that we have not as yet identified and clarified.

Discussant: As I remember your technique book (Langs, 1973), you advocated the active recognition of the prior session as a basic leg, as you put it, on which each session stands, and you suggested that the present hour would be based on the previous session and on the intercurrent realities that took place between the two hours.

Langs: Langs quoted against Langs. That particular position is one that I have now partly revised, for the reasons that I have just stated and also because I now feel that it is crucial for each session to unfold on its own terms, and to create its own understanding and interpretations. This approach promotes discovery and reformulation. The foundations of each session remain the prior hour, the intercurrent realities, and the patient's intrapsychic responses to them; it is only the approach that is different: I now stress passive recall, allowing the patient to direct your remembering and even your forgetting.

It is important that you experience the extent to which you readily and without effort recall or have difficulty in recalling a previous hour. Implicit to the patient's style of associating is the degree to which he fosters in the therapist the experience of links between each session, or destroys or obliterates the connections, the conscious or unconscious flow of themes, and the like. In addition, there is the therapist's capacity for open and unencumbered remembering and recall—a factor that is open, of course, to countertransference-based difficulties. He may fail to remember or may instead focus intensely on the area to the exclusion of others. Deliberate efforts to remember the previous hour, and notetaking of any kind, interfere with the experience of these important dimensions of the therapeutic interaction, and with the basic listening attitude of the therapist.

Well, let's get to the clinical material so that we can develop our further discussions with some clinical data at hand.

Therapist: Okay. The patient comes in and starts relating how she feels. It's bad. She can't get over being rejected by Leslie, even though Leslie is now making some advances toward her. She feels terrible, she still feels rejected because of the ambiguity built into the situation.

Langs: I interrupted the presentation at this point. Does anyone have any additional thoughts about this brief opening excerpt?

Discussant: It's not the same theme that she started the last hour with; she's turned it around.

Langs: No, this is the same hour. Isn't it interesting that you heard it that way, that you thought she had said something quite different than she did previously? This experience can help us to recognize that the listening process leaves a precipitant within the therapist, that he carries around consciously and unconsciously with himself until the next session. At times, this residual can be quite distorted and prejudicial. All of this demonstrates how important it is to give the patient a fresh start, to allow her to generate a new communicative interaction, and to provide you with an opportunity to check out the silent hypothesis that you have been carrying with you all that time.

Would anyone else like to comment? Any other associations, or perhaps another hypothesis?

Discussant: I am reminded of what I said last week, that this material may be related partially to her relationship with the therapist, and we should listen to the material on that level.

Langs: Yes, related to the therapist. That is, indeed, a silent hypothesis that we developed last week, and we will see just how far it takes us as we hear additional material. Now,

although we very much want to maintain the kind of openness
that will allow the material that we hear to generate new
hypotheses and permit us to avoid premature closure, I must
nonetheless attempt to identify some general principles, and
trust that we will not allow them to bias our listening.

We do have to recognize that the statement of a technical
principle, for all its value in generating order out of chaos,
tends to stultify original thinking and creative listening.
Seemingly or falsely validated principles—especially those
that become a part of what I have termed the mythology of
psychoanalysis and psychoanalytic psychotherapy (Langs,
1974) carry with them the danger of preventing the discovery
of that which is truly new or idiosyncratic in the material from
your patients.

Therapists tend to stick with known principles as a means
of managing their anxieties and of maintaining a false sense
of safety; this often leads them to develop forced formulations,
based more on accepted but erroneous theory than on a
sensitive listening to the material from the patient. Throughout this course, I will make every effort to keep these dangers
in mind and to maintain an attitude of skepticism and
openness, an insistence on rediscovery, and, who knows, we
may indeed find from time to time that the material presented
here will actually generate new general hypotheses about the
listening process.

There are different ways in which we could listen to this
material. I will summarize and begin to extend some of the
concepts we developed last week. We could listen in terms of
manifest content—the relationship with the boyfriend. We
could also look for latent content, Type One derivatives,
searching for unconscious implications related to the patient's inner mental world, especially for reflections of
possible psychopathology, intrapsychic conflicts, disturbed
object relationships, pathological unconscious fantasies, and
the like. We would search for genetic ties and, if we are
especially sophisticated, would make use of Type One
derivatives related to possible unconscious perceptions,
perhaps in her relationship to her boyfriend but mainly in her
relationship with the therapist.

I think you will find that there are many therapists who would address this material on the manifest level alone. It is an approach that is extremely common in the papers that I receive for the *International Journal of Psychoanalytic Psychotherapy*, even among so-called sophisticated analysts. Some would listen with the therapeutic relationship in mind, though few would consciously attempt to generate what I have termed Type Two derivatives and specific adaptive contexts. Still fewer would accept as validated the clinical observations that I have described that lead me to suggest that almost all of the significant adaptive contexts will lie within the therapeutic relationship, and that even those that are apparent in outside relationships will have some meaningful connection to the therapeutic relationship.

So, as a gentle but I hope useful guide to subsequent listening—a tentative principle open to validation and revision—let me suggest that we regard all the patient's associations as in some way what I like to call a *commentary* on the therapeutic relationship. And within this commentary we can distinguish both fantasies and perceptions.

To state a second principle that applies directly to the listening process: we will maintain a consistent effort to listen in terms of all three levels, manifest content Type One derivatives, based on our reading of the implications of the surface of the material, and Type Two derivatives, based on a continuous search for the specific adaptive context (or contexts—there can be more than one) for these associations.

I will attempt to document clinically every one of the basic principles that I offer in this course, and I am well aware that I have taken only a small segment of material and generated some rather profound principles, but I want to identify as quickly as possible the issues with which we will have to struggle again and again. As this course proceeds, we will have repeated opportunities for validation and, I hope, a chance to observe interventions in keeping with these principles.

In turning now to these initial associations, I hear something new, either because I have further sensitized my own listening or because you have now added a bit more

material. I can now show you something of the interplay
between Type One and Type Two derivatives, in the context of
the patient's comment that the situation is ambiguous.

In terms of Type One derivatives, one tries to listen for key
words, bridges from manifest to latent content—an aspect of
listening that I will soon specify. I think first, in a general
way, that this is a clinic patient, that we know nothing of how
the therapeutic situation was defined, the ground rules and
how they have been explicated, directly and indirectly, though
I know very well that I have never seen an exception to the
finding that psychotherapy in a clinic situation occurs with
an altered frame, and with a set of ground rules that often
have significantly ambiguous elements, that are ill-defined,
poorly explicated, and inconsistently applied. And when we
include the therapist's neutrality among these rules, as we
must, we then recognize that such an association can
unconsciously allude not only to the basic structure of the
treatment itself, but to the deviant nature of the therapist's
interventions as well—an aspect that we discussed in some
detail last week.

We must always apply the listening process to the
therapeutic relationship in two basic but interrelated realms.
First, we monitor the material in terms of self- and object-
representations, along what I term the *me–not-me interface*;
we look for condensations, in the patient's associations, of
allusions to herself and the therapist. Second, we listen in
terms of the therapeutic situation itself; we consider direct,
and especially indirect, references to the framework and to the
therapist's formal, usually verbal, interventions—essentially,
his interpretive efforts and management of the ground rules.
Now when these interpretive and management endeavors are
in error, they will tend to modify the therapist's anonymity
and neutrality, and will involve both basic frame issues and
the image of the therapist, so the distinction is largely a
heuristic one, though nonetheless extremely useful.

This principle will help you to understand the experiences of
your patients. Every patient, will consciously, and especially
unconsciously, monitor the state of the framework, of the
therapist's hold, and, to extend it a bit, of his containing

capacity, and will respond quite sensitively and intensely, largely in derivative form, to any alteration in the ground rules.

And so I offer an hypothesis that this allusion to ambiguity refers not only to the therapist's actual intervention, and to the uncertainties in her unconscious perceptions of his interventions and his inner mental world, but also that it refers in some way to the ambiguities of the bipersonal field and its frame. Perhaps too the boundaries between the patient and the therapist, as she is experiencing them, and as the therapist is encroaching upon them—we will always attempt to distinguish such possibilities—are also ambiguous for the moment; we shall see.

Incidentally, the framework is essential to what Searles (1965, 1970, 1971, 1973) terms the *basic therapeutic symbiosis;* it includes, as I stated, the therapist's neutrality, anonymity, appropriate management of the ground rules, and the use of interventions geared toward neutral interpretations. I am well aware of the limitations and possible misreadings of the metaphor of the frame or framework. I am referring to a largely human frame, or to a human container, and there is a danger of stressing the nonhuman elements of the ground rules, such as the set and established fees, hours, and spatial arrangements, when, of course, it is the human elements that are so crucial. There is also the danger of undue rigidity, although many therapists do indeed need a more rigorous and more functional image of the ground rules than that which they presently apply. Despite all of these limitations, though, I have found it an extremely useful metaphor.

We maintain, then, an effort to identify the specific adaptive context for the patient's material—a search that is to some extent shaped by the patient's ongoing associations and by our own listening process, as well as just a little bit by theory and important therapeutic principles. Remember, that part must remain secondary and open to revision. We will endeavor to allow the patient to direct us anew every time, we allow the associations to direct our search for the adaptive context, and at the same time we monitor the material in terms of Type One derivatives related to the patient herself, her relationship with the therapist, her experience with his interventions, self-representations and therapist-introjects—the me–not-me interface—the status of the framework, and the state of the bipersonal field.

You can begin to experience again how complicated and burdensome the listening process is, but the patient will provide clues that will enable you to move between a very broad and a rather narrow listening approach and to shift freely from one sphere to the other, attempting to locate meaning or to experience its absence, allowing clues to impinge that will then lead you to focus your listening process in a particular area which, if valid, will begin to lead to a coalescence of meaning. We will always, of course, maintain in addition an openness that allows the patient's material to redirect our focus and that permits our own subjective responses to redirect us as well.

You can also see that each major area of listening implies an important area for intervening. Your hypotheses, derived from the listening process, crystallized, and silently confirmed, will become interventions when the patient's material provides the necessary indicator or bridge. We will focus on that aspect of therapeutic work much later on.

One final point that will bring us back to this material and to the specifics of the listening process: you will notice that my comments about the ambiguity of the situation touched first upon the realities of the therapeutic situation, and valid unconscious perceptions, and that for the moment I did not suggest that the patient's sense of ambiguity may be based on some type of inner psychopathology or mental disturbance; I think that would have been an injustice, largely because I can myself validate an unconscious perception of ambiguity in the therapeutic situation on several levels. This patient may well have a sense of inner cloudiness and a disturbance in processing incoming information, but I hope that you can see that such problems could not be identified so long as the therapist has created an ambiguous therapeutic situation and is conveying messages to the patient that unconsciously are contradictory and confusing. This is a small example of what I mean when I state that the patient's psychopathology will be hidden and embedded within the therapist's countertransferences so long as their influence exists unrectified within the bipersonal field. I do believe, however, that the appropriate rectification and interpretation of experiences of this kind can also serve the patient therapeutically.

It is paradoxical that when a therapist intervenes erroneously—when he realistically puts into the bipersonal field countertransference-based interventions and misman-agements of the framework—the patient's communications will be primarily veridical, in the realm of nontransference, even focused unconsciously on the actual psychopathology of the therapist, and only secondarily distorted and in the realm of transference. In contrast, when you have a secure field, a proper communicative medium, and make a correct interpre-tation, the patient's communications will fall primarily into the realm of self-pathology, fantasy, and transference, and you will be in a position to analyze the intrapsychic distortions and pathological introjects. The realities will still be present, but secondary.

Therapist: Something must have been bothering me since the last time—not only bothering me, but I'm not clear on it. In respect to the intervention that I made last time, you said there was one part of it that was empathic in nature, and that the second part was confronting—you remember, the second part being to the effect that it's interesting to me that you continually denigrate therapy, but work on the outside. Doesn't confrontation play a role as an intervention, or was the juxtaposition of a confrontation and a more empathic statement bothersome to you?

Langs: It isn't a question of bothersome to me. It's going to be bothersome to the patient. That's my prediction.

The issues that I raised were not really based on the formulation that one part of your intervention was empathic and one part was confronting. No. What we will get to—and this again is more in the area of intervening than it is of listening—is that what is crucial is not the manifest nature of an intervention—silence, clarifications, confrontations, inter-pretations, reconstructions, and questions—but the uncon-scious communications that they contain. That's really what I tried to identify, because the adaptive context for the session we're about to hear would be not only the manifest message, but the latent message as well.

Confrontations play a role in therapy. However, I would say that they should really play a relatively minor role. I think there are very few indications for confrontations. Most interventions should be interpretive, and I think that most noninterpretive interventions are not valid, that they have a measure of countertransference. A major pathological aspect of confrontations is that they serve therapists as a primary vehicle for expressing aggression against their patients, which is not out of phase with our formulation of your confrontation. They tend unconsciously to be a justified way of attacking a patient, for whatever reason.

Therapist: So you're just really conceptualizing the field, rather than talking about the practicalities of interventions?

Langs: Yes, for now, at least. While you can see that it is difficult for me to restrain myself and not get into a wide range of side issues, largely because they are also quite pertinent to the listening process, for the present, we will focus on listening. It bothers me a bit to make statements without documenting and validating them, and I promise to do just that later on in this course, but I don't think that we can entirely ignore these other issues. Ultimately, we are attempting to generate a conception of the therapeutic situation as a whole, and the more complete and accurate that conception, the more valid your listening will be. Let's get back to some more material.

Therapist: She said, Furthermore, he's not a good person, he's a bad person. I . . .

Langs: See, it's interesting. You were expecting to get further than that in your presentation, were you? You haven't learned yet.

Therapist:Well, I hoped to.

Langs: I suspect that you'll quickly learn that I really believe I have a lot to say, that I hear an enormous amount in very tiny segments of material. You can be certain that I will interrupt you as soon as I hear something that is pertinent to the listening process, and to the validation of the concepts I have been developing.

You will find that I always apply the listening process to my own silent hypotheses and, more broadly, to the general discussions that are generated by the material from both patient and therapist, and that I intend to validate this particular discussion.

I just finished stressing that there are two basic areas to monitor within the therapeutic situation: one, the field or medium and its framework, and two, the therapist and what he communicates. If you have been following this material, this patient had just said that the situation is ambiguous, alluding unconsciously to the field and frame, and now she says that he's actually not a good person, he's a bad person— referring unconsciously to the therapist. In this way, in sequence, she has addressed the two very areas that I have touched upon, and in terms that support my specific formulations. I take this as a form of validation of my discussion and hypothesis, through indirect Type Two derivatives.

I am always impressed with how a patient, in a sentence or two, can quite unconsciously and pithily condense what I have said consciously and in elaborate form.

The therapist, she implies, is manifestly trying to be a good person but nonetheless comes across—as a therapist—as a bad person. That comment leads me into another lecture that I have often given: the means through which a therapist is a good person to his patients are distinctly different from the means through which he is a good person in social relationships. A good-therapist introject is derived from the therapist's capacities to maintain the hold of the patient—the framework—to contain and interpret the patient's projective identifications, and to interpret as well the latent contents of the patient's derivatives. All other efforts—deviations in the framework, noninterpretive interventions, and such—while well intended as a rule, generate bad or destructive introjects.

Without pursuing that concept further, I would like briefly to establish the nature of the validating process, since it is such an essential component of the listening process. Here again, there are few papers in the analytic literature on this subject, and I refer you to my own earlier writings (Langs, 1974,1976b,—chapter 18—and 1978a); in these places, I have summarized the previous literature and have attempted to delineate the validating process in some detail.

In brief, the whole sequence entails listening to the patient's communications and receiving his projective identifications, processing all of this information, including your subjective responses, toward a silent hypothesis, listening further to the material from the patient for validation, rectifying or managing the frame or offering an interpretive intervention as seems necessary, and then listening for confirmation, essentially through the communication of what Bion (1962) has termed the *selected fact*—a bit of material that provides an entirely new means of organizing and understanding what has previously been known. This I term *validation through Type Two derivatives*. In addition, confirmatory responses involve the appearance of derivatives of positive introjective identifications with the therapist who has intervened correctly.

Each of these steps is related to the listening process and is quite complex. So far, we have been focusing not only on the intaking aspects of the listening process, but also on listening to our own interventions, and to some extent on listening to the patient for validation or its absence.

I am well aware that the basic model that I have offered stresses the role of the patient, and emphasizes the extent to which the patient shapes the therapist's listening. I have done so largely because there has not been, in the past, sufficient emphasis on the importance, technically, of allowing the patient to do just that, on the interactional qualities of listening, and on the patient as a positive resource within the therapeutic relationship. But as an interactional product, the listening process is also open to active influences from the therapist, which can shape and even evoke much of the patient's output. We are dealing with an endlessly circular or spiraling process with, at best, an ill-defined beginning. Though we must arbitrarily identify an evocation and response in order to organize the material, we must nonetheless recognize that a particular evocation has its own previous evocative history, and may have been prompted by a prior communication.

The point, then, is to recognize, for example, that the therapist may well evoke certain communications and projective identifications from the patient, and that this will, of course, influence the experiences to which his listening process is subjected; he is by no means entirely passive. Similarly, the patient's communications evoke reactions in the therapist—here, in the form of dealing with the framework or intervening verbally—so that what the patient listens to is also very much under the influence of his own evocative efforts.

Discussant: There are sessions that I have had where a patient has gone on a whole session and I've said almost nothing, and at the end of the session I get a feeling that the patient is aware of the fact that I've said nothing, and in a sense is looking at me, as though, at least, let there be acknowledgement, let there be something. And I often feel bad, if there is nothing in particular that I have formulated, that I'm going to comment on, if I don't think the timing would be right for some sort of interpretative comment. I feel bad about the silence—I'm not giving anything—and I can sense in the patient the desire for something. Now to what extent is that to be used?

Langs: There is no way we could formulate the basis for the patient's response to your silence. That is, silence can be valid or invalid and it can be giving in important ways, or depriving. If it is valid and appropriate because there was no interpretation to make, it is a positive communication to the patient. I really believe that we can listen to a session and decide whether or not there is a valid interpretation that could be made, and I think we can state its nature, and can confirm our assessment. I think the field is much more definitive than most people believe.

Discussant: Do you include matters of timing?

Langs: Yes, including timing. On the one hand, the session may have been such that you did not pick up the appropriate adaptive context, did not hear the derivatives that you should have heard, and did not make a necessary interpretation, and the patient is responding to that. On the other hand, your silence may have been quite appropriate, and the patient's reaction carries other implications. We would need the specific material from that session, to which we would apply the listening process, to make this distinction. Without that material, you are describing a direct complaint—manifest content—and asking for an explanation that can only be made on the basis of the preceding material, manifest and latent. You must understand the unconscious meaning of the complaint.

That is why I feel that your sincerely offered summary is a form of noncommunication—a variation of the psychoanalytic cliché—mistakenly suggesting that such manifest experiences demonstrate that the patient must be offered something specific each session, and that the good therapist intervenes in every session, and only the bad therapist is silent. Bear in mind what I just said—that the good therapist conveys those qualities in a manner that is different from what it is in a social situation. Socially, if you are silent all night, something is usually the matter. In psychotherapy, if you are silent in a session where the patient has not communicated interpretable derivatives, especially related to the prevailing resistances, so that the silence is quite appropriate to the material of the session, you have behaved as a good therapist, holding, containing, and waiting. Had you intervened, you would have been a bad therapist, commenting because of some countertransference-based need and because of some distorted perception of the material. In part because of countertransference influnces, it takes therapists a long time to learn the distinctive properties of valid therapeutic work, especially those qualities that run contrary to the socially accepted standards of behavior and interaction. Sadly, some therapists never ever learn this distinction, while every patient unconsciously appreciates it and needs to be treated accordingly.

In principle, any protest from the patient should direct you to reformulate the material, to explore your counter-transferences, to search for missed interpretations or a mismanagement of the frame, and if nothing else emerges, or as a final step in the process, to consider some inappropriate basis within the patient for the protest. Remember: reality before fantasy, and the therapist before the patient—although eventually everything. Let's hear more now.

Therapist: Okay. She said, He's a bad person. I really don't want to have anything to do with him, but even though I don't want him, I still feel rejected. I don't know why rejection hits me so hard—maybe it has something to do with other experiences, as you suggested. But it's certainly difficult for me to see that, if it's true. Not only that, it seems that whether I reject or am rejecting, it's almost the same—it's almost the same. And she was quiet for a time, and then she said, Of course, as we talked about it, I did have that episode with my father, which was a severe rejection. And then I asked her, Could you tell me something more about that episode?

Langs: Okay. What I like most about you is that you are the typical resident, and you're making the typical interventions. (Laughter.) It's marvelous, because it gives me a chance to give the typical lectures—that is, to give the ones that everyone really needs. This is interesting, because she had already told me my suspicions were well founded when she quoted an earlier intervention of yours. Now you make a similar comment, here in the session, and we can work it over.

So let's begin again by taking this from the vantage point of the listening process. You've heard the material, you've heard the intervention. Of course, the intervention reflects what the therapist has "heard"; what is that? Has anybody heard anything else?

Discussant: I think she's questioning whether or not the therapist is being helpful to her. And she's sort of saying, You are suggesting that maybe this has something to do with the past, but I'm not so convinced that that's the case.

Langs: Yes. Now reflect upon what you've just said. How have you formulated this material?

Discussant: In terms of the relationship with the therapist, and the framework.

Langs: Well, you've just added something—the framework—but can you identify what you are doing?

Discussant: I'm formulating in terms of her experiences with the therapist.

Langs: Right. So what have you done with this material? What type of formulation are you offering? Were you working with manifest content, Type One or Type Two derivatives? (Pause.) Allow me to lead you: have you addressed the manifest content?

Discussant: No.

Langs: No. Well then, have you given me a Type One derivative, manifest content which you read for latent content, without a specific adaptive context. Type Two would be formulated and organized around a precipitant, a day residue, an adaptive context.

Discussant: I believe that I was offering a Type One derivative, that is, a formulation based on inferences from the manifest content, involving the therapeutic relationship.

Langs: Yes. Your formulation demonstrates that we can conceptualize Type One derivatives in a variety of ways, ranging from a rather general impression or formulation to a far more specific conception.

Your formulation was rather general, a broad suggestion that this material related to the therapist, rather than an attempt to identify possible specific unconscious fantasies and perceptions. You alluded to some dissatisfaction with the treatment, but did not attempt to make use of or translate the additional, specific derivatives. It is important to be as specific and as precise as possible; once you have identified the more general themes you must attempt to be more definitive. This will be reflected in the nature of your interventions, which will vary from those that are quite vague and general, to those that are quite specific. There is a tendency among therapists to listen for general themes and to disregard specifics, especially as they relate to unconscious perceptions of the manifestations of their countertransferences, and to the patient's instinctual drive expressions. Therapists tend to generalize painful and specific material as a means of detoxifying it and rendering it essentially without meaning.

These attitudes and countertransference-based needs will be reflected, of course, in the therapist's interventions. Some therapists might listen to this material and point out to the patient that she seemed to have some conflict about men—a general intervention based on the manifest content of this material and a very minor degree of inference. Others might suggest that the patient stays with men who are punitive, while those therapists who inappropriately like to use technical jargon might suggest to the patient that she is masochistic. They would be working with manifest content, adding superficial or relatively apparent inferences, and actually offering psychoanalytic clichés (Langs, 1978).

Had your comment been offered as an intervention—and technically, we would wait until the patient offered derivatives more closely related to or openly referring to the therapeutic relationship, and, then utilize those associations as a bridge that would permit us to connect all of the earlier material to the therapeutic interaction—it might have been to the effect that the patient seems to be questioning whether treatment and you, the therapist, are being helpful. This would constitute a general interpretation or confrontation based on the use of Type One derivatives. Considering this simply as a model intervention, I can suggest that it lacks specificity, especially ignores the fact that the patient represented her relationship with the therapist in terms of her relationship with her boyfriend, and does not attempt to define what the patient means by rejection as it pertains to the therapeutic relationship.

In general, it is characteristic of interventions based on Type One derivatives to be rather superficial generalizations, open to countertransference-based influences, selective in the contents that are addressed, incomplete, and perhaps concealing a more important truth that would have been derived if the therapist had used the adaptive context to organize the material. This type of intervention probably should be restricted to those situations where the therapist lacks an adaptive context, and wishes to play back as Type One derivatives, selected manifest themes and inferences with the expectation that the patient would then provide the adaptive context, which, as a rule, would be related to a repressed aspect of the therapeutic relationship.

Some of this, I suspect, may be a bit vague and confusing, and we will return to these issues again and again in subsequent meetings. For the moment, I am attempting to show you how the level at which you apply the listening process influences the nature of your interventions, and having said quite enough about that subject for the moment, I will ask for further comments. Does anyone wish to add another formulation or intervention or to evaluate the therapist's intervention further?

Discussant: The thing that I sort of hear is that the therapist missed an interpretation when the patient said that whether she's rejected or whether she does the rejecting, she ends up feeling the same. I would have to feel that she wanted him to ask her about that—that she feels rejected.

Langs: Please, if you are proposing an intervention indicate as clearly as you can exactly what you might have said to the patient. This is often difficult to do, but it will help you to crystallize your own thinking in your work with your patients.

I very much appreciate your having introduced the concept of a possible missed intervention. It is an important and neglected area, and we will propose from time to time in this seminar that particular interventions have been missed, formulate them specifically, and listen to the subsequent material for validation.

You are suggesting that you might have intervened at a particular point in this session. What would you have said?

Discussant: I would have intervened, especially if she were silent after she brought up that point. Let me see. Perhaps something like this: When you say you end up feeling the same whether you reject someone or you are rejected, I wondered why you feel that happening?

Langs: There seems to be a preference for offering your own interventions, rather than evaluating the intervention that the therapist made. I am, in fact, quite pleased that both of you proposed alternative formulations and suggested interventions that the therapist may have missed. It deflects me a bit from the comments that I will make about the therapist's actual intervention, but it provides us an opportunity to study the precipitates of your own personal listening process.

Your intervention is, formally, a question, but that is undoubtedly among the least significant of its communicative properties. This intervention addresses itself to the manifest content; it lacks entirely any sense of consideration of derivatives, either Type One or Type Two, and there is no attempt whatsoever to identify an adaptive context.

You'll notice too that the communication that you have commented upon is, itself, quite vague—it's about being rejected by someone. You accept its vagueness and ask a question that is also rather ambiguous. While ambiguity certainly has its place in the therapeutic process, here, I suspect that it will promote rumination and intellectualization, sheer speculation, and avoidance of specific fantasies and perceptions, especially as they pertain to the therapeutic relationship.

Your intervention bears some similarity to the last intervention that the therapist made, even though the particular distraction offered to the patient is rather different: you proposed that she consciously wonder about why she feels the same whether she is rejected or does the rejecting, while the therapist proposed that the patient talk more about a time in the past when her father rejected her. Now, neither of these proposals has much immediate relevance, and I suspect that only when the patient responds with material that does not meaningfully illuminate the intervention or lead to truly new understanding of her conflicts, and becomes even more defensive and resistant, that you will be convinced that listening and intervening in terms of manifest content, whatever it may be, will not further the therapeutic work, but will instead offer the patient a set of underlying interactional defenses (Langs, 1976a, b).

You can readily see that your particular question addresses the surface of this material, and you might also sense that these associations may be alternatively formulated as derivatives containing unconscious perceptions and fantasies relevant to the therapeutic relationship, prompted in part by the therapist's interventions in the previous hour. Your proposed intervention is an effort to simplify a complex situation, have the patient ruminate about why she feels a particular way. You are narrowing the communicative field rather than allowing her to associate freely in a manner that might offer additional derivatives that would soon begin to coalesce. This is why, as I said, your comment would push the patient toward the development of an interactional, obsessional or ruminative defense, generated by the two of you, and designed to protect both of you from her unconscious fantasies and feelings toward you.

Your decision to ask an isolated question about rejection and rejecting shows that you are not attempting to allow the patient's associations to coalesce, to accumulate around images, to develop into themes and variations, to generate silent hypotheses about unconscious perceptions or fantasies, or to reveal their possible connections to yourself as therapist. Instead, you appear more interested in her thinking about why she feels in a strange and unusual kind of way; you are more interested in her speculations than her actual feelings and fantasies, her direct associations, rather than indirect communications. You show that you wish her to ruminate about abstract issues rather than deal with more defined, instinctual drive-related, and disturbing concerns that would ultimately involve the therapeutic relationship.

So your seemingly innocuous question turns out to have many important unconscious functions and meanings, some defensive, for both yourself and your patient. If her confusion about rejecting and being rejected is of significance, there is no need for you to ask any specific questions about it; the unconscious meanings and functions of this bit of confusion will emerge quite naturally and spontaneously through the patient's subsequent associations. I want to stress that point because many therapists feel that when the patient begins to communicate something important it is essential that they ask questions. They fail to recognize that such queries direct the patient to the surface of her thoughts, and will interfere with the spontaneous flow of derivatives of unconscious fantasies and perceptions—her use of the crucial indirect communicative mode. The best mode of questioning, in terms of effective psychotherapeutic technique, takes the form of the therapist's silence. Such a silence implies: Tell me more— associate further—give me the links to this particular conscious fantasy, anxiety, symptom, or whatever. Direct questions actually interfere with that type of unfolding. They tend to be based on misconceptions of the therapeutic process and psychopathology, in which work with manifest content is erroneously seen as useful and there is a general ignorance of, and difficulty working with, derivative communication of both types.

Much of this anticipates the comments that I want to make about the therapist's actual intervention. First, does anyone else wish to add anything?

Discussant: I would have made an intervention at the same point that he made his intervention, but I would have made it a little differently. When she's talking about rejecting—"It

hurts whether I the therapist do the rejecting or someone else
does the rejecting"—the thought that comes to my mind is
someone who rejects to avoid rejection, who rejects first
because she feels an incipient rejection and thus, almost
prophylactically, it is better that the relationship should be
terminated from her point of view, rather than her being
rejected.

Langs: So how would you have intervened?

Discussant: In terms of the adaptive context, I think it had
to do with what she said before, from last session. I don't know
what happened at the beginning of this session, but she had
said last session that she didn't think they were getting
anywhere, she didn't know if he could help her. In other words,
what I think is going on is that she's perceiving, or worrying
about, a certain rejection on the therapist's part, and she's
going to try, in a sense, to provoke it or to bring the issue to a
head, by rejecting him first. I would have intervened at that
point . . .

Langs: By saying?

Discussant: With a question: Is it important who makes the
first rejection? Or, Is it important who is rejected and who does
the rejecting?

Langs: Yes; thinking again that your particular question
would lead her into further material related to the therapeutic
relationship. I have just commented on my evaluation of such
questions, and stated my preference for silence as an
alternative. I might add now, in view of the popularity of such
questions, that the use of silence also permits the patient to
convey a wide range of indirect and seemingly unrelated
derivatives that will bring with them important surprises,
connections that you might not otherwise discover.
Again briefly, in respect to your particular intervention, let
me say this: you first talked about how she defensively rejects
before being rejected. If you had stopped there, and I want to

do this as a model, once again, what you would have been suggesting is that it is important, in and of itself, in isolation, to show her that she defends herself against a threat of rejection by rejecting first. There is a tendency among therapists to think intrapsychically about the patient and to divorce contents and even mental mechanisms from interactions, especially the therapeutic interaction. They're listening only for intrapsychic contents and defenses, they don't connect it to the therapeutic relationship and interaction, and they isolate these communications in terms of intrapsychic processes.

This is a style of therapy characterized mainly by work with manifest contents or Type One derivatives, translating the manifest content into some unconscious mechanism, often on a very general level, and then playing it back to the patient. All of this serves, of course, to keep the patient away from the therapeutic relationship and offers interactional defenses as well.

Now, when you go on to say that you feel that this is what was going on in the therapeutic relationship, then we enter a more specific realm of meaning. We then look for a definitive adaptive context within the therapeutic relationship. You just formulated that she anticipates being rejected, so she's thinking of rejecting him first—that is a Type One derivative. Now, where would that come from? Can you convert it into a hypothesized Type Two derivative?

Discussant: Her feeling of intended rejection by the therapist.

Langs: What does that mean? Based on what?

Discussant: To avoid anger.

Langs: Well, it could, on some level, have to do with avoiding anger, but there's a specific adaptive context that I have in mind.

Discussant: Do we have a vacation coming up or something?

Langs: A vacation, or what else?

Discussant: Termination.

Langs: Yes, termination. Clinic patients are always preoccupied with the ultimate and usually forced or premature termination of their treatment. Since this is your final year at this center, whether she specifically knows that or not, she must be concerned on some level that there are less than six months left to her therapy here. Now, whether you've told her anything about that as yet or not, patients know what's going on.

Therapist: I could take her into private practice. (Laughter.)

Langs: She should only stay around that long—but that's what this course is about, helping you to do just that.

You can see how the detection of a general theme can often lead you toward a specific adaptive context, and that somewhere within your mind you keep a catalogue of potential adaptive contexts, especially those related to the frame and to your interventions. You will find that at the beginning of every calendar year, with the anticipation of a forced termination in the coming June, this rather traumatic modification of the framework will have a considerable impact on all of your patients.

So, she has said the situation is ambiguous, and she's now getting around to one aspect of that ambiguity: possible rejection, though it may well be that, in addition, your interventions have a kind of rejecting quality and the patient is specifically concerned with your ultimately rejecting her. This is a silent hypothesis, derived from the listening process, that we will leave open for confirmation.

You suggested a rather open-ended question about rejecting and being rejected, and it does leave room for the possibility that she will get around to talking about her relationship with the therapist. However, as I said before, I would rather maintain that question as a silent hypothesis and allow the patient to continue her associations, permitting her to shape the flow of the material, and convey to me more dimensions of the meanings of her communications.

Still, your suggestion that a question might help her to communicate brings us back to the issue I discussed just a moment ago: the listening process is not merely a passive process; though it entails an essentially passive attitude, it does not by any means simply imply silent expectations. Let's now review this aspect: the material that a therapist gets to listen to is influenced not only by his silences, but by two other major factors—what are they?

Discussant: His interventions.

Langs: And? You haven't caught on yet? What's the other area?

Discussant: The nonverbal level?

Langs: In what area? Our interventions have verbal and nonverbal qualities.

Discussant: Confirmation?

Langs: No. Confirmation is a different type of concept. What's the other area?(Pause.) You see, it's interesting; this group is typical. This is where almost everyone else has a blind spot too. I identified for you two spheres. How quickly we forget.

Discussant: The framework?

Langs: Yes, the ground rules. Don't you think that the nature of the framework, the conditions of treatment, are going to determine important aspects of the patient's communications? It is every bit as influential as your verbal interventions, and more basic too. What you hear from the patient and what it truly means will depend on your interventions, silences through reconstructions, and your management of the framework. As I said, the influence of the management of the framework supercedes the role of your interventions; there's a whole area for discussion there.

Discussant: Could you give us a quick idea about what you mean by the management of the framework?

Langs: The way in which you handle the ground rules. I'm using the term *framework* to allude to all of the ground rules of psychotherapy: the basic ground rules of set fees, hours locale, and the patient, let's say, face to face. I assume that's how most or all of you see your psychotherapy patients, though I don't now believe that's an essential ground rule. What is necessary is to define the position as part of the frame, and to maintain it as established. Many therapists see psychotherapy patients on the couch. I had said earlier (Langs, 1973) that I thought this was disastrous, but I no longer think so. I have found that one can do very effective psychotherapy with the patient on the couch. We'll leave that as an open question. Maybe you'll provide us with some data some day. So, set position, either face to face or on the couch, the patient's free associations—the fundamental rule—and the therapist's basic neutrality, anonymity, and use of interventions that are neutral and geared toward interpretations. There are also many implicit ground rules, such as not touching the patient, the understanding that communications occur only in the office and within the time limits of the session—things of that sort.

I have explored this area in a concentrated way for at least six or seven years (Langs, 1973a, 1975b). I have tested these ground rules explicitly, and have validated them using psychoanalytic methodology again and again. Remarkably enough, I cannot suggest a new ground rule that should replace any of the basic tenets that are now established. I have found that their total accumulated effect creates a viable medium for therapeutic work in both psychoanalysis and in psychotherapy. I have concluded, for the moment, that we are using an optimal set of ground rules, and I have tested this hypothesis against Freud's own case histories (Langs, 1976c, in press a, b), and found that there too, when Freud deviated from his own standards, and from those of present day analysis and therapy, there were disruptive responses similar to those observed in today's patients.

You'll find, as Viderman (1974) so nicely described, that every patient will test the ground rules: ask for a change of hour or for an extension in a session, or want to go away on a unilateral vacation. Or he'll become frightened and attempt to evoke nonneutral interventions. The manner in which the therapist handles these tests of the frame quite significantly reflects the state of his own intrapsychic balances, his own inner capacity to manage, and the degree to which he does, indeed, wish to create a truly communicative bipersonal field.

While there is considerably more that I could say about the ground rules, allow me simply to add this because it is specifically related to the listening process: for classical psychoanalysts, as reflected in the writings of Greenacre (1954, 1959) and Greenson (1967), for example, and as first stated by Freud (1912b), adhering to the ground rules is related to safeguarding the transference, that is, to allowing the patient to express his neurosis in derivative form on its own terms, without contamination from the analyst. In addition, these analysts imply, and Milner(1952) and Tarachow (1962) explicitly stated, that the ground rules are essential to what has been termed the *transference illusion.* In essence, these rules are vital to the communication of the patient's unconscious transference fantasies and derivatives in analyzable form. An alteration in the ground rules was seen as a means of gratifying the patient's transference wishes, fixating them as actual and verified in external reality, and interfering significantly with their analytic resolution. Freud made the point several times, especially in a paper on the psychoanalytic movement in 1914.

I trust that you can sense from this brief review that in one form or another, classical analysts have recognized that the framework is a critical factor in determining the nature of the communications from the patient. When it is maintained, these communications take on an "as-if quality" and constitute what I have termed analyzable derivatives of unconscious transference fantasies and perceptions (Langs,

1976b); but when the frame is modified, the patient's communications, in some way not entirely specified by these analysts, no longer maintain their as-if quality. The underlying neurotic wishes have been gratified, and their analysis precluded.

The concepts that I am developing in this course are, in part, an extension of these initial ideas. In respect to the listening process, one of the issues, then, that underlies these tests of the framework involves the nature of the communications that will unfold within the therapeutic bipersonal field—the properties of the communicative medium and interaction. For reasons that I will soon detail, patient and therapist may both welcome and dread the communication of Type Two derivatives and the unconscious fantasies, memories, and introjects that they convey, especially as they are related to the therapeutic relationship, since they evoke a strong sense of regression and anxiety which is nonetheless potentially therapeutic in quite important ways. Still, the dread prevails, and efforts are made to resolve the underlying anxieties through what I have termed *framework cures,* modifications in the ground rules that provide immediate but maladaptive relief for patient, therapist, or both.

You can see that I am indicating that the framework determines the attributes of the communicative medium, which, in turn, determines the nature, meaning, and function of the communications from each participant. Before we get into the different types of communicative bipersonal fields, though, I want to be sure that we understand the nature of manifest content, Type One, and Type Two derivatives first, since those concepts are fundamental to the delineation of communicative fields.

We've all heard such aphorisms as "the medium is the message," and I am saying that the medium also determines the message, and that the medium must be uncontaminated and free flowing; when it is disturbed, it must be rectified and interpreted as a necessary and insightful prelude to the exploration of other messages—contents and defenses. This all has important implications for the listening process: we attend not only to contents and indications of intrapsychic and interactional defenses and resistances, we must also monitor the state of the communicative medium itself, and the factors that influence that state—a level of listening that has been quite neglected in the analytic literature.

Now, I want to come back to the intervention made by this therapist. A great deal of discussion has taken place since you presented the material that preceded your intervention and the intervention itself; perhaps it will help if you would repeat that segment of the session once again.

Therapist: Okay. She was saying, I don't know why rejection hits me so hard—maybe it has something to do with other experiences, as you suggested. But it is certainly difficult for me to see it; whether I'm rejected or I'm doing the rejecting, it's almost the same. Of course, I did have that significant episode of rejection with my father. Then, after a brief silence, I say, Tell me more about that episode.

Langs: Okay, so this is a directive—a kind of question or effort at clarification. It indicates that the therapist has heard this material in terms of a manifest theme of rejection and that he is now attempting to develop some genetic material related to that theme—solely, for the moment, in terms of the intrapsychic processes of the patient and her personal past history, divorced from current adaptive context or the therapeutic interaction. I'm going to teach you that this approach is never effective, and that it is always in the service of countertransferences. But before I say too much: what function is this inquiry into her genetics made to serve? What's the main unconscious message in this intervention? Apply the listening process to the therapist's comment.

Discussant: It seems to me that she's perceiving that he doesn't want to listen to her talking about him.

Langs: Right. He is saying, Let's talk about your father in the past, rather than about me in the present. So it's really the offer of an interactional defense. He's proposing to her the use of displacement and intellectualization too, because I predict that her response will, in part, be rather intellectualized, as a defense against talking about the therapeutic relationship, directly or indirectly. This is an effort to preclude the expression of further transference and nontransference derivatives.

You know, some analysts (e.g. Kanzer, 1952; Szasz, 1963; Chertok, 1968) have taken a hard look at the concept of transference as discovered by Freud, and have concluded that for him, the concept served some defensive purposes; and many analysts since have also seized upon the genetic transference hypothesis as a means of denying that they actually were behaving in a seductive or hostile fashion that recapitulated earlier traumas for the patient.

Racker (1957) indicated that it is very crucial to distinguish the actual repetition of past traumas in the therapeutic relationship from the patient's fantasy that this is occurring. Margaret Little (1951) commented that every interpretation of transference implies a denial that the therapist has actually behaved in that particular way. And therapists do not consider reality first and distortion second: the relationship is called the transference, and the patient is always distorting; it turns out, of course that often this is not the case.

The main function, then, of this intervention is, I believe, to move away from the therapeutic relationship. And I predict that the patient will comply initially, share the defense and misalliance (Langs, 1976a), and share, too, what the Barangers (1966) call a *bastion*—a split-off segment of the communicative field—here referring to the sealing off from this communicative field of derivatives, and especially the build-up of more direct references related to the therapeutic relationship. I also predict that eventually she will try to cure you of your countertransference and help you to rectify your errors, bring them to your attention in some unconscious way, and even work them over for you through unconscious interpretations based on her introjected experience of these communications.

Now I don't mean in any way to imply that I do not accept the genetic point of view or that I reject the importance of genetic material, reconstructions, and interpretive work in this area. But I do suggest that such efforts may, when ill-timed, serve the defenses of both patient and therapist, rather than the resolution of the patient's neurosis through the meaningful analysis of its genetic basis. You must always be alert to the possible defensive use of genetic exploration, and attempt to understand the connections to the here and now, especially in terms of the therapeutic relationship. You must be quite certain that the genetic material is unfolding spontaneously from the patient, that it can be understood in terms of a current adaptive context, as well as of past relationships, and that it is meaningful material, rather than intellectualized and defensive.

In the situation that we are discussing, the therapist heard a series of associations and for reasons of his own decided to select the genetic material for conscious exploration, on the basis of a single allusion to her father. This, in a sense, is a modification of neutrality, of open listening to all material, falsely justified by a theoretical recognition of the importance of genetic material that is nonetheless inappropriately selected for the moment. It leads me to encourage you once again to sit back, to allow the patient to shape the session, to allow material to cluster and coalesce—to agglutinate—rather than working with a rather flat segment here or there. Now please continue.

Therapist: Okay, so she said, It's difficult to remember. You know, it's been so many years, so much has happened; it's difficult to recall.

Langs: Yes, so much has happened, and so much is happening now. Actually, she's not so ready to join in the misalliance as I had anticipated, but we'll see.

Therapist: So anyway, she says, I thought I was pregnant, and the guy and I went over to his father, and he hit the roof, a big scene. Then we went over to my father with his parents, and my father also hit the roof. After that there was . . .

Langs: Okay. Now what aspect of the frame does this touch upon? How nicely she adds to what I have already discussed.

Discussant: It sounds seductive.

Langs: Yes; anything else?

Discussant: The framework—the therapist's hostility.

Langs: Right. But anything else? Something basic to the ground rules. (Pause.) Well, she describes something that has happened that is very personal and secretive. It reminded me that I did not mention before that among the basic ground rules of therapy is the one-to-one relationship and total confidentiality, which again, never exists in a clinic, so it always comes up as an issue, usually quite indirectly, as is true here.

Therapist: Right! (Laughter.) And not only that, it's actually a real issue, because I had to talk to this patient's family to get her into therapy when she made her first suicide attempt. And when she came into psychotherapy with me, there was an issue of confidentiality, which has continued to be an overt issue, not only a latent issue.

Langs:What did you do with the family?

Therapist: I had to tell the family that she hadn't come back after being seen in the emergency room.

Langs: How did you contact them?

Therapist: There was a phone number left on the chart.

Langs: So you called the family because the patient had not come back for her sessions—there was a specific break in the frame, justified because she was a suicidal patient who had not come back to treatment.

Therapist: Yes.

Langs: And they then pressured her into coming in.

Therapist: Yes.

Langs: So this is a very specific issue. In detecting its presence, I have demonstrated several facets of the listening process. I have already told you that we should monitor the material from the patient for allusions to the therapeutic interaction and to the unconscious nature of the therapist's interventions and the state of the framework. I have suggested that patients are exquisitely sensitive to any alteration in the frame, and that such deviations generate specific adaptive contexts to which patients respond intensively. Here we touch upon the ground rule of the one-to-one relationship and total confidentiality, and the theme of everybody knowing, of third parties to sensitive information, arises. This new piece of history quite nicely converts these derivatives from Type One to Type Two, though only in terms of a past aspect of the therapeutic experience. I should alert us to her detection of a related, current deviation as well.

You have, then, a demonstration of the way listening to general themes can alert you to specific adaptive contexts, and how we make use of Type One derivatives for their discovery. At the point at which we identify a specific adaptive context, we can then reexplore the same derivatives as Type Two derivatives built around the particular precipitant. The patient gives an extremely lucid description of your need to contact the family in order to continue her treatment in the face of a suicide threat. That is an apparently necessary modification of the frame that nonetheless contains significant unconscious hostility and seductiveness. In fact, I would stress that it is important to be aware of the extent to which that telephone call unconsciously had such qualities, and how it was an invasion of the patient's right to privacy and total confidentiality. Despite its necessity, the patient will undoubtedly respond to these additional dimensions as well.

This emphasizes again how important it is to know the unconscious communications conveyed in your manifest intentions and efforts, and ultimately, to know yourself. Otherwise, you will hear these communications from the patient primarily or almost entirely as unconscious fantasies and distortions, while a more accurate description would be that they contain unconscious perceptions, which the patient may or may not modulate in keeping with the additional realities of the situation. These are qualified truths, then, that should be regarded to some extent in the light of an appreciation of the dangers for the patient.

So, her concerns about hostile seductiveness, her sense of ambiguity, her not knowing where she stands are all rather appropriate responses to your alteration in the framework at the beginning of this treatment. We could only identify as entirely inappropriate in this context the patient's failure to recognize that there were mitigating circumstances. It would be quite unrealistic for you to think of this material entirely as distorted, without recognizing the impact of your telephone call—the veridical core. You can see that the therapeutic work with this material depends on a very sensitive application of the listening process and a very keen appreciation of the nature of the realities.

Once again, we see how absolutely crucial it is to realize in some concrete way the extensive influence that the framework has upon the therapeutic interaction, and upon the actual meanings of the patient's associations. In their preoccupation with unconscious fantasies and their implications, and in their constant search for material from the patient, analysts have tended to forget that there are qualifying factors such as the state in which such material emerges—factors that determine not only the analyzability of that material, but also the extent to which the entire experience either essentially repeats a past pathogenic trauma, confirms the patient's pathological inner world, and further fixates her neurosis or emerges in a setting and relationship that is distinctly different from those elements, and therefore permits the development of cognitive insight and new, rather positive introjects that are health-promoting.

We can no longer think of material as material, and we can no longer think of the listening process as simply a matter of determining the presence of derivatives. We must measure these communications against the nature of the medium, and against the state of reality that prevails, both consciously and unconsciously. So you can see that our search for meaningful material from patients cannot simply be a matter of identifying derivatives, but that it must contain considerations of actuality, especially within the therapeutic interaction, and that this distinction between reality and fantasy is quite crucial in determining whether analytic work or reinforcement of the neurosis will prevail.

Too many analysts utilize as a defense the notion that reality doesn't matter; so long as the material is present, they argue, it can be analyzed. This is in no way true; reality is crucial, just as the patient's unconscious fantasies and introjects are crucial, and reality takes precedence as well. It must be determined in order to understand the degree to which a segment of material is not reality, but distorted fantasy. And for the patient—and forgive me for emphasizing this again, but it is a point that is quite misunderstood—so long as the realities of the therapeutic relationship unconsciously repeat or reinforce past pathogenic, traumatic relationships, so-called analytic work on a verbal level will have no salutary influence, and will not only be confusing, but will also reflect an actual distortion of the patient's communications and a misunderstanding of their unconscious meanings and functions.

There is another quality of these associations that we should all appreciate. I pointed out that the therapist's questions seemed designed to keep the patient focused on early genetic experiences, and away from himself. Nonetheless, you can see the patient's unconscious creativity, and her need to communicate what is bothering her, far more than sharing defenses with the therapist. As I said earlier, this will not always prevail; often, patients will indeed accept a sector of misalliance and bastion, and adopt for long periods of time a series of interactional defenses designed to avoid the crucial, prevailing, adaptive context.

Here, the patient follows the therapist's lead rather skeptically, and goes back to a genetic interlude through which she is able nonetheless to communicate Type Two derivatives related to the therapeutic relationship.

This implies too that if the therapist sits back and listens freely to the material that follows his intervention, he is in a position not only to seek validation but to reformulate. He should apply the listening process to the associations after his intervention in a rather open and free way; he should not remain fixed in his hypothesis but should be open to new manifest themes, to new Type One derivatives with clues to unexpected underlying themes, and to the appearance of an unrecognized adaptive context and a new constellation of Type Two derivatives. When the patient responds to your intervention, think of her as not only letting you know whether you have been correct or incorrect, but also of attempting to expand on your thesis, if it is valid, taking you in as a positive introject but also working over those areas in which you have been in error. If you are listening to the patient in this type of framework, you can learn a great deal, not only about her, but about yourself as well.

We keep coming back to the frame. I have suggested that the framework should be maintained securely, and that the only exceptions are truly dire emergencies. Possibly your telephone call here is such a situation. Beyond that need, we should restrict alterations in the frame to those that the patient truly imposes upon us, such as by being late or something of that sort. Therapists often express an unconscious need to inappropriately modify the frame in many situations that extend beyond these indications. I have demonstrated repeatedly that under these conditions, the patient suffers rather than gains, and though she may consciously express appreciation, her unconscious communications will be filled with anger, feelings of having been seduced, rage at losing her autonomy, and many other negative derivative expressions.

On one level, here, the patient may appreciate your having attempted to behave in a life-saving manner, and to continue her much-needed treatment, but on another level, almost entirely in derivative form, she will express her anger about the invasion of her privacy and autonomy, and of the destructive impact that this will have on the very therapeutic field that she so desperately needs. These modifications in the framework, however justified in an emergency, actually alter the communicative properties of the bipersonal field, and therefore impair the therapeutic work that is so necessary under such circumstances.

Even in an emergency, then, it will be best for the patient if you maintain the therapeutic hold and the communicative properties of the field in "pure" fashion, without modification. When you modify the communicative qualities of the field, you shift the patient toward manifest content and away from unconscious communication; you alter his image of you, and there tends to be a sense of continued and utter chaos, something akin to the kind of material that we are hearing now.

Your interventions will have a great deal to do with what you wish to hear from the patient, and often, this is strongly determined by unconscious factors. Should you dread primitive inner mental contents, the patient's regression, anxiety, unconscious fantasies and introjects, and fear what they will stir up within your own inner mental world, you may so intervene as to modify the communicative properties of the bipersonal field, restrict the patient's communications, and narrow the field to which you apply the listening process. Our influence on the patient's communications is not only determined by our theoretical position—for example, recognition of the importance of derivatives of unconscious fantasies, memories, introjects, and perceptions—but is also open to major countertransference-based influences.

Perhaps some of this seems a bit extended, based on this very small segment of material, but it is my intention to take interludes of this kind as models for extensive discussion, although the validity of the model will certainly depend on my validating my formulations of the therapeutic situation itself. But I have found again and again that when the framework has been modified in some significant way, the patient will come back to those issues repeatedly. Please continue.

Therapist: She said that after that point, there was constant bickering. She had a miscarriage; there was some question about the medical care she received. Her father paid for everything, and still there was constant bickering. He called her a tramp, and there was just no contact in the house.

Langs: You hear again an image of a third-party payer, of accusations against the patient, of questionable medical care. You see how the entire situation changed the way in which the patient communicated with her father, and generated tremendous hostility; eventually, they broke contact. All of these are derivatives to be monitored as both Type One and Type Two derivatives, to be related in general to the therapeutic relationship, specifically to the way in which the therapist has been intervening and to his earlier modifications of the framework. They are, as I have now said quite often, to be monitored in terms of both unconscious fantasy and perception. Please continue.

Therapist: Well, the patient went on: Finally my younger sister arranged a meeting for us—the patient was living out of town at the time, but not too far away, and the father drove there and had dinner with her. The patient remembered being so hungry that she ate for more than an hour before she would even talk to her father. He paid for dinner, and they had a long discussion.

Langs: It is most interesting to apply the listening process to this material. You experience yourself searching for meaning, checking out the material against the adaptive contexts that we have already identified, searching for connecting links that would generate meaningful Type Two derivatives, and you really go nowhewre. You listen to the manifest content; you take this material as Type One derivatives and look for general themes, or for clues to unconscious threads; and again, you meet with frustration. The material is not organizing; it's getting flat and ruminative, and you can sense that the patient is in a state of resistance.

Such a conclusion, however temporary, is most difficult to reach with any degree of confidence. It requires a repeated application of the listening process—of efforts to hear broad themes, to identify adaptive contexts, to organize the material, to allow it to run free, and to attempt to reorganize again. Still, you must develop a capacity to feel confident when at best you decide that there is a lack of meaningful or coalescing derivatives.

I must stress, too, that in making such a decision you must search for your own contributions to this communicative style, and not simply conclude that the patient is using a variety of obsessive or other defenses. As I had predicted earlier, this patient has now accepted the therapist's offer of an interactional defense, and is no longer communicating meaningfully beyond the manifest level. In some ways it is far more difficult to conclude that the patient's associations do *not* have central and important meanings for her neurosis, than it is to discover meaning—a point that I will be discussing with you in our next seminar.

Incidentally, I want to mention, since the patient brought it up, that modifications in the framework, and especially premature terminations, are often experienced as miscarriages and abortions, as failures in the therapist's holding capacity and containing ability, and as disasters for the therapeutic bipersonal field. I shall continue to make efforts to apply this genetic material to the present therapeutic situation. Please continue.

Therapist: She said, he laid down these guidelines for my coming back, for my continued living in his house.

Langs: Developed a set of ground rules?

Therapist: That is, I would have to be in by a certain time. I was to be allowed only this degree of freedom. I told him that he could shove his guidelines up his ass.

Langs: That's fabulous! That's the first patient who's ever told me that. We really must understand why she said this. I think she's saying it because they're a destructive set of rules, a poor frame, as is the case with her therapy. But I must say, really, in all my work with the frame, the unconscious communication has alwaye been enormously positive, so I accept the challenge, in face of all my critics.

Therapist: So I told him I would not live in the house under those guidelines.

Langs: They need restructuring, because they're not viable. This treatment wasn't established under viable conditions. Please continue.

Therapist: So I left the house and after that I moved into an apartment of my own, instead of staying with friends.

Langs: She created her own ground rules, her own setting and hold.

Therapist: Then I mentioned to her that it was in fact she who made the decision to leave the house.

Langs: Time is short, so I will be brief. On the manifest level, this intervention is a confrontation, and you'll notice that while it derives from the patient's material, it is not she who has shaped it or who has communicated derivatives through which it could be developed. I would suggest that the intervention functions as a means of conveying your own unconscious hostile and accusatory attitudes, and reflects further efforts on your part to deflect her manifest communications away from the therapeutic relationship. On another, interactional level, through the countertransference qualities of this intervention, you will mobilize more intense derivatives concerning her relationship with you. Please continue.

Therapist: She said, Yes, but he was in control of the continuing harassment; he wouldn't let up on me.

Langs: Well, that's a rather prompt validation of my silent hypothesis. I will, therefore, make a few additional comments, and I trust that you will continue with this session at our next meeting.

You can see how important it is to take each intervention as an adaptive context for the patient's subsequent communications, and how meaningful it is to organize this material as Type Two derivatives around the latent content of the therapists intervention, deriving in that way an expression of the patient's unconscious perception of the therapist and her introjection of his harassing qualities.

This specific interlude also affords me an opportunity to demonstrate a point that I had mentioned earlier in a more theoretical way. In this situation, where the therapist is in reality, however unconsciously, behaving in a manner that is psychologically identical or similar, on some level, to the behavior of the patient's father, no amount of verbal, so called interpretive work could help her to modify the pathological father introject and related unconscious fantasies and memories that reside within her mind and contribute to her pathology. This material did not reflect essentially transference-based communications, but nontransference. An interpretation—for example, a statement that the patient in some distorted way perceived the therapist as harassing her on the basis of fantasies and memories displaced from earlier experiences with her father—would actually constitute an inappropriate denial of the actualities of the therapist's behavior. It would in no way modify this patient's pathology, but would, instead, enhance or substantiate it.

So you see, it's not the material per se, but the dynamic state of these communications and their true implications that are so essential. This does not imply, by the way, that there is no intervention available to the therapist under these conditions. To the contrary. Technically, this is a modification of the therapist's neutrality and of the framework, and if the therapist became aware of his harassing interventions, either through self-analysis or by monitoring the patient's material for allusions to himself—first in terms of actuality, and only secondarily in terms of fantasy and distortion—he would then rectify the frame, which in this instance implies that he would no longer make hostile and harassing interventions, and then interpret the patient's unconscious perceptions, their extensions in fantasy, and their genetic links to her.

It is here that you can also see quite clearly that nontransference has important genetic counterparts, and that the appearance of genetic material does not necessarily imply transference, but may imply either transference or nontransference. Here, then, the correct interpretation to the patient would be to the effect that she perceived his interventions as somewhat harassing, in a manner that reminded her of her father—a perception that then led to such and such reactions. We would define that latter aspect on the basis of the patient's continuing associations. So, in the adaptive context of the manifest and latent content of the therapist's intervention, we decipher a series of Type Two derivatives and utilize them for an intervention that stresses unconscious perception and its genetics rather than, for the moment, unconscious fantasy-transference and its genetics.

Interactionally, it appears to me from both my own listening to your intervention and from the patient's responses, that your comments had qualities of a countertransference-based projective identification into the patient, of some type of hostile, accusatory, and manipulative introject, which you are placing into the patient for containment, metabolism, and response, possibly as a means of evoking a proxy, that is, in order to evoke adaptive resources that you yourself are unable to mobilize in the face of certain inner pressures. You will notice how nicely it is possible for the therapist—as is true for all human beings—to make use of the material from the patient as a vehicle and even invitation for projective identifications. All interactional mechanisms unfold in this kind of way: unconscious facilitation by the object, unconscious needs within the subject, unconscious effort by the subject to shape the object in a particular way, unconscious response by the object either in the form of compliance or resistance, further reactions by the subject, and so on. These are always active and passive interactional processes, and the object can not only facilitate but also invite projective identifications, just as the subject can unconsciously and actively shape a relationship in a manner that will also promote the discharge of such interactional projections.

I hope that you now have some sense of how, exactly, we listen; if you have begun to develop a sensitivity for this basic tool—and I will have more to say about these processes as we go along—then I have contributed already to your capacity to listen to your patients, and to yourselves.

Discussant: Before we stop, may I ask a final question? In these first two seminars, you've talked a good deal about unconscious fantasies, unconscious memories and introjects, and derivatives. I have some idea of what you're talking about, but I wonder if you couldn't clarify those terms a bit more, since they seem so important.

Langs: Yes. I should not actually assume prior knowledge or consensus of meaning, and those are basic concepts related to the listening process that I have not fully defined. Since time is short, I will outline an answer, and the rest will be clarified as we go on.

If we take the term *unconscious fantasy* as representative or all-inclusive—that is, as alluding to unconscious fantasies, memories, and the related introjects—if we take, then, unconscious fantasy as our model, my basic postulate is that neuroses, again used in the broadest sense of the term, are based on the influence of pathological unconscious fantasies, even in patients with whom ego defects or dysfunctions are postulated. Now, I will refrain from clarifying any side issue, even one as important as the neglect of the role of unconscious fantasy in psychopathology, and especially so-called "preoedipal syndromes"—a problem recently discussed by Slap (1977) in terms of the erosion of the concept of intrapsychic conflict. There is little doubt that one of the unconscious motives for, and consequences of, an overemphasis on developmental defects in recent writings on psychopathology has been avoidance of the effects of primitive intrapsychic conflicts, and the disturbing unconscious fantasies, memories, and introjects on which they are based.

So, I use the term *unconscious fantasy* in a manner first described by Freud (1908, 1912c, 1915b), and later elaborated by a number of analysts such as Beres (1962), Arlow (1963, 1969a,b), and more recently Brenner (1976). In essence, unconscious fantasy activity is conceptualized as a form of day-dreaming, taking place at various levels of conscious availability, expressed in terms of varying degrees of defensive disguise. As with all fantasy activity, unconscious fantasies are a synthesis of expressions from external reality and the id, ego, and superego, speaking structurally. As a rule, they contain elements from various periods in the life of the patient that are often concentrated around a hierarchy or sequence of significant, usually traumatic, experiences.

In my own definition of an unconscious fantasy (Langs, 1976a), I have described it as the unconscious working over of a current adaptive stimulus and its echoes into the past through displaced mental activities and, sometimes, behaviors. That is, an unconscious fantasy is an adaptive effort, in derivative form, related to a particular primary adaptive task. Here, of course, I come to the concept of derivatives—a term that is used to describe manifest thoughts, fantasies, and behaviors that represent, in some disguised and altered way, underlying (that is, unconscious) fantasies which are, as a rule, both pathological and pertinent to the patient's neurosis, though there are, of course, nonpathological unconscious fantasies as well.

The basic model is derived from Freud's description of dream formation and the structure of dreams (Freud, 1900). He applied a similar model to the development of neuroses: namely, that a stimulus in the present serves on some level as a reminder or reinstigation of a past traumatic event related to the patient's psychopathology—to use one basic model of the onset of neuroses for the purposes of this discussion. As for the dream: he argued that some reality event—day residue— evokes the recollection of earlier traumatic experiences and stirs up the unconscious fantasies and memories connected to that earlier trauma, leading to an unconscious working over of the total constellation. Then, as we would now more broadly state it, through the influence of the ego's defenses in response to an id expression, and at the behest of the superego, a manifest dream is produced, containing in some disguised form the pertinent day residue, its earlier genetic counterpart, and the ego's unconscious fantasies and memories—with, for example, representations from the ego, in terms of its defenses; from the superego, in terms of its psychic representations and influence; and from the id, in terms of the aroused instinctual drives.

This is the basic model of unconscious fantasy formation and representation, though, as both Arlow (1969a) and myself (Langs, 1971, 1976a) have noted, we must also leave room to include in our conception the extent to which the patient unconsciously seeks out such reality precipitants, creates them, or interprets them in terms of his own needs and conflicts. We must recognize that here, too, there is a continuous, spiraling interplay betwen reality and fantasy. So, derivatives are the surface communications within which unconscious fantasies are embedded, and unconscious fantasies are a means of working over psychic trauma—adaptive contexts—in displaced and disguised form. They are one of the crucial determinants of neurotic symptoms—again, used in the broadest sense to refer not only to the whole continuum of psychopathology but to the entire range of symptomatic expression from discrete symptoms to characterological disturbances.

How is this relevant to the listening process? It is clearly crucial to have a means of developing the conditions under which unconscious fantasies may be communicated by the patient, and their presence and functions detected and identified, so that the therapist may be in a position to interpret them and thus provide the patient with insights through which the effects of these pathological fantasy formations can be sufficiently modified to provide lasting symptomatic relief. Interventions of any other type, then, do not get to the heart of the problem, and while it is possible to provide momentary and sometimes lasting symptom relief through other means, the avenue that I have just described is clearly the most adaptive, secure, and potentially stable route to symptom alleviation, though we must not neglect the anxiety and disturbing therapeutic regression which accompanies such a process.

Discussant: I am a bit confused, and I have a question. I have the impression that some analysts think of unconscious fantasies as the central organizing factor in neuroses, and while I can see that you place considerable importance on their function, it seems to me that your emphasis is on external realities—primary adaptive tasks or adaptive contexts, as you call them—and that they seem to be the central organizers of the neuroses for you.

Langs: That is an excellent question. Your characterization of the classical position is accurate, and one with which I agree—though I have supplemented it in some ways. The Kleinians, in particular, have seen primitive introjects and unconscious fantasies as the initiators of, and basis for, neurotic disturbances. Only recently are they, and some classical analysts, beginning to acknowledge and explore the influence of external realities.

There are several answers to your question. First, I have been stressing the organization of the listening process, rather than that of neuroses, and there is an important distinction there, especially in regard to organizing the material that will ultimately reveal the nature of a neurotic response. I have often thought about this very issue, and have wondered if I could organize the listening process, not around an adaptive context, but around the central unconscious fantasy active at the moment, or perhaps around a key unconscious perception. Theoretically, it should be possible to do it either way since both are crucial. But that also touches upon another issue, related to the role of introjects in psychopathology. I obviously find my approach clinically meaningful, and it helps to avoid the basic technical fallacy of failing to append unconscious fantasies, memories, and introjects to current realities, especially, to the therapeutic interaction, and treating them as isolated contents, and therefore essentially as dynamically meaningless communications. Actually, both the relevant external realities and intrapsychic contents and mechanisms are essential.

However, unconscious fantasies, memories, and introjects do influence the patient's interpretation of reality, the experiences that he may provoke, and the like. I do not wish to disregard the essential role of these unconscious contents and mechanisms in neurotic reactions. Wherever we begin our study of the patient's material, however we try to sort it out and conceptualize it, we must take into account a continuous interaction between inner and outer—another version of what I call a spiraling interaction. I have been aware that my emphasis on the adaptive context has led to a criticism, which I believe to be unfounded, that I neglect the intrapsychic influence. I term my approach *adaptational-interactional* because I endeavor to take into account both inner and outer factors in neurosogenesis. Still, those who have adopted my approach are sometimes seen as developing a paranoid-like system which could easily overstate the influence of reality and underestimate the intrapsychic factor, and it's a danger of which I am well aware. On the other hand, those who begin their study of the continuous spiral with the intrapsychic realm have a depressive-like system, which runs the danger of overstating the inner influence and neglecting the outer. However you organize the communications from the patient—whether your key organizer is an external stimulus or internal fantasy—this continuous and mutual influence between inner and outer should be constantly recognized and developed. Wherever you begin, you must take into account both spheres, and I find that beginning with the adaptive context enables me to do just that.

Well, there is more to be said on these subjects, but I see that our time is up. We can keep these questions in mind as we go on.

Chapter Three

THREE TYPES OF
COMMUNICATIVE STYLES
AND FIELDS

Listening to the therapist's interventions and the patient's responses to them • Listening and openness to creativity • A classification of communicative fields • The Type B and Type C modes of communication • The communicative qualities of erroneous interventions • Transversal communications • Projective identification and containing functions

Langs: Today I suggest that we move directly to the clinical material. We'll continue to forgo, for now, listening to the continuing presentation without desire, memory, or understanding (Bion, 1970)—the session has been fragmented too much by the interruptions for comments and discussion. So, why don't you begin by briefly summarizing the session up to the point where we had left off, and we'll pick it up from there.

Therapist: First, you might recall, we started off discussing the patient's feeling of ambiguity in the situation with her boyfriend, and her statement about feeling rejected and rejecting—how they strike her in the same way, and affect her similarly. I had intervened, and she went on to suggest that her father...

Langs: Since you are picking up in the middle of an hour, we will accept this review. But please repeat your intervention. It's remarkable to see how defensive therapists are regarding their comments to patients.

Therapist: Okay. She mentioned that she had been rejected by her father and I asked her for more information on that—sort of a general, diplomatic point. In any case, she went on to describe how she had been pregnant and then had bickered constantly with her father. And that a meeting had been arranged with her father for a reconciliation. The father said, I will get off your back if you do X and Y and Z. And she said, Forget it. That's not exactly what she said. I then pointed out to her that it was in fact she who responded by leaving the house. And she said, Yes, I was the one, but you must remember that he was continuing his harassment; and he wouldn't let up on me. So I made the comment, Nonetheless it's interesting that all through the therapy you presented this as your father having kicked you out of the house, but in your actual account of the events, it seems that you made the final decision to leave.

Langs: Okay, that's about where we were—the point at which you had made that first intervention, and we've heard a bit more now. Just as an orientation, it seems to me important again to raise this question: if I don't impose certain kinds of organizing methods upon you, can you formulate this material without them? Can you generate meaning without, for example, the adaptive context? I don't know how to prove to you that you need that context every time. I guess what we'll do is see if anybody can produce validated formulations without it. We can evaluate each formulation offered here, particularly from the therapist. You see, that will be a nice test, because you already have finished the session; you can't change your intervention. We'll then see how those interventions that are formulated without organizing principles related to the listening process work out—how they are assessed by us, consciously, and unconsciously by the patient.

So we will be developing a methodology here. In the context of this material, I would like to emphasize again that in listening to a session here, or as it unfolds with our own patients, we have to do as much analysis, as much listening to our own interventions—"listening" meaning, then, all the processes of taking in, responding subjectively, experiencing, metabolizing, formulating, trying to understand—as we do to the patient's material. The literature on the listening process—whatever fragments exist—has focused on listening to the patient, and acknowledges only in passing that we should also listen to ourselves. But I am saying we really have to do it with equal openness and perceptiveness.

Now, you've heard this particular intervention again, and its elaboration. For the moment, rather than allowing the material to generate in some insistent way a restatement of a set of principles related to the listening process, I will suggest, as I did last week, that in addition to adaptive contexts that lie within the prior session, and secondary contexts that relate to intercurrent realities that take place between sessions, each communication from the therapist becomes an immediate adaptive context for the patient's subsequent associations. So, even though I briefly discussed this intervention toward the end of our last meeting, let's identify its nature and formulate the unconscious communications involved, and let's see if it doesn't help us to predict the material that shall follow or, for the moment, since we've heard a bit of that material, let's see if it doesn't help us immediately to understand in some depth, and to organize, the patient's response.

So, what's the nature of this intervention and what does it communicate?

Discussant: Could the therapist repeat his remarks?

Langs: Yes, I will make an exception and allow repetition, largely because I tend to make such extended comments. Just remember, as I said before, that in principle we do not ask that of our patients, and we analyze within ourselves any failure to recall and any listening block as it occurs in the therapeutic interaction.

Therapist: The gist of it was, it's interesting that she had presented herself as having been thrown out of the house, because that in fact was not the case—that she had decided to leave.

I don't know if you would classify that as an interpretation.

Langs: No, I wouldn't. How would you classify it formally?

Therapist: An observation.

Langs: Which goes under the heading of which of the basic interventions?

Discussant: A clarification.

Langs: It could be a clarification; it could also be a...

Discussant: Confrontation.

Langs: Exactly. It would have formal qualities of both a clarification and a confrontation. What are its—well, not informal—but unconscious qualities?

Therapist: Well, you said last time—I don't know if I believe it completely—but you said that there are aggressive, unconscious qualities, that confrontations tend to be used in that way.

Langs: You mean, confrontations in general?

Therapist: We were talking about confrontations in general. Oh, you're talking about this particular intervention?

Langs: Yes. Your thought is that confrontations, according to me, are often aggressive, but you don't know if that applies to this intervention. Or are you saying that you would like to think that it doesn't?

Therapist: I would hope not.

Langs: Hoping against hope doesn't establish clinical facts, or self-knowledge.

Discussant: It would have to be by its very nature, because it's really a contradiction. You're saying, You say your father kicked you out, but actually it's not so; you decided to go yourself. But since that isn't what the patient just said, it would be an aggressive act to state that, to contradict her.

Langs: Some would feel that at certain times a therapist must be aggressive. The question is whether or not this is in the service of the treatment and coincidental to the main thrust of the intervention—that is, whether such aggressiveness is needed here.

Therapist: I would agree that it's aggressive but "aggressive" is different from "hostile."

Langs: All right, we'll do it in terms of that distinction. "Hostile" would imply an inappropriate quality, and an attack. "Aggressive" could be part of an appropriate intervention. It seems to me that you're telling her that she contradicts herself, that what she said at one time actually wasn't true. I would say, again, and I'm not going to belabor it because I want to continue with the details of the listening process, that this is a hostile intervention. This is an intrusive, you-are-a-liar kind of comment. If you cut through all of the niceties, it reads: Isn't it interesting that you lied to yourself and to me, and why don't you pay attention to that? It lacks a sense of neutrality.

What basic element does this intervention fail to utilize? Have you caught on enough to what I'm teaching? If you make a really valid intervention, what's going to be one of its basic properties? What will it always have? Have you picked that up yet? (Pause.) It will always have an *adaptive context.* You will know and state what's organizing the patient's communications in terms of their unconscious meanings.

If the intervention lacks an adaptive context, it will foster the working over of the material in terms of its manifest content, and this is typical of confrontations. It is an intervention that deals with the manifest content. There have been many attempts to dignify such work as meaningful, and repeatedly, I'm going to raise questions about that contention.

Your comment keeps her on the surface of this material, the

manifest content. Her inconsistency is not treated as a
derivative, as an indirect expression of something else; it is a
direct expression of a direct problem in memory or recall, or
representation, stressing manifest content. Now this will
promote certain qualities in the communicative field, which is
an aspect that I don't want to get into until we've really
worked over the basics of listening. For now, we can say that it
will promote communication on the level of manifest contents.
It's your way of saying, That's where I think the important
themes and psychic mechanisms lie; that's what I listen to;
that's what I want to hear about; and that's what we're going
to work over. I tried to say in our first meeting that this is not
the realm of psychopathology, which has to do with unconscious processes, unconscious mechanisms, unconscious
contents; so, it is precisely these psychotherapy must deal
with.

Discussant: How would you identify here an adaptive
context for his intervention? You said that that was what was
missing.

Langs: That's hard to state. You see, there's no adaptive
context for this intervention, that's the point. The adaptive
context that I've developed in our previous discussions of this
session consists of his interventions in the previous and
present sessions, through which he is being hostile and
pressuring the patient, directing her away from her relationship with him, and into all sorts of side issues. His comments
also entail a denial of what he is putting into the patient, and a
projective identification into her of a hostile introject.

If that is my adaptive context, I would never make this
intervention, which is totally unrelated to that context. This,
too, is my way of saying that this is an intervention that is
almost a total falsity. It's wrong to say to the patient, This is
what's meaningful, even though you do it in the name of
identifying her falsehood. It's my belief that this is not at all
meaningful in the manner suggested, and your intervention
invites the patient to continue a fiction. I shall elaborate upon
this way of putting it later.

Therapist: What would you have said?

Langs: I would have been silent. I would let the dust settle, and allow her to get back to derivative communications. You see, patients will come back to the adaptive context. If I'm right, the patient will get back to it on some level; there will be passing references to the therapeutic relationship or the derivatives will become clearer. In disguised form, they will more strongly suggest allusions to the therapeutic interaction, to the way the therapist is intervening. I would let her reorganize the session, the field, the material. I'd be silent, I'd reformulate, and I'd wait and see.

Remember, too, that this intervention is really a further elaboration of earlier comments. It is offered in the absence of confirmation of the initial intervention, which should have taken the form of something new, original, and genuinely different that would reorganize the material. Many therapists just continue along their merry way—they've got an idea and they continue to intervene, regardless of whether or not they get genuine confirmation. Instead, you should listen to the patient for the adaptive context and for derivatives. You should generate a silent formulation; if it's confirmed, then you intervene—that's the first part of listening. The second part follows the intervention. It involves the patient's commentary on what you said, and the search for confirmation. You organize listening a bit differently before and after intervening. Confirmation will then lead you into new material, and you start a new round of listening, confirming, intervening, seeking new confirmation.

Therapist: With all due respect, I really must disagree with you on that point.

Langs: Please do.

Therapist: I don't feel as you do. I really feel that I am not leading the patient on. This is a crucial bit of information in this therapy. This patient has been saying for two months that she had been kicked out of the house by her father, and he had never gotten over it. And now she relates these events in detail, albeit perhaps because of a maladaptive intervention, but nevertheless, she relates this information, and it turns out that lo and behold, she wasn't kicked out at all—she left. And I can't see how—well, maybe I'm asking; I'm not going to insist upon the point, but I'm saying—I don't understand, I just don't know how I could not have said something at that point. It's such a flagrant contradiction in the material. I'm not really challenging you; I am genuinely confused. If that's a point I would be quiet on, I just don't know where I would intervene.

Langs: You make it necessary for me to say something more, and I'm going to try to shape it around the listening process. I'll say three things about your comment. Number one, you shouldn't agree with me unless you see validation of the point that I'm making in the material from the patient. You should state your disagreement so that we can now let the patient be the arbitrator—which the patient always is. The patient unconsciously knows when she's been given a correct intervention, or an incorrect one—that is the outcome of her intaking processes, her listening process. I am suggesting here that you have made an incorrect one.

Therapist: Right.

Langs: I've also suggested what the correct intervention would be, and the patient is now going to tell us who's right. I'm not worried about that at all. In other words, everybody here is entitled to their own formulation. This is the distillate of your listening process.

Therapist: Not that this is confirmation, but I'm just curious about other people in the room. I'm not saying that this proves if anyone is right or wrong, but what would people do if they were presented with that material?

Discussant: Some of us would do exactly what you did, so don't be uptight about it.

Therapist: No, I'm trying not to be uptight. I'm just curious about the nature of the therapeutic process, because your suggestions are much different from the suggestions that I've been given in supervision, or maybe I'm not assimilating things properly.

Langs: Oh, no, they're often quite different. You're going to learn that I feel there's an entire, different world of psychotherapy that exists other than the one that has been what I call fictionalized by psychoanalysts. You can then apply the listening and validating processes to each position, and with the unconscious help of your patients, decide on the truth for yourselves.

Therapist: So, you do have a different point of view. It's important for me to discover it.

Langs: There's no question about that.

Therapist: My internal monitoring state really picked up differences between you and everybody else.

Discussant: Tell that to our supervisors. I made one of your points to a patient I presented in supervision yesterday and I really got taken to task by the supervisor. In some ways you make some very different points.

Langs: You now know more clearly what you're in the process of experiencing. This is going to happen in all kinds of ways. It's a concomitant of learning truly new concepts in this field, especially those that challenge hallowed shibboleths.

Discussant: It's a bit hard to bear.

Langs: That's true, but if you can't tolerate this—and some won't—you will be unable to learn. It does get to be very tough, not only because of other supervision, but also because of your own therapy; whoever is in therapy is going to have the same problems there too.

The point is this: we're searching here for the truth, and we must stand with it. Now obviously, I believe—I'm convinced—that I have now discovered a whole set of interrelated observations and formulations that do not exist in integrated form in the current literature and in today's therapeutic work. And much of it came out of discoveries related to the listening process. I'm going to show you their validity, their utility, through the material that you present, but you're going to have the problem of being taught elsewhere and treated in one realm, and being taught here in another, and being confronted with those discrepancies again and again. But I also promise, as I said, to help you develop a listening and validating process through which you can psychoanalytically assess these varying positions.

Therapist: See, the differences I can take. It's just that I thought you were teaching a course on traditional technique, which is what's confusing to me. Apparently you're not doing that solely.

Langs: I can't do that. I'm going to teach you the basics of technique. I'm going to derive them empirically. I'm going to teach you the truth about technique. I cannot teach you untruths.

Therapist: Okay, but your truths don't match other people's truths.

Langs: But they're going to match the patient's truths, and that's all that I ask you to try to remember.

Therapist: But you know what's very disturbing—well, I don't know if it's disturbing, but it's certainly apparent: you can prove with your system and your beliefs that this is what the patient will do, but when we raise some of the points you have made when we talk with other supervisors, they take us to task on this.

Langs: Some will. Others may listen.

Therapist: They will show us in the material how the opposite is true.

Langs: But I am going to teach you the validating process—that is the key. You will find that those supervisors will not truly use the validating process. They speak through fiat and dictum, or in terms of manifest content. Here we will restrict validation to the communication of selected facts (Bion, 1962) and Type Two derivatives, through indirect material that truly sheds new light and reorganizes what is already known.

You're going to have to filter this out, learn to think for yourselves, learn to have the courage to express what you'll become slowly convinced about, and to deal with the inevitable conflicts and all. It will get complicated, but I hope that over the year, what will precipitate out will be an appreciation for valid methodology and for valid technique, and for what can be confirmed.

This is no sleight of hand on my part, and what is involved are not differences in viewpoint. I am absolutely convinced that there is only one true means of validation—in terms of Type Two derivatives, and that there is only one valid clinical method, not two or three or four. I'm not saying that I am entirely right, but I am saying I am one of the few analysts who properly test out clinical psychoanalytic hypotheses, and that is a tool I hope to develop for each of you. You can bring in, if you want to, for the purposes of learning, material where you tried to apply something that I said, and the supervisor said it was entirely different, and give us a chance to go over that session and see what the material itself dictates. We'll do anything that you need to help clarify the situation for yourself.

But what you're about to embark upon is very crucial, because it has to do with responses to creativity, in your field, in your patients, and even in yourself. Creative ideas generate tension and uncertainty; they disrupt your equilibrium. In psychotherapy, to the extent that they're valid, creative concepts disturb your pathological defenses, reawaken unresolved conflicts, and impinge upon unresolved counter-transferences. I don't want to get into too much of the details, but ultimately it's a personal problem, a personal disequilibrium which, if you can tolerate it, enables you eventually to discover the truth and to grow. If you don't tolerate the anxiety, you'll just try to shut it off, to obliterate the creative idea, and you cannot grow.

Yes, these are all things that are absolutely inevitable, so long as we are touching upon truths that others have denied. I no longer apologize for them because my ideas are valid and constructive. They're going to have to create these problems for you, and you have to benefit from their resolution (see Langs, 1978c).

All of this is quite relevant to this material, in that this discussion comes up in response to this particular intervention because, you see, you said that here she tells you that something she has presented as the truth turned out to be a fiction. That is, indeed, a crucial communication, but I would suggest that the manifest contradiction, and the apparent implication that she has been misrepresenting or deceiving you, is merely the surface of this communication, a ready implication that has meaning but need not be the central meaning at all. It may well contain a more important latent content. In principle, once the therapist has heard an important communication, it is essential not to intervene, but to allow the patient to continue to associate, so that the subsequent material can establish for you the pertinence of the manifest content, as well as the indirect links, and the constellation of unconscious meaning contained in that particular seemingly nodal association. This is what I mean by allowing the patient to put into you all of the material that you will need for your interventions. This shifts the quality of your therapeutic work from the surface, and from some type of flat and staccato effort, to the depths.

Your acceptance of this material on a manifest level once again can serve a defensive purpose, because here you ignore the me–not-me interface, the monitoring of this material for allusions to qualities not only in herself, but also within you, as her therapist. Now, you'll notice that the *not-me dimension*—speaking from the patient's vantage point, as I will—her introject or object representations of you, which entails an entirely latent thread, readily organizes as Type Two derivatives around the adaptive context of the unconscious nature of your intervention. There is striking unconscious meaning there, a point that I will develop in a moment.

So, let me propose an alternate hypothesis for validation from the patient's subsequent material. We must always maintain the basic methodology and use of the validating process.

I believe that a more valid appraisal of the latent content of this material—as Type Two derivatives in the adaptive context provided by the unconscious nature of your intervention and her perceptions and introjections of these qualities—conveys her experience that you have been deceiving her with each of your incorrect interventions. As you may remember, I said that I would clarify the nature and meanings of incorrect interventions, on a number of levels. An incorrect intervention is, on the interactional level, both a pathological projective identification and an effort to evoke a particular inappropriate role and image in the patient. Here, for example, you are implying that she experience herself as the "bad one," that this be her self-image, that she contain your criticisms of her badness—in one sense, your condemnation of her deceptiveness—and that she immediately experience and confront this deviousness, for reasons that I believe to be related more to your countertransference-based needs than to those of the patient, and to be connected with your own discomfort with her lie to you.

The only analyst that I know to have written on the lie is Bion (1970). He considered it in terms of efforts to destroy meaning, to break links with the analyst, disrupt the analytic work, and serve as a defensive barrier to more disturbing underlying contents.

Well—I knew that I would find a ready way to introduce a new set of concepts, and it happens that the lie is characteristic of one dimension of the subject that I planned to explore with you today. The lie is a property of one of the three communicative fields within which psychotherapy and psychoanalysis take place. The identification of these communicative fields is a matter with which I have been concerned over recent months (see Langs, 1978b). And here, this patient and my evaluation of your interventions begin to tell me that the interactional amalgam that constitutes this communicative field is what I call a *Type C field*, in which the lie is a communicative vehicle, as are noncommunication and deception.

I think that in this particular sequence, the patient is protesting against your deceptions, against your falsities, against the things that you're saying to her that are really not substantiated, and perhaps secondarily against her own deceptiveness. As I said, I can only offer that as a hypothesis for the moment, but it's equally or more valid than yours, because it derived more complexly, in more convoluted form, from the patient's associations. It is a hypothesis to be validated, but it shows again why you need to be silent in order to see what the unconscious meaning of all of this is. Is it really that she wants to tell you something about what's happening currently between you and her, or within yourself, or is it really more important that it has to do with the way in which she communicates? I think that she's talking about the way in which the two of you communicate—that you have been really deceiving each other—and she wants to try to work that over, perhaps, in order to modify the communicative medium and to make it more viable.

Therapist: That's going to be validated.

Langs: Please don't tell me in advance.

Therapist: Let me go over this, it's very interesting in light of what you just said—now I understand it better.

Langs: I have to tell you one other thing, just very briefly. We'll get into this later on. I can perceive three kinds of therapeutic fields. This discovery is for me a major payoff of my ideas and my listening methods, and it will show you significant ways in which I differ from the usual classical analyst, though I remain one in basic spirit, and how the therapeutic work becomes shaped somewhat differently. I'll mention it now, so we can begin to identify some specific communicative qualities of this particular field.

The Type A field (see Langs, 1978b) is the one that has generally been written about and thought of, especially by classical analysts. It's the field in which symbolic communication prevails. Type Two derivatives are available, and the field is similar to what Winnicott (1951) calls the transitional space. It's a play space, and a creative space, a field in which illusion is also present. Words are used to represent unconscious meanings, by both patient and therapist.

The Type B field is what I call an action-discharge field. It's a field of action and projective identification, which has to do with taking contents within yourself, placing them into the other person, not for the purpose of understanding but to get rid of them, to stir that other person up, to achieve goals other than cognitive insights through symbolic communications—to get rid of what's disturbing you as patient or therapist. It is a field characterized by riddance and discharge mechanisms, unburdening, and it is not designed for understanding, though this may be imparted by a therapist capable of containing and symbolically interpreting such efforts.

And the Type C field is the most fascinating of all because it's really not been identified before. The Type B field is implicit in the Kleinian literature, and both the A and B fields have been described in a paper published in 1973 by Masud Khan.

Discussant: What is the difference between projection and projective identification?

Langs: Projective identification is an interactional mechanism. Projection, if it does exist at all—and some feel there is always an interactional element—is intrapsychic: I within my mind attribute to someone else something that's part of me or mine, some part of my inner mental contents or defenses. In projective identification, I actualize that mechanism; I effect it in the interaction, try to have you experience what I am identified with.

Some discussion of this is a necessary prelude to so much of what will follow. The word *identification* is used in a very unusual way in projective identification. Usually identification is an intaking process: I take in from you something of yours, an attribute or whatever, usually unconsciously, and modify my own self-representation, psychic structures, and self based on this incoming identification. Projective identification is an outgoing process, in which I attempt to have you identify with me, I evoke in you something of my own inner state so that you will experience it and identify with me. But in addition, I remain identified with whatever I'm projecting into you in the interaction.

There's a literature on it (see Langs, 1976b), and we'll get to it bit by bit. But I call it "interactional projection." That is, in addition to attributing something of myself to you, I really want you to experience it. Martin Wangh (1962) calls it "the evocation of a proxy" because one dimension is: I want you to help me with it. Hanna Segal (1967) describes it as getting rid of some aspect of your own inner state in order to be able to better manage it in the other person, outside yourself. Let's leave it at that for the moment; Malin and Grotstein (1966) have also discussed this subject rather lucidly. It's an interactional mechanism that is very crucial. It means again wanting to stir up and evoke responses in the other person.

Now, in the therapeutic interaction, some of that could have to do with wanting insight, but a lot of it has to do with getting rid of this inner tension state, not in order to understand it, but more just to get rid of it. That comes as a shock to analysts and therapists—their patients not wanting to understand—but they very often don't. It's even more upsetting when they discover that they themselves, while manifestly proposing what they believe are valid interpretations, turn out, when one applies the listening process, actually to be using language primarily for projective identification, rather than for symbolic communication designed to impart insight. But remember, for now, that this mechanism is most characteristic of what I have termed the Type B field.

The Type C field is another field that comes as a great surprise to most analysts. I call it the static field, and it appears to be what we're confronted with here for the moment. It's a very interesting field, in that noncommunication is the medium. Language is used in order not to communicate. In the other two fields, positive communication is still present. One is symbolic and the other is interactional and through action, but in a Type C field, all language is used as a barrier. There is no depth, no substance. Interpretation of contents, and of Type Two derivatives is, by and large, impossible.

When a resistance occurs in a Type C field, you do not have the derivatives with which to interpret it, as you would in a Type A field, and in general you can only establish its presence, and make use of the patient's tendency to represent the Type C field metaphorically, with allusions to its falsifications and barriers. As a result, you are limited to a general interpretation of the metaphor, a rather flat intervention related to the patient's massive use of barriers and his efforts to destroy communicative meaning.

In a Type A field, by contrast, resistances occur, of course, but they can eventually be interpreted because the material, the Type Two derivative, is there, as is the patient's effort to communicate analyzable expressions. In contrast, the Type C field has very flat qualities, and language is used for the purpose of obliteration. Analysts, in general, have never really thought about this, because they are, by nature, so interested in meaning, and in giving language meaning in depth, and a Type C field is one in which meaninglessness is the model, the lie is the mode, and deception is the goal. The Type C field is a facade; communications are something like the images in a mirror, if you try to take hold of them, you find that they are entirely without substance.

My preliminary observations suggest that the Type C field and Type C mode of communication—that is, the effort at noncommunication, the destruction of meaning and of interpersonal links, and the creation of massive, impenetrable barriers—constitute an attempt to seal off a psychotic core, an inner catastrophe, intense psychic pain, as Bion (1977) put it. Often these barriers are so well constructed that these patients are able to function reasonably well socially. They are capable of ruminative associations for long periods of time in their therapy, providing only an occasional clue as to their underlying disturbance and to the presence of falsifications and barriers. As you would expect, a Type C communicative mode—this is true of the Type B mode as well—may be characteristic not only of patients but also of their therapists, who, at present, are not really aware of their own communicative preferences and style. I do not have the impression that this particular patient prefers a Type C communicative mode, though she does shift toward it a bit at the behest of the therapist. I hear efforts at Type A communication, primarily related to the alterations in the frame, including those evolving from the therapist's nonneutral interventions. On the other hand, I detect distinct signs of the Type C mode in the interventions from the therapist.

Therapist: You definitely don't think that this girl is a Type C patient?

Langs: I would say that that is a difficult determination for the moment. The communicative field is an amalgam developed through the interaction between the patient and the therapist. It is sometimes difficult to determine an individual preference because the interactional factors may overshadow them for the moment. Here, there is considerable influence exerted by your own tendency to utilize psychoanalytic clichés such as your confrontation with her contradictions, which served, in part, further to obliterate and bar underlying unconscious perceptions and fantasies about yourself. We will attempt to identify the nature of the communicative field, and then try to conceptualize the contributions of each participant to it. From there, we will try to identify the preferred communicative style of both patient and therapist. I suspect that she is capable of Type A communication, in that I have heard a number of Type Two derivatives related to her unconscious perceptions and possibly to unconscious fantasies vis-á-vis her relationship with you, but she may also have strong needs to utilize a Type B mode—action and projective identification. But there are also Type B qualities to your interventions. I sense that they create intense interactional pressures and introjects.

Discussant: Can a Type C patient be worked with in psychotherapy?

Langs: Oh yes. What you work with is that very kind of defense and effort to destroy meaning. You then generate interludes during which the underlying psychotic core gets expressed, the defenses are softened and modified, and eventually the inner chaos gets worked through, analyzed, and detoxified. Defenses become less rigid, less pathological. Often, these patients don't change their basic communicative style. I thought initially that the goal was to make everyone a Type A, symbolic communicator. Everybody does communicate at times symbolically, and these patients can be helped to do more of that and to use a less pathological Type C mode, but the basic style may not change. I think communicative style is something very basic and is probably related to family communication, very early experiences, heredity, and all.

It is well to realize—and this was a most marvelous experience for me—that patients evincing each of the three styles undergo charactistically different courses of treatment. The goals are different, the working through process is different, and the indications that termination is at hand are different. This is very crucial. As an analyst, I was waiting for my patients to communicate symbolically and I thought that I had failed with patients whom, otherwise, I really thought I had analyzed to a point of successful termination, but who had not changed their communicative style. And now I know, in retrospect, that I can rest easy—that there had been enough of a change to resolve their symptoms but they're not necessarily going to become another kind of person.

These are complicated issues that in one sense take us beyond listening, but they're all related to the listening process as well. I wanted to establish a framework for future discussion, and, you see, both listening and interpretive work differ in each field.

Since you brought up the differences in my position as compared to other analysts: in today's thinking, as far as I know, all analysts, even the Kleinians, have believed themselves to be working in a Type A field. Some people, like

Khan (1973), who is, so far as I know, the single exception—
and I've never seen a reference to his paper—recognized that
there was another kind of communicative interaction, which
is quite different. That is the field I term Type B, and it is one
with which the Kleinians are quite conversant, though they
are far from appreciating all of its implications. But aside
from Khan, and certain inferences in the writings of Bion
(1977), classical analysts think of patients as—well, either
they're Type A or they can't be analyzed. My concept permits
you to work therapeutically with two other major groups of
patients who turn out, I suspect, to constitute some 80 percent
or so of your patients. Type A patients are few and far
between, and Type C patients, and therapists and analysts,
are far more common than anyone would imagine.

Therapist: Kernberg (1975) works with Type B and C
patients. He talks about the silence and the unproductiveness
of the borderline in therapy.

Langs: Yes—the borderline and narcissistic patient. This
cuts across a lot of the literature. There have been efforts to
work with such patients, but it's never been written about as a
distinctly different communicative field—a view which lends
a lot of perspective. Now remember this: there's nothing that
I'm saying here that is unprecedented or doesn't have a
relationship to a certain segment of the literature, which now
becomes, I believe, much clearer. I don't want to get into all of
the different ramifications and sources of these ideas;
everything has its antecedents. The reorganization, though,
brings to light some very significant differences too. Okay.
Let's get back to this material.

Therapist: After that intervention, she just responded yes.
She didn't have much more to say about my intervention.
Then she went on to describe...

Langs: So we're listening to her response in the realm of
primary confirmation: yes or no. It's to be considered with
caution, because it may be meaningless. Yes is often

insignificant, while no may have more meaning. It's really the area of *secondary confirmation*—the indirect derivatives— that now will tell us something of how she took this in.

Therapist: She said, After that, I didn't see him for years, until one day—it was about a year ago—he called me and said he had been hemorrhaging from the bowel, and that he didn't have long to live. He said, buy a coat and a dress, and come home to see me. I want to talk to you. So I bought the coat and dress, and I went home to see him; it was seven years I hadn't seen him. To be perfectly honest with you, I didn't really believe that he was seriously ill, and I didn't believe he had a short time to live.

Langs: That's beautiful—the Type C field!

Therapist: Yes, I said that there was confirmation...

Langs: This is fascinating in a number of ways, though I do not believe that they entirely decide the dispute between your formulation and mine. You see, if we take, as we must, your intervention as the adaptive context, these are Type Two derivatives, and they suggest her responsive use of the Type A communicative mode, though the inferences could be inter- preted both ways. For example, you might say that your intervention is being validated because the patient has now proceeded to clarify aspects of the genetic factors in her own propensity to be deceptive—the role of her father's behavior— to which she is adding allusions, through indirect derivatives, to some seriously destructive inner disturbance—the bowel hemorrhage—that is within herself and which she wishes to deny or negate. And there may be some truth to such a formulation, though I suspect that the patient's subsequent associations will tend not to support that thesis as primary and central for the moment. We'll have to see. It develops the "me" part of the me-not-me interface, focuses on her pathology, and would be easier for you, as her therapist, to formulate and accept than my thesis.

The same material, however, tends to support my formulation fully: that the patient is making use of these recollections of her father to communicate her unconscious perceptions of you and to state that, in reality, your falsifying interventions are being experienced by her as a repetition of past pathogenic traumas in her relationship with her father. There is some support for the idea that unconsciously this material alludes to you in derivative form, in that she had been skeptical and somewhat disbelieving of your interventions. All of this alludes to displacements from you onto her father, and to the not-me part of that interface, in that her father at this level is not a self-representation (and separate object), but an object-representation of you, her introject of you, and her struggle with some image of the possible disease inside of you—the more disquieting aspect of this communication.

Actually, this material seems to exquisitely condense both spheres—the me and the not-me; it alludes, therefore, to both herself and the therapist, to transference and nontransference. My point, then, would be that we must deal with the nontransference elements first, before we can validly interpret the transference aspects.

In any case, she now goes on with a rather exquisite description of a Type C communicative field, that can give you a sense of what it feels like to grow up in the presence of parents who communicate in the Type C mode, and to live with lies and deception. Remember too—even as we formulate this—that since we constantly monitor this material for unconscious allusions to the nature of the therapeutic interaction, and now, I would add, to the nature of the prevailing communicative modality, we must consider this material as a reflection of the patient's unconscious appreciation of the existing communicative field, allowing, once again, for contributions from both the patient and therapist in proportions that we are attempting to determine.

So this patient is representing, metaphorically and even rather concretely, some specific qualities of the Type C field. There is no sense of truth; the lie prevails. If you treat the lie like a truth, you feel deceived, and you can never quite get hold of the substance of what is being communicated. Language is being used here to destroy meaning; even as her father expresses his wish to communicate with her, he does so in a form that destroys the link between them, destroys any bond through consensual communicative sharing, and generates uncertainty and confusion. There is a manifest communicative effort, but it is based on lies or the possibility of lies. Falsifications prevail—at least, as this patient experiences the relationship.

Incidentally—to expand my comments about the me–not-me interface—you hear the patient wondering unconsciously whether there really is something seriously the matter within you as her therapist, and hoping that your destructive communications are actually a facade for a more intact or benign underlying attitude or existence. That is, you convey an inner disturbance that she hopes does not really exist.

Falsifications, as you would expect, are often used for denial, and they may serve wishes both to preserve and to destroy the object. Here, they function more as the former—as an unconscious effort to maintain an idealization.

Notice, too, how the patient returns to the theme of death, to denying that there is only a short time to live—a variation on the theme of rejection. All this tends to confirm some of the formulations that I made last week regarding these anxieties within the patient, especially as they pertain to the anticipation of a forced termination of her therapy, although it still does not, for the moment, link up to a specific and immediate adaptive context that would give it definitive meaning as a Type Two derivative; it remains, in that regard, a Type One derivative in terms of the current material, and a more remote Type Two derivative in terms of her possible anticipations; for the moment, it reinforces and gives added meaning to other similar derivatives.

But coming back to the Type C field: on the level at which the patient is unconsciously communicating her experiences of your intervention, you can very vividly share with her the dilemma of a patient confronted with a Type C therapist. Actually, I believe that there are two kinds of Type C therapists: one who constantly obliterates the meanings of his patient's communications and repeatedly offers massive, impervious barriers, and the other, which is more in keeping with the present situation, who works with psychoanalytic clichés that are experienced as deceptions, and for whom, unconsciously, the active lie or narrative deception is more pertinent. I must say that I am still very much attempting to organize my observations in this area, and as recently as two weeks ago, I wasn't sure that the Type C field wasn't merely a variation of the Type A field, until I realized that the defensive structure is really so different, and I started really to hear Type C patients presented to me and observed Type C fields. As Bion (1962) says, once you catch on—identify a selected fact—the material you need is always there. And then suddenly you realize its meaning—it's all in the listening and formulating.

And for her to come so quickly to an elaboration of this theme of deception and not knowing what to believe, and not believing, is fascinating, though, of course, your intervention in several ways helped to evoke it. Listening to material in terms of the communicative properties of the field takes on meaning now, and it has some very—well, almost poetic qualities. Please continue.

Therapist: She said, I called his doctor and in fact he really wasn't telling the truth. She went on to describe that he had had a polyp, and that he could have lived for years—that was what the doctor told her. So in effect she felt he was being provocative with her, that he had lied to her.

Langs: I hadn't realized until I got into this area that patients experience erroneous interventions in that way. You see, I had emphasized that the incorrect intervention is a projective identification of the therapist's problems into the patient, and I hadn't understood until I got to the Type C field that it's also a lie. It's stated as a truth about the patient, but is really a truth about the therapist, and a lie about the patient. This opens up a whole area; over the next six months, we will find out much of what it means. I don't know all that it means as yet, but I can now sense that the communicative fields idea is filled with important implications.

So she's saying that what you said is partly true—Yes, I did it, I decided to leave home—but the essence of it, the real heart of it, is not true. This is what she's saying about your intervention—that it was stated in a most provocative and deceptive way. This is why I said earlier that in listening, we must not assume—and this is another characteristic of the classical position—that we're going to hear fantasy and distortion. We must listen to this as a *commentary* on what we have said, in which we will find a great deal of truth and, depending on many factors, some degree of distortion; and we must realize that we must first discover the truth, before we can determine what is distorted and invalid.

Discussant: But you also say that he's identifying parts of her that relate to her own need to lie, and that she's responding by talking about her father's dealing in deceptions. I kind of intuitively appreciate what you're saying, but it's not clear to me that it's necessarily related to the therapist's intervention.

Langs: Exactly. I said that earlier. The only way there could be any such a conviction for the moment involves the fact that I made my statements before she got around to the theme of lying—I had already implied that this intervention was a deception and a lie.

Discussant: The content of the intervention was also in that area.

Langs: Okay, so we're going to have to hear more. You're saying that her associations also reflect the very area in which he had intervened. All right, we're going to have to hear more material from this patient, and other incorrect interventions, to see if we find clearer validation of my position. Yes, the manifest content of the intervention promotes associations in this area. There are other possibilities, and in time, we'll have to sort them out. It will be an excellent opportunity to apply the listening process. We'll have to now see if there is anything that would convince us that her associations have to do with her feelings about the therapist or whether her relationship with her father is the area of true meaning, or both. For the moment we could be quite unconvinced that the image of the therapist is central—I would agree with that.

Therapist: She said, He could have lived for years, the only thing was that he got bad medical care. That's the only reason he died very quickly.

Langs: So there's her commentary, her answer to our debate. What do you think now? Are you convinced? Bad medical care—you can see what I mean by indirect validation via Type Two derivatives.

Discussant: All right; that seems to do it.

Langs: If you ask a good question, the patient will answer it, because whatever is troubling you should be troubling the therapist, and most certainly is troubling the patient. Who was this really all about? So this is her first answer, and you can see again that it takes the form of a Type Two derivative given meaning in the adaptive context of the unconscious nature of the therapist's interventions. I am reminded once again of the importance of identifying the adaptive context— a truly crucial dimension of the listening process. Please continue.

Therapist: So she says, In fact, he was murdered.

Langs: So it's a lie and an assault.

Therapist: Here, I said, Murdered?

Langs: Okay—what about that intervention?

Therapist: You're saying that I'm accusing her of lying again.

Langs: Anything else?

Discussant: It seems this is focusing on a detail of what she's saying, rather than on the communication involved: the father had been done in and done wrong by his doctor, the murder may just be secondary; it may be a detail, rather than the essence of the communication.

Langs: Well, you're approaching something.

Discussant: The therapist finds it more striking than everything else that she's saying; that obviously would have some unconscious ramification.

Langs: What do you think it is? What do you think is the unconscious communication in that seemingly innocent question?

Discussant: Don't tell me that you want to murder me?

Discussant: Yes, she's afraid of the therapist, or she feels that the therapist is afraid he's going to murder her, as her doctor.

Langs: Yes; here once again we find that a question has a variety of unconscious functions and meanings. It's not only that you are challenging her somewhat, and implicitly, as you yourself said, possibly accusing her again of lying, but it also shows something about the listening process on both the cognitive and interactional levels. Let me clarify.

On a manifest level, you are questioning the surface of her communication, but that is the least of it. On a latent level—let me begin on an interactional plane, since we have not been systematically addressing the interactional dimension of the listening process: the experience of roles and images imposed upon us by our patients, and the projective identifications that they place into us, and us toward our patients. Here, after talking about being lied to and deceived, the patient gets around to the poor medical care that her father received, and to her feeling that he had been murdered. The manifest content that you seem to be concerned with leads you to treat this communication implicitly as a distortion, something that you have a need to question.

Your unconscious need to question her is clarified if we shift to the interactional level. Listening to this material as Type Two derivatives in the adaptive context of your interventions, we find that the patient is communicating an unconscious perception of your destructiveness as a therapist. Actually, that is a cognitive formulation that has interactional attributes—that is, it is an effort to identify the contents of these Type Two derivatives and to give them specific meaning in the adaptive context that I just mentioned. As a response to her unconscious perception, your question constitutes a denial of its validity, and a repudiation of the murderer image she is unconsciously imposing upon you. Your question is a remarkably condensed, single-word expression of a transference interpretation, offered, however, unconsciously rather than consciously. Actually, both you and she are discussing you sub rosa.

To bring it out into the open here, if you had been monitoring this material in terms of the therapeutic relationship, you might well have suggested that the patient had some kind of distorted perception of you as a murderer, based on these earlier experiences with her father and his physician, or with other physicians in the patient's past. The more recent experience with her father would, of course, have additional genetic roots that would relate the material more directly to either the patient's father or mother, but as long as it was treated primarily as transference and distorted, the emphasis would be on the inappropriate displacement from the past rather than on a valid appreciation of the present. Consciously, your question: "Murdered?" implies something along these lines.

Having established that much, I think we can now proceed to identify the distortion that is present, following our tenet of identifying reality before fantasy. After all, you are not attempting to kill her, though your countertransference-based interventions could evoke suicidal fantasies or behaviors— primitive destruction is her idiom—but you are not behaving maliciously. It is this type of derivative that I would term a *transversal communication*. It has unconscious truth, yet it is a truth that is distorted and instinctualized—aggressivized— by the patient. It condenses a pathological unconscious fantasy with a sensitive appreciation of unconscious qualities in your communications to the patient, and in intervening, it must be treated as a *commentary* which mixes reality and fantasy in proportions to be determined by further use of the listening process. The key point in this context is that her communication must be treated as containing both realistic elements and distorted elements. Both are significant and both must be acknowledged.

Interactionally, you can see that both she and you have contributed to the development of a particular image of you to this point. In addition, this challenging question keeps the patient at the manifest level, which is another way of keeping her from eventually relating much of this to yourself, and it encourages her once again to continue this displacement into the past—upon her father and his doctor.

To the extent that this communication is a projective identification by the patient of an introject of yourself as a murderer—and let's trace that aspect—the patient has expressed herself through interactional pressures. You had processed her material and had made a number of interventions that, in part, constituted a destructive projective identification into the patient. She took in this projective identification, contained it, serving as a *pathological container* (Langs, 1976a), and then worked these contents over, metabolized them, and connected them to her father and her father's doctors. She is now reprojecting much of it back into you, actually in a more toxic and blatant form.

We can characterize your response as a refusal to contain this projective identification from the patient. You immediately shut it off by challenging it, you do not permit the patient to expand upon this image, nor do you allow time for yourself to work over the projective identification internally, to metabolize it and to then interpret it to the patient. Instead you refuse to contain her projective identification and immediately place it back into herself, unmodified. In terms of unconscious image evocations, you are, quite without realizing it, attempting to defend yourself against a view of yourself as incompetent and murderous; it is, indeed, a difficult image to accept—and to process and interpret.

In all, then, we've been talking about two avenues of listening: the cognitive and the interactional. By the latter, as you can see, we mean first, the realm of object relationships, role pressures, and pressures to experience particular images of yourself, and second, the realm of projective identification—interactional mechanisms. In this sequence, the experiences derived from each of these levels or forms of communication tend to coalesce, and each supports a silent hypothesis that you have indeed been intervening so as to place destructive and possibly even murderous projective identifications into the patient, trying to cast her into the role of the victim—that last is your own unconscious role and image evocation. The therapist too, of course, creates pressures on the patient to experience particular self-images and roles, as well as certain projective identifications. Alternatively the patient may evoke them, and in addition, will process them in keeping with her own inner needs.

This touches upon important aspects of listening, so I will elaborate a bit. You could utilize all of this information to generate a silent hypothesis to the effect that the patient has unconsciously perceived and introjected the therapist's interventions as destructive, deceptive, and even murderous, and that this has reminded her of qualities of her father and his physician. Had you allowed the patient to continue to associate unencumbered, I very much suspect that her derivatives would have moved more closely toward disguised, indirect communications involving the therapeutic relationship, and that she would have provided you a bridge to her relationship with you and a clear-cut opportunity to intervene in the manner that I described.

Having touched upon those aspects of this interaction regarding which the patient has been quite sensitive and perceptive, I must now turn again to a further examination of any possible distortions based on pathological unconscious fantasies within the patient that are also influencing this material. This is a suicidal patient; her perception of erroneous interventions as murderous contains some element of distortion, though I would be very cautious in identifying the degree to which that is so, since there is also truth to the fact that erroneous interventions increase the risk of suicide in this patient, and are in some true sense potentially murderous. Still, it appears that the patient intensely aggressivizes the nature of the therapist's errors, just as we had clues earlier in the session that she sexualizes them. There are both hostile and seductive kernels of truth to her perceptions, but there is evidence that the patient exaggerates and instinctualizes these elements of truth, leading to some degree of distortion. For these reasons the term *transversal communication* seems apt.

In addition, this interactional approach may help you to realize that suicidal tendencies are by no means based entirely on intrapsychic conflicts; they include conflicts with pathological introjects. Suicidal impulses, like any other symptom, have both an interactional and intrapsychic basis.

Discussant: You're saying that there is a correct unconscious perception, on her part, that is casting doubt upon the therapy. In other words, she is responding unconsciously to some real aspect of his intervention—which is a destructive one?

Langs: Yes. Actually, that is part of what I am saying, that there is a valid core here and that any aggressive intervention can be experienced unconsciously as a murderous attack. Remember, the therapist too has an unconscious—these are unconscious meanings that are colored and intensified by the patient, but there is an essential truth to it all: an incorrect, attacking intervention has qualities of murder, which then take on specific added meaning for the patient. And we could never interpret this as just some displaced distortion from the other doctor, without really being aware that it contains a certain element of truth that the therapist must face. This is a suicidal patient, experiencing the therapist's unconscious provocations as pressures on her suicidal propensities, and you're going to have a difficult problem sorting out what is valid and what is distorted, but you now know, I hope, that this is a very important determination to make. We take it first as a transversal communication, and then we apply the listening process, including our knowledge of ourselves and the patient, to our subjective reactions and the patient's continuing associations. Let's hear more.

Therapist: She said, Yes, he was murdered. In the hospital they gave him a transfusion and the blood was contaminated; it was too much for his body to handle, and they killed him, and he was dead within six months after that first phone call.

Discussant: They placed into him more than he could handle.

Langs: Yes. I am quite pleased that you are listening on that level—a cognitive representation and validation of a formulation related to an interactional mechanism. The therapy destroyed him by putting into him something that was too much for him to handle, to contain, and that eventually killed him. Many therapists ask: What is projective identification? Does it exist? Is it relevant to this session? It has been quite amazing to me to hear from patients symbolic representations of projective identification, metaphors and the like, that follow upon my formulation of its active presence in the therapeutic interaction. You hear in this material allusions to a transfusion, putting into, the father unable to contain it, to the point where it destroyed him. Here too we have validation through indirect communication—Type Two derivatives organized around the adaptive context of the therapist's interventions.

Now Bion (1962) and, more recently, myself (Langs, 1976a,c) have written about the container's fear of the contained, fears of denudation and annihilation. Many therapists have wondered what this could all be about, and I think this patient is rather exquisitely telling you just what we mean by those metaphors. These striking communications yield an enormous amount of indirect meaning. At this point, I really don't see how it very much illuminates her father's propensities toward lying, although I guess that some would conclude that this was, in her mind, his final punishment for his badness. For me, that is rather simplistic, though I do not doubt that it is true on some level; it seems to me that the more immediately meaningful, beautifully convoluted level is an elaboration of the formulations that I have been developing.

You can see too that this dread applies equally to the patient and to the therapist, to both sides of the me–not-me interface, in that the patient has unconsciously perceived and experienced the therapist's dread of containing her projective identifications, his fear of being destroyed by them—a formulation that I had outlined just a moment ago, and which this patient now confirms so remarkably. Again, as I hope you can now appreciate, and as I now repeat: this validation unfolds entirely in terms of indirect and derivative communication, Type Two derivatives. This is what I mean by true validation: this is not an empty echo; it is the patient's own unique way of unconsciously communicating the very hypotheses that I consciously defined for you just a little while ago. Unconsciously, this is her effort to generate a selected fact (Bion, 1962) through which she could comprehend her experiences with the therapist, and oddly enough, it involves some conception of projective identification.

At the same time, of course, this communication expresses the patient's dread of being destroyed by the therapist's murderous projective identifications, her fear that they will intensify her suicidal impulses, and in some way lead to her own annihilation. It would be difficult to identify the point at which the patient begins to distort, since there is so much unconscious truth to these communications. This unconscious image of the therapist is quite disturbing and you can readily understand why the therapist would turn to counter-transference-based defenses in order not to hear this material as referring in some valid way to himself, and endeavor to maintain the fiction that this material essentially relates to the patient's relationship with her father. Here, a genetic truth is being used as a defensive barrier, and this, as I said, is characteristic of a Type C field.

It seems to me that here we are seeing qualities of each of the three communicative fields that I have identified. I am certainly not surprised that there can be intermixtures. First, there is the patient's Type A symbolic communication of derivatives of her unconscious perceptions of her therapist, and in addition, her Type B projective identification of disturbing introjected contents from the therapist, and I must add, undoubtedly from other pathological introjects as well—introjects that have been projected into her and reprojected back into the therapist—the hallmark of a Type B field. Lastly, there is the therapist's offer of defensive, fictional barriers. It would be interesting to follow this therapeutic interaction to see the type of field that eventually emerges and persists. In my experience the patient initially often accepts the barriers proposed by the therapist, and becomes depressed and gives up on her unconscious curative endeavors and her unconscious efforts to alert the therapist to what is disturbing her, and accepts the Type C field, at least for some time. Because of the patient's suicidal potential, and tendencies toward Type B communication, however, these barriers might not sustain her for very long.

In terms of another facet of the listening process, I believe that you can see that the patient is expressing what I have termed closer and closer derivatives related to the therapeutic relationship (Langs, 1973a). That is, while the material continues to be displaced and disguised, even as Type One derivatives, it is becoming more and more evident that on a latent level she is alluding in some way to the therapeutic relationship—as seen, for example, in the mention of a doctor and a hospital. At this point, then, the most common error would be not to organize this material around the traumatic adaptive contexts that have evolved from the therapist and to think of this material largely in terms of transference and distortion, eliminating the crucial veridical core.

Let's see where she goes now.

Therapist: She said, I took care of him during those months when he was ill. I took him to doctors.

Langs: What can you make of the material? It has to do with the listening process, which is so much an interactional process, not only what the patient is actually saying, but what you can experience as the latent content, using empathy, intuition, and all such subjective aspects, which we will discuss later on; listening has both shared and personal qualities. For example, this communication—what do you experience from it? What does it mean to you? What are you hearing? Anybody? (Pause.)

Discussant: I did hear something: she's trying to help the therapist, I think. She mentions going along with the father, trying to help get further care for him by going to other doctors. I get a sense of compliance, that she's trying to salvage their relationship.

Langs: What you did is interesting: you took a theme and you changed it. Instead of tracing it out, extending it—trying to help the father—asking then what it could mean with her therapist, you veered away. You are right on some level, but you are missing a more pertinent and less disguised derivative. Could you try it again?

Discussant: Well the way I thought of it was that she was the father who was being murdered by the doctor, and she's going to have to go out and help herself. The doctor can't help her.

Langs: Yes, that is more in keeping with the kind of listening that I am trying to teach you: taking the adaptive context of the therapist's intervention, and tracing out the material from the patient in terms of Type Two derivatives; first, attempting to delineate Type One derivative themes, and then trying to connect them to the actualities of the therapeutic interaction. Yes, this material could imply some type of realization that she's going to have to cure herself; that is well taken.

But in addition, I heard the patient unconsciously expressing a lecture that I will offer much later in this course. When the therapist places a pathological projective identification into the patient, the patient then unconsciously realizes that she must become the doctor, and that she must undertake curative efforts directed toward the introject—and therefore, the therapist—and of course, then, on some level, herself, as you just said. At such junctures, the interface of the bipersonal field has shifted toward the therapist's pathology, and the communicative line contains more of his pathology than that of the patient for the moment. Here, the therapist becomes the patient, and the patient is therapist, much as Searles (1965, 1975) described and I elaborated upon later (Langs, 1975a, 1976a).

Discussant: That's what I meant—some fear of the therapist, in terms of her needing to help things along by not fighting him, but by trying to maintain the therapeutic situation.

Langs: Yes. She is certainly endeavoring to maintain a therapeutic quality to this bipersonal field—a therapeutic alliance, if you will—but I think that it is important to also understand this on a more personal level, in terms of unconscious curative efforts. In terms of the listening process, the manifest carrier of the derivatives of her curative endeavor alludes not only to a treatment *per se,* but quite personally to the father. As Type Two derivatives, they should be translated not so much in terms of the therapeutic situation, but quite specifically in terms of the patient's relationship with the therapist. It would be defensive to leave out that personal element, and the patient would sense a certain type of anxiety should the therapist intervene in terms of the treatment situation without alluding to himself as well.

So, the patient is saying that as long as the therapist continues to behave in these ways, and to have some degree of inner pathology, it is necessary for her to take over the curative role. But in light of the therapist's rather uncharacteristic silence while the patient was conveying this material, the reference to her curative efforts may also be some type of positive introject, through which the patient is expressing her appreciation for the therapist's silence, which is far more therapeutic than his disruptive interventions; this may well be a commentary on the therapist's shift to a more neutral listening attitude. You can see that in principle, we monitor not only the therapist's interventions but also his silences, using them consistently as an adaptive context for the material from the patient.

In our concern with responses by the patient to the therapist's interventions, I have been focusing, perhaps excessively, on their relevance to validation, largely because it had become increasingly clear to me that there is too great a neglect of the validating process. So, initially, I stressed the interplay between listening and validating, and until now I may have failed to specify fully the many other implications of the patient's responses to interventions and to identify the many other dimensions to which we must apply the listening process at such moments in a session. This includes, as we now see, such matters as the patient's unconscious perceptions of the therapist's unconscious communications, her reactions to these communications, her unconscious curative efforts, unconscious introjects, and the like. I certainly have spent considerable time writing about these processes (see especially, Langs, 1976a) and relating them by implication to the listening process itself. So, I want to stress, specifically, that assessing the material after an intervention from the therapist in terms of its confirmatory qualities is but one task among many.

Here, then, we hear something of the patient's unconscious appreciation of the need for her to take over the curative role.

Therapist: Yes, but look what she says next. She says, I took care of him for those months, but if he had lived, I wouldn't have stayed with him because he was a son of a bitch.

Langs: You're sure you want me to hear this?

Therapist: She said, Whether it's true or not, I feel that he rejected me.

Langs: That's a last little dig at you, back to your first question—and your doubting her. She's also saying that she wonders if she can cure you. She's saying, You're a son of a bitch and I don't know if I can do it. She's afraid she's going to fail, that it's not going to work, because undoubtedly she's been trying to help you throughout this treatment. If this thesis is valid, which obviously I believe it is, then she has been attempting to let you know these things throughout the therapy.

Now, who among therapists is willing to recognize that the patient becomes therapist to the analyst or therapist? Margaret Little wrote this in 1951, but nearly everyone else has ignored it completely. Searles (1975) picked it up, and he didn't even know about Little's paper. It is a concept that had been expressed in a number of his earlier papers (Searles,

1965) and then he crystallized it in a contribution published in 1975. I've written about it too (Langs, 1975a, 1976a,b). Many analysts are very skeptical.

Therapist: There's a little bit more to this session. Then she said, Anyway, I've been reviewing all of this and we should stop talking about that. I've been reviewing all of this and I'm really interested in how talking about this can help me. How can it help? Then she said, Oh, don't bother to answer me. I know. I'll link the past and the present, and we'll work out my problems.

Incidentally, I never told her that.

Langs: That reflects very important qualities of the field generated by Type C analysts and therapists, and, often of course, their patients. She says, at first, rather accurately and quite consciously, though it is modified by a kind of sarcasm, that all of this kind of talk can be of no help to her; it is an isolated review of earlier genetic experiences that have not been connected to the therapeutic relationship, and that remain dead within her and within this communicative field. You have helped to push her into the position of a *Type C narrator,* whose tale is told for now without essential meaning—a position that she herself may have welcomed for reasons of her own.

And she goes on to characterize the qualities of the application of psychoanalytic theory on which such efforts are based; she uses a hollow statement, words without essential meaning, to convey her perception of the emptiness of these efforts. You can see that the cliché quality of this statement lies not in the statement itself, which is certainly true and could be quite viable under certain conditions, but in the timing of the statement, in its dynamic function in the therapeutic interaction, and in the nature of the communicative field.

In a sense, I will paraphrase an observation made by Gill (1963) and others: yesterday's viable insights become today's defenses, and when today's defenses are emptied of derivative meaning, they become Type C defenses, empty, flat, barriers.

It seems to me that the patient is attempting to take a clue from you, and that she's trying to mobilize some Type C defenses against a very fragile and potentially catastrophic situation, both within treatment and within herself. The hour is drawing to an end and the interpretation that the patient needs—the intervention that would link this material to the therapeutic relationship, largely in terms of her unconscious perceptions—has not been made. I think, in retrospect, that at the point where the patient had begun to talk about destructive and murderous doctors, the therapist could have played back the major themes to the patient, selecting derivatives in the hope that she would then directly or indirectly communicate, or even consciously realize, that an important adaptive context for this material pertained to her relationship with the therapist. At that point, the necessary specific intervention could have been made, in the form of a true interpretation, even though it would have dealt primarily with unconscious perceptions. One could then readily add genetic links, as long as their nature was properly formulated.

Because of the disruptive nature of these interventions— their role as a traumatic therapeutic context—the therapist should have made every possible effort to intervene as soon as he began to recognize, either through self-analysis or through clues from the patient's material, the modification in his neutrality and the pathological qualities of his interventions. Possibly, had the patient not provided a link to therapy, he might have had to forgo a basic tenet of intervention that I will discuss in detail later on: that we intervene regarding the therapeutic relationship only when the patient provides the necessary bridge. Occasionally—most often in crisis situations related to unneeded deviations in the framework and missed interventions—one can make the bridge for the patient, though only after playing back the relevant derivatives, especially when there are such close derivatives as we have heard in this session. An intervention of this kind would be of considerable help to this patient in understanding what she is feeling, and in recognizing some of the genetic overtones. It would help her to realize that she's not entirely crazy, and to modify the very destructive therapist introjects that are being derived from the present interaction.

Is there more?

Therapist: Yes. She was quiet, and so I made an intervention. (Laughter.) I said You seem to be very skeptical about
this whole process. And she said, Well, you know it's pretty
hard to pin all my problems on one incident that happened
many years ago. And she added, In any case, how can you
reverse all those years? And then she said something to the
effect, Oh dear, what the hell, I've said this all before. And that
was the end of this session.

Langs: We can see then that you did make some effort to
bring the patient closer to dealing with her relationship with
you, but that you stated the intervention in terms of her
skepticism about the process, instead of using the Type Two
derivatives reflected in her associations, organized around
specific adaptive contexts related to your interventions.

To be brief, because it would be well to hear the beginning of
the next session, you'll notice that the patient asks how all of
this can reverse the problems that have developed throughout
the years of her life. This touches upon my comment that so
long as you behave in a manner comparable to the patient's
father, no such reversal is possible. Nor is it feasible in a Type
C communicative field. You also may have noticed that the
patient said: What the hell. I said all of this before. I made a
hypothesis just a moment ago that the patient had undoubtedly been involved in unconscious curative efforts of this kind
before, and now she quite indirectly but rather clearly states
this herself, with a sense of hopelessness, as if she feels she
must now give up because you have not heard the specifics of
her unconscious communications.

All right, let's hear the beginning of the next session.

Therapist: The next session began. She said, After that
session the other day, I was thinking about my father the
other night, and I threw up. (Laughter.)

Langs: So many classical analysts think the Kleinians are
crazy. It's just astounding when you wonder how much is

metaphor and how much is actuality, and how it gets expressed somatically—a form of communication quite common in the Type B and C fields. And here she says, I was thinking of last session, and I just vomited out the whole damn thing.

I myself become quite perplexed, because I know about concrete thinking, about energic language, which is often validly criticized. When I find myself using a metaphor that begins to sound too concrete I know I'm open to criticism, but clinically it just makes sense. I can immediately understand the unconscious meaning of this vomiting and what she's trying to do.

She ends the previous session by saying she's depressed, and that everything seems hopeless; there seems to be no way to cure the situation or the therapist. Now she adds that all that she can do is vomit everything out. Here, I wonder, are we dealing with an unconscious perception or fantasy, or some somatized expression of a mixture of both? She really seems to feel that the therapist has put into her some very toxic and poisonous projective identifications—if I might add a bit of fantasy of my own to all of this—and certainly, that he has put into her some very bad stuff. She adds that her only defense is to get rid of it, to save her life, to protect herself from murder, by vomiting everything out.

It seems to me that this patient, whatever her own propensities, is in a way being forced, through the nature of the therapist's interventions—his failures at symbolic interpretation and his own use of projective identification—to use projective identification herself, to use discharge and ejection mechanisms to get rid of the disturbances within herself and within this field, because cognitive interpretations directed toward insight are not being utilized as the vehicle of cure. And even though there are efforts toward symbolic communication by the therapist and certainly by the patient, there seems little question that they do not characterize the communicative medium of this bipersonal field. You can see, too, how projective identifications convey meaning—they are efforts at communication—and do not represent an attempt to obliterate meaning and create barriers.

Discussant: Must the therapist deal with her language, with the level at which she does communicate?

Therapist: You're saying that she has a limited means of communicating—she's a sick patient and she has a limited communicative capacity?

Langs: Actually, that is not what I am saying. Her communicative style is so greatly under the influence of your own communicative pressures—it is such an interactional product—that I cannot truly characterize the patient's propensities for the moment, and my view has fluctuated. I can, however, identify contributions from you that have forced, as I said, a shift in this patient toward the Type B mode, or reinforced her own tendencies in this direction.

The other question—how the therapist should deal with the patient's communicative style—raises many important issues that we will be discussing as we go along. In brief, the therapist's first responsibility is to establish a secure framework for the bipersonal field and therapeutic interaction, and then to both listen and interpret, ultimately on a symbolic level. It is, as you can readily sense, another psychoanalytic myth that every analyst is by implication a symbolic communicator. Many analysts and therapists use language for discharge and projective identification, and not for communication on a symbolic level. Many use language to erect meaningless barriers and to destroy communication.

In principle, when you are dealing with a patient in a Type B or Type C field—or with a patient who utilizes a Type B or Type C communicative mode—we cannot pursue directly the interpretation of unconscious contents and introjects, but in a Type B field, must contain and eventually symbolically interpret the patient's projective identifications and behaviors, and in a Type C field, we must interpret the metaphors that the patient generates regarding the use of defensive and interpersonal barriers. Projective identification also can be utilized defensively; this use must be interpreted for meaningful contents to emerge for analysis. Similarly, one must help the patient to modify Type C barriers and destruction of meaning in order to have a field within which contents can be meaningfully interpreted. So, in brief, the answer is yes. We do deal with the patient's communicative style. But I am now moving toward a discussion of interventions; let's try to maintain our focus on the intaking side of the therapist's work.

Therapist: She continued: I was thinking of the conversation that we had.

Langs: Now in terms of listening, what does this direct us to as the adaptive context for this particular session? What is the primary adaptive task, as I had first termed it (Langs, 1974)?

Discussant: Her reaction to the past and her reaction to her relationship with the therapist.

Langs: I would stress the latter. She is really directing us very quickly to the therapeutic relationship. It's as if she were saying, I was thinking of last session; this is what set me off. She also offers material about her father, so that you could kind of either see it in the way I stated, or go on and on again about the father. We'll see, though, which organizes the material better. So, she immediately gives us an organizer in this session—let's see how it helps in listening.

Therapist: She said, The conversation I had with you the other night...uh, other day. (Laughter.) It was the darkness. That's what it seemed like. The conversation that I had with you the other day was really upsetting. And she said, In some ways I feel that I'm just getting worse.

Langs: Which is in keeping with what I said. She didn't say she's a sick patient who doesn't know how to communicate. This is confirmation of my earlier formulation, that she feels that therapy—the therapist—is making her worse.
Now this may or may not be so. This is a conscious statement. It is not true validation, though it does conform to my silent hypothesis; indirect confirmation is what I'm looking for as true validation. Let's see where it goes.

Therapist: She said, I'm certainly doing no better. I'm making no more progress on my research, but I am dwelling a lot, thinking a lot more about this idea of rejection. She said, You know, when I first went to a lesbian club several years ago, I told you that I was living with a girlfriend, not a lover. Anyway, as I said, she went to California to live. The patient had had a depression—a very severe depression—at that time.

And then she repeated, She went to California to live, and said, Well, that was certainly proximal—maybe it was a cause—I just don't know. But my latest downturn happened when I considered coming back to therapy again. Several weeks after that, I made the suicide attempt and I've been in a fog about it for all this time.

Langs: Now, can anybody organize this material, in any way?

Discussant: She feels that she's getting worse and therapy isn't helping. It may even be causing more pain; and she says, I remember rejection and I got depressed at that time. So she's saying she feels depressed over the results of the prior session, the interaction. I guess.

Langs: Can you, in terms of the three kinds of communications from patients—the three levels of listening—tell me what you just formulated? Manifest content? Type One derivatives, reading inferences into material from the manifest content alone? Or Type Two derivatives, unique meanings based on an organizing adaptive context? Your formulation was of what kind?

Discussant: Well, it sort of veered toward Type Two derivatives; it included part of the adaptive context of the session.

Langs: Yes, you were trying to move in that direction, but you failed to make use of a clearly defined adaptive context, and of the patient's specific derivatives. By confining yourself to generalizations, you were either using very general Type

Two derivatives or Type One derivatives, and some of your remarks, as you seem to be aware, were related to the manifest content.

Now, when you say that she's talking about rejection, and it probably means being rejected by the therapist, that's an evaluation that is based on a Type One derivative. It is important that you recognize that you stayed very close to the surface, because I have found that many therapists tend to apply the listening process in a very generalized manner, and fail to get around to specifics. Often these avoided specifics are related to instinctual drive needs, to painful unconscious perceptions by the patient related to the therapist; this need to generalize, to be global and vague, can occur almost at a perceptual level and can serve the defenses of the therapist. Can anyone else offer a formulation of this material?

Discussant: I would take the formulation just offered and extend it to a Type Two derivative. I would say that there is an adaptive context, namely, in the last session the therapist gave her more than she could handle, and she might not be able to help him and he might not be able to help her. Therefore, she might have to separate from him and that particular separation will precipitate a depression like the last separation.

Langs: You're moving toward a more precise formulation, but the Type Two derivatives that you have developed are given meaning more through that first communication—her vomiting—than through the rest. I'm talking now about the subsequent material, and I think your emphasis was really on the initial communication, to which you've added something that I think is rather shaped by your own impressions and fantasies, which is fine, so long as you know it—though some of it is also derived from the later associations.

Discussant: Could she be saying, I became so depressed and suicidal when I was abandoned by my friend, and I feel abandonment now?

Langs: Yes, but again, that's a Type One derivative. My point is this: the material lacks depth. It has a quality of strongly invested fragments, but they do not lend themselves to organization. I want you to realize that as residents, psychiatrists, therapists, and analysts we're always looking for meaning. The last thing that we look for is the absence of meaning. And this is related to a facet of the listening process that I had just begun to address: the need for the therapist to be aware of the extent to which his own impressions, fantasies, and possibly even distortions contribute to his shaping of the material from the patient; the need to recognize that the listening process is, as I have stated repeatedly now, always interactional, and that the product is always an amalgam of contributions from both the therapist and the patient. And it turns out, of course, that the therapist can contribute creatively or in distorted fashion to every step in the process, from his basic perception of the patient's communications, and his initial experience of the patient's projective identifications, evoked roles, and evoked images, to his formulation of the material, his responsive associations and fantasies, and his eventual synthesis into a silent hypothesis.

We are so steeped in the tradition of searching for meaning in the patient's material, of understanding derivative communication, of seeking implications—fantasies, memories, introjects, self-representations, object representations, and so much more—that we have not as yet, for whatever reason, fully considered the problem of non-meaning, of facade, and of situations in which it is essentially impossible to organize the patient's communications around a specific adaptive context in order to derive a definitive unconscious meaning—fantasy or perception.

Certainly, the recognition that the patient's material could be serving essentially as a defensive barrier, falsification, and facade creates new issues for the listening process, and new potential for countertransference expression. For example, the therapist may well conclude that the material lacks meaning when, in fact, he has missed a crucial adaptive context, and an essential unconscious communication. But that should come as no surprise, since every aspect of psychotherapeutic technique is open to countertransference-based influence, and must be safeguarded by the validating process, and ultimately by the therapist's self-knowledge.

For the moment, this material lacks a specific adaptive context, and I do not see the derivatives of such a context, except in the vaguest sense—that is, that perhaps something is disturbing her about treatment, that it's taking place in a fog, that there's the danger of abandonment or a sense of loss, and perhaps even that there are some unconscious sexual qualities (the reference to the lesbian club). But at this point, it is important to recognize that the material is not organizing around a specific adaptive context and has not coalesced. It is essential to experience this vagueness and uncertainty; then, after having appied the validating process to your efforts, and explored your own inner feelings for possible counter-transference-based influences, you can for the moment accept, as a definitive silent hypothesis, that the material from the patient is not generating clear-cut meaning.

We will have a chance to study therapeutic interactions in which the absence of meaning is far more evident, but it is not uncommon in psychotherapy to have sessions in which there appear to be all sorts of clues—bits and fragments that seem to point in diverse directions—and in which the material does not coalesce, while at times, even the adaptive context itself remains uncertain. Often, by the way, this mode unconscious-ly is designed to destroy the therapist's mental capacities, his ability to organize the material. It is a disorganizing projective identification.

Now at such times, the most relevant and basic silent hypothesis is that the patient is splitting and fragmenting her associations in order to deprive them of clear-cut meaning—in the language of this patient, to maintain a foglike quality to the situation. In forming such a hypothesis, we must always be prepared to identify our own contribution to this communi-cative style—the fog-promoting qualities of the therapist's interventions—and we make efforts, then, to understand the communicative style as an interactional product; but it is important to be open to experiencing and understanding interludes of confusion and uncertainty in psychotherapy.

Many therapists would attempt to formulate this material in a manner not unlike the discussants who have commented here. They think of suicide as a response to separation and loss, as a reflection of depression. But you can see that such a concept is rather manifest and obvious; it is flat and generalized, a psychoanalytic cliché, which must then serve primarily as a falsification and barrier to the more painful underlying truths. Despite the intensity of this material, it stays quite close to the surface. The themes are that if someone leaves her, she's fragile, becomes depressed and suicidal. It implies a hope that the therapist will not abandon her. There's something also about returning to treatment and becoming suicidal, but again, I would just continue to cite some additional fragments. For the moment, I would hypothesize that this patient is attempting to maintain the static, Type C field through a Type C narrative which contains many seemingly interesting elements but lacks organization and meaning.

Discussant: But there's an implied threat in what she's saying.

Langs: Yes, perhaps even a suicidal threat. For the moment, that is a projective identification into the therapist that he might have difficulty in metabolizing and understanding. It could generate feelings of confusion, perhaps even of guilt. Certainly he would need further material so that he could understand, metabolize, organize, and eventually interpret the meaning of this projective identification. But he is more than likely experiencing a sense of threat without, for the moment, a basis for understanding its unconscious meaning, although you could sense that this is, in part, a reprojection of the therapist's threatening projective identification. Nothing seems certain, and nothing builds—perhaps only an anxiety-provoking sense of danger.

It is so important in the listening process to realize that if you pick up a truly crucial theme, it will eventually be shaped through Type Two derivatives, will be part of an accumulation of meaning. Derivatives will add to your understanding in surprising ways, through one variation and another—theme and variation—something like the vomiting in terms of the formulations that I had offered. There really can be no substitute for experiencing moments of confusion like this; they are contrasted with interludes in which you suddenly discover an adaptive context that beautifully organizes the material from the patient, where you have an adaptive context that renders exquisite meaning to a series of associations that now take form as Type Two derivatives.

Discussant: Maybe the threat is: If you reject me—in the sense, if you reject what I say, like you did last time—I'll become suicidal.

Langs: Yes, but it's still a very obvious statement, however moving its content. She's saying, If you are not good to me, if you are hurtful, I would not want to live. It's all right there on the surface. Later in this session, I suspect she'll give us something with more depth, and we can then contrast it with these associations. She's trying desperately to mobilize some very surface-oriented defenses here to keep things under control and to alert the therapist to some sense of danger or threat. What lies beneath that is, as yet, unclear.

Discussant: Are you saying that the adaptive context that is most meaningful has to do with the patient's attempt to adapt to the therapist's misinterventions, in a sense?

Langs: Well, at this point, probably yes. The material is not, however, organizing clearly and meaningfully around that issue.

Discussant: In this case, you're not making that as some general statement.

Langs: Well, as a general statement, whenever the therapist makes an error, that becomes the most significant adaptive context for the patient.

Discussant: That gives you less information about the patient, more information about the therapist.

Langs: Not at all. You learn a great deal about both of them.

Discussant: It doesn't necessarily lead to progress in the treatment and your understanding of the patient, since you're really then dealing with an artifact created by the treatment.

Discussant: I get the feeling that for teaching purposes, you are kind of emphasizing that part of it. I can see where all of that would help to understand the patient a lot more, because you get different kinds of feelings for different patients. You have to understand the part that comes from you. But it is different with each patient, isn't it?

Langs: It will be different with each patient, and it will be different with each therapist. But you are not recognizing the fact that therapy is always an interactional unfolding, that the influence of the therapist, even when it is counter-transference-based, creates not an artifact but a particular set of conditions to which the patient responds in terms of his assets and liabilities, his healthy and sick parts.

Certainly, countertransference-based interventions impose particular burdens on the patient, influence her perception and introjections of the therapist, and disturb the communicative qualities of the field, and the therapeutic work as well. It is not the optimal approach to therapy. But I have been trying to stress, as a counterbalancing factor, that the recognition of these disturbances, their rectification, and their analysis with the patient can be quite therapeutic for the patient and, secondarily, for the therapist as well. It is true that the therapeutic experience and the communicative relationship have different qualities when the therapist's countertransferences have not imposed themselves upon the bipersonal field and the patient, but you should be learning that in reality, countertransference-based influences are ever-present. They are to be minimized through self-analysis and through self-curative efforts when they emerge in the treatment situation, but when they are more blatant, they have a distinctly significant influence on the entire therapeutic experience.

In addition, it should now be evident to you, as therapists-in-training and as individuals who have had only a small amount of analysis or therapy, if any, that it is quite likely that there will, indeed, be significant contributions from your own unresolved counterfransference constellation in the interaction with your patients. It is more than evident from your reactions that this is a quite disturbing truth, and you are, indeed, protesting a bit against recognizing it. I should hope that after you get over the initial disturbance and anxiety you will welcome it as an important insight that will better enable you to understand your interaction with your patients. Remember, I bring them up not only for teaching purposes, but because your own patients unconsciously are confronting these issues with you all the time. In a sense, by the very nature of your reaction, it appears likely that you have found it necessary to make these efforts at silencing and suppression not only here in this seminar, but with your patients as well.

Perhaps this helps you to understand what I said earlier about creativity. If you cannot tolerate truly new and disturbing ideas from me, you will certainly have a similar difficulty with your patients. Quite specifically, if you cannot tolerate recognizing the extensive influence of countertransferences in the work with patients presented in this seminar, you will certainly not tolerate their recognition, however unconsciously, by your patients, nor will you be able, yourselves, to identify their manifestations and to deal appropriately with them. They will remain as silent disruptive influences on your therapeutic work and, as I said earlier, on our essential search for the truth. I hope that you will not become too personally defensive to the point of not wishing to know the truth. I've seen it happen.

Discussant: But aren't we learning more about the mistakes of the therapist than progressing in our knowledge of the patient?

Langs: Once again, you separate the two, as if they were unrelated. Clearly, the more you learn about the mistakes of the therapist, the more you'll learn about patients; the more you learn about yourselves, the more you learn about your patients.

I am trying to teach you a basic model of psychotherapy, a bipersonal field in which we are prepared to accept vectors from both the patient and therapist. In applying this model, we allow the data to direct us, and if it directs us to the pathological inputs of the therapist, we should be prepared to explore their ramifications, just as we are equally prepared to explore the ramifications of the patient's pathological vectors. It really can be no other way. Ultimately, it should matter little for this course whether we trace out the effects of the patient's pathology or those of the therapist's pathology. We are dealing with an interactional product, and are endeavoring to conceptualize the vicissitudes of that interaction.

Actually, we will study the therapist's errors in greater detail when we consider the therapeutic relationship. But it seems now that I must say this much: one of the criticisms of my work is that I am preoccupied with the therapist and his pathology, and that I tend to neglect the patient. This is not at all true as any careful reading of my writings will indicate. Furthermore, I am, I believe, presenting a really fair and unbiased view of the therapeutic interaction, explicitly stating in some detail the contribution derived from the therapist's countertransferences while delineating the patient's assets and capabilities in her relationship with the therapist along with the effects of her pathology. This approach stands in contrast with the usual attitude of psychoanalysts, where the therapist is seen as healthy and functioning quite validly, though suffering occasional, isolated, countertransference-based disturbances, and the patient is seen as sick and distorting, almost without any acknowledgment of her unconscious resources. My more balanced and accurate description of the therapeutic situation disturbs this more defensive and prejudiced view, and I believe that your questions indicate that this is very much the way you have been taught. Incidentally, this is a position that no one openly espouses, though many maintain it implicitly.

In principle the therapeutic work occurring in the biperson- al field will tend to concentrate on that vector of pathology that is the greatest, be it from the patient or the therapist. That appears to me to be a simple and basic principle that allows room for the patient's unconscious therapeutic efforts, as well as those of the therapist. It does not prejudge the situation, and is derived from empirical observation based on a sound and unbiased use of the listening process.

I have no personal need to be preoccupied with the pathology of the therapist, but if the patient is so preoccupied for the moment, one must recognize that fact. In any situation where the therapist is not contributing significant pathologi- cal inputs, we will have far less to say about the realm of countertransference, and far more to say about the realm of transference in its true and narrower sense.

For the present, in studying so-called contaminated bipersonal fields, which are characteristic of those generated by most trainees and training situations, we will find that the patient will largely work over the disturbances in that field— the pathological inputs from the therapist—camouflaging or concealing much of his own pathology within that of the therapist. That is where we will have to do our work, and that is how we can learn.

After all, it is impossible empirically to conceptualize psychotherapy by ignoring the actualities of the therapeutic interaction. Let us learn directly from these interactions, and if certain types of material are not available to us for now, we can fill in the gaps in a more hypothetical way through principles derived from the material that we have observed. Let's follow the data and accept where it takes us, and once we have absorbed that, we'll see what remains to be done.

Discussant: I'd like to make a suggestion. It seems to me that most of the presentations that we're going to be dealing with will relate to very contaminated fields. At some point, could you bring in a session or two in which you feel that the therapist was not in a contaminated field, and in which countertransference factors were not important?

Langs: I'm hoping that you'll produce that for me. I maintain total confidentiality, never reporting or using in any way, shape or form, any of my own work. I am not now in a personal analysis and I'm not here to learn from you through presenting material from which you can teach me, and those are the only two conditions under which I feel confidentiality should and has to be modified.

Let's get back now to some more clinical material.

Therapist: Okay. She talked about her latest downturn. She said, It's a mystery to me why the other time I went down the tubes, it was a clear loss. She said, I have no idea about what precipitated this thing, but you know, I was thinking about this suicide attempt. Then she went blank, I'm not sure why. She just said, Wait, just hold on. I just have to collect my thoughts. Then she went on again. She said, At the time I went into the latest downspin, that was a few months ago, I had broken up with this Korean artist for the second time. (She had lived with this guy, this forty-nine-year-old guy before.) As a matter of fact, she said, I was living with him off and on, but I didn't want him any more. I was just tired of the relationship. It wasn't right, and I told him that it was off, that it just wasn't right, but still I felt very rejected, but I just blocked it out. I didn't remember the incident until the other night—that was the first time I remembered for a long time that it had even happened at all. It was with that—that spirit of the breakup of that relationship that I moved into my girlfriend's apartment. I just can't understand it. I forgot that whole episode.

I made a comment here: I said, The way you seem to deal with many painful episodes is by blocking them out.

Langs: Okay. So again, this has to do with what you heard, and it reflects something about the nature of the communicative field. Any thoughts about this material and the intervention? (Pause.)

I would suggest that this is a confrontation, and that it deals with the manifest content of these associations and with a surface kind of defense. You can see that the intervention really lacks a meaningful adaptive context, once again, although it attempts to use a rather general adaptive model by stating that the patient deals with painful episodes by blocking them out. The intervention, nonetheless, lacks a specific immediate adaptive context and it is without an effort to deal with derivative communication.

It seems evident—and I believe that this intervention also reflects these qualities—that the patient's material continues to be ruminative, that she does not develop a specific adaptive context, and that there are occasional hints of some type of unconscious fantasy or perception—something sexual, or the end of a relationship. There are bits and pieces that suggest a Type C communicative field and a fairly massive defensiveness without derivatives that illuminate these defenses and their unconscious meaning; her associations also fail to indicate in derivative and interpretable form the unconscious contents that the patient is warding off.

The same evaluation can be made of the therapist's intervention. It is, despite its manifest intention to identify a mode of defensiveness that the patient utilizes, a psychoanalytic cliché, offered in a nondynamic manner to maintain the patient's focus on the surface of this material, and probably, as I have suggested repeatedly today, designed also to discourage the communication of derivatives related to the therapeutic relationship. You will note, in this respect, that the patient's efforts to block out painful episodes—reflected in associations that can be conceptualized along the me-not-me interface—could apply with equal validity to the therapist, and that I am in a sense implying just that by characterizing both the patient's and the therapist's communicative style as in the Type C mode for the moment. Both are using language to obliterate meaning and as a facade.

One final point: your intervention reveals that you are unable to conceptualize the unconscious basis of this patient's depression, suicide attempt, and present state. You're left with her surface communications: somebody left her; she got depressed; she wanted to kill herself; and this is reflected in the surface level intervention: When she has a painful episode, she tries to block it out.

Therapist: I don't know why she attempted suicide; if that's what you're saying, it's true.

Langs: You know nothing of the inner mental contents and of the unconscious interactional inputs at all.

Therapist: I know nothing; you're right.

Langs: This is a sealed off field. The blankness is a representation of the Type C field. This is now an empty field. Her words, and yours, are empty too. I would be thinking about intervening in regard to the blankness; I would be developing her images of the communicative field in terms of the way in which she's trying to obliterate its communicative qualities, and how the therapist is contributing as well, but I wouldn't have intervened as yet. I would have been silent, though this would be my main formulation. Let's just hear what she said next and we will stop.

Therapist: She said, I do forget a lot, yes. It's true.

Langs: Your intervention keeps things on the surface. This is going to reinforce her own defenses through which words without functional meaning will help her to seal off whatever does have meaning.

Therapist: She said, But I go through these motions all the time, and what exactly is the benefit for me in doing all of this?

Langs: Where is that benefit? I go through the motions. She now takes all of the blame, and becomes depressed. She also uses a metaphor for the Type C field: going through the motions—the absence of meaning.

Therapist: I made the comment again which I made several sessions ago. I said, You seem to be working on these associations outside of the session, but you come in here and say that it's not doing you any good.

Langs: Yes, so again, you are noninterpretive. It's accusatory, you introduce that old theme, not her, and you continue to intervene along the same line even though you did not get confirmation. You blame her for the lack of confirmation, rather than both you and her—and silently. Typically, what you're going to have to learn is to ask yourself, What did I do to contribute to this defense? Defenses are essentially interactional, you see. So now you're dumping all of the blame into her, which will increase her depression; that's a disturbing intervention. What you're saying to her is, You're doing it outside of here, you're not doing it here—and you're complaining about what we're doing.

Therapist: Yes, that's what I'm saying.

Langs: It's very blaming, very hurtful.

Therapist: Well, the next session she comes in.

Langs: Is that the end of the session?

Therapist: Yes, but I just wanted to add into the hopper that the next session she comes in—I just never know what's going on with this woman and all—she comes in and tells me she's been taking a tranquilizer all the time she's been in therapy, and she hasn't been telling me. She got it from another doctor. It turns out that it is the same drug that she used to make the suicide attempt—that, and gas.

Langs: So, she was taking in this destructive stuff from the other doctor. There is concealment, some sense of deception, a different attempt at cure that is linked to her efforts at self-destruction. My observations to this point indicate that the use of medication is characteristic in a Type C communicative field. It is an effort to avoid meaning, and to create a truly amorphous, concealing barrier.

Now, even though we will not be able to hear any more of this session, let me tell you that in general, patients turn to medication when they feel that they are not being helped through the therapist's interventions, and when they feel threatened by an uncontrolled therapeutic situation and therapist. They modify the frame by taking drugs, and effect a "framework cure," which is, as she implies, inherently quite destructive.

It seems to me that some crucial problems in developing your skills in using the listening process involve the way the therapist learns to get beyond the manifest content of the patient's material. How does he learn to generate interventions that will promote Type A communication in the patient, rather than Type B or Type C? How does he learn to process the cognitive material, and the patient's interactional communications, beyond the manifest content and obvious inferences in order to derive truly unconscious meaning?

I have outlined the necessary methodology, but I think that it's more than evident that this is not simply a matter of cognitive learning, and that the ability to utilize this methodology is intimately related to your capacity to master your own countertransferences. That seems as good a note as any to end our meeting for today. Thank you for such a candid and interesting presentation.

Chapter Four

NEUROTIC AND NONNEUROTIC
COMMUNICATION

Monitoring the material in terms of the therapeutic relationship • Three basic steps in arriving at Type One derivatives • The me-not-me interface • Limitations to formulating without an adaptive context • A selected fact and its ramifications • The anxieties in learning to do psychotherapy

Langs: Today we begin with a new presentation, through which, I hope, we will further illustrate and clarify the basic principles that we have so far developed. Perhaps you can begin with the session before the main hour that you will be presenting.

Therapist: It's not too concise, because I didn't put it together. Do you want something about the patient?

Langs: Sure, briefly.

Therapist: I'll give you one sentence. She's a thirty-four-year-old Ph.D. in economics and business administration, whom I have been seeing for about a year, who completed her work for her doctorate about a year ago, and who is now working at a job at a rather low salary, and at a level that is quite beneath what she ought to be able to do. She has an apartment of her own, but she spends most of her time in her boyfriend's apartment. Okay?

Langs: How frequent are your sessions?

Therapist: Twice a week. She had recently passed a licensing exam; I think she told me about it two or three sessions before this one. She was sure she was going to fail, convinced of it.

Discussant: I wonder if there's anything you can tell us about what she's like in the therapy?

Therapist: Yes. She always goes off on tangents, saying that she doesn't seem to be able to get anything together. Her complaints are always very vague.

Langs: These are reasonable questions, and yet, we'll see how relevant they are to the material we are about to hear. One of the criticisms of my work has been to the effect that I don't give enough background about the patient, enough material. I have learned, though, that much of that material is really noninformation—it falsifies and distracts.

There is information that is important. You'll fill us in as we go along—offer us some perspective. The patient will clue us in too. If something alludes to something else that happened in the previous session, an explanation would help us too. We'd like to have some notion of this patient and why she's in treatment. But I do think to the extent that it's a relevant question, we will soon hear about it in the session. There's a kind of silent—or not so silent—chief complaint for each session, if you will, and often it's related to the adaptive context. In all, for now, let's develop what we will need for the listening process, and try first to experience a need for what seems to be missing. So we have a little bit of background. Go ahead.

Therapist: In the previous session, she told me she was planning to meet with her boss, to ask for more money, but that she was afraid that she would appear too demanding. That led to a discussion, I think instituted by me, about the fact that her parents didn't like it when the kids were demanding—they always said that adults take care of themselves, don't ask other people.

Langs: I'm sorry—this is a bit too condensed to follow.

Therapist: All right, I would have to tell you the session...

Langs: Oh yes, in sequence. You can read it through quickly.

Therapist: All right. She came in saying that she was going to ask for more money, but she's afraid that she'd seem too demanding, and that she tends to inhibit herself to avoid these aspects of herself, which she doesn't like. And also that she feels very stunned when people see parts of her that she doesn't like herself. She said that her parents were strikingly intolerant—that she and her two brothers were strikingly undemanding—but went on to say that her dislike of this part of herself is very much a part of her mother's attitude—that adults don't act that way, are not demanding. She went on to say how angry she was that she's in that whole situation— originally, when she took the job—that she would accept the job with so little money. How could she have done this to herself? She always does things like this to herself.

Langs: Now, let's pause for a minute. Because inevitably, we have a session without the previous session—that's this session, the one we're just going to go over briefly. Tell me now: what you hear? What can you do in the way of the listening process with this material?

Discussant: The basic thing she's saying is, I'm afraid that I make too many demands on people, or that I'm going to be too demanding. I would wonder, is this in the context of what happened with this boss? Is that the main context? Or does it have to do somewhat with her relationship with the therapist, who is a woman—the reference to her mother.

Langs: Any other thoughts?

Discussant: Perhaps in the previous session the therapist had said something in some context to the effect, Don't make any demands on me. Perhaps that's what the patient is reacting to.

Langs: Just again, for our clarification—you accepted my suggestion, but moved along a bit too quickly. Let's hear a bit more of that material.

Therapist: Just the business of her being uncomfortable with men and not wanting to show parts of herself—saying that she always avoided confrontation because she got into so much trouble with men, and when she was demanding, people didn't like it. Somehow the atmosphere in her home—there was a lack of demandingness that sometimes led her and her brothers to become increasingly demanding. And that she doesn't like these parts of herself, but that she recognizes that that statement comes right out of her mother's mouth—that adults don't act that way, in other words, demanding.

Langs: Okay.—Anybody else hear anything in this material, for the moment? (Pause.) Let's say a bit more about it. First of all, let's clarify what the two discussants did. I'm one for really attempting to identify the nature of what we're doing, rather than just leaving it to "instinct" in its broadest sense. That is, you both listened to or monitored the material in terms of the possibility that it contained some commentary on the therapeutic relationship. That's the first job; you were taking this material as a displaced commentary on the therapeutic relationship, and you related it to possible past transactions—to a possible prior adaptive context. Both of you were really saying that it might be based on something the therapist did; you're even now leaning more toward that contingency than to the possibility that it might be based on some fantasy the patient had, and I'd just as well see you lean that way: it might be based on something that happened, because you'll have to determine that, before you can determine anything about what the patient elaborated in terms of her own fantasies. Yes: reality before fantasy—I'm pleased to see that you're picking that up. So, you're monitoring the material in terms of the therapeutic relationship. And we'll have to see whether that works with every presentation we have. My hypothesis is that it will, without exception. It's something I will have to demonstrate again and again; perhaps we can even find an exception and understand its basis.

But I want to identify an aspect of what you did that is related to another dimension of the listening process: You took certain concrete associations; you then identified their thematic content, the more general themes. You carrried out a process of abstracting from the particular. This is a very important concept for which kind of derivative? Anybody remember?

Discussant: Manifest content, Type One derivatives?

Langs: You condensed two concepts. There are three levels: manifest content, Type One and Type Two derivatives. Type One derivatives—indeed that's what we are dealing with here for the moment. We don't have an adaptive context. That's really what you were telling us in the comment you made. You were saying, You know, maybe something happened in the past with the therapist that could have prompted this material. But you were admitting that you don't know what it is, and that not knowing it, you're not really sure what to make of this material. But what you can do is develop some Type One derivatives that go beyond the manifest content. What's the manifest content—I mean, what's its main theme? It's very obvious.

Discussant: Asking the boss for a raise.

Langs: What else? So it isn't so obvious. What other theme?

Discussant: Demands.

Langs: Yes, demands as a theme—demands, demands, demands. In fact, when you hear so much of the same word, you begin to wonder what's going on—because surface repetition without an adaptive context conceals far more than it reveals, at least until we know the context. It does not promote knowledge. It maintains ignorance. Repetition hints at a Type C communicative field. If she just keeps talking about demands and not being demanding throughout this session, you will learn absolutely nothing about this patient, even though she gives you genetic material. For the moment, even the genetics are really used for deception, because she's trying to tell you that her problem is that, in her life, she never learned to be demanding, and her mother told her not to be, and that's why she isn't making demands on her boss.

Now, is that the nature of a neurosis? The answer is no. Even a preoedipally determined neurosis—and I use the term *neurosis* in this course in its broadest sense—has unconscious elements to it, is based on unconscious factors, has intrapsychic reinforcement based on unconscious fantasies and introjects and is not founded on conscious knowledge. If it were simply a matter of conscious knowledge, the next sentence would be: Now I know it, and I won't do it any more. And of course, that's not how you cure or resolve an emotional problem, because the unconscious factors remain untouched and, essentially, are not revealed here. What's revealed here is a conscious chain—not a convoluted, derivative one, at least to the extent that we can formulate it without knowledge of the prior hour and the adaptive context, which does not seem to have been conveyed as yet.

Therapist: Well, that's not exactly what she's saying though. She's saying that she senses that she is very demanding, but she's uncomfortable in being that way and she tried to squelch that tendency.

Langs: All right, it's a little bit more subtle. She's saying that nobody was demanding in her house, and that she and her brothers became demanding because of it. Now people don't like her when she's demanding. It's still the same thing; this is a conscious thread related to her fear of being demanding—because she was demanding and people didn't like it. It is based on a model of conscious learning. It touches upon her problems in a direct and linear way, and it is what I would term *nonneurotic communication.* It will not, as formulated, reveal the unconscious basis for her neurosis.

Therapist It involves her fear of men too.

Langs: But it's the same point. It's a series of manifest links, all of which yield nothing in the psychoanalytic sense—at least, nothing without a specific adaptive context.

Discussant: I think there's another schematic content to it, and that's justifying her own sense of self-worth. How does she do that? In a number of ways, but she has to do it externally and those are the ways that have been devalued by her parents.

Langs: So, at what level is that formulation? We have manifest content, Type One and Type Two derivatives. What have you just identified?

Discussant: It seems to be more of the latent content of what she has said. She hasn't brought any of it back to her sense of self worth, whether she gets her job or not. She may, but we haven't heard enough to know whether she will or not.

Langs: You're saying that this would be a Type One derivative, an implication that you derive from the manifest content, leading you to organize the material around the theme of self-worth. As you can see, it's rather close to the manifest themes of the material, and it is, at best, a readily implied Type One derivative—an implication that you can easily read into these associations and in a very general and even vague way.

Actually, I am very pleased that you offered this particular formulation, because it is characteristic of a type of psychotherapy that is quite prevalent, as far as I can determine. It illustrates what I have been referring to when I allude to efforts to work with Type One derivatives, and it will provide us with an opportunity to identify the value of such work, if there is any, and many of its liabilities.

I would characterize your formulation in this way: you are taking as the adpative context the actual situation between the patient and her boss—an adpative context that is, for the moment, unrelated to the therapeutic interaction—and you are considering it in terms of its rather direct implications: there are issues of self-esteem in the patient's approaching her boss for a raise. There are distinctive features to this type of adaptive context: it is an evident stimulus for an inner response; the reaction is rather direct; she is dealing with an apparent trauma or anxiety. But it evokes an intrapsychic reaction with many straightforward qualities—much of it conscious, some of it even genetic. This differs from a response that we would characterize as primarily occurring in derivative form, based often on a somewhat disguised adaptive context, and which includes indirect allusions to significant unconscious fantasies, memories, and introjects.

It is sometimes difficult for therapists to distinguish between varieties of adaptive context, and to identify those that contain more realistic concerns which, while they clearly have intrapsychic and unconscious ramifications, evoke responses that are largely conscious and direct. These adaptive stimuli must be contrasted with those often less evident precipitants—and those contexts with apparent manifest elements, to which the patient is responding largely in terms of their latent implications—that evoke immediate pathological defensiveness, derivative communication, intense pathological unconscious fantasy activity, and with which the patient tends to deal largely on an unconscious level, through indirect means.

To put all of this another way: with the first type of adaptive context, the patient's associations are directly relevant and immediately illuminating, linear and often flat, while with the second and more significant adaptive context the patient's associations tend to veer away, to move toward indirect and derivative communication, and they have to be organized and linked back to the adaptive context in order to generate true unconscious meaning. The latter has qualities that can be described as unexpected, rich, convoluted, deep, creative, and imaginative.

In fact, in the face of a seemingly significant adaptive context that is intrapsychically and interactionally relevant to the patient's unconscious conflicts and fantasies, when the patient continues to ruminate directly we should have reason to suspect either that the adaptive context is in some other area, or that the patient is utilizing an intensive Type C barrier-defense. When we come to accept the finding that the most significant adaptive contexts in psychotherapy are almost always contained somewhere within the therapeutic relationship, and are often embedded in the material and not directly stated by the patient, we soon learn the important qualities of these intrapsychically significant adaptive contexts and are in a position to contrast them with the more reality-oriented contexts.

So for the moment, I am suggesting that the patient's concern about asking her boss for a raise is a *direct adaptive context,* one that is more linearly evocative and whose intrapsychic implications are rather evident from the manifest content and from Type One derivatives. With that in mind, we will have to wait for more material in order to identify a possible *indirect adaptive context,* one that is intrapsychically meaningful and that evokes indirect responses characteristic of unconscious fantasy activity, unconscious conflict, and the like. Once we have the other adaptive context—and my prediction must be that it will lie somewhere within the therapeutic relationship—we will be able to contrast its nature with the present adaptive context, and I hope that this will clarify this very important technical point: a direct adaptive context is often alluded to quite openly and extensively by the patient, while the indirect context tends to be embedded in the patient's ongoing associations, well disguised, and at times, entirely repressed.

Let's extend our characterization of these two types of adaptive contexts, and the type of therapeutic work that may be done with each. In the first situation, exemplified by your formulation regarding the patient's concerns about self-worth, the therapist confines himself to the manifest content or Type One derivatives. His inferences are based on psychoanalytic theory and his comment is characteristically a generalization that lacks specific personal qualities. This type of effort generates formulations that could be stated about every human being, and they do not include specific unconscious fantasies, memories, and introjects, that would characterize this patient alone, even though quite often, they have, like the present situation, genetic underpinnings.

That is, in this situation you are attempting to suggest that the patient's mother did not permit an integrated system of self-esteem to develop, that she interfered with the patient's feelings of self-worth and with appropriate avenues for achieving such feelings. This, again, is based on the patient's conscious and direct description of her mother and her relationship with her, and it contains no elements of unconscious fantasies and the like. In a sense, it is based on a notion of cure to the effect that becoming aware of the ways in which the mother interfered, and recognizing their present influence, will lead to some type of internal readjustment, and to an adequate sense of self-esteem or an adequate means of achieving it.

As you undoubtedly recognize, there is a great deal of work in the area of narcissistic disturbances that is done on just this very basis. Such efforts, I believe, actually deny the influence of unconscious processes and mechanisms, restricting them to some type of mechanistic view or to a level of generalization that totally excludes the specific intrapsychic processing of earlier experiences and the fantasies and introjects that they generate. I really can't stress this point enough. There is no sense of intrapsychic mediation in such work, no true sense of intrapsychic processes, defenses and fantasies, no use of Type Two derivatives, and massive use of intellectualizations and generalizations as Type C barriers designed to destroy more disturbing underlying meanings and the kind of specific therapeutic work that such patients really need. In fact, were it not for the finding that such efforts can actually create or reinforce Type C barriers, and in that way provide the patient with momentary noninsightful symptom relief—a misalliance cure—they would have been discarded long ago, because they do not lead to true resolution of intrapsychic conflicts, to the modification of pathological unconscious fantasies, memories, and introjects, and to true adaptive inner change.

In a general way, I would contrast such an approach with that which utilizes the indirect adaptive context, and which organizes the material as Type Two derivatives around that adaptive context, generating an understanding of indirect communication, of the expression of unconscious fantasies, memories, and introjects through the interpretation of disguised, convoluted, coalescing derivatives, leading to specific understanding of the patient's intrapsychic conflicts and anxieties, of the precise and now unconscious genetic basis and the specific unconscious processing to which the patient's earliest experiences and traumas were subjected. This approach utilizes as a basis for intervening not an intellectualized theory but the derivative communications from the patient. It recognizes that it is in that realm that the patient's emotional disturbance has developed, and that it is work within such a context that can provide the patient with insights into the nature of his pathological conflicts and fantasies, and with a means for inner, adaptive change. And incidently, I should also stress that such work will always evolve from the present dynamics of the therapeutic interaction, and will always include links to that interaction.

We wish to analyze unconscious communication rather than conscious communication, unconscious fantasies rather than conscious fantasies, unconscious introjects rather than conscious identifications. These are the underlying basis for psychopathology, and psychotherapy must be designed to gain access to these unconscious processes and contents. This is feasible only when one works with an adaptive context and Type Two derivatives. I hope to demonstrate repeatedly in this course the difference between surface-oriented work which—as I say, by and large generates misalliance cures and Type C barriers, and deals with what I term—*nonneurotic communication* and work with Type Two derivatives that deals with the patient's often primitive unconscious fantasies and introjects, and the related anxieties, in a way that permits their true adaptive resolution—work with *neurotic communication.*

Forgive me for having made such extended comments at this point, but this is such a basic issue, and the distinction between work with manifest content and Type One derivatives on one hand, and the Type Two derivatives on the other, is so crucial and that I have attempted to define it in some detail. At some point in this session, I hope that we will finally discover the indirect adaptive context, and be able to reorganize this material in terms of Type Two derivatives, so that you can see the element of surprise. You will see that we are not dealing with simple extensions and inferences of the patient's manifest associations, and will be able to discover a *selected fact* (Bion, 1962)—the adaptive context that suddenly provides an explanation of the material that is entirely original, and that explains its unconscious meanings in a manner that was previously totally unknown.

It is this discovery of new meanings, indirectly conveyed, this sense of indirect communication, this recognition of scattered elements that are suddenly organized through an adaptive context and through a unique integration—all these generate valid therapeutic work with the crucial unconscious fantasies, memories, and introjects that relate to psychopathology, whether oedipal or preoedipal.

That last distinction has also been another source of confusion, and I will not discuss it now to any extent, except to emphasize that preoedipally based disturbances, and even symptoms that were initiated preverbally and were subsequently reinforced, must, in therapy, ultimately be worked over in terms of unconscious fantasies, memories, and introjects. In addition to identifying the manifest nature of an acute or cumulative trauma, true intrapsychic resolution of psychopathology must be based on a comprehension of the unconscious meanings of such traumas and the analysis of these additional unconscious mental contents and the pertinent unconscious defenses. Defenses themselves are founded on unconscious fantasies, memories, and introjects, and an interpretation to the patient that he is using repression, or isolation—or undoing—is mechanistic and insufficient. It is based as a rule on manifest content or Type

One derivatives, and is distinctly different from identifying the unconscious contents embodied in defenses, the interaction through which a particular defense was formed and structured, and its representation in the correct therapeutic interaction. These give that defense its definitive unconscious meanings.

Discussant: I think some therapists might look at this material as involving ego derivatives regarding which there was conflict—mother's demanding this and that and so on—and they might want to work with that as a preliminary or shallow phase, and feel that eventually through such work they might get to what you might feel is more on the money, and involves unconscious id drives and what we think of as the real heart of the neurosis.

Langs: Be careful about suggesting that unconscious processes or contents equals id, because it doesn't. There are very important unconscious processes in the ego and superego. What you're describing is the work of those therapists who would deal with this material on the level of manifest content, and I've already established my position in that regard. Work on manifest content is not psychoanalytic; it is a denial and negation of unconscious processes. The same is often true for work with Type One derivatives; it really denies the unique, unconscious processes within the patient, and the effects of a specific adaptive context, and it utilizes generalizations and timeworn psychoanalytic clichés, the main function of which is to obscure what is being perceived or imagined. So that while such therapists would rationalize their efforts, and say that they are working on the surface to get to the depths, an examination of such an interaction will reveal that the unconscious message to the patient directs him away from unconscious processes, away from primitive inner mental contents, toward the surface, and away from meaning and understanding, toward the absence of more catastrophic meaning and the absence of understanding. That is the way patients unconsciously experience it; it is how it actually functions for the therapist, despite his rationalizations, and it is how I would characterize that particular kind of work.

Let me state explicitly that nonetheless I still hold to the principle that we work from the surface toward the depth, with the ego before the id, with defenses before content, and with interaction and reality before unconscious fantasies and content. Their explication, however, is developed around specific adaptive contexts and Type Two derivatives, even in respect to the ego's defenses. Such efforts stand in contrast to your proposal that this material be interpreted generally in terms of the manifest content and Type One derivatives, at the very moment when I am postulating that there are more important unconscious issues—fantasies and perceptions— which would be totally neglected by such interventions.

Discussant: Are you saying that you never direct a comment or direct attention at the level of manifest content?

Langs: Yes, with rare exceptions perhaps; for instance, when I play back surface themes in search of an adaptive context. When we get to interventions, I will tell you that I never ask questions...

Discussant: Just because they shift the patient to the surface. On the basis of what you're saying, it's actually hard for me to formulate what type of interventions you do make.

Langs: I'm glad to hear that, because you've been offering interventions now for some time and what we're discovering is that by my criteria—and I dare say, the patient's, which is where mine came from—you don't know what you should be saying. That's excellent. That's the kind of state I want to create—where you start to lose confidence in what you're doing so you're open to new ideas and techniques. Yes, I'm saying that I essentially would not intervene on a manifest level. I don't even want to get into exceptions—it might be necessary in a Type C field, where I would address a particular kind of defense, and even there, I would probably use Type One derivatives, and try to approach Type Two derivatives as well. The kinds of interventions that I make are quite different from those you're accustomed to.

Discussant: I hope we'll get to hear them...

Langs: You will, I promise you. I always try to offer at least one intervention for each hour presented to me, even when we talk about listening, because I want to show you how listening shapes your interventions. I don't have an intervention at this point, and I can't hypothesize one. Right now, I hear a lot of noncommunication, repetition, some unclear, Type One disturbing derivatives possibly related to the therapeutic relationship, because I always monitor the material for such commentaries—actualities and fantasies. I know that I can't organize it yet; I can't really tell what has gone on.

For the moment, I'm taking concrete themes, generalizing, trying to find new particulars. You've left out some of the general themes, and this is very crucial, because much of the work that we do as therapists has to do with this process of categorizing, generalizing, and particularizing as we listen. For example, you may start with the concrete manifest themes, shift to more general themes, and then come back to a different concrete theme.

Here, the concrete subject that you identified relates to being demanding—different references to requests, demands, and asking for things. You then generalized in one direction to references to demanding people, and next came back to a new specific theme: the therapist may have been demanding. That's a very crucial process, even when you work without knowing the specific adaptive context, because it helps you in your search for that context. What you are looking for is the adaptive context that would enable you to organize divergent themes. You see, the adaptive context itself would then be a selected fact (Bion, 1962). Here, for example, it would be an organizer that would give new meaning to each of the themes that you've been working over from the concrete to the abstract, and back to the concrete. What could have happened which, if known to us, would bring new meaning to the theme of demandingness? Or it would relate it in some special way to the other themes in this material.

There actually is another theme that nobody mentioned, one that you should always be thinking of, which always suggests something about therapy. She said: I don't like to see parts of myself that I don't care for—that she doesn't like herself, and that she's stunned when others see those parts.

Now, we could extract from those concrete allusions general themes related to being seen, to seeing, and to exposure. In particular, since we monitor this material as Type One derivatives related to the therapeutic relationship, we can select the theme of exposure, link it to the treatment situation, and recognize that in general the patient does indeed expose herself in a clinic situation—actually, overexposes herself, since often these revelations are available to persons other than the therapist, such as supervisors and members of seminars of this kind. So, if we are sensitized to themes of exposure in all patients in psychotherapy, and recognize that it is an especially sensitive issue for patients in a clinic, we would feel some likelihood that this material could relate to the therapeutic relationship though, lacking a specific adaptive context, we would be at a loss to give it definitive meaning—they are, for the moment, Type One derivatives.

I want also to show you that we should derive impressions from these themes—reality or fantasy—related to both the patient and the therapist. That is, we should make use of the me–not-me interface in carrying out this crucial exercise in listening: shifting from the concrete to the abstract and back to the concrete. Here, the patient talks specifically about not liking to expose herself by making demands on her boss. We then abstract a theme: exposing oneself, using the word *oneself* so that we can apply the theme equally to patient or therapist, and we wonder if either or both has exposed herself in some inappropriate way, and whether something has happened to generate anxiety and unconscious perceptions or fantasies in this area. As you can see, this process would direct us to search for a particular adaptive context that must fit this configuration. In Bion's (1962) terms we are generating an unsaturated *preconception* that can only be filled by the relevant adaptive context—which would then produce a saturated *conception*.

This is a very important point. In actuality, the relationship between these different aspects of the listening process is rather complex, but essential to clarify: we can begin again with the shifts from the concrete to the abstract and back to second-order themes—the concrete—and the search for a definitive adaptive context. Each will exert an influence on the other. That is, you may identify a particular adaptive context early in the session, and it will play a major role in respect to the first-order themes that you identify—the generalizations that you make from them—and the specific second-order themes that you subsequently derive from this process as they allude, then, to the disguised derivatives contained in the manifest content. The danger in that situation is in allowing the adaptive context to overwhelm your listening process, to the point where you are not open to the recognition of other adaptive contexts, and of apparently unrelated themes that might direct you to search for some alternative or additional, still unknown context.

The situation that we see here is of the other kind: one in which we are listening to the patient's concrete themes, abstracting and making generalizations, and then attempting to apply them in some specific and particular way to other situations. In this case, we are taking specific themes in the patient's relationship with her boss, generalizing them, and deriving new specific themes that we connect tentatively to the patient's relationship to the therapist. And as we work over each theme—demandingness, exposure, and actually, there are many others as well—it prompts us to search for an adaptive context which would give them unique and immediate meaning, and synthesize them into an entirely unanticipated whole, itself filled with pressing dynamic implications.

In this type of search, it is important to undertake this exercise along the me–not-me interface, so that we are monitoring this material for Type One derivatives related to the therapeutic relationship. Here, for example, we would wonder about the possibility of the therapist being overdemanding, of her exposing herself inappropriately to the patient in some way; and we would be asking comparable questions about the patient. By applying the me–not-me interface, we search for adaptive contexts within the patient's experience in treatment, as well as the therapist's, and we are open to discovering adaptive contexts based on the therapist's valid interventions, or, as is more frequently the case in the work that we will be studying here for now, based on erroneous interventions, missed or incorrect interventions, and mismanagements of the framework.

I'll grant you that this material could be utilized in still another way: these themes, derived from the patient's relationship with her boss, could be applied genetically to the patient's experiences with her parents, or to her relationship with her boyfriend. At times, this yields currently alive, dynamic meaning, though I must stress that it is, as a rule, secondary, and has vitality only so long as it is appended to the therapeutic relationship. In general, the most significant second-level or second-order concrete theme—taking the manifest content as the first-level concrete theme, alluding then to a first-level abstraction or generalization, and finally back to second-order concrete themes—is most often related meaningfully to the therapeutic relationship, to transference and nontransference. Allow me to say it again: in listening cognitively, we go from the particular to the abstract to the particular, adding in vaguer impressions and the rest all along the way, generating themes that then direct us to search for an adaptive context that will give the divergent thematic content a specific meaning as Type Two derivatives. This is the process of formulating, if you will, a series of Type One derivatives, since this three-step process shifts us from the manifest content to a possible latent theme. On the other hand, in situations in which we know of a specific indirect— neurosogenic—adaptive context and use it as our guide for what I shall call the—*abstracting-particularizing process,* we can shape our listening into Type Two derivatives.

This has been an important exercise, and if this particular bipersonal field is a Type A field, and the patient is utilizing symbolic communication, we will eventually discover a definitive adaptive context that will serve as a selected fact. Incidentally, for those of you who are, not unexpectedly, concerned about interventions, I would suspect that as this session moves along we will be collecting a number of such themes—utilizing this generalization-particularization process, and at that point at which the adaptive context emerges—if it does—I would more than likely make an interpretation in which I utilized the adaptive context to organize the material as Type Two derivatives and interpreted to the patient the newly discovered meaning.

However, we must recognize that if this is a Type B field, the patient will then frustrate the therapist and talk about demands, demandingness, exposure, and whatever— scattered fragments—and just wear the therapist down, trying to contain, trying to organize the material, and unable to. She will put a sense of frustration and disorganization into the therapist, a sense of pressure that constitutes some type of unconscious projective identification, and the focus will be on the interactional aspects. But here, too, it is essential to know the primary adaptive task, the context, since the interactional cycle may have been initiated by some projective identification by the therapist. If this is the case, you could then interpret the entire sequence: that the therapist did such and such, and that the patient responded in this type of a way, that the patient felt dumped into, and dumps it all back into the therapist, using the specific contents and mechanisms reflected in the material. Or if this is based on some type of external frustration, you could then identify its nature and point out to the patient that when she has been dumped into in a particular way, she handles the internal disorganization and distress by attempting to get rid of it, placing it into the therapist.

Now, I must add that I would not offer such interventions unless they were also shaped by the patient's associations; I always validate interactional experiences and formulations with the cognitive material, just as I attempt to validate the cognitive material with interactional impressions. I have tried to offer a generalized intervention in order to demonstrate to you the symbolic interpretation of a projective identification—another whole realm that we will consider far more carefully later on in this course.

Now, if this is a Type C field, the static, noncommunicative field, this patient would continue to talk on and on about demands and demandingness, about exposure and the like, and she'll never give us the adaptive context. You'll never be able to intervene unless you decide that the material presents us with a metaphor of the Type C field—the empty vacuum, the armored truck, the grave, the sealed-off place, the walled-off person. Then you might intervene to point out that something is disturbing her, but she's sealed it off. We often approach major defenses in a Type C field based on Type One derivatives. But without such a metaphor, I would have to just be silent and, as it were, hold the patient, contain what she said, and not intervene.

So, there's the orientation. And that's what we can hear for now. We hear the clues that this might be a Type C field, but we don't know yet. It is for us, because we do not as yet know the adaptive context. Let's hear some more.

Therapist: As best I can figure out from my notes, somewhere in here I said something to the effect that it's as if she thinks that thought and action are the same thing at times, and judges both of them as bad. But I haven't told you what she said that made me say that.

Langs: If you want to, go ahead, though I must say, it probably won't really matter. My assessment of that intervention would be the same no matter how much of her material you gave me to justify it. It has a particular set of characteristics that speak for themselves.

Therapist: I think you're probably right. She had been ruminating about these thoughts as if they had been spoken, but it all was kind of empty.

Langs: Now, we're hearing what the patient is listening to and what the patient is working over. The intervention, in essence, was that she seems to think that thought and action are the same; she doesn't make the distinction.

Therapist: And judges them both as bad.

Langs: And judges both of them as bad. Any brief

comments? (Pause.) Well, in terms of the principles I've been developing here, there's one tenet that we'll always come back to when we hear an intervention. First of all, let's identify its formal nature, and then we'll see what you can add. What is this intervention formally, in all likelihood?

Discussant: A confrontation? Or perhaps a general interpretation?

Langs: Yes, we're not exactly sure, but it sounds like a confrontation.

Now, what's the second thing we want to identify whenever we look at an intervention? What do we want to look for, in terms of what I've been teaching? (Pause.) We're going to look for its unconscious communicative qualities, but in order to determine that, what do we need? (Pause.) You're not with it yet.

Discussant: At its manifest level, its superficial contents?

Therapist: You need the adaptive context.

Langs: Yes—you need the adaptive context. That's the second answer to everything I'll ask you about interventions.

Discussant: For the therapist as well as the patient?

Langs: For both, of course. In order to understand what the patient is saying, we have to have the adaptive context. To understand what the therapist is saying, we need that element too, but we already have the material from the patient that forms the adaptive context for his intervention.

Now, for the moment, I'm talking about a different level. We have to see whether the therapist has made use of an adaptive context. That is, in evaluating an intervention, the first principle is: Has she used an adaptive context? All therapeutic work should be done in an adaptive framework, and with an adaptive context, and you will have to explain why you would make an exception. Does this intervention have an adaptive context?

Discussant: It's hard to define the context.

Discussant: In terms of what she's been saying, I couldn't hear how she related what she said to what the patient had said.

Langs: Well, the patient was saying something that indicated her fear that when you think something, then it will just happen—and all the rest. Is that the adaptive context?

Discussant: It's isolated from the overall adaptive context; it's focusing on one aspect, apart from the issue of the context that she brought up.

Langs: What you said wasn't clear, but there is an important point contained in it: that *there's a distinction between the material on which an intervention is based and the identification of an adaptive context.* Let's say that the entire intervention was based on things the patient had said, that still doesn't tell us whether it contains an adaptive context, an allusion to a primary adaptive task, a defined day residue or precipitant.

You know, I think that identifying this distinction helps to sharpen the definition of the adaptive context. Please be clear that we were just a moment ago using the term in two senses: first, to indicate that the material from the patient, whatever its nature, constitutes the adaptive context of the therapist's intervention. It is the patient's associations that prompt adaptive responses in the form of interventions, as well as in other forms, of course, from the therapist. That use of the term *adaptive context* must be distinguished from our use of the very same concept in evaluating the therapist's actual intervention. Here, we are not studying what happened to prompt the intervention itself, but the formal and communicative properties of the intervention. And as I have indicated, a most crucial property of every intervention is the presence or absence of a reference to a particular adaptive context, and, of course, since it refers to the material from the patient, our study of this aspect of the adaptive context implies an

investigation of the material from the patient through which
we would identify the adaptive context for the patient's
associations. Then, in keeping with that evaluation, we would
determine whether the therapist has referred to that particular adaptive context in her intervention.

Let's remember that we are dealing here with the indirect or
neurosis-related—neurosogenic—adaptive context: the significant, specific stimulus for the patient's derivative responses
and her pathological unconscious fantasies, symptoms,
intrapsychic conflicts, unconscious perceptions, introjects,
and the like. It is the reality stimulus that is most relevant to
the realm of psychopathology. Remember too that it has
manifest and latent content, and that these then form the nub
of the therapist's interventions.

I am certain that you can all readily recognize that this
intervention lacks an adaptive context. Almost without
exception, in this seminar, such interventions will be treated
as essentially incorrect; the adaptive context should be clearly
stated or readily implied in every intervention. By this, I do
not mean to offer an arbitrary conclusion. Instead, you may
infer the prediction of the absence of confirmation, determined when we apply the validating process to the subsequent
material from the patient.

We will do that here, of course, in order to demonstrate that
this intervention, which is based on the manifest content of
the material from the patient and on rather superficial and
theoretically determined—intellectualized—Type One derivatives, will in no way evoke a confirmatory response—neither
through new, truly original and elaborating new material
in the cognitive sphere, nor through the presence of derivatives of a positive introject in the interactional sphere.

On the basis of the material from the patient to this point,
and the nature of this intervention, I can identify a number of
communicative qualities in the therapist's comment. This,
too, can serve as a prediction related to the material that will
follow from the patient, because, in essence, I am attempting
to identify the unconscious communications that the patient
will be subjecting to her own listening process, and this
should, of course, be reflected in the subsequent material. In

essence, this constitutes the offer of an interactional defense. It is an obsessive and intellectualized intervention, something that could be said about almost any patient at any time, and especially about so-called borderline patients, schizophrenics, and those with severe character disorders. It is therefore a statement without specific meaning for this patient in the context either of her specific past life experiences or of the details of this therapeutic interaction, except for one important quality: it sounds very much like her mother's use of clichés, and may generate the actual repetition in therapy of a past pathogenic interaction.

On the basis of my typology of communicative styles and fields, I can add more to my evaluation of this intervention. You have here an excellent demonstration of what I have termed earlier, a psychoanalytic cliché, and it is the type of intervention from a therapist that promotes the development of what I have described as the Type C field—an effort to utilize what Bion (1977) describes as the "statement known to be false" as a barrier to underlying statements which are both true and the source of considerable emotional turmoil.

Lacking a specific adaptive context, we are not in a position to make statements with any degree of certainty, but it may well be that these associations from the patient reflect her own propensity to generate a Type C field; and she may be what I have termed a "Type C narrator," who describes in endless detail a particular experience or set of experiences, without a significant adaptive context, and with the main function of creating a static and meaningless interaction to generate impermeable barriers and emptiness, and of breaking or destroying all meaningful links to the therapist. I offer this formulation as a model, and I repeat: if we know the adaptive context, we might recognize powerful Type A communications, many Type Two derivatives.

On the other hand, it seems quite certain that this therapist, working without an adaptive context and offering this type of intervention, is promoting a Type C field, for reasons that are apparently unconscious in herself and certainly unknown to us for the moment. Still, it is my hope that we will soon obtain a selected fact with which to reorganize and suddenly understand both the material from the patient and this intervention from the therapist. Without that the best that I can do is to evaluate this intervention in a rather formal way, and to characterize its properties on the basis both of my conception of the therapeutic interaction to this point and my general knowledge of patient-therapist interactions.

One final point: both the patient's material to this juncture and this intervention are, in my opinion, fictions designed to cover the truth. They have no significant depth, no complexity of form, and it's all something like the use of mirror images: if you try to grab that image, you have nothing, even though you see something there. I am well aware that this intervention has been influenced by the teaching that you have been exposed to. This is a comment that Bion (1977) also makes: it is the therapist's use of interventions of this kind that constitute a pretense at doing therapy in the service of creating impenetrable barriers to what I have termed the *psychotic core* or the psychotic part of the personality—barriers to what Bion has called catastrophe or unendurable mental pain. As you undoubtedly recognize, that statement could well constitute a commentary on much of the therapeutic and analytic work that is done today.

Therapist: I must say that you are describing something that I really feel during the sessions with this patient; there is something unreal, something missing. I have a feeling that I don't know what's going on, and that was my feeling during this entire session, and I had felt that there was something wrong about what I had said, but I couldn't get out of it.

Langs: Well, no. In one sense, of course, you can't get out of it once it is stated, but in another sense you can get out of it. What I mean is that the patient will probably now exploit your intervention to ruminate further, but that eventually she will shift to derivative communication. And if you take these derivatives in the adaptive context of this intervention, as commentaries containing perceptions and distortions, you could first rectify the situation by not offering another intervention of this kind, and you could then interpret the patient's unconscious perception of the intervention, and her reading of its unconscious meanings, adding, to the extent that it is available, something about the ways in which she then attempted to exploit the very nature of what you said to further or to reinforce her neurosis. There are ways to rectify and interpret such errors and the communicative fields they create, and we'll get into those techniques eventually, especially when we discuss interventions.

Therapist: Let me tell you what happened in the rest of this session. She talks some more about how she's very angry at herself because she was in this situation, that she should have asked for the right amount of money when she started, when she took the job.

Langs: See, again: The right amount of money. She didn't get enough money, she's angry at herself, she should have done something different. Now these again are specific manifest contents, first order particulars, and if we abstract some general themes from them—anger at the self, being self-demeaning, not asking for the right amount of money, and the like—we can then continue to monitor this material vis-à-vis her relationship with the therapist, along the me–not-me interface, as possible references to the low fee, to her feelings about being seen in the clinic, and perhaps, to the therapist's feelings about the fee that had been set. However, these continue to be restricted to Type One derivatives and they are, in effect, speculative silent hypotheses. We still lack a specific adaptive context, and because of that, as you can see, our thesis keeps shifting about.

Now, considering this material in terms of the hypothesis that I offered a moment ago—in the adaptive context of the unconscious communications contained in the therapist's intervention, I would say that these associations appear to confirm my hypothesis, while they do not validate the therapist's intervention. I say this because first of all, there is nothing new and original. It is the same old stuff. Secondly, the material from the patient continues to lack definition, and there seems to be more qualities of the Type C field than ever before.So long as this patient goes on and on describing her job, and her feelings about her salary and her wishes to ask for a raise, you will never know what's happening in the unconscious realm. This is a barrier to the truth, a fiction, a falsification.

And in this context, I must mention that some aspects of my delineation of the communicative properties of the bipersonal field—a conceptualization that I am presently in the process of elaborating—may create some havoc, especially because they will touch upon unresolved countertransferences. But I want to share with you the anticipation of discovering its utility, its function as a new means of mastery, the rewards. I very much hope that you will find this exciting and, especially, useful clinically.

For example, in this context I would stress the lack of derivatives through which we could clarify the patient's defenses and those of the therapist. The delineation of three types of communicative field helped me to understand that defenses and resistances, as defined in the classical analytic sense, imply the presence of derivatives through which their unconscious meanings can be analyzed and the material being defended against can be detected and, in turn, analyzed.

But in the Type C field we have a different type of defense: it lacks depth and derivatives; it is an impenetrable barrier. No meaning is detectable beneath it, and as Bion (1977) pointed out, analysts, in their search for the truth, really hadn't discovered the need of patients to destroy the truth, to destroy meaning, to become noncommunicative, to lie, in a sense, and in their intense search for derivatives and for unconscious meaning, analysts failed to recognize those interactions in which such meaning is truly absent.

It's quite crucial to recognize that the major defenses in a Type C field are somewhat different from repression and denial and that, in fact, our interventions must be distinctly different as well. In the Type A field, we will be able to discover an adaptive context and Type Two derivatives through which we can interpret the unconscious meanings and functions of a defense and resistance, while in the Type C field, we will be restricted often to Type One derivatives, to confrontations with the patient's metaphorical representations of these defensive barriers and efforts to destroy truth and meaning. In the Type A field, the patient will confirm our intervention with further elaboration of Type Two derivatives, while in a Type C field we may have only a fragmentary validation—either through a further elaboration of the unconscious meaning of the barrier, or through the momentary breakthrough of underlying primitive contents.

Discussant: That has the same quality that a narcissistic kind of defense has, where the meaning shifts in order to defend against awareness. And I don't think it's entirely unprecedented.

Langs: No concept is entirely unprecedented—but I don't know what a narcissistic defense is.

Discussant: That's the same way Horowitz (1976) talks about a narcissistic defense—as being something that's sliding things, shifting, in order to avoid knowledge or awareness.

Langs: Yes; there's no question that other people have written about this to some extent. The ramifications, you see, are far more extensive than merely that. We know patients will communicate in order to avoid awareness, that they will shift meanings. We'll see if you get a feeling for some of the differences though. You are still describing something that should be understood and analyzed. What I'm describing cannot be understood in the same sense—the only intervention available is that there is no meaning, and that the intention is to deprive the experience of meaning. That has a different quality.

Discussant: But then you have to ask yourself, What is the meaning that is being hidden, that's so important? It is a defense in the sense that it avoids a meaning that does exist—that she's not worth the raise, that she's in some way not entitled to it—to what extent does this reflect that she's going to have to pay more to the therapist, and what does that mean about her relationship with her?

Langs: The point that I'm making is that in the material from the patient, if it is a Type C field those meanings will not emerge, though they're there somewhere. They will unfold in a Type A field; you will get the derivatives that will tell you what is being defended against. I'm trying to tell you that there are therapeutic situations where you will not get those derivatives. The problem—and I thought that's what you were going to bring up—the difficulty is in being sure that meaning is absent; that's where you have a very tricky technical problem and you'll need to know how to listen, but this kind of issue will come up again and again.

Discussant: I think you're confusing meaning and communication. Meaning is not absent; communication is absent.

Langs: The only meaning is that all is to be rendered meaningless, if you want to consider that a meaning. Communication is not entirely absent—there's a communication of nonmeaning. Meaning and communication do have different implications; we'll get to that as we proceed.

Discussant: I still think all you're saying is that the adaptive context is being hidden from you.

Discussant: I would agree, but it seems to me that you're suggesting that in a Type C field it is characteristic to be unaware of the adaptive context.

Langs: Yes, that's part of it, but there are other forms. You could have a Type C field in which you have the adaptive context and no derivatives.

All of this has to be demonstrated clinically. As I said, we're a little bit ahead of ourselves. Later, we will study various kinds of communicative fields, and we'll see if you can begin to appreciate the distinctions. For the moment, I'm trying to emphasize the listening aspects. I know I get into other issues, when they're there, but I don't wish to get too far into them.

To come back to this material: it seems that she does then go on to ruminate in a seemingly meaningless way, and we do not get any new selected facts. We get no new material, so that tends to confirm what I had anticipated. Please note again the contribution of the therapist to the Type C field—it's an interactional amalgam. Interventions like this generate a Type C field.

Therapist: She went on to talk about how she likes things to go well for herself, and she prefers not to make demands. She tries to present herself in that way, as accepting and not demanding. And I said something about how, often, when children are rewarded only for being good, they come to feel that they always should be rewarded for that.

Langs: What kind of an intervention is this?

Discussant: Sort of an obsessional kind of comment.

Langs: What is its formal nature?

Discussant: It's not clearly a confrontation.

Langs: It really would be called an educational intervention—a type that I didn't even cover in my technique book (Langs, 1973), unless it belongs with so-called supportive interventions. It's an attempt to educate the patient, and its contents extend beyond the material from the patient. It's not an interpretation or a confrontation. Someone might say, Well, it implies a genetic interpretation. But I think that that could be true only in the crudest and most vague sense of that concept.

As for the unconscious communications—you had started to say?

Discussant: It offers her the opportunity to give more intellectualized genetic material and to continue to avoid whatever the adaptive context is.

Langs: Yes—excellent. What else?

Discussant: It's communicating to the patient that perhaps the therapist feels she should be rewarded for her nondemandingness, which is not in any context, but it communicates that attitude, I think.

Langs: Yes, that's part of the educational effort. See—once again, this is an intervention without an adaptive context, it's a generalization, and it treats the patient as if she were nonexistent. This is not specifically about this patient at all. It says to her: Rather than talking specifically about you, we will talk about anybody. But everybody is nobody. It has that particular quality, which again is a Type C attribute, which would further the disruption of meaning, and of personal relatedness in this field. So it does offer an obsessional, interactional defense. It does address itself to the surface of the material, and there's no notion of unconscious processes.

But it is also an attempt to keep the patient from organizing her associations around something specifically meaningful. It suggests that specifics and whatever is immediate could be very frightening, so let's be sure to keep away from it. And that would really create a Type C field. Go ahead.

Therapist: She said, You know, I really am very upset that things don't get worked out for me automatically. And I said, It's as if some of the anger that you feel toward yourself in the situation, not having asked for more money, is really directed toward your boss.

Langs: You're really working on a manifest content level, and that is characteristic of a Type C field. Your listening process is on the surface entirely.

Next, you're taking as a kind of adaptive context her anxiety about talking to her boss, but it is not a psychologically significant adaptive context in this session. It has direct valence, but not indirect impact. It's not filled with the kind of unconscious meaning that relates to neurosis. It certainly is imbued with some type of unconscious meaning but again, it's

all very straightforward and very much involved in that
immediate outside situation. You almost never get truly
significant material in that kind of a way. Human beings
function by displacing and representing symbolically,
through derivatives, whatever is really meaningful to their
inner mental world and their inner psychic struggles. Dealing
with these associations directly falsifies the situation in that
you're saying, Look, if we work this over, this is going to
resolve your problem. But this is simply not the case.

Another point: after you made your first intervention, you
did not get genuine confirmation. She just went on to offer
more stuff about being angry and about the job. That should
always be a signal to reformulate: when you're not getting
something new and you're not getting validation, stop. Please
stop intervening, start listening again. See if you can begin to
reorganize the material.

Now, another message from you here is very strongly to the
effect that you and she will not consider this in any way as
derivatives related to the therapeutic relationship: let's really
exclude that once and for all, let's really create a bastion, and
this patient is going along with it. I can see that she's really in
a tight grip in that respect. But sooner or later she's going to
have to give us one derivative related to how the therapist is
intervening—this can't go on like this indefinitely. The
patient also wants to get to where her suffering is. She wants
to resolve it, though she also will accept this kind of
defensiveness for long periods of time. But sooner or later,
she's got to say something meaningful in this context. Please
continue.

Therapist: Here it is: She says, That stops me.

Langs: That stops me. See, there's a metaphor for the Type C
field, the static field. See the patient's language: That stops
me! It really does.

I am notoriously long-winded; and patients are notoriously
brief and to the point. It's remarkable to me how they can say
in one sentence what I just got through saying in twenty
minutes. I'm not sure that I want to express myself entirely in

that way, because I think I have to teach in a more elaborate fashion. But here again the patient is functioning as supervisor to the therapist. When you develop a clinically useful concept, like the Type A, B, and C fields, you consistently find metaphorical representations of the particular field at hand, or of the communicative style of either participant. Often, that's when I intervene. See, I might intervene now. If I suddenly woke up and realized what the hell I was doing, I might say to her: Yes, so you're experiencing my interventions as just stopping you, as immobilizing you.

That would be an attempt to identify the interactional qualities of the Type C defense.

Discussant: Wouldn't the patient hear that as blaming? it's like saying, You're taking what I'm saying in a way that's causing you to stop working in treatment. In other words, what's implied there is: If you were hearing my interpretations correctly, you'd make use of them better.

Langs: No, because I said nothing about distortion. I implied that this was a perception that I accept as true. You'll hear the difference when I talk about distortions. I really feel it implies the exact opposite: that the patient has experienced this quite validly, but I don't confess. I don't overstate it. The patient gets to know that if I say, This is how you've experienced my comment, and I don't qualify that statement, then I'm accepting that particular experience as having a significant kernel of truth.

Discussant: With other therapists, perhaps, who don't have your style, I think that may be taken rather differently.

Langs: Yes, right, but other therapists don't make the continuous distinction between reality and fantasy, and so we can't judge their work in this respect. When you hear me interpret a transference fantasy, if we get to a distortion this year, because we're going to be working over so much in the way of valid unconscious perceptions and introjections, you then will see that I allude to the distorting elements, and realize that when I don't allude to distorting elements, I am saying: This is how you've experienced what I've done. I don't deny it, and it's brought you to a dead stop. Interventions like this will get true validation through Type Two derivatives, surprising forms of validation. It will be something remarkably original. I can't create it for you for the moment, but I've experienced it, and it's really quite exciting. For the patient, it is really quite effective of inner adaptive change.

Discussant: Your intervention also sort of places almost the entire responsibility for maintaining the Type C field on the therapist, rather than on the patient who originally was doing that herself.

Langs: But we're still not certain of the patient's communicative style. Yet if this is the model of prior therapeutic work, this static field has been an interactional product all along. I place the first responsibility for the field on the therapist, because if she pushes toward a Type B or C field, the patient will move in that direction. If she doesn't do that, and becomes a container and symbolic interpreter in the true sense, as all too few therapists are, then the patient's responsibility will loom very large, and it will be the patient's responsibility, because you will be prepared for a Type A field and will be ready to analyze the patient's Type B and C communicative propensities. A Type B and Type C patient may never become a Type A patient, but he will, with effective therapy, communicate more and more in the Type A mode, and you can detoxify and resolve much of the pathology that has to do with the Type B and C modes as well. The goal of therapy need not be to make everybody a symbolic communicator. These are very basic, longstanding patterns, but you can modify them so that they are no longer severely pathological and the patient then experiences more insightful symbolic moments.

Discussant: You say then that the comments so far have a very intellectualized quality and that in general, intellectualized interpretations are Type C communications.

Langs: They will tend to promote a Type C field. I say this because I have learned that beyond intellectualization is falsification. These are related to what I at first called the myths of psychotherapy (Langs, 1973), in the sense of reassuring falsehoods. These are interventions designed as truths, that are really not true at all—that are designed to maintain a field of deception in which it would appear that patient and therapist are working over the patient's sickness, but they're never touching it. So it's more than just intellectualization or defensiveness. It has a very falsifying quality. Okay, go ahead.

Therapist: She was silent for a while. And then she said, You know, I seem to have this inordinate need for approval recently, especially during the past couple of years. That was at the end of the hour and I offered another cliché, or something: I said I thought that was something we needed to understand more about, but that we had to stop.

Langs: Okay, let's go on to the next session. At least, we now have our context for the session we're about to hear.

Therapist: This session—Oh, I should tell you because it might be related. . .

Langs: This is classic. I won't even wait. Before she says anything, I will tell you all that this will be the adaptive context for the session. This is what I call the Oh-by-the-way comment, and it almost never fails to be significant.

Therapist: I know I kept looking for it in the material, but couldn't find it. But in any case—she has a habit of coming late to sessions, and she was late to this one. Oh—this particular session was a make-up session.

Langs: That's the real Oh, by the way. Embedded in the first is the one that I'm waiting for: this is a make-up session. Please explain.

Therapist: All right. I had canceled a session with her on this Thursday and I offered to reschedule it—to a Friday.

Langs: You see her on which days?

Therapist: I see her on Tuesdays and Thursdays.

Langs: The session you just gave us was on which day?

Therapist: It was on a Tuesday.

Langs: Okay. You had then—when did you cancel the Thursday session—before the session you just reported, or during it?

Therapist: Before that session.

Langs: Before the session we just heard, you had already canceled the second session for that week—actually, you had changed the hour.

Now you've delivered it to me. I've been waiting for this since we began this seminar—to say nothing of this meeting today. What did she just deliver to me? She changed the hour, and this second session now is on a different day—a Friday.

Discussant: The adaptive context.

Langs: The adaptive context! Yes, I hope you are all experiencing the selected fact, which is now the organizer of the previous hour. How, then, does it organize it?

Discussant: There's the question of whether she could demand to be seen on regular days, stand up to the therapist and express her feelings about it.

Langs: Okay, so you're trying to develop one aspect, one theme. I don't think it's exactly on the mark. Somebody else try. (Pause.) Now, we're trying to organize this material around an adaptive context, which again—lo and behold—happens to be a frame issue.

While you are thinking about how else you could organize this material, let me point out that the first discussant really offered a fantasied response to the change in the hour. He tried to formulate a responsive wish within the patient, and suggested that the material contained Type Two derivatives of that wish within the patient: to be seen on regular days and to be able to stand up to the therapist. And this is so typical, to think first of the patient, to make no use of the me–not-me interface, and to think in terms of fantasies long before perceptions. My point will become clearer as we continue this discussion. How else could someone organize this material for us?

Discussant: I also would wonder if in the same way that the boss didn't value her enough to offer a raise—the therapist in some way is shunting her aside and making her less important than whatever it is she had to do on the other day. There is the question of how the therapist values her.

Langs: Yes, now you're moving toward the side of this material that I want to develop first: the actual implications of the therapist's behavior, contained in this material in the form of Type Two derivatives. So, the patient may well have felt devalued. What else?

Discussant: Wanting something more.

Langs: Well, let's be a bit more specific. In terms of this material, the cancellation was experienced in what way by this patient?

Discussant: As a demand.

Langs: Yes. It was a demand that the therapist placed on her patient. That's what I was trying to get at. You see, you're taught to think about the patient's fantasies, and not about the patient's unconscious perceptions and introjects. You know, all analysts would agree that such a distinction is important, and would wish to believe that they continuously make efforts along such lines, but in actuality, as reflected in the papers they write and the case presentations they give, this is seldom the case.

We are seeing how the patient experiences what we may call an introject of the demanding therapist who forced her to change the day of her session, and that the genetic components of this material are not to be organized primarily around transference, but nontransference, around the manner in which the therapist's actual behavior is repeating in some form a past pathogenic interaction, probably with the patient's mother. I hope that point is especially clear. Even though we will study that issue more carefully when we consider the therapeutic relationship, it is also crucial to the listening process.

I hope too that you now see how exciting the material has suddenly become; how it has taken on a quality of meaning that was entirely lacking before, how it now possesses a convoluted, disguised, derivative quality. What we had, of necessity, considered a bilaterally established Type C communicative field seems now to have been a field in which the patient was attempting to communicate in a Type A mode, conveying unconscious fantasies and perceptions related to the alteration in the framework—to that particular adaptive context. So, we must recognize now that it was indeed the therapist who was making, as I stated at the time that we heard the material, repeated efforts to destroy the unconscious meanings of the patient's communications.

I hope that this convinces those of you who have remained necessarily skeptical, that interventions of this kind, that are addressed to the manifest content of the patient's associations and to isolated Type One derivatives, and that are rationalized as efforts to deal with the surface as a means of approaching the depths, are in fact not endeavors of that kind at all. The so-called depths are actually at hand in the available material, if we simply recognize the adaptive context and organize the material around it as Type Two derivatives.

So, you can now see that all of these efforts at surface listening and intervening represent interesting examples of the work of a therapist who is endeavoring to protect herself from the patient's unconscious perceptions of the meanings of her shifting an hour, and who is, indeed, attempting to create clichéd and virtually meaningless barriers to the true unconscious meanings of this material, barriers to ward off the turmoil within both herself and the patient that had been generated by the change in the hour. This is extremely important material for you to consider quite carefully in terms of the kinds of communications or interventions that can serve as Type C barriers, and the use of the psychoanalytic cliché as a defensive barrier beyond which no threatening derivatives should be available.

There are other elements of this material that now take on previously unrecognized meaning. The adaptive context, as a selected fact, is truly generating new conceptions and giving this material previously unknown implications. For example—the reference to the mother who wasn't demanding could well represent an unconscious therapeutic effort on the part of the patient, who offers the mother as a positive model to the therapist. Of course, the material related to the patient's boss—the dread of approaching him, the feelings of lowered self-esteem—rather than being considered in an isolated and intellectualized manner as representing some type of inner problem within the patient and some struggle with the actuality of her job, once again takes on dynamic meaning as Type Two derivatives related to the patient's unconscious perceptions of the therapist and her anxieties in approaching the real issue of this hour: the change in the session.

You can see too that the patient's fear of the therapist who modifies the frame prompts an avoidance of the specific adaptive context which is nonetheless conveyed in derivative form in this material, through the references to an agreement, a work pact that is a cover for the therapeutic pact, that the patient regrets having made, that she wishes to modify, and which means, by implication, that unhappily it has been modified by the therapist. This manifest content, then, contains derivatives of the adaptive context itself, as well as of the patient's responses to it. As long as the therapist's interventions obliterated that adaptive context and addressed this material on any other level, they encouraged the generation of a Type C field, the use of interactional defenses, the creation of a misalliance and bastion, and a strict avoidance of the issue of the changed hour. This then is an interaction that would clearly reinforce the patient's neurotic functioning, avoidance of issues, obliteration of symbolic representation, and would promote the working over of anxieties and conflicts in a displaced form that will distort the patient's perceptions of, and reactions to, her boss—the second situation. All of this would lead to pathological personality and characterological traits, and inappropriate reactions to reality situations to which she responds unconsciously in terms of the therapeutic relationship. This interaction can offer you all a very sensitive feeling for the manner in which neuroses are generated intrapsychically, especially by "errors" within the interactional elements of an important relationship—of course, in its most basic terms, that between the mother and child, and of almost equal importance, later on in the relationship between patient and therapist.

I apologize for being so straightforward here, but this adaptive context, as a kind of punch line, fills the material with meaning, and fills me with understanding—a tension-filled preconception is now a saturated conception (Bion, 1962). I think it essential that I expand on a number of major themes and topics. When you have identified a true adaptive context, and have heard the material in terms of Type Two derivatives, this is the kind of excitement that you will experience in your session with the patient—tapping the patient's creative efforts, appreciating them—all of which is another subjective hallmark of valid therapeutic work, though it must be validated itself through other avenues, such as the continuing material from the patient and confirmatory responses to interventions based on the formulations generated in this way.

Since I want to focus on the listening process, I will just briefly offer a couple of technical points. For one, I make every effort not to cancel sessions except for dire emergencies—which means that I almost never do so. Should such a situation arise, I would never offer an alternative hour, but would simply cancel the hour, maintain the framework as agreed upon, and work over the material that followed, with the cancellation as my adaptive context. I will not expand further on this issue, since we will soon focus on it when we discuss the ground rules and framework.

Secondly, I can now tell you how I would have intervened: I would have been silent, and if the patient finally got around to mentioning something about the changed session, I would have used that as a bridge, and suggested to the patient that she apparently has been quite concerned about the shift in the session, and that much of what she has been talking about throughout the hour seems quite connected with it—that she's been talking about people who have been demanding and manipulative, and about her dissatisfaction with the nature of her basic agreement with her boss, which must imply a similar dissatisfaction with the framework of the therapeutic situation. I would comment that she has seen this request as unreasonably demanding and manipulative, and that the entire experience has reminded her a great deal of her childhood, and of earlier experiences with her mother.

I am omitting some of the details because our discussion has placed me at some distance from the material. In essence, I would have developed an intervention built around the adaptive context of the changed hour: her experience perceptions, and introjection of the psychological implications of this request. I most certainly would have referred to the possibility that this shift in the hour seems to have made me, as her therapist, into a threatening figure whom she fears to approach regarding her own needs. The entire intervention would have implicitly accepted her perceptions of this alteration in the framework. For the moment, I would not have included any reference to additional distortions from the patient, although after having made my initial intervention, it is this area to which I would then give the most attention.

Both aspects of the intervention—the nondistorted and ultimately distorted—are crucial. These are transversal communications that will require transversal interpretations that reflect an appreciation for both reality and fantasy. This is important therapeutic work. Since you cannot rectify the frame except by not repeating the change in hour, the pathological introject can be modified only through these interpretive endeavors. Therapeutic work of this kind evolv-

ing around deviations in the frame and pathological introjects, is every bit as important as analyzing additional
distortions based on displacements from earlier figures. That
is, it is therapeutically important to rectify and analyze an
actual repetition of a past pathogenic interaction and its
genetic counterpart as expressed in the therapeutic interaction to modify and analyze a current traumatic interaction
and with it something of the past genetics that it repeats. Such
work supplements therapy as it usually conceived—though
who knows how often it actually unfolds in that way—as
working with a relatively nontraumatic or nonpathological
current reality within therapeutic interactions, and analyzing
the distortions that the patient brings to it. The latter, as I am
sure you realize, is a condensed way of stating the ideal
concept of analytic therapy; the former has been alluded to by
an occasional analyst, such as Racker (1957), but has not been
recognized as an essential component of analytic therapy and
psychoanalysis itself. It is probably, as I am implying, far
more common than realized, and deserves to be established as
an important means of cure, so long as it is properly handled:
rectified and analyzed.

Discussant: But what does it accomplish for the patient to
introject the therapist's demandingness? Is it a way of
communicating to the therapist, I will demand of you and
others as you have demanded of me?

Langs: Introjections are not primarily accomplishments.
They may be used secondarily in that way, but they should
first be seen in terms of what the environment unconsciously
imposes upon the subject—here, the patient. It is true that the
patient may unconsciously invite projections and projective
identifications into herself, and I am not suggesting a
simplistic notion here. It is always a circular and interactional
process. I do ask that we attempt for the moment simply to
recognize the basic elements, and that we save for later in this
course, when we discuss the therapeutic relationship in detail,
a more careful consideration of the particulars. As I have said
before, if we talk in terms of the subject and object, the subject

may invite projections and projective identifications, may refuse to contain them, and the like, but for the moment, we simply want to stress that these incorporative processes on the part of the patient (invited to some extent, and imposed upon, as well) are all part, on one level, of her own listening process, conscious and unconscious.

Returning once again to the therapist's listening process, we can see how a seemingly minor element of the situation— the oh-by-the-way element that the average therapist would tend to put aside—does indeed generate the type of indirect meaning that I have been trying to describe to you. The average therapist would certainly not use that alteration in the framework as the key adaptive context and organizer of the patient's material. I hope that you can see the difference between organizing these associations around the fear of confronting the boss regarding a raise, which produces a linear and flat sequence, and organizing this material around the pending shift in the hour—a complicated, rich, and disguised sequence filled with byways and implications pertinent to derivative communication and to the generation of unconscious fantasies and introjects, and immediately clarifying for us the very nature of neuroses and how they are developed. Oddly enough, many therapists have held one theory of neurosis and a different theory of listening; the two must have a common basis.

You can see in this material how bastions, misalliances, and unconscious collusions develop, and you can see that the contributions from each participant to the bastion can actually be quite distinctive. For the patient, the collusion was filled with derivatives pertinent to the true adaptive context and underlying meaning of this material; these were really efforts at Type A communication. For the therapist, the interventions totally ignored the pending change in the hour, and contained no readily identifiable derivatives related to it. I suspect that if we went back over these interventions, we could suggest some extremely well-hidden allusions to the change in the hour, but essentially, they were impenetrable barriers, and we were totally unable to detect the true meaning of this material from them.

I hope this helps you to sense the difference between a Type A defense and a Type C defense. The Type A resistance of the patient had analyzable derivatives, the Type C interventions of the therapist were entirely lacking in them. Think on that; it is one of the clearest examples of that distinction that I have seen. In general, the usual trend is for the patient soon to begin to give up, to become depressed, to accept the therapist's Type C barriers and mode of communications—the falsifications and all the rest—until she gathers strength once again for renewed Type A communication. You can sense now that patient and therapist are, so to speak, in different *communicative spaces*, using different message media, and perhaps you can also experience the destructiveness of the Type C mode: unconsciously it is designed to destroy the true meaning of the patient's words and the link between patient and therapist. With Type C patients you will experience much more than emptiness; it is a form of psychic assault.

Remember, too, that I am attempting to accumulate data that will justify my thesis that it is crucial to monitor the material from the patient, in terms of the therapeutic relationship—along the me-not-me interface—and of allusions to the conscious and unconscious nature of the interaction between patient and therapist. Clearly, it turns out that the key to the session that we just heard lies in that very realm. The patient was indeed working over her relationship with the therapist in displaced form. The frame issue unconsciously took precedence over all else, as it always will. On this basis, I would like to stake a claim—so to speak—that in the first two presentations that we have heard in this course, these very principles have been validated as essential to the listening process and the therapeutic work necessary with these patients. Now that is certainly not definite proof, even though it is the very means through which I arrived at these principles—through repeated observations—but it certainly is an excellent beginning.

Therapist: It was in the context of what you said at our last seminar that I picked this session. This is obviously not a session that ordinarily I would have picked to present, because she is a very difficult patient. Now I know why I selected it—I wasn't clear about that until now.

Langs: Often, quite unconsciously, students select for presentation to me sessions in which they sense that important countertransferences are prompting their contribution and difficulties, and it gives them a chance to clarify the issues. It's part of your effort to work something over in your relationship with this patient. You may remember, I had made a statement that this patient should be working over her feelings toward you in some form, and I said at the time that I could not see clear evidence of that. It turns out that she has been working over her relationship with you throughout the session, but I had no way of knowing it so long as I did not have the adaptive context. It's no wonder that she didn't validate your interventions, because they were really defensive barriers and she was struggling with a very painful introjective identification.

Actually, we could now hear this preliminary session once again, knowing the adaptive context; I am sure that we could generate a much more elaborate discussion, based on a far more sensitive application of the listening process. Instead, I would like to move on. I've already attempted to predict some of the unconscious implications of the material from the patient that we are about to hear. She now will be working over the adaptive context of the change in the hour. The material we are about to listen to will involve the change in the session, the make-up session, and the therapist's interventions in this session that we just heard.

In general—to offer a few comments with predictive implications—a make-up session implies to the patient a need to control and manipulate her, to make her helpless and dependent, and a belief in her inability to manage. In other words, the therapist fears that the patient will go crazy without her. We'll see if there are derivatives of those unconscious perceptions in this session. Remember too that the patient will be working over the interactional defenses and bastion that she has developed with the therapist, and will be dealing with the therapist's efforts to generate a static Type C field. So, if we have now this kind of adaptive context for the session that we are about to hear, the material should be quite lively and meaningful. Still, with all of this, let's try not to be too prejudiced, however difficult that may be. Let's remain open to the possibility that despite all of the evidence, there might be major flaws in my formulations and that some other adaptive context may take precedence. In any case, the adaptive context has brought the material to life, and actually has shifted us from a Type C communicative mode in this seminar to a Type A mode—at least, it has most certainly done that for me.

Discussant: If a patient cancels a session—for example, a student has intersession and goes on vacation, but he's in the area and would prefer different hours—would you make such changes?

Langs: No, but you see, that would not be my decision, but the patient's. I would simply not accede or refuse—I would explore the material long before intervening, and would allow the patient's material to direct the interventions. His derivatives will function in just that way, and the decision is then made essentially on the basis of the patient's own answer—especially his indirect answer. I never arbitrarily introduce a directive in therapy, and I am confident that the material would indicate that it is inappropriate to change the hour—but that has a lot to do with understanding the functions of the frame.

I know that these are important and intriguing issues, but I ask that you hold off such questions until we quite carefully study the framework of psychotherapy.

I see that we are near the end of the hour. We will begin next time with the session that the therapist intended to present to us.

Discussant: You know, you are actually raising a number of crucial questions regarding clinic policy. After all, so long as the patient gives us advance notice, he is never held financially responsible for a session that he misses.

Langs: There are many aspects of the framework that are approached by clinics in a manner that is quite destructive to the patient, the therapy, and the therapist. But please, let's hold off a bit on those issues until we have developed the framework within which we could consider them.

Returning to the listening process—I hope that I have shown you today how absolutely vital it is to attempt to reformulate when the patient's responses to your interventions do not contain selected facts and true validation.

Therapist: I must say that I find this process extremely uncomfortable.

Langs: Yes, I can appreciate that. I can both empathize and sympathize with you, but there really is no other way of truly experiencing and learning from new concepts.

Therapist: I had decided to present this patient because I thought that there were elements of the Type C field in evidence, and I am quite interested in that kind of a field. I see some very important concepts in what you're saying, but even though I am aware of them, this process, and the way in which you are developing it, is making me quite uncomfortable.

Langs: I'm really sorry, but I think that I can honestly promise you a strong sense of growth once you begin to master it, though the initial phase can be quite discomforting. I do try to take these disturbing effects into account, but it is also necessary to develop some very difficult, valid concepts with you even though they activate countertransference-based anxieties. I hope that you can see that without these insights, you could not effectively treat this patient. So while I can appreciate that you're feeling somewhat helpless at this point, because I am undermining some of your more treasured but unfounded tenets and techniques, and am disturbing your defensive balance without offering either therapy, which I can never do, or functional substitutes, which I hope to do in time. For the moment, it must be somewhat confusing and anxiety-provoking, but please try to bear with it, because much of it will eventually fall into place and, you will as a result be a far better therapist and far more pleased with your therapeutic work—and yourself.

Discussant: In some ways, you are negating aspects of the technique that we were taught, but not entirely. There is a feeling, though, that we're identified with what we do, and this becomes a negation of us, rather than of our technique. That's just another thing that we have to work with. Some of us are in treatment, and many questions come up.

Langs: Yes, I understand. I am quite sensitive to these issues, and that is why I am trying to go slowly, and have begun with the listening process rather than elsewhere; I have also attempted repeatedly to document and validate each of our formulations. I think that you're all a bit shaken up because of today's seminar, and I suspect that you are beginning to appreciate the validity of the concepts that I have been developing. There's an impact from today's session that you are now trying to work over. I will encourage you to do just that. We'll all be the better for it. I really hope that my words don't sound trite and empty. I am trying to offer you some hope and perspective. This is all a reminder of just how personal the learning of psychotherapy is, and of the extent to which revolutionary new ideas really impinge upon a falsely established equilibrium, on countertransferences and the like, and generate what I call, in the therapeutic situation, a potentially *therapeutic regression*—chaos in the service of positive change and true learning. This type of learning is by no means simply a cognitive process, and we should all try to remain appreciative of that fact. It's painful for you as my students and it's really painful for me as your teacher.

In field language, you are now experiencing something of the anxieties generated by a Type A field, and by my repudiation of a Type C Field—my attempt to forego any possible use of the psychoanalytic cliché or the development of falsifications and barriers. I know that this can impinge in very threatening ways upon you, but I hope that you will all be able to tolerate the necessary anxiety and disorganization that will promote the growth and reorganization that will serve you so well. Often, supervisees feel so threatened that they have a terrible need to leave the seminar or to blindly attack my method of teaching. I will try to not be overdefensive, and I am really hoping that this will not become too disruptive here—at least, not to the point where any of you decide to leave the seminar before you've had a chance to hear me out. Such a step can only imply that you cannot tolerate new ideas and concepts in your patients, and the chaos and anxiety that is necessary for personal growth. That would be tragic for anyone, but it is especially sad for a psychotherapist or psychoanalyst—someone who is committed to the search for truth, and to the toleration of the personal anxiety that it entails. Much of this has to do with the choice of analytic versus more manipulative therapy as your mode of work, and my paper on this subject (Langs, 1976c) may help you gain additional perspective.

I have also just completed a study of responses to creativity in psychoanalysts (Langs, 1978c). It was quite a therapeutic paper for me in the writing and I think that it might offer you a helpful perspective regarding the anxieties that we all experience in response to innovative ideas. Incidentally, much of this has been stated in very imaginative and perceptive form by Bion (1977), a psychoanalyst that I hope you will some day study quite carefully; he is, in my opinion, among the most creative analysts of our time.

Discussant: I am not experiencing this seminar as especially destructive, but I do, at times, feel overwhelmed by how much you say we still have to learn. Here we all are about to finish our training, and we would like to leave here with some sense of competence. Your teaching certainly makes us feel, if not incompetent, still a need for a great deal more training.

Discussant: I also think that you take a particular vantage point that we would sometimes rather strongly disagree with. I really wonder as I listen to you whether I could adopt your approach with many of my patients, because I feel that they would not tolerate my being so intrusive with them as you are with us, to the extent that an interpretation is intrusive.

Langs: First: I do not believe that it would be unfortunate if you complete your training with a feeling that you need still to learn a great deal more. In fact, should you think otherwise, that would be both sad and untrue: a Type C barrier. Psychotherapy has a way of making all of us humble and aware of our limitations, and we must all remain open to new ideas and to learning.

As for your concern about being intrusive with your patients: every interpretation is intrusive in some way, and is an act of creativity to which your patients will respond in a manner not unlike the reactions that you are describing here today. Your own experience can help you to empathize with these responses and understand the threat that a valid interpretation always contains. I am a very active supervisor and seminar teacher, and a relatively inactive and silent therapist—believe it or not—who intervenes quite selectively. Be careful not to place your own anxieties and defenses into your patients intrapsychically via projection or interactionally via projective identification. It may well be that your patients could tolerate such interventions, while you yourself would have difficulty in offering them. Still, every effort will be made gradually to provide you with the means through which you will be able to make sound interventions to your patients, and I am certain that your patients will find them quite helpful, and that the experience will be gratifying for yourself.

Discussant: While I think that I can now see otherwise, my initial reaction was somewhat persecutory. It seemed to me that you were blaming us as therapists for everything that happened in the therapy. Here we felt that we were trying to use correct technique, and that we were being helpful, and I heard you saying that the treatment situation was stalemated and negating, and even hurtful. I am beginning to appreciate that you were simply trying to describe the true nature of the therapeutic situation, and to call to our attention aspects of the relationship between ourselves and our patients that we tended to miss.

Langs: I'm glad to hear you say that. Often, my postion is misunderstood as attacking the therapist and as ignoring the patient's pathology—as a statement that therapy unfolds through virtue of the therapist's pathology. I won't belabor the point—this is not the case at all. We are here to establish the truth about the therapeutic interaction, and to let the chips fall where they may. If we learn to listen, a valid model will be produced.

Discussant: But there's another way to look at what happened: the therapist referred to the patient as a child, and if my therapist did that to me, I would be mad as hell about it. She also said that the patient expected to be rewarded, and if I'm understanding this patient, it seems to me that the last thing that she expects is to be rewarded. So that would have stopped her in another sense.

Langs: Yes, these are all important unconscious communications, and they may reflect the misunderstanding of the therapist, and be hurtful as well. Here, the issue would be that of listening to the most important adaptive context—and recognizing additional adaptive contexts that are for the moment secondary.

But remember, too, that this patient actually was rewarded. Here you may have touched upon what I alluded to earlier— some unconscious communication contained in the therapist's interventions that unwittingly and quite obtusely alluded to the cancellation of the session and the make-up hour. A demand was placed upon the patient; she felt demeaned, attacked, and placed aside, but she was then offered some type of seemingly inadequate compensation through the make-up session. As I stated before, the session that we will hear next week should clarify just how the patient unconsciously experienced this entire sequence, and those aspects which took on the most meaning for her.

Discussant: Well, it is true that the therapist's interventions seemed to have stopped this patient, but I think there may be other interpretations of why this woman said that she was stopped.

Langs: I would welcome an alternative formulation.

Discussant: I'm not sure that I could add anything to what has already been said, at least not for the moment.

Discussant: I think we should remember that the therapist may have had some other objective in mind, in terms of what she was trying to accomplish with her interventions, which may not have been stalemating in itself.

Langs: You are now raising questions about my formulations that I cannot address because the hour is late. All that I can say for the moment is that the material that followed those interventions were nonvalidating, and it was on that basis that I found support for my hypotheses.

Therapist: I must say that I feel that this treatment is stalemated, and this is one of the reasons that I wanted to present her to you.

Langs: Perhaps I will be even more helpful next week when we hear the session that you wanted to focus upon. Well, this has been a dramatic seminar in more ways than one. Thank you again for your presentation.

Chapter Five

THE ADAPTIVE CONTEXT AND
THE ME–NOT-ME INTERFACE

**The intricacies of the adaptive context • Organiz-
ing the listening process • Qualities of the adaptive
context • Relating to two adaptive contexts • The
me-not-me interface • Listening and the frame •
The embedded derivative • The not-me part of the
interface, and introjection of qualities from the
therapist • Manifest references to the Therapist as
derivatives of unconscious fantasies and perceptions**

Langs: I suggest that we move directly to the clinical material that we began last week, and that we use it to rework and clarify our developing conception of the listening process. Let's get to it, without a summary of the previous hour. We can begin without desire, memory, or understanding (Bion, 1970) and see where it takes us.

Therapist: She came in and said, Well, it went terribly; it was a failure. I didn't even get a chance to speak my mind, to express myself. She said, Well, I met with my two bosses, and they talked very rapidly and I couldn't even get a word in. I don't know what I'm doing. They said they could give me a token raise, but that's it. So I'll have to go and find another job. I don't even want to return to work for the rest of the week, but I know I have to. I know I can't make any waves there, because I'm going to need letters for my specialization certification. I have worked for them for a while since graduation.

Langs: Let's stop here to formulate. How are we listening to this initial material? What processes are involved? How are you receiving and organizing it?

Discussant: Maybe what she's trying to say is that she felt that she had tried to talk to the therapist about her feelings about the missed session, but the therapist, by offering a make-up session, had made that impossible; somehow the therapist had cut her off.

Langs: Let's identify the procedure you used. You've taken this manifest content, you've made use of the adaptive context of the change in the hour, and you have taken the specific themes from this material that related to her job and produced a selected set of general themes. Then you came back to a set of new specific themes—derivatives, contents related to the therapeutic relationship and to the adaptive context.

So, we could start off with a specific manifest content: her asking for a raise. We pick up some additional themes—being unhappy, not being heard, being given something as a compromise, feeling that she should just leave, that she really has no choice, no say, because of the conditions. We hear those first-order specifics, we generate a set of related, general themes, and we now have Type One derivatives. And then we turn to the adaptive context as a key. It's like a template or a genetic organizer, I mean here, like a biological gene. It's a form of linkage. You go into the general themes and you pull out the ones that fit the adaptive context. You did that with a few of the themes, and it shows again how crucial it is to identify the adaptive context, because it's going to determine the way in which you pick out and shape those first-order and general themes.

So, you're now raising some questions about the extent to which she has unconsciously perceived the therapist as responding in appropriately, as offering a poor compromise in arranging this alternate hour.

Can anyone develop a different thread or do a different kind of linking, and hear anything in addition? (Pause.) While you are thinking, notice too that when we are picking out the second-level specific themes from these general themes, we are not making the basic assumption that Freud (1912a) and most other analysts have made—that they will fall primarily into the realm of unconscious fantasy. Our assumption—my assumption—throughout will be that the derivatives from the patient fall into two realms: unconscious fantasies and unconscious perceptions, that they contain both distortions and valid elements. Once we pull out the derivatives that we want, specific to general and back to specific via adaptive context, we then have to evaluate them. Are they valid and appropriate, or distorted, fantasied, and therefore transference-based? What is our main instrument in making that crucial evaluation that some many therapists set aside?

Therapist: Our knowledge of ourselves?

Langs: Exactly. Ultimately, it is self-knowledge, our own capacity for reality testing, and especially our ability to understand our own unconscious communications to our patients. That is the backdrop for every aspect of the listening process, and it is especially relevant in sorting out the realistic and distorted aspects of the patient's communications. This refers not only to the content of the patient's associations, but also to our comprehension of the nature of the patient's defenses, the extent to which they are appropriate and nonneurotic, and the degree to which they are quite inappropriate and pathological.

While we are now covering territory that we have discussed to some extent in earlier seminars, I hope it will bear repetition, and that it helps you to further organize the dimensions of the listening process. Another aspect that I have commented upon before—and one that tends to be overlooked by many analysts, though none would disagree with it—is that the therapist's communications to the patient also have manifest and latent contents: they are filled with derivatives which are present despite our efforts to communicate primarily consciously and directly to the patient. We must determine the nature and function of these unconscious elements that are embedded in our conscious intentions, and hope that the proportion of valid components will far outweigh those that are distorted and countertransference-based. But we will apply the same exercise in listening to our own interventions that we apply to the patient's associations,

and to their responses to our interpretations and managements of the framework.

There's a general tendency to be rather more defensive in
applying the full listening process to the therapist's own
subjective experiences, formulations, and interventions than
to the patient's material. Doing so means overcoming
continuous and basic resistances, and maintaining a consistent search for countertransference elements. In all, it is quite
a humbling experience that leads one to develop a reasonable
degree of caution as a therapist, though it should not totally
paralyze you. The listening process is there to serve you, and it
will serve you well, even though it might appear at first
somewhat overwhelming.

The adaptive context—here, the cancellation of one session
and the offer of a make-up session—is filled with unconscious
communications, and the patient appears to be quite sensitive
to some of them, such as her lack of control of her own destiny,
and her feeling of being demeaned and vulnerable. Much of
this, you realize, is based on the therapist's need to offer the
make-up session.

I hope that the concept of derivatives has now become quite
clear to you. To review the concept briefly: a derivative, and it
may be of either unconscious fantasies, daydreams, or
unconscious perceptions, is an expression of some inner,
mental contents, affect, or defense contained in the manifest
content of the patient's associations in some disguised form.
As Freud (1900) pointed out for the dream, the manifest
content is in some sense a disguised communication of the
latent content. In analyzing manifest content, we, in turn,
seek to discover the derivatives contained within it. It is
through derivatives that manifest contents function as
indirect communications, and it is in this realm that neuroses
are developed and resolved. In one sense, a neurotic response,
however pathological—and remember, I'm using the term
neurosis in this course to refer to the entire gamut of
psychopathology from true neuroses to psychoses—is inappropriate to the stimulus—the adaptive context—on a
manifest level, but is understandable on a latent level.

The concept of unconscious fantasy need not be especially mysterious. Quite practically and clinically, it refers to the working over of a particular adaptive context in some displaced manner, in latent and derivative form. Once you know a particular adaptive context, the unconscious fantasies and perceptions contained in the material from the patient become quite evident. The latter, by the way, are the valid working over in displaced form of a particular adaptive context—nondistorted indirect responses to, and perceptions of, that adaptive context. So, both unconscious fantasy and unconscious perception are processes that involve derivative communication—disguised expressions—always present in some form in the manifest content.

By contrast, if you have only Type One derivatives, how are you limited in developing specific, first-order themes, general themes and abstractions, and second-order specific themes determined by a particular adaptive context?

Discussant: It seems to me that you could relate this material only to the patient's conflicts about her boss.

Langs: Much of that would be on a manifest content level. I didn't go into that restriction, but obviously you would not be able to undertake anything but the identification of individual themes if you confine yourself to the patient's relationship with her boss, and to what I have called real conflicts (Langs, 1973a): linear conflicts, stresses that are worked over largely in direct rather than derivative form, however unconsciously—the realm of nonneurotic communicative mechanisms.

Discussant: It seems to me that we could also make some generalizations on that basis, but I think that the answer to your original question is that Type One derivatives include the first two steps of the process you have been describing— the identification of specific themes, and the derivation of a set of general themes—I guess you would say general themes that are implicit to the specific contents.

Langs: Yes, you are quite right. Type One derivatives are essentially the generalizations and inferences made from the manifest content of the patient's associations. However, there is a considerable difference between Type One derivatives confined to the patient's relationship with her boss and Type One derivatives developed around the therapeutic relationship. This is another way of stating a tenet I have been trying to develop in different forms throughout this seminar, and it is essential to understand its implications, if you are to do psychotherapy in the realm of unconscious fantasies, conflicts, introjects, and the like.

Neuroses do not arise from a straightforward working over of realistic conflicts and their unconscious repercussions. They occur when the individual shifts to derivative communication and then responds to a different situation quite inappropriately—neurotically, as we say, because the unconscious fantasies and perceptions that are determining her reaction have arisen in connection with events at one scene, and are being incorrectly applied to a second scene.

While you can generate Type One derivatives in a kind of linear fashion around the patient's relationship with her boss—I believe we did some of that last time—discovering implications for her feelings about herself (her system of self-esteem, her sense of depression, her ability to speak up, her fears of being demanding, and even some genetic connections to her mother), all of this is in the realm of linear nonneurotic communication, and is not essentially related to neurotic behavior, symptoms, or characterological disturbances on that particular level.

On the other hand, you will find that Type One derivatives monitored in terms of some other situation outside of her relationship with her boss—as a rule, monitored in terms of the therapeutic relationship itself—will bring you right into the realm of indirect and neurotic communication and will provide you the crucial derivatives—unconscious fantasies and perceptions—that are the essential components of this patient's neurosis and symptoms. And all of this is really another and I hope clearer and more practical way of stating that it is the analysis of the so-called transference, of the therapeutic relationship, if you will, with its transference and nontransference components, that provides that patient the most meaningful cognitive insights and positive introjects, the best opportunity to understand her neurosis and resolve it adaptively.

It happens that the situation that we are observing here is typical: the manifest content will tend to revolve around some outside relationship, while the latent content pertains to the therapist. It is this latent content that must be understood and interpreted. Still, at other times, the manifest content will pertain to the therapist, and the missing link would be a specific adaptive context which gives that material its derivative qualities and gives you an important arena for interpretation—here, also, at a level beyond the manifest.

Without the adaptive context, the whole communicative field is equipotential. It's impossible really to know what's important. You are left with manifest accents when it is the latent valences that are crucial. Without it, you hear one theme, then another, and they keep slipping past you, because you don't have a way of really capturing them, organizing them, and generating special meaning. So you're stuck with generalizations and certain speculative particularizations until the adaptive context suddenly appears, and now you have derivative and real meaning.

The primary adaptive task should not be seen as some kind of panacea for all of your problems with the listening process. As I have mentioned, there are patients who will offer important adaptive contexts and yet will provide you little if any derivative communication in response to them. Sometimes, in the presence of a clear-cut adaptive context, there are few derivatives to work with. Often, this is an aspect of the Type C communicative field, and you will then need a somewhat different approach than you would use in a Type A field. Still, despite such experiences—and you will have many of them—the adaptive context quite often is the key to the listening process and to the understanding of your patient.

Remember that I am stressing the cognitive aspects of the listening process for the moment, and that there are important emotional dimensions that must also be experienced: empathic, identificatory, and other ill-defined responses, projective and introjective identifications, and other interactional pressures. But we can take only one component at a time and attempt to understand it fully and, eventually, to link it with the other dimensions of the listening process to give us a very serviceable totality.

Therapist: I recall now another patient with whom I had to cancel an hour, and while she did respond by first saying it was perfectly all right, and then, later, by stating that she wondered if I was ill, she quickly changed the subject and went on to something else and seemed to ignore it entirely. I had the impression, though, that she was quite angry that I hadn't made up the session.

Langs: You are implying that you have provided us enough material to work over and to derive validatable conclusions. But I hope that upon reflection you will see that your brief summary is devoid of specific material, and that it is impossible, on the basis of comments you have just made, to make any type of evaluation in the terms being developed in this course.

I have made this particular response to your comment because this is how analysts and others generate myths. Another form of the Type C field involves generalization to the point at which no true meaning can be perceived. While you might want to present this other session for us to listen to and evaluate, for the moment we should continue with the particular presentation you have been developing.

Therapist: So she said, They could only give me a token raise.

Langs: I had asked a question. I suggested that there was another way of organizing this material, and I wondered if anyone could identify another cluster of derivatives from these initial associations in the light of the adaptive context.

Therapist: She seemed to feel rather depreciated, as if I didn't trust her to function well and didn't respond appro-

priately to her capabilities. On the basis of the discussion that
we have been having, this would imply that I should simply
have canceled the hour and allowed her to have her independence.

Langs: There is truth to that, but you can see how all of you
are formulating a series of second-order specific themes built
around the patient's unconscious perceptions of the implications of the therapist's management of the frame and largely
centered upon the patient's self-image.

Now, when I talk about taking first-order specific themes
and generalizing, I am well aware that there are many
possible levels of generalization. Only one aspect of this
process has to do with the therapist's ability to recognize the
largest variety of themes, though it is certainly true that the
creativity that distinguishes the better therapist from the less
adequate one involves, in part, his ability to listen, to tolerate
ambiguity and disorganization, to be able to detect adaptive
contexts, to make the most imaginative and meaningful
generalizations from a set of specific themes, and to develop a
similarly sensitive group of second-order specific themes
around a particular adaptive context. Some of this is
cognitive, some of it is affective, much of it is unconscious, and
yet it must be scientific as well, subjected to the validating
process—an alternating between creative imagination and
empathy, and the ability to organize and formulate, a point
first specifically developed by Ferenczi (1919), and reiterated
by many others (see Langs, 1976b).

But I now want to turn to another level of generalization,
one therapists characteristically tend to set aside, even
though it's related to a formulation of this material that has
already been developed: the me–not-me interface, and especially the not-me part of that interface, which refers, of course,
to the therapist. This is the level at which the patient's
unconscious sensitivities to the therapist's countertransferences are most often expressed. And we should note here the
extent to which these communications, with their self-
demeaning qualities and allusions to low self-esteem and to
not functioning well—to select one interrelated cluster—could

refer not only to unconscious perceptions, but, to be more precise, to the patient's introjective identifications, based on his unconscious reading of the implications of this particular modification in the framework.

It is here that you see the outcome of the patient's listening process, and I have little doubt that much of this stems not only from this deviation in technique, but also from the nature of the therapist's verbal interventions. I have not included the latter area in my discussion to this point, because I wanted to focus on a single adaptive context—but matters are never that simple in psychotherapy.

I want now to come to another dimension of the me–not-me interface that I have not stressed as yet and which I delayed considering for a very specific reason—namely, because it is so often used as a defense. I have, to this point, been emphasizing the need to monitor the associations from the patient in terms of Type One derivatives related to the therapeutic relationship and as Type Two derivatives involving specific adaptive contexts involving that relationship. And I have stressed the use of the me–not-me interface: all of the material alludes, both validly and with possible distortions, to both patient and therapist—with a focus on the not-me (not-the patient) elements particularly.

And now I want to point out that these associations must therefore entail self-representations, that there is some truth to formulations offered on that basis, and that we must be sensitive to this dimension as well. In fact, as you already know, the patient will at times say things ostensibly about the therapist or some other outside figure, while the primary unconscious meaning of such remarks, especially as Type Two derivatives, may well lie within the realm of self-representation. I have played down that dimension to some extent because introjects and object-representations (if you will, introjects from and reactions to the therapist based on the actualities of the therapeutic interaction) must be rectified and analyzed before self-representations related to psychopathology.

It has never been my intention to imply that we do not deal with both sides of the me–not-me interface. We most certainly do. But in the initial part of this course I have played down the self-representation side—the "me" part of that interface—for a number of reasons. First, because therapists tend to project and projectively identify their own pathology into their patients and to neglect their actual, traumatic effects on the patient. As a result, they have difficulty monitoring the patient's material for valid unconscious perceptions and introjects of their difficulties. For narcissistically gratifying and defensive reasons and as a means of denying expressions of their countertransferences, they tend to consider the material from the patient as reflecting the patient's pathology—fantasy, self-representations, transference, and the like—much to the neglect of the not-me aspects of that material—the introjections of the pathology of the therapist—and at times, I should add, the positive functioning of the therapist.

Still, we should not ignore this important dimension. We must learn to use it nondefensively and must learn when to shape our interventions in that particular direction. And as I have tried to stress, this is not really possible or effective until the introjective disturbances are recognized and brought under control—until you have rectified the field, reasonably managed and self-analytically resolved the expressions of your countertransferences, and come across to the patient as a rather kind, understanding, managing, containing, holding, and interpreting therapist. Under those conditions, the transference component will loom large, and the patient's self-representations can be meaningfully explored and interpreted. They will share the focus of our listening along with the not-me part of the interface: we will have balanced listening and an openness to both "me" and "not-me."

I must also stress that I am referring now not only to the patient's manifest comments about herself but also to her comments about her boss. I am trying to develop Type One and Two derivatives, and here, too, we do not confine ourselves to manifest contents. It is important that you realize that the monitoring of the me–not-me interface applies not only when the patient is talking about herself or the therapist but equally well to all the communications and representations in the patient's associations. Once we turn to the "me" dimension—to her self-representations—we recognize that the allusions to the boss—his being critical, attacking, insensitive, demanding, and the like—could all represent split-off parts of herself. As Freud (1900) said, every person in a dream is in part a self-representation. Similarly, on some level, every person to whom the patient refers, and every segment of material, is a representation of some aspect of the patient's inner mental world and should be considered such: first, in terms of manifest content and Type One derivatives, searching for broad implications regarding both the patient's image of herself and the state of her inner mental world; but secondly, as Type Two derivatives, considering all this material as self-representations that have unfolded around the specific adaptive context—the change in the patient's hour.

So psychotherapy is really a complicated business, and you can see how easy it is to simply wed yourself to one aspect of the listening process, let's say to the cognitive sphere, to the neglect of the interactional realm; or to manifest content and Type One derivatives, to the neglect of the adaptive context and Type Two derivatives; or to introjects of yourself to the neglect of the self-representations of the patient. The reverse of this last is also possible: listening to the material only for the patient's distortions, fantasies, and self-representations, to the neglect of her object-representations and valid introjects of yourself as therapist. The potential effects of countertransference are everpresent. I can only assure you at this time that those influences can be managed, and that it is possible to generate a basic understanding of the listening process that provides you a really sensitive therapeutic instrument.

It's interesting to apply the listening process to what I have just been talking about, because this material has apparent meaning (open to validation, of course) when applied to either patient or therapist. It relates, I suspect, to the sense of helplessness experienced by every beginning therapist, as well as by many throughout their careers. This patient, again in terms of the listening process, communicated a series of images that coalesce as Type One derivatives into a theme of helplessness. And if we were to take that general theme and apply it to the therapeutic relationship, along the me–not-me interface, in terms of both the specific adaptive context of the changed hour and the more general adaptive context of the ongoing state of this treatment, I would suggest that these communications embody the patient's experience of the helplessness of both participants to this therapy. Reversing the usual order of discussion first there is her own helplessness in the face of the therapist's modifications in the framework and, more broadly, her noninterpretive interventions, a sense of weakness that is intensified because the patient is being seen in a clinic at a low fee and has almost nowhere else to turn—which is probably part of why she so severely constricts and disguises her sense of outrage and anger. So, on this level, these are self-representations, portrayed manifestly in a situation with her boss, that are receiving a strong impetus in her relationship with the therapist.

At the same time—and here you see a good example of the process of condensation—this theme applies to the patient's unconscious perception and introjection of the therapist as someone who feels (by the latter's own admission—and it is important to have such insights if you are ever going to resolve the underlying difficulties) quite helpless in the face of this patient's pathology, and perhaps also in the face of her work with a particular supervisor regarding this patient. There have been a number of references to third parties in this material, and I have been wondering about the patient's conscious or unconscious fantasies—or, for that matter, direct knowledge—about a supervisor. But in any case, this material points up the therapist's sense of helplessness as reflected in this deviation and in the nature of her interventions. And you can see too that this then generates another unconscious motive that prompts the patient to inhibit and disguise the expressions of both her aggression and, more broadly, her craziness. This motive is her fear of overwhelming and destroying the therapist, whom even as much as she wishes to destroy she wishes to preserve as a good object—and even to

cure, in order to enable the therapist to function as the good
object she so very much needs: an adequate therapist.

And you can see how monitoring this material at this last
level, the not-me part of the interface, provides reminders of
your own sense of helplessness and inadequacy, a good deal of
which is quite realistic and extremely difficult to modify
quickly, if at all. Such listening can generate an anxiety-
provoking experience that can very readily prompt defensiveness, avoidance, and the wish to maintain a bastion and
misalliance with this patient so that material of this kind is
somehow excluded or, at the very least, that the connections to
the patient's unconscious perceptions of the therapist are
obliterated.

These are among the motives in therapists that prompt
them to psychoanalytic clichés, to unneeded alterations in the
framework, and to erroneous interventions as a means of
allaying their own anxieties. It prompts them also to offer the
patient interactional defenses based on anxieties shared with
the patient, and even on shared unconscious fantasies,
perceptions, and the like. All these efforts turn out, however,
only to intensify anxieties and a sense of helplessness in both
participants, as well as their mutual need for pathological
defenses.

It is indeed a complicated business, very difficult to sort out.
And I must say that as I have been developing this seminar
and listening myself to the concepts that have been emerging
in our discussions, I feel that I am coming to realize why there
has been what I might term, perhaps hyperbolically, a
conspiracy of silence as regards the listening process and its
companion, the validating process. To address these facts
head-on requires considerable mastery over one's countertransferences and a strong capacity to contain and tolerate
painful awarenesses and conflicts. And still—I was talking a
moment ago about the need to eventually alter the therapist's
realistic sense of helplessness—it is undoubtedly the listening
process, more than any other tool besides your own therapy or
analysis, that can pave the way for an outcome of that kind.

Now, I have gone on quite a bit, but I still must cover two
more topics. First, regarding the need to enter a session

without desire, memory, or understanding, it seems evident that most of you can sense just how strong the links are between the last session and this one. Indications are that virtually everyone immediately began to recall fragments of that previous hour as we listened to the initial part of this session, much of it because the manifest content was almost identical. In addition, at least based on our formulations, the latent content also remains pretty much the same. Here, then, the material fosters recall, though it also encourages further listening at the manifest level—at least on the part of this therapist—in the sense that it does not suddenly, or even shockingly, shift the contents in a way that would either interfere with recall or evoke reformulations on the part of the therapist—new hypotheses that might well be directed toward the latent contents.

I say all of this because it is evident that the evaluation of the links between one session and another is a complicated matter. There are, of course, many implications when such links are in fact readily evident and yet have been subjectively obliterated by either patient or therapist. When recall is difficult, an exploration of the possible factors involved is in order. In fact, we search continually for these determinants of the presence or absence of evident links, and look for them within the patient, the therapist, and the material itself—especially in the latent content of the material and in the therapeutic interaction.

So you can see that the striking surface link here is probably due, first, to the nature of the reality situation between the patient and her boss, and, second, to the fact that this is a make-up hour and the patient has an intense need on the one hand to continue to work it over (this material so far lends itself nicely to that effort—in derivative form) and, on the other, to avoid direct allusions to this modification in the frame. Thereby, relatively disguised derivatives are provided that can maintain the bastion established with the therapist in regard to the frame issue. Perhaps too in listening to this material it might be possible to detect some degree of hollowness and to use this as a directive to reformulate and to discover whatever it is that needs interpreting—basing this effort on what is indeed contained in derivative form in this material. Clearly, it is only when we no longer take notes, no longer make efforts at active recall of the previous hour, and bring our own desires and understanding to an absolutely minimal level that we can work over these aspects of the listening process—and often they prove especially significant.

↘   The second major point that I want to discuss involves the whole area of empathy, intuition, and trial identification—various automatic and unconscious processes and interactional experiences that are very much a part of the listening process. This material suggests to me that it is time now to obtain a perspective on these processes—areas in which a considerable literature exists—and I have included the main references on the reading list that I prepared for this course (see also Langs, 1976b). In this regard, as we listened to the last session and to the beginning of this hour, I would expect us to respond with empathy for how the patient was feeling, with temporary trial identifications (see Fleiss, 1942) with the patient, which would have heightened our own experience, as this patient's therapist, of her pain, demeaned self-image, and sense of helplessness—to focus on one set of interrelated qualities. You might momentarily share her pain, her frustration, feel identified with it, while maintaining a sense of your own separateness (Schafer, 1959; Greenson, 1960). There exists, as always, the possibility of countertransference-based misapplications, such as a loss of separateness and overidentification with the patient or, on the other hand, a lack of empathy and a dread of trial identifications that lead to undue distance and insensitivity on the part of the therapist (see also Beres and Arlow, 1974). Misapplication of this aspect of the listening process can lead to blind spots—failures to understand—and, of course, to errors in intervening. Still, the proper use of empathy could serve to generate a particular type of selection process, one based on empathic understanding, trial identifications, if you will, that would foster a particular cluster of first-order themes. The point I would stress, however, is to treat these empathic experiences as first-order data, and to further process the understanding so derived—eventually using the me–not-me interface—so that you have an opportunity to tune in with qualities ultimately related to yourself, as well as to the patient.

In addition, the therapist might respond intuitively, with a sudden, seemingly insightful thought, with a hunch which he would then, of course, need to subject to the validating process. Some might intuit a relationship between this material and the patient's earlier experiences with her mother—there's a clue in that direction—while others might suspect that this material somehow involves something about the therapeutic relationship. They may even suddenly experience a particular formulation in that regard.

Up to this point, I have been emphasizing trial identifications and empathy with the patient and her self-representations, but there is, in addition, a second level of empathic and identificatory responses. These were first described by Helene Deutsch (1926) and later discussed by Racker (1957) and Beres and Arlow (1974). They are identifications and empathic responses with the patient's objects: active or passive efforts—they should be mostly passive—to sense, empathize, and identify with, for example, what her boss is experiencing. Does he feel that he is trampling all over her? Is he dominating her? Does he feel guilty for what he is doing? Responses of that kind. That level of empathy and trial identification is often more difficult for a therapist to experience, largely because as a rule he tends to identify more directly with the patient and, though countertransferences can enter into any identificatory process, he sees greater countertransference-based dangers in identifying with the patient's objects.

Now in terms of the aspect of the listening process we have been outlining, where would you place empathy, intuition, and trial identifications? On what level of the listening process would they seem to operate?

Discussant: Well, I can see a contribution from unconscious aspects of the therapist's functioning, but in the formal sense of your question, it seems to me that they mainly involve Type One derivative.

Langs: Yes, actually they can relate to the manifest content or Type One or Type Two derivatives, but must of their realm is on the manifest content and Type One derivative level. Only rarely will an intuition involve the recognition of an adaptive context, though it certainly may do so. Most often, however, these responses involve the surface of the patient's feelings—and the therapist's as well—empathic and identificatory reactions related to the manifest material, such as, in this particular presentation, the patient's relationship with her boss. And it is crucial to recognize that they create a sense of identity and knowing that must not be experienced as having closure, that is, as a saturated conception, to use Bion's term (1962). Instead they should be experienced as unsaturated preconceptions that need additional inputs for closure and validating.

So these subjective experiences of the therapist, while often unconsciously motivated and unconsciously in tune with aspects of the patient's experiences, both inner and outer, should not be thought of as constituting organized insights or direct revelations of unconscious processes or contents, but rather should be treated as input clues: first-order themes which can be generalized but which need further processing, most often in the form of the search for the adaptive context that will permit the transformation of these inputs—combined with the direct material from the patient—into Type Two derivatives. In all, then, these are important intaking sources, very much under the influence of both patient and therapist, which contribute to the many ways in which we take in the patient's communications—their contents, mechanisms, and affects. But these first-order themes constitute only one phase, which must be followed by formulating, by synthesis, and, especially, by validation.

Still, if you are aware of the particular adaptive context, empathy, identification, and intuition may then serve to comprehend the patient's responses to that primary adaptive task. These processes might also help you to better formulate the me–not-me interface and may, in a roundabout way, help you to tune in on yourself as well. Your identifications and empathic focus may shift about: one moment with the patient, another with her objects, next with yourself in the patient's material, even with your own objects, and often with the patient as your object. These are all dimensions of the therapeutic interaction.

Perhaps the major danger in using these tools is the failure to explore the source of a seemingly empathic or identificatory reaction. Does it stem largely from the patient's communications or does it have an idiosyncratic, countertransference-based primary source within yourself? It is essential always to treat your own subjective experiences as interactional and to make efforts to evaluate their veracity. In keeping with that, it is crucial to validate emphatic, identificatory, and intuitive responses and to overcome the apparently natural and narcissistic tendency to take such moments of apparent insight or seeming sensitivity as gospel truths—a position that fosters their relationship to manifest content and their use as Type One derivatives, as well as a failure to generate Type Two derivatives in terms of the therapeutic interaction. Thus all these experiences must be subjected to the validating process, in terms both of the patient's continuing associations and of your own ongoing subjective responses. These experiences must also be seen in terms of their derivative qualities and be consistently monitored in terms of the therapeutic interaction.

I will have more to say on these aspects of listening as we go along. I think that now it is time to hear more material.

Therapist: She said, I'm getting a token raise, but that's it. So I'll have to go and find another job.

Langs: Okay. Let's take this as a first-order specific theme: a token raise. We can abstract and generalize: an inadequate gesture, something that's simply not enough, inadequate compensation. And we can take the other bit of manifest material: the specific theme of the starting to find another job. General themes: Changing positions. Making a change. Searching for something better. Being forced to do something. Being disappointed. Having to better herself.

It's valuable to do little exercises of this kind with a single communicative element. It helps to clarify the listening process and this particular phase of it. And if you attempt to do this on your own with sements of material from your own patients, it will enhance your ability in this regard. Soon it becomes quite automatic. Certainly in the session itself this association flits by very quickly, and you have to develop a quiet sort of processing in which you do this kind of exercise with segment after segment of the material: attempting to bring together sequential specific themes, coalescing them into a set of repetitive general themes, and then, of course, generating a new set of specific themes around a particular adaptive context. This on the basis of monitoring this material in terms of the therapeutic relationship and of the me–not-me interface.

The complexity of the process may seem staggering, and it certainly renders it remarkably vulnerable to countertransference-based influences, pressures that lead to voids in what you hear in the first place, blockage in respect to important general themes that impinge upon your countertransference-based anxieties, and difficulties in recognizing their function as derivatives related to specific issues in the therapeutic relationship. But it is precisely because the listening process is so very fundamental, and because it is almost never carefully defined and organized, and because it is such a complex process—and I say this knowing that we have hardly begun to study its interactional dimension—that we will need a good bit of repetition and reworking in order to enable you to slowly become proficient in this sphere.

So. I have identified some general themes here—and you'll notice that I dealt with both phrases. We must be careful to apply the listening process to all the material from the patient. And by the way: while we may discover that this material tends to coalesce, that we are hearing certain repetitive general themes and are able to formulate with considerable reinforcement a particular set of second-order specific themes around the adaptive context of the changed hour, please understand, first, that this should not serve to exclude an openness to other possibilities, and, second, that this sense of synthesis will not always pertain. At times, the patient's associations defy meaningful generalization. They lack a specific adaptive context, and turning to the therapeutic situation in some general way as a rule proves insufficient. That is, we need specific adaptive contexts, and it will be insufficient to organize the material around some general sense that a patient has that the treatment is not going well or that the therapist is not being helpful. In fact, let me emphasize that point, because often therapists will take as the adaptive context this kind of general sense of dissatisfaction and it will serve as a defense against the recognition of a more specific and acutely traumatic adaptive context—the context to which the patient is responding in her immediate associations. Try to be as specific as possible in identifying the adaptive context, as well as in formulating first-order specific themes, general themes, and, especially, second-order themes as they apply to the therapeutic relationship.

So. I have offered a number of general themes, and we want to go from them back to the particular. How would you do that?

Discussant: The change in the hour was an inadequate gesture. It doesn't compensate for the mistakes that the therapist has been making, and the patient is thinking of finding another therapist.

Langs: Yes. Here you have focused on unconscious perceptions and self-representations, on the "me" side of the me–not-me interface, and you might have added something of the patient's sense of disappointment and suspected that possibly too there is an underlying sense of anger. When dealing with material in the cognitive or interactional spheres, it is well to identify the actual or potential affects involved. Now what must we do next?

Discussant: Determine something about whether this is valid or distorted.

Langs: Exactly. Is this a distorted or valid unconscious perception of the implications of the change in the hour? Of the state of the therapy? And is her response appropriate or inappropriate? Is it a senseless and pathological flight and defense, or does it appear to be reasonable and adaptive? These are neither value judgements nor moral judgments. They are clinical judgments, and inevitably they are based on your appraisal of reality. They are based, as we said earlier, very much on your own knowledge of yourself, because I think that you can now see that without a rather full understanding of how you have been working with this patient, and of the unconscious meanings of the cancellation and make-up session, you would be bound to misunderstand the implications of the patient's response.

So. Is this distorted or nondistorted?

Therapist: Well, I guess I should say it. She seems to be very much in touch with the inadequacy of what I am doing, but still, I'm not entirely clear as to whether it's realistic for her to seek another therapist or not.

Langs: Yes, these are difficult evaluations, and on a very personal level, like it or not, the therapist has a great deal at stake. These are not matters of contemplation at a distance. The therapist inevitably is quite involved in the interaction itself, in what the patient communicates, and in the evaluation of those communications.

And I would agree with you: your interventions have been well-intended gestures—but mere tokens of the kind of interpretations the patient really needs. And you must accept the painful truth that it really has not been enough to satisfy her therapeutic needs. And again: this is why I consider associations to be commentaries, transversal communications, and maintain an openness for the truth as well as for falsifications and distortions.

As for her thoughts of changing therapists, what can we say? Perhaps the treatment is not actually being helpful. If you are, indeed, being overwhelmed to some extent by her pathology and communications, and if she recognizes that she is too much for you to handle at this time, it may well be that the most sensible resolution would be her leaving treatment and searching for another therapist—with whom we can only hope she will fare better. But feelings such as that—conclusions of that kind—are very painful for us as therapists. This is reflected in the fact that there is virtually no literature on stalemated analyses and therapies—on indications for referrals to a second therapist—except for some preliminary efforts by Greenson (1967) and myself (Langs, 1974, 1976b). It's the kind of experience that can be so shattering to our self-esteem, to our image of ourselves as therapists, to our goals and aspirations—to just about every aspect of our feelings about being psychotherapists. And yet, without seeming maudlin, I really want to emphasize that it is only through experiences of this kind, allowing them to impinge upon you, and to generate inevitable anxiety and chaos, that true resolution and growth can occur. It's really a difficult field that you have chosen, and it's quite unfortunate that much of your growth can only occur in this way. But so it is, and on this basis I hope that you will all maintain a sense of hope and, even, of positive expectation. Please continue.

Therapist: She said, I don't even want to return to work the rest of the week, but I know I have to.

Langs: In the adaptive context of the make-up session, and as a commentary upon it, you could see that the patient feels quite poorly treated and responds rather negatively. This is a reminder that being nice as a therapist is not enough. Often such gestures are experienced unconsiously as rather destructive interventions despite the conscious good intentions. You are not dealing with a social situation, and kindness takes a very special form in psychotherapy, in terms of maintaining a secure framework and the capacity to contain and interpret. The rules of therapy are distinctive.

Discussant: It seems to me that this material reflects a kind of ingratitude on the part of the patient to the therapist's really kind gesture.

Langs: That's a most interesting comment, because many therapists would indeed feel that the patient was simply being ungrateful, that she was not receptive to your kindnesses. That she has some kind of transference-based unresolved hostility. And actually, I don't think that I can fully respond to that point until we have carefully studied the framework of the therapeutic situation and heard more material from this patient. But I would say that whatever elements of that kind do exist, they are for the moment quite secondary—because I happen to agree with the patient. I don't remember now, but earlier I must have predicted some type of negative response to this alteration in the frame, and if I hadn't I should have. If we had been discussing the frame itself, I would have delineated in some detail the inappropriate and destructive qualities of this deviation, despite the therapist's seemingly good intentions; and I seem to recall doing some of that last week.

You see, it is here again that knowing the unconscious implications of your interventions is so crucial. If you simply see the change in the frame on a manifest content level as a kind gesture—a concept, by the way, that would in itself suggest underlying hostility, a demeaning of the patient and her helpless position by sort of throwing her a bone, by being nice to her and making up the hour, something of that sort— but in any case, if you simply adhere to the manifest level of this intervention, this alteration of the framework, you would indeed fail to appreciate the patient's unconscious sensitivities in this regard. The patient is communicating here in derivative form, on an indirect and unconscious level, while you are experiencing the situation directly and on a manifest level. It is this kind of discrepancy in the application of the listening process that places patient and therapist worlds apart, in different communicative spaces. And this is a rather typical situation: the therapist remains with the manifest content of his interventions, while the patient is responding to the latent content, their unconscious meanings and functions.

Discussant: I'm not sure I follow your comments about the make-up session.

Langs: Well, the therapist made up the session. She modified the frame. I'm concentrating for now on the listening process and what the patient tells us indirectly about that decision. And the patient is not expressing gratitude. Don't forget now, I'm talking about Type Two derivatives and, actually, I'm trying from this indirect material to validate some hypotheses I formulated last week and to do it through Type Two derivatives. This is the model of validation I have presented to you.

So she may have come in and said, Thank you for making up the session. That's her conscious and direct response. But now she goes on: My boss is so insensitive and he makes inadequate token offers, and it's very demeaning, and I'm going to have to leave him. These are Type Two derivatives related to the adaptive context—making up the session. We know that whatever else this material relates to, it is a commentary on the cancellation and making up of the session.

Now in contrast to this type of derivative material, if you do something truly constructive, like offering a correct interpretation, she will talk about how kind and perceptive her boss is—or it won't be her boss, she'll find somebody else: On, a neighbor did something so nice for me. People are so constructive. Someone did this marvelous thing. She'll find a way of showing you the positive introjects derived from your valid intervention. Here we're hearing derivatives of the negative introject based on a manifestly well-meaning but latently destructive alteration in the frame. These are not the rules of social intercourse, though they probably relate more to social relationships than many realize. There's probably a lot of falsification in the social sphere too. But in any case, these are specific rules of the therapeutic situation and what is good or constructive in that situation has to be defined in terms of the needs of the patient, and in terms of derivative responses to your interventions.

Discussant: Couldn't we theorize that the adaptive context for this session is the canceled session rather than the make-up session?

Langs: Right. I've suggested it's both, but we're going to have to sort that out. I'm basing my emphasis on the clues from some of her derivatives and perhaps on prior clinical experience. Let her shape a derivative where you will say, Ah! Now I'm tuned in; that must be it. So I leave it to the patient. It's an excellent question, and you're right. I'm saying it's both, and you have to sort out the influence of each—the cancellation and the make-up. The total combination is generating this reaction for the moment. Now we'll see if she provides us derivatives that help us be more precise—and I believe she will. Go ahead.

Therapist: She said, But I need not to make any waves because I need letters for my certification. I have worked for them since graduation. I don't want to have to chase people around to get them to write those letters, especially if I've left the job with bad feelings.

Langs: Here the fear is the specific theme. Now, who can give me the general theme? You asked a good question. We expect the patient to answer it. We are sorting out the effects of two adaptive contexts—the cancellation and the make-up session. What clues lie in this material?

Discussant: What strikes me is the general theme of being frustrated, of having someone meet her needs but nevertheless being tied to that someone—unable to leave, unable either to get what she wants or to break away. Stuck with someone who won't satisfy her needs properly.

Langs: Right. And then, particularizing from these general themes once again, we wonder if this is her perception of the therapeutic situation: the bind, the bond—the bondage, really—that she's experiencing. But she also says something else in here—about how she feels about stirring things up, pursuing people. She doesn't want to leave with them feeling angry. Now, what would you connect that to?

Discussant: Rejection. She's afraid of her anger toward the therapist.

Langs: All right. Afraid of her anger—that's the self-representation. And as I said, that will usually come to your minds first—until we work that over enough. So the first thought is: she's afraid of hostility toward the therapist. Now give it to me the other way around; give it to me as an object-representation of the therapist, as an introject.

Discussant: That the therapist will reject her if she does get angry.

Langs: No, that's still part of the first formulation: that if the patient does something provocative, others will reject her. That's one whole theme. Now, give it to me in terms of an introject of the therapist or an object-representation of the therapist. Clearly that's more difficult for you to conceptualize: the not-me part of the condensation.

Discussant: If the therapist canceled the session without offering something else right away, the patient will go away angry. So the therapist did not want that to happen.

Langs: Exactly. Hear it as an introjection: if the therapist were to say, I cannot make that hour and cannot make it up, the patient would then get angry. The therapist is afraid of the patient's aggression, so she makes up the hour. So that begins to shape our sorting out process. Again, it's in the listening. If you listen to it in that way, if you use the me–not-me interface, it begins to shape an understanding of how the patient perceives the make-up session: as an effort by the therapist to prevent a hostile response in her patient. (Pause.)

You're not convinced yet, we'll get more evidence. But still that's a model of how to monitor this material in terms of the incorporative aspects—the unconscious perception of the therapist, the object-representation. It's much easier to listen in terms of the self-representation; that's why I waited to explore that aspect with you. Therapists often use it as a defense: She's talking about herself and not about me. I'm not afraid of frustrating my patients, and I'm not afraid of their anger; I did this because I'm really a very nice person. But unconsciously, the patient believes that the need to make up the session has something to do with the therapist's fear of her aggression. And to take the final step: is it reality or fantasy? I think she's right about it; it's probably a valid commentary, a perceptive Type Two derivative. Of course, that is open to validation. Please continue.

Therapist: She says, My boss called me from Baltimore. His daughter had been hospitalized in a psychiatric hospital in New Jersey, and he called to tell that she had been transferred to Chestnut Lodge. So I guess he was upset when he was speaking to me about it. He apologized for not letting me talk, and offered to talk again when he returned. He also said he realized that the money isn't enough. But basically he was saying he is not willing to pay me more than a particular client will pay him for my services.

Langs: What do you hear now? There's so much.

Discussant: You wouldn't deny that she's also talking about her boss and her job? You won't deny that, will you?

Langs: Please don't deny that!

Discussant: That there are two levels to which her productions refer: to both the therapeutic situation and the way her character acts *she*—acts—in extratherapeutic situations.

Discussant: Why is she bringing in the extratherapeutic information unless she wanted the therapist to do something about it?

Discussant: Wait. I'd like to finish my question. The way I see it is that almost everything—all the material we handle— is handled by exploring it transferentially. Can you also explore it in extratransferential situations?

Langs: Well, I see we still need to work over that basic issue. How would you do that with this material? What would you say? What's your pending interpretation? I have an interpretation I'm developing, a silent hypothesis which I've been spelling out. See, in the listening comes the intervention. The hypothesis is, that the patient has perceived the make-up session—I haven't even finished developing it, but up to this point it seems that the patient has perceived the make-up session as based on the therapist's fear of the patient's hostility over her canceling an hour, and the patient felt demeaned because of it.

As you can see, I have made use of Type Two derivatives around the adaptive context, rather specifically, for the moment, of the therapist's decision to offer a make-up hour. And as I said before, I am making use of derivative communication and intervening in the realm that is pertinent to the development and sustenance of neuroses. Let's compare it with the intervention that you would propose. And we can see too what it reflects in regard to the nature of your own use of the listening process.

Discussant: No, you are proposing a perfectly sensible intervention.

Langs: Thank you.

Discussant: But will you, in general, make extratransference interpretations at any time? Because you see, with your theory you tie all productions to the therapeutic situation.

Langs: Well, not because of my theory, but because of the listening process. It's a difficult question to answer at this point, but I'll give you a very general response. This question cannot be answered convincingly until we study the therapeutic relationship and hear many more presentations. What you have to do is produce a session where you're absolutely convinced that meaningful interpretations can be made outside of the therapeutic relationship. Then we could see if your thesis holds up. In principle, I'm saying that in studying material from patients, you will find that this is true about once every thousand times and the other nine hundred and

ninety-nine times, it is not true. And that even that one time,
there is a connection to the therapeutic relationship which
should not be neglected. You might not want to intervene at
that moment in regard to it, but you should eventually make
that connection. Now...

Discussant: Can I tell you why I'm so curious?—though it's
a bit personal. I mean, I'm in therapy, a lot of people are, with
training analysts and all, and I'll bet one out of every fifteen
hundred interpretations has anything to do with the transference situation, with the therapeutic field. This analyst is a
reasonably competent psychiatrist, but I would imagine that
if I were in therapy with you, your interpretations would very
much be stilted in the other direction. Now, I'm asking you:
How can two analysts work so differently?

Langs: It's an interesting slip you made—you said "stilted."
That's beautiful—you just answered your own question. I
don't even have to answer you. (Laughter.)

Discussant: But I do have a valid question.

Langs: Of course you do, and I will neither sidestep it nor try
to interpret your slip of the tongue. All I can say is that I am in
the process of teaching you from empirical data concepts
related to therapy and analysis that are, for whatever reasons,
going to be different from what you've been taught or have
experienced in your own therapy. And this is something that I
can't spare you. It's not deliberate—it's based on simply
following the implications of the data. It's going to create
turmoil, out of which I promise you, if you're at all constructive, growth will occur. And it's not going to be easy. But I will
only answer from the material being presented to us, from
data that I can formulate and validate.
   Incidentally, you keep saying "transferential," "transference relationship," when actually you are referring to the
therapeutic relationship and its transference and nontransference, countertransference and noncountertransference
aspects. You subsumed all four dimensions under the term
transference.

Discussant: I'm not really challenging you. I'm confused.

Langs: That's fine; that's inevitable, too. After all, no one else has written an article about the adaptive context and its function in listening—just me (Langs, 1972, 1973a)—and I have only recently organized this process even better, in terms of manifest content, Type One derivatives and Type Two derivatives. If we all agree—and I don't think anyone would disagree—that psychopathology, however it's formed, on whatever level, has to do with Type Two derivatives, and that the cure has to be in the realm of Type Two derivatives, then we should not be interpreting what the patient is working over manifestly. Yes, that's part of her problem, part of her life, but it's not part of what will help her in therapy. It is too direct...linear...realistic...and the like.

Discussant: Oh, that's what you're saying. Okay.

Langs: That's what I'm saying. Because the conscious and manifest do not have to do with the realm of her neurosis.

Discussant: Okay, that makes it more sensible. Now I understand.

Discussant: I think the thing that confuses me—and I'm not exactly in the same boat as he is, but in a nearby boat anyway—is that to the extent that her relationship with the therapist continues her neurosis as a direct manifestation of her underlying character, you try, by your process of working through the transference aspect, to disengage yourself from her neurotic attempts to use you in the same way that she gets involved with these or other people.

Langs: Now you used the word *transference* again, which I would ask you to not use in that way in this seminar. Because it's the relationship, and you seem to be talking about transference and nontransference. But it's not only the patient wanting to use the therapist; that happens and it would be analyzable in a standard way. But it's the therapist actually behaving in ways that lend themselves to, and truly repeat, the past traumas. So long as you're doing that, therapy is stymied. It isn't only that the patient wants this to happen, which she does, but also that you impose it upon her.

For example, the make-up session, as I hope to demonstrate, may have repeated something from her childhood that had to do with her mother's infantilizing her, or with her mother's avoiding her daughter's hostile feelings. So long as you're actually doing that sort of thing you can't analyze what is now an intrapsychic introject: part of her character and her self-representations or her introjects that are pathological and thereby disturbing her handling of the realities of the job and whatever. You can't modify that pathology because you are fostering it, reinforcing the introject and repeating the processes through which it first developed. Even though you are saying words that are designed to do something else, the patient still is experiencing that repetition.

So yes, I say that first and foremost, you must be a different object. Then the rest of therapy unfolds. And that's why so much work that I do has to do with helping you realize the implications of not being a different object, and the ways in which that is present, however unconsciously, in alterations in the frame, errors in intervening, and the rest. And when you get that under control, then the interface of the bipersonal field shifts to the pathology of the patient, almost entirely as the patient's responsibility, not as an interactional product developed equally by both you and the patient, but as an interactional product to which you contribute only minimally—there is always an interactional amalgam.

Discussant: This is the first time I've really understood what you're trying to say.

Langs: We're going to review this over and over again.

Discussant: So what you're saying is that there is material outside the bipersonal field that is part of the person's pathology, but that interpreting it is not curative. What's curative is interpreting within the bipersonal field.

Langs: Yes, but we do so because the manifestations of her pathology, the contents of this session, do not give you responses to the outside relationship in derivative form that lends itself to interpretation. It isn't that I insist I'm going to interpret it in terms of the relationship with the therapist. Rather, this patient is telling me that if I interpret the outside relationship, I will be dealing with manifest content or, at best, Type One derivatives. And by definition, that is not psychoanalytic therapy, especially in the case of dealing with the former. I don't think anybody objected to that statement— that psychoanalysis and psychopathology involve unconscious processes and concepts. This is mainly manifest content, which you could stretch into some general inferences. But they would not be true unconscious derivatives, in contrast to contents that are displaced from, and derivative of, something that is truly unconscious, where the roots of pathology exist: something that has to do with her early childhood, her inability to deal with the therapist directly, and all the rest. The patient is telling you this, and I'm going to try to convince you that she is my source for these concepts and principles. I learned all of this from patients, and patients insist on it being done this way. I can't tell you how many times therapists have intervened in terms of the outside manifest conent, and the patient has indirectly, through Type Two derivatives, said, Will you cut it out already? This isn't helping me one bit. That isn't what I want, it isn't what I need. Thanks a lot for trying, but will you do it right already?

Discussant: You're working differently now than you did ten years ago.

Langs: Yes, different in many respects from the work reflected in my books on technique (Langs, 1973a 1974), but similar in many ways as well. Those volumes express the basic position of a classical analytic approach to psychoanalytic psychotherapy, and they deal with how to listen and validate. But I would extend and revise them considerably today, and I would write much of it on a different level, some of it reflected in *The Bipersonal Field* (Langs, 1976a). Still, those technique books contain the seeds of most of what followed.

Discussant: Perhaps it won't change further now.

Langs: I very much hope that you are wrong. For me, that's tantamount to being dead. So long as we are alive as therapists, it is the nature of the therapeutic interaction that its ultimate unconscious contents and functions—its secrets, if you will—are of a proportion approaching infinity. And I think that every viable therapist should be in an active state of learning and changing—sometimes in major ways, sometimes in minor—and I must say that that continues to be my experience. While, most recently, this has been happening in smaller ways, I have certainly gone through some major transformations in the past.

To state all of this another way, no therapist ever fully resolves his countertransferences. But he should actively, and sometimes even rather passively, pursue their resolution throughout his career, doing so largely as bits of his underlying countertransference fantasies and introjects are expressed occasionally in his therapeutic work. And each new bit of insight and adaptation should in some way further his understanding of the therapeutic interaction, of himself and his patients, and of his technique. And that too should be a never-ending process. In general, the valid core should remain stable, though never ossified, and the rest can and should change. To be alive as a therapist really implies momentary periods of chaos and disorganization, reorganization and reintegration, and of course, growth. You should worry when it is otherwise.

So, this is the best that I can offer for now, and I think that it has certain qualities. I've become more and more convinced that these new concepts—or this reintegration of, or different emphasis on, old concepts—that they make a very crucial difference. But do you realize that virtually every graduate analyst goes around with the basic assumption that he knows analytic technique and there's nothing really new for him to learn in that area? Oh, they may accept some new concepts such as those of Kohut (1971, 1977) and Kernberg (1975) on narcissism, borderline syndromes, and the like; but often enough such ideas are simply used to rationalize deviations or alterations in fundamental technique. But in terms of basic ways to listen and to intervene, their often unconscious assumption is that nobody can teach them anything significant or genuinely novel. Almost every experienced therapist or analyst feels that way, though I do want to add that there are exceptions.

But to get them to think otherwise, especially if they have been in practice for a while—the resistances are almost excruciating. To act otherwise seems to entail a risk of opening up and disturbing unconscious countertransference-based defenses and fantasies, risking chaos—as you all now know quite well—and unfortunately, too few therapists and analysts are prepared to risk that. It takes an enormous amount of pressure to make them do so. And the more that I feel that there are crucial differences for the treatment of their patients, for their own satisfaction in their own work, the more frustrated I become when I encounter these resistances. On some level, of course, and to some degree, we all harbor these resistances: they are in fact the very factors that disturb the listening process with your patients. They make it difficult for you to hear material in truly unexpected and unique ways, and especially, they make it difficult for you to appreciate the patient's unconscious creativity and curative efforts on your behalf. Let's leave it at that.

Now, coming back to this material, there is more for us to discuss. It touches upon an aspect of the listening process that I term an *embedded derivative*—that is, a derivative that is quite well disguised and kind of set into the material in a manner that can easily lead you to overlook it; it seems so very incidental to what is being said. And in fact, this particular embedded derivative has a good deal of relevance to the adaptive context of the canceled and make-up sessions, as well as to some of the postulates I developed toward the end of our discussion last week. Has anyone picked it up?

Discussant: I think that what she was saying is that whatever the therapist was doing was more important to her than her patient was, and that she feels that the therapist is less available to her even in a make-up sense, in the sense that this other thing was more important: that this boss is going to call her back when he finds out about his daughter.

Langs: All right. Those do constitute possible Type Two derivatives organized around the adaptive context of the canceled session. But that is not the theme or area I'm looking for. What else? (Pause.) I said it was embedded—disguised in a way—easy to overlook. You've picked up a general theme from a number of first-order specific themes, and have generated a second-order specific theme using quite a bit of this material. You've worked with some of the more evident manifest content, but what is another theme that was neatly tucked away?

Therapist: The transfer of the daughter.

Langs: Yes. The daughter who is what? (Pause.) The daughter who is mentally ill, who is hospitalized, who is crazy—right? Okay, now I've identified a specific segment of manifest content that was, indeed, easy to miss—something just mentioned in passing, somewhat peripheral, it would seem, to the main theme of the patient's communication, to the main point the patient was making in regard to the telephone call from her boss (the manifest content), and seemingly unrelated even to the second-order themes (the latent content) that we had been developing—an embedded derivative that is easy to bypass.

But if we're not lulled into missing its presence, we can take it as a first-order specific theme and attempt to generalize from it, generate a second-order theme as either a Type One or a Type Two derivative, and thereby generate a silent hypothesis. Would someone give it a try?

Discussant: Well, the transfer from one psychiatric hospital to another could bring up feelings about termination.

Langs: Yes, but that's another issue, another possible level of this material concerned with an additional adaptive context related to the patient's presence in a clinic, and to her anxieties, fantasies, and perceptions related to the possibility of a forced termination.

But notice what you did: I had selected one aspect of the reference to the daughter—her mental illness, her sickness or craziness, to use a general term that can evoke a number of different associations which could be relevant to the patient's unconscious communications—while you focused on the shift from one hospital to another. You can see, then, that in the course of the listening process the effort to identify first-order specific themes entails making a variety of readings of the manifest content itself, of each particular segment of manifest content. Each aspect of an anecdote that the patient is reporting, or whatever the material may be, has a variety of immediate implications, and in the course of the listening process we endeavor, optimally, to sample each of them. We try to remain open to the various leads while also, as I said before, selecting those implications that enable us to begin to build a constellation of themes—a coalescence of seemingly related themes—and the connections may be on the conscious or the unconscious level. And either we develop a group of themes that call for the identification of an adaptive context that will fit them together, or we make use of a known adaptive context as a basis for selecting relevant themes.

Once again, we have complexity, and it can be no other way. Remaining open to all possible implications and, at the same time, attempting to organize are seemingly contradictory tasks which must be carried out alternately, if not virtually simultaneously; and neither should ever be neglected.

If we pursue the implication I have been developing, the embedded derivative related to the mentally ill daughter—what more can you say?

Therapist: Oh, I know—you said it last week.

Langs: Yes, I did.

Therapist: You said that the patient will feel, in my making up the session, that I feel she can't manage without me.

Langs: Yes, that's exactly the area that I have in mind, and this patient found a beautiful way of saying it—through an exquisite embedded derivative that contains still more meaning than you just identified. This association reminded me of similar situations, described in my technique books (1973a, 1974), in which the therapist would offer a make-up session and the patient would talk about crazy people, losing control, her feeling that no one trusts her, and things of that kind.

And here, we can see once again how marvelously the patient unconsciously selects reality incidents and finds a particular way of shaping and presenting them that enables her to communicate unconscious meanings, perceptions, and fantasies. The telephone call with her boss was a way of bringing up the issue of craziness, which we can now study a bit further along the me–not-me interface—as a commentary on the changed hour and, in addition, on the therapist's failure to analyze its implications.

We'll start with the patient this time—her fear of going crazy. It's embedded there as a derivative and is related to the adaptive context of your canceling and making up the session in ways that are, for the moment, somewhat unclear. Conflicting messages, perhaps, or maybe a response to other adaptive stimuli. In any case, as a Type One derivative at least, and perhaps Type Two, she's saying that she is afraid of losing control, of going crazy. So this is a self-representation. And what does she do with it? Something very typical: she splits it off. This is a nice example of splitting and projection, if you want to call it that, and she disposes of these fears by alluding to her boss's daughter. This is all so anxiety-provoking for the patient that she does this beautiful job of splitting it off and getting rid of it—externalizing it through a representation that is quite a distance from herself, one that could not, for the moment, be interpreted at all. That's why I called it an embedded derivative—it's so incidental to what she was talking about.

Therapist: Yes, it's funny, because I remember my reaction when she said it. I said to myself, Ah, she's afraid of going crazy. Then I looked and there was nothing else there; I couldn't substantiate it.

Langs: That's the cleverness of her defenses, their strength: a way of conveying meaning that cannot be immediately substantiated.

So—that's her. Now who are we going to do this to next? (Pause.) The therapist, the not-me part. And here the Type Two derivative would be to the effect that this intervention, of canceling and making up the session, is based on some fear that the therapist has of managing her own inner mental world and her patient's reactions. In other words, it was done as a protection against *your* going crazy, in addition to your fears for the patient.

Therapist: My going crazy?

Langs: Yes, that's what she's saying. I'm just talking for her, translating her derivative communications into direct statements. That's the second level of meaning here, and with both—the "me" and the "not-me"—you must then ascertain how much is valid and how much distorted. We have to monitor the material for allusions to herself and you, including your inner state, and her perception and distortions of its contents based on the meanings of your interventions.

Let me elaborate: for herself, she's afraid she will go crazy and afraid you will go crazy too. For you, based on your behavior, she experiences, validly or not, your fear that she will go crazy and your fear that you will go crazy. All of these are possible, all are contained latently, and, as the material unfolds and as you get to know more about yourself, you can then select what is really the most relevant thread. The most obvious and easiest one would be that you are afraid she will go crazy and, rather than interpreting something relevant to this concern, you modified the frame, which conveyed your lack of faith, both in her ability to manage and in your capacity to interpret. That would be easier to take; the other is more painful.

So why don't we stop here, since you have to leave, but let's hear the rest of this session next time, because it's really very, very meaningful and gives us a chance to work over the listening process.

Discussant: As regards the main adaptive context: why did it have to be the make-up session? Why not the cancellation of the regular hour? We could interpret that what she's referring to—in terms of this tokenism, being unable to express the anger, of needing something from the boss—is that she's very upset, very angry about the missed session. However, she knows that if she expresses that anger, expresses her upset, expresses the hostility she's feeling toward the therapist, then she won't get what she needs from the therapist, which might, in fact, be the make-up session itself.

Langs: Yes, we have already touched on that thesis, and, if you remember, we have been trying to determine to what extent the material centers around the adaptive context of the canceled hour, and to what extent around the make-up session. For the moment I have been stressing the influence of the replacement hour and the patient's unconscious fantasies and perceptions related to it—regarding both herself and the therapist. The same communication—the reference to the boss's very disturbed daughter—could be organized around the adaptive context of the canceled hour. If I may continue to focus on the theme I have been developing, at least for the moment, I would suggest that the cancellation itself could be viewed as a danger to the patient, who, on that basis, fears losing control and going crazy. But it can also be viewed as a reflection of some loss of control by the therapist—an image which could be quite distorted, since the therapist may have had a very rational reason for canceling the hour— but this image might nonetheless be somewhat reinforced by the therapist's decision to replace the session to be missed.

Now in regard to your own formulation, this too involves an aspect of the listening process that we must identify, in that you are postulating that we organize this material around Type Two derivatives related to the canceled hour. The formulation includes a silent hypothesis that the patient dreads expressing her anger about the cancellation for fear of antagonizing the therapist to the point that the hour will not be made up.

Two comments seem pertinent to your formulation: first, the therapist offered to make up the session at the same time that she indicated her need to cancel the hour, and, while the patient might have had some anxiety that the therapist will not keep her word, it seems likely that the patient will accept the situation as one in which the hour will indeed be made up, and that she does not especially fear such a reprisal as canceling the make-up session in response to expressions of hostility.

Second, I would like to offer a somewhat revised formulation, suggesting the kind of restatement that you yourself might make as you continue to listen—largely when you discover that one aspect of your silent hypothesis does not seem to make much sense or does not seem particularly compelling. Here you might turn again to the theme of being crazy and suggest that the patient fears expressing her hostility toward the therapist because of anxieties that she herself might lose control in so doing, and that the therapist too might go crazy under these conditions. That formulation is more in keeping with the material and is rather interesting as a model, since it makes use of various fragments of the first-order specific themes and their generalizations as a means of creating a new whole that has had to be pieced together: a construction quite different from the more linear reading of manifest content for readily available implications in the form of Type One derivatives.

I very much hope that you see that last point. I have just used a number of fragments in the manifest content that were not connected on the manifest level and have generated a formulation regarding the patient's unconscious fantasies and perceptions, that has been shaped by the adaptive context of the canceled hour. These scattered fragments I have brought together as you would the disparate pieces of a puzzle. Many Type Two derivatives are formulated and completed in just that fashion, taking a bit from one part of the patient's associations, and another bit from a different segment of the associations—and this is where unconscious sensitivity and creativity can serve you well.

It seems to me that we have taken this material as far as we can for the moment. Perhaps next week we can validate some of these formulations so that they will be more convincing. After that, we can review the listening process through which we generated them and hopefully bring you to a new level of conviction regarding the basic concepts I have been developing with you. In this specific instance, too, you will continue to listen to the derivatives to determine the adaptive context which fits best—an important and practical exercise.

Discussant: I'm beginning to see something of what you mean by this matter of fit, and how the fear that the patient would not be able to manage without the therapist, without the make-up session, could tie into this mention of someone who has been hospitalized psychiatrically. On the other hand, I still get some feeling that you have stretched matters a bit, strained them, so to speak, when you say that the material is a reflection on the therapist—that the patient is saying something about the therapist's own inner state.

Langs: Oh, I understand that. This is an aspect of the monitoring of this material, and of the me–not-me interface, that is most difficult to tolerate and accept. For the moment, I can only hope that it opens your mind to such considerations, that you will begin to make efforts to monitor the material from your own patients in terms of their introjection of your own inner mental state and unconscious communications, and that you will begin to investigate what you can learn from such efforts. In this presentation much will depend on the patient's subsequent associations. I will try to keep this issue in mind and see if I can validate my formulation. We'll just have to wait and see.

Therapist: I must leave now, but I will continue next week.

Langs: Yes—and thank you. Now. Has anyone any material he would like to present in the time we have left?

Therapist: Yes, since we do have a little time, I wonder if I could present a couple of sessions with a patient with whom— well, a number of problems came up. Actually, I've had a lot of difficulty in treating her. But in particular, I had a question about the listening process, largely because . . .

Langs: Well, we have enough time to hear some specific material, so I'll ask you to not tell us what troubled you. We will accept the presentation on good faith and expect it to raise an issue that was, for you at least, important. And I expect it will be for your colleagues and me as well. Just provide us a brief introduction and moderately condense the sessions you would like us to hear.

Therapist: Okay. This is a young woman in her late twenties who lives with her parents, who has been depressed and at times very confused, who has not been able to settle into a long-term career, and who has not done well with men. I've been seeing her twice a week for over a year and recently, largely under the influence of this course, I have begun to realize that I was much too involved with her, that I had been making far too many noninterpretive interventions. So I began to sit back a bit, trying to identify the adaptive context and trying to organize the material around it. I can't say that I've been especially successful with all of that, but I've been trying.

Let me quickly summarize the session before the one or two that I would like to describe in a bit more detail. She spent most of the beginning of that session ruminating about her job—she's now training to be an assistant manager at a department store—and she doesn't know whether she wants to work in the children's wear section or in women's wear. She had been given a special opportunity for advancement in the children's section and had taken it, but then felt unhappy and was in a terrible quandary. So, she was ruminating about that, said something about feeling better, but her mother ruined all that by calling her an old maid and attacking her for not getting married. There was some mention of a friend of her mother's who had died, of the friend's daughter, who is married and has had children, and of the patient's guilt in depriving her mother of the things that she wanted. Her mother had been vicious, called her a lesbian, and the patient told her she was crazy. She went on in some detail about all of that.

She then compared that interplay with a mother she had waited on at the department store, who had been quite loving with her son, who had been upset, and she went on to talk about thoughts of leaving home once she finished her training period at the department store. At times she feels she can do it, but at other times she panics, and is terrified of being along— and of being murdered, raped, or molested. She ended the session saying that she believed that I could say something that would make her troubles disappear and expressing hope that she could change. In the next session . . .

Langs: Does anyone wish to make a comment focusing on the listening process as applied to this session?

Discussant: Well it's hard for me to determine an adaptive context. I really don't see any, unless maybe it has something to do with the therapist's becoming silent. I noticed that he didn't report an intervention for this session.

Therapist: Yes, that's right. I was silent, and I felt that the patient was alluding to that toward the end of the hour.

Discussant: Still, even with that it's hard for me to organize this material and to make any sense of it.

Langs: Yes, that seems to be the case, and I think we should leave it at that since we have not heard the previous session and will therefore be unable to identify any specific adaptive context that might be derived from that hour. I am quite pleased that you did not consider the patient's conflict with her job as the adaptive context for this hour, and that you also did not suggest that her problems with her mother served as the adaptive context—although on some level that may well be evoking a great deal of intrapsychic conflict and pain.

In that regard, it might prove necessary, since this patient is living at home, to monitor this material in terms of her relationship with her mother—the original pathogenic object, and she certainly sounds just that—in addition to monitoring it in terms of the patient's relationship with the therapist. It will be necessary to intervene in a way that would connect the two wherever possible, aa, aa, and to attempt to sort out, on the basis of the unconscious implications of their communications, the similarities and differences between the therapist and the patient's mother.

In order for us to get to the main issue that the therapist wants to present, let me just formulate that in the adaptive context of the therapist's relative silence—whether it is the main context or not—we can monitor this material along the me–not-me interface. Let me also suggest that the patient is somewhat frightened by the sense of abandonment that she's experiencing, quite uncertain as to the implications of the therapist's silence. Is it the beginning of some good parenting and holding, or a silent and destructive abandonment that will render the patient helpless and vulnerable? These are some of the main threads.

In terms of the related introjections of the therapist, the patient seems to sense some uncertainty about his decision to modify his therapeutic approach. She is wondering if he is, indeed, becoming unconsciously destructive and attacking, an unconscious perception that—so long as there has been no indication for an intervention—could be a distortion based on a misreading of the therapist's silence. And based on my limited knowledge of this session, I would have to say that I see no evidence of any such indication.

Allow me to pause for a moment with that. It's an important model, and this may well be one of our few opportunities to observe a possible unconscious *mis*perception: an introject that is distorted rather than valid, one based here on an unconscious fantasy—an unconscious transference fantasy, as I have defined it for you—derived from the patient's experiences with her mother. While we cannot evaluate this material or validate the point I am making, it serves nonetheless as an excellent model of what might very well be a distorted image of the therapist based on the patient's own pathological introjects, her own unconscious fantasies and memories.

Toward the end of the session—with her thoughts of leaving home—the patient seems to be sensing a possible hope for relative independence based on the change in the climate of the therapy. But she soon shifts back to unconsciously perceiving the therapist's silence as an abandonment, as rendering her vulnerable, and somehow she seems even to suggest that it is an attempt at rape or molestation—which is difficult for me to understand since we are dealing with silence rather than overactivity. Perhaps this relates to the therapist's earlier style of intervening.

Well, rather than going further with these speculations, let's hear more material.

Therapist: Well, here's where the problem began. I had to make a special case presentation and the conference began some twenty minutes before her next session would end. I had decided to extend the session as long as I could, and to stop five minutes early and make it up the following week.

Langs: This takes us immediately to issues of the framework. Without elaborating, let me state that any time you put your own needs above those of your patient there will be extensive repercussions, some of them impossible to resolve. In fact, your decision to stop five minutes early, to not see the session through, suggests some kind of countertransference. After all, it would have taken only five more minutes to have maintained the frame. The patient will certainly be sensitive to that aspect. Still, I should not overly bias our listening process, so please proceed.

Therapist: She began the session by saying that things were going well at her job, and I quickly told her that I had to end the session five minutes early, that I was sorry, and that I would give her the extra five minutes in the second session the following week. (By the way, I couldn't extend the first hour of that week.)

The patient said that I shouldn't worry about it and then ruminated in some detail about now feeling that she preferred to be with women's wear rather than in the children's department. Soon she said she had nothing more to say and asked me directly if I were going to talk. Becoming silent herself and occasionally ruminating about her job, soon she was pressuring me to speak, complaining that I hadn't been talking for weeks now, and saying that she was getting sick and more anxious, and that I had to talk. She soon said she couldn't take it, that it was better when I spoke, and that this new business of my being silent was no good. Eventually she stood up and said that she was leaving.

Langs: Well, can anyone offer a brief formulation?

Discussant: I'm a bit confused. I can see that the adaptive context must be his telling the patient that he has to end the session five minutes early, but it seems to me that in all of our previous discussions, when the therapist had done something traumatic, we found that the patient took it out on someone else, worked it over in some outside relationship. Here she is directly attacking the therapist.

Therapist: Yes. That's why I decided to present this material. It seemed to me that the patient was telling me that my silence was not helpful to her. And actually, I felt that I was under pressure here, though it's hard for me to define just how.

Discussant: I can't quite formulate it, but it seems to me that in some way her complaints about your being silent has something to do with your leaving the session early.

Langs: Yes, exactly. Let me briefly unravel this for you, because this is very important material and shows how therapists can misapply the validating process and come to quite erroneous conclusions in regard both to their shortening a session and to their use of valid techniques about which the patient directly complains. Let me do it in terms of the basic steps in the listening process that we have been developing. We have two principles through which we identify the adaptive context of this session: first, every intervention is to be taken as an adaptive context. Here it is a modification in the frame. Secondly, we can sense for ourselves that a decision by the therapist to shorten the length of the session must have an impact upon the patient. So, there seems to be complete agreement that the adaptive context for this material is the therapist's decision to leave the session five minutes early.

Now, we listen and monitor the material in terms of the adaptive context and find that on the manifest level the patient reassures the therapist that she's not at all concerned about his shortening the session, though she soon says that she has nothing more to say. But then she attacks the therapist for his silence, and soon demands that he speak. Here we have an opportunity to formulate the listening process on both the cognitive and the interactional levels.

To begin with the one that we are more familiar with for the moment, the cognitive: in the adaptive context of the shortening of the session, the patient's anger that the therapist is not talking to her—the first-order specific theme— can be generalized to reflect anger at the therapist and rage over a feeling that he is depriving the patient of something that she very much needs. This material can then be organized, as Type Two derivatives, around the specific adaptive context we have identified, so that we arrive at the formulation or the silent hypothesis that the patient's rage over the therapist's silence is a derivative of her fury over the deprivation and hurt involved in his shortening the session.

Here I would stress the following: first, that there is a characteristic split within the patient in response to seemingly innocuous or even supposedly helpful deviations in the frame: manifestly, she accepts the shortened session; latently, she is furious and attacks the therapist for the loss and all that it implies. Second, so long as we did not organize this material around that particular adaptive context, we would not be aware of the true unconscious meaning of these communications—their functional capacity for the moment. We would then be inclined to conclude that the therapist's silence had been destructive and poor technique. We would ignore the implications of this material for the alteration in the framework—something that a therapist who had both conscious and unconscious needs for this decision might be quite prone to do. All of this would also lead to a sector of misalliance and a bastion in which the patient's unconscious reactions to his deviation would be split off and repressed and denied. And, in general, this is exactly how therapists have failed to realize the important ramifications of the framework—that a patient experiences a deviation of this kind as an infuriating rapture of the therapeutic hold and that, as the patient so poignantly says, this is experienced as a pathological effort to disturb her equilibrium and make her sick: in Searles' terms (1959), to drive her crazy.

Now very briefly, since we will soon consider this area of the listening process in far greater detail, we will view the situation interactionally. The therapist's decision to end the session five minutes early can be viewed as a projective identification into the patient of some unconscious counter-transference fantasy, some difficulty in holding and containing the patient and her communications, and some countertransference-based need to harm, reject, or drive this patient crazy. These are the elements the patient seems unconsciously to have detected. Here the therapist is using the patient as a pathological container and, at least on one level, she seems relatively refractory. On another, she introjects the pathological communications involved, begins to feel sicker and more anxious, returns the projective identification with its rageful qualities back into the therapist, and demands that he contain her disorganization and sickness. What we have here is a pathological reprojection that the therapist experiences as pressure on him—a likely sign that the patient is projectively identifying disruptive contents back into him.

Remember, however—and this is true too in the cognitive sphere—that these interactional impressions must be validated, especially through the patient's further associations. You don't want to lay yourself open to the charge that your validating process rests solely on "subjective impressions." Further, not everything that the therapist experiences subjectively is prompted by the patient—he must always seek out sources within himelf as well as in the patient's material.

You will also note how important it is, when dealing with interactional pressures, to recognize a circular quality: to not simply see this, as do many Kleinians, as being generated wholly within and by the patient, but to recognize that in this particular sequence the pathological interactional projections have been, for the moment, initiated by the therapist—who nonetheless, in keeping with the endless spirals involved, may have been provoked into this kind of reaction because of unconscious pressures and projective identifications from the patient. These may in turn have been evoked by the therapist's behaviors. Still, it is well to realize that whatever the sources of these interactional pressures from the patient, the therapist, rather than dealing with them by altering the frame, should have better managed, better contained, and better metabolized them.

Briefly, in terms of the other interactional level—role and image evocations—the deviation seems to have generated a self-image in the patient as someone who is sick, deprived, frustrated, neglected, and demeaned. Her role—again, determined both by the input from the therapist and by inputs from within herself—soon became that of someone making demands upon the therapist and attempting to provoke him as well. The patient became both victim and victimizer.

In defining all of this, I cannot help formulating that much of this must derive from projective identifications from the therapist and must reflect the placing into the patient of many of his own pathological introjects. And it may be that this is the way in which the object relationship and interactional mechanism levels tend to come together. Often, the role that the therapist evokes in the patient is based on his own introjects, just as the patient's efforts to evoke images and roles within the therapist depend in part on her own self-representations and introjects. Of course, in keeping with the principle of spiraling processes, the patient or therapist may invite various roles and images. It is also true, as reflected in this example, that many therapists enter the profession because the patient can be established as the sick one and can be expected to play out roles in keeping with that image.

Returning to the material, these interactional pressures culminate when the patient is about to leave the session. It is here that she produces the derivative closest to the therapist's decision to leave early. This validates the initial silent hypotheses (one) that the patient was unconsciously responding to the shortened session and (two) that she was experiencing it as a hurtful projective identification, a role and image evocator which she was unable to metabolize or handle, and which she attempted to reproject back into the therapist in virtually the same form.

Incidentally—I won't go into detail because time is short— all of these formulations could have been used as the basis for interpretations to the patient at the point at which she was about to leave, or even a bit earlier. Though here I hasten to point out that I would have begun by suggesting to the patient that, while she consciously accepted my need to shorten the hour and consciously denied any anger or other response, she soon became enormously agitated and seems to have experienced it in the manner I defined a moment ago. I would also point out her impressions and reactions in both the cognitive and the interactional spheres. And I would add this much: on the basis of this patient's agitation and these communications, I would probably have decided to restore the full session, to immediately rectify the frame, accepting her associations and behavior as a directive in that regard and realizing that these interpretations could by no means heal the wounds involved in such a sudden and seemingly senseless desertion. After all, it was only five minutes. Nor would these wounds be accepted and integrated in the face of my continued plans to abandon her.

Again, let's be content with these basics and hear a bit more.

Therapist: Here I suggested that the patient sit down and told her that she seemed to want to avoid something, that she was running, putting me in the role of hurting her, of inflicting something monstrous upon her, and that she seemed to feel deserted and alone—a feeling which in last week's session she equated with the danger of being raped and murdered—and that this connected up with her need to keep intruders out and reflected her feelings that something terrible was happening to her. Finally, I said that she was placing it into me and was seeing my silences as doing these very terrible things to her.

Langs: Well, we could spend an entire session discussing that intervention. But because of the hour, let me just offer a couple of highlights: first, you bring up an experience of role pressures—interestingly enough, in terms of the patient's influence on you. Still, that too is an interactional dimension of the listening process. The patient in leaving wants you to experience yourself in a particular way and in a particular role—here, as hurtful and destructive. But, as Sandler (1976) has pointed out—and as I have already stated several times— the experience of image and role pressures must be sorted out in terms of contributions from both patient and therapist. And here, you speak as if this was initiated entirely by the patient, although you later suggest that in some small way it was related to your silences. You might rather acknowledge that than recognize that all of this stems directly from the actual hurt involved in shortening this patient's session, and that perhaps the greatest pathological role pressure in this session has been placed by you upon the patient. You have made her your victim and the target of a psychological rape and murder—to use the kernel of truth in your own intervention— and she is actually attempting to evoke in you something of what you have stirred up in her.

Second, you of course denied, along with the patient, the immediate adaptive context—the shortened hour—and did indeed join her in a bastion and sector of misalliance. This response further suggests that there were indeed important countertransference factors in your decision to modify the frame.

Third, your intervention implies at the outset that the patient is misperceiving, that this is primarily a transference-based response, one based on unknown genetic factors and on the patient's conscious displaced fantasies of murder and rape. And although you do eventually link her reaction to your silences, you still imply that this is a rather distorted and inappropriate response to them. Rather than taking this reaction as a transversal communication containing truths about you, mixed perhaps with some distortions, and rather than regarding her leaving as both appropriate and inappropriate, you stress the distorted aspects to the neglect of the more reasonable side.

And this is how, in still another way, patients experience themselves being driven crazy by their therapists. They are told directly and by implication that their reactions are distorted and pathological, when a true appreciation of the adaptive context and its unconscious implications reveals that their responses are far from that: they contain large, rational segments, and we would have a great deal of difficulty in validating the impression that it is quite insane and inappropriate to leave a therapist who without apparent reason suddenly shortens your session by five minutes.

We could perhaps suggest that there is a clear element of pathology in the fact that the patient did not respond with direct anger, did not question the therapist, and did not make efforts to ascertain whether there was some truly emergency reason for the loss of the five minutes. Clearly, she could have responded in a more adaptive and controlled manner, and we would have to suggest that this response reflects some degree of proneness to action, loss of control, and uncontrolled rage—though we would have to feel somewhat sympathetic to this patient's plight, because the therapist himself has behaved in exactly these ways, placing exactly that kind of introject into the patient who might otherwise have handled the experience somewhat better and whom we cannot simply see as the therapist's victim. You can see here how we experience transversal communications.

To summarize: there do appear to be pathological elements in this response, but we have an entirely different perspective on them when we recognize the true adaptive context for the patient's reactions. And our intervention would certainly be different from that made by the therapist, if it were based on the formulations I am developing now. We would probably simply point out some of the seemingly inappropriate aspects of the patient's reaction within a context implicitly acknowledging the many valid perceptions and responses—both conscious and unconscious—to the true nature of the therapist's decision.

Finally, let me emphasize an aspect of the listening process that can now be made much clearer. You can see that this patient, instead of responding to the adaptive context of the shortened hour by displacing her reaction to an outside relationship, has in fact continued to talk about her relationship with the therapist and has kept her response within that relationship. However, the following point is what I want to stress, because it is here that her neurosis—again, used in its broadest sense—emerges: she does not deal directly with the therapist's decision to shorten her session but instead responds through derivatives involving her relationship with the therapist. She shifts the focus from an immediate hurt to his silences, which may have been hurtful, or may have been constructive; since we have not heard the material, we cannot know.

So, in responding in derivative fashion, the patient may use either another aspect of her relationship with the therapist, or allusions to an outside figure, as a vehicle for indirect communication. But the principle that neurotic and inappropriate responses develop along derivative lines, rather than along conscious and straightforward lines, remains valid, and this material is an excellent opportunity to demonstrate that very point.

Therapist: Well, she responded by saying that she knew that I wasn't a murderer and that I didn't mean to hurt her. And she spoke at some length about how painful my silences are, how she needs to hear my voice, how helpful it was for me to talk, and the rest. Finally she went on to say that her mother yells at her and hurts her, and that silence is also her weapon, that it just cuts the patient off. This is why the patient needs to provoke her. She also spoke about her father, who also is silent. And I suggested that her parents inflicted pain on her by being silent, and that she wanted me to undo that by talking, even if I had nothing pertinent to say. I suggested that when I was silent, she saw me as her mother and father, and therefore had a need to force me to talk. The hour was at an end, and she smiled and said that she had a good weapon there.

Langs: Yes, here you organize the material again around the adaptive context of your silence, rather than around the shortened hour. You accepted and worked with the manifest material and interpreted the patient's responses to your silence as transference-based, as distorted and inappropriate, and as connected genetically to her parents.

On the other hand, I would have suggested that the shortening of the session was an actual repetition of her parent's traumatic behavior—of their cutting her off—and you can see that there I use that particular derivative as a bridge between the manifest theme of your silence and the latent theme of your shortening the hour. And I would have pointed out to the patient that she was experiencing the shortened session as an actual repetition of the destructive and abandoning behaviors of her parents. I therefore would deal with this reaction first as a form of nontransference, and only then would I turn to any transference aspects.

And, while I cannot validate this using the me–not-me interface, I would take her comment about the good weapon as referring to your use of the transference interpretation; it is a good, defensive weapon indeed, and is often used as such. So the actualities should have led first to a nontransference interpretation, an effort to help the patient understand the actual trauma she was experiencing. In general, therapists do use transference interpretations quite often as a weapon against the patient, rather than as a means of affording them valid insights.

Tell us briefly about the next session.

Therapist: Well, she came in and said she wanted to continue the discussion of the previous session, that my silence was an abandonment, hurtful and painful, and yet she felt that if she were drowning, I would give her the support that she needed. She said she felt that I was suggesting that she had to get sick—or sicker—to get me to talk.

She then described a panic attack over the weekend, a fear that she would die, and how, through some breathing exercises, she got it under control. I intervened here to suggest that this was her model of cure—breathing exercises and rational control—and that it was different from my model, which was based on talking and understanding. I said I thought she was disappointed in what was happening between us.

Langs: Well, time is short, so, briefly, I would suggest that you have again made use of a Type One derivative, introduced a great deal from your own subjective responses, and failed to sit back and allow the material to unfold. You are not—and you should be—awaiting for further reactions to the alteration in the frame, or for a new adaptive context to emerge. In fact, here you are inviting a shift away from the shortened session and are not attempting to monitor the material for derivatives.

Therapist: The patient said she felt better before I had become silent, that she needed to hear my voice, that she had a fantasy of revealing herself, but that she feared she would go crazy. She saw the silence as punishment and again likened it to her parent's behavior. Here again I suggested that she felt that I wanted to punish her—much as her mother and father had done—and since she had mentioned that her mother gets irrational, acts irrational, I said that she saw my cutting the sessions short as a punishment and abandonment.

Langs: Well, you're in the right area, but your intervention is rather premature. It invites denial because it reflects difficulties in containing and metabolizing the patient's reactions to your deviation. It would have been best to sit back and allow the derivatives to direct you, to permit the patient to put into you the elements you would need to eventually interpret her reactions to your deviation.

Incidentally, if we are monitoring this material along the me–not-me interface, you hear again a theme we heard earlier in today's seminar in response to another deviation in the framework—the theme of the fear of going crazy—as it applies to both patient and therapist. And it is a very common theme when the therapist modifies the frame, because that alteration is experienced as irrational behavior, a kind of craziness, and as an attempt to manage inner craziness through what I have elsewhere termed a *framework cure* (Langs, 1976a, b). This is the closing off of disturbed inner mental contents through a modification in the ground rules. The patient, for her part, becomes threatened by the introject derived from the deviation, as well as by fears that she will be unable to manage and contain her own disturbed mental contents at a time when the therapist is unable to hold and contain them for her.

Therapist: You're right. She denied that she had reacted to the shortened session, claimed that she planned to talk about my silences in that session anyhow, and again said that when she was sicker I would talk. And now that she's better, I've become silent, and yet she feels that I'm pushing her to grow up.

Briefly, in the next session she was depressed, and ruminated about her job and her fear of speaking up and asking to be transferred to women's wear, and to stay there. If she said something and got the transfer, she feared making mistakes and looking like a fool—as well as going around in circles. She had seen an old boyfriend and he had seemed happy; he was dating a lot of other women and she was jealous and furious. She had thoughts of leaving home, saw her mother as attacking, and my only intervention was to suggest that she seemed to feel imposed upon at work, victimized and afraid to speak up, and that her complaining of my silence had followed my telling her that I would end the session early. I said I felt she still felt imposed upon and hurt. Her response, in essence, was that she speaks out more in therapy than anywhere else; that she knows that she can't destroy me; that she trusts me and has had a long-term relationship with me; and that she knows I don't want to get rid of her. She ended the session by saying that when she looks in a mirror and takes her glasses off, she doesn't recognize herself; she feels like a different person—bland, and empty—when instead she wants to be active and gutsy.

Langs: Well, we would certainly be hard pressed to validate any of the formulations regarding this patient's responses to the alteration in the frame. And my hypothesis about this lack would be that the modified frame has disturbed the communicative properties of this bipersonal field and generated both Type B and Type C communicative modes. The former are rather prominent in the projective identifications that we saw in the previous session, and the latter are characteristic of the present hour. For me this session is largely an exercise in relative nonmeaning, through which I see occasional meaningful threads—bits and fragments—but no whole.

I can see something of the patient's concerns about going crazy, about her therapist's stability, something of her need to cure herself in the face of the therapist's difficulties in assisting her in that regard, and something of her envy of the therapist who is able to speak up and make a demand upon the patient—something that she is quite unable to do, and a factor that has, I think, greatly modulated her response to the deviation. For me, the qualities of this session are expressed in the patient's final communication—there is a facade with emptiness beyond it— and this may well be how the patient experiences both herself and the therapist, as well as the bipersonal field, at least for the moment.

Still, this material has enabled us to refine an important aspect of the listening process and to deal with a common situation, one in which the relatively immediate adaptive context, one related to the therapeutic situation—a context that is stirring up considerable anxiety for both patient and therapist—is placed into a bastion. The patient associates instead around a different, usually less traumatic, and often more remote adaptive context involving treatment, and the therapist has difficulty in understanding the derivative nature of the material, in rectifying the frame, in modifying his countertransference difficulties, and in interpreting adequately to the patient. This is a model experience that should serve all of you quite well, but since our time is nearly up, let me ask if there are any questions.

Discussant: What would you do at this point?

Langs: In principle, I would sit back and allow the material to redevelop, knowing that in the next session the frame will be rectified, the five minutes made up, although the hurt and the seemingly irrational quality of the experience will not disappear. Still, if I am able to sit back as the therapist, and can contain the new set of derivatives and projective identifications from the patient, can maintain the deviation as a tentative adaptive context, and can link it to any new adaptive context that might arise in the therapeutic relationship—then once the frame has been rectified it should be possible for the patient to again communicate meaningful derivatives, through which the necessary interpretations could be made.

I would not suggest directly reassuring the patient that you will not modify the frame again—we really can't make such promises—so I would make an inner resolve not to do so unless there is a dire emergency and would implicitly convey that to the patient through my interventions. So my answer, however simplistic, is, in essence, that I would work over my countertransferences, rectify the frame, and turn to the listening process in order to permit the expression of—and interpretation of—the material related to this traumatic incident.

Thank you very much for a very well presented and nicely condensed presentation.

Chapter Six

COUNTERTRANSFERENCE AND LISTENING

The therapeutic context • The functional properties of the patient's associations and the therapist's interventions • The therapist's subjective reactions • Reformulating • The patient's responses to interventions • Further considerations of the Type C field • An evident countertransference problem and the listening process

Langs: I suggest that today we get directly to the clinical material and allow it to direct us once again toward a further delineation of the listening process.

Therapist: May I summarize the brief segment of this session that I presented last time?

Discussant: It was very short; it would help.

Langs: Well, we won't be purists. I need the data to establish principles related to the listening process, but you need opportunities to begin without desire, memory, or understanding.

Therapist: It was fairly brief.

Langs: Just recognize the anxieties that have to be mastered in letting go of notes and such. For now, present as you wish.

Therapist: She came in and said that things were going terribly, or that it went terribly, that she was a failure, that she didn't even get a chance to speak.

Discussant: Now this is the make-up session—we're still in that session?

Therapist: Right. She said she met with her two bosses, they talked very rapidly, and she couldn't even get a word in. They told her that they're not so satisfied with what she's doing, that they could give her a token raise but that was all. So she thought she'd have to go somewhere else and get another job. And though she didn't even want to go back to work for the rest of the week, she knew she had to. She knew, or felt, that she'd rather not make waves, because later on she was going to need letters from them for her certification. She didn't want to have to chase around after them if she quit the job, especially if she left with bad feelings. She then said the . . .

Langs: Identify the point at which you stopped presenting last time.

Therapist: I'm going to do that. The boss had called her from Baltimore. He had gone up there because his daughter was transferred to Chestnut Lodge from a psychiatric unit in New Jersey, and he said he guessed he was upset when he spoke with the patient the other day and kind of apologized for not letting her get a word in. He offered to talk to her when he returned and said that he recognized the money wasn't enough. But she said, Basically he was saying he's not willing to pay me more than one particular client will pay him for my services. So she said she'd have to look for another job. I think that's as far as we got.

Langs: Okay, I want to add one other dimension to the listening process, and it's relevant to this material. I'll ask it first as a question. In doing psychotherapy, there is a concept that certain work should be done, with certain goals and purposes, and this applies also to each session—that is, while there are some sessions in which we're not aware of an immediate or well-defined goal, there are others in which the patient makes us aware of an immediate purpose. Now what might be an indication for some particular kind of therapeutic work? Do you follow what I'm saying? What kind of things would require some therapeutic work on our part?

Therapist: You mean in general or in this session?

Langs: No, in general for the moment; later we'll get to it for this session.

Therapist: An increase in some kind of symptomatology.

Langs: Yes, that is, if the patient comes in and reports new symptoms or an intensification of ongoing symptoms, then it should occur to you, though you're not bound to it, that it would make sense if you could intervene meaningfully in that session. I mean, we talk about timelessness of therapy and all, and about not having therapeutic ambition, but if a patient comes in and says, You know, I developed a symptom this week, then you would like, in the course of the session, to be able to help him understand something of the unconscious factors in that occurence; you'd like to do some interpretive work if you could.

Now what other indications are there for therapeutic interventions? Let me offer a definition: I call this the *therapeutic context* (Langs, 1973a) because it is a context, an organizer. It is both an organizer of the material from the patient and an indication for an intervention—recognized with the understanding that you will wait for the necessary material. But in sessions in which the patient reports symptoms, you will be inclined to organize the material in a manner that might illuminate their unconscious meanings and functions.

In brief, then, the adaptive context is the organizer of the patient's adaptive responses and gives basic unconscious meaning to the material, while the therapeutic context expresses the patient's need for understanding; it is a second-level organizer. In all, then, the material is comprehended first, in terms of the adaptive context and the patient's derivative responses, and then that, in turn, is used for the second evaluation, which is designed for the understanding of a particular symptom.

Now, what other kinds of therapeutic contexts occur to you?

Therapist: I think, a change in the flow of the session. Sometimes a patient who has been able to speak very easily will suddenly come in and there will be periods of silence, some change in the direction of the flow of the material.

Langs: Right. To generalize, what concept does this fall under?

Therapist: The patient's style of communication?

Langs: Yes, but what aspect of communicating is involved? Anybody else have a thought? (Pause.) You're describing resistances, a form of resistance, and the appearance of resistances is a therapeutic context.

Therapist: I thought that you discarded classical terminology.

Langs: No, I don't discard any of the classical terminology. I've simply added to it. I don't believe I've discarded anything. That's quite an image you have of me—an interactional product, of course.

Therapist: Transference.

Langs: Transference?

Discussant: You discarded the concept of transference.

Langs: I never discarded it; that's an interesting comment.

Therapist: You said you don't use that word, didn't you?

Langs: No.

Discussant: Do you use the term anymore? We thought you said you didn't.

Langs: No, that's not what I said. You didn't hear the communication correctly—the listening process in seminars. What I said is that I do not use the term *transference* for the patient's total relationship to the therapist. The patient's relationship to the therapist is a totality with both transference and nontransference components. So I use the term *transference* but restrict its meaning.

But in any case, you're describing resistances, and that remains one of the basic indicators for an intervention. The analysis of resistances is the bread and butter of therapy, as well as of analysis. And it is a prime therapeutic context. So we hope to analyze anything we sense as resistance, which is a subjective evaluation inasmuch as resistance is ultimately an interactional concept.

All right. Common therapeutic contexts include resistances and symptoms, and, among symptoms, a very common form is what I call *living out* (Langs, 1976b), any kind of enactment, what's usually called acting out and acting in. But there's one more indicator, which is always the one we get to last, and it happens to apply to this session. What is the therapeutic context for this session? What are the classic indicators that we have omitted?

Discussant: Any change in the framework?

Langs: Yes, and the general category would be what? The three we just named—resistances, symptoms, and living out—all reside in what realm? And where does a change in the frame reside? Which realm? Do you see what I'm trying to get across? Resistances, symptoms, and living out: to whom are we referring?

Discussant: The patient.

Langs: We're referring to the patient. And the change in the frame in this instance: to whom are we referring?

Discussant: The therapist.

Langs: The therapist. So, yet again, the last thing we got around to is the fact that the therapist can do something that would create a therapeutic as well as an adaptive context for the patient. This category would include any unnecessary alteration in the framework undertaken by the therapist and, more generally, all of his errors in technique. So, to state this as a broad principle, an important group of therapeutic contexts pertain to any disturbance in the transaction between the patient and the therapist: on the patient's part, unneeded alterations in the framework, resistances, living out, and the like; and on the part of the therapist, all of his technical errors as well as, in some sense, his tendencies toward resistance, living out, and symptom formation within the therapeutic interaction. Thus, if the therapist has erred, he will want to organize the material around his error and will also be inclined to intervene in that hour if at all possible. This will enable him both to rectify his mistake and to analyze the patient's responses to it.

Discussant: I'm not clear on what distinguishes the therapeutic context from the adaptive context. Can't they at times be the same?

Langs: Yes, certainly. In this instance they are, but sometimes they're not. If the patient comes in with a symptom—let's say that this patient came into this session and said, I've had headaches all week, since you told me you were changing the hour. Now, the headaches would be a therapeutic context. The adaptive context would be the therapist's change in the hour, and that would be another therapeutic context as well. You would want to intervene in respect to what you had enacted as well as to what the patient might enact or experience as symptoms. Or she comes into this session and says, I quit my job. That too would be a therapeutic context, but it would not be the adaptive context. The adaptive context would still be the change in the hour. So they could be identical. For the moment, in this session, they are. We don't have an additional therapeutic context for the moment, though there's a hint in her own thoughts of possibly living out by quitting her job. But for now we have no indication of other symptomatic responses in this patient—but we will keep an open mind.

So the therapeutic context is any indication for an intervention. This we will discuss in greater detail when we consider that aspect of psychotherapy. Here I am presenting it as yet another organizer of the listening process. And, if you think about it, any intervention in this session that would avoid the therapeutic context of the alteration in the frame or that would, if the patient had presented with headaches, failed to unconsciously illuminate that symptom, would not only be of little value to the patient, but might even be, in essence, the offer of a Type C barrier.

Discussant: What about a patient who comes in with a symptom, but the symptom is a frequent therapeutic context for the session—extreme anxiety, for example, or anxiety attacks. Now does that remain the therapeutic context after it comes up in ten out of twelve sessions and the patient keeps talking over and over about the symptoms?

Langs: Yes, though we would hope to hear indirect material.

Discussant: Would you still see that as a therapeutic context or would that then become a defense? I'm thinking of a patient who has the same symptom that he keeps hammering away at every session, that he sees as the significant theme to discuss.

Langs: You are now confusing two concepts. Anxiety or an anxiety attack reported in the session is always a therapeutic context. This is quite a different statement from stating that the repetitive description of such anxiety attacks can be used as a resistance—which is certainly true as well. As I said a

moment ago, your intervention must be shaped by the
material from the patient, and you might want to point out to
such a patient that he is utilizing the repetitive description of
anxiety attacks as a means of destroying all meaning in the
sessions. Alternatively, you might develop some other type of
intervention to identify the nature and unconscious motives
for the patient's resistance. Such an interpretation might well
help to resolve the symptom by illuminating an aspect of its
unconscious functions. But the point that I am making for the
moment is that the appearance of references to the anxiety
attack would direct you to organize the material around that
symptom, as well as around any adaptive context you might
also identify. In fact, this particular symptom might later be a
response to a whole series of different adaptive contexts
emerging in succeeding weeks—its functional capacity or
unconscious meaning can vary considerably. Often it is quite
illuminating to study the relationship between the adaptive
and the therapeutic context—an interrelationship that is
usually part of the intervention you make to the patient.
    Let's now hear more material.

Therapist: Okay, at this point I said something.

Langs: Please read the last associations from the patient,
and then your intervention.

Therapist: She said, The boss called. He apologized and said
that he understands that the money isn't enough and that
he'll talk to me when he comes back. But basically he was
saying that he's not willing to pay me more than his client
would pay him, so I'll have to look for another job. I then said it
said it wasn't clear to me why she felt the situation was so
hopeless after the second call.

Langs: Okay. So we now pause to identify the formal and
communicative-functional—I'm adding the term *functional
properties*—of the intervention. So help me with that. What's
its formal nature?

Discussant: It was a question, but it sounds kind of like a confrontation, because the patient said something, made a statement, and you were kind of saying you didn't understand what she was saying. So you're kind of confronting her.

Langs: Right. There's another term that applies here. It's an effort at what?

Discussant: Clarification.

Langs: A clarification. That's in the Bibring (1954) lexicon.

Discussant: It also deals with the manifest material.

Langs: Right. It's directed at the manifest content and communicates a wish for the patient to stay with the manifest content. Now, having established our contexts in earlier discussions, how does this intervention relate to the adaptive and therapeutic contexts we've hypothesized for the session? What would its function be in that respect? Would it help the patient—I'll say it even more clearly—will it move the patient toward these contexts or away from them? Toward or away from the change in the hour?

Discussant: Away.

Langs: Yes, away. I mean I've loaded the dice, of course, but I want you to see that, in the terms of my thesis, if there exists the possibility of an unfolding based on an adaptive context, and if that context can be a constructive organizer, then certainly we can say that the present intervention not only does not relate to an adaptive context, but that it actually moves away from the specific adaptive context we've defined. At best, it is an effort to deal with the direct context of the patient's problems at work, but it does not approach an indirect and neurosogenic context at all.

And again I'll say it: most questions have this function. While there are, of course, questions that unnecessarily direct the patient toward the therapeutic relationship—ill-timed questions which prematurely try to force the patient in that

direction: Tell me something about your feelings toward me—
in my experience as a supervisor, most questions function in
the opposite manner. There's an adaptive context related to
the therapeutic relationship that the therapist is either
unaware of or has decided is unimportant, and he asks
questions designed to move the patient away from that
adaptive context, away from himself or herself, away from the
therapeutic interaction and toward manifest content related
to some outside situation.

Therapist: Are you interested in any further information
about this intervention, other than what the words were?

Langs: If you would like to add something, please do.

Therapist: Because I can tell you: I thought of it as a kind of
confrontation and a clarification when I said it. This patient—
her chief complaint and what she's doing in this session is
that she continues to present a hopeless situation. And often,
I'll just sort of listen to it, and here I felt the need—it was
almost like I was saying to myself, Maybe I'm really not
following her closely enough. Maybe she's sort of saying a lot
of contradictory things here that I'm not hearing and maybe
there's some disguise here. And I'd better find out whether
there isn't something else going on here that she's sort of
glossing over or disguising with all of these words about how
hopeless everything is. So that was what was going on in my
head.

Langs: That's quite clear, and I would like to react to it for
two reasons: because it's an excellent description of your way
of listening, and because you introduce the realm of the
therapist's subjective reactions to the patient's material.
    First, let me talk about this subjective sphere in a broad
way. As you know, as the therapist is listening to the patient,
he responds with a whole range of feelings, fantasies,
thoughts, efforts at organization, symptoms, and the like:
impressions and responses that are intermixtures of cognition
and affect, and that in addition reflect the experience of

interactional pressures from the patient (a dimension that I will set aside for the moment). These reactions also involve the therapist's needs, propensities, inclinations, and the like. In short, they are interactional products.

Now, there is some literature on the listening process related to empathy and intuition, and I have provided you a bibliography so that you may do the relevant reading. I have discussed some aspects already and will review this area again in this context. In brief, empathy is a kind of emotional knowing, a temporary identification with the patient within which you maintain your separate identity while experiencing something of the patient's inner state (Schafer, 1959; Greenson, 1960; and Beres and Arlow, 1974); intuition is a form of immediate knowing that need not include any special identificatory process (Beres and Arlow, 1974).

In approaching this area, I would emphasize, as have most of the authors who have written recently on this subject, that empathy and intuition—and, in fact, all the subjective experiences of the therapist—are interactional products. They are manifest experiences which develop in a manner not unlike the basic listening process that we have developed for attending to the patient. And they are to be organized around the various adaptive contexts facing the therapist, especially in his relationship with the immediate patient—although sometimes, in regard to outside relationships as well—and they are to be explored and validated within the framework of such adaptive contexts and the search for unconscious meaning.

So I am attempting to establish at least two important technical principles regarding the therapist's subjective reactions: First, they are to be recognized on the manifest level as such and then explored subjectively for latent content using the adaptive context and the concept of Type One and especially Type Two derivatives. Second, they are interactional products that reveal important information about both the patient and the therapist; that have to be sorted out for contributions from each; and that have to be used in arriving at formulations, which must then be subjected to the validating process. There is a tendency among therapists to treat their subjective responses on a manifest level and as singularly valid. This is a narcissistic approach to one's subjective reactions that is fraught with countertransference-based difficulties. So long as you approach your subjective experiences as another form of communication—within the therapeutic interaction and handle them accordingly—they can yield extremely important information about the patient and, of course, yourself.

Now turning to this particular situation, you describe yourself as confused, as experiencing contradictions, and there is also some latent implication of a bit of annoyance or impatience with the patient because she so repetitively describes hopeless situations. Now, quite rightfully, you wondered where the confusion was coming from. Was it that you hadn't listened properly, or hadn't understood? Or was it—to state your subjective reaction in somewhat different terms—that the patient wished to confuse you? It is quite important that you recognize that your confusion is an interactional product and that it may tell you something about the patient as well as something about yourself. You should also recognize that you would like to sort all of this out. Now in principle, this sorting process should take place subjectively within yourself, rather than imposing it upon the patient.

Therapist: Well, I really wasn't sure of where this confusion was coming from; that's why I intervened.

Langs: Yes, but my point is that for the moment, this is best asked as what I call a *silent question*—something that you ask of the patient to yourself. And in allowing the patient to continue to free associate, you will have her indirect answer to this very question, so long as it is pertinent and meaningful, which here I believe it is. The important answers to questions in psychotherapy are contained in derivative form, through indirect associations, and not in direct and conscious responses.

By intervening the way you did, you are implicitly confessing your own confusion to the patient and are stressing a direct and manifest search for clarification rather than allowing the patient to continue so that she could possibly communicate the crucial adaptive contexts that could suddenly help you to understand and organize this material—that could resolve your confusion and help you find meaning in this material in the form of Type Two derivatives.

Therapist: The problem is that I didn't have a concept of the adaptive context when I held this session.

Langs: Yes, I understand. And as a teaching exercise it helps us to learn what the implications of therapeutic work without an adaptive context are, as well as how resourceless the therapist is without such a concept. After all, if you think about it, the confusion in this material has at least two important qualities: first, it is based on your failure to recognize the vital adaptive context that would give the material meaning—I would identify that as your contribution to the experience of confusion; second, it involves an unconscious effort by the patient to confuse you, to projectively identify into you her own state of confusion, which you were experiencing at that time subjectively. You can see then that the confusional state is truly interactional: that there are significant contributions from both the patient and yourself, and that you would be in error if you intervened without considering both aspects—it is a transversal experience.

Left to your own devices, you felt that the patient seemed hopeless, and that her hopelessness did not seem derived from the material she was communicating—at least not on the basis of its manifest content. You hoped that by asking her a direct question, she could consciously clarify what it was that was making her feel so depressed and hopeless—with the notion, I suppose, that you could then kind of play it back to her and give her a perspective.

This approach is on the surface and linear, and implies some type of unconscious content only in the sense that something seems to be missing. The assumption is that the patient could directly provide that missing link or that you could determine it through some ready effort at inference.

Compare this with the approach I have been developing. Suppose we do that as a kind of exercise in listening: where, in terms of the adaptive context I have defined, is the hopelessness coming from?

Therapist: The change in the hour.

Langs: Yes, the change in the hour. And what else?

Discussant: The therapeutic relationship.

Langs: And the patient's response to it: that something that is going on between the two of you is making her feel hopeless and misunderstood. So, if you had taken this inner state of confusion you were experiencing and viewed it as both a communication and a projective identification from the patient—and possibly as a signal that in some way you yourself were confused—you could have initiated a search for a selected fact, a crucial adaptive context, that might have helped you reorganize and understand this material. You could have taken your inner state of confusion as a directive to reformulate. To state this still another way, it could have led you to reexamine the therapeutic relationship and see your experience as a reflection of the inner state of both yourself and the patient. On that basis, allowing the patient to continue to associate might aid you in discovering the adaptive context you so desperately need, as well as in ascertaining the basis of your confusion. So by being silent, by not asking the question or directing the patient to the manifest content, you would have had the greatest opportunity to initiate a fresh listening process and to engage in continued self-exploration as a means of understanding the truth contained in this interlude: the actual basis for her confusion and yours. You can see now that asking her to play back the manifest content is asking her to play the same broken record, and that it will never get you onto the other record, into that other communicative medium or space.

Therapist: It goes along with the obsessional defenses I've been struggling with in her sessions.

Langs: Yes, you told me that this patient is always talking about hopelessness and that you wanted to help her with that symptom—another therapeutic context, by the way—by helping her to define its source. But your quest really did not include the possibility that there is an unconscious source of this hopelessness in the actual therapeutic interaction with yourself—and of course, as therapists, that's always our last thesis.

Therapist: I disagree with you about that.

Langs: Yes, go ahead.

Therapist: Because the way I've worked with her in the past—this session is very different, which is kind of why I chose it. It's different from the way I usually work with this patient. But for some reason, and now I would say that it was possibly because of my own feelings about changing the hour, but whatever, I was feeling unusually pressured, that maybe there was something that I wasn't doing that I should have been. Usually I work with the relationship and ignore a lot of this rumination, because I have to, because there really isn't an answer to it.

Langs: That's exactly the point.

Therapist: But in this session I felt differently. Okay. So the whole session is really different.

Langs: Right. But when you feel a difference in any session—and this relates to the listening process, and listening to yourself, monitoring your subjective reactions—when you feel anything unusual in any session, you should search for its underlying basis: in the material from the patient, in your interventions, and in specific adaptive contexts. Monitor your subjective reactions along the me-not-me interface, as applying to both yourself and the patient, just as you monitor the material from the patient along that dimension. If you have a conscious fantasy, attempt briefly to associate to it, to seek out its latent content in the particularly pressing adaptive contexts you are faced with. And then sort it out as an interactional amalgam with interrelating contributions from both yourself and the patient.

We'll get into this aspect in greater detail when we study the therapeutic relationship more definitively—the entire realm of countertransference and noncountertransference—but as a rule, any unusual feeling, any disturbance within yourself, the patient, or the interaction, should be taken as a possible indicator of a countertransference difficulty. Your subjective feelings and thoughts, as well as the material from the patient, should all be utilized as a resource for the investigation of the countertransference problem, both its manifestations and unconscious basis. This must be done as quickly as possible, since it takes precedence over the investigation of the patient's pathology. And without going further into this area, when you feel a sense of pressure, ask yourself what it could be based on. *Silently* ask the patient where it's coming from and scrutinize your own and the patient's subsequent associations for the relevant adaptive contexts, for the unconscious basis for your disturbance, and for the unconscious fantasies it contains. This is valid both cognitively and interactionally: how much from whom? It's often not so easy to do, but it is essential to try your best.

And remember that analysts and therapists have tended to look away from alterations in the framework as a possible reflection of countertransference difficulties. And while this is a subject that we will get into in a few weeks, remember that in principle the manner in which you handle the frame reflects your way of holding the patient and of containing what she is putting into you, as well as your contribution to the boundaries of the therapeutic relationship and the communicative nature of the bipersonal field. All listening takes place within a framework, within a bipersonal field that has been clearly or sometimes quite poorly defined. And in this way, the frame influences not only the nature of what you will be hearing, but its very meaning to your patient and to you as a therapist. This is what I now term the *functional meaning* of her associations. In a sense, then, a secure frame permits the widest latitude to the listening process and its ultimate expression, while alterations in the framework can very much hinder or skew the available material and the listening process, as well as your capacity to process the material you are taking in.

Therapist: What occurred to me also as you're talking about this patient is another one of those things I've kind of forgotten: this lady had been canceling sessions. And while we had dealt with it, perhaps we'd not dealt with it completely—because she always had a good reason.

Langs: Yes, as compared to dealing with it interpretively.

Therapist: So, if you're going to talk about errors, I was probably in error there too.

Langs: Yes, we'll soon be dealing in some detail with frame issues. For the moment, I'm trying to develop a model of the listening process, as it applies to listening to yourself, and the directions it may take. The listening process includes self-awareness and attending to internal cues, and the outcome of this processing—and this is what the patient will experience too—is reflected in your ability to manage the framework, to hold the patient, to contain her projective identifications, and to tolerate her role and image evocations. In essence, a relatively unencumbered use of the listening process relies on your capacity to manage your own inner mental state, inner anxieties and conflicts, disruptive introjects, and unconscious fantasies and memories. Technical errors are experienced by the patient in terms of difficulties in each of these realms.

Here you're feeling a sense of pressure, and your effort should be toward silent mastery rather than toward intervening—which is often not easy, of course. It actually requires a great deal of you.

Discussant: What do you mean: toward mastery?

Langs: Mastery within yourself: discovering the source of

the pressure and understanding what you and the patient each are contributing to it rather than intervening in a way that says to the patient, Look, I'm under pressure; I don't understand; sort of tell me what it's about, but make sure we do it with a bastion related to the make-up session. That is, we'll seal that off, we'll try to search in some other area, and that in itself is going to create a good deal of confusion and a further sense of hopelessness.

You see how the model I'm developing is very important in terms of understanding her symptoms. You want to resolve this sense of hopelessness. The first level on which this can be achieved has to do with giving her a sense of hope in the therapeutic relationship, and in rectifying and interpreting the basis for this depression as it has unfolded within that relationship in terms of the altered frame. From there, you could be in a position to analyze other sources of those feelings.

Let's now get to some more material. Let's see how she responds to this intervention, and let's see again what we can hear.

Therapist: Okay. What she said was, Well, I didn't tell you everything that was bad in the conversation, but the conclusion is that I won't get any more money. Every decision that I make doesn't work. I should never have taken this job for this amount of money in the first place, and I'm sure when I look for my next job, that the next decision is going to be just as bad as the one I made this time. This is her chief complaint—that she makes poor decisions.

Discussant: Can I ask you a question, sort of out of context? When she took this job, was her clinic fee raised?

Therapist: No, it was not, and as a matter of fact, I should have talked to her about it and didn't. As it turned out, she's paying what she would be paying if it had been adjusted. She was paying too high a fee initially, but it wasn't really dealt with. She was overpaying, but the amount of money she's making at this job doesn't make her much better off than she was unemployed.

Langs: Okay, that's another sad truth. But notice again now: we've heard an intervention and what do we do? We take the intervention as our immediate adaptive context and listen to her response both as a commentary and for validation. We've got a basic adaptive context—a change in hour—but each intervention becomes an additional adaptive context for the subsequent material, as well. You give the patient an input; you've created a stimulus to which the patient must respond. Now, we monitor the material accordingly. Is it going to give us what we hope for? A new revelation that will help us understand the patient's sense of hopelessness? Or is it going to give us something else? What does it give us for the moment? As we hear this initial material, what's the communication?

Therapist: The communication to me is a negation of what I said. And there's a sense of further hopelessness.

Langs: Yes, that's right. In other words, she just says, You know, things are really, really hopeless; I make wrong decisions. But at this point, this is no longer simply a repetition of what she has already said; now it's a further response to her perception and introjection of your intervention. Here again I can stress the importance of understanding the *functional meaning* or *functional capacity* of a repetitive manifest communication. We do not treat material *qua* material; we deal with it as serving communicative and defensive functions, especially in terms of the therapeutic interaction.

We have to consistently realize that whatever is said now is a response to your conscious and unconscious communications to the patient. We apply these principles in endless cycles; it is an essential dimension of the listening process. And incidentally, its application will help you learn not to intervene so actively and indiscriminately, because you begin to realize that these negative responses are reactions, quite often, to erroneous interventions. Here, by using the me–not-me interface we can postulate that the patient is implying an experience of an unhelpful introject—of repeatedly poor decisions involving how to intervene and what to intervene about—and it is, of course, contributing significantly to her sense of depression.

In general, it has been through failures to take a change in the frame, such as a shift in the hour, as the adaptive context for the patient's associations, and through failures to listen to this material in terms of Type Two derivatives, as I have just done, that has led to so many misconceptions regarding the frame and the consequences of errors in technique. Here the adaptive context is the therapist's question, her effort at clarification; and the patient's response, her mention of repeatedly making poor decisions on the job, is taken as a concrete, first-order theme, from which we can derive the general theme of error making. From this we then generate the specific second-order theme, in the adaptive context of the intervention, as a Type Two derivative: the theme of erroneous interventions.

Once again, this is the patient's effort at supervision. This is what I mean by taking her responses as commentaries that contain valid perceptions as well as distortions, as possible transversal communications. This is what I mean by the search for indirect validation. It is really quite interesting to find that it is largely through the neglect of the identification of the critical prevailing adaptive context that therapists have maintained their defensiveness and their blindness to their influences on their patients—especially to their negative influences, though also to the actual sources of their positive effects. On the other hand, if you adopt these principles, you'll learn very quickly of the powerful consequences of your interventions for your patients and you'll discover a great deal about your own psychopathology and assets as well as those of the patient, and in more realistic and meaningful terms. You'll especially get in touch with the much neglected adaptive resources of your patients—and of their curative efforts on your behalf.

Therapist: During all of this, she was talking in a low voice. It was very monotonous and it was hard to hear her at times.

Langs: Yes. Well now, when you describe her low, monotonous voice and say that material is repetitive, that she's really not elaborating very much, what sort of field do you think this is? Actually, this brings up another point about these interventions that I might as well make. What type of field do we seem to have here?

Therapist: A Type C field.

Langs: Yes, it's a Type C field now—as I believe I predicted it would be. There's a little bit of an effort to work over her feelings of distress about being manipulated, but not much more than that. And these are not very rich derivatives at all. And as the Type C field is an interactional product, this material may help you realize that I'm not being pedantic when I analyze in such detail the unconscious communicative functions of your interventions. Because here you are asking her to repeat herself, and I used the image of the record being played over and over again advisedly—it is a typical representation of a Type C field. You're really asking her to communicate in a Type C mode: to repeat the same thing over and over again as a barrier to the truths that have to do with you, with her, and with the change in the hour.

So once again, you're offering her a kind of Type C barrier, and your intervention then falls into a category I have mentioned before. It is really very common and I have, in part, borrowed the concept from Bion (1977): I call it the *psychoanalytic cliché*. Here questions and other interventions, including seeming interpretations, are used in a hollow manner so that they function actually to destroy meaning and genuine relatedness.

Discussant: You're saying that even if the therapist obtained clarification of what she was trying to understand, it wouldn't apply to anything meaningful. It wouldn't go anywhere.

Langs: Exactly.

Discussant: It was not on target in the terms of the real context and issue that concerned this patient.

Langs: This is not a particularly good example of what I mean by the cliché, but you'll soon see. You make all kinds of interventions, very fancy ones based on analytic theory, on seemingly accepted clinical practice, and an analysis of their unconscious functions reveals that their main purpose is not to further communication but to establish barriers to communication. Please continue.

Therapist: She said, You know, I always avoid making decisions. Excuse me, she said, I'm sure I'll be just as unhappy two months after I take this new job, if I get a new job. And she went on like that, like a record. Then she said, I always avoid making decisions, I prefer to avoid making decisions rather than to actually make them. But in itself that's a decision, and I wait until I'm forced to make a decision. This must sound very boring.

Langs: So. I trust you all hear what's happened and can sense how this is an interactional product and one form of the Type C field: boring, repetitive, obsessional, and the like. You ask for manifest content, and that is what you will get; you ask to avoid the adaptive context, and that too will be done. And so on.

As you listen to this material, I hope that you can also sense something else that I have found to be characteristic of the Type C field. And Bion (1977) has implied its presence as well. These are not only boring communications; they are now confusing. As the therapist said earlier, they are now empty to the point of emptying the therapist of all possible constructive and functional thoughts—or at least they have that potential. And I suspect that material of this kind is an unconscious response to the unconscious destructiveness contained in the therapist's diverting interventions. It constitutes, unconsciously, an attempt to projectively identify a void into the therapist, or actually, since it is another spiral, to reproject that void. It is an exchange of relatively unmetabolized projective identifications, much of it in the form of destructive voids. At this point, the emptiness is being placed into the therapist, and an image of helplessness is being evoked, designed unconsciously, I would postulate, to destroy the therapist's capacity to listen, think, integrate, and the like. Underneath all of this there is something quite destructive going on—on both sides, I fear.

Allow me to pause with that comment. It is derived largely from my my own listening process, from my own feelings of emptiness and boredom, and from my own incapacity to generate fresh or exciting ideas—or any sort of positive meaning—from this material. I feel that my capacities as a supervisor have temporarily, I trust, been destroyed, and this suggests the presence of a parallel or reflective process that is taking place in the actual session—a point made by Searles (1955) in a paper on supervision.

Now, having experienced something of what I would term a *negative projective identification,* a sense of interactional pressure and a subjective response, I would maintain it as a silent hypothesis open to coalescence and validation. As you have seen, I often verbalize in seminars silent hypotheses that I would otherwise keep to myself if I were with a patient. I would not, as would many Kleinians, intervene on the basis of these subjective experiences in an effort to interpret the interactional meaning of these associations. Such an effort, of course, would of necessity include some allusions to my own contribution, as this patient's therapist, to this communicative style. I would not intervene, but would wait for validation, for some supportive material from the patient, primarily in the cognitive sphere. It is quite crucial to the listening process and to therapy to be able to develop such silent hypotheses, to use your subjective feelings and impressions, your sense of interactional pressure, positive or negative, your empathy, intuition, and the rest—but sound technique calls for independent validation before experiencing confidence in regard to your formulation, and certainly before intervening to the patient.

Discussant: I was going to ask you if you would have made an intervention at that point.

Therapist: Well, let me say that she looked upset, and she said, It sounded boring.

Langs: I could say this: as I am listening, I'm doing two things which are clearly very much interrelated. I've already described to you that I'm consistently forming what I call *silent hypotheses*, formulations as to the adaptive context, as to available Type Two derivatives, projective identifications, the absence of meaning, or whatever, and including the type of communicative field. I form these hypotheses around the relevant adaptive context and then look to the patient's communications to see if they fit and add to the construct that I am developing. If they do not, I try to reformulate. I look around—what else could be going on—always starting with myself, and the actualities of the therapeutic interaction. Is there something I put into the field and into the patient that I'm not aware of? And once I've worked myself over, I then look to the patient for possible reasons for her defensiveness. This is the first process.

Now the second and related process is that of generating and formulating a tentative interpretation. I'm always thinking interpretively, because I confine myself almost entirely to such interventions. And I'm trying to shape an interpretation which is really relevant to my main silent hypothesis and which is the ultimate representation of that formulation. So, the interpretation that I'm formulating here is what? You should all be doing this. Let's try it. Who would formulate an interpretation, a tentative interpretation? Just briefly.

Discussant: Something about the therapist feeling that things are hopeless.

Langs: In presenting your intervention, please say it as you would to the patient. That's how I like to work. We can talk theoretically here much more easily than we can talk directly to our patients for some reason. Your ongoing formulations also should take form in terms of what you'd like to say to the patient, so please just put it in that form for us too.

Discussant: Something like: You seem to be saying that a lot of the issues that you keep going over and over in the session are not actually relevant to what's really going on in terms of your feelings of hopelessness.

Langs: All right; that's one possibility. Any other tries?

Therapist: You're describing a lot of feelings of hopelessness about your life and capacity to deal with it, and I wonder whether some of that hopelessness doesn't also apply to the way you're experiencing your therapy.
Unfortunately that leaves out the specific adaptive context.

Langs: Exactly, that's the point; it leaves out the specific adaptive context, it's too vague and general, and it omits a specific allusion to her feeling that you're contributing to that sense of hopelessness.

Also, if this is a Type C field—and though this is true of any field, it's especially true of the Type C field—you have to approach the defensive aspect first, the barrier. That is, the intervention should first address what we call resistance—and this is what I have termed an *interactional resistance,* one with contributions from both of you—and it must be interpreted as such. In addition, resistances in a Type C field are very special barriers, a unique form of resistance.

So, all of this considered, my silent formulation or interpretation would be something like this: In the context of my having changed the hour, you're feeling especially hopeless. You also experienced my offer to make up the session as conveying a lack of faith in you, and this too adds to your sense of despair. As you try to communicate some of this sense of hopelessness to me, you experience my interventions as reflecting my failure to understand where the hopelessness is stemming from, as if I too felt hopeless about being able to help you. And you then feel even more hopeless. It's as if you

feel I have put something depressing and destructive into you
and are attempting to place it back into me. And as a result of
all this, you shift away from relatively meaningful communication to repetition and noncommunication. You distance
yourself from me, as you feel I have done with you, feeling that
in some way I have also responded to you in a kind of non-
understanding way.

You see? I used the adaptive context—the sequence of
adaptive contexts in the two sessions—and referred to the
sense of repetition and monotony, both as I contributed to it
and as the patient did. And all of this silently, all quite to
myself and tentative—and addressing both the cognitive and
the interactional spheres. And I deal first with the communicative medium and resistances. I could add more, but take this
as an initial sample.

Discussant: I grant you the fact that, yes, unconsciously in
the patient's material, we can see—in terms of her unconscious communication—that she may be dealing with the
hypothesized important subject of the changed session. But if
your interpretation were to be made, given the fact that the
patient had not given us any very direct derivative of that
subject, in terms of what she had said—her associations— do
you think she could really hear and accept your interpretation?

Therapist: I would feel confused by all of that if I were the
patient.

Langs: But that's why I emphasized to you that this is my
silent interpretation, my *silent* hypothesis, and I even said it
as I would initially experience it—in bits and pieces, using her
associations as much as possible, establishing links, approaching the interactional resistance and communicative
nature of the field first, elaborating from there into all spheres.
I could add my having helped to make her feel hopeless—a
countertransference-based image evocation—and more. But I
would soon become more selective, based on her further
associations. I am prepared, still open and waiting, and

continue to listen, to allow her to further shape and refine my formulation.

Therapist: Oh, I see.

Discussant: You need an in, and would wait for it before intervening.

Langs: Yes, I'm listening also for the necessary bridge. This has to do with the timing of interpretations, of course. Now I know that she hasn't given me that bridge, but I wanted to offer a small sample of the results of my listening process.

Discussant: This is a silent hypothesis—an interesting concept.

Langs: Yes, a silent hypothesis and, for the moment, a silent interpretation. Now in certain sessions the patient comes right along, joins you and gives you the crystallization and bridges you need, and those are easy sessions, if you have the right interpretation.

Discussant: What do you do if, in the whole session, there's no bridge.

Langs: That's exactly the point: there are sessions when this does not occur. And that's where you need another principle of technique. It has to do with playing back the relevant derivatives, themes, in addition to recognizing that the therapist's intervention promoted this rumination—a contribution that has to be rectified, interpreted, and undone. So I hope ultimately to intervene in that regard, to keep these needs in mind. It also has to do with recognizing that, even on a manifest level, this is a changed hour, and the patient has not alluded to it at all. It is possible to point that out or, as I prefer, to lead the patient toward that omission and eventually interpret the defenses involved.

So, there are several possibilities. The first one is to play back the themes that unconsciously relate to the change in hour. If the patient then . . .

Discussant: Not the themes that she gives you on a manifest level?

Langs: Themes are manifest themes, but they are selected because of their relevance as derivatives related to the adaptive context of the change in the hour. You might say: You're talking about feeling hopeless, feeling misunderstood, and feeling misused. Period. It's said in an ambiguous way so that the patient, with her listening process, can now take these generalities and shift to a specific context—as she often will. Later, you could suggest that she's not at all mentioned something rather evident; if necessary you could say, Something related to therapy.

Therapist: That's what I've been trying to do in what I've said.

Langs: Yes, but not successfully and ambiguously enough, and not so it is unmistakably implied that you are working with the adaptive context of the changed hour.

Therapist: Okay.

Langs: You want to invite a connection to yourself. And most patients would then say something about the therapeutic situation. This has been my experience. Let's say that the patient then doesn't. In the face of your having changed the hour (a strong therapeutic context) I think then you could say: Now you're talking about repeating the same things over and over. Perhaps in some way you're alerting us to the fact that you have not at all mentioned something that is different. And toward the end of the session, if I had important derivatives of unconscious perceptions and fantasies to interpret, I would come quite close to mentioning that this is a changed hour and that the patient has not addressed this fact directly.

There's a nice bridge, even though I know it's a bit forced: she talks about sameness, and I'll point out that she's using sameness to avoid something that's different. That's an interpretation of the Type C barrier and an implied invitation to talk about the change in the hour. In fact, it's a nice piece of timing and a nice intervention. We'll study this aspect more carefully later on in the course.

Discussant: In your first intervention, where you were playing back the theme of hopelessness, would you merely stop at that point and see if she made any connection, or would you go on to make the bridge for her?

Langs: No, no, it's a matter of just playing back themes, without any bridge, without any reference to therapy at all. I try not to bypass defenses. But I didn't confine myself to hopelessness; I pointed to other themes as well.

Here again you can apply the process of identifying important manifest and concrete first-order themes; shifting up to general themes; and attempting now to promote the shift back to new specific themes centered around a definitive adaptive context. The intervention of playing back the general themes to the patient is an unconscious effort to encourage her to search for the selected fact, the adaptive context that would give these associations meaning and organization. You create a preconception—actually, you reinforce one that is already present in the patient—a preconception and state of tension that can be adequately saturated and resolved only by the correct adaptive context.

Perhaps the analogy between the adaptive context and the gene might also be helpful: the gene is an organizer—it gives meaning, and actively organizes and directs—and the adaptive context functions in a similar manner.

But in working over this aspect of the listening process, remember again that your defenses can enter at any step along the way. Countertransferences can intrude. You listen to the manifest content and you don't pick up the important general themes. That's one level of defense. You pick up the general theme, but you don't link it to an adaptive context. That's another level.

Now I will select those general themes that are most pertinent to what I believe to be the unconscious meanings she's experiencing in respect to the change of the hour. So I would not simply say hopelessness; that's why I mentioned, if you remember, her feeling manipulated, feeling misunderstood, feeling that her needs were not being taken into account. I mentioned unreasonable demands being placed upon her, her feeling demeaned. I'm inviting the bridge, I'm leading her to it. I'm giving her the general themes and we want to see now if she can pick them up and work toward the adaptive context.

I'm inviting a transition that the patient defensively hasn't made: maybe because I haven't allowed her to make it in the past, or maybe because of her own defensive needs. If I've been working with manifest content and generating Type C barriers all along, that can do it. If I haven't been prepared to symbolically interpret Type Two derivatives around adaptive contexts and because of this change in hour she feels very threatened by me, then I'm too dangerous to communicate to directly. She uses a derivative form and, with my help, soon destroys most perceptible meaning. All of that can contribute; there could be many factors. I'm always looking for my contribution, and then for hers.

Play back the themes, first shaping them in keeping with the postulated adaptive context, and then let her work it over. Here, with the specific therapeutic context of the change in hour, you have a nice bridge in her saying: It's the same old stuff; I must be boring you.

You see too how I say it, by the way. I have a picture of the patient which I find almost absent in the literature: that the patient is your supervisor, and your supervisor's supervisor too. The patient is also in some sense our therapist, in an unconscious and unobtrusive sense which we're entitled to, so long as it's secondary. This I think now is a necessary and inherent part of the therapeutic situation; it helps to make it viable. But in addition, the patient is our ally and a great resource. The patient will shape our interpretations, will give us in disguised form what we need to give her directly.

And I want the patient to realize that. I constantly intervene in a way that lets her know she's unconsciously aware of something: You're aware of something, but can't say it directly, but here is how you've said it indirectly. And that's why I shaped the intervention in the particular form that I did: that this was her way of reminding us that she's repeating something over and over again, and that it kind of calls our attention to the opposite—to what is new in this session. Here too, I tend to make a type of intervention that is as ambiguous as possible, but I don't bypass defenses. I don't at first just mention the change in the hour that she has avoided. I attempt, rather, to allow the patient to experience her resistance and its manifestations, and I let her work over the defenses and analyze them to the extent possible.

Okay, let's hear this out.

Therapist: During all of this I was feeling extremely tired.

Langs: Yes. It can be an exhausting experience—another subjective clue to be analyzed, understood, and related to the Type C field.

Therapist: She went on and said, Well, I'm also depressed about going home for the holidays. My family will never be the same.

This is also another old theme, because her mother died about three years ago. She said, I go out of obligation. If I don't plan the holiday dinner, if I don't call my father and tell him what food to get, and so on and so forth, then the whole thing just won't come off.

Langs: You know the adaptive context, and this is the manifest content. And we've established two sequential adaptive contexts. So how would you shape this into a Type Two derivative? Give me the manifest content, the general theme, and the new specific theme connected to the adaptive context. Because she does shift a bit, there is definitively Type A communication here; she does come back to it; she does not stick with Type C barriers.

Discussant: Did she say she feels obligated to go home?

Therapist: Yes.

Discussant: She felt obligated to come to the make-up session.

Langs: That's one part of it—a bit narrow, but well done. What else? I almost introduced the subject just a moment ago.

Therapist: About things not being the same?

Langs: The theme of deadness often comes up when communication is being destroyed. It's a metaphor for the Type C field. I'll say that much. But I have something else in mind. What else, in terms of what I just said? I had in fact just made this very point in my own idiom; that's what's so fascinating. What is she saying?

Therapist: She says she has to call her father in order to tell him what to do, and if she doesn't do this, he won't do it.

Langs: Right, that's the manifest content. Now give me the general theme that will then apply specifically to the adaptive context at hand.

Therapist: I have to do it, you won't do it—referring to her and me.

Langs: Yes, in treatment. If I don't get around to bringing up that this is a changed hour, we're never going to get to it. If I don't feed you the derivatives and interpret them, it will never get done. Remarkably, de Racker (1961) used the feeding idiom in writing a paper on this very subject.

Therapist: Then she says, I didn't do it this year.

Langs: She didn't do it, so nobody did it, and it didn't get done.

Therapist: She's saying, I just don't want to.

Langs: Yes, she expresses so much of this in terms of food, of feeding, just as de Racker formulated the patient's contribution to the analyst's interpretations in similar feeding terms. The patient will feed you the ingredients that you have to digest in order to generate an effective interpretation; it's a most fascinating model that she has offered.

Therapist: She said, I'll go, but I'm not looking forward to it. No one else will plan it if I don't.

Langs: Again, if you use the me–not–me interface as part of your listening process, you could take that specific theme, generalize it, and monitor it in connection with the therapeutic situation. Monitor it not so much in terms of what the patient is now failing to contribute—though there is some truth in that respect, since she really did stop feeding you derivatives for a while and works herself over for that—but also in terms of your own contribution. You could ask, What is it I am failing to feed her, to do with her? What is not being accomplished? And the like. It could lead you to reformulate, to search for the key ingredient—the adaptive context— and more.

Therapist: Yes, but I don't think she's referring to the missed session or to the change in session. I think she's referring to the make-up session itself. I'm not going to tell you; we'll see what happens.

Langs: Yes, we'll see. Go ahead. I would have to maintain for now the hypothesis that relates this material to the change in hour and to your recent noninterpretive interventions.

Therapist: She says, You look very sleepy to me.

Langs: Okay. But now see again, what I mean about the development of a closer derivative: you're asleep on the job, and she comes directly to you now.

Therapist: But that was true.

Langs: I know; it was true in more senses than one. It is

important on a manifest level but is also important as a derivative.

Therapist: She says, You look like you're going to fall off the chair.

Langs: So you see about bridges; she does get around to the therapist, after all. And that is not only a very nice bridge to the therapist, but her comment that the therapist looks like she's going to fall off the chair is a very interesting representation, a rather interesting metaphor related to the Type C field, because again, the basic hypothesis is that the patient or therapist who utilizes the Type C mode is involved in an effort to maintain very strong barriers against disruptive inner turmoil and destruction. This is a specific thesis that I developed earlier in our discussion, to which some of you had raised initial objections. So this is both a metaphorical representation of a dimension of the Type C field and a Type Two derivative in the adaptive context of your recent interventions. It is for the moment a valid perception, both conscious and unconscious, and, I would add, it contains as well an implied unconscious interpretation.

I am sorry to so often get ahead of myself in regard to the areas we will be covering, but I feel that there's something constructive in calling to your attention different dimensions of the therapeutic interaction as they become pertinent to the material being presented. So, in regard to your capacity to contain the patient's projective identifications, I am speculating that this is her view of your response to her sick or bad stuff. She has not said that exactly, but she is saying that she perceives you as losing your equilibrium in response to whatever she's putting into you, and is suggesting that this prompts you to defensively become sleepy, to shut out all perceptions, and to close yourself off as a container for her pathological contents. This includes your avoidance of the most pertinent adaptive contexts for this hour. There is a dread of containing and of the disequilibrium and damage that such contents may cause for you. Bion (1962, 1970) has a concept for that phenomenon, by the way; he calls it the container's dread of the contained—the container's fear of denudation and destruction.

Therapist: But you see what I'm having trouble with. I can see very much that I was disturbed by the unconscious meanings, the sense of hopelessness, the depth and all the rest of it. It's very disturbing, and that's really what's coming through to me loud and clear in the session. And I can see that much of this had to do with the specific adaptive contexts—my conflicts about changing the day of the session

Langs: The underlying source of anxiety and threat.

Therapist: Yes.

Langs: I will soon, perhaps next time, say a great deal more about the interactional dimension of the listening process, but I must mention this aspect at this point because it seems so pertinent. You appear to have been experiencing at that moment the hopelessness and sense of death that the patient was putting into you—whatever other sources may have contributed to your sense of sleepiness and anxiety. In a sense, the Type C void—her negative reprojection—did indeed damage your capacity to function adequately.

We must postulate an interactional pressure which you were unable to consciously understand and metabolize, and which was proving somewhat toxic to you, so to speak, and which you felt was dangerous and which you felt you had a need to protect yourself against—all of which constitute important subjective feelings that could have been identified, analyzed, formulated, taken as hypothetical images, fantasies, sensitivities, and theses, and eventually validated from your further subjective reactions, and especially through the material from the patient.

This material shows the great importance of a conception of the interactional dimension of the listening process—a term which pales when used to describe such a broad area of internalizing on the part of the therapist. And I think that it is a crucial dimension for the patient as well. She appears to have picked up your anxieties about containing her projective identifications, to have consciously sensed your anxiety about being harmed or thrown by them—your inability to metabolize the negative projective identification that she generated in the last few minutes of this session—and to have recognized certain aspects of your problem quite consciously.

Therapist: Yes. So she said, You know, your eyes look like they're closing, and I recognize that. You're sort of moving around in your chair the way I move around when I'm struggling to keep awake. Do you want to stop?

Langs: Do you want to stop? Do you want to bring it all to a halt?

Therapist: So I said, No.

Langs: In brief, I don't make this kind of intervention.

Therapist: Well, you may not, but I'll tell you what I did.

Langs: I'm just trying to establish some principles. The patient is working this over, and you should listen, and try to understand, to rectify, and to analyze your countertransference.

Therapist: And not say anything?

Discussant: What do you mean? You don't make any sort of intervention at such a point?

Langs: No, I would simply let her continue, and for the moment just let her say whatever comes to mind.

Discussant: Nothing at all ? You'd be silent?

Langs: I wouldn't say anything, but I would continue the session. That's all. I wouldn't respond to her question.

Therapist: But if she said, You look drowsy, and asked me if I wanted to stop?

Langs: I would simply continue to treat this as her associations and try to understand their manifest and latent meaning. There are both, you know.

Therapist: Well . . .

Discussant: What if she says, Do you want to stop? And she looks at you and waits for an answer.

Langs: She'll continue to associate, and, if not, I would offer the best possible interpretation at the moment. Or, if under direct pressure, and only then, I might simply suggest she continue to say what is coming to mind, implying: Of course, let's continue. Look, she's discovered a clear-cut indication of countertransference difficulty, and she's going to try to exploit it for a while, and shift the focus on to you, and work you over. And rightly so. Now your silence implicitly acknowledges the validity of her perception and, in the meantime, you begin to explore this problem and try to identify its basis—within yourself and in the communications from the patient—and you search for the meaning and functions of your drowsiness.

She's picked it up, she's perceived it and referred to it directly. But even here, despite the manifest truth and validity of her perception, we must continue to search for unconscious meanings in her communication: for example, we might make the hypothesis that on the latent level it refers to the therapist's failure to detect the crucial adaptive context for this hour and to her own need for a Type C communicative field. Please do not misunderstand my position. Just because I've emphasized the importance of identifying valid components of the patient's perceptions and reactions, I don't give up the search for distortions and unconscious meanings. I let these unfold too, and the more material that I have, the more precise my intervention can be.

You know, I can well understand your anxiety and your need to answer her directly; it is a very difficult moment. But if we continue to concentrate on the listening process, you can see, first, that in psychotherapy listening is always an emotionally laden experience; and, second, that it is quite easy, when under pressure, to set aside the basic principles of the listening process, and of technique, out of a need to allay your own anxiety, or even in the rationalized service of diminishing the patient's anxiety, which, in actuality, such responses will only intensify.

Your intervention serves to modify the frame a bit further; it is a self-revelation and a failure to contain the hostility and disruptive effects of her question. Silence, on the other hand, along with rectification and, ultimately, an effective interpretation, will show and implicitly allow the patient to introject your capacity to recover, to manage your own inner turmoil, to return to meaningful communication, and to contain her disturbing projective identifications. In addition, and here too the listening process comes into play, it is important that the patient have a full opportunity to communicate her unconscious perceptions and introjections of this experience, as well as the inner turmoil it is creating for her, and I don't want to interfere with that communication.

Incidentally, McLaughlin (1975) has written a paper on sleepiness in the analyst. He discusses it in terms of depletion states and underlying countertransferences and adopts a somewhat interactional approach in that he suggests that certain patients tend to generate sleepiness in their analyst or therapist. I believe also that he mentions the obsessional patient in that context. Still, he stopped short of the kind of circular interactional approach that I have been developing here.

As you can see, the therapist herself set the stage for this sleepiness with the change in the hour and the Type C mode interventions she offered the patient, who then obligingly adopted that mode of communication herself—a most interesting sequence, to be sure. And sleepiness does, indeed, tend to occur in the Type C field. In respect to the listening process, I must add here that it requires a normal state of consciousness, because the full application of the listening and validating processes are feasible only in such a state. Sometimes therapists become confused, and because they recognize that they are searching for unconscious contents and functions and are interested in primary process mechanisms, they seem to believe that an alteration in their state of consciousness that approaches sleep will facilitate their listening to, and understanding of, the material from the patient. This is a conceptual confusion at best, and, beyond that, a rationalization for a countertransference manifestation.

Discussant: I don't know if you could respond, because you don't have the full material, but a very similar thing happened to me in a session. A patient said to me, I saw such and such a movie, and he was starting to tell me about it. And he said, Oh, did you see the movie? And I gather you would have remained silent.

Langs: Yes, and it's much easier to do it under those conditions. And if you feel obligated to respond, just simply say: Let's see where your thoughts go, or, Just continue to say what comes to mind. That's an appropriate response, particularly early in treatment. Because, don't you see, you're feeling guilty now, you're feeling badly about what you've done. You feel a need to apologize. When that becomes your need, you can no longer place the therapeutic needs of the patient uppermost.

There are those who say, Oh, you must respond, that it is inhuman not to do so. But they are misguided in their concept of how the therapist conveys his humanness—it must be communicated within his appropriate role as a therapist. Now, you don't deny her perception or do anything to destroy her valid experiencing; you implicitly acknowledge that aspect of her functioning. At the same time, you maintain both your search for distortions and your stance as therapist. She wants to know that, when you're under pressure from within yourself and from her, you can manage without falling off the chair. And it is important to convey this to help her indirectly. Go ahead.

Therapist: So I said no and apologized for becoming so sleepy. And she started to laugh and said, That's okay. So I said, On the other hand, I wasn't so tired at the beginning of the session, so we'll see if it's related to anything that's going on here.

Langs: Yes, this is a common technique, which I don't utilize—because again it implies that the patient has more responsibility for what happened than you do, or that your contribution is to be quickly set aside. But it's also asking her to stick with what is manifest and conscious. You don't have to say that to the patient; it would be implicit in allowing her to go on associating. And that would be more valuable— permitting her to proceed on her own—because you don't want to direct her and she is quite unaware of the basis for this incident in herself or in you. She can't turn around and say, Well, I was talking about this and that and it meant such and such. In other words, you're asking for her conscious scrutiny, when what you want is unconscious communication in terms of Type Two derivatives. She has the answers, but unconsciously, not consciously. Oddly enough, for the patient, both the continuation and the modification of her neurosis lies in the sphere of unconscious processes and communication.

Therapist: Yes, I see that now.

Discussant: Are you saying that the patient may be tired? Is that what you're implying by that intervention? Or that she's inducing the countertransference?

Therapist: I wasn't implying that I experienced drowsiness in her; rather, I was asking her to investigate her contribution to my drowsiness. I was saying, Let's see what may have happened in the session to have done this.

Discussant: You wouldn't have done that?

Langs: No, I wouldn't have. I would simply have said nothing, and if she didn't continue speaking, I would have said, Let's hear what's coming to mind, which is a way of indicating to her: Yes, I want to continue. Let's try to understand. Let's see where your thoughts go, as freely as you wish to shape them. Period. This is the area of listening that I have termed *role evocation*: you must not assume that your response is the patient's wish; you must sort out her wish from the therapist's own needs. Okay, but let's now see how she responds to this.

Therapist: She said, Well, what do you mean?

Langs: Yes. Does anyone know who identified what is happening here? (Pause.) Sigmund Freud (1912b). He said that when the analyst modifies his anonymity, the patient will try to turn the analysis into the analysis of the analyst. He said it in his basic papers on technique—papers I will ask you to read eventually.

So, she's trying now to exploit your apology—your self-revelation, your countertransference—and she siezes this opportunity to help her move more and more away from her own pathology and more and more toward yours.

Discussant: Can you imagine a situation where acknowledging countertransference would be helpful?

Langs: Implicit acknowledgment is almost always necessary. Explicit acknowledgment is a deviation in the frame and I don't think it's essentially helpful. I think the former satisfies the patient's need for reality testing and his need to realize that you're human and that you are aware of your errors. So it is best to acknowledge errors implicitly. When the error is self-evident, such as starting late or forgetting a session, a brief explicit acknowledgment may be in order.

Discussant: Then explicit acknowledgment would have been termed a realization of the therapist's need to confess or absolve herself of guilt? How would you have intervened?

Langs: The implicit acknowledgement will come when I can

give you an interpretation from her material: You perceived me as tired and drowsy—that's how the intervention would begin. So this is a new adaptive context, and we'll use it in listening to whatever follows.

Therapist: But saying it that way—doesn't seem to acknowledge the part that's coming from me.

Langs: Well it must be contrasted to how I state a transference interpretation.

Therapist: You know, it's saying, her perception of my being tired. Well, I was sitting there very tired and falling off . . .

Discussant: It's too ambiguous.

Langs: Again, that's the essential model. Please accept it for now, at least until we discuss countertransference and errors, and until I can demonstrate the various kinds of interventions involved. This is impossible to resolve without such clinical data.

Therapist: To me, it contradicts what you're saying.

Langs: No, not at all. I know that you're saying that "you perceive" could mean that it may or may not have been true.

Therapist: Yes.

Langs: The point is that when it's distorted I intervene in an entirely different way: You believed I was tired. When it is valid I would say, You perceived me as tired, or, You saw me becoming drowsy, I mean you could say it in just that kind of way, without saying, I was drowsy and I'm sorry. You saw me becoming drowsy, and then we do our interpretive work from there. It depends on the situation, very much so. But what I'm trying to offer for now is an essential model of acknowledging the patient's perceptions, rather than also adding: Yes, I was this or that, but I'm sorry, and all the rest. That overburdens the patient with your problems and invites her to shift the communicative focus to your pathology. It's like asking her to say, Now let's hear *your* free associations. You've made that fair game.

Therapist: So then I said, Well, I wonder if there was any reason why you'd want me to feel tired. And she said, You mean more than it just being an expression of how I feel, very drained? Well, I could spice it up a bit to make it more interesting.

Langs: She's now going to wake you up. And also, she's prepared to accept your drowsy state as an introjective identification with her own inner state. It's an interesting comment, one which reflects, first, her depressive pathology— she'll take the blame, both hers and yours—and, secondly, she conveys an image of projective identification: she put her inner emptiness into you, though she again leaves out the rest of the spiral—your having put your inner emptiness into her. But here you can discover a cognitive representation of projective identification, and you could use it judiciously when you intervene. This is a small bit of cognitive validation of an hypothesis formulated in the interactional sphere.

Notice too, in regard to your asking her to identify her need to make you sleepy—to evoke in you a response or role—you are placing a great burden on her and neglecting your own proclivities. Role responses call for an exploration of contributions from both patient and therapist, using the indirect communications in the patient's material and judicious self-analysis. Every aspect of listening requires a balanced approach of that type, especially in the face of evident countertransferences.

Therapist: Right, she did wake me up. And I said, I'm not asking you to do that, just that we try to understand why this has happened.

Langs: Now she suddenly wants to give you something, to do something for you, and you tell her, No, not that. You're interfering with the flow of communication, and you're still taking it all in on a manifest level. You can see the kind of trouble you get into when you start listening solely to the manifest content, which therapists often do when they're laboring under a sense of guilt or other countertransference pressures.

Therapist: I think it's more that. I felt confused, and didn't know how to set things straight.

Langs: And you get a little bit afraid too, of how she might spice it up. You're saying again: Oh, I don't want to contain it.

Therapist: Right. She said, Well, I'm avoiding putting feelings into what I'm saying because I want to get rid of my anger. I don't like it and it's not going to help anyway.

Langs: That was *your* model too; she's picked it up: Let's get rid of the spicy stuff—the feelings—don't put them into anything.

Therapist: And I said, Perhaps you're feeling that you would like something from me.

Langs: Well, this must have been a very difficult interlude for you. And you can see the extent to which you were under pressures of guilt and countertransference. You detect her feeling that she's not being helped, and you do try to intervene in that respect. But it's disconnected from even the most recent adaptive context, at best a Type One derivative, and, while it's an heroic effort, it's too flat and linear.

In general, I've found that therapists have difficulty maintaining their listening capacity when they are experiencing the influence of acute countertransference difficulties and dealing with openly recognized technical errors. They tend, in general, to modify the frame under such conditions, and much of this occurs because of their guilt and their need to offer immediate reparation—not through an interpretation which would be a valid form of repair, but through some deviation which unconsciously extends the destructiveness of the situation and continues to express the underlying countertransferences. As a basic principle, you should attempt to maintain the frame and to utilize the listening process in the adaptive context of the technical error, as a means of delineating the patient's unconscious perceptions and introjections and their extensions into fantasies and into connections with her past life experiences. It's difficult, but it reflects a sound ability to contain, at a critical moment, both your own inner disturbance and that of the patient—an ability to maintain your hold on the patient even when you, yourself, are feeling rather disturbed and inadequate—and it expresses, as well, your capacity to interpret under stress. This not only generates important cognitive insights but provides the patient adaptive introjective identifications and a positive hold that will serve her well.

Therapist: She said, Well, I guess I do want you to say something, to be supportive. (This is the first time she's ever said anything like this: that she wants anything from me, for me to be supportive, to jump in and ask questions, to tell her if she's not saying anything.) She said, I guess I do want some advice, just to help sort this all out, because so often I decide on the basis of emotion and my wish to avoid, rather than really because I want something.

Langs: You see, you *did* insist on a Type C field—not the exciting stuff, not anything with meaning—and now she starts to ruminate again and asks for further alterations in the frame: direct gratification, so-called support.

Therapist: What I did was this: she said, Maybe I put some of my anger into all of this, and I said no, that I didn't think her anger made me sleepy.

Langs: I'm not clear what the patient meant by her remarks, even on the surface, and while there is some rather superficial reference to anger and some indication that it unconsciously involves her own anger, and yours based on an introject, you are shutting her off far too quickly, listening on the surface and closing off any development of conscious or unconscious themes by intervening too rapidly and prematurely. You haven't been taking each intervention as an adaptive context, haven't been listening to her associations as unconscious commentaries, as transversal communications with valid truths as well as distortions. Anxiety and guilt have led you to close yourself off and to do the same to the patient.

I'm sure that she wishes to convey something quite specific in terms of unconscious fantasies and perceptions, and I'm also certain that both instinctual drives are represented, anger and sexuality. I'm also sure that in this field, and the way you're shaping it, your communications—and soon, hers too—will serve as a very effective barrier to the instinctual drive derivatives, to the point where you're going to hear nothing sexual or truly aggressive, just some ruminations and clichés about anger, about wanting to know, at a time when she begins to realize again that you don't want to know at all. And she'll go along with that, and not want to know herself. That's the way it has to be, that sort of reaction. But all that could suddenly change, once she wishes to modify the sector of misalliance.

Therapist: She said, Well, I'm not comfortable with this part of myself—the part that wants somebody else to decide for me. I think it's terrible that I decide on the basis of emotion. It would be better if I could assert myself and say how I feel to my boss—tell him that I'm angry—but I get this physical reaction that stops me from doing it and I don't understand it. I'm also ashamed of it. And she described it: her heart pounding, becoming short of breath, and so on. She said, It also seems to prevent my taking any initiative at all, and I don't see why. I can't make decisions, and I always make bad decisions and never succeed. That's the end of the hour.

Langs: Let's hear the beginning of the next hour. This should be interesting.

Discussant: What would your prediction be?

Langs: That it will relate to the frame and in some way to this whole destruction of meaning in this particular field—to their mutual discomfort with inner sick parts.

Therapist: Okay. She came on time for this session, which was unusual for her. She said, I want to pick up where we were last time. She took off her coat; that's also unusual. She usually sits there all wrapped up.

Langs: So, she wants to do some work to open things up.

Therapist: She said, Why do I always see myself as failing? I did it with my thesis exam, but I passed it and now I'm doing it with jobs. She said, I wouldn't go so far as to say that I've set up failure, but it's also hard to convince myself that I don't. She said, This all seems to be related to self-esteem and somehow needing to be perfect. I'd like to...

Langs: I just learned how difficult it is to predict themes in a Type C field: there are some threads but nothing definitive at all.

Discussant: Well, I just wondered, would you—I don't know if it's true or not—are you saying that she's wanting to maintain a Type C field?

Langs: For a moment, yes. Can you identify an adaptive context and Type Two derivatives? Do you sense any interactional pressures related to a Type B field?

Discussant: Well, the context that I can see is that the therapist asked her in the last session: What happened? I wasn't as tired at the beginning of the session as I am now. And now the patient is saying, Yes, you're right, I make you tired and I'm also a failure.

Langs: Well, there is more of a Type One derivative quality to what you said, namely we can recognize themes:

that treatment has failed—and, yes, has she created the situation of failure? There is a Type Two derivative quality there, but it's tentative for the moment.

Discussant: Yes, I'm saying that, in terms of the way the therapist has presented this woman, it seems to me that she went away blaming herself for the fact that the therapist was unresponsive to her, just as everybody else is. The fact that the therapist did not interpret the issue of the missed session I don't think was the beginning of this feeling in relation to her therapist. I think what she's talking about in terms of her self-esteem is a hope that here again she's going to begin to get into the ways in which she allows other people to rule what she does and how she feels.

Langs: No, I don't think it's quite that. I would amend what you're saying in this way: the therapist really did put something into the patient. As I said to you, her intervention would imply that the patient is responsibile for the failure of that hour.

Therapist: Which she then accepts.

Langs: Yes, right. And she took that in, and it's related to what she's feeling now. This is an introject of the therapist's failure to interpret, and I don't mean only the meanings of the changed hour now but also the patient's responses to your sleepiness and to your interventions. And it is an introject that is also based on the therapist's insistence that the patient be burdened with this sense of failure and the therapist's inability to interpret in that area as well. But she's now expressing all of that in a rather ruminative way. That's all I'm saying.

She does participate in the misalliance because of her own needs, but this is not to say that it was not also imposed upon her. You have to see both factors. Another patient would protest in some way. As a depressive, she takes in the bad introjects and allows them to reign supreme, if you will, allows them to influence and intensify her depression. There is an interaction here between the patient's—let's call it masochistic, self-punitive needs—and the therapist's need to dump the bad stuff into her. You see what I mean? Think of both sides. All right, tell us a little bit more.

Therapist: She says, I'd like to be able to talk with somebody else about decisions that I make, because often my perceptions are off and it isn't really such a huge failure. And I need somebody else to tell me that it's not such a bad failure and that I'm just distorting because I'm caught up in all these panicky feelings. And I want somebody else to check out these perceptions. They're colored by anxiety and so on.

The notes that I have are not complete, and it was hard to follow what she was saying in this session.

Langs: Right. You see, in my prediction, as I said, I underestimated the intensity with which she had been pushed to a Type C communicative field. She says, I want to go back to where we left off, which at least confirmed a bit of what I said, but then she picks it up mainly in terms of the hurtful introjects.

Discussant: In your book *The Bipersonal Field* (1976a), there were three terms that came up, and I think it would help us greatly if we talked about them more at this point: *holding, containing,* and *metabolizing*. From my own experience, those three characteristics of what I'm doing seem to dominate how well the patient is able to talk about his inner mental life. I constantly have this sense of holding and containing with the kinds of patients that we see. They seldom feel at liberty to really express their feelings and need constant reassurance to do so.

Discussant: They get that indirectly by how we manage the frame and how we intervene.

Langs: Direct reassurance? If you mean by that the indirect holding and containing capacities that are reflected in proper interventions—actually, indirect reassurance—then I can follow you.

Discussant: But I'm saying, for me, in that session, that's what didn't happen. That sense of holding and containing didn't happen, and the therapist's ability to do it needs development. I would like to hear more about this metabolizing function, in the sense of sampling what the patient is trying to say. Here, it got cut off too soon.

Langs: Right. *Metabolizing* is a term that I borrowed from Fliess (1942), who wrote about the analyst's trial identifications with the patient. It has to do with experiencing, sampling, working over, and ultimately making conscious not only the direct experience but some of the unconscious implications of a projective identification. It entails understanding directed toward interpretation. It can involve the processing of cognitive material too, though I tend now to use the term mainly for the internal processing of introjected projective identifications. You're going to present next week. We'll try to work over these concepts with your material. It is relevant here, but I just want to hear how this session ended. These topics will come up when we deal with the frame and interpreting.

Therapist: I don't know the order in which this was all said, but there were two other things that came up. One of them was, she said, For instance, if I go for an interview, I'll feel much more comfortable, uh, I feel uncomfortable if I show myself too much, or if I show all of these panicky feelings. It would be much easier for me if I could know there is even one other person there I know already.

Langs: See, that is related to holding and containing functions, to a secure maternal-like hold and the safety it would afford her, and her own incapacity in that regard.

Therapist: Then she said two other things. She said, When I get anxious all I can think about is getting out of the situation—either separate from myself or I get suicidal. But I know the panic will stop if I don't act, so I don't. And she also said, I feel so intimidated because I don't want the other person to see that I feel that way and I want to appear perfect.

Langs: So you see again, she gives you enough Type Two derivatives to recognize the introjections. These general themes are connected to your having gotten sleepy. These associations constitute what I call an unconscious interpretation: that you became frightened, became overanxious, and withdrew to protect yourself from self-destructive impulses. You implied some blame for her so you could feel perfect. Somehow, it doesn't jell, though.

Therapist: But you know what's fascinating—skipping all of this—I said something like that to her. I did make an interpretation. Again, I don't have the exact words I used, but I played back some of those themes in terms of my getting sleepy in the last session.

Langs: Yes, how did she respond?

Therapist: No, no. I didn't even say that. I just asked if it connected to anything that happened in the last session, because I wasn't sure if she was reacting to my getting sleepy or to my laying the blame on her, both of which I felt, but I didn't know. But in response, she paused and she said, The only thing I could think about that happened in the last session was when I talked about my family. It was really an incredible response on her part.

Langs: You're amazed at the patient's defenses, her use of barriers.

Therapist: And she looked kind of teary, and she said, I feel like I was complaining about a situation I can't change. And then she said, Well, I just assumed you were tired. (I guess I had mentioned my falling asleep and her forgetting it.) And she added: But that is typical of me, that I would just deny it, and maybe I was angry, but I can't imagine getting angry at you. And then we got into a discussion about that. And after another week, finally she's gotten to talk about how she's afraid I'm going to stop therapy with her if she gets angry at me.

Langs: But recognize this much: it is difficult to listen when we do not have a clear, sequential presentation. This is the manifest content, which you have quickly summarized for us. Embedded in all of this material is the latent and derivative content, which is usually much more meaningful. And much of it is lost in a general condensation of an hour. Still, there is the whole business of you protecting yourself against suicidal impulses, of using somatization defending against the impingement of disturbing communication from her—that's all indirect and represented as an introject. Comments about herself and her panicky qualities could also apply to you. This is what I mean by Type Two derivatives, indirect communications, and the me–not-me interface. Notice their qualities—much more frightening, much more perceptive, much more dynamic than the manifest threads: Yes, I'll finally admit I was angry, I'll finally admit I'm afraid you're going to kick me out if I say too much. Those communications are rather obvious, and are easier to manage. The embedded stuff, the derivative stuff, is the really frightening stuff, for her and you, especially the not-me aspects, her introjects of you.

Therapist: Right. Because the other embedded thing that came out at the beginning of the last session was that we'd been missing a lot of sessions at this point and therapeutic work had been impossible, because of the holidays. And when we talked about that directly, embedded in that was her feeling: If I don't come here, I feel so alone, and I can't deal with my feelings about being alone.

I would have to reorganize my notes to add anything further.

Langs: Well, we must stop soon, but I hope that this material gives you a feeling for the difference in the impact and ramifications of the various levels of the patient's communications and, for that matter, your own communications as well. There are differences at the manifest and the latent levels. Indirect and derivative communication is rich and deeply meaningful, but it can be quite anxiety provoking and therefore often poses a problem in listening.

The form of communication is also important. In a Type B field, the patient is getting rid of contents and alleviating her anxieties in a manner that can generate considerable threat to the therapist; the Type C field, on the other hand, is flat, dead, and static, while the Type A field is quite alive and filled with potential for both threat and cure.

In a Type A field, the therapist has much more to contain and fewer avenues of inappropriate discharge for himself. He has to manage the framework and maintain a hold under conditions that can be rather disturbing for him. Analysts have not appreciated this aspect of the Type A field as yet, a field in which they open themselves to the patient's symbolic communications. The impingements relate to suicide, to murder and destruction, the terror of losing control, and the like, much of it involving unconscious introjects of themselves. These are a part of the regressive qualities of the Type A field, and, while they provide a unique means for adaptive mastery, they also contain intensely threatening qualities— in our praise of symbolic communication, we have tended to neglect its burdens. As a result, therapists unconsciously endeavor to generate Type B, and especially Type C, communicative fields. With clichés and nonmeaningful interventions they protect themselves from these regressive threats, and, for the same reasons, they accept the patient's manifest associations.

In my teaching I find it extremely important, though sometimes quite difficult, to characterize the crucial differences, for both patient and therapist, in working with manifest content and Type One derivatives, with readily available inferences, as compared to working with latent contents and derivative communication. And this is why I am trying to stress the difference between what you experience in processing this material on the manifest level and in doing so in terms of latent themes. The impact is quite different when the patient says, Well, I don't get angry at people and I don't allow myself to get angry; I'm afraid you'll kick me out, and the like. Contrast this with such communications as, I'm afraid you'll go crazy, that I'll go crazy, that you're afraid of my inner mental contents so much that you dread going insane, losing all control, and fear becoming totally helpless. Images like that are far more distrubing. They impinge on anxiety provoking truths about ourselves; they disturb our falsely maintained equilibrium; they stir up our countertransferences; and they're a hell of a lot more to handle.

Therapist: But you see, I am in touch with that, and I sensed what was going on in the beginning of that session. But I don't know how to work with it.

Langs: Yes, it requires so much of you. That's the point. You're saying that doing psychotherapy properly seems almost impossible because it's so threatening. How can you possibly achieve mastery under those conditions? That's true. And that is why I take so seriously the conceptions that I am attempting to develop with you here—because I believe that they, and I must say, they alone, constitute the essential tools of mastery that can make you into effective therapists. But as you now already know, this is not simply a cognitive process; it gets entangled in your emotions and unresolved pathology. But that, hopefully, becomes the realm of your personal therapy, while here we can continue to develop the cognitive tools that you very much need to have.

Therapist: Between her anxiety and my anxiety...

Langs: Yes, and that's just why therapists shift to clichés and Type C barriers or unconsciously begin to projectively identify pathological contents and defenses into their patients. They thereby protect themselves, inappropriately, against their mounting anxieties, all of which, unfortunately, deprives the patient of an opportunity for true mastery.

And you can see too that the Type A field, in which all these disturbing contents and defenses are most openly and symbolically expressed, while it would afford the patient and yourself the most effective level of cognitive insight and positive introjects, requires of both of you the greatest possible mastery and controls to begin with. It means you must stop living out, control your pathological projective identifications, manage your unconscious wishes to destroy meaning and create impenetrable barriers, and open yourself to the primitive contents within your patient and yourself as well. It's pretty scary, and yet if offers something incredibly valuable and unique that can truly last a lifetime—once again, for both you and the patient—so long as your own gains are indirect and secondary.

Therapist: She's been especially troublesome for me.

Langs: Yes, so you appreciate what I mean.

Therapist: But that still doesn't help. I mean, I don't expect to ever be able to reach a reasonable point of mastery—at least, not with her.

Langs: Well, be patient. The potential is there. What you do now is let the dust settle. You've rectified the frame as much as you can, and can try now to intervene with an adaptive context as your fulcrum. Allow such contexts to emerge and permit her to begin to communicate in derivative ways—even if it impinges upon your areas of vulnerability and anxiety.

Therapist: See, what isn't clear to me is what makes this more manageable for the patient. And it's obviously not clear to me, because it's not manageable to me.

Langs: What makes what more manageable?

Therapist: All of these feelings, and derivative communications.

Langs: What will make it more manageable is your capacity to contain and interpret them. Yes, it can only be put in a general way for now. We'd have to then get to some further material to be more precise. In the main session that you presented, you would have had to tolerate allowing her to get around to derivative communications related to how she really felt about your changing the hour, which would have led into this whole business about fears of going crazy—hers and yours—and her being treated insensitively and things of that kind. And the same would apply to your having become sleepy.

Therapist: But what she would have talked about, if I hadn't cut her off, is her suicidal impulses and fantasies.

Langs: Yes. So perhaps this is your way of saying that you were frightened by the depression that you would have evoked in her by simply canceling the session that you had to miss, and that you felt unable to contain and manage her suicidal fantasies and impulses and their repercussions within yourself. So in order to protect yourself from that material you offered a makeup session, and that generated a great impetus toward a Type C field. And you then felt protected—while the patient felt both protected and upset.

But perhaps you can now see why therapists so often modify the frame unnecessarily. And even though I will not attempt to validate the thesis we are discussing in regard to this particular unconscious motive for the makeup session, let it serve as a model to all of you. It is exactly these kinds of unconscious motives that prompt unneeded deviations in the framework and errors in intervening, as well as and unconscious efforts to shift the patient away from the Type A communicative mode.

So you can see too that simply canceling the hour, a move that in itself would promote the continuation of a Type A field by maintaining a secure frame, and then listening to the material from the patient in what would then be an easy adaptive context—the missed session—you could have then worked over her unconscious and derivative reactions, linking them interpretively at some point to her psychopathology and thereby offering her both a positive introjective identification, based on your capacities to maintain your hold and to contain her disturbing reactions, and cognitive insights that would have accrued to her under those conditions.

And the same principles apply to her reaction to your sleepiness: managing your guilt and other feelings, containing her responses, allowing her to continue on with indirect derivatives, and interpreting the painful stuff that would have emerged. There too, you have a clear-cut adaptive context, and the identification of Type Two derivatives—at least cognitively—would have been quite easy, however painful their contents might have been for you. For her, the incident became almost a matter of life and death, sickness or cure, and that's pretty awful to work over, especially in the face of a clear-cut expression of your contertransferences. But then again, that's the nature of our work, and there is great consolation in knowing that when an incident of that kind is properly managed—rectified and interpreted—there can be enormous growth for both your patient and yourself.

Thank you again. It was a most interesting presentation.

Chapter Seven

THE THREE BASIC REALMS
OF LISTENING

Identifying possible adaptive contexts • Confidentiality and the listening process • Listening in the cognitive, object relational, and interactional mechanism spheres • Levels of listening and levels of intervening • Factors in therapists who listen on a manifest level • Listening to the therapist's projective identifications

Langs: Today let's move toward the presentation of a single session which we will take by itself with an absolute minimum of information regarding the patient. The goal will be to see the extent to which this restricts our application of the listening process—or perhaps facilitates it—in any case, to see its effects on our capacity to listen and formulate.

Therapist: This is a thirty-six-year-old divorced woman who sought therapy because she was having problems in her relationships with men and was somewhat depressed. Just prior to the session I will present she had missed two sessions because of holidays. She is being seen twice a week and I've worked with her for over a year.

Langs: Apparently you felt it necessary to give us some preliminary information—here, about the prior missed sessions. We'll take it as you present it, but I will ask someone else to present an hour with just a word or two of introduction, and then the details of a particular session without any other preliminary remarks. You seem to be telling us by implications that we need context for adequate listening. In any case, please continue.

Therapist: Well, this patient has had chronic cystitis since she was seventeen and first had intercourse. A few months ago she had a surgical procedure for some vaginal polyps which at the time were thought to be the cause of the infection. She was symptom free for about four months. However, while in the hospital she had an acute episode of urinary retention and managed to so antagonize the urologist that he virtually kicked her out of his office.

This patient had a severe fall about four years ago, suffering a concussion with vertigo and other complications, and there's some question of neurological complications. Several weeks ago, she was again hospitalized for a workup, and she had been angry at me for not visiting her, especially after her arteriogram, though she had called me several times. She felt that I hadn't offered her much support.

There was some evidence of a neurological lesion, a benign tumor or something, rather small, but they felt it had something to do with the urinary retention. The surgery was not done, and she left the hospital feeling that she had not received any help.

Now, to get to the session. She came in and said she had had a nice holiday. She didn't depend on anyone. She was by herself. She goes on to talk about how her bladder has continued to be a problem, and asks me, what did I tell her neurologist? She'd been to see him. Parenthetically, I had talked with him on the phone. I said, Why do you ask? She said, He was playing the psychiatrist. He was telling me about all sorts of reasons why I might not want to urinate because of an anniversary reaction about my father's death. He seemed to act at first as if he didn't know about that, even though I had told him about it before. He started treating me as a nut.

Then she stopped for about ten, fifteen seconds. She says, Maybe I brought it on myself. I feel like my body is falling apart—any sense of control that I had built up about myself and my life is gone. I didn't interpret that, although it's something we talked about in relation to the death of her father when she was about two years old. Her mother had had a psychotic depression around that time. I said, What does it mean to you that the doctor treats you like a psychiatric patient? And she says, How I present myself may cause him to dismiss me. She didn't answer my question.

Langs: Let's say something now about listening, because you've intervened twice. What can anyone say about the listening process as applied to this material? (Pause.) What are we looking for?

Discussant: An adaptive context.

Langs: Yes, we're looking for an adaptive context. Is one identifiable in this material?

Discussant: On the surface, we have the meaning of what she may see as the therapist's violation of her confidentiality.

Langs: So one possible adaptive context would be the violation of her confidentiality, a modification of the frame. That may prove central; it's been alluded to in the session. We have to see where it goes. Any other possible adaptive context?

Discussant: She began by mentioning the holidays and being by herself, and went on to her illness and treatment.

Langs: What adaptive context do you identify there?

Discussant: Feeling abandoned by the doctor, by her therapist. His not visiting her in the hospital, her view of doctors as unsympathetic and not taking her problems seriously.

Langs: So there are two ways of putting it, and it involves another possible adaptive context. There's a number of them. Let's identify and sort them out. Yet another is the holiday, which could refer either to her missing the session or to her being alone, without family, divorced, or whatever, that is, something outside of the therapeutic relationship. The therapist's not visiting her in the hospital hasn't come up in this session specifically, in terms of an immediate adaptive context, but it may be in the background. We'll see. What other adaptive context can we mention?

Discussant: You could really combine all three: the experience of his not visiting her in the hospital, the violation of confidentiality and the doctor's not caring about her.

Langs: Well, an adaptive context must be linked to a specific event, at least as a definitive starting point.

Discussant: It could be linked to the therapist's talking to the neurologist about her and her feeling that the therapist doesn't care about her, doesn't bother to visit her when she's sick, doesn't recognize her needs, and the like.

Langs: See, but here you're confusing the adaptive context with dynamics. I'm trying to get you to organize your thinking. The two are related, but try to first isolate the adaptive context itself; then develop dynamic meanings from the additional associations. The adaptive context is a specific event or set of events that sets off all of this, and as a rule you can see that they are interactional events, external events, though it could be an internal experience as well, say her menstrual period. That could be an adaptive context. But we want to separate that from the meanings the patient gives to it, from its latent content, and from the fantasies or perceptions it evokes. It really helps you to sort out your thinking a lot better. But you're coming back to her feeling traumatized by the way the doctor treated her.

Discussant: I think I'm focusing on three adaptive contexts: number one, the break in confidentiality; number two, the therapist's not visiting her in the hospital; and number three, though it doesn't have to do with the therapist directly, the neurologist's treating her like a psychiatric patient.

Langs: Right, that's three. You see, now you are identifying separate primary adaptive tasks. Next you can assign them manifest and latent meanings, and then you can define the relationship between these contexts. Finally, you can organize all of these associations around each context and derive separate and clustered meanings, fantasies and perceptions. Now, can you identify any other adaptive context?

Discussant: I was thinking of the missed sessions.

Langs: Yes, we said the missed sessions on the holidays.

Discussant: There's also her illness.

Langs: Yes, the illness and the hospitalization could also be an adaptive context. I wanted to show you that there are many possibilities, and that as this patient goes on her material will guide us toward the one or two that are most significant and immediate. We're going to let her direct the way, unless one thing happens, which is already happening. Which is what?

Discussant: The therapist interferes.

Langs: Yes, unless the therapist interferes. It's like a compass: if you let her go free, she'll get around to it. But if you keep a magnet around, you'll have trouble, you'll fix her bearings, her focus. You're going to be distorting the natural flow.

So by and large, it's our place initially to not intervene, at least not until we begin to sort out these possibilities. And recognizing that there are many possible adaptive contexts, you can see that the therapist's interventions are somewhat arbitrary—he has made no effort to utilize any of the adaptive contexts. His interventions reflect his listening to the material on what level so far?

Discussant: Manifest content.

Langs: The manifest level: "Why do you ask?" is a question.

What could it communicate unconsciously, in terms of what
the patient hears, in terms of the patient's listening process?

Discussant: His question could imply: You're not entitled to
know all the privileged communications between doctors. I
mean he's not going to give this information to her as readily
as he gives it out to the neurologist.

Langs: It could mean that. What general qualities does it
have?

Discussant: It's defensive.

Langs: In terms of unconscious communication, defensive
and what?

Discussant: Condescending.

Langs: Yes, there's a certain degree of condescension, of
anger and annoyance. Even though it's well-meaning. If you
want to know why the patient asked, what would be the
appropriate "intervention"?

Discussant: Tell me what you're concerned about in my
talking to the neurologist?

Langs: No. It would be silence. The patient will tell you why.
Again, we're after Type Two derivatives, not manifest
content. If you want manifest content, you will ask this kind of
question. And if you don't, if you want her to build the
important adaptive context for you, to organize the derivatives for you, you'll just sit back and let it unfold. You'll ask a
silent question, to yourself. And you'll then find out: Is Langs
right, that a modification of the frame will be more important
than any other adaptive context, or is he wrong? We'll see. We
want the communicative field to be as open as possible.

Discussant: When she asks him what he said to the

neurologist, you're suggesting that the therapist should first sit back and let her go on.

Langs: We have to get into the whole issue of whether he should have modified the confidentiality of the therapy. We'll discuss that when she tells us what it means to her. The answer will be evident.

Discussant: What about the persistent patient who's going to look at you and say, "Well…? Tell me"?

Langs: If you have indeed given information to someone else about the patient, your responsibility should be to share it with the patient as well. I didn't even bring that up, because obviously I feel that it's your responsibility not to share information with *anybody* else; that there's no constructive reason to do so. None whatsoever. So the whole question of should you reveal what you say or not becomes irrelevant, because it should not, on principle, be done in the first place. Ever. I don't want to get into that issue until we have enough material from the patient to shape a response, and until we begin to discuss the frame more specifically.

Therapist: Somewhere in here I did say to her that I would tell her what I said. I had spoken to him with her permission, but I said to her that I thought it was important as to how she was feeling about me right now that she tell me what she felt I had told him, and that I'd answer her question later on.

Langs: Yes, to let it unfold. This is generally the way in which it is handled by therapists, and we'll see how she actually responds to it so we can decide for ourselves if this is the right approach. Now, the second intervention was also in the form of a question.

Therapist: Yes. I said, What did it mean to you that he treated you like a psychiatric patient? I was asking her if she thought I had told this guy she was nuts.

Langs: Yes, she already said that she thought so.

Therapist: No, she said he treated her like a nut. He did the same thing to me on the phone when I spoke to him.

Langs: Manifest content, latent content. He treated her like a nut, and she asks, What did you say to him? I don't think we have to go very far to say, What did you tell him, you must have told him I was nuts. That is an evident inference.

Therapist: I told him that there was no possible...

Langs: I don't want to know...no...no...I don't want to know that. She doesn't know it, I don't want to know it right now. I want to know what she's working over. She doesn't know what you said to him. She just knows that he treated her like an insane person, so she figures that you had something to do with that. That's pretty obvious. But you asked her, What did it mean to you?

Therapist: Trying to get her to say just that.

Langs: Yes, you're trying to get her to explicitly tie this to you.

Therapist: To bring it into the transference ...

Langs: Don't use that word that way.

Therapist: In relation to the relationship.

Langs: In relation to her relationship with you.

Therapist: With me.

Langs: You're going to have major nontransference components here, I can promise you.

Therapist: Its already been a big part of her therapy.

Langs: But wait, let's not get ahead of ourselves. You wanted her to say something. You were leading her to say something specific about yourself. Let's see if your intervention will do that. It's a question. What kind of unconscious communication will the patient hear?

Discussant: You think I'm crazy too.

Langs: Please clarify.

Discussant: That the patient is crazy, or that the therapist thinks she is. The therapist is saying to the patient, Well, what did you mean, what did you think? He seems to be saying—implying, that is—that the patient is misperceiving reality; that's she's crazy.

Langs: It may be an implied question, something about the therapist's wondering what she has picked up from the neurologist, and you believe that the patient may feel that the therapist is raising the question so he can tell her how wrong she is.

Discussant: Yes.

Langs: That may be part of it. What general qualities does this question have?

Discussant: Denial, exonerating himself...

Langs: Yes, it could lead to that; that could be implied. It is treating her something like a nut already, in a certain sense. What else though? (Pause.) It's evident in the intervention, which is very controlling and manipulative: I want you to say something, I'm going to lead you to it. It has a very forceful, controlling, and manipulative quality. You have to know that, as I said earlier, in order to understand the material that's going to follow. If you don't realize that your intervention has those attributes, you'll never relate it to the subsequent associations or to any of this material.

So we're beginning to hear something of how the patient communicates. We're also hearing something of how the therapist listens and communicates, and that has to do with what we have to scrutinize about ourselves and our own interventions.

Therapist: I must apologize. I see that I did not write out my notes for the balance of this session. If I may, I would like to go on to the next hour. Many of these themes reappear.

Langs: Well, that's unfortunate. We were beginning to develop some important silent hypotheses, but so be it. Let's continue with what you have.

Therapist: She comes in and wishes me a happy new year. She starts in talking about this neurologist again, feeling he had dismissed her as a nut. She tells me she's gotten some books on neurology. She thought it was information she was entitled to but wasn't getting from the doctor. I said then, It seems that this is one way of dealing with being dismissed by people, that by going to try and find the information yourself, you try to turn a bad situation into a good one and try to keep yourself from feeling bad about yourself.

Langs: Yes, here too we hear an opening fragment, the crystallization of the therapist's listening process. And without spelling it out in detail for the moment, the intervention suggests that the therapist is operating almost entirely on the cognitive level. Just a moment ago, as we heard the initial fragment of the previous hour, I had begun to think in terms of the interactional sphere, of these forceful interventions as some form of projective identification into the patient. I had begun to think about both spheres: the cognitive and the interactional.

I would like to pause a moment and share some thoughts with you. For one, I would be very happy if someone could generate a different title for this book—something besides *The Listening Process*—because the area that we are exploring really involves all intaking processes, in both patient and therapist. And while I am, of course, using the term *listening* in its widest sense, it would help to have a more apt term for this aspect of the therapeutic interaction: the intaking process, the incorporative process, incorporation and metabolism—something of that sort.

There are many limitations to the term *listening process*. First of all, the intaking process actually includes all sensory modalities: not only the auditory, but also the visual, sometimes touch and kinesthetic, and even pain. But second, listening is primarily a cognitive term and it reflects the emphasis in classical psychoanalytic theory on the cognitive sphere. It thereby tends to place the interactional aspects to the periphery, leaving much of it to the Kleinians and neglecting the processing of projective identifications and role and self-image pressures as well.

So we are actually dealing with all intaking processes. On the part of the therapist, we think of him as attempting to experience all of the dimensions of the patient's communications: whatever the patient is putting into the therapist; whatever the patient is saying or conveying cognitively; whatever pressures exist in the relationship, including all thoughts, fantasies, and affects, as well as all interactional vectors.

Finally, I can think of one more objection to the term *listening process*—namely, that it suggests a basically passive image for the therapist. And while this has its relevance and is primary, actually, for both patient and therapist, it would tend to lead us to neglect the active qualities of listening: the ultimate efforts at synthesis and even the immediate unconscious selectivity that may be involved. It also disregards the ever present spiraling effect, the manner in which the listener evokes the very communications and interactional pressures that he is experiencing from the other person, and the inevitability of subjective coloring in all aspects of listening.

All of this is a way of saying that I am well aware that my previous discussion of projective identification, introjective identification, and containing and metabolizing is relatively incomplete. As a classically trained psychoanalyst, I have tended to stress the cognitive realm, although I have, from time to time, attempted to define the object relationship dimension, role and image pressures, and what I would term the *interactional dimension*—the influence of the patient's and the therapist's projective identifications and the introjective identification process. The listening process defined in its totality reminds us again of its remarkable intricacies. It requires much of the therapist, who, as you would expect, must monitor each of these levels, must discover the most meaningful dimension for a given interlude, must determine both his and his patient's contributions, must validate each silent hypothesis with communications (not only within the realm he considers dominant, but also in the other two realms, to whatever extent feasible), and must then shape an appropriate intervention.

So you can all see why it is taking so much time to delineate the listening process, not only to identify its components, but also to put it into practice and develop some proficiency with it. It helps me to understand why my own concepts have been evolving and expanding with each presentation, and with each week's discussion. And whatever my inevitable initial biases may have been and, certainly, we have to begin somewhere—I hope that we will arrive at a relatively complete conceptualization before we finish this phase of the course.

We will now apply the listening in each of these basic spheres. Shall we term them two areas, cognitive and interactional? Or three?—cognitive, object relational, and interactional mechanism. The latter seems most sensible and it is an approach that would, by the way, be in keeping with some recent remarks made by Sandler (1976), who insisted upon a firm distinction between, on the one hand, projective identification–introjective identification and, on the other, unconscious efforts by the patient to evoke self-images and role responses in the therapist or analyst—an aspect of listening that he felt pertained to the object relations sphere and not to the Kleinian theory of projective identification.

We won't split hairs, and I think it would be best to consider these three basic realms—cognitive, interactional mechanism, and object relational—and to include each dimension when we are listening to and experiencing communications from either patient or therapist. In our own work we must apply it both to our own listening process as therapists and to our understanding of the patient's listening process—responses to our communications. As you would expect, it is in this latter area that we would be most inclined to develop blind spots and to bypass the possibility that we are generating projective identifications—especially pathological ones—or that we are attempting inappropriately to evoke a role response or self-image in the patient based more on our own countertransference-based needs than on any other factor.

And throughout this course, as I have said often now, we will think of the listening process as a spiraling process, as essentially interactional in each of these spheres, in that we will acknowledge the possibility of unconscious promptings and evocations, of responses with their own qualities of provocation, and of second-order responses that are a mixture of further evocations and passively received communications. We know, then, that though we may select a particular point to initiate our investigation of a given sequence, there are always prior factors. And there is always a mixture of activity and passivity, reality and fantasy, consensual truth and idiosyncratic distortion—all of which we will endeavor to sort out.

Now let's apply these principles to this material in regard to both the patient and the therapist. Perhaps if you read this segment again, your colleagues can help you to work it over in terms of the listening process.

Discussant: Before we do that, I wonder if you'd be willing to go back to the situation I described last week—where I left a session five minutes early. Could you identify these three components in my intervention, as you see it, and in the patient's reaction? I mention it because I sense that there is some meaning in each of these areas in what both the patient and I did.

Langs: Well, perhaps briefly—the material isn't fresh. But what do you have in mind?

Discussant: Well, I begin to sense now that my informing her that I would have to end the session five minutes early was a way of dumping into her—if I can put it that way—the anxieties and pressures that I was experiencing from my own superiors regarding the presentation I had to make and my feelings about their unreasonable demands that I cancel her session or leave twenty minutes early. I can see that I kind of frustrated her, behaved in a seemingly unreasonable way, and that maybe too—and this was quite unconscious at the time—this might have been my way of doing back to her some of what I felt she was doing to me in the session.

Langs: Yes, here you must rely heavily on your own subjective responses to your intervention and use a sorting out process in terms of influences from outside relationships, especially the relationship with the patient. The announcement that you would be shortening the session undoubtedly constituted a projective identification into the patient and generated interactional pressures that I believe we discussed last week. So, we would suspect that the patient experienced interactional pressures—here, our subjective sense of pressure is an important indicator of the presence of a projective identification, thought it must, of course, be subjected to validation. Do you—or does anyone else—have any idea as to its influence in the other two realms I have identified?

Discussant: Yes, if I may continue. I can also see now that cognitively—and this we certainly worked out in her associations—I was imposing a deprivation, a hurt and a rejection, and it was a kind of aggressive act—all of which she worked over in regard to my silences, if you remember.

Langs: Yes, and further self-analysis would reveal that the decision reflected a series of specific pathological unconscious fantasies and memories, and also introjects, which you would have to work toward identifying on your own and self-analytically resolve. That's an excellent piece of preliminary analysis. What, then, about the object relationship sphere?

Discussant: Well, there I must confess that I hadn't really given the matter any thought. It's not really clear to me.

Discussant: I think we said something last week about making her into the victim. In any case, it seems to me that the image imposed upon the patient is that of someone who is unwanted, some sort of demeaned self-image, and, as I said, some role as victim, as someone who is helpless. Something along that line.

Langs: Yes, that's quite true, and all these images and roles are actually quite inappropriate for the patient vis-à-vis the therapist. That is, they are imposed upon her based on the therapist's countertransferences rather than as a result of inevitable roles and images that would derive from valid interpretations and the proper management of the framework—as well as from just being a patient.

That particular incident lends itself well to this kind of analysis and, as I recall, the patient herself went on to speak of feeling somewhat demeaned and mistreated. Of course, with this kind of summary you can't expect to develop validation; let's just accept it as an exercise for the moment. Now what about the patient's response?

Discussant: Well, as I said last week, I felt considerable pressure when she stood up to leave, and I experienced it largely in the area of self-image and role evocation. I felt that she was trying to make me look bad and destructive, hurtful and dangerous, and the like.

Langs: Your comment leads to an important point: each therapist will have tendencies to experience the patient's and his own communications in one of the three realms, and to formulate in a particular area, and there may be tendencies to neglect other spheres. You respond on an object relations level, while another therapist might stress interactional mechanisms. The goal, of course, is to be open to all three levels of experience and conceptualization.

I want to point out that it is here, as I believe I said last week in regard to self-image responses in the therapist, that you must carefully sort out the contributions from both yourself and the patient. That is, Was her getting up to leave an effort to make you feel that way based largely on some inappropriate and pathological need within the patient? Or was it a reflection of your actually having behaved in those ways and therefore an attempt to help you to become conscious of the implications of your behavior? That is, there may have been some awareness on the part of the patient that you were acting somewhat blindly.

Remember: in identifying a role pressure or evoked self-image, you always have the additional task of determining the circular interaction involved—what you have contributed as distinct from any pressures from the patient—and then you still have the responsibility to sort out how much of what you have experienced is distorted, and how much is valid and perceptive.

In regard to self-images, therapists will often repudiate pressures of this kind from patients, either because the particular self-image is incompatible with their idealized self-image, or because the self-image involved touches upon countertransference-based vulnerabilities. And often the two go together. So let's remember that, as is true also for the cognitive sphere, in the interactional mechanism and object relationship spheres it is our goal not only to properly identify the nature of the relevant unconscious contents and mechanisms but also to evaluate the extent to which they are pathological or nonpathological.

So, to finish this exercise, on the cognitive level the patient was letting you see what it feels like to suddenly be deserted. Well, perhaps I put that too interactionally; cognitively, the unconscious communication is that the patient wishes to leave you, to hurt and abandon you, to express aggression toward you—undoubtedly, in part, as a means of alerting you to the unconscious implications of your own intervention. There too, however, we would want to trace out the specific unconscious fantasies, memories, and introjects involved on the cognitive level, and not simply settle for these general impressions.

Finally, on the level of projective identification, you could sense that the patient is creating interactional pressures upon you—a point that I believe you made last week—and it is important to recognize that the delineation of a projective identification is based on a subjective experience of interactional pressures, of fantasies and other contents being pressured toward you, being evoked within you, though not in some simplistic sense that excludes your own misidentification, as well as processing, of these pressures, or even your refusal to be open to them, and to contain them. The concept implies, rather, a sense of interactional pressure that can then be validated both subjectively and through the patient's additional material, and in the other basic spheres.

So this action is in part a postulated projective identification of contents and fantasies related to your own decision to cut the session short. It is a pathological reprojection into you of the very frustration, pressures, hostility, and the like that you had placed into the patient. Eventually, all of this must be identified in terms of specific unconscious contents and mechanisms. Here, for example, we detect a shift toward action, the defensive use of projective identification itself, and some degree of denial. In all, then, we would see her behavior as an effort by the patient to interactionally project back into you these disturbing contents and mechanisms which she was unable to contain and metabolize, to consciously understand and adapt to. She now wishes to reburden you with them and to have you metabolize and reprocess them, hopefully toward—well, here, I would believe that it would have been toward the rectification of the frame, toward seeing her for the full session, as well as toward the necessary appropriate interpretations.

Well, even though we did not go back to the specific material, I hope that as an exercise this has proven helpful, and that it shows the need for the therapist to be open to experiencing the patient's communications in each of these spheres, and the need to empathize with the patient as he or she experiences your interventions in each of these areas.

During this discussion, I've been trying to remember Bion's term for the listening process. I came across it recently in reading his commentaries in a volume of his collected papers called *Second Thoughts* (1967)—it's *intuiting*. So it would be the *intuiting process*, a term he prefers to listening because the latter is in the sensory realm while the most important psychoanalytic experiences and communications are nonsensual, related more to intuiting than to listening.

But you can see that here too, while his term frees us of certain misleading penumbras of meaning connected with the term *listening*, the intuiting process has its own, however different, set of drawbacks. It would tend to set aside the important cognitive aspects of the intaking process and would perhaps suggest an almost exclusive use of intuition, which would indeed be a most unfortunate inference. So perhaps the *intaking* process is most accurately descriptive, though I will continue to use the term *listening process* because it seems to me to be best understood by others, and because I am defining its qualities in a way that would include empathy, intuition, the entire nonsensual realm, and many other qualities as well.

Well, enough. Please review again the opening segment of this session so that we can apply the listening process to it.

Therapist: What I read earlier really went on over the course of about five or six minutes, during which she talked about this neurologist and how he didn't answer her questions but continued to ask her if there were some reason why, psychologically, she might have this urinary retention problem. And she had said afterwards that she had gone to the library and checked out some books on urology. And so on. We had been talking about this previously, about her attempts to reverse bad situations and make them into good ones to avoid her painful feelings.

Langs: And your intervention was?

Therapist: And so I turned this back into that and said that I think here again is one way you try to deal with feeling dismissed. You then try to turn the bad feelings about this doctor into good feelings about him, so that you won't feel that you're losing him in some way at a time when you need him.

Discussant: What specifically had she just said prior to your intervention?

Therapist: She said something about information that she felt she was entitled to, which involved whether she thought that I had told him that she was crazy. She said that's the way he was treating her and how she had been treated previously by another neurologist.

Langs: Okay, let's do this as a mini-exercise with each segment. At this point in the course, I would like to help you synthesize some of the concepts we've been working over and to expand them wherever we can. So. What do you hear in this material, and in this intervention?

Discussant: In the context of the last session, in which it came up that the therapist had spoken to the neurologist, I hear her still dealing with that issue. She seems to be saying that doctors don't give you the information you need to have; there's a question of trusting them. She goes to look it up in the book, rather than just taking what the doctor has to say. She doesn't feel that the neurologist took her seriously, and with all this talk about the neurologist I wonder if she's not displacing onto him her concerns about the relationship with the therapist and confidentiality, as well as other issues she brings up in talking about the neurologist.

Langs: Now, if you were to talk in terms of the facets of the listening process, what have you done? And what has the therapist done in his intervention? And where are the differences? You've given me a kind of loose formulation, a silent hypothesis about this material. Can you identify some of the technical tools you have used in arriving at that formulation?

Discussant: I'm not sure what you mean by technical tools.

Langs: Well, I always want to hear your assessment in its natural state at first—your ideas and how they are shaped. But if we're going to derive general principles from them, we then have to identify the principles or concepts you've used. The tools, as it were.

Discussant: The initial thing that I was listening for was that we know from the previous session that there was a modification of the frame in terms of confidentiality.

Langs: Right. And how are you using that—as what?

Discussant: As an adaptive context.

Langs: Yes, so the first step you took was that you identified an adaptive context. That is, you found it helpful to organize this material around the adaptive context of the previous session in terms of a modification of the frame. That gave you a way of organizing these associations which led you to feel that the material was displaced from the therapeutic relationship onto the neurologist.

All right. Does anyone else have anything to say about this initial material? (Pause.) Then I'll try to be very brief. There are two comments I would make: one is that just this morning, with another presentation, I generated a principle which I think is very important here—one we have already seen in operation in earlier seminars here. It comes up again because I have been giving a good deal of thought to the failure of psychoanalysts to write specifically about the listening process. Now it is true that there have been some papers on such matters as empathy, intuition, trial identification, and the like (see Langs, 1976b), but I refer here to specific investigations of the details of how we listen, of how we formulate the material from the patient, and of how we validate these formulations. Clearly this is a most crucial aspect of our work as therapists and analysts. So when you find a blind spot of this proportion, when you discover what seems to be a tacit and unconscious agreement to develop a form of therapy without identifying its most basic tool, without sorting it out and reaching consensual validation, then you have to try to understand this avoidance. And of course, it's true about human beings in general that we avoid whatever causes us anxiety and disorganization. For psychotherapists and psychoanalysts, that whatever is preeminently the realm of countertransference. So you always look there, and there are some very interesting discoveries to be made. You find, over and over again, interventions of the sort made here. And you learn why we prefer to accept the notion that you can listen to this material in all sorts of different ways, that there really isn't one basic and correct way of listening, but many; not one basic model of therapy, but many. This easy eclecticism.

As you now know, I do not subscribe to such notions. I believe—no, I have found empirically—that there is one basic model for listening and for therapy, that it can be adapted for all patients, and that all patients unconsciously express a need for it again and again.

So we hear a set of associations about the neurologist, about his insensitivity, his not giving her the information she wants and needs so that she has to go to other sources to obtain what she feels she's entitled to. And the therapist then responds on what level? (Pause.) We know that this could be listened to in terms of the manifest content, which I just played back, or could be listened to in terms of some hunch we have about it, some inferences we could make in terms of Type One derivatives, and if we're getting more and more sophisticated our main Type One derivatives would always refer to the therapeutic relationship and the me–not-me interface. So we might also suggest that she's saying something about herself. We very often treat associations as if they were dream elements—each segment regarded as a self-representation. You could listen like that, monitoring the material for representations of herself, something about her not communicating, her not being forthright, her needs for defensiveness, her nastiness. That's one level: The "me" part of the me–not-me interface. But then there is the other level, the not me–not-me. Here we find the therapist's not communicating, his not telling her things, his not providing her what she needs. So we could, through Type One derivatives and without knowing a specific adaptive context, get some notions, make some inferences. Maybe all of this refers to the therapist. Now, as we become more precise we can take the next step, too, and not think, as most therapists rather self-servingly do, that this is all just some transference fantasy. We'd ask ourselves, Is this partially or almost entirely a valid perception? To what extent is it distorted, a fantasy? We could consider both aspects.

So we could do all of that. But then, if we have a specific adaptive context such as the alteration in the frame, we could then derive very specific meanings in terms of her references to books and readings and what is made public, and could relate it directly to her sense that her needs are being disregarded in her therapy. In other words, we would take these as *commentaries* on how she perceived the therapist's sharing information about her with the neurologist, and would then try to sort out how much is realistic and how much distorted, as well as how much the therapist was doing consciously and deliberately, if we can decide that, and how much he was doing without being aware of it. Certainly the therapist should get to know all that. He meant to do well by the patient, and it comes out, of course, as a compromise. Which has to do with the input from the therapist, the input from the neurologist, the input from the patient. It is an amalgam of that kind—with the emphasis, for now, on the therapist.

Discussant: Could we discuss what is appropriate within the therapeutic context for the therapist to have done, given the fact that—was it your referral to the neurologist or did she go to him on her own?

Therapist: She had a neurologist before, but this is somebody that she had gotten when she had her fall.

Discussant: Because there are very hazy situations like, a patient that you see—it may not be as much in this case—who say, has chronic headaches, which probably have some psychological basis, who then is requesting a referral for more evaluation. What do you consider the appropriate stance for the therapist?

Langs: That's the next segment of the course: the ground rules. I'll just say, in brief, that I've learned first of all, that I can't fully trust any physician, therapist, or analyst. I've seen too much damage done. I don't make specific referrals. I will interpret to a patient who has somatic symptoms his fear of going to a doctor, which I know nonverbally communicates by implication some kind of directive, but it does so only through an interpretation of the defenses and anxieties involved. And I would expect him to take it from there. Patients have many more resources within themselves and in their lives than therapists give them credit for. So I just do the necessary interpreting and the material will fall along such lines. If the patient has, let's say, a recurrence of his headaches and just keeps coming to his therapist and doesn't go and have it checked out, he will be communicating derivatives having to do with his wish to believe that it's entirely psychological and his dread of finding out that it could be a tumor or something like that. I don't make a commitment either way; I just do the analytic work. I maintain as true a sense of neutrality as possible and don't make the referral.

Discussant: Suppose the patient says to a doctor he has consulted, I see Dr. Langs for psychotherapy, and this doctor is then set to wondering about the psychiatric component in the patient's condition. And he gives you a call on the phone, with the patient's permission. What then?

Langs: I don't modify confidentiality under any circumstances.

Discussant: What would you tell this physician?

Langs: It depends. There are a few physicians who don't get angry; there are some now who understand the need for confidentiality a bit, but many of them just get angry and furious, and think you're crazy and all the rest. But I will not under any circumstances modify confidentiality. In fact, most of my patients would know in advance, just from having worked with me, that it's inconceivable that I would talk to another physician about them. So it's seldom an issue. And if it does come up, it's being used to try to modify the bipersonal field and its frame, and to modify the nature of the communications and the therapeutic work. So we analyze it.

I know that these are important and pressing questions, but for the moment they're not central to the listening process. I promise we will soon go over all of these issues. We couldn't deal with the framework until we knew how to listen, because the patient is going to teach you what to do with the frame. You would know the answer to your question if you had been able to listen to your patients in terms of their derivative communications. This is all that I'm playing back to you.

I want to make one other point about this intervention, one bipersonal field and felt that she was saying something about the prevalence of a Type C field where communication has been damaged. It may also have Type B qualities, because it sounds like there's been a lot of damage and chaos effected through projective identification, through both patient and therapist putting things into the field that are disturbing and disruptive. So the problem is not entirely one of damage through obliteration; it's a mixture I want to sort out as I listen.

So I have a silent hypothesis: there's something damaging the communicative flow between patient and therapist—and then the therapist intervenes. And he intervenes in a way that tells me immediately that one of the factors disrupting the communicative qualities of the field is precisely his interventions. I have an hypothesis and am collecting data for it from the patient as well as from the therapist. He happens to intervene at that point, and it really sheds light on how she's experiencing the therapeutic relationship.

Once again we have an intervention without an adaptive context. Earlier, I had started to formulate an hypothesis that I have now validated many times over regarding this blind spot, this unconscious conspiracy of silence among therapists and analysts in respect to the listening process. I had raised the question as to why therapists would rather not use the concept of the adaptive context; would rather not organize this material rigorously, in terms of Type Two derivatives; would rather not make full use of the listening process itself. Perhaps you can begin to sense the drift of my argument. Empirically, when a therapist misses the adaptive context, what is it usually related to? (Pause.) Would you expect the adaptive context to fall within the therapeutic relationship or outside of it? I know that's a loaded question.

Therapist: I'm taking a little objection to this because of the next remark I made. This is a girl who uses a lot of denial. To me the issue was to establish a context—not the adaptive context, but a context related to me—that if she were to agree that she was feeling dismissed by the other doctor, she would then agree she was feeling dismissed by me—which was my last interpretation from the previous hour, as I now recall.

Langs: Look: I'm not addressing myself to this specific intervention in isolation; I'm using it as a model to establish some concepts. You're giving us a look ahead. What I'm doing is freezing the situation at this point and identifying what the patient is experiencing. If you then went ahead and rectified the error I will define, that's all well and good. We'll have a chance to hear how the patient responded to your initial intervention and we'll then have a chance to hear how she alters her reaction with your second comment. I'm simply asking that you let it stand as the patient heard it for the moment. You may be heading somewhere; that's fine. But for the moment this is where you're at, and it gives me a chance to make some remarks that are open to validation.

Most adaptive contexts significant to the patient in psychotherapy are within the therapeutic relationship. This is especially so when the therapist does not use the listening process to the fullest extent. This is an empirical finding and a repetitive clinical observation. In essence, then, therapists work with manifest content and Type One derivatives in many therapeutic situations as a means of avoiding adaptive contexts and Type Two derivatives related to themselves—as an expression of unresolved countertransferences and their defensive counterparts in the listening process. And I suggest that therapists have neglected to learn how to listen for the reason that if they did so they would discover that their patients know far more about them than they want to realize or can tolerate; that they have many more problems than they wish to acknowledge; and that their patients unconsciously perceive and work them over far more than they are willing to recognize. And this is absolutely typical of an intervention without an adaptive context: it is almost always made about an outside relationship and it includes an unconscious invitation to exclude the therapeutic relationship—to create a bastion. And it turns out this way again and again.

The patient plays his role in this too. He unconsciously welcomes the bastion, since it momentarily alleviates his anxieties. He fears communicating openly and directly to you, partly because of his own inner need for defense and partly because of your therapeutic approach. But in any case, especially when he has been traumatized and you become a fearful figure, he will avoid a direct confrontation unless the situation becomes so intense that it is grossly disruptive. But in most instances he will be afraid to tell you directly that you're making a mistake—that you're hurting him—because he fears your reaction, because you have become an actual threat to him. And this actuality is then elaborated upon on the basis of his own unconscious fantasies and introjects. It is, as always, a circular, spiraling process, one with mixtures of both reality and fantasy.

So the patient is more than willing to communicate manifest contents that you can refer to directly, thus joining him in a kind of denial mechanism—Type C mechanisms— and you'll both talk about some outside relationship and obliterate the therapeutic relationship. And sometimes, if you're a little bit more sophisticated, you'll take it all as a displaced fantasy—a Type One derivative. But still, if you're prepared to deal with yourself and where your patient is really at, you'll take it as Type Two derivatives and you'll discover yourself.

Discussant: Where are the Type Two derivatives in this material?

Langs: Here, Type Two derivatives could be developed around the adaptive context of the therapist breaking confidentiality. This would lead to the formulation that the patient experienced this as a kind of hurt, betrayal, and insensitivity—as her needs not being attended to—and that she felt that he hadn't been listening to her. Also, that unconsciously she's been telling him, despite her conscious sanction, that this is something destructive and inappropriate. These associations take on very specific meanings as a commentary on that deviation—as perceptions—and, while there may be some of her own distorted fantasies mixed in, we can't determine them as yet.

Discussant: Doesn't that overlap with Type One derivatives? With ideas we would get if we monitored this material in terms of the therapeutic relationship by itself?

Langs: Yes, that's what I said: that if you are sophisticated enough, this is how the listening process would go. Let's say you don't happen to know the adaptive context for the moment. You then monitor the manifest content in terms of Type One derivatives as self-representations and object-representations—especially of you, as therapist. You're doing all of that and you emphasize the you-as-therapist aspect. And you're taking these communications as what I like to call "commentaries" so that you don't initially say they are mere fantasies. They are commentaries that contain fantasies and perceptions. We then turn to the sorting-out process, based, as I said before, largely on self-knowledge.

Now if you're sensitive enough, you've already taken in a lot that you have applied to yourself. Then, when it suddenly occurs to you what the adaptive context is, or when the patient suddenly reminds you of it or mentions it for the first time, you can organize that material in an extremely immediate, meaningful, and beautiful way. The Type One derivative is preliminary and lacks the specificity you must have to intervene.

You see, the listening process generates interventions in a way that I really had not seen before. What I've said in principle to you is that if you don't have the adaptive context, sometimes you play back the themes for the patient— especially in the presence of a strong therapeutic context. And that's exactly what Type One derivative listening produces. You've got some themes, you don't have the adaptive context, you sense some meaning in the relationship with you, you as a rule identify a therapeutic context, and you play back the relevant themes to the patient—hoping and expecting these to give you, as they often will, the specific adaptive context.

So, coming back to the therapist's intervention, it is, for the moment at least, on a manifest level, accepting the displace- ment away from the therapeutic relationship onto this other person. It deals with qualities of badness: it is not you, but the patient who is bad; it is this doctor who is bad, and this is how you—and the patient—are dealing with it. In a kind of general way, I must say that if you had stopped with this intervention I would have categorized it—I have a new favorite term—as a form of *psychoanalytic cliché*. That type of communication is the single most important contribution from the therapist to a Type C field—which may well be the most common communi- cative bipersonal field around. I have begun to realize that one of the things that must absolutely drive therapists crazy is the Type C field with its negative, vacuumlike projective identifi- cations, its absence of meaning, and the destruction of meaning in general and in the things you say. I had not fully appreciated this particular threat to our integrity as thera- pists. Previously, I had stressed the disruptive effects of the patient's pathological projective identifications, his efforts to drive the therapist crazy (Searles, 1959), and the dangers and anxiety evoked by material from the patient that corresponds to the therapist's conflicts and vulnerabilities. But the Type C mode unconsciously is designed to destroy your basic functioning and your capacity to integrate and understand— to function as a therapist.

Bion (1977) said, and I'm just learning to understand it, that the Type C field—the term is not his, but he does address some of its communicative properties—is based on envy and the need to destroy the object for various reasons. He's the only one I know who has ever described these qualities, doing so in his own idiom and around different, but related issues. As you may know, the Kleinians believe that there's a certain degree of inherent or inborn envy. However, you don't have to consider it inborn; it can be a basic and early emotion to which more and more is added through the years. But for the Kleinians, envy is a central emotion. In addition to the object evoking envy, there are internal and fantasied sources of envy, and I'm beginning to realize that there's a lot of truth to that and that in the seemingly innocuous boring Type C field, there's a tremendous amount of destructiveness. Unconsciously, the patient is trying to destroy your capacity to think, formulate, and function, and much of this may well derive from unconscious envy, a thesis that I am presently attempting to explore.

Isn't it interesting? I had said to myself earlier today that I was going to get to that lecture about not using an adaptive context and its connection with the denial of countertransferences. And your first communication provides me that opportunity.

Another dimension that I have been mulling over relates to interactional mechanisms, the use of projective identification, in particular. And in this material, there are some qualities of projective identification, largely by the therapist for the moment. And I think that the patient has been conveying her experience of these projective identifications unconsciously in the material related to the neurologist. As you may recall, she had described him as rather forceful, probing, offering unfounded comments, withholding information, and, overall, placing into her a sense of attack, of confusion, and the like.

In a way, these verbal associations could be used to confirm a subjective impression that projective identification is in operation, and I would suggest that these last interventions— the therapist's questions and other comments—will also be experienced by this patient as pathological projective identifications, possibly as some type of disorganizing assault, a formulation that I will attempt to validate from the subsequent material. And I stress the need for confirmation, because the Kleinians do have a tendency to subjectively experience projective identifications from their patients and to respond rather quickly on that basis. Their published work indicates that they do not make efforts to validate these subjective experiences. There is always some temptation within the therapist when he experiences an affect or introjection from the patient to accept it at face value and to not attempt the necessary validation.

Implicit in these comments is my belief that we can learn to identify the presence of projective identification, based on experiences of interactional pressures, and to process these experiences in order to determine how much stems from the patient's efforts, and how much is idiosyncratic within the therapist. Some classical analysts have rejected the concept of projective identification entirely. They say they have never seen it. Well, that can hardly be the basis for the refutation of a psychoanalytic concept. These are abstractions drawn from interactional experiences, and abstractions are not visible. Have you ever seen a defense? Have you ever seen an unconscious fantasy? Bion (1977) makes a related point very clearly. In analysis we are not dealing primarily with the sensory mode; rather, we're dealing with the nonsensory— nonsensuous experience—what he calls the unknown. And he feels that you have to have special techniques for appreciating that realm.

Discussant: Would you say something more about how we experience projective identification?

Langs: That has to do with sensing what I call *interactional pressures*. Let's now take it from the patient's side. She comes in disturbed, there's disorganization, there's a lack of clarity. She feels she's being hurt and she's not understanding things. She goes on and talks in a kind of fragmented way, begins to confuse you and all, and you experience that confusion. I would formulate the presence of a projective identification at such a point. I would see it as having been initiated by the therapist. She feels it has been put into her, and now she's putting it back into the therapist. And I don't think this is all hocus-pocus. I don't think it's magic. I think that we can make that formulation and then validate it in the cognitive realm. That's the point: if you're right in the interactional sphere, you will get confirmation in the cognitive. If you're right in the cognitive, you'll get some interactional confirmation. That's the safeguard.

We won't adopt the approach that projective identification sounds kind of crazy, or primitive, so we'll just use cognitive stuff in psychotherapy. No. We can define some of its qualities, we can delineate some of our subjective experiences when faced with it. These we can use as criteria, along with some qualities of the patient's material, and can understand that we're going to validate any formulation developed primarily in one sphere in each of the other spheres.

So if you're feeling kind of oppressed, if you're feeling some sense of pressure, something being stirred up in you or something being taken away, suctioned out, or emptiness and lack of meaning, or whatever—this last is what I call *negative projective identification*, which may be a poor term, but I'm trying to describe that empty vacuumlike quality. So we process these experiences and try to understand them. That's the process I call *metabolizing*. I got the term from Fleiss (1942), who noted that we temporarily identify with the patient, metabolize that identificatory experience, separate ourselves once again, and make an interpretation. And we do that both cognitively and in the interactional sphere. That's really the essence of the listening process. And we consistently sort out how much comes from the patient and how much from ourselves.

So I think that here, there is some sense of projective identification, something the therapist put into her that she's putting back into him. Now, if you don't become conscious of the nature of the patient's projective identification, you may then unconsciously reproject it. Grinberg (1962) gave that a name: *projective counteridentification*. It sounds rather complex, but it means that you dumped it back into the patient without understanding it, and now she's got even more of a burden to carry.

We'll see now if any of this helps us understand the material. Go ahead.

Therapist: What I said then was that I think the same situation exists here, that...

Langs: No, no. She responded to you, you had finished your intervention. She must have said something.

Therapist: She just tried to take issue with it.

Langs: Yes, describe it, please; what sort of things did she say?

Therapist: She disputed my comment, said it wasn't really that way.

Langs: All right, so she kind of disagreed with you.

Therapist: She did disagree with the interpretation, and I said, I think the same situation exists with me. You felt in my not visiting you in the hospital and in our missing a session each week for the last two weeks that I've dismissed you in some way. She's talked about this, about her being a clinic patient, saying I don't care about her, and so on in relation to my not visiting her. But this is a distinct change from her previous feelings that she owed me considerable gratitude for having to pay only five dollars a session.

Langs: Okay now, is that the end of your intervention?

Therapist: I said, It's the same situation with me, that you feel that I dismissed you and that I didn't care about you.

Langs: I would like to comment on your intervention. There's one very important point which I have mentioned before but haven't really spelled out. You say these are things that you had worked over previously with her. All right. What about this intervention in terms of the listening process? Let's do something very simple here. How do you feel it reflects back what the therapist heard?

Discussant: I'm still not clear how the patient had responded to the first intervention.

Therapist: After the first intervention about the neurologist, she had sort of tried to deny it on the basis that to the extent that she read the books it allowed her to reconstitute him as a good object, and that the interpretation was no longer really true. She was trying to deny that she had felt that he had dismissed her, she just sort of pushed it aside. I said that I think this is an area where you've succeeded, but I think there's a situation that exists here between us, and that we have to recognize that something very similar is going on here with me.

Langs: I trust you are all experiencing the difficulties in listening to a presentation when it is not explicit and sequential. You wish to add something?

Therapist: And then I went ahead and said what I said: that she was feeling that she would lose him if...uh...she would lose me at a time when she needed me, that I wasn't available to her, and that now she was trying to avoid the pain of thinking about that fear of losing me.

Langs: Okay now, I want to ask a very basic question, which we should always keep in mind. To what extent do you feel that this intervention reflects having listened to the patient? Let's see if it corresponds to what the patient said.

Therapist: I said that she was trying to avoid the pain of feeling angry and dismissed by me, and that she feared that if she did talk about it, she would lose me at a time when she felt she needed me.

Langs: Yes, and I may add that you alluded to the missed sessions and to your not visiting her in the hospital.

Therapist: Right. I said, it was not just the hospital, but now we had also missed sessions.

Langs: Any comments about this in terms of the listening process? (Pause.) Well, if not, let me just point out that I would like you to appreciate that a great deal of what the therapist just said had not really been said by the patient. His point was that these are things that she had said before. I want to make two comments in response to that. Number one, you'll notice...

Discussant: Didn't you say that there were second-order Type Two derivatives present? That some of that was reflected in this material?

Langs: Yes, something of that sort had been formulated by us. But let me point out to you that we had identified an immediate adaptive context for this material which had to do with his recent telephone conversation with the neurologist. Was that true?

Therapist: It wasn't recent; it was about a month and a half ago.

Langs: Oh, so there wasn't a recent conversation. Okay, so we were in error. We must reformulate. Let's say that we have not identified an immediate precipitant related to the frame in this session. This is now quite confusing. Let me try to organize things a bit. You decided to address two issues: one was the recent holidays.

Therapist: She's been to the other neurologist recently and he treated her like a nut.

Langs: Right, but what I want to get across is that at this point in the session—I can say it correctly now—we do not know the adaptive context at all. She has not told it to us. You have made two assumptions about the adaptive context that are open to question and possible error. One context is the sessions missed recently because of the holidays; the other is that it still goes back to your not having visited her in the hospital.

So my first point is that she did not as yet allude to either of the postulated adaptive contexts in this session. These were silent hypotheses developed by the therapist that the patient had not as yet confirmed in any manner, and they were introduced by the therapist rather than by the patient. This leads me to stress a principle that I have mentioned before, namely, that each session should be created on its own terms. Bion (1972) said that we should enter the session without desire, memory, or understanding. We should allow the patient to recreate our understanding, and evoke our memory and recall. And I am adding the tenet that we should allow the basic communications to unfold on their own terms so that each session is a creation unto itself, so that any intervention that we would make in that session would then be based entirely on the material from the patient in that hour.

Now, I will say that occasionally, when you have a very important connecting link that the patient has omitted, when you are intervening based on a strong accumulation of derivatives from the hour at hand, you might well add the missing component, often stressing the patient's defensive need to avoid allusions to it—though that element is often the least vital and least often confirmed aspect of such an intervention. On the whole, the basic effort should be made to keep each session a separate creation. That it is an hour that is part of the continuous treatment situation is certainly true, but we would permit the patient to indicate the points of continuity rather than presupposing them. In this way—and again, it is Bion (1977) who has stressed this—we are more open than otherwise to the discovery of new truths, to new material and formulations that we might miss if we are too embedded in our preconceived ideas.

The second point is that while some of this material can be monitored as Type One derivatives related to the therapist, the patient has not as yet bridged the gap from this manifest material to the unconscious communications regarding the therapist. This link should also be allowed to unfold during the session. You formulate it as a silent hypothesis, and allow the patient to guide you, to move toward it, with...or the therapist, rather... therapy or the therapist, with the closer

derivatives and even a manifest to move toward it, rather
manifest reference to therapy or the therapist, with closer
derivatives and evan a immediately suggesting that the
material must relate to yourself long before the patient has
indicated such a connection, whether directly or indirectly. If
you are right about such an hypothesis, by the way, the
derivatives will become closer and closer to referring to
yourself, less and less disguised, and often the patient will get
around to saying something about you directly, though,
typically, not in a way directly involving that central adaptive
context. It's at that point that you can intervene if the patient
has given you all you will need. And if, in contrast, the
derivatives do not move toward her relationship with you, you
must spend your time reconsidering your hypothesis in
addition to considering the possible presence of resistances
within the patient, or of unconscious pressure from yourself to
avoid allusions to the therapeutic relationship.

Discussant: I'm not clear. You're talking about listening
and nonintervention, and that can be confusing. You so often
talk about the second-order Type Two derivatives that we
sometimes lose sight of the fact that the patient is not thinking
on the same wavelengths. And you do have an inclination—if
you think in the fashion that you are describing—to make
interventions based on Type Two derivatives which are not
conscious as yet to the patient. And yet, you say that is a
mistake.

Langs: No, no, I think the patient *does* think along Type
Two derivative lines. I think that when you make the proper
interpretation, when you have the adaptive context and the
derivatives, they understand exactly what you're talking
about. But that's because I wait for them to convey such
derivatives. Remember, we had agreed that we don't have an
adaptive context in this session. So we're going to take back
our initial formulation entirely now; it's a revision that we
should be prepared to make when any new light is shed on the
situation. We don't have an adaptive context for this session.
These are only Type One derivatives now. We cannot make a

definitive intervention here. We cannot make up the adaptive context for the moment. We should let the patient tell us what it's about.

Discussant: Aren't there some patients who are always skirting around this sort of thing, never quite making the bridge, where sometimes you have to become more active?

Langs: In my experience, more therapists than patients engage in such skirting around. In other words, if you learn how to listen it turns out that the patient really has been alluding to an adaptive context related to therapy, but you haven't recognized it. I find the opposite extremely rare, though it does occur in a Type C field. It is possible to have a patient who has defended and sealed off the adaptive context. But even your Type C patient lets you know from time to time what's prompting an intensification of their defenses or anxieties.

Discussant: But there are situations sometimes where you can guess pretty clearly what the adaptive context is, where you know that something happened in a previous session, and the patient will come in and be talking in rather obviously displaced terms but never comes around to the context. In such cases, do you think you could then mention, as an interpretation, what seems to be fairly clear, just to give the patient a clear adaptive context?

Langs: It is under those conditions that you should play back to the patient the derivatives most meaningfully related to the unmentioned adaptive context. Sometimes, if need be, it should be suggested that something has been set aside. In general, I've almost never had an experience with an obvious adaptive context, especially an alteration in the frame, where the derivatives did not come pouring out. Patients universally work this over very intensely and, as a rule, in the form of Type Two derivatives. But yes, certain adaptive contexts are kept out of the material, at times as a kind of conspiracy— misalliance and bastion—between patient and therapist.

Let's say you extended the hour five minutes. The patient
will work that over in the next session and will almost always
never mention it directly. So now it's up to you. And yes, you
can approach it by first playing back the derivatives, as Type
One derivatives, and the patient might then put it all together.
But when it's a major alteration in the frame, and the patient
avoids it, you might then also have to point out to the patient
that he's saying this and that, but that it seems that
something's being left out. You approach it from the side of the
defenses, of the avoidance. He'll always give you a lead;
patients always communicate unconsciously about these
things. So you say, It seems like you're leaving out something.
And you might add: something that actually happened. You
don't directly allude to it as yet, and, almost always, the
patient will then get around to it.

This is a matter of technique, but if the avoided adaptive
context did not entail a major alteration in the frame, I might
not introduce it myself at all. Instead, I would introduce all the
derivatives and would accept the patient's need to destroy
meaning in this session. I would interpret things about
destroying meaning, dealing with the defenses first—
assuming the relevant derivatives were available. This brings
up another point of technique which is becoming so much
clearer to me of late. There is a hierarchy of therapeutic tasks.
The basic classical statement is defense-resistance before
content, and ego before id. I would add: form before content;
communicative style and mode before content; reality before
fantasy; therapist before patient. We spent the first hundred
years of analysis studying contents and defenses, but when it
turns out that you can have content without available
meaning, and contents designed as fabrications and as a
means of destroying meaning and relatedness, you have to
realize that you have to get to the form of communication first.
That is, of course, a variation on the tenet, defense before
content, but it contains a somewhat new approach. You have
to have truly meaningful material before you can interpret
contents.

Discussant: That's interesting. This is a little bit off the
subject, but it's interesting because people from other

psychotherapeutic disciplines have been saying that for quite a while. For example, family therapists often emphasize that form is often more important than content, while analysts have accentuated content much more.

Langs: Yes, I have been apprised of some of this literature—family therapists are obviously in an interactional situation—but for the moment I want to do this empirically on my own. Then I will read.

The search for content is still the model used by many analysts, and often it's the patient's model of treatment as well: if you just tell me the right thing to talk about, if I just get the right memory and work it over, everything will be okay. They don't at all realize that such an approach—talking about topics the therapist has selected—will not generate a Type A field, but instead a Type B or C field. I've seen the most marvelous genetic material that could not be interpreted at all because, at the time, both patient and therapist were communicating in a Type B or C field.

So, medium before content, defenses before content, and all the rest. We must learn to look for opportunities to interpret the patient's communicative style and mode and to be patient enough to know that such interpretations are every bit as important for the resolution of his neurosis as interpretations of the specific derivatives of his unconscious fantasies, memories, and introjects. In addition, in keeping with what I said about the frame, the therapist's contributions to a distorted communicative mode, when present, must be rectified in actuality, and interpreted first. In fact, that step is fundamental to the interpretive work and to the insightful resolution of the pathology contained within the patient's communicative style.

So our goal is to allow the patient to create the session and our interpretations, knowing that our silence or other interventions contribute. Nonetheless, we permit the patient to shape everything that takes place within the therapy, a point rather nicely made by de Racker (1961) in a paper on the use of the patient's communications to shape interpretations with severely disturbed analysands. And patients will put

into you everyything you need for an interpretation, as well
as, in fact, everything you need to rectify a disruptive reality.
They will provide you the ingredients, and all you need do is
recombine them through the development of Type Two
derivatives built around the appropriate adaptive context into
a new whole—giving them a new shape that reveals their
unconscious meanings beginning with the nature of the
patient's communicative mode and resistances and extending
from there into intrapsychic contents.

Therapist: Well, my comment was directed toward a
constant theme that I have been hearing from this woman,
which has to do with her feelings that she's always the bad
one. She's constantly trying to rectify whatever field she's in,
in a way that she looks bad, so that it's never the other
person's fault. They're simply too busy, or whatever. I'm
trying to get her to the point of realizing that this is what she's
doing, so I have to be more directive and I don't like to be.

Langs: No, no, that's untrue, it doesn't follow.

Therapist: Well, I disagree with that.

Langs: Fine, please do. But allow the patient's responses to
these interventions to decide which of us is right.

Therapist: You talk about what is an analyzable derivative,
but I'm saying that I've worked with this woman for over a
year and I know how you have to speak with her in order to get
her to say something that's analyzable. She goes on and on
without analyzable derivatives and it would not change
unless I intervened.

Langs: I can't dispute what you just said. We don't have the
data. I can just tell you in principle that I don't believe that
any of it is true or valid. Your intentions are good, but your
methods are open to question.

Therapist: I don't ask you to believe it. I'm just telling you
what my experience has been.

Langs: Allow me to say this in terms of principle. Number one, I do not think of resistance as lying entirely within the patient. And I already hear enough in the way in which you're intervening to see your likely contribution to her feeling that she is the bad one, as well as to her possible resistances, the nature of which are unclear to me at this point.

Therapist: I'm not denying my own possible contributions here.

Langs: I would think of all of that as interactional products—interactional resistances. Number two, I don't believe that we have as yet any evidence whatsoever that this patient is incapable of producing analyzable derivatives. I know that you're saying you've already decided that that is the case, and that's why you intervened rather prematurely. But that is a prejudgement. Let the material of this session demonstrate or convey that quality. I know of no patient with whom there is an indication to intervene noninterpretively. Understand this in principle: even the actual absence of analyzable derivations must be understood and interpreted, and not pushed aside or bypassed.

Discussant: And yet, a lot of analysts—I'm not saying they're right—a lot of people do intervene directively, with suggestions and extraneous comments.

Langs: I understand that, I know.

Therapist: But I wonder if you're not referring here to a certain type of patient that you work with?

Langs: No: *in principle*. This applies to all patients, though it will be explicated differently with each patient.

Discussant: You mean in analysis and therapy?

Langs: We're talking about psychotherapy here. Yes. I'm saying that no patient truly benefits from directives. They are usually very destructive and disruptive for the patient, who

will communicate such reactions and perceptions unconsciously. He will split his response: conscious gratitude and
unconscious rage. What he needs is interpretations. There are
patients who will force you to make noninterpretive interventions. A patient could end a session and say, You know, I'm
going to go out and kill myself. And even if a secure frame is
best, you must respond by extending the frame in such
emergencies. I would not sit there and say, See you next time.
No. The patient then forces a deviation in the frame which I
am prepared to deal with, and you can be sure that if such a
session happened to me, I would spend considerable time
thinking about what I did to contribute to that crisis. Only
then would I think of what the patient had done and explore
the extent to which the crisis derived from his pathology and
other factors within him. But as a rule, I would suspect that I
had missed something; that maybe I had made a serious
technical error; that I had unwittingly altered the frame
myself; that I was in the throes of a serious but unrecognized
countertransference problem. I would work the situation over
from that viewpoint first.

So the therapist damn well better carry out lifesaving work
when it's necessary and deviate when it's called for to save the
life of the patient. Then he must restore the frame as soon as he
can and accept that crises of this kind come up from time to
time. Frame issues are everpresent. But I won't pursue this
problem further, since we'll soon be dealing with the ground
rules and can bring it up then. We do, I notice, keep coming
back to frame issues, confirming my belief that it should be the
next topic we cover.

Returning now from general principles to this particular
therapeutic situation, I see no indication for modifying a
basically interpretive approach.

Discussant: If I may say something, it seems to me that if
you really screwed things up, made an error, you're implying
that it would not be appropriate to use directives in order to
correct the frame?

Langs: Well, in rectifying the frame some type of implied
directive might be used—but not necessarily an explicit one—

or, at least, such directives should be kept to the minimum required to secure the frame. Then, in addition, you would analyze and interpret the patient's unconscious perceptions and fantasies related to the entire experience, and this will require a proper use of the listening process. So perhaps we can get back to that area at this point.

Discussant: It is a bit difficult for some of us to understand what the listening process means in terms of interventions.

Langs: Yes, it is hard to integrate the various components of the therapeutic experience and the relevant techniques into a smooth whole. As we have been going along, I have tried to identify the kind of interventions that would be derived from the type of listening process that we have been developing. I plan to spend several weeks on the subject of interventions, but I can appreciate your wish to clarify that aspect as quickly as possible.

In essence, then, I would say that the listening process is best seen as a route to a proper interpretation through the identification of an adaptive context and the organization of the patient's material around Type Two derivatives, usually in the form of unconscious perceptions and fantasies related to the therapist—and their genetic underpinnings. Once a silent hypothesis that has been developed early in a session is validated by the patient's ongoing associations and a bridge to the therapeutic relationship has been presented—in general, that would be a point at which you would intervene, largely in terms of communicative mode and resistances before unconscious contents.

As I outline this, I realize that I must offer an insufficient answer, because there are many issues—of timing, precedence of material, indications for intervening, indications for silence, and the like—which we simply will not be able to discuss at this point. I would only add that the listening process also entails the metabolism of projective identifications toward silent hypotheses which, when validated, can lead to interpretations, and that a similar effort also takes place in regard to processing pressures from the patient to evoke responses and self-images within the therapist, which can also be worked over through the development of a silent hypothesis, subsequent validation, and, only then, interpretation.

Discussant: Isn't it possible for the patient to do something pathological, to have pathological ideas and fantasies, that are based on his own pathology rather than that of the therapist?

Langs: Yes, your comment touches upon a familiar criticism of my work. It is as if you are asking, isn't the patient sometimes the sick one rather than the therapist? Of course that is true, and I have never been unmindful of it.

Discussant: For example, in the illustration you gave us, isn't it possible that the patient is suicidal because of his own pathology, and that it isn't necessarily related to interventions the therapist has made?

Langs: Yes, of course, but perhaps you didn't hear what I said a moment ago: that I would examine myself *before* the patient, not *to the exclusion of* the patient. I'm just establishing an order of importance that I think crucial, because I think you'll discover that in most of the chaotic situations in therapy, when you might roughly estimate percentages of responsibility—I'm thinking particularly of the suicidal patient—it will never be one hundred percent the patient's responsibility. It might be five percent therapist, ninety-five patient, but from there the patient's share can shade downward toward greater contributions from the therapist. Empirically, I've found that in most disruptive therapeutic situations, the therapist turns out to hold a significant share of the responsibility.

I am well aware that in your presentations, because of the fact that you have not been analyzed and that you are still in the process of learning psychotherapy, there will be a high percentage of pathological input from your side, based on your countertransference difficulties. And since we are working from your clinical material, that very much influences the specific formulations that I make. It influences also the specific assignment of unconscious contributions to a given interlude, and even to a given experience or symptom within the patient.

But that does not mean that the situation is so distorted that it is useless to attempt to draw general principles, or that it is useless to compare it with the work of therapists who have been analyzed. It merely means that we must recognize the influence of the source of our data, that we must be careful with the generalizations we draw. And I would add this: it also means that we should use our understanding of the consequences of these blatant countertransference expressions as a means of sensitizing ourselves to the more subtle expressions that occur in the everyday work of every analyst—no one is ever totally free of countertransferences.

All of this came up in regard to my *The Bipersonal Field* (1976a). That work was sometimes misunderstood as representing my total view of therapy and was caricatured as a position that therapy is an unfolding based on the therapist's pathology. But as I think you can see in *The Therapeutic Interaction* (Langs, 1976b), I do indeed have a quite balanced view of the therapeutic interaction. I am well aware of the contributions from the patient's psychopathology and of the need to focus the ultimate therapeutic and analytic work in that realm.

But empirically—and I described this too in *The Bipersonal Field*—the patient characteristically conceals his pathology inside that of the therapist. Now, in terms of the listening process, the material from the patient under such conditions will not have primary—functional—meaning in terms of his own pathology. It will not be traceable and analyzable in genetic terms until you have brought your own inputs under control and analyzed their implications for the patient. This for two reasons. First, your input has disturbed the communicative flow and the properties of the field so the patient won't give you the material you need. Second, because the patient will, of necessity, be working over a current introject based on your pathology and will not move on to the sectors of his own pathology except as it interdigitates and exploits your difficulties.

So that's the problem. That's why I say I think we should monitor our contributions first, and only then the patient's. I'm not in any sense overlooking the latter. Look, when you're in the process of teaching therapy and supervising, you know there are going to be many disturbing inputs into the field. And this is where I do much of my teaching, but it has served me well. In a well-managed therapy, the percentage of pathological inputs from the therapist into the field can shift down to five percent or so. It will happen. The principles will be the same, but the form of communication and interaction will be different. The major vectors into the field are going to be different, and you'll be doing far more work with the patient's pathology, much of it the patient's input, some of it yours.

But the model we are developing here will serve you no matter who you're studying, yourself or the patient. I'm trying to be entirely unbiased for the moment: these are the bipersonal fields we're studying. Let the patient and therapist direct us; we can learn a great deal about therapy and ourselves from all of this, I assure you. So this is not a statement about how therapy will be done optimally, though it touches upon it. It's not a statement about the patient's pathology, though it also approaches that to some extent. It's a statement about the nature of the interactions that we are examining and it leads to general conceptions that apply to both patient and therapist, to the nature of the neuroses and to a valid means of modifying their influence.

Discussant: I understand what you're saying, but it sounds—you know—when you say that most of the patient's manifestations are primarily derived from the therapist rather than the patient, it sounds like you feel that most patients would be better off either not being in therapy with most therapists or being in therapy with another patient.

Langs: No, because I am not saying that the patient's symptoms will always derive in significant measure from the therapist's errors. This is only true when there are major countertransference-based inputs from the therapist. Nonetheless, you should be clear that I am indicating that, even under those circumstances, the patient's own pathology contributes significantly. In addition, the patient is always responsible for his own reactions to disturbances in the therapist.

I am simply trying to delineate a truthful empirical description, one that will direct us to the necessary therapeutic measures. Here, for the moment, these would begin with the rectification of the therapist's countertransferences and their expression in the interaction with the patient. We would then turn to the patient's reactions, accepting those that are appropriate to the therapist's unconscious communications, while analyzing those that express the patient's pathology.

So your first impression—that I feel, deep down, that most patients would be better off not being in therapy with the typical therapist—may or may not be valid. I don't really know. I do know that a great deal of so-called therapy serves patients largely through the development of misalliance cures and the offer of Type C barriers, and that this enables patients to rigidly reinforce massive defenses that seal off their inner disturbances. It provides them with some degree of relief, however fragile. Your second, alternative impression, however—that I perhaps think patients would be better off in therapy with another patient—reflects a different kind of misunderstanding. The patient is, as a rule, therapist to his therapist almost entirely on an unconscious level. He lacks the capacity to do conscious therapeutic work and in this respect differs from the actual therapist, who must be able to offer conscious interpretations, and who cannot function adequately on the basis of the unconscious interpretations characteristic of the patient.

Now, in the face of what you are clearly experiencing as the bad things that I am saying about therapists and analysts, recognize that there is something good in what I'm saying. It implies that, unconsciously, all of us are gifted therapists, and that the goal of your own personal treatment and of your training is actually to free up these unconscious gifts and to dispose of the defenses and other barriers to their expression so that you can make use of your unconscious sensitivities, your curative needs and capabilities.

Discussant: But that's a peculiar conclusion, that everyone could be empathic if they weren't sick.

Langs: Well, I really wouldn't have put it that way, but there is some truth to that.Modification of pathology does enhance empathy and other interpersonal sensitivities. But I am also saying that even though you identify sickness in a given person, on an unconscious level there is considerable evidence of empathy and understanding despite the surface disruptions. You will find this is true when you work with schizophrenics. As a matter of fact, Searles (1975) discovered the patient's unconscious curative efforts toward the analyst in his work with schizophrenic patients, but you will find as well that this aspect of the therapeutic interaction exists with every single patient you treat.

Well, we have wandered a bit from the listening process but, as you can see, everything we have discussed has a bearing on that process. We have in fact again brought up the role of empathy in the therapist's intaking efforts, a subject I have deliberately postponed considering until late in this segment of the course because it is a capacity that is readily subjected to misuse and abuse—though empathy, immediate emotional knowing, is an important means through which the therapist comes to understand his patient.

As I said earlier, most of the literature on aspects of the listening process has been devoted to such matters as empathy, intuition, and trial identification with the patient— to the virtual exclusion of the more cognitive and interactional dimensions I have been stressing. I think it has been essential to establish those details before turning to the less well-defined qualities of the listening process, but we will try to consider them in more detail in our final three meetings on this topic.

So, we'll continue with this presentation next week and then conclude this part of the course with one session presented in isolation and with another in which the patient reported a dream. Thank you.

Chapter Eight

INTERACTIONAL
CONSIDERATIONS IN
LISTENING

The function of premature interventions in evolving images and as projective identifications • Listening and faith • Further consideration of projective identification • The therapist's empathy and intuition reconsidered • Evaluating symptom relief

Langs: Perhaps today we can begin without desire, memory, or understanding.

Discussant: Last week was so confusing, we could hardly follow the presentation. Perhaps you can allow a brief summary.

Discussant: Yes, we really have little to go on.

Langs: Well, soon we'll have to discipline ourselves better. There is a conflict between the need to learn this approach to listening and the needs of the course. You'll often have chaotic previous sessions, and it's well to experience the confusion that follows—the sense of dislocation...

Therapist: Actually, I see now that I had left out some material.

Langs: Well, in that case, please proceed as you will.

Therapist: She's going through this thing with her neurologist about having felt he dismissed her as a nut. This is a man she's seen for about two years since her fall—which is connected with her own father's death in a fall when she was an infant.

Langs: You've added that.

Therapist: She blamed herself for his death at one time. He'd been paneling her room.

Langs: And what does this have to do with her present illness?

Therapist: Not much, just in the sense that she's had constant vertigo and a radicular type of back pain, and then she got into this urinary retention problem and whether these were sequelae to her accident or not is unclear. But her accident occurred soon after she left her husband.

So, she had gone and gotten some books on neurology in order to try and understand her symptoms and to get this guy into her good graces, the neurologist we've been talking about. This also seems to relate to her fear of my seeing her as sick. And my first real intervention was to say that it seemed to me that this feeling that he was dismissing her was similar to her feeling that I had dismissed her when she was in the hospital, and because I had seen her only once a week the last two weeks due to the holidays. She tried to dimiss that interpretation and say that it was the same old story, that we had talked about it before in relation to this other doctor. And I said, But it's a different situation and one that I think you feel is more important to you, also.

Langs: She feels which is more important?

Therapist: I am. She said, I've always felt that...

Langs: This is kind of where we were. I recall now that when we left off, I wanted to say something more. I think there are some interesting models here, which I had started to develop last time and should extend for you.

You had said to me last time—I worked it over a bit, but some of these principles are clearly well worth repeating—you said that you had been working on this area with her and you used that to account for your early intervention. Now, taking that as our model, let's recognize that it's very easy for a therapist to become strongly invested in a particular formulation in a selected area of working over, and to use the slightest clue from the patient as an opportunity to rework it and to continue to press home a particular point.

The listening process is really an interactional product. I mean, you influence what you will hear from the patient almost as much as the patient himself, and here, too, the proportions can vary considerably. There are always inputs from both sides. The patient's communications are an interactional product. Clearly, the therapist's silences affect the patient's communications, as do his interventions—as does the entire treatment setting. And while the patient's associations, again, are his own responsibility, we must not fail to recognize the extensive influence of the therapist in this regard.

After all, as you have seen in the presentations we have discussed, a therapist may consciously or unconsciously see to it that the patient excludes certain kinds of material; that he includes or even concentrates on other types of associations; that he repeats certain things, and all the rest. On the other hand, the patient does have some degree of independence and will have his say as well. In fact, in a typical sequence in which there is a countertransference-based input, the patient will tend to join in a misalliance or bastion with the therapist and will shape his communications accordingly. Only later on will he attempt to express his own needs and to direct his communications on that basis, often, I must add, giving up and becoming depressed if the therapist does not then consider them.

All of this is why we have the validating process, why we make silent hypotheses and validate them before we intervene, and why, as well, we attempt validation once again *after* our intervention. If the hypothesis is valid, the patient will give you Type Two derivatives that relate to it, that expand it, and that give you meaningful surprises that can be readily integrated into both the adaptive context and your main formulation—both in the course of his initial associations and after your intervention. And when you find that you are lacking this kind of buildup and decide to intervene despite the absence of any coalescence of meaning, you are more than likely going to be using a psychoanalytic cliché, a formulation that would function as a Type C barrier, as a falsification interpersonal barrier, and cover for what is really disturbing both you and the patient for the moment.

Now much of this applies as well to the identification of the adaptive context. It is important to discover new and fresh adaptive contexts and to link them to past adaptive contexts to which the patient is still responding. Interventions that relate exclusively to old adaptive contexts tend to take on clichéd and Type C barrier qualities.

And much of this discussion applies to the therapist's intervention at this point. Your comments about it imply a rather fixed view of the patient and her material. They certainly indicate that you did not enter the session without desire, memory, and understanding, and that you had a need within yourself to work over two particular adaptive contexts that were now somewhat dated: your not visiting the patient in the hospital and the missed sessions. As soon as you saw some material that hinted at connections to your formulation, you intervened.

You can see that this type of intervention is not made out of the blue. It is not unrelated to the patient's associations, and there is probably some truth to what you said—a burned-out truth, if you will. Its main function, however, is to destroy the living truths of the moment. You've not permitted the patient to lead the way and to put the necessary elements for your intervention into the field and into yourself so that you could merely reshape them in pointing out a particular unconscious concern or fantasy or defense. And if I may stick with the listening process here, I would stress that your intervention reflects your inability to recognize that listening requires a buildup, that one derivative does not generate a validated hypothesis or intervention, and that coalescence and preliminary validation are essential.

Bion (1972) calls this approach to listening one of "faith," and I find that a very sensitive term. Faith in indirect communication, faith in the patient's wish to express herself. Faith that the patient will convey the unknown, the unexpected, whatever is necessary to shape an interpretation. Faith that the patient will help you remember and will enable you to create something new in the session. Faith: a waiting, mildly expectant attitude. Listening and having faith.

So all this does mean sitting back, and it does mean waiting for the patient to generate hypotheses instead of coming in with a defined set or plan or predetermined issue. By contrast, your remark suggests that you came into this session with desire, with understanding, and with memory. You had the desire to interpret this area that you thought you understood and that you remembered working over with the patient. But I am emphasizing the extent to which that can exclude the expression of, and the ability to listen to, fresh material. It obviously can interfere with your listening process, because it biases and prejudices you terribly.

So, developing an attitude that's much more passive, that's imbued with faith in the patient, fully recognizing that your very passivity will influence what you will hear—such an attitude opens both you and the patient to a much wider range of possibilities than otherwise. You have no idea how much therapists wish to hear what they already know, how often they repeat that which is known to them, and how much they dread the unknown, the ineffable, the nonsensuous "O" which Bion (1972) has written about—especially those elements of the unknown which they dread. Bion (1977) has been especially sensitive to this as a major problem among therapists and analysts, and, while its resolution must ultimately rely on the self-analysis of residuals of countertransference, there is little doubt that one can at least develop principles of listening that will minimize the influence of these countertransferences and create an atmosphere within which the unknown can be expressed, recognized, appreciated, and analyzed.

So your reference to having certain goals in mind, particular areas to work over—your sense of determination, which is characteristic of a whole group of therapists—these enabled me to generate these very importa t comments. And you even convey this determination in your intervention, which can then have very interesting effects. For example, when you say that you're more important to her than her neurologist, and that it's more important than anything else that you and she get into this area, you're determined that this be so. This gives her something that she will then be forced to either work over or massively refute. And you can sense the nature of the projected contents as well as the interactional pressures to which the patient has been subjected.

And you can see here something else that's rather interesting about projective identification. It does not occur in vacuo; it makes use of a facilitating environment. Here the patient promotes that particular projective identification by communicating something related to it in derivative form. So, in some way, her relationship with you is unresolved in her mind, too, but you get way ahead of her. Still, this is how the object facilitates a projective identification from the subject, just as the object facilitates projection. We don't project into the wind. We find people who will help us to project into them things that we don't want to own up to ourselves, and the more a person facilitates that process, the more you feel that you're not projecting at all, and the more effective the defense seems. Here you might say: She really brought it up in derivative form; it had nothing to do with what was disturbing me. Clearly, it's bothering her.

This is the way in which projective identification really operates, and this is how we rationalize its presence. So you have to keep reflecting upon that. But you put this powerful stimulus into her: Look, you're upset about me, about what I've done, and this is more important than anything else; we've got to work it over. But you do this long before she defines this as an issue. And initially she's sort of refractory. She knows it's the same old stuff. She doesn't want to contain all of that. We'll soon see how she works it over from there, but on the surface she refuses to contain it.

Therapist: She's trying to deny that she's depressed, you see, which is why she does what she's doing. And you're saying—I understand what you're saying right now—but she's talking about terminating therapy, which means to me that this is something we still have to talk about, which she has avoided, and she's talking about it indirectly in connection with the neurologist. She's talking about changing neurologists.

Langs: Yes, but don't you see—again, what you say is so marvelous, because what you're trying to do is justify getting to these issues directly, when my answer to you would be that it's this very approach of yours that is discouraging her about treatment. You see, that would be my hypothesis. She is trying to fend off a depression, one based not only on things disturbing her in her life but also on things disturbing her about treatment and about you. This is an interactional depression. And any statement that you make about her I will turn around and apply to her perception of you. For example, I would postulate that part of what you're putting into her is a struggle within yourself around some kind of depression, at the very least, over the threat of losing her as a patient.

But the very techniques you apply modify your neutrality, because if you have a need to work over a particular area, you're no longer neutral. You are not using evenly hovering attention; you're selecting and are biased. It's these very pressured efforts, you see, that are actually unconsciously discouraging and disturbing her. So it's this very problem that leads me to encourage you to return to basic techniques: to sitting back, listening, waiting, formulating silently, validating, and all the rest. Yes, so you hear an implied threat in the material. But the threat is stemming from the nature of the interaction—that would be my hypothesis. Let's get some more material from the patient.

Discussant: Would you call that a manic defense?

Langs: Do you mean by the therapist or by the patient?

Discussant: No, by the therapist.

Langs: By the therapist. That's interesting—good, very good. Yes. I would say that this has a certain manic quality. Yes, that is an excellent point, especially in light of the reference to the patient's depression and my formulation that this is an interactional depression that contains aspects of the therapist's struggle against depression. Your hypothesis supplements mine and adds an important dimension to the interactional mechanisms here, because you are postulating that the therapist, through his excessive activity, is attempting to create a manic defense against his own, and the patient's depression. So that as an interactional projection— as a projective identification—it constitutes the unconscious offer of a manic defense against a postulated shared depression. And in that way too, you can see the unconscious curative wish contained within this pathological projective identification from the therapist.

In addition—and please understand, this is entirely in the realm of hypothesis—as a model, this shows you that the unconscious meaning and function of a projective identification can be quite different from the manifest communication through which it is expressed. That is, the therapist here is making a series of interventions and raising a series of questions: Isn't her anger at the neurologist in some way displaced from him, the therapist? and doesn't it reflect her disappointment in him? and the like. And here, we are postulating that beyond the content of his interventions is a quality of extensive activity, of pressure and excitement, that is being placed into the patient unconsciously as a possible means of resolving her depression through a manic-like defense.

So here, the form of the communication has a different function than the contents, and our stress for the moment is on the projective identification of a defense, rather than a set of unconscious fantasies and introjects—which, of course, are present on another level. This is really quite interesting, and I hope that you are able to follow these formulations, because they relate to the listening process in an important way. They show you that you must respond to projective identifications not only in terms of the contents involved but also through an appreciation of the timing, the form, the affect, and other such qualities if you are to metabolize them toward conscious understanding.

And here, of course, we are formulating that the patient projectively identified into the therapist some sense of her depression, perhaps through her threat to quit treatment—an interactional effort to depress the therapist and make him feel hopeless—and that, unconsciously, the therapist's reprojection is a *projective counteridentification,* as Grinberg (1962) would term it, which took the form of an unconscious manic defense which the patient is initially refusing to contain—though we may expect her to work it over subsequently.

I always worry when I develop such extended formulations as this, particularly in the area of projective identification, a concept that is so alien to most American therapists and analysts. I fear that the words will lose their meaning, and yet, to anyone who is sensitive to this dimension, I very much believe that the comments I just made are extremely valuable clinical metaphors that can afford us considerable insight into the unconscious nature of this therapeutic interaction. All of this implies, of course, the presence of a Type B field. We'll see if we can validate that thesis.

Incidentally, there is an excellent paper by Winnicott (1935) on manic defenses. It's a concept well worth understanding, because depression is such a pervasive illness. You're going to see a lot of manic defenses.

Well, let's hear some more material now. Pick up from the point of your intervention: you told her that you are more important to her than the neurologist.

Therapist: I said I felt this was her usual way of doing things: that she was trying to withdraw in order to insulate herself from the pain, and from her anger at me for not being there when she felt she needed me.

Langs: You added all of this to your intervention to her?

Therapist: Which I then said to her, yes. She said that her purpose was not to be dismissed. And I said that I thought that was true also, but that it was like when she was with her mother and her mother always rejected her or hit her. I suggested that at times she took on her mother's attitude and felt that her mother was justified, and said that I thought that was part of what was going on here. So as not to make this an issue, she wanted to feel that I was right. In order to not feel angry with me.

Langs: Okay, let's say a couple more things about the listening process in terms of this intervention. What would you say about this intervention vis-à-vis the listening process? Any comments at all? I'll ask it in a very general way, then we'll be a little more specific. What are we looking for? How do we organize our listening?

Discussant: I just haven't heard enough material from the patient. I guess I'm a little confused. I know the therapist brought in the references to her mother, but it was a little hard for me to tell what was from the patient and what was from the therapist.

Langs: Well, you're touching upon one aspect of the intervention that eventually I wanted to get to. Again, we seem to be applying the listening process to the therapist's interventions as much as we are applying it to the patient's material; I guess that's inevitable—the two are so closely tied to each other. Incidentally, you must take your sense of confusion—the specific uncertainty as to who's who—as subjective data, and treat it as you would any dimension of the listening process. How much from you? How much from the therapist? How valid? What does it mean? And all the rest. Now, what sort of intervention would you say this is— formally? It attempts to be—what?

Discussant: A confrontation.

Langs: It tends to be a confrontation, with some qualities of an interpretation—a genetic interpretation. This is really an effort to say that her reactions—in fact, it's really an attempt to generate a *genetic transference* interpretation. Let me show you how. It's an effort to say that her reactions to the therapist are derived from the patient's relationship with her mother, and that she is trying to use the same kind of defenses with him that she used in that earlier relationship.

Now, beyond the formal qualities, how do we assess its communicative properties? What are our criteria? What have we been developing? What properties does it have? (Pause.)

I'll go over it again. When you're assessing any intervention, there are some basic principles to be used. Perhaps I haven't spelled them out one, two, three, but I'll do that right now. Number one, the adaptive context—does it have an adaptive context? Number two, does it use manifest content, Type One derivatives, or Type Two derivatives? Three: What are its unconscious messages? And four: What type of communicative mode is involved and how does it contribute to the overall communicative field in terms of Types A, B and C? Do we have respectively, symbolic communication, projective identification and discharge, or barriers, static, and falsifications? There's more, but let's leave it at that for now.

Discussant: Can the therapist repeat what he said?

Langs: Yes, if you want to hear it again. We'll make an exception. A sense of uncertainty and confusion continues to prevail. Using Searle's concept (1955) of the reflection process between therapy and supervision, it seems likely that the patient is quite confused too.

Therapist: She said her purpose was not to be dismissed. And I said that I thought that was also true, but that I felt that there was also the element that she was seeing me as being like her mother when she went to her, and her mother would either reject or hit her. And in a way she'd seen me in the same way: as being rejecting when she felt she needed me.

Discussant: Before she said, I'm not trying to be rejected, what had you said?

Therapist: I had said that she needed to work through this new situation and I thought it was very important.

Discussant: The new situation being...?

Therapist: Me. She felt I was dismissing her by not having gone to visit her when she was in the hospital.

Discussant: I hear the therapist pounding away at this point, but I'm not sure that the material has brought her to that concern.

Langs: You really can't refrain from characterizing some of the interactional qualities of this intervention, and I think that's important to pick up on. This is your listening process here in this seminar, and what you're conveying—it's an excellent opportunity to see it—is that you hear something with such a powerful interactional thrust that you don't want to be bothered with classifying or organizing it cognitively. You just want to react to it emotionally, because you feel something very strong has been put into you, something powerful, and, I would add, confusing. Your request that he repeat his intervention could have been stated more directly as: this is a somewhat disjointed and perplexing intervention, in which the therapist has added a great deal to the patient's material—and it packs a disorienting whallop.

All right, let me address myself to that for a minute; we'll get back to the formal aspect a little bit later on. The listening process, if we're really going to organize it in terms of all intaking processes, can be nicely divided up, as I said, between the cognitive and the interactional realms. And as for the cognitive realm, that's the realm I'm trying to address with my question regarding formal attributes. Well, you're saying that this material doesn't really work in that area, doesn't permit a primary cognitive formulation, because it commands consideration interactionally—which is very interesting because this is the kind of thing that you have to experience and do as a therapist. You start off kind of listening openly— experiencing, taking in—for the cognitive nature of the material and for the interactional pressures. And then the material intrudes in one primary realm, and you must remain open enough to follow along.

Now let me show you: cognitively, you're listening for adaptive contexts, to the kinds of derivatives. You're listening to manifest content and to derivatives you can read from it: Type One derivatives. And if you identify a specific adaptive context you generate Type Two derivatives as well. And you're working all of that over.

Now at the same time, you're feeling the pressures of what the patient is conveying and how the patient is expressing it. And these interactional pressures occur on two levels. We've just begun to sort this out systematically. Sandler (1976) has written a paper on role responses. And he says that in addition to free-floating attention, the analyst or therapist should engage in a free-floating role responsiveness, because the patient expresses himself on that level too. And he doesn't quite go back over the history of his concept, because Freud said this in "Remembering, Repeating and Working-Through" (1914) and in *Beyond the Pleasure Principle* (1920). The patient tries to actualize his unconscious transference fantasies in his interaction with the analyst; he tries to get the therapist to behave in a fashion that is identical or comparable to those earlier figures, the parents. He tries to experience the traumas and actualities once again, and he tries to induce in you the feelings and behaviors of these earlier objects. It has to do with identificatory processes and with evoked self-images in the therapist, all of which I'm going to get into again in a moment.

So, you have to be aware of the role that the patient is imposing upon you, to which I would add—the self-image he imposes as well. Because it's not only that the patient wants you to behave in a certain way, but also that he wants you to experience yourself in a particular way, very often in a way that's contradictory to your idealized self-image, and this of course may evoke defenses. Me: angry, destructive, nasty, seductive. No. I'm just a nice listening therapist, trying to do some good therapeutic work. So, interactionally, on what I have termed the object relational level, you have role and image pressures. That's one interactional sphere.

Discussant: That's all very different than projective identification, in that it's not projecting the patient's feelings, but he's trying to give the therapist the feeling of the earlier objects. So it's not coming from the patient's feelings, but from what he perceives as those in the earlier objects.

Langs: Well, you are quite right that this is a different realm than projective identification—the other interactional sphere—although I'm not sure that I can fully accept your formulation regarding role and image evocations. Your comment does, however, lead me to stress one other aspect of these object related interactional pressures, namely, that unconsciously, the patient will attempt to evoke identifications within the therapist that are related both to himself and to his earlier objects. You can see then that these evocations also involve interactional efforts to arouse empathic responses in the therapist—which is a way of stating again that the therapist's use of empathy is, as is any phenomenon in the bipersonal field, an interactional occurrence.

But in respect to the patient's role and image pressures, it was Helene Deutsch (1926) who first suggested that the analyst unconsciously will identify with certain portions of the patient's ego—to which we may add, self-image, inner mental contents, psychic structures, and the like—a phenomenon that Racker (1957) later studied and termed *concordant or homologous identifications*. She suggested, in addition, that the patient will evoke unconscious identifications and behaviors, and images, in keeping with his earlier objects—his so-called transference objects, what Racker termed the patient's *internal objects* or *introjects*—an identificatory process that both termed *complementary identification.*

So, in the object relational realm, the patient may actually attempt to evoke roles and images that are in keeping with his self-concept, his own behaviors, self-image, and the like, as well as attempting to have the analyst behave or experience himself in a manner that is comparable to important early figures. Once again, you can see that this area is quite complex, and that the therapist must be sensitive to it, must attempt to analyze his subjective responses—his images and his hopefully controlled impulses toward inappropriate action, for example—and that, ideally, the therapist should confine himself to signal experiences—pressures to behave in a particular way, a tendency toward a particular image—rather than being caught up in the evoked response to the point of living it out or experiencing it as an accepted part of his self-image.

Then, based on these subjective experiences and signals to act, the therapist can generate a cognitive formulation of the patient's unconscious intentions, fantasies, perceptions, and the like, and can use it as a silent hypothesis to be validated based on the patient's further communications in any of the three basic realms I am describing. While validation is necessary for silent hypotheses developed in any of these realms—the cognitive, the object relational, or that of the interactional mechanisms—it is especially so in the latter two. In these realms part of the listening process entails the specific sorting out of the sources of the therapist's subjective feelings and impulses—fantasies, images, tendencies toward action, and the like—a process through which he identifies the contributions from the patient and those from his own inner propensities.

This is an important step in the listening process that is comparable to the sorting out of the patient's unconscious fantasies and unconscious perceptions in the cognitive scheme I developed earlier for you. I suggested that we listen to the material from the patient along the me–not-me interface and then sort out the second-order themes—Type One and Type Type Two derivatives—for valid unconscious perceptions and distorted unconscious fantasies. Eventually, it is necessary to determine the realistic and distorted elements of these role and image evocations and to determine how much alludes to the patient and how much to the therapist. But there is, additionally, a particular need to identify the source of a given experience, and, as I think about it, it occurs to me that this need exists in the cognitive sphere also, since you must, as a basic step in generating a formulation, determine how much stems from the patient's material and how much from idiosyncratic responses within yourself.

So the basic procedure is pretty much the same in each sphere. It seems that I am accenting one or another task based on the special problems that are likely to arrive in a given area, but each of these considerations must be developed in each of the basic realms of the listening process. And you could see again how crucial self-knowledge is as a determinant of the course of the listening process and its outcome.

Now, I want to mention again the second realm of interactional pressures: the one I have identified as the area of interactional mechanisms of projective and introjective identification. I must say first off that I could not immediately respond to the question implied in your comments regarding the differences and possible similarities between object relational pressures and interactional pressures, though I will state that I consider it quite important to delineate the relationship between these two interactional realms. Certainly, it is possible to projectively identify into the therapist introjects that are based on earlier relationships; so, interactionally, we can create active projections based on earlier object relationships.

But it seems to me that you are dealing mainly with different levels of conceptualization. In the sphere of object relationships you are alluding to object-representations, self-representations, roles, self- and object-images, and the like, and these are based largely on the vicissitudes of early and later object relationships. Projective and introjective identifications, on the other hand, are interactional psychological mechanisms that are based only in part on the nature of one's object relationships. What is stressed is the placing of inner mental contents, defenses, and states into the object—a particular type of psychological mechanism, one with definitive interactional pressures and whose influence need not be confined to roles and images but may be extended to all kinds of internalized contents and defenses.

These brief comments must suffice, because our main focus must be on defining each of the realms. As you can see, I am still in the process of clarifying each sphere and of considering the relationship between them. We could raise similar issues as to how the cognitive sphere relates to the interactional; but for now I'm going to concentrate on the practicalities of the listening process.

So, in the interactional realm, we listen in two kinds of ways, one having to do with what's being put into us for us to contain, the other having to do with what's being evoked in us in the way of self-images and inappropriate tendencies toward action. Now though they obviously interrelate—what you contain, you respond to—I think there's reason to separate the two conceptually, because they involve different kinds of introjective experiences in the therapist.

All of this brings me back to literature. I have noted the virtual absence of any literature on the cognitive aspects of listening, or on the processes of listening itself—taking in, formulating, determining the presence of derivatives and adaptive context, and the rest—and except for Reik's suggestively titled *Listening with the Third Ear* (1948), a volume I have not read but am now tracking down, I know of little that has been written in this area.

The same applies to most of the interactional aspects of listening. There is the recent paper by Sandler (1976), to which I have referred, but the Kleinian literature on projective identification simply assumes that the analyst has the capacity to identify and metabolize the patient's projective identifications and, so far as I have been able to determine, makes no effort to offer criteria or to describe in any detail the nature of those listening processes.

So most of the literature relating to the listening process is involved with empathy and intuition, two processes within the therapist, and within the patient as well, that for several reasons I have scarcely mentioned: first, I wanted to concentrate on the neglected areas; second, these are only two of many tools that the therapist uses in his intaking processes; and third, there is not a great deal that you can say about empathy and intuition on the level of practical clinical work (most of the literature pertains to the genetic development of empathic abilities and involves rather general, ill-defined descriptions of its clinical application). But both are certainly important to the listening process and perhaps at some point one of our presenters will describe an empathic or intuitive reaction for us to evaluate and discuss. For now I will make my remarks rather brief, largely because I have devoted considerable space to this subject in *The Therapeutic Interaction* (Langs, 1976b, chapter 14).

As you may know, the term *empathy* is sometimes used so broadly as to be synonymous with the listening process, while its more specific meaning, as defined by Schafer (1959), Greenson (1960), and others (see Langs, 1976a), is that of a form of emotional knowing, or of sharing within oneself, and understanding, the psychological state or inner mental world of another person. Writers describing empathic experiences have stressed the role of introjective and projective mechanisms, temporary identifications and introjections while maintaining ego boundaries (see Beres and Arlow, 1974), and have defined it as an interactional occurrence considerably influenced by the patient. They have emphasized the need to restrict empathic experiences to signal types of reactions (Olinick, 1969) and have stressed as well the need to validate all so-called empathic reactions (see Langs, 1976c), noting that these subjective reactions may arise primarily from valid temporary identifications and introjections or may stem largely from countertransference-based needs within the analyst, with only a minimal degree of valid introjection. Reactions of the latter sort constitute idiosyncratic responses that are mislabeled "empathic."

Incidentally, as you undoubtedly know, empathic reactions may take the form of most any type of subjective experience, ranging from affects to conscious fantasies, and entail responses to the conscious and unconscious communications from the patient. I make this point in order to stress the need to recognize that empathic reactions are manifest responses that must be subjected not only to validation, but also in order to yield latent contents, to self-analysis. The same principle is applied to intuition, although that experience tends to take the form of some kind of immediate knowing (Reich, 1966; Beres and Arlow, 1974), a subjective experience that either may be based primarily on a pathological projection by the therapist into the patient, or may constitute the development of a sudden insight of considerable validity derived from unconscious processes of which the therapist is unaware. Again I must stress the need to validate all such inner experiences—a point that Olinick and his associates (1973) neglected to seriously consider in their use of such sudden but uninterrogated insights. Kanzer (1975) presented this criticism in some detail.

I am well aware that much of this is more theoretical than empirical, and that is why I will not elaborate. There is a considerable literature on the analyst's or therapist's use of his own unconscious sensitivities and capacities, writings in which both conscious and unconscious identification play central roles, both in regard to their positive potential, and in respect to possible countertransference-based disturbances. It is, however, a literature still in need of careful clinical documentation. We have learned (see Langs, 1976b) that there are kernels of understanding in every subjective response to the patient, a point initially stressed by Racker (1957), so that we seek out nuclei of affective understanding of the patient in even our most disturbed and countertransference-dominated reactions. We endeavor to minimize the pathological component so that these nuclei come to dominate most of our reactions to the patient and his material.

So once again we have an opportunity to experience the complexities of the listening process, both as an actual experience by the therapist in his interaction with the patient, and as a constellation of responses and endeavors within the therapist whose theoretical understanding requires conceptualization on many levels. Listening is cognitive and noncognitive, intellectual and affective, sensory and nonsensory, thoughtful and amorphous, and certainly distorted and nondistorted. It is subjectively interactional, with pressures to feel and respond, but also introjective and containing, and sometimes even projective. And you can see, too, why the validating process is so essential: countertransference-based influences can be introduced at any point, and yet even they, while their effects are always disruptive, can be turned to good account in the service of understanding the patient—but only if one makes use of the validating process.

Now, coming back to this session, it stimulated this discussion because each of us seems to be experiencing the communications from this therapist with strong valences in the interactional realm. His interventions have qualities of projective identification and, in addition, seem to have been unconsciously designed to generate particular images and role responses in the patient. It led us, as observers, to experience contents and interactional pressures that had to be contained, as well as creating in us the impression of some type of role response.

If we attempt to formulate the patient's experience—her listening process, which also takes place in both the cognitive and the interactional realms—in terms of the three major divisions I have outlined for you, we would develop the silent hypothesis that the patient has experienced the therapist as endeavoring to place into her the working over of a group of problems that have been bothering him—for example, his not visiting her in the hospital. Certainly we have been impressed with these inputs, and I suspect the patient has been as well.

Incidentally, the intensity of these interventions is reminiscent of certain patients who utilize projective identification rather pervasively, constantly creating interactional pressures and contents and defenses that you must contain and metabolize. Much of the therapeutic work with such patients must be conducted in the realm of interactional mechanisms, a realm in which such defenses as denial and splitting are rather prominent. The therapist assists in the repair of their egos, as Bion (1977) has put it, largely through his own capacity to contain—to identify and interpretively modify the massive use of these projective mechanisms, and to generate meaningful cognitive understanding.

So, in this particular session the therapist has introduced a number of his own associations. And while these would be valid as silent connections and as a possible basis for a silent hypothesis, early interventions of this kind are not in keeping with the principle I presented earlier, to the effect that each session should be permitted to unfold on its own terms, to be its own creation, and that each intervention should be shaped from the material from the patient in that hour.

Discussant: That's one thing I was wondering about—why you were saying this. I didn't understand your point. The therapist has been with this patient for more than a year, so it's conceivable that the material he's introducing is not foreign or alien to the patient. She knows this is part of her past associations or similar material. But you wouldn't introduce any of this and I'm not sure why.

Therapist: I am also terminating with this patient in a few months.

Langs: Even if this were the last session, basically I would not change my approach. These principles have been derived by consistently observing what is destructive and what is helpful to the patient.

Discussant: But do you know what I mean?

Langs: Yes. Termination doesn't lead me to deviate. It does lead a lot of therapists to do so, for instance: We'll have dinner together. We'll be so-called equals now. None of that is in keeping with the principles that I will develop for you.

You see, my answer to your question is that if you develop a correct silent hypothesis—by all means this should be a *silent* hypothesis—the patient's material will come around to it and you will obtain support in some derivative form. And in that way, you can safeguard against the very tendency that I identified earlier: to repeat what you already know, to avoid what is truly unknown and anxiety provoking, and to generate Type C barriers based on psychoanalytic clichés, premature interventions, and the like; or to generate a Type B field, based on your own countertransference-based needs to projectively identify into the patient your own unresolved inner anxieties and fantasies.

As you can see, your question actually contained its own answer: your point that, after all, this material the therapist is introducing might be old and familiar stuff. Well, it may be expressed again in a fresh form in this session, and then we could intervene meaningfully. But it is also possible to use this all-too-familiar material as a Type C barrier to a more immediate and compelling truth that could disturb both patient and therapist. Again, it is a matter of faith, a matter of learning that the patient will put into you what you need for an interpretation, will help you build the interpretation or rectification of the frame that is required. And therapists must also learn that it is not helpful to be too far ahead of the patient, to respond too much in keeping with their own needs, rather than his. Sit back, have faith, learn to listen. It will keep you quite busy. Formulate and validate before you intervene.

Discussant: I would like to mention a patient that I am now beginning to terminate with because he will soon leave the area. It seems to me that when I got to the middle phase of his therapy there appeared certain core themes—streams of the therapeutic process—repeated themes that I found myself forced to respond to, forced by the material to keep making the same interpretations, pointing out examples of his defensiveness against his aggressive feelings, and the like. Now my supervisor has encouraged this kind of reinterpreting, and there *is* the concept of working through. So it seems to me that some repetition is necessary.

Langs: Well we certainly cannot evaluate the therapeutic situation that you just described without hearing the details of a session or two. Still, I certainly accept the principle of working through and the need to interpret repeatedly the various dimensions of a given intrapsychic conflict, unconscious fantasy and introject, or the like, and to deal with it from many different angles, both within the current therapeutic relationship and in terms of its genetic underpinnings. All I am suggesting is that such work is viable only when there is an immediate and pertinent adaptive context, only when the material is alive and in the form of Type Two derivatives, and only when it has been meaningfully recreated in each session. That would characterize true working through, while the kind of premature interventions and repetition I was addressing a moment ago is more a defensive Type C barrier than an insightful process. It would be a falsification to consider that a form of working through, although many therapists do indeed carry out such work.

Discussant: Well, this patient works in this medical center, and I often feel that I am under considerable pressure to intervene and be helpful.

Langs: Well, the bipersonal field may be contaminated to the point where the patient is no longer communicating viable derivatives for analytic work. The frame may be so modified that you have a Type C field that cannot be altered and, as a result, both of you are repeating the same old stuff again and again. You are also in a situation where you enter the session with intense desire, and, unconsciously, the patient will exploit that as well. So there can be many underlying reasons for a Type C field, and for repetitive, clichéd, and empty therapeutic interactions.

Discussant: Yes, I'm beginning to see that. And I feel quite uncomfortable when I find myself repeating what seems now to be a rather hollow intervention.

Langs: When you find yourself repeating, it is best to just sit back and ask yourself, What's causing the repetition? You're now undoubtedly in a Type C field, using clichés and facades. It's meaningless stuff and you've got to sit back and see if you can begin to identify sources and factors. And I will guarantee that if you sit back and become silent, the patient will bring up derivatives related to the frame, if that's the key issue, and to other pertinent dimensions—within himself, you, and the therapeutic interaction—that are contributing to this stalemate. Here too, often after participating in the misalliance with the therapist, the patient will eventually generate the derivatives necessary for understanding and interpreting this unproductive repetition. The patient, unconsciously, will guide you.

Before hearing more material, I would like to add one or two comments. First, you can see the importance here of including in the basic listening process a continuous assessment of the source of the therapist's impressions, fantasies, feelings, thoughts, subjective reactions, and formulations. We could call this the therapist's me–not-me interface and it is a crucial determination, founded ultimately, as I have said before, on the therapist's self-knowledge.

My second point is the following: we have been stressing the extent to which the therapist's interventions create an adaptive context for the patient's subsequent associations. Implicit in this discussion, however, is the other side of that principle: the patient's material is, of course, the adaptive context for the therapist's interventions. Beyond that broad principle, you will find it extremely important to identify the communications that immediately precede the therapist's intervention. Often, this is the immediate precipitant of the therapist's communication to the patient, and especially when there is a countertransference influence, that segment of the adaptive context often provides important clues regarding the underlying disruptive fantasies and introjects within the therapist.

This is a dimension of the listening process that I developed in some detail in *The Bipersonal Field* (1976a), and we can apply it here by suggesting that the patient's contact with another physician, her turning to reading, and her feeling deprived have evoked some sense of disturbance within the therapist that he is attempting to master through his rather premature interventions. It would be well for us to keep this principle in mind, and I will illustrate its applicaton to you as we go along.

Therapist: But, she's trying to avoid these feelings, and I'm trying to say that they're there. Now, I could interpret that in the sense of her not wanting to go back and look at these feelings—I could have made that intervention. Approaching it from the side of her defenses.

Langs: I'm suggesting that you shouldn't have made any intervention at all. You should just have sat back and let her develop this session for you. But I want to hear her reaction to all of this.

Discussant: Would you say that when a patient evokes a strong reaction in the therapist, assuming that it's not coming from the therapist...

Langs: No, no. *Never* assuming that it's not coming at all from the therapist: assuming, rather, that the therapist's contribution is relatively small.

Discussant: Okay, you're dealing with an interactional frame. You are suggesting that that framework has to be operational all of the time. I'm thinking of one patient who always—well, I get the feeling that I'm being intimidated, and he has a way of doing it. He forces, pressures me. He maneuvers me into situations where I have to think very quickly, make snap decisions. Would you say that in that sort of situation you'd have to deal with the interactional aspect first, before you get to the cognitive?

Langs: Oh yes, there's no question that the interactional realm takes precedence, for every human being, and must be understood first. And I would suspect again that there is more of a contribution from yourself than you realize. It must be understood, first; your contribution must be rectified. It must be analyzed implicitly in terms of the patient's reactions and then analyzed in terms of the patient's need to evoke it. Yes, that realm must be worked over and interpreted before contents.

You see, it turns out that there are many jobs to do in therapy before interpreting unconscious contents—fantasies, memories, and introjects. And the interactional dimension really implies the immediate reality as well, and that has to be worked over in terms of implicit and explicit meanings. The communicative mode has to be worked over too. All of these actualities must be analyzed before inner contents, and it's very meaningful therapeutic work. It's not secondary at all. It means revising our concept of the development of psy-

chopathology, viewing it as an interactional development—
which analysts are doing. Freud presented us with the
intrapsychic aspects, and the whole field now is learning
about the interactional contributions, though this really has
not quite caught up with the way in which we're doing
therapy.

Discussant: The primary emphasis is always on making
that very fine genetic interpretation—that has been the
ultimate goal.

Langs: Yes, the golden egg, the award winner. The
interpretation-of-the-month award. Yes. And I've been aware
of this. This is a very personal struggle too. That is, as I got
into unconscious perception, for example, I had to set up my
own value system, because it was totally discordant with the
value system I had been taught. Yes, a good interpretation of
an unconscious perception related to the framework of this
therapy—that would really be, I think, prime stuff. You'll get
my award.

I am not, by the way, devaluing reconstructions, or genetic
and transference interpretations; I am simply trying to
develop a perspective on their role and importance in
psychotherapy and psychoanalysis. I'm attempting to
counterbalance an overriding emphasis on that type of
interpretation with the recognition of the importance of many
interactional realities and fantasies—mechanisms and the
like—that prevail in the therapeutic interaction, that require
rectification at times, that need consistent interpretation as
well—from which the patient derives enormous therapeutic
benefit. It would seem now that the ideal interpretation would
begin with an aspect of the present communicative interaction, in terms of a specific adaptive context, and more from
there into Type Two derivatives related to the pertinent
unconcious perceptions and fantasies—and their genetic
repercussions.

Discussant: How about people who are trained in institutes
outside of those under the aegis of the American Psy-

choanalytic Asociation? How do they work with their patients?

Langs: Look, we are now moving into the realm of impressions without data. And as you know, that can be treacherous. I can say that I have read many papers as an editor of a journal, and that I have heard many presentations from therapists and analysts who have experienced all types of training. And the book that is unfolding from this course indicates my impression: there are major flaws in the prevailing listening process and, of course, there are therefore major defects in their management of the ground rules, in the communicative fields that they develop with the patient, and in the nature of their interventions. Most therapists are working with manifest content, a smaller number with Type One derivatives; occasionally, intuitively, they work with an adaptive context and some Type Two derivatives, but the capacity to listen to projective identifications and to role and image evocations appears to be extremely limited, and work in the cognitive sphere is quite restricted as well.

But let's tend to our own problems: we have enough to do in learning how to listen properly. And from this we can readily learn from our patients how to do proper psychotherapy. Now, let's hear some more material.

Therapist: She tried to deny the interpretation.

Discussant: It's been a while since we heard that intervention; could you repeat it briefly?

Therapist: I had said something about her trying to withdraw to insulate herself from the pain and anger she is feeling toward me for not being at the hospital when she felt she needed me. I had been saying that her reaction to the neurologist really had that as an underlying meaning and that her purpose was to not be dismissed. It was like when she was with her mother who always rejected or hit her. I also suggested that she sometimes took on her mother's attitude and felt that her mother was justified. And I related that to her not making my failure to visit her an issue in the sessions. I said that she wanted to feel that I was right in order to not feel angry with me. So, as I said, she tried to deny the interpretation. She says no, but just stops, waits about ten seconds, and says, You mean my feeling unlovable? And she's about to cry.

Langs: My feeling unlovable. Now what could that convey? Let's carry out the exercise which I never finished: his interpretation was offered around an old adaptive context—his not visiting her in the hospital—and it was an attempt to generate Type Two derivatives in terms of distortions and fantasies based on her perception of his not coming to the hospital. The main fantasy was experiencing his absence largely in terms of her early experiences with her mother. As I recall it, you alluded to her mother rejecting and hitting her, and I must admit that you were stressing the genetic roots of her reaction to your not having visited her far more than you were, for the moment, emphasizing distortions. And that's rather important, since some therapists might have implied or even directly stated—or at least, implied more forcefully—that her feelings of rejection were rather crazy, or that she had no right to feel hurt. Or whatever. But I do think that your intervention implied that she overreacted, based on those earlier incidents with her mother.

Therapist: She's *under*reacting. Her mother is schizophrenic.

Langs: Yes, but I mean that her reaction was determined in part by distortions derived from those earlier experiences that there was a transference-like quality to it. She was overly defensive because of genetic factors.

Therapist: Overreaction to me, underreaction to her mother.

Langs: An overreaction to you in terms of the past. And my assessment is that your intervention is not based on the material of the session. Nor is it derived from an immediate adaptive context. It's an attempt to deal with the relationship in the realm of transference, when there are many pressing and more immediate actualities that are being split off, sealed off, by these interventions.

So she says no, and then she says, You mean, my feeling unlovable? Let's do a quick listening exercise with that. How do you hear it? Now we're listening to a piece of material from the patient.

Discussant: In the context of what's gone on in the session, we could say that she's wondering why he's not allowing her to go on with what she wants to say, as though he doesn't consider it important. And that may mean to her that she's unlovable: he can't accept her on her own terms, her own feelings.

Langs: Let me formalize what you did. You took, as the adaptive context, the therapist's specific interventions—which you should always do. See, I realize here that initially my main approach to the patient's responses to interventions has been built around the validating process, because that aspect has been so enormously neglected. Now that I have done the work, I recognize, of course—and it's been implicit in everything I've said—that in response to interventions we get not only validation or nonvalidation, but we get as well a whole set of unconscious perceptions and feelings, their extension into fantasies and distortions, and all the rest—commentaries.

"My feeling unlovable" some therapists would take on a manifest level: you mean you felt unloved by your mother. And that's what you're talking about. That's what you're trying to get me to understand. So some therapists would take this as a statement that she felt unlovable in the past, and that she therefore felt unlovable when the therapist didn't visit her in the hospital. That would be manifest content, maybe a little bit of a Type One derivative, in terms of reading in some latent meaning to that, but basically it's focused on a past transaction between the patient and the therapist.

But as a Type Two derivative based on the adaptive context

of the therapist's immediate interventions it takes on a different implication. It takes on the meaning that the therapist sees her as quite unlovable. This is just paraphrasing what you just formulated, and the way that he's intervening conveys that to her. In other words, it suggests that the therapist's interventions have an impact on the patient on many unconscious levels—and this is just the other side of it, which tends to be neglected. The therapist imposes cognitive material on the patient, as well as images and roles and projective identifications. The patient listens—often more unconsciously than the therapist—listens and incorporates cognitively and interactionally. And what I'm pointing out here is that the patient is saying that a particular image of herself is being imposed upon her by the therapist's interventions: an image of herself as unlovable. This is a different level of experience and meaning from what you intended consciously. She's experiencing your pressured interventions as a reflection of your finding her unlovable. Despite its genetic referent, the first formulation deals with nonneurotic communications. It is linear—being abandoned is being hurt—while the second is disguised, convoluted, and in the realm of neurotic communication. It is interactional and is probably meaningfully tied to the patient's past with her mother—as an actual repetition, based on the nature of these interventions rather than as a basis for distorting the present.

On another level—what other level do we have? (Pause.) The monitoring and sorting out processes are seemingly endless. I haven't included one final dimension here, and that is the me–not-me interface—everything that we hear from the patient is evaluated for how much is about her and how much is about the therapist. And the patient does the same thing: everything we say to the patient has to be monitored for how much is being said about the patient, and how much about ourselves. So when she says You mean, my feeling unlovable? that first level I just formulated is stated in terms of her self-representation and how she's experiencing the pressures from the therapist—image evocations. Now, the next level is this: Is there something that she's perceiving about, and introjecting from, the therapist, who feels unloved, unlovable, and has a need to try to evoke concern, a loving response from his patient so he can feel better about himself?

You see how incredibly complex it gets. In each of these realms—cognitive and interactional, both role and image evocation and projective identification—every communication has to be sorted out to identify and distinguish the following: me, not-me; self, not-self; self-representations, object-representations; introjections, projections. And you have to be doing this constantly, though as you gain experience, it becomes a bit easier And also, by the way, the order of precedence must be: me as therapist, before her as patient; reality and introject before fantasy and projection. I always do it in that order: I want to know where I stand, and what she's picking up from me. What's left then is what's going on inside of her. It's a nice way to approach it, instead of the usual way: patient first, therapist second or never; patient sick, therapist healthy. Both are human, so both are both sick and healthy. It is a matter of proportion. So we must sort it out again and again.

One other point. I think that this material and the formulations that I have developed enable you to see that there are different implications in the two interactional spheres: role and image evocation (object relational), and projective identification. That is, in terms of the image that the therapist's interventions evoked in the patient, there was a stirring up or intensification of the patient's feelings that she is unlovable—undoubtedly, an aspect of her self-image intensified by the therapist's comments. In the other interactional realm, there is a projective identification into the patient of what I have postulated as the therapist's own self-image of himself as unlovable, and related unconscious fantasies, conveyed, as you see, not through some direct reference to being unlovable but through a series of communications that the patient unconsciously experienced as an introject containing an unlovable self-image of the therapist and efforts to evoke a loving response.

It seems to me as I develop this analysis that the two are interrelated, and that the object relationship sphere has intensified the patient's own negative self-image and those related introjects with which she is identified, and which she experiences as part of her self-representation. Meanwhile the projective identification creates a somewhat different but related kind of introject, one that remains identified with the therapist unconsciously while touching off the patient's self-representations as well. Also, the therapist's image of himself as unlovable prompted a similar projective identification and image evocation. So the two spheres are related in that way too.

In terms of technique, attention to the object relational sphere would lead to interventions related to feelings that the therapist is trying to evoke in the patient. The other sphere, in which projective identification is a primary mechanism, would involve aspects of the therapist's own inner state that he is in some sense placing into the patient in order to have her contain and work them over. So, although these are interrelated formulations, there would be some differences in the interventions that one would make, depending on which level is being considered. The same would apply when the therapist would listen to, experience, metabolize, and interpret interactional pressures from the patient. I very much hope that this brief comparison has proven illuminating. The object relations and interactional mechanism formulations do seem to be two related though somewhat different ways of considering interactional phenomena.

Discussant: In regard to his two interpretations, it seems to me that the first one was in the cognitive realm, and the second one was more of a projective identification.

Langs: Would you please clarify what you mean?

Discussant: Well, I am really comparing the two formulations. When you say that the patient is experiencing herself as unlovable based on the therapist's interpretations— well, I would now ask it as a question: whether that would be cognitive, or interactional. While I can see that the second interpretation that you made of the material, in which there is a kind of introject of the therapist and his own feelings that he is unlovable—there I can see the interactional mechanisms, the projective identification, more clearly. The other seems to have more cognitive qualities.

Langs: I think you're right. The first formulation does have both cognitive and interactional—object relational—aspects, while the second pertains to projective identification. Here the patient's feeling that she is unlovable is an introjective identification based on a projective identification by the therapist, whatever other factors might be involved. Do you follow that?

Discussant: Yes.

Langs: The therapist put into her, in this indirect form, some sense of feeling unlovable, distressed, whatever, and she then worked it over. That's interactional, but it's formulated cognitively. It's based on interactional mechanisms. And when I speak of metabolizing a projective identification, part of what I mean is translating it from an interactional experience—conscious and unconscious—into conscious metaphors, fantasies, perceptions, and the like—that is, into conscious symbolic and cognitive terms.

So, much of this has the qualities of a Type B field in which there is an exchange of projective identifications. There's a lot of interactional pressure here—lots of pressure toward action and discharge—and even some refusal by the patient to contain the therapist's projective identifications, to negate or fend them off, though she eventually accepts them and becomes depressed. She accedes both to his interactional pressures and to her own depressive tendencies.

Perhaps the complexity of these formulations will encourage you to sit back and listen, to put less into the field, to be more selective in your interventions, to sort things out and generate silent hypotheses to be validated before you intervene, so that you increase your chances of offering a valid intervention and decrease the extent to which you put disturbing vectors into the field. I hasten to add—and, actually, every single statement that you can make about psychotherapy should be accompanied by a caveat, a reference to how that particular principle can be abused or pressed into the service of countertransferences—so I must add that silences are by no means a protection against countertransference, since inappropriate silences, failures to intervene, are also based on the therapist's psychopathology. The real protection lies in the validating process and in self-knowledge.

Discussant: Are you saying that you confine yourself to just one or two interventions in any session?

Langs: Well, I do not have such a game plan, so to speak, and I do intervene flexibly and in keeping with the patient's needs and communications. But on the whole, I do average about one intervention per session, zero to one, although there are sessions in which I will be considerably more active. This might occur with a patient who intensely utilizes projective identification, with one who is depressed, or where the patient is communicating so meaningfully that a whole series of interpretations are indicated. Another such situation is one in which the frame has been modified and interventions, both rectifying and interpretive, are necessary.

Discussant: I gather, then, that you tend to intervene toward the end of sessions.

Langs: Yes, as a rule toward the end rather than the beginning, because there is so much to listen to and process. But please believe me, that's not a rigid rule. Nor is it a reflection of any other kind of rigidity. There are sessions in which meaningful communications—and here I am referring to the whole range of communications: fantasies, perceptions, defenses, contents, interactional mechanisms, and the rest— there are sessions in which they coalesce quite early in the session and I am able to develop a silent hypothesis and find confirmatory derivatives early on. Then, as soon as—and if— the patient gives me a communicative bridge, I make the intervention. After that, I may not speak again in the hour; or, if the patient adds significant confirmation and new slants, I may intervene a second or even a third time.

In situations in which there are crises, I am prepared to develop silent hypotheses and to identify the adaptive context as quickly as possible. And while I would look to be more active, I must stress the importantce of sitting back initially so that you can deal with it in terms of unconscious meanings rather than through manifest contents which will prove relatively ineffective.

And as you would expect, virtually every intervention is essentially interpretive. I do work from defenses toward contents. I interpret the metaphors of barriers and efforts to destroy meanings in Type C fields; the meanings and functions of projective identifications in Type B fields; and symbolic, Type Two derivatives in Type A fields. And almost always, the most valid unconscious meanings pertain to the therapeutic relationship even with significant and traumatic outside adaptive contexts, I will, as a rule, establish the unconscious links to the therapeutic relationship as well. And I do this not because of some type of bias on my part, but because that is where the Type Two derivatives lie, where the psychopathologically meaningful adaptive contexts reside. It is where the patient's most intense disturbance is expressed, as well as his soundest capacities to function.

And I do keep in mind the importance of establishing genetic links: the history of a symptom or characterological disturbance—or whatever the pathology may be—and the introjects and unconscious fantasies and memories on which it is based. I attend to all of that, proceeding from the surface to the depths and always intervening from the adaptive context outwards.

Discussant: I would just like to be clear that you are referring to psychotherapy as well as to psychoanalysis.

Langs: Yes, to both.

Discussant: So it makes no difference whether the patient is in therapy or analysis?

Langs: It is here that my position is often misunderstood. There is little or no difference in terms of the basic principles of technique to be applied; the basics of the listening process, for example, are clearly the same for both, as are the fundamental qualities of the patient's communications. On the other hand, there will be differences in the nature of the patient's communications, their depth and other qualities related to the frequency of sessions and, at times, to the use of the couch. But there will also be differences based on the patient's pathology, his ego capacities, and many other factors, not the least of which is the therapist's or analyst's pathology—the extent to which he has resolved it—and his positive capacities as well. So it is my contention that there is one basic model of therapy and that one applies it sensitively and judiciously to each therapeutic situation—whether analysis or therapy—in keeping with the patient's communications and needs, and all the rest.

Discussant: So you're saying that the patient will have a long therapy.

Langs: You see, it's quite easy to misrepresent what I said. When I speak of basic principles, many hear me saying that everything is identical: the depth of the material, the solidity of the curative process, the degree of working through, the length of treatment—whatever. And I am not suggesting that this is the case at all. There are differences between analysis and psychotherapy which I will not attempt to detail here. Those of you who are interested can look at the first chapter of my synthesis in *The Therapeutic Interaction* (1976b), where I have expressed my thoughts on that issue.

Discussant: But sometimes I get the feeling, as you're describing your technique, that because it is so taking in and listening, and staying with the patient, that you would have a therapy that went on and on and on. Because there would always be so many derivatives and things.

Langs: No, that isn't the case. You left out the goal of

therapy, which is to do all this interpreting around the therapeutic context of the patient's symptoms, to resolve them and know when to stop. The unconscious is infinite and endless, but therapy isn't.

Discussant: Then symptom resolution is your goal?

Langs: Sure.

Discussant: Because that's not what a lot of analysts would say. They say that sometimes symptom resolution occurs in the first three months of treatment, but that that's a defense— or a flight into health.

Langs: Symptom resolution based on cognitive insight, adaptive structural change, and positive introjects. The modification of pathological defenses and interactional mechanisms: symptom resolution or characterological change on that basis, not symptom resolution per se. I mean it in that specific sense. That's my goal.

Discussant: So you're not interested in personality "reorganization"?

Langs: If it's a symptom, then I'll work on it. Or it will occur in the course of such work.

Discussant: You mean it as a very broad concept.

Langs: When I say symptom, I again get into a lot of confusion. To me, a symptom is any emotional disturbance, characterological or whatever, just as when I say *neurosis* in this course I really mean anything from neurosis to psychosis. I mean any type of disturbance, addiction, character disorder, psychosomatic syndrome, or whatever. I just use these terms as a kind of shorthand.

These are important questions, but for now let's hear a little bit more material.

Therapist: This me–not-me kind of Sullivanian idea is primary to her. There's a whole sort of unwillingness or inability on her part to own up to things because she gets so afraid of her anger. She is afraid to talk about these feelings, or of her depression, or of her feeling unlovable, which is really what I've been trying to get to.

Langs: You are talking about a defensive denial, projection, or locates outside of herself. I'm using the term me–not-me in a different way. That's the trouble with all of these terms. Me–not-me, as you're describing it, has to do with a form of externalization that tends to be characteristic of certain Type C patients who communicate about their own terrible inner distrubance by talking about someone else. The me–not-me interface that I talk about is different. It is a theoretical construct that allows us to state, as a principle of listening, that no matter what the patient is saying, whatever she is talking about, it refers both to herself and to you as her therapist; and it should be monitored as such—at the very least, in the form of Type One derivatives and, wherever possible, around specific adaptive contexts related to the therapeutic interaction, that is, as Type Two derivatives. The term implies nothing about the kind of defenses the patient is using; rather, it describes a condensation of communicative meanings contained in the patient's manifest associations and gives rise, as I have said, to an important principle of listening that should be applied to everything that either the patient or the therapist expresses.

Therapist: Well, what I was trying to do was to focus more and more on which parts were coming from me, and which were coming from her, so that she could own up to some of these feelings rather than just see them as being a reflection of my neglect.

Langs: In principle, certainly one must analyze and interpret denials, projections, and externalizations. At issue is the technique involved: the contrast between your efforts at direct and seemingly premature interventions, and my principles of sitting back, listening, allowing her material to express metaphorically the nature of her defenses—and to shape your intervention. But now, please give us a bit more.

Therapist: But she does this thing, that she frequently will do, and says, after saying something that I thought very meaningful, that it has no meaning. Though I can see it from your point of view also.

Well, to continue: she feels unlovable; then she says, I'm feeling good about myself. She had almost cried, and now she tries to say she's feeling good about herself. And I said, And I'm trying to take that away by making a comment that links how you're relating to me with how you felt about your mother.

Langs: Yes, that has a kernel of truth in it. This is something else I want to get into: the nucleus of truth in an erroneous intervention. See, you're very close to the immediate interaction and to the surface qualities of it, and you intervene very quickly about it. And in terms of the listening process, the session is difficult to understand, because there are so many active inputs from you, and so much from the patient...

Discussant: Isn't each intervention a new adaptive context?

Langs: Yes, each one. Well, let's see how she responds to that; let her guide our discussion a bit.

Therapist: She doesn't respond to it; she starts talking.

Langs: She doesn't respond directly, you mean.

Therapist: She doesn't directly.

Langs: You can see what that says about how you listen. But this is indirect, derivative communication; by and large, it is just what we are searching for. Let's see where it takes us.

Therapist: She says she's decided that the best way to deal with things is to love herself and to not care about how other people feel about her.

Langs: See, it's so interesting, because I really try not to be nasty. I say seemingly nasty things, but not to be nasty. I say them only because it happens to be that this is what the patient's experiencing or saying. So I said to myself, Okay, I won't say anything about her feeling good for the moment. After all, somebody should have said to me: Look, if this is all a commentary on the interaction, how come she feels good now? You're telling us how many bad inputs there are—what's going on? And I would have welcomed that challenge.

Discussant: She feels good by saying, The hell with what you're saying. I have to make myself feel good because you're not going to help me.

Langs: Yes: I'm going to just seal you off, use a manic defense against all these destructive inputs.

I didn't want to say it prematurely. I didn't want to sound nasty, saying that this reference to feeling good is really a form of denial. You'd then say, Look at Langs, he's so arbitrary. Whatever he says is right. He says this is bad stuff. She says it's good and he's going to decide arbitrarily that it isn't. I would have let you in on my silent hypothesis, but I felt it would seem too prejudiced. So I waited, and now she says it for me.

And this is related to our discussion of cure. I'm not talking about momentary symptom alleviation based on this kind of mechanism: give me a bad therapist and I'll feel better because I'm better than he is; I can fend him off, seal him off, deal with him, and let him be the sick one, and I'll be the good or healthy one. On that basis, she'll have to spend her life finding sick, destructive people to live with so she can feel better. That is maladaptive.

But I also want to use this material to show you what I mean about applying the listening process when you hear something about symptom relief. Don't take it at face value—on a manifest level—but listen to the next derivatives. Recall the antecedents, examine them as a commentary on the symptom alleviation, and determine the underlying basis for the symptomatic change. Many therapists simply accept symptom relief as such, and have no interest in determining its unconscious structure. The patient feels better, they're satisfied, and they're ready to terminate. There are countless ways through which patients momentarily, or even more lastingly, find symptom relief. I just recently discussed this issue in a paper (1978a), if any of you wish to pursue the subject.

Discussant:You're saying she's able to feel better, in part, by saying she's going to shut out the therapist and not allow him to intensify her feeling unloved.

Langs: Right. She going to seal off all of these assaults and interventions.

Therapist: But that isn't what happened. She's been kind of pushed to that point.

Langs: She's been pushed, but...

Therapist: Pushed *in her real life* to that point.

Langs: This is in part her tendency too. You see, she starts off by saying No, that's not right, I don't want to hear about it. And you kept insisting and insisting, and you can see that she's at the mercy of these onslaughts. She can barely handle them. So that becomes her resource: Okay, I feel fine. I don't feel unloved.

Therapist: That's what she did with the neurologist. He didn't give her what she wanted, so she got the book out of the library.

Langs: The neurologist, right. She went and generated her own sense of goodness there too. You keep seeing this as a product of the patient's defenses and psychopathology. I keep seeing it as an interactional product, an alloy derived from both of you. It is difficult to shift one's frame of listening toward the interactional side. It means, again, confronting your countertransferences, whatever else it might entail. So can you give us a little bit more?

Therapist: This is pretty much the end.

Langs: Oh?...

Therapist: A few more things get said, she goes through this whole list of things that she tries to do. Cook well, look nice, have pleasant friends and a home...

Langs: Yes. So she shifts now to a manic defense and a Type C barrier: do the clichéd things and that's how you get to feel better. A facade. And I said that the Type C defense is directed against a very disturbing, turbulent inner world. We can see now that it can also be used as a defense against a very turbulent set of interventions. So she's erecting some very nice barriers. That's very interesting.

Therapist: She then said that she had no home.

Langs: "No home." Somehow this material is rather fragmented—at least that is the way the presentation is coming across. I can only treat it as roughly a Type Two derivative in the adaptive context of these provocative interventions, and suggest that it expresses a longing for a home, a place to be contained and held—and a perception of the absence of these qualities in the therapeutic situation.

Therapist: Well, I thought of it in terms of the patient's history. Her mother had been married several times, and each marriage and divorce had been stormy. There were many men too.

Langs: Yes, but I would still suggest that you begin with the immediate therapeutic interaction and trace the genetics from there. In that way, you can distinguish between, on the one hand, the influence of the patient's past as it distorts her perceptions of you, and, on the other, the ways in which your manner of intervening constitutes, on some level, a repetition of her turbulent past. That is an important distinction, since the latter calls for rectification and for a different type of intervening. It will vitiate any effort on your part to interpret this material in terms of transference, fantasies, and distortions based on earlier genetic experiences.

In addition, this material calls for monitoring along the me–not-me interface. Since time is late, I will only suggest briefly that the patient's use of clichés is an introject of the therapist's defensive use of psychoanalytic clichés— premature interventions designed as barriers to the disturbing truths related to the therapeutic interaction—and to himself—and which unconsciously convey, as the patient perceives it, the therapist's wish for a home, container, and hold—considerations that merit serious consideration and self-analysis. Please finish up.

Therapist: Well, her last comment was something to the effect that she tries to present herself as best she can.

Langs:Well, you can see what I mean by a Type C cliché. But, as I said, it's also an unconscious message to you, and it involves both your use of clichés and a suggestion that you present yourself in the best possible manner.

Therapist: Well, I didn't think of it that way and I said: Your presenting yourself as best you can pushes away the bad feelings about your childhood, and now about me. It's your way of dealing with those feelings.

Langs: I'm very pleased that you added, "And now about me," even though your formulation differed from mine. If you had mentioned only her bad feelings about her childhood, you would have left her with the unacknowledged total residue of the badness in this session.

That's another thing that many therapists do all the time. The sick patient is the bad patient, you know, the one with all the bad, sick stuff, and they're the good therapist with all the good stuff. Patients get very depressed on this basis, very overwhelmed with the badness, and they feel terrible. But again, that's one of the unconscious motives for becoming a therapist: you're going to get rid of all your bad stuff and place it into your patients. Therapy is misused for pathological projections and projective identifications. The therapist works over his problems and puts them into his patients (see Langs, 1976c).

So, the fact that you included a reference to yourself, even if it wasn't specified, is very helpful here. It may spare her an unbearable depression. Is there anything more?

Therapist: I had more to say: I then tried to link it up again. I said, And you talked about this through the course of this year, that as a child you felt unloved, and then you went through a phase where you tried to find men to replace your mother but found they didn't care for you either, not in the way you wanted. You had a real problem of feeling unloved by your mother, but from that it seems you developed a tuff and place feeling of being unlovable.

Langs: Yes, so now you shift away from the present interaction, back into the past again.

Therapist: Although in referring to her trying to find men to be loved by, there is an indirect reference to therapy.

Langs: A kernel of an unconscious reference to the therapist. But, remember, I said that as a therapist, you're going to have to express yourself directly and consciously, not unconsciously. The genetics here again are being used in a way that I discussed several times before—as a defense against the immediate relationship—and of course it becomes a means by which you fend off the patient's unconscious perceptions, and possibly your own unconscious perceptions, of the intensity of your activity and your interventions.

There's one other thing I wanted to say about this material in terms of the basics of the listening process: you lose sight so quickly of any immediate adaptive context. You speak in generalizations so quickly. It really offers her reinforcement of her Type C defenses—the use of what's called intellectualization, of genetic psychoanalytic clichés—and this is reinforced by your having been taught to try to interpret genetics. So you keep introducing them, again and again, and it now promotes a bastion and misalliance, a barrier to the tumultuous interaction of the present session.

In stressing the genetics, in treating this as transference, in tracing her response to you to her childhood, you are denying that you're actually behaving in that way on any level. As I said, Margaret Little (1951) has made that point. The transference interpretation implies: I, the therapist, have not behaved that way; you are distorting.

Winnicott (1965) also said something that's helpful here: the patient has no use for the therapist's knowledge when it's way ahead of what he can fathom and use. So often therapists and analysts intervene with ideas and concepts that the patient has not generated in the session at hand, and such comments, even if true, are way ahead of the patient. The patient absolutely cannot integrate them and he will react mainly to being overwhelmed by the therapist's need to be brilliant.

Discussant: Sometimes we make an interpretation to a patient and he gives us this puizzled look, as though we're speaking a foreign language, and he doesn't know what the hell we're up to.

Langs: And here you thought it was so creative and so helpful. Yes, that's another way of stating this point, of getting too far ahead of the patient, but I think it also has many dynamic meanings. Is there anything more to the session?

Therapist: Yes. She talked about this some, and although I did not write down what she said, it was basically her restatement of what I said.

Langs: Right, just a playing back of what was said. Which is all that you get—surface repetition.

Therapist: I said, The pain of feeling unloved and feeling bad about yourself, because you felt unlovable, has a lot to do with your reactions now, and that same sense of being unlovable affects what you feel you can say to me and how you feel about what I say to you.

Langs: Is that how the session ended?

Therapist: She works over some of those things.

Langs: Do you have any notes on that part?

Therapist: Yes. She goes back initially to how she felt I treated her when she would call me on the phone from the hospital when they were doing those tests. She said she felt I was unavailable.

Langs: Again, let's organize this manifest content around the adaptive context of his recent interventions. What does this mean as a Type Two derivative? The manifest content is, You weren't available when I called. As a Type Two derivative in an adaptive context, what would it be?

Discussant: You're not available to me now. You're not listening to me.

Langs: Yes. Your interventions are of no use to her. I just said that; now she says it. I just gave you the lecture about what the patient can't use, and now the patient gives it in her own, derivative way: The manner in which you intervene renders you absent, not here. You're not of any use to me at all.

This is a different level, more immediate and much more painful. You could accept it about the phone calls, but about all these very nice interpretations? And yet, this is her evaluation of them. You can see why you've avoided conceptualizing those derivatives in this way, and that's why I want the specific material. Anything else?

Therapist: She said, I know that much of my not asking for things from other people has to do with other people, that my reaction is to not need people, but it is the best I feel I can do. I wish someone would say to me that these feelings aren't true about myself. She's admitting that she's denying all these feelings at that point. And the final thing...

Langs: Let me just say this: you're about to make another intervention?

Therapist: Yes.

Langs: See, now she's reduced again to using clichés, generalities, vagueness, and this is an interactionally shaped outcome. You used the psychoanalytic cliché, the genetic; she's using the clichés about how to get better: Somebody should tell you it isn't so, and all of that. It all now has that Type C quality, I think quite strongly.

Therapist: But this is what I'm trying to change though, and this isn't unusual when you're dealing with a patient who uses a lot of denial.

Langs: What I'm saying is that you can't change it until you master your own use of that communicative mode. Do you see my point?

Discussant: There's also the implication in what she's saying—it's as if she's asking for an interpretation: Tell me that I'm not unlovable.

Langs: Ultimately, that must be stated through a valid interpretation; that would be the way she would experience it. One viable interpretation could do that. Your final intervention?

Therapist: I said, I think that all of this concern about what your feelings are, or are not, is still related to your feelings about what you did as a child that made your mother not love you.

Langs: Okay, you're married to the genetic stuff. Read the first lines of the next session. Do you have that?

Therapist: Yes.

Langs: Just read the opening remarks, they're always so interesting.

Therapist: In light of the discussion, you'll be happy to hear she canceled the next session.

Langs: I'm never entirely happy to hear that. So, the next communication was that she canceled the session.

Therapist: Due to the flu.

Discussant: When a patient comes in, do you think that, while we have many hypotheses for the adaptive context for the patient, there is usually one main adaptive context? Or can it be three or four?

Langs: It could be several, but usually it's one or two. Most often, just one.

Discussant: And they will usually emerge during the session? Or will the patient deal with one at a time?

Langs: Oh, they'll work over all of them; if there are two, they are often interwoven. It depends. It can be more than one, but even then, one stands out.
What was the first communication in the session after the missed hour?

Therapist: She comes in talking about being sick. She had been sitting in the waiting room reading a book by Horney on Feminine Psychology. She's done to me what she did to the neurologist.

Langs: Yes, so she brings in a book...

Therapist: And was very obviously reading it.

Langs: Yes, in the waiting room. Now there again, using our adaptive context, about the way you've been intervening, which she may well be moving toward—she's reading in the waiting room—you could then take all the material that follows as Type Two derivatives and could eventually intervene about how she's perceiving your interventions.

Discussant: The message there may also be: Since you don't understand me as a woman, I'm reading about it.

Langs: The book is also the Type C field. It's the public, written stuff, which is ultimately a cliché, because it doesn't have personal meaning.

Discussant: The fixed, written word?

Langs: Exactly. It's the cliché that lacks personal meaning.

Discussant: But there's the other sense: if she can't feel good in an interactive way with the therapist, then she'll cure herself.

Langs: Right, she'll do her own containing, her own therapy. These are initial silent hypotheses.

Therapist: In the next session, she first said that she was feeling not understood in relation to the book she had read, and she hoped I wouldn't catch her cold, she'd been very sick. She then clarified for me what was not wrong with her on the basis of having read the book, and then said, at one point, that she felt like she was flunking a test with me, like she felt when her mother would scream at her as a child.

Discussant: It brings it back to the last session; it fits in with that adaptive context.

Langs: Yes, as Type Two derivatives, she saw your

interventions as screaming at her, as attacking her. And again, I'm not saying these things just to be nasty; it's really just my effort to characterize the truth of what you're doing, so that you can begin to come to terms with it. And the business of catching her cold: you see, I can postulate an interactional quality in that, the putting into her of your sickness, your failure therapeutically to hold and contain her pathological projective identification. All this made her ill with the flu. These are the conditions under which I have found physical illness to occur in patients.

Notice too that the patient insists, though through Type Two derivatives, that you are in actuality behaving like her mother. This is primarily nontransference. The functional meaning of the genetic link is clearer now.

Discussant: She's also saying to the therapist: I must have been such a sick person I made you respond this way in the last session.

Langs: Oh, she'll take all the blame. He's putting the badness in to her, and this kind of depressed patient will invite it, accept it, contain it.

Therapist: And I said—to stop her—What would happen if you didn't take on the blame?

Langs: Well, I see that our time is nearly up. In brief, your intervention addresses the manifest content of these communications. It does not treat them as Type Two derivatives related to the adaptive context of your interventions in the previous session—even though she may have alluded to them in her initial associations-(her reference to not being understood was ambiguous)-and had missed a session. You may be implying that she is inappropriately accepting blame with both her mother and yourself, although I think, from your earlier interventions, that you probably have the genetic past in mind. But so long as you unconsciously blame her for the badness in therapy, and in yourself, these interventions will be of no avail. By the way, unconsciously, this intervention is an effort at a curative projective identification: the offer of an unconscious introject that encourages the patient to no longer contain blame, and to refute your efforts, as well as those of her mother, to blame her. And while it might offer some temporary relief, it is by no means an interpretation that can lead to insightful structural change. And it also runs contrary to your unconscious communications to her.

Lastly, your interventions suggest to me the presence of problems in being empathic. You are too focused on your own formulations and insufficiently sensitive to the patient's feelings and communications. Your own needs seem to outweigh your attention to hers. And in a way, I believe she is trying to tell you just that. Discussions of empathy can get very personal, so I will say little more. I just wanted you to see that considerations of empathy can be very difficult to make. It is one dimension of the relationship that is always present, for better or worse.

In general, there are elements of empathy or their lack in every phase. The therapist may be open empathically in its fullest sense, or only with certain patients or with certain types of material. His capacity for empathy is an interactional product too, under consistent influence from the patient. It is an important part of the poorly defined receptiveness of the therapist to the many unconscious qualities of the patient's associations and behaviors, an aspect of the ill-defined unconscious intaking processes that includes intuition and other unconscious sensitivities that are so important in the therapist. They are difficult to specify and important to monitor, and countertransference influences are often hard to detect.

This discussion provides me an opportunity to stress the importance of these more indefinite aspects of listening, and of the more amorphous and unconscious qualities of that process, in contrast to the more explicit aspects of listening and formulating that I have been concentrating on in this course. Actually, there is little that I can teach you regarding the use of empathy, intuition, unconscious sensitivity, and the like. As therapists you must be free to use these tools of listening, to do so as responsively and openly as possible, and to maintain a capacity to validate the inferences derived from these sources. Well, I see our time is about up.

Discussant: Just one final question: How would you define projective identification?

Langs: I define it in *The Bipersonal Field* (1976a) and in *The Therapeutic Interaction* (1976b). Projective identification is an interactional mechanism through which you attempt interactionally to place into the object an aspect of your own inner mental world—your own fantasies, defenses, conflicts, introjects, and all the rest—and you do it in a way that's communicative. Some analysts feel that there's no such thing as pure projection—that projection always has an interactional element even if it is done solely to an introject. But projection is usually thought of as an intrapsychic mechanism: you, within your mind, attribute to another person something that belongs to yourself. And that person may not be there, and you may not try to get him to feel that part of yourself at all. With projective identification, that person is there and you're doing something to have him feel that way.

Discussant: Is projective identification an attempt to get the other person to know where you're at, so they can now feel a camaraderie?

Langs: It can have many functions: the evocation of camaraderie, of proxies. Martin Wangh (1962) says it is used to place things into another person that you can't manage. It can be used to get rid of bad contents or store safe contents, but you really need clinical material to demonstrate its presence.
"Identification" is used idiosyncratically here.

Discussant: That's what I didn't understand.

Langs: Identification usually means: I take on some aspect of your inner state, qualities, or functioning. In projective identification it means I'm identified with what I'm putting into you. That's the first meaning of identification. Number two, I want to evoke in you an identification with parts of me. Identification usually means a process occurring in the exact opposite direction.

Discussant: It can be used both ways?

Langs: It turns out that identification can go both ways; it's a fascinating mechanism. There's no question we're going to have to learn more and more about it.

Well, I see that our time is up, and I can see that you are teaching me the value of working and reworking, of defining and redefining. We will have two more exercises in the listening process: next week, with a session that will be presented without introduction, and, two weeks from now, with a session in which a dream was reported. Thank you for your presentation.

Chapter Nine

AN EXERCISE IN LISTENING

The need for adaptive context • Listening and intervening • Processing subjective responses • Applying the listening process to the therapist's interventions and the patient's responses • Conscious versus unconscious, and nonneurotic versus neurotic communication • The Type A and Type C communicative modes • The functional state of the patient's associations

Langs: Today, as an exercise in listening, we're going to hear a session cold. Perhaps you'll just tell us the age and sex of the patient, the chief complaint, how long the patient has been in treatment, and the frequency of visits. Then start right in and let's see what we experience.

Therapist: This is a twenty-four-year-old woman, a laboratory technician here, who has been in treatment for a year and whose complaint was that she's depressed. I've been seeing her twice a week.

Langs: Okay. Please begin.

Therapist: She comes into the session, and the first thing she says is, Were there any mixed messages regarding last Thursday's appointment?
Do you want me to explain?

Langs: Well, does anyone have a comment?

Discussant: It's kind of like a mixed message. Without

knowing what happened with last Thursday's appointment, we would be at a loss to understand any aspect of this communication.

Langs: That's exactly the point.

Discussant: It sounds like she starts this session with the adaptive context, and perhaps with some issue related to the ground rules.

Langs: Yes, we can see that there is some question regarding what apparently was her last session: either something that happened during the session or something surrounding it. And it is rather undecipherable without at least knowing what had actually happened. Perhaps this shows us that the patient's associations are not to be treated merely as fantasy vehicles; they have to be measured against actuality in order to distinguish elements of fantasy from elements of reality. We quickly see that we cannot meaningfully treat an association in total isolation.

I think we can sense too that the patient initially establishes a continuity here between the last session and the present one, that she immediately mobilizes the therapist's memory in a particular direction, and that her remark pertains, of course, to the therapeutic relationship.

Discussant: I think it would help if the therapist would at least offer some clarification as to what the patient meant.

Langs: Yes, now that we have established that information as something we will need.

Therapist: Actually, this does give you some aspect of the adaptive context, and I'll make it brief. I see her on Tuesday and Thursday. This was on a Tuesday. On the previous Thursday she was away on vacation—that is, she was away the whole week. She wasn't sure she'd be back Thursday and was going to call me Wednesday to let me know if we would have a session. If she didn't call, I was to assume that the session was canceled. That's how she had left it before going on her vacation, and it was clear to me that something was being set up.

Langs: I believe you've told me that clinic policy is that she's not responsible for the session if she's on vacation—as far as the fee is concerned.

Therapist: Yes, and employees don't pay any fees at all. It is covered by the hospital as part of their health care.

Discussant: Plus, when you miss a session, you're not responsible. If you have an appointment and miss the session, even if you don't call or anything, you still don't pay.

Langs: You know, what you've done is interesting. You've really made it very clear that it's almost impossible to just listen to a session without knowing anything at all about the conditions of the therapy or about what happened in the previous hour. I guess, now in retrospect, that I should simply have said, No, don't tell us anything at all. But look, it doesn't have to be a pure exercise and, as such, would have been impossible. Perhaps we should have experienced that quality; our need for clarification may well reflect an intolerance for ambiguity, and even chaos. Still, this does show how much we need a context in order to understand the patient's material.

But, this also shows you, as I said, that in regard to the listening process the patient may bring back certain events and experiences, very quickly in some sessions, though obviously there are many other ways in which the session could begin, including some where there would be no specific reference at all to the therapy or the ground rules. Or to the prior hour. The patient would start to talk about something extraneous, or whatever. Still, you'd be surprised how often an hour begins with a continuing working over of a frame issue when it is present.

You did not tell us whether she called you—whether there was a session the previous Thursday. It may become obvious in a moment, but don't tell us for now. We'll see if it becomes apparent from the material. Let's tolerate a bit of uncertainty for the moment.

So I want to do a number of things. I want to have you experience what happens with a session where you know very little—although with this session, you already know something very significant that set the stage for the hour. So we really don't have a blank session. We already know something that is undoubtedly part of the adaptive context for the session, so we're not going to be listening without an adaptive context. We don't know if there are additional adaptive contexts; we'll get into that a little bit later on.

I also want to concentrate on what you experience subjectively, because we want to continue to study, in these last two sessions on listening, the role of empathy, intuition, and other subjective responses. The basic point with such inner experiences, as I said last week, is that they must be validated. We try to make use of our subjective experiences, but we also try to validate what we derive from them. And we don't take an empathic or intuitive experience as a form of gospel; we are prepared to distinguish essentially sensitive empathic or intuitive responses from those that are contaminated by significant countertransferencers and that contain, for example, pathological projections from the therapist onto the patient—a point made by Beres and Arlow (1974) and Shapiro(1974) among others. Please continue.

Therapist: So she had asked if there were any mixed messages regarding last Thursday: Was there any confusion about it? And I said, No, were you concerned that there were?

Langs: Okay. Briefly, how would you assess this intervention?

Discussant: The first part was simply an answer. Well, perhaps not simply—I'd rather not use that word in this seminar. It was an answer to the patient's question. The second part of the intervention was itself a question, asking the patient about her feelings.

Discussant: I think that the first part reflected a certain pressure that the therapist must have felt as a need to answer the patient.

Langs: Yes. We will, of course, study the nature of the therapist's interventions, in regard to both the management of the framework and verbal interventions—ultimately, interpretations and reconstructions—later in this course. Still, as I respond to the interventions that have been detailed during these initial presentations, I realize a number of things regarding the classification offered in my technique book (1973a). Some of these things I was unaware of at the time of writing.

For example, while I did include questions among the interventions that I identified and discussed, basing my considerations on Bibring's basic paper (1954), and while I also included silences, confrontations, clarifications, interpretations, and reconstructions, I now very much suspect that had I undertaken an extensive empirical study of interventions I would have offered a considerably different classification, more in keeping with the actualities of the therapist's communications. Instead I offered a relatively idealized and intellectualized categorization. In addition—and my initial discussions did begin to move in that direction—I would now include a far more extensive delineation of the unconscious communications and unconscious functions of the therapist's interventions. And, as I have already pointed out, much of it would revolve around a basic twofold classification: management of the framework, and interventions directed toward understanding. The latter would deal both with cognitive aspects and with the metabolizations of projective identifications.

Discussant: Could the therapist repeat his intervention?

Langs: Well, I think it's now time to exercise the principle of listening in these seminars without repeating the presentation, unless I happen to develop an extended discussion. I think that it's important for you to experience a failure in listening—which includes, of course, remembering—and to develop some sense of how to deal with it. In your sessions with patients, this may occur, as we have said, on the perceptual level or while accepting vague impingement. And it may happen later in the course of listening, not only as you attempt to exercise the formulating aspects of the listening process, but simply as you try to recall the patient's associations, actively or passively. And when you experience blank spots, failures in recall, it is certainly inappropriate, in principle, to ask the patient to repeat herself. Instead, you should attempt some type of effort at comprehension and of self-analysis: Is the problem in your relationship with the patient? The nature of the material? Or is it in some outside distraction, or some combination of these factors? Anyway, you should sit back and have faith that whatever is important, the patient will repeat in some way. Her subsequent associations will help you rediscover what has been lost.

I could also take this as a model. Your subjective response to this material is possibly one of confusion; you have forgotten what the therapist said. You may, in your sessions with patients, even have difficulty remembering what you yourself said earlier in the same session, just as here you couldn't keep hold of the therapist's intervention. We can take that as a subjective response and can ask if it reflects something of a state of confusion in the therapeutic interaction. Perhaps the intervention was confusing, or unmemorable. Maybe you were distracted or the intervention evoked some kind of anxiety within you. Maybe you just don't listen well in my presence. Whatever. These responses are always an interactional amalgam, and, especially when there is evidence of blockage or some other difficulty, you must begin to investigate them. And you work over all of this along the me–not-me interface: How much is coming from the patient—here, we would add, from the presenter or myself—and how much from within yourself? And you'll find that whatever the contribution from your own inner difficulties your confusion bears some relationship to the material at hand.

Now it is evident that other members of this seminar have remembered what the patient and therapist said so we are immediately faced with individual differences in subjective reactions and responses to material from patients. Still, it should be possible to filter out these individual differences and to arrive at a consensus in respect to the meaning of the patient's and therapist's communications—though we know full well that there will always be some individual and stylistic variations surrounding any particular validatable core.

Now, returning to the formal and communicative properties of this intervention, the first part is actually a declaration from the therapist in the form of a self-revelation: something he thought, or felt, or experienced. It's not derived from the material from the patient in the sense in which I have used that concept; it is, instead, a direct reaction to that material. It is not an approach to the interpretation of the unconscious meanings of these initial associations, but rather a description of an aspect of the therapist's own subjective state; it's as if he were saying, No, I was not in the state of confusion.

In hearing that, I was immediately struck by the way in which I had organized and categorized the therapist's interventions in my technique book (1973a). There I actually delineated a series of formal and supposedly neutral interventions geared toward interpretations and, while I now doubt that questions, clarifications, and confrontations can be offered with an aura of neutrality, I had not classified a whole category of interventions that are clearly and fundamentally *not* neutral—interventions that are self-revealing and, possibly always, countertransference-based. Typically for our field, I avoided a detailed study of erroneous interventions—though I did approach the subject.

So the first part—the No—is not a neutral intervention, and it also modifies the therapist's anonymity. The second part is a question of the patient, about her feelings. What are its communicative qualities?

Discussant: Well, I guess the feeling I had was that the therapist must have felt a certain pressure to answer, in order to relieve her confusion, to put less confusion into her.

Langs: To alleviate her confusion. Anything else?

Discussant: Maybe his own confusion.

Langs: Well, to relieve his postulated sense of inner

pressure, his need to answer the question. So it communicates a way of getting rid of tension, through a self-revelation. There is some sense of tension and demand in the patient's asking you whether there was a mixed message: Were you confused? Your way of dealing with that tension was to simply respond, No. Let's dispose of the tension—the question—of how the patient might feel if you don't answer her question, or whatever.

Now such responses can also be listened to in the interactional sphere, in terms of a projective identification made by the patient quite unconsciously, of her own inner tensions and unconscious fantasies regarding the possible missed session. And your intervention reflects a refusal to contain those tensions, a failure in your containing function, and your need to dispose of them through a tension alleviating projective identification. Clearly, I am postulating a transaction in a Type B field and an exchange of projective identifications without processing toward insight.

So, we've seen some of the cognitive qualities of the patient's communications and the therapist's response, and we'll soon get to a bit more in that regard. I have formulated this material in terms of projective identifications—in the realm of interactional mechanisms—sensing interactional pressures that must be subjected to validation. Now, to complete the picture, would anyone respond to this material by listening in the other interactional realm—that of role and image evocation?

Discussant: Well, I see the therapists as subservient here, as sort of humbly answering her question and as needing to clarify.

Langs: Yes, if we were the therapist we might experience an immediate role pressure to shift away from an interpretive stance to the direct answer of a question, and to allow the patient to control the situation and ourselves—rendering us passive and in some sense subservient. Here too we would process these subjective feelings and pressures, attempting to sort out the me–not-me interface: how much is stemming from the patient's pressures, and how much from our own inner sense of vulnerability? We would try to identify those qualities that do indeed derive from the patient and to formulate their basis in terms of the recent therapeutic interaction, including both our own contributions and the patient's internal psychopathology.

Now, what does this intervention reflect in terms of the therapist's listening process?

Discussant: Are you talking about the first part now?

Langs: Any part—the entire intervention.

Discussant: Well, this is not a direct response to your question, but it seems to me that the second part of his intervention was something of a suggestion. In other words, it wasn't just asking her about her feelings about it: it was suggesting that she was concerned.

Langs: Yes, it's leading her and that may narrow the range of her associative response. But in terms of her material, the therapist intervened on what basis?

Discussant: Manifest content.

Langs: Manifest content. He addressed the manifest content of the material. Okay. Now, the other basic property of an intervention is what? The question we always ask about an intervention? (Pause.) We've given it a formal identity. We're starting to discuss its communicative qualities, and the first thing we need to know when we consider its communicative qualities—and that is where I should have begun my discussion—is...what?

Discussant: The adaptive context.

Langs: The adaptive context. Right. Does this intervention have an adaptive context?

Discussant: We don't know, but maybe the adaptive context

is the issue of the communication related to the session that occurred or didn't occur. Perhaps his comment is related to that adaptive context.

Discussant: I would say no. The way he intervened really didn't deal with that adaptive context.

Langs: Don't you see, it's tricky. It implicitly addresses the adaptive context of the missed session, but not explicitly. I see that I am assuming the sessions were missed based on my impression of this communication from the patient. But this is not an intervention in which the adaptive context alluded to in the patient's question is addressed interpretively. As I said, it seems likely now—and this is not in the manifest material as yet—but it seems likely that she missed both sessions and is raising the question, did you understand that I was not going to be there?

But the therapist is not saying, You missed two sessions and now you ask me a question in order to do such and such about that, for example, to put me under pressure, or to have me feel the pressures involved with your absence, or to set aside some concerns you had about how we handled it, or whatever.

Now please understand that I am not suggesting that I would have intervened in that way. I am simply offering a model with which you can compare the therapist's actual intervention. His response was not an effort to generate an understanding of the patient's unconscious reactions to a particular adaptive context. It did not utilize Type Two derivatives. And so, while it certainly involved the adaptive context, it did not attempt to analyze anything related to it.

And here you can also see that the therapist's intervention can be understood, listened to, by determining the immediate precipitant in the patient's material for his comment. And in this regard, the adaptive context of the missed sessions remains in the background. And if this intervention is not interpretive, if it turns out to be largely countertransference-based, we would see it as a maladaptive reaction to that same adaptive context and, in addition, to the patient's initial communication, in which she asks a direct question and calls the attention of the therapist to the ambiguity of the arrangements they had made. So I trust that we can see again that the adaptive context concept serves us in listening both to the material from the patient and to the therapist's intervention. Every communication from the patient and therapist must be considered in terms of the ongoing therapeutic interaction and in terms of the adaptive qualities of each response.

It's interesting too, if you think about it, that we are dealing with a situation in which the frame is apparently basically unsecured. The patient's initial communication is, unconsciously, an effort to further modify the frame, and her wish in this regard is immediately gratified: the frame is, indeed, further modified, though then the therapist attempts to recover and to reconstitute. So here in rapid succession, in an intervention, you have a deviation and an attempted rectification. He deviates in the first part, by answering her direct question, and then, in the second part, tries to rectify the frame by asking her was she concerned about it. Still, as a question it lacks full neutrality. At best, then, it is an attempt to move toward the restoration of one part of a damaged frame.

So this now is what she has heard. She probably will recognize that he's under some pressure, that he has a need to answer , that he addresses the manifest content, and that he then tries to begin to rectify the situation. And we'll see how she picks it up and works it over.

Now, he has addressed this on a manifest level. He's asked a question, and questions are almost always geared to manifest content, and away from derivative communication—even though the conscious intention is to elicit derivatives. Let's see how it gets worked over. This is an early intervention, one that has already become a part of the adaptive context for the patient's associations. Let's see how it unfolds.

Therapist: Okay. She said, No, but she realized that it was a complicated message that she had given me, and she had been under the pressure of exams (she's doing postgraduate work) and so she wasn't sure whether I would have gotten the message clear.

Langs: So, there's the theme of being under pressure and of doing things in a confusing way. They come up partly as a response to the intervention, partly because of other factors. But you can be sure that there is an important introjective element here. Certainly, when the frame is ill defined, when there is no fee, when the patient can cancel at will while the therapist is still available—you see, the whole situation is chaotic.

Now what I'm already doing—I slip into it so quickly—is that I'm taking specific first-order associations manifestly related to an aspect of treatment. I'm abstracting from them more general themes—two of them, pressure and confusion—and generating specific second-order themes as Type Two derivatives around the adaptive context of the treatment conditions: the recent missed sessions and the therapist's initial intervention, and their latent contents. I do not, as many therapists would, suspend the listening process in the face of a direct question from the patient. And I see the patient's response to the therapist's comment as Type Two derivatives which validate the silent hypothesis I had just offered—the appropriate reward for valid listening.

The hypothesis that I made based on the opening communication of this session—that there was a projective identification by the patient of her own sense of inner pressure (and, I should have added, a projective identification of an inner state of confusion). In retrospect, that is now quite evident. My formulation regarding the interactional pressures the patient seemed to be experiencing is now validated by these additional associations—on a cognitive level. Had I also postulated an inner sense of confusion based in part on the insecure frame, that too would have found validation here.

Next, as a Type Two derivative monitored along the me–not-me interface in the adaptive context of the altered frame and this last intervention, this material implies that it is not only the patient who is confused and gives out complicated messages. The therapist himself has done just that—offered complicated and confusing interventions, a chaotic therapeutic situation, and a pressured, confused response to the patient's question. Failures to interpret and self-revelations are, unconsciously, typically experienced and introjected by the patient in this way. So our hypotheses regarding the interactional inputs from both patient and therapist—their spiraling interplay—have been validated through Type Two derivatives from the patient.

In terms of the details of the listening process, you'll notice that although the manifest content is about one aspect of the treatment situation, it contains derivatives related to other dimensions of the therapeutic relationship. That is, the first-order theme involves the manner in which the patient told the therapist about the missing session and then shifts to a reference to the patient's exams—a situation outside of therapy—and her feeling confused and under pressure. The general themes are situations of chaos and confusion, pressures of examination—and take note of that theme in the light of supervision and of the fact that the patient works in this hospital and is probably quite well informed—as well as themes related to complex messages and uncertainty, to name those that are most salient. And the second-order themes, organized around the adaptive contexts I just identified, allude to the basic nature of the ground rules and framework of this treatment, an issue which would arise at this time because she had just missed two sessions and was able to exploit the situation by leaving the therapist in a position where he was waiting to hear from her, holding the time open. He was at her beck and call. There are additional Type Two derivatives related to the sense of pressure conveyed in the therapist's premature intervention, as well as a Type One derivative monitored around the therapeutic relationship, in terms of the patient's possible belief that the therapist is being supervised and examined, and that this is the source of some of the pressure that he is experiencing in this therapeutic relationship.

But in principle we start with one particular issue in treatment, generalize, and organize the resultant around another and related treatment issue, using the most imme-diate adaptive context. We then develop additional specula-tions based on possible Type One derivatives. So, she spoke of one problem with the frame, and I'm suggesting that the latent content alludes to several other frame issues, including the therapist's nonneutral interventions. In all, you can see how rich this very brief segment of this session is in terms of interactional mechanisms, unconscious contents, and all the rest. And you can see the complexity of the listening process that we must apply to this material.

Discussant: Could you also say that this patient, then, tried to put her confusion into the therapist?

Langs: Yes, that was part of my initial formulation and, as I said, this material seems to confirm that thesis. Now for me it is a tentative confirmation. I will see if there is additional material that coalesces in derivative form around that theme. But remember too, this is a circular interaction, and it will be hard to determine who initiated the sense of confusion. Probably, the best hypothesis is that there has been a variety of exchanges of projective identifications of confusion, and that it exists as an inner state in both the patient and the therapist.

So, remember that once you have intervened you listen to the material from the patient as a commentary on that intervention. And the least of its content will be the patient's efforts to consciously clarify. We must continue to utilize the full listening process and to understand the material on every possible level. In fact, her comment about her own complicated message is really a version of the extensive evaluation that I developed for the therapist's intervention: that, too, was a complicated message. And in terms of the patient's listening process, she may well have sensed the variety of unconscious messages that it contained. And I say this despite the fact that I am well aware that there is a logical sequence here, a clear-cut surface meaning, but that too is only a small segment of the listening process, and it should not prompt us to disregard the inevitability of rich unconscious communications beneath that realistic surface. Please continue.

Therapist: She then went on to say that last Tuesday night, this fellow Al—and she asked me, Do you remember him? I'm not sure if I mentioned him here. This was a guy I knew in high school; he was interested in hospital administration. I liked him. He was very unemotional. She was asking me, Does it ring a bell?

Langs: One of the principles that we will get to in regard to the frame is: one deviation begets another. And Freud(1912b) actually said this, in one of his papers on technique. He said that if the analyst begins to reveal himself, the patient's appetite will be whetted, and it will soon be the analysis of the analyst, rather than that of the patient. So, having answered her once, now she has another question. You see?

Therapist: And I slipped right into it. I said, Wasn't he the fellow you called before going to Atlanta?

Langs: So, not only do you acknowledge that you remember him, but you add—well, this is another intervention, we might as well classify it. What's the nature of this intervention?

Discussant: It's a question.

Langs: It's a question. What else is it?

Discussant: It's a self-revelation.

Langs: It's a self-revelation, and it's one that extends the patient's associations, by adding a particular association from the therapist to the material at hand. This is self-revelation, and it represents the need, again, to directly reassure the patient that you understand her, that you listen and remember. And you do it inappropriately: that is, not through an interpretation, but via a direct, noninterpretive response. This reaction is designed to ease the pressures that she is creating in you, and it reveals a special need on your part to exhibit certain seemingly positive qualities.

The intervention also implies—and communicates—a need on your part to continue to relate to the patient on the manifest level, to explore manifest contents, and to use them as Type C barriers against more disturbing latent contents. You imply that you prefer that the patient not develop fantasies—transference or nontransference, distorted or nondistorted—of you as confused or uncertain, as unable to remember, and you intervene in order to remove such speculations from the patient's mind. I am reminded here of a principle espoused by Tarachow (1962) to the effect that at the point the therapist shifts to a consideration of the realities of the patient's communications and takes them as manifest or real, the transference illusion—its "as if" qualities—disappears.

To put this all another way, in terms of one important underlying dynamic that is being obliterated through your offer of Type C barriers, these endeavors carry with them a sense of falsification. That is, the patient's uncertainties and doubts about your capacities as a therapist are to be directly modified into feelings of confidence to the point where they are to be obliterated of falsified. Unfortunately, this intervention will only heighten those concerns. In any case, these associations can be organized as Type Two derivatives around the modifications in the framework and the considerable chaos that this is creating for the therapeutic interaction—within the patient and, I suspect, within the therapist as well. The frame, after all, offers ego support for both patient and therapist. And here, through derivatives, the patient is attempting to work over that area.

And your response is not exploratory; it disregards the unconscious meanings involved, and directs the patient not to work over such anxieties and concerns—to set them aside. Your intervention therefore constitutes a refusal to contain the sense of uncertainty and chaos that exists within the patient and, once again, is a projective identification of a defensive denial, of the model of an impervious barrier, and, in its extreme, of a delusion that everything is clear. This, rather than a preparedness to face the actual chaos which exists in this therapeutic situation, and which is typified by the kind of arrangements you accepted in regard to this patient's vacation. You have our sympathy, because much of this is imposed upon you by clinic policy, though some of it undoubtedly expresses your own countertransferences. You are trying to impose a false sense of certainty upon a patient and a therapeutic bipersonal field that actually is characterized by uncertainty and chaos. And she will take that in, hear it, introject its implications, perceive you on that basis, experience it as a role evocation—let's pretend that everything is clear and fine—and work it over accordingly.

Discussant: I know when I do that—when a patient asks me, Do you remember so and so, and I say yes—when I look back on it, sometimes it's a feeling of proving to the patient how good a therapist I am.

Langs: Yes, how smart you are, how much you remember—which again, is an attempt to generate a specific image of yourself for the patient to present his having a different, more threatening image. It is a way of disposing of an image evoked by the patient that runs contrary to your ideal image, a way of responding to a subjective feeling that the patient thinks badly of you by contradicting it. Instead, you should use the evoked image as a means of understanding what it is that the patient is trying to create within you, and then attempt to trace out its implications and meanings so that these efforts can eventually be interpreted. It is here that you may understand what I mean by utilizing subjective reactions as signal responses, experiencing in some limited way the image that the patient has evoked and then responding with efforts to understand its sources and meanings, rather than with behaviors designed either to contradict or to further support it.

It's rather interesting to realize that you can put together the patient's initial associations in terms of the image that she has of you and is attempting to evoke within you. They're filled with allusions involving confusion, uncertainty, unreliability, doubt concerning your capacity to remember. Things of that sort. And you can see that consistently you responded by refusing to contain and metabolize the projective indentificatory elements and to process the images as well. Manifest refutation is substituted for efforts at interpretive and insightful alteration. And as I said, manifest efforts of that type are generally experienced by the patient as an unconscious communication of further confusion; there is a split

between the manifest and the latent message, but, unconsciously, the patient experiences both.

Discussant: Could the therapist have responded differently? That is, couldn't he have said, Yes, he was the one who
called you before he went to Atlanta—saying it affirmatively.

Langs: Well, either way, as question or affirmation, the form
it takes is a minor aspect of the communication involved here.
It would still convey the needs and meanings I have discussed.
But you see, again he's listening on the manifest content level;
he's not allowing an adaptive context to develop. And you
have to remember: this is an employee here. It's probably an
impossible therapeutic situation to begin with—an employee
with a resident, both from the same hospital. It has to be
chaos. So he's trying to prove to her that he's a good and
remembering therapist, that she shouldn't have bad images of
him and all of that, and he's doing it because of the pressures
that this kind of situation is bound to create, whatever else is
going on.

So again, in terms of the material, he addresses the manifest
content and responds with a self-revealing intervention. And
again we learn that work on a manifest level—here, direct and
realistic responses to the patient's questions—tends to involve
misalliances and bastions designed to seal off unconscious
aspects of the therapeutic interaction that are creating
unresolved difficulties for the therapist and, usually, for the
patient as well. Insufficient use of the listening process stems
from countertransference-based needs, whatever other contributions may be involved.

And you can see how this patient attempts to exploit the
ground rules on one level, while on another she tries to call the
absurdity of their application to the attention of the therapist.
The next thing you know, she is attempting to exploit them
even further. And unconsciously, the therapist continues to
participate without interpreting, without rectifying the frame
to the greatest possible extent, and without interpreting the
nature of the unconscious interaction.

Discussant: I must say that I have had similar difficulties in treating employees at this medical center, and I have really questioned the advisability of having such patients in therapy. They often learn a lot about our personal lives, they know that we're in training, and the pressures from them and within ourselves are often quite unbearable.

Langs: It's good to know we all share the same problems; that's why everybody presents in this seminar, you know. Go ahead.

Therapist: So she goes on to talk about him, saying that they got together Tuesday night, and she said that he opened the door and came in, and she hugged him and gave him a kiss. And immediately he tensed up, and she felt terrible.

Langs: Okay, so that didn't take very long, you see. Isn't that marvelous? So now, we see again that whatever went on in the past—in therapy and in the patient's life—the present interaction so overshadows it for the moment that it must be dealt with first. So what do we hear? Let's formulate this communication. Let's do the listening exercise, if I may call it that, with this association.

Therapist: I think it refers...

Langs: Well, you speak last. Therapist last, because you're closest to it. Anybody else want to try? (Pause.) Well, they seem to want to leave it to you.

Therapist: I think she's referring to her coming back to treatment—to me. And she comes back in and greets me—well, I'm not exactly sure about the details, but it refers to her coming back to me and this whole issue of the vacation. That's the way I hear it.

Langs: See: as therapists and human beings we're absolutely marvelous. We always find a way of removing the impact just a bit. It's such a representative formulation. Let's do it this way: when we formulate associations, where do we start? Do we have an adaptive context? (Pause.) Okay. I'll do it now in a very formal way. Do we have an adaptive context for these associations?

Discussant: The canceled session, and then, her coming in and the therapist's giving his interventions.

Langs: Yes. For the moment, which of the two seems more important?

Discussant: I won't go out on a limb—okay, the second one.

Langs: Yes, exactly. You're on a very safe limb. There are two adaptive contexts: the first is the cancellation of the sessions and anything else that went on between them before that. The second is what's already happening in this session.

Discussant: What I heard in that—I wasn't exactly sure what you asked for, the way you formulated the question—but what I heard was that she came in and greeted him, kissed him in a sense, and he tensed up. And she felt bad.

Langs: Yes, greeted him and kissed him. How did she do that?

Therapist: She asked me questions.

Langs: Yes, as Type Two derivatives coalesce around the immediate adaptive context of her communications and yours at the beginning of this session, the patient now unconsciously reveals that for her, at least, and perhaps for the therapist as well—applying the me–not-me interface—her question was a greeting, a kiss—and a seduction. Now how much of that is unconscious actuality and how much is fantasy? This is very much a transversal communication that must be treated as such, and it is an unconscious communication that shows you what happens when you deal with manifest content alone. You respond directly to the surface of the patient's material, yet often you are on another level reacting unconsciously to crucial, unrecognized unconscious meanings, and you get into a lot of difficulty.

So you can see that I don't make up this stuff about modifications in the frame; they are filled with unconscious meaning, and the patient will reveal them if we simply apply the listening process to the material that follows even the most minor deviation. And you can see too that the most seemingly innocuous associations and interventions can be—and usually are—filled with unconscious implications.

Now, when we attempt to arrive at a formulation of a particular sequence, we begin the listening exercise by identifying the adaptive context, if available, and we then take the specific first-order themes and generate general themes. We then shift back to second-order specific themes organized around the adaptive context. This is a training exercise in how to listen, the detailing of a process that you will soon be able to carry out rather automatically. But the more you dissect and understand its nature, the more you will properly use it. Start by being open and loose. Allow free impingements. I must emphasize that again, because I say so little about that part, because of the need to clarify the many neglected facets of the more formal and organized aspects of listening. Remain open to all possibilities and impingements, but at some point, too, shift to processing and conceptualizing, then back to openness, and so on.

So, what the therapist did here in formulating the material for us was rather interesting—and very human. Therapists do it all the time. He chose to obliterate the specific adaptive context derived from the immediate interaction between himself and the patient in this session and considered, instead, a more general adaptive context related to the patient's having been away and returning—a context that immediately excludes a significant contribution from the therapist himself, and especially from his underlying countertransferences. Also, he left out his specific interventions in this session, and we can sense his need to do so for defensive reasons.

And we can generalize that this is exactly how many therapists formulate material: without an adaptive context at all, nondynamically, in terms of contents suspended in air so to speak, defensively avoiding the dynamics of their immediate interaction with the patient, in which, as I say, their unconscious countertransference fantasies may exert considerable influence. At best, if such a therapist were to monitor this material in terms of the therapeutic interaction, he would think of this material as the erotic fantasy of a patient who had been away a while, and who now returns, wants to love her therapist, and is concerned that he will be frightened away. That is a transference formulation: the immediate displacement is from the therapist onto the patient's male friend. And we would anticipate, as well, genetic links to the past, to her father or brother, or whatever. This reflects a consideration of the patient in terms of her fantasies and isolates the material from the actual therapeutic interaction and the unconscious communications from the therapist. And while it pertains to the therapeutic relationship, it does so in a singularly one-sided way. It also illustrates a function of transference formulations and interpretations identified by both Szasz (1963) and Chertok (1968), to the effect that such efforts may well function as defensive barriers to an awareness of the contributions of the therapist's counter-transferences—and to the nontransference aspects of the patient's responses to the therapist.

As you would expect, I would formulate this material quite differently. I would note the background adaptive context: the missed sessions, the arrangements that were made in that respect, and the manner in which it had been handled in the sessions prior to the patient's vacation—an aspect regarding which we have no information as yet. And I would then identify as the second adaptive context the initial interaction in this session, especially the therapist's interventions. And with this as my potential organizer, I would take this material about being seductive and frightening the boyfriend who then pulled away as the first-order theme. I would generalize to themes of seduction on one side and fear on the other, leaving it open so that I can apply the me–not-me interface. I would then derive second-order specific themes around the adaptive contexts of the vacation constellation and the therapist's interventions, thinking of it all as a transversal communication, a mixture of unconscious fantasy and unconscious perception, and developing two separate formulations: one in which the patient is the seducer—the more apparent level; and one in which the therapist is the seducer—the more concealed level, and the one the therapist is most likely to avoid.

Let's take that first level and spell it out. Unconsciously, her vacation arrangements were seductive, as were her questions in the initial part of this hour. And your direct answers were perceived as responding in kind, while your attempt to rectify the frame by asking her to explore her question further was seen as a kind of frightened withdrawal. Similarly, your describing your recollection of this boyfriend was seen as your participation in a seductive misalliance initiated by the patient, while your subsequent listening was seen as a pulling back. And you may recall that I had, especially in connection with the first sequence, already formulated and predicted the presence of such unconscious meanings. And so I would suggest that there are strong elements of unconscious perception here, and that the extent to which the patient's pathological unconscious fantasies are contaminating these perceptions will be unclear until the frame is rectified and you no longer participate in the sector of misalliance.

In addition, it strikes me that I had also suggested rather strongly that you were pulling away from the unconscious implications of the patient's communications. And the patient's associations at this point in the session suggest an unconscious perception of your fear and avoidance of the underlying meaning of these derivatives. And I see this again as her brief unconscious lecture on technique, her unconscious supervision: therapists who wish to remain at a manifest level are frightened by the meanings of the underlying derivatives. That is a point that I have made repeatedly, and, unconsciously, patients will make it too.

Now in regard to the therapist, some of this is perhaps based on his interventions in the session prior to the patient's vacation, but some of it must be founded on the arrangements that he accepted in regard to the missed sessions, and on his need to further modify the framework by directly answering the patient's questions, in a manner that also was self-revealing. In that way, he too—and you can see the circularity of all of this, the never-ending spirals—he too can be seen as initiating a seductive interplay. And the material suggests that the patient unconsciously is aware of her own initial tendency to join in responsively, and of some additional underlying anxiety. This formulation is, of course, based on an introject of the therapist within the patient. And for the moment, because of the countertransference-based input from the therapist, he would find it extremely difficult to determine which level and meaning of this material is most central— although we should keep in mind every possible implication as we listen to further associations. The patient will help us sort it out.

So, allusions to manifest content by the therapist do not appear to be experienced by the patient as preliminary work geared toward an ultimate understanding of unconscious processes. They tend instead to function as barriers, to constitute a breaking of closeness and relatedness between therapist and patient—a form of pulling back, or the breaking of links, as Bion (1959) has termed it—and are a means of creating falsifications designed to conceal unconscious fantasies and perceptions related to the therapeutic relationship.

And you can see too that, in so many ways, it's all in the listening. Every session can indeed be its own creation. All you need do is apply the listening process in its fullness. If there is an important antecedent, more often than not the patient will allude to it on some level and it can be readily included in your silent formulation and, then, in your intervention. In fact, everything that I have just said could be treated as a set of silent hypotheses. And because of the presence of modifications in the framework—an important therapeutic context—and the related need to rectify and interpret in this area, I would be more than prepared to intervene once the patient offered me a suitable bridge that made the connections between this material and the ongoing therapeutic interaction unmistakable. Since she has already alluded to therapy, all I would wait for is a full coalescence of derivatives. I already have much to say.

Discussant: What would you say?

Langs: Well, I might start by pointing out that the patient is now back after having missed two sessions; that there had been an arrangement, as she was now recalling, that I would wait to hear from her as to whether we would have the sessions; and that she also had asked several questions in this hour. I would then point out that I had responded by accepting her arrangements and by answering her questions rather directly, and that she has now gone on to talk about her boyfriend and used that as a means of telling us something of what was going on unconsciously in all of this. I would point out that she is saying that she was being rather seductive, that she perceived my responses as acceptant of that seductiveness, and that the effort that I made to restore the session to an exploration of what was going on in her mind had been experienced by her as my having been frightened off and pulling away from her. But as I say, that is a very tentative and model intervention—part of a silent hypothesis—and I would wait for the further coalescence of derivatives, in particular, for a major organizing or meaningful derivative, before offering it. There are already sufficient derivatives and clear-cut therapeutic and adaptive contexts. There is no doubt that I would intervene in this session. The patient is so actively working over these issues, there can be no other response, and it would include implicit rectification of the frame and an interpretive intervention.

Now, I hadn't wanted to get into the details of intervening, but, since you may be using these techniques, notice that my intervention implies a nucleus of valid perceptiveness on her part and yet leaves open the possibility of distortion and sexualization there too. It is what I now term a *transversal interpretation*. My proposed comment also implies some degree of error on my part—my participation in her seductiveness through agreeing to her arrangements and by responding directly to her questions—and also approaches the rectification of the frame. It does not treat her view of me as joining her in some kind of intimacy as if it were totally distorted and based on some early seductiveness on the part of her father or brother. It does not treat it even as displaced for the moment from her relationship with the boyfriend. It is also not a confession, though it implicitly acknowledges some sense of error and a wish to rectify the situation, as well as to interpret the patient's perceptions and, eventually, her fantasies.

And I must add, since this is often a point of confusion, that it will be possible to deal with the patient's unconscious transference fantasies, her own essential psychopathology, only to the extent that it can be relatively isolated. And this can be done only when the therapist's contribution to the patient's sexualization—to take that as an example—has been rectified, that is, when essentially it is no longer in existence and these unconscious perceptions no longer have a valid basis. Only then, and only after interventions that implicitly accept the perceptive nature of these communications, can you get at the kinds of derivatives that you have heard a great deal about, in terms of transference and pathological unconscious fantasies and introjects. I am not proposing a neglect of that sphere but am simply adding another and more primary sphere that must first be understood and dealt with through both rectification and analysis before this other area can be explored and analyzed.

And certainly, the fewer errors, misinterpretations, and unnecessary framework deviations, the less your own pathology will contribute to the field, the more your patient's pathology will contribute, and the more the therapeutic work will focus in that area. Let's leave it at that for now; we will certainly come back to this issue many times during this course. Please continue.

Therapist: Okay. She felt terrible. She knew that it wasn't all her. She knew that she wasn't really trying to seduce him, but that he felt that way. She said, We talked about it; I told him that I had feelings about him a few years ago, at which point he totally tensed up and just felt very uptight.

Langs: "She knew that it wasn't all her." I hope you all heard that. That is her condensed version of the lecture that I gave just now, the part about the distinction between transference and nontransference, the part about everything being an interactional product. And she even adds something regarding the possibility that the therapist might distort—though of course we must also recognize that she too can misunderstand and distort. And it would really be quite sad if the therapist had intervened in a manner suggesting that it *was* all her, that these were merely her fantasies and distortions, perceptions, and all the rest.

You'll notice too—and we might connect this to the issue of manifest versus latent content—that the patient is talking about the surface, and about implications, and about being misunderstood—all of which may reflect wishes to confuse the therapist, but may also very much convey the patient's sense that she is not being understood and that the therapist is too tense to appreciate the implications of her communications. I would say it this way: in the face of these rich Type Two derivatives and the patient's effort to create a Type A field, the therapist's adherence to the manifest content and to Type C barriers may well be disrupting her efforts at symbolic functioning. There is a most interesting, recent paper by Fiumara (1977) devoted to the development of symbolic functioning, and it's well worth reading in this context.

Discussant: If what this patient is relating about seeing this guy was a significant event that occurred in the interim, say between sessions, or whatever, and is something she thought was significant to bring up in therapy, do you not think that she would have been talking about this same material, in a similar way, regardless of the therapist's response?

Langs: I'm glad you asked that. It's one area I have to come back to over and over again to make convincing the point about the functional state of derivatives, the functional meanings of associations vis-à-vis the ongoing therapeutic interaction—not thinking of material as material, as static and fixed. And it also brings up again the difference between an intrapsychically significant adaptive context in terms of neurotic or psychotic mechanisms and processes, which is the realm of neurosis in the broad sense, and significant events—contexts—that evoke intrapsychic responses but not unconscious fantasies and introjects in their derivative and pathological forms. There are, then, two basic issues here: the distinction between different types of adaptive contexts, and the nature of the patient's associations—the claim by some that material is just material and needn't be related dynamically to the ongoing therapeutic interaction.

As for the first point, her reactions to the boyfriend are manifest. And while they are undoubtedly in some way related to the patient's psychopathology, they are in this particular session *not* connected to the unconscious meanings and functions of that pathology, but are serving rather as a means of representing an aspect of the relationship to the therapist that *is* so connected. The best way that I have found to describe this distinction is that the material about the boyfriend is on the surface, linear, a form of nonneurotic communication, while the implications for the therapeutic relationship are convoluted, derivative, have a sense of depth, and constitute neurotic communication. To put it another way: for the moment, the true source of pain and even inner catastrophe within the patient centers around her relationship with the therapist; the pain with the boyfriend is secondary and not immediately connected with the patient's essential inner disturbance and its representation. Interventions related to that outside relationship would in no way help to illuminate and resolve the patient's psychopathology, while interpretations that pertain to the therapeutic relationship, if accompanied by necessary rectifications of the frame, would very much do so.

Now as for the notion that material is just material—that the experience with the boyfriend was important to her and would have come up anyway in the session and, by implication, that it would have had the same meaning regardless of the therapeutic interaction—I must say that this is a major misconception among psychoanalysts and psychotherapists. This material comes up at this particular point in the session, saturated with the particular set of meanings that I have been outlining throughout this discussion, largely because it unconsciously serves as a vehicle to convey the very meanings, perceptions, and fantasies that the patient has a need to express. It is an exquisitely, unconsciously selected transversal communication. And, in general, the material from the patient always contains meanings derived from the actualities of the therapeutic interaction, as well as from the elaborations within the patient of that interaction.

There is no such thing as material per se. Among the factors in the emergence of the patient's associations is the ongoing therapeutic interaction, specifically, the therapist's interventions or failures to intervene. If the therapist had responded to the patient's vacation and to her initial questions differently, this material might not have come up at all, or might have come up in a different form—that is, the patient might have selected a different set of associations based on the actual incident. After all, she cannot detail every single thing that happens to her, and unconscious selectivity is inevitable. Another possibility is that the material might have come up at a different point in the session, conveying a considerably different unconscious message and meaning and serving a different unconscious function. It is the manner in which the material is embedded in the patient's associations and in the therapeutic interaction that gives this material its most crucial meaning, it's functional capacity or state, and much of the failure to recognize that crucial dimension is, once again, based on defensive countertransference-based needs.

Discussant: And the patient would not be describing it in the same way, depending on the therapist's treatment or interventions. I gather that is what you're saying—that his interventions will shape the way in which the patient reports a particular incident.

Langs: Yes, and his interventions will give each communication a specific meaning and function, and will determine the extent to which it conveys reality and unconscious perceptions, fantasies, and distortions. The determinants of the functional state of these associations lie within both patient and therapist—don't overlook either side. And the determination of how much derives from whom cannot be made so long as material is thought of simply as material, by which one usually implies that it is mainly composed of fantasied elements derived from the patient. The analytic notion that material will come up, no matter what, has to be revised. There's all the difference in the world, depending on whether this material comes up after the therapist has been seductive and has withdrawn out of fright, or if it comes up after a valid interpretation which the patient then unconsciously misperceives and misunderstands, experiencing her own seductiveness and fear of it. To put this another way, it matters greatly whether, unconsciously, the therapist has behaved in some actual way like the boyfriend or the patient's father in her childhood, or he has not. The meanings and implications of this material will vary accordingly, and this is true in principle about every communication from the patient—and, I might add, from the therapist as well.

Discussant: Are you saying that this would be so even if the patient makes the same associations, reports the same material?

Langs: You're talking here about manifest content, and I believe that you are at least beginning to sense what I am saying. Yes, the same manifest content will serve all sorts of different, unconscious meanings and functions and will have distinctive unconscious communicative qualities depending on the true actualities of the conscious and unconscious therapeutic interaction. Yes. I'm trying to say that the same material, under different conditions, will have an entirely different dynamic meaning or function.

Discussant: That might be the case here, okay. Let's take this question one step further. In other words, in this case it isn't such an overwhelming issue—her relationship with this boyfriend—so we can say that the fact she's bringing it up now is probably because it refers to the therapist's interventions. But what happens when a patient comes in with material that could be reflected in the adaptive context, but very clearly is such overwhelming material that she would have brought it up no matter what. For example, let's say a patient comes in and says, I was raped on my way here. Okay. Now isn't that clearly a case where it came through it as the material in itself, and not in terms of the therapeutic interaction?

Langs: Well, I believe these questions reflect an inherent need within therapists to divorce the patient's material from the therapeutic interaction, and especially from themselves. It may well be that in an extreme case, large segments of material can be based primarily on a recent and intense trauma, but the therapeutic interaction will nonetheless still shape both the way in which the patient communicates its contents and the dynamic meaning of those communications at the moment. The rape situation may present itself as an immediate reality through which the patient is able to convey her unconscious perception of the therapist's inappropriately penetrating interventions. There will be no way of knowing that unless you apply the full listening process, monitor the material in connection with the therapeutic interaction, make use of the me–not–me interface, and explore these associations in the light of specific adaptive contexts related to recent interventions by the therapist and other dimensions of the communicative interaction. I am well aware that a full application of the listening process may indicate that any vital connection to the therapist is primarily fantasied, or that the connection is minimal. I would not expect, however, at any time, that the material will be entirely dissociated from the therapeutic relationship. I would always investigate that dimension of the material first, while you, on the other hand, are attempting to establish the case for not having to do so.

As for this particular sequence, we had already identified a number of adaptive contexts, and the patient's communications regarding outside realities coalesce very meaningfully around these adaptive contexts as Type Two derivatives— second-order themes—that contain unconscious meanings in keeping with the predictive formulations I had developed earlier. Of course, we must apply the validating process to these formulations and see if the patient's subsequent associations offer further support. But for the moment it is important to recognize the possibility that the patient is side-stepping the most significant adaptive context for this material—the details of the recent therapeutic interaction—and is defensively addressing herself to an outside context communicated in derivative form. That is, this is not an impervious barrier but a derivative related to the therapeutic relationship that can be deciphered for its unconscious meanings. These are analyzable defenses in a Type A communicative field.

Actually, while I will not elaborate, we can learn a great deal about neuroses and psychoses from the listening process. And there is something very important about neurotic responses— using the term *neurosis* in its broadest sense—contained in this delineation: not all unconscious processes, fantasies, and the like are neurotic. In the nonneurotic situation, the reaction is direct and linear and the unconscious repercussions rather evident, while in the neurotic situation defenses and especially displacement are consistently at work: the response is convoluted and derivative, and there is an essentially inappropriate element. This is seen perhaps most clearly when a patient has been unconsciously attacked by a therapist and goes home and breaks up with her boyfriend. That is neurosis; that is an indirect response. The true meaning is quite concealed, and I can only hope that you are beginning to sense the distinction I am trying to make.

Discussant: The concept is clear, but how it relates to actual material is not so clear.

Langs: Much would depend on self-awareness. Say the therapist thought, I don't like the way I intervened; I think I revealed a bit too much; I pulled back. And say he began to realize what he had done. Then he'd recognize that she's picked this up and that the situation with the boyfriend is a way of conveying her perceptions of what had actually happened on one level. He could then begin to sense how she's working over her feelings toward him—the therapist—in this indirect way. You can see the dynamic state of this material. This notion of material as just material is an attempt to defend against countertransference-based inputs.

Discussant: One question that always troubles me. Let's say you realize you've made a wrong intervention. How do you rectify it without showing that you goofed?

Langs: I've tried to clarify that question already, emphasizing implicit acknowledgement of errors and intervention in terms of the patient's perception without suggesting distortion. Sometimes the error is out in the open and is referred to without dispute. Other times, it is implicitly accepted in your comments to the patient. We will consider this issue again when we discuss the ground rules, as well as in our study of interventions. But for now, let's hear more material.

Therapist: So he tensed up and felt uptight. She went on: He said that he had mixed feelings toward me. It made me feel hurt and angry. I felt rejected.

Langs: See what's so marvelous? The typical split in the patient's reaction to the therapist's deviation: consciously, it's Oh, thank you for answering me. But, what's the derivative response? It's, You're afraid of me, you're pulling away from me, you have mixed feelings about me. I'm hurt and angry. She's making what I call an *unconscious interpretation* to the therapist: You're very conflicted in your feelings about me. That's why you answer these dumb questions, these false questions. That's why you're so defensive. You're really quite uptight about me.

Now she's working over your problem. She's saying, The problem is not me, it's in the therapist. And this is not a projection, although it could be. The reality facilitates the projection to the point where the patient's pathology disappears inside the therapist's and hers is now blurred and indeterminant. This is always the case when there are disturbed inputs from the therapist.

She may well be conflicted in her feelings about you. I can't evaluate that at this time because she doesn't have what's called a neutral field to put it into. She has a conflicted therapist to very readily put such thoughts, in the form of perceptions, into. And she may have conflicts about her boyfriend too, but as long as he behaves that way, she can say, No, No, I just want to be very nice and sweet, and he's scared as hell. So she's already offering some kind of unconscious interpretation, and her saying, Look, it's his problem, has a certain very important degree of truth to it, whatever may lie beyond.

Discussant: One of the things that seems to come up here that I'm not clear on in terms of your method of operation is how to approach a situation where perhaps you haven't been seeing someone for so long and the same kind of seductive thoughts seem to be emerging, the same kind of perceptions and errors. To some extent you have to let these feelings emerge over time, and certainly most of our patients have been in therapy with us for quite a long time. Obviously, we screw up sometimes, and then we begin the process of rectifying the situation and trying to interpret it. But it's not at all clear to me how you would broach a subject like this in an early phase of therapy.

Langs: I'd make the same type of intervention, though probably with greater care and tact, and perhaps interpreting upward to some extent, in that I would use more general language. But I would develop this kind of intervention in the first or second session, if that was when it came up, because the material is readily available, quite on the surface and with derivatives of unconscious perceptions and fantasies that can also be easily identified to the patient. And if I had modified the frame in these ways early in therapy, only rectification and interpretation along the lines I have described could restore the frame. It could influence positively the pathological introject of me as therapist that the patient had derived from these experiences, and could help the patient understand her perceptions and fantasies. These insights, I expect, could then be extended into areas related to her pathology. In fact, such interventions—and they would pertain to early interactional resistances—are the only means of truly creating or restoring a sound therapeutic alliance and communicative field.

However, to clarify my response would take us into basic issues related to how to deal with the therapeutic relationship early in treatment. It would require the establishment of a series of basic principles that are quite different from those commonly expressed by analysts in regard to psychotherapy. Such an exposition will have to wait until later in the course; for now, I trust that you can see that such work is crucial to establishing a sound framework for the psychotherapy and to the development of a strong therapeutic alliance and a sense of trust in the therapist. And it would be quite inappropriate to neglect such work for any reason, because the patient will experience this as a lack of insight on your part and will not have a therapeutic setting within which she can safely and unconsciously reveal and express the derivatives of her psychopathology.

Discussant: But it seems to me that to the extent that you talk about the patient's feelings, especially feelings about the therapist, that early in therapy the sense of trust hasn't been built up. You can contain the impulses or whatever feelings they have about you, but a sense of trust hasn't built up.

Langs: But this is how it gets built up: through the patient's realization that you can pick it up, can rectify and interpret the situation. That experience is bound to be an entirely unique and positive one for her.

Discussant: So you're saying that a lot of that sense of containing is built up through the actual process of making the patient's unconscious feelings conscious.

Langs: Hanna Segal (Langs et al., in press) first said this to me: the best container is a good interpretation. She's marvelous. And that's really the way to put it. That shows that the ultimate expression of the containing process—and of the therapist's concern and goodness—are rectifications and interpretations. Please continue.

Therapist: She said: He tried to woo me. I decided I would go along with it, and see what would happen.

Langs: See: "He tried to woo me." Now comes another derivative. Notice again how many valid unconscious readings of your interventions, your deviations, she can make. You're afraid, you pull back, but you also answer her questions and reveal yourself. So you're being seductive. She'll accept the misalliance for now; she'll go along with you, and with your problems.

Therapist: I decided to go along with him and see what would happen. I had always felt that there were emotions here, on his part, that he cared for me and that I could change him. It was awful. I felt...

Langs: The unconscious quest for the cure of the therapist. Listening with his interventions as the adaptive context reveals some exquisite Type Two derivatives: "That I could change him."

Therapist: I felt even more hurt. It was terrible. I just felt I didn't want to be there, wished I were somewhere else.

Langs: I must tell you that Searles (1975) says that the most destructive thing that you can do with patients is to not understand and appreciate implicitly their curative efforts on your behalf. And the entire setting of this therapy promotes this therapeutic wish on the part of the patient. You're a resident, a trainee. It's a you help her and she'll help you kind of thing, which has to pervade this treatment. And on an unconscious level—and I think rightly so, based on the interventions I've heard—she feels she hasn't made you into the kind of therapist she wanted to. She feels sad that you haven't appreciated these efforts. Okay, go ahead.

Therapist: I didn't want to be there. I wished I were somewhere else. I never felt like that before. He didn't have any consideration for my feelings, although at times in the past he would relate, and at other times he didn't. I couldn't express my anger at him. I was angry, although I did say that I was angry at him, and at me as well. I should have trusted my feelings, which were mixed about him. I realized that I had made a lot of demands on him to relate and to show and express emotions to me that I needed from him. It was painful. I learned about myself. And then she said: The next night, at a party, we were friendly, but I really didn't give him much attention. Unfortunately, he had to stay over at my apartment. Some way to turn over a new leaf. Although on the other hand, I learned a lot and have understood things better.

Here, I said, You know, it sounds like what you're talking about could be related to our relationship. And she cut me off.

Langs: All right, don't tell us what she said. Okay, what about this intervention?

Discussant: I guess it's an interpretation.

Langs: Yes, it's an attempt, in a very general way, at an interpretation, which may—you don't know where he was going to take it, but in general we would expect him to approach something in the realm of transference, her fantasies. We'll also see whether he acknowledges any perceptions as well. But it's an effort to develop an interpretation. Now what about the communicative qualities?

Discussant: There hasn't been a bridge back to therapy or the therapist, so this seems premature to me. I guess it should have remained a silent hypothesis.

Langs: Well, we haven't heard the whole intervention, so we will wait and see whether he uses a specific adaptive context. But in terms of the listening process, the patient started the session by saying something about treatment. She then went on to say something about her relationship with the boyfriend. The therapist is now about to intervene and connect that material to treatment, and to himself.

Now, it would be nice to wait for the patient to come back to the therapist once again, but she's already set the course enough by having mentioned treatment initially and then going on to the boyfriend. So you can show her that she went from one to the other. You do have enough of a basis on which to intervene and relate this material, one theme to the other, because of the way the session went. Yes, it would be nice to have an immediate bridge, but you wouldn't need it since the session began with a reference to treatment. So we're okay, we could do that. It will depend, then, on how you heard and formulated the derivatives. Let's hear what happened.

Therapist: I started to say something, and then she said, Yes, you know, I've thought about it. I have demands. At first I didn't realize them. I thought I wanted you to talk, not because I had feelings about it, but something in me needed it. Then she was silent. And she said, I'm not expecting you to say anything, you know. (Laughter.)

Langs: Why do you laugh? What's the experience?

Discussant: The opposite.

Langs: In what sense?

Discussant: It's the opposite of what she really does want.

Langs: Well, I think that she's really afraid of what he might say. She cut him off so that he wouldn't say more, so he would leave his intervention at this general level and talk about demands. You see, this patient is saying, Yes, let's talk about demands, not about seductiveness and boundaries, and his staying in my apartment, and meeting him again at a party, and all of that. Let's just keep it at this level.

And the therapist was, indeed, kind of put off; whether he was scared off or not, he was put off, in that he had planned to say something more, the nature of which we don't know. But once she interrupted him, he sat back again. But at least she's connecting one part of the material to the other, though she uses it defensively and avoids the specific adaptive contexts and her unconscious perceptions and fantasies. In any case, we do have a disguised derivative: she refers to what he has failed to say—his failures to rectify and interpret—that is often the unconscious referent in such a complaint.

We laugh, I think, because we sense a kind of contradiction. So again our subjective response is to feel something of her discomfort, her uncertainty—her sense of absurdity, perhaps. We empathize with her struggle, and try to sense and intuit the elements involved.

Therapist: Then she said, One of the residents assigned a patient to me who had leukemia, to do the lab tests by myself. This is the first time that I would be acting independently. I asked him to come along with me, not to draw the blood or talk to her—I would do that—but just to be there. I felt bad—I made demands on him, in a sense, but I'm becoming aware of it. Yes, this was the first time I was going to be doing this by myself, but I still wanted some attention from him, and of course he said yes. Probably because he realized I was afraid. But it is really my own insecurity. Yet I was afraid maybe he was pissed off at me. Maybe he was angry at me for demanding his attention, for demanding his time.

And I just looked puzzled—I wasn't sure what she was saying—and didn't say anything. Oh no, I'm sorry, I did say something: I said, I wonder if this could be related to your concern about the mixed messages and your demands on my time, your keeping me waiting.

And she said, Well, maybe I thought that you would expect me to call and since I didn't you would be angry with me. And I think I said, That sounds like the way you describe Al and your interaction with him. You can just substitute me for him. And she said, Yes—again, she cut me off, she didn't let me go on—she said, Yes, I thought about it, but it's different. At times you do smile. I thought over the weekend of your smiling—during this episode with Al.

I thought of you and remembered, at one time you smiled. And she said that she thinks I am connected with her, but she's afraid that maybe I'm not—although there have been times when I would smile or give nonverbal cues. She says she has trouble with that, that it's difficult for her at times to interpret that kind of nonverbal communication. Then she said she knows that she can do certain things to draw me out, things she's noted in the past that could make me either say something or nod, or something. But she's beginning to realize that it's in her, that she has these needs that's she's either denied or repressed. And that was the end of the session.

Langs: All right, any comments about this material, particularly in terms of the listening process?

Discussant: She said that her needs were denied or repressed?

Therapist: That she either denies or represses them.

Discussant: It sounds like there is this in-between point, that she has this need to talk about the therapist and a need to get closer to him. And there's a certain point—almost like two protons, two electrons—at that certain point there's an attraction, and beyond that point, a repulsion. And every time the therapist tries to make an intervention, if he gets too close to her, then she sort of pushes him away a little, by interrupting him. And she wants to know that she's connected to him, but she doesn't want to know how connected she is.

Langs: Yes, but your comment focuses entirely upon her anxieties, her needs and fears, and again it doesn't address the specific sequence, only selected parts of it rather than the whole series of interventions which played into a good deal of this. I mean, there's no question that she herself—and I think one can sense this particularly toward the end of the session— she herself is quite conflicted and quite uncertain. But there's more here—the me-not-me interface, unconscious perceptions, etcetera. Are there any other comments?

Discussant: The other thought that I had was that she decided to be the therapist to the therapist, to analyze him. She speaks of what he communicates.

Discussant: But I think even that smile is an ambivalent sort of message. Here she's missed two sessions, and I think that she's trying to reinstate him as a good object in some way for her so she can come to him and talk about her feelings. But this is getting all involved in her sensitivities, her feelings about him, as well as her wondering whether he can tolerate hearing the fact that she has all these feelings about him.

Langs: What's her major defense at this time? As you listen to this material, consistently try to identify the prevailing defenses. In what area do they fall, and what form do they take? What is being defended against, and how is it being done.

Discussant: Are you talking about the patient?

Langs: I asked it in exactly that ambiguous way to let you tell me who you want to talk about.

Discussant: Displacement?

Langs: In what sense?

Discussant: She's displacing her feelings about the therapist onto the disappointing boyfriend.

Langs: Yes, that's there, but that I think is rather obvious. The defense in the field—the interactional defense—is a bit different.

Discussant: She won't let him intervene. She cuts him off.

Langs: Yes, but what is she trying to cut off? What doesn't she want to hear about?

Discussant: Seductiveness.

Langs: The seductive. Sexual material. What is defended against involves two major areas and the defenses are shared by both the patient and the therapist. They are *interactional defenses*. The first area involves the way in which she experienced the therapist's initial interventions and his management of the missed sessions, both of which had distinctively seductive qualities. The second area arose when she got around to some seductive material, with clear-cut sexual overtones, which was immediately put away, tucked away into a bastion—in part because all that the therapist said was, Look, this all has something to do with your relationship with me. He omitted the specific details, omitted the derivatives. And the patient was able to acknowledge that point only so long as they didn't consider it as really sexual, but just a matter of making demands, a matter of knowing whether the therapist was with her or not. This is a not uncommon outcome of a listening process that is under pathological pressures in the therapist or the patient: getting rid of the specific derivatives and instinctual drives.

Discussant: What defenses are involved? How would you categorize them?

Langs: Well, there's repression, denial, displacement, splitting—to name a few. There's a bastion—that's an interactional defense. These comments about demands and about the general relationship are being used as a defense against specific instinctual drive-related derivatives. It's a very common form of defensiveness, and it can occur at any level of the listening process. You can listen to the material and just not even hear the sexual references. Or if you've heard them you may forget about them very quickly, and just talk about the relationship.

But in addition, the therapist's intervention was stated in an ambiguous form in regard to the issue of how much of this material—formulated as Type Two derivatives around the specific adaptive context related to the therapeutic interaction—is essentially unconscious perception, and how much is unconscious fantasy. How much has to do with the actualities of this therapeutic situation and the unconscious meanings of the therapist's interventions, and how much involve aspects of the patient's psychopathology?

You see, in a situation in which there are major elements of countertransference and significant uncertainties regarding the framework, the implications of the patient's communications, their essential meanings, and for that matter the implications and meanings of the therapist's interventions—his interpretations and efforts to manage the framework—are inherently ambiguous. The communicative qualities of the bipersonal field are chaotic and it is impossible to know how much derives from the patient and how much from the therapist; how much of the patient's psychopathology is in evidence, and how much the therapist's problems predominate or contribute; and how much is reality and how much fantasy. Despite the most sensitive application of the listening process to the material from both patient and therapist, this chaos is essentially unresolvable because of these factors. And in principle, I trust you can see that the rectification of countertransference-based influences and alterations in the framework is a sine qua non for a viable therapeutic situation and that truly constructive therapeutic work depends on insightful rectification and interpretation in these areas, as a basic step toward dealing with other dimensions and expressions of the patient's psychopathology. There is, among therapists and analysts, so little understanding of the functions of the ground rules, the framework, that I could not refrain here from emphasizing these points, so evident in this material, even though it anticipates discussions that will undoubtedly unfold in greater detail in the next segment of this course.

I see that our time is almost up and I will leave it to each of you, and especially to the presenting therapist, to review this material in terms of Type Two derivatives that should be organized around the series of specific adaptive contexts we have identified. There are so many meaningful derivatives, easily monitored as Type One derivatives, and even a good deal of manifest content involving the therapeutic relationship. And this provides me still another opportunity to emphasize that the manifest communications pertaining to the therapist and to the treatment situation are functioning here as derivatives for important latent contents—unconscious perceptions and fantasies—that are detectable only through a recognition of the essential adaptive contexts. Too many therapists would work with this material in terms of the manifest themes and, perhaps, with some Type One derivatives—that is, with readily available inferences—and far too few would do consistent work around the adaptive contexts that we have identified. That is, far too few, hearing material related to the therapeutic interaction, would view it as disguised in derivative communication.

There are many such derivatives here, and they can be very nicely applied to the me–not-me interface as well, since they contain allusions to therapist-introjects as well as to the patient. Both object- and self-representations are present here: the doctor who assigns patients; the patient herself, who is learning and about to become relatively independent; the need for supervision; the third party as a protector; the patient's ability to draw the therapist out; her repressed or denied needs. All are allusions to both herslf and the therapist, all culminating, on one level, in a fashion typical of depressed patients: the patient absorbs all of the badness, accepts all of the blame, and identifies herself with the bad introjects.

Discussant: It seemed to me that toward the end of the session this therapist felt some pressure to repeat his interpretations, to get back to the mixed messages, and to try to rectify something about the frame—although I did sense a certain vagueness to his intervention.

Langs: Yes, and here you can see the positive nucleus contained in these somewhat defensive interventions. They are, in part, a sincere effort to deal with the unresolved frame issues and with the patient's unconscious perceptions and fantasies about the therapist. And I think that this is an excellent attempt at this point of your development, because you were trying to deal with very crucial adaptive contexts and had correctly located the necessary locus of the therapeutic work. I would therefore not be too discouraged by your failure to have been specific—that will come in time. There is a lot of promise in what you have done.

I really can't think of a better note on which to end today's seminar. I want to thank you again for a most excellent presentation.

Chapter Ten

LISTENING TO A DREAM

A review of the more unconscious and ill-defined aspects of listening • The four basic steps to the listening process • Efforts at Type A communication • A Type C communicative field • A long dream: nonmeaning in the face of excessive content • Applying the listening process to dreams • Dealing with outside, traumatic adaptive contexts • A review: monitoring the material in terms of the therapeutic interaction and the me-not-me interface

Langs: Today's seminar will be our last formal session on the listening process, and I very much hope that you will be able to apply the principles we have developed over these first nine weeks to the material you will be hearing. As we all know, somewhere in the body of the main session to be presented today we will hear a dream. I thought it would be helpful to conclude this segment of the course by applying the listening process to a session in which a dream occurred, not only as a final exercise in listening but also as a means of deriving some initial perspectives on the use of dreams in psychotherapy. That subject, itself extensively debated, we will not consider in any detail—though one of our goals today should be to see whether a sensitive application of the basic listening process to such material can lead us to some hypotheses in that regard.

Now, before we get into the presentation, I do want to share with you the fact that I was finally able to obtain a copy of the Reik book, *Listening With the Third Ear (1948)*. And you might find this work an interesting supplement to this course, because it does constitute a sensitive and extensive effort to study the means through which the analyst takes in and

comprehends unconscious processes. It focuses especially on
the analyst's use of his capacities for unconscious sensing and
observing, his self-awareness, and his global capability to
understand unconscious communication. Reik emphasizes
such factors as temporary introjection of the material from the
patient, unconsciously determined conjectures, the use of free-
floating attention, the importance of self-knowledge, the use
of what he terms *poised attention*, the tolerance of chaos, and
the surprising qualities of sudden insight—the point at which
the analyst comprehends and integrates previously chaotic
communications. Reik does not attempt the kind of detailed
study of many of the conscious and unconscious aspects of the
listening process that I have tried to develop here, but his work
nevertheless stands as a unique attempt to understand a
critical component of the therapeutic situation, one that Reik,
too, felt was remarkably neglected in the psychoanalytic
literature.

One final comment in regard to this book. It served as a
reminder to me that I should say again, quite explicitly, that
the effort that I have made to identify the various elements of
the listening process should not be misunderstood as a
suggestion that the major components of listening take place
on the conscious and intellectual, cognitive level. It should not
be seen as showing any disregard for the many unconscious
processes and sensitivities involved. I have attempted to treat
these quite ill-defined aspects as systematically as possible in
this teaching seminar, and to concentrate my studies with you
on the much-neglected organizing aspects of listening. But I
am well aware that unconscious sensitivities are crucial to
this process, and that much of the work that must be done in
freeing up these tools must take place in your own personal
therapy.

As you know, it is the goal of psychoanalytic theory to
meaningfully understand unconscious processes, within
patient and therapist alike. And that has been my intention in
regard to the listening process. I am very much in agreement
with Reik and others, such as Ferenczi (1919), who have
viewed the listening process as occurring largely in two
phases. The initial phase is characterized by free-floating
attention and role responsiveness, an openness to projective

identifications, a tolerance for expressions of primary process mechanisms and thinking, and the full use of a wide range of unconscious sensitivities including identification and introjection, empathy, intuition, unconscious perceptiveness, and sudden insights. It is in this phase that the analytic instrument, to use Isakower's term (1963), is quite unguarded in its receptiveness, and I have tried to identify the qualities of this phase throughout these discussions. There is little doubt, however, that in this seminar I have stressed the second phase of the listening process, which, like the first phase, entails a certain degree of looseness and unguardedness, momentary periods of unconsciously guided thoughts and feelings, but which relies ultimately on the application of cognitive, intellectual, conscious efforts at organization and formulation. And I have done so not because I overvalue this aspect of the listening process, but because I think that it is the least defined in the literature, the most open to teaching and learning, and, for the moment, the aspect that can be most readily developed and extended.

In addition to the Reik book, I was able to find a pioneering paper by Peterfreund, published in 1975, on the specific subject of how the analyst listens. His thesis has to do with the working models, open to revision, that we use as a means of understanding our patients and through which we comprehend the unconscious meanings of the communications. He offers criteria for a good analytic hour, stressing the emergence of genetic material, affective understanding, and similar elements, and includes a concept of error-correcting feedback by the patient—though conceived of largely on a conscious level. He also identifies a number of different models within the analyst, including models relating to people in general, to the analyst and patient specifically, and to the analytic process.

This leads him to delineate the types of strategy used by the analyst in the psychoanalytic process. Here he includes a group of general strategies, as well as those that pertain to the analyst's role as a participant observer, and to the patient's role as well. He also includes some general comments on strategies related to the establishment of meanings. He emphasizes that the analyst must work very close to experience, must empathize and temporarily identify with the patient, and must allow himself to be open and then be capable of evaluating what he has experienced. He also offers a series of concepts regarding how to sort out the material from the patient and includes a rather general notion of both prediction and validation.

I will not offer a critique of this important effort, except to suggest that you review the paper and develop your own appreciation and criticism. I will, however, simply comment that you will find that much of his effort is on a manifest level and is divorced from the ongoing analytic interaction. There are many differences between his formulations and those that I have developed with you in this course. I will not go into detail, since I prefer to develop our thinking not so much through a comparison of my position with others, but essentially through the case material that we have been hearing each week.

I suggest that we now turn to the clinical presentation. Perhaps you can briefly summarize the previous hour in order to orient us and to provide us a means of applying the listening process as extensively as possible.

Therapist: Okay. The patient is a thirty-year-old, white, unmarried female. She comes once a week. The session I will be presenting is her twenty-fourth. She had been seen previously—for evaluation—by another resident, who referred her to me for therapy. In the previous session...

Langs: Her chief complaint? My first inference from what I have heard would be depression.

Therapist: Yes, dissatisfaction with the quality of her life. In the previous session, she started out by discussing her feelings about Christmas. She was somewhat serious, somewhat facetious.

Discussant: What religion is she?

Therapist: She's Catholic, I believe. She then discussed her plans—or lack of them—for New Year's Eve.

Langs: This is the session before New Year's Eve?

Therapist: Right. And then she started talking about what had happened in the session before that. The previous week she had mentioned for the first time that she had had two abortions. She had never mentioned that previously, even though we had gone through a pretty thorough history at the beginning.

Langs: What do you think might have brought it out at this time?

Discussant: Well, just Christmas.

Langs: It could be Christmas. What else? (Pause.) All right, we'll see. The turn of the year often brings up the anticipation of the end of therapy in a clinic—forced termination.

Therapist: She said—this led to my first intervention—she said, I got the impression that you expected me to be very upset. She was referring to the discussion of her abortion the previous week and said, I got the impression that you expected me to be very upset. My intervention was: Why? And then she went on, discussing her feelings about the abortions at greater length, and spoke a bit of the first abortion. She really didn't want a child. She was talking at great length about this. And then she said, With the last one, I don't know. And she started crying. Right before this, she had started getting upset, and my intervention was, The thought of it seems to upset you. That was the point at which she started crying. And then she started talking about feelings of hopelessness—hopelessness and helplessness—and she ended the session with a story about a friend of hers who has a baby. That was the session before the one I want to present to you.

Langs: You know, I just thought of myself as Diogenes with the lamp, searching for the resident—or, for that matter, the therapist—who truly wishes to be open to unconscious fantasies and memories. I should teach first-year residents, because this way of working seems to be drummed into you in your supervision and to have reinforced your natural proclivity to address the surface, just manifest contents and readily evident inferences. Perhaps there are first-year residents who are really interested in unconscious processes and contents and who then get spoiled by their supervision. I would like to find just one such person, who really spontaneously moves the patient in that particular direction. Because you can see that each of you, as you have presented case material here, have rejected the same model of therapy. What I never tire of emphasizing is the importance of distinguishing between work on this manifest level and work with derivatives, what I truly believe to be the realm of neuroses—of neurotic communication.

So we've heard the previous session and lack a clear-cut adaptive context. We have a rather striking manifest theme from the patient, some so-called supportive but actually rather nondescript interventions from the therapist, and a possible silent hypothesis from me that might give this material unconscious meaning in terms of the present therapeutic interaction. For the moment, however, there is little more than my general experience with which to support this hypothesis, which I trust you will recognize was derived from a monitoring of material in terms of the me–not-me interface and the therapeutic relationship, and from allowing the manifest themes to suggest a possible adaptive context. This is an effort that should always be made when there is no readily identifiable context for the moment.

So the themes are loneliness, abortions, a girlfriend with a baby, possible implications of envy, wanting the first abortion, and having mixed feelings about the second: these are first-order themes that suggest rather pessimistic second-order themes related to therapy—a sense of helplessness and hopelessness, qualities that she may unconsciously be perceiving in the therapist, whatever other sources may reside within herself. There is a sense of bleakness and perhaps if we now hear the material of the next session, all of this will take on more specific meaning.

Therapist: I feel like a baloney facing the slicer. (Laughter.)

Langs: I'm sorry. I do try to make the issue one of general principles, rather than anything more personal, but I am well aware that there is no possible way to remove those personal anxieties. Let's just see if we can help you to generate a different kind of fantasy, and we'll try to avoid fulfilling that particular one. Incidentally, and I will not pursue it in the least, I can't help but point out how your particular fantasy relates to the material from this patient—the references to the abortion—though I know it also has a good deal to do with the anxiety you are experiencing in presenting to me for the first time. I just thought it would be of interest to demonstrate the multiple potential sources for any communication related to a therapeutic interaction.

Well, enough of that type of commentary. Let's get to the session.

Therapist: This session was after New Year's Eve. There was a TV monitor in the hall—the resident next door to me was using it—and she sort of looked at it and smiled as she walked in. And she started out by saying, Oh, they're putting people on TV here? And I smiled. So she said, there were some people from a TV station at my library—she's a librarian—and this is my chance to be a star. But they didn't tape me; I missed my chance to be a star. I got a letter from Frank with a present. That cheered me up.

Langs: Please clarify a bit.

Therapist: Frank is the man she lived with for a few years. He's also the man who got her pregnant twice. He lives in San Francisco, and she lived with him there for a year or so.

She went on: The present was for Christmas, it cheered me up. The letter didn't say very much. The present was a kind of urn—a pre-Columbian piece in which the ashes of the dead were buried.

Langs: Talk about unconscious communication—that's some gift. (Laughter.) You can imagine their relationship—he impregnates her twice and she has two abortions. The gift

actually says a great deal about both him and her—and
perhaps the therapist as well. We shall see.

Therapist: Then she showed me a locket and tells me that
this was a present he gave her a few years ago. It's in the shape
of a heart. Then she explains that she has only one gold chain
with which to wear it and that she can never wear it with
silver. She makes a big fuss about that, so I (addressing the
unconscious) made an intervention: Why only gold? (Laughter.)

Langs: Let's stop for just a moment and apply the listening
process. I would like to do this as an exercise. As you conceive
of the listening process, how can you apply it to the material to
this point, including the therapist's intervention? What are we
looking to identify? What are our basic tools?

Discussant: Was this session after New Year's Eve or
before?

Langs: After. But what are you looking for? How have you
been listening to this material?

Discussant: For manifest and latent content, and looking
for the adaptive context.

Langs: All right. We're looking for an adaptive context.
That's our first step in the listening process. Do we have one
for the moment?

Discussant: It's not clear.

Discussant: No.

Langs: I agree: I can't find one; nobody else can for the
moment. Okay. In terms of the manifest content, what themes
do we hear? In listening to the manifest content, we search for
specific first-order themes. The first step in the listening
process is looking for an adaptive context. The second step is

looking at the manifest content and identifying what I have called first-order specific themes. Then we make generalizations, and then maybe something more, which we'll get to in a moment, second-order specific themes, based on some monitoring process. That's the next whole step.

And when we don't have an adaptive context, we have to limit ourselves to what I have called Type One derivatives. We monitor the material for Type One derivatives—inferences regarding possible latent contents, not organized around an adaptive context for the moment—and we also allow these derivatives to direct our search for the adaptive context. Now the monitoring process: we'll monitor the material around what? She's talking about an outside relationship; where would we do our monitoring?

Discussant: Around the therapeutic interaction.

Langs: Yes, the therapeutic interaction, the therapeutic relationship. So we can do that here, as a monitoring exercise. And what interface would we use for that? (Pause.) I know you won't believe it, but this is our tenth week at this.

Discussant: It's something about the language.

Langs: Yes, it is new, but I'm trying to give you a language that we can use throughout the course and that I think will be very helpful to you. I must say I'm much sharper with the listening process myself since offering this course. I really have it organized now—that is, the parts of listening that can be categorized and systematized—and I want to see how much you have organized.

Discussant: I'm not sure what you want.

Langs: The interface.

Discussant: The interface—I guess I'm not sure either what the definition of interface is or what the organizing principles are.

Langs: It's a term I used before: the *me–not-me interface*. In other words, the steps that we have so far are: search for the adaptive context; identify the manifest content in terms of first-order specifics, generalizations, and second-order specifics; and monitor around the therapeutic relationship, along the me–not-me interface, in terms of the self-representations and object-representations of both patient and therapist. Now I'll finish the steps in this process, and since I can see that you're kind of lost, I will soon have an outline for you (see Appendix B). The final step occurs once we have identified second-order themes and have sorted them out, attentive to both aspects of the me–not-me interface. We then try to determine how much is essentially realistic and how much is fantasy.

Discussant: I don't quite understand what you mean by the "me–not-me interface."

Langs: We'll get to that in the specific material.

Discussant: Could you illustrate now?

Langs: Well, we're listening to this material, and she's talking about herself and her reaction to this boyfriend...

Discussant: So you want to know what part is referring to herself—what is a self-representation—and what part is referring to the therapist—an object-representation?

Langs: Yes. Another way of putting that second part is, What meaning do these communications have based on an introjection of the therapist? For instance, let's take the first-order theme about presents, and let's first take the "me" part of the interface. There are two aspects: first, the patient as the recipient of a gift, which is in fact the manifest content and which generates Type One derivatives related to the nature of the gift. Here we have a connection to themes of death and love—if we consider both gifts—and other ties to pregnancy and abortion, and all of this is latent to the reference to the gift or, if you will, is connected to that theme. If we then monitor this material along the same lines in terms of the therapeutic relationship, we would wonder if the gift theme in some way relates to the therapeutic interaction. And here we would apply the last step of this process: sorting out reality and fantasy. We might wonder if in some way the patient has actually received a gift from the therapist, on some level, or if there is a fantasy and wish for a gift, perhaps even a baby, or something like that.

The second aspect of the "me" part of this interface would be the patient's unconscious identification with the boyfriend who gives her a gift—her image of herself as gift-giving. Here we must process the references to him as self-representations. Now, if we then monitor these derivatives around the therapeutic relationship, we will ask if the patient on some level has actually given a gift to the therapist, or if she has such a fantasy or wish.

Now we shift to the most difficult step in the listening process: monitoring all of this material along the "not-me" part of the interface. It is difficult because it is in the area of these introjects that the therapist's countertransferences are contained and the most painful truths about him communicated. Again, as with the "me" part, there are two aspects involved. Here we are essentially monitoring this material in terms of therapist-introjects, and, to consider the first aspect, we would ask if on some level the therapist had asked for or received some type of gift from this patient; or whether the patient has detected an unconscious wish for such a gift; or whether, in some form, this wish has in fact been actualized. And please take note of that last issue, because it is especially crucial to our efforts to sort out the derivatives. However, since this particular area impinges upon our countertransferences, we will have a biased need to believe that much of this is distortion rather than truth, and we will therefore have difficulty in identifying levels of truth, preferring to focus on manifest content rather than unconscious meaning. After all, it seems unlikely that the therapist has accepted a gift from this patient in a direct and manifest way, though he may have on other, more derivative levels. This is the realm of the transversal communication which contains unconscious truths and surface untruths.

Therapist: No, I have not accepted a gift so far as I know.

Langs: Yes, so viewing one aspect of the not-me part of the interface, we think about the therapist as the receiver of a symbolic or unconscious gift, and about possible connections to pregnancy, abortion, and love. Now, about viewing the second aspect, we can think of the therapist as giving the patient a gift. This derivative we would arrive at through a second means, by wondering if the boyfriend in some way represents the therapist, though here, in terms of a possible introject within the patient. We would therefore wonder if unconsciously the patient perceives or imagines that the therapist has some wish to impregnate her, abort her, or love her. My earlier comment, that the pending forced termination has certain of the actual qualities of an abortion—a premature termination—touched upon one aspect of this part of the listening process, one of my silent hypotheses—of which, at this point, there are many.

Again we are faced with the complexities of the listening process. But I think that if you begin to recognize these levels of listening, the importance of monitoring the material along the me–not-me interface and in terms of the therapeutic interaction, it will soon become quite automatic for you—perhaps as unconscious and as sensitive as the initial intaking part of the listening process—though you can always go back to identifying these basic steps when necessary.

There are, then, four essential steps to formulating: one, the search for the adaptive context; two, the identification of first-order manifest themes, derivative general themes, and, at this point, the development of Type One and Type Two derivatives; three, the monitoring of the material along the me–not-me interface as it pertains to the therapeutic interaction; and four, the assessment of all manifest and latent themes for the proportions of reality and fantasy.

Discussant: And you do this as you listen to a patient.

Langs: Yes, I know that the intricacies may still seem staggering, but it is possible to maintain an open listening attitude and to alternate between free-floating responsiveness and efforts at organization. It is possible to freeze moments in each session and to apply the listening process here as an exercise. With your patients, you can't ask them to stop while you formulate, but it is possible to make sound use of the listening process—though in another sense it is impossible to do it without a hitch, which is why Freud (1937) called psychoanalysis "that impossible profession," a phrase echoed by Greenson (1967). And yet, much of this can be sorted out and properly applied.

Discussant: You have also said something about various types of communicative fields. How is that arrived at?

Langs: That is a second-order inference derived from this entire listening process. In brief, we would conclude that we have a Type A field when the patient is communicating in terms of Type Two derivatives organized around a particular adaptive context or, at least, does that often enough, even when in a state of resistance and in regard to the underlying factors in that very resistance. And in this field, when we monitor the interventions from the therapist, we discover valid, cognitive interpretations filled with symbolic meanings.

When we discover that a patient is impinging upon us with projective identifications and is prone to action-discharge, or when we find that the therapist himself is communicating in that manner, we have evidence of a Type B field. Finally, a Type C field is characterized by very flat material and either the presence of a clear-cut adaptive context, without derivatives that organize meaningfully around it, or a flood of derivatives without an evident adaptive context—a style I characterize as "the Type C narrator". We observe in such a field massive resistances that cannot readily be understood in terms of underlying derivatives, and our evaluation of the therapist's interventions, if they are contributing to the communicative mode, is that he is using psychoanalytic clichés, that he is intervening without an adaptive context and actually generating falsifications and barriers rather than true insight. Instead, he should be interpreting the metaphors of the Type C field to help the patient understand the nature of his defenses and to foster their modification..

In regard to the session being presented, we can not yet determine the nature of the communicative field, and let me just say, since we know that the patient will report a dream, that such a report is in no way a criterion for any particular type of communicative field. Dreams can be reported for the purpose of symbolic communication, as a means to projective identification, or to generate Type C barriers. The latter two functions have, by and large, been relatively overlooked, although Bion (1977) has had some interesting things to say about dreams as a form of projective identification—a point that Segal (1977) has clinically documented in an interesting paper. But for now, let's concentrate on the basic steps of the listening process and remember to apply the four basic steps: the search for the adaptive context; the particularization-generalization-particularization process; the development of Type One and Type Two derivatives; the monitoring around the therapeutic relationship; and the determination of reality and fantasy. And we will apply this process in each of the basic realms I have identified: the cognitive sphere; the realm of interactional mechanisms, projective identification in particular; and the object relational sphere—efforts by either patient or therapist to evoke roles and images. And all of this will lead us to generate *silent hypotheses*, tentative interpretations that we're attempting to build and confirm through *silent validation*, another crucial component of the listening process.

To complete this cycle: eventually, when the patient has validated our initial main silent hypotheses, when the material has coalesced, and when silent validation has occurred and the patient offers a meaningful bridge, then we intervene interpretively or through an appropriate effort to manage the framework. We then sit back, listening to the material that follows as a *commentary* on our intervention and applying both the listening and validating processes to that material. We are seeking validation, new insights, positive introjects, and an understanding of the patient's unconscious perceptions and introjection of the unconscious nature of our intervention—as well as any distortions of what we have conveyed.

Now, in my discussion of this material to this point, I have stressed the cognitive level. For the moment, I am not experiencing interactional pressures to any large extent— either projective identification or role pressures—although one might sense a bit of that in the patient's allusions to the television equipment in the hospital. You know, the notion of televising patients, exhibiting them. It may also be present in the patient's reference to the therapist's expectation, as she experienced it, that she should have been more upset in discussing her abortions. There are role and image pressures there, and perhaps a bit of projective identification, first from the therapist and now, more subtly, from the patient: You are exploitive, you should feel guilty for exhibiting or capturing your patients on film. You're a voyeur. These are hints, and we can monitor this realm further and see whether the associational material and later interactional pressures begin to coalesce around such clues; it is possible they will fade to the periphery. We'll see.

So coming back to this initial material, we have agreed that we do not seem to have an identifiable adaptive context. On the manifest level, what additional specific and general themes do we hear?

Discussant: On the manifest level, she's talking about the presents she's getting from Frank.

Langs: Yes, about gifts, about having received gifts in the past, which she shows to the therapist. She talks about having some problems wearing them, about hearts, which chain she can use, previous love relationships. All this.

Now, some of the material connected to this manifest content is that Frank has impregnated her twice and is involved in the abortions. You see, that's inference from the manifest material, links you are likely to recall from the previous session's material. And monitoring it a bit more in terms of the therapeutic relationship, you can interrogate it along the following lines: Is there some issue of a gift? Is there something that isn't quite right? Is there something about boyfriend, girlfriend in her mind, or in the therapist's mind? Is there anything about abortions in either of their minds? And how much is reality, how much fantasy?

These are all fragments we can wonder about. Derivatives are fragments that we attempt to put together into meaningful wholes. Notice here that the material is not coalescing, it remains fragmented. And part of the fragmentation comes from her own need to scatter, and part of it from the therapist's interventions, which keep directing her to the surface and to insignificant details. They ask her to elaborate on something relatively meaningless, offering her an interactional defense: let's move away from anything that might shift us closer to the derivatives that are disturbing you, particularly those that would relate to the therapeutic relationship. Let's destroy meaning in the field. Such interventions are strong invitations to develop a Type C field, a field of nonmeaning.

Any questions about all of this? (Pause.) Let's leave it at that so we can get to the dream—that's why I've done so much of it for you this time. You can see too—ten weeks—it took all of this time to generate, even for me, a solid conception of the listening process. And you can see how difficult it really is to keep it together. Go ahead.

Therapist: Shall I explain why I said, Why only gold?

Langs: If you wish. You didn't tell her, but you can tell us.

Therapist: The way I schematized it was that the manifest content was her discussing the gift. The latent content was her feelings about Frank, which she wasn't discussing. And why my question about why only the gold? Well, Frank had said something about gold being special and silver being dead, flat, and I was hoping that by asking the question in terms of the manifest content she would get to the latent content—in other words, that she would say something more about Frank.

Langs: So your hypothesis was that her neurotic conflicts, in her relationship with Frank—and in regard to the abortions, and life and death, and whatever else—were somehow central and latent.

When we get to interventions, I will stress that if you have such a silent hypothesis, you should wait. Ask the question silently—to yourself— and allow her to continue to associate. Let her direct you to the derivatives to which the manifest content and your silent question are related. You see, you're narrowing the field far too much. If you're right, she'll get around to such feelings. And if you ask her to address it consciously, it would actually interfere with that flow.

See again, it has to do with the whole concept of the level at which we wish to work in psychotherapy, and with appreciating the importance of derivatives and wanting to work on that level, primarily with Type Two derivatives rather than manifest contents. And then, we have to decide how to get the material we want to listen to, at a level at which interpretations are generated that will be truly insightful and symptom-alleviating for the patient. And this is a very crucial point, because therapists very often ask questions and attempt to direct the patient, and such efforts contain very mixed messages: manifest level: Let's explore this area further. Latent level: Let's do it in a narrow way, directly rather than in derivative form. And let's really be quite defensive with it all.

If instead you raise questions silently to yourself, develop silent hypotheses and allow the patient to associate, eventually she will change the subject, the manifest theme, and direct you to the derivatives you need. In this way, you let her build the session and your intervention, and you sit back and apply the listening and validating processes. In fact, the most resistant form of communication here would be for the patient to continue to talk manifestly about these gifts, without changing the subject. That would become a Type C narrative designed as a barrier against more painful underlying meanings. Please continue.

Therapist: Okay. She responds, I don't know. I'm allergic to silver, it makes my neck look strange, distorted somehow. After this there is a long silence. Then she says, I was very pleased. I really like that heart, it's beautiful. I really, really like that brooch. And then she's silent. And then I made another intervention: What are your feelings in terms of Frank?

Langs: So, having obtained no validation whatsoever, you decide to bring him up directly, asking for manifest associations to Frank. And you can see how easy it is, in listening to the material that follows an intervention, to think of it in terms of a particular silent hypothesis or a direct set of thoughts in response to your question. And how very difficult the alternative is: to take all responses to any intervention as a commentary on that intervention, and to explore it for its latent contents and validating qualities.

Here, we hear something about allergic, strange, distorted, liking the heart—commentaries difficult to organize as Type Two derivatives around the adaptive context of your intervention, and commentaries that present a mixed image. Something is not right and is being distorted, while something is providing her with gratification—perhaps it's some type of manic defense and denial. It is really too early to tell.

I am describing these formulations so that you can see how we listen after an intervention, and what it means in the actual clinical situation to take each intervention as an adaptive context for the material that follows rather than simply pursuing a particular question or a particular line of manifest thought. So it is well to sit back after you have intervened, in order to study the patient's commentary and explore the extent of validation. And when confirmation seems lacking, it is essential to attempt to reformulate, rather than to insist on the pursuit of your own unvalidated hypothesis.

Incidentally, in terms of the communicative properties of this field, much of this sounds more and more like a Type C field now, and it seems almost a miracle when we realize that the one thing we know in advance about this session is that the patient reported a dream—but it may well turn out to be a dream embedded in a Type C communicative field. Please continue.

Therapist: She answers that her thoughts about Frank are what they always were. There was a little pause. What they always were. Pause. He loves me, he wouldn't let that change his life at all. He wishes I were in San Francisco.

Langs: He wouldn't let that change his life." He wouldn't let it change his course. I would take that as a nicely condensed commentary on the therapist's interventions that expresses the mini-lecture I just offered. And that, by the way, is what I mean by validation through Type Two derivatives: the intervention reflects the therapist's stubbornness and inflexibility.

Therapist: There's a pause between each phrase: He loves me. Pause. He wouldn't let that change his life at all. Pause. He wishes I were in San Francisco. Pause. But he wouldn't marry me. Pause. He's accustomed to his life. Pause. But doesn't want to be disturbed. At which point there's a long silence.

Langs: That's very nice in terms of my formulation. See, again we're monitoring this material in terms of the adaptive context of the therapist's interventions. What do you think is her main commentary? Monitor this as Type Two derivatives around his interventions. We'll set aside validation for now, since there's certainly little of that.

Discussant: I think the response is that his questions are extraneous: She's saying, Things are as they always have been, and I'm not talking about that.

Langs: Yes, and what else could you say?

Discussant: Kind of, the therapist doesn't want to be disturbed by whatever she wants to talk about. He has his own ideas about what that should be.

Langs: Right. In other words, what she's saying is that she unconsciously feels that your interventions are designed to maintain your equilibrium, your stability, and that that entails a disregard for her needs and what's disturbing her. Your interventions are self-protective, which is what I had said earlier in terms of the invitation for a Type C field, an invitation to create barriers to more painful truths and relatedness that would be more disturbing for you and, possibly, for her too.

Discussant: How would you assess the field—what she's giving now?

Langs: Well, in the adaptive context of what the therapist just said, I would suggest that she's trying to symbolically communicate to him the way she's experiencing his interventions: her mode is Type A, while, for now, his is Type C.

Discussant: I mean the material—manifestly, it is bland.

Langs: No. It's bland only on one level. It would seem bland if you didn't understand it to convey her reactions to the intervention. It has depth if you know the context. Intervening without the context would be to empty it of its underlying meaning.

Discussant: What field is this, then?

Langs: Well, as I said, it's a mixed field. I think there is some effort at Type A communication on her part and some effort at Type C communication on the therapist's. You're seeing a compromise.

Therapist: At this point, after she says, But he doesn't want to be disturbed, there's a long silence. I fortunately don't say anything. (Laughter.)

Langs: Good move.

Therapist: After two minutes, she says, It's not the way it should be, but I understand this. Another silence. It's not so much marriage as children. Pause. He adamantly does not want to have children. Another pause. He survives only because he owns his tiny little apartment. All of this was coming very slowly, very painstakingly. Finally: He still works at his miserable job. As a valet at a women's hotel. (Laughter.) Which is where I met him. At this point there is a silence, then: I assume he's seeing other women. Pause. They would always ask him out. At one point I had some doubts but I don't know. I've never asked him, because I didn't want to know. She's referring now to, ostensibly, to during the time she was living with him.

Langs: Right. See, it's becoming more of a Type C field. She has accepted the misalliance and interactional defenses offered by the therapist. And she represents the Type C field metaphorically: a relationship in which she does not want to know the truth, in which there are things she wishes to obliterate, because the truth would be too painful. You can also continue to monitor this material around the therapeutic relationship in general—specifically in terms of the therapist's interventions—and leave open possible meanings to such themes as not wanting to have children, surviving in one's own small quarters (the therapist's office perhaps), and being unfaithful. You can listen along the me–not-me interface, wondering what is reality and what is fantasy, but it's really rather difficult to synthesize for the moment. Continue.

Therapist: She says, If I knew, what would I do? I was never very jealous.

Langs: See: the theme is not wanting to know the truth, which would create turmoil, which at least one of you could not handle (the me–not-me interface). See again how you can pick out, from the specifics, a general theme that you could use in connection with the adaptive context. Notice how it's helping me to select general themes and how I now feel we must address the communicative mode before contents, the Type C barrier before the derivatives—largely because of the therapist's interventions, which must be rectified. Again, the context is a template, a gene, the organizer. It leads me to pick out certain themes and to state them in a particular way that is in keeping with the adaptive context. At the same time, I remain open to new contexts, to other themes, to any sense of nonmeaning. Here everything is at a low level of—how to put it—of intensity. It's low key. Go ahead.

Therapist: She says, I was never very jealous. And at this point, she's starting to get upset. And she says, I always felt very secure. And she starts crying. She cries for a while, and while she's crying she says, I always felt he really cared. Still crying, silences in between: I trusted him. He would never do anything to hurt me. I still think it. And then she brings up the dream.

Langs: All right. You can see that you can have strong affects in a Type C field. But now, based on our listening to this point, let's try to predict the dream—at least what the dream is about in general. Any thoughts at all? (Pause.) How would you go about doing that? What principles would you use to try to determine the underlying meanings of the dream? In the field we have before us, I'm not too confident. I've done this in the past with a hell of a lot more confidence than I can with this material. But give me some avenue of thinking that might help you predict the latent content of this dream.

Discussant: Well, obviously, if you could identify the latent content of whatever had gone on before, you might expect some kind of extension of those themes.

Langs: Right. And how would we go about determining that? What would we think of first?

Discussant: You mean specifically with this patient?

Langs: Or in principle. How would we do that? In other words, you're saying we would search for the latent contents in this session, and in the last session as well, and expect that in the dream the patient would work them over.

Discussant: I would think of going through the same thing that you said before, which is: looking for the manifest themes, and generalizations, and new specifics, and monitoring the material around the therapeutic relationship.

Langs: And where would you start? You went through all of it, but you didn't mention where it begins.

Discussant: With the adaptive context.

Langs: With the adaptive context again. If we can correctly identify the adaptive context, we could predict that the dream will be an attempt to deal with that context—that it would be the day residue for the dream. So let's all try it. Where do you think the adaptive context for this dream is. See, Freud (1900) interestingly enough started with the dream and discovered the day residue. That's led to some confusion, because he really should have discovered the day residue first, and seen how it leads to the dream, which of course, was part of his theory of neuroses—he saw the link between reality and fantasy, between reality and the intrapsychic. We'll get into dreams at some point more carefully, but if you start with the right adaptive context, we're going to get to the latent content of this dream. What's the adaptive context?

Discussant: The adaptive context—I think you described it before—is the therapist who is not open, who wants to guide the line of associations in his own direction. And the patient is angry about that.

Langs: Well, not only angry. She's also rather submissive to it.

Discussant: Passively angry.

Langs: Yes, she's hurt, but yet she submits and feels that he really means well, this therapist who is trying to guide the material based on his own defensive needs, who seems to be shutting out her wish to communicate her unconscious fantasies and perceptions, and conflicts and all. So. Does anybody want to add to our hypothesis or offer another possibility?

Discussant: Well, I think we should mention something about her feeling insecure and alone. I don't know if she really feels chaotic inside—that may be—or there might be more disruption in the treatment than she's able to say.

Langs: Okay, so you propose another possibility. That maybe she won't be working over the therapist's covered-over chaos and his effort to keep her communications constricted. It could be more a working over of her own sense of chaos. We'll see. I would say that so long as she's experiencing this intense defensiveness against chaos on the part of the therapist, she will not really be able to convey her own sense of chaos—which of course will lie concealed within his. Anything else that you would want to add? (Pause.)

The timing of the appearance of the dream in the session can be used as another clue as to what the dream will be about. The dream could represent a compromise between her wish to communicate symbolically, Type A, and the pressures she's feeling within herself and from the therapist toward a Type C field and defenses. I think it comes up at a point in the session where she's had enough of this rumination about the boyfriend. The patient may want to do some therapeutic work.

Now that brings up the third possible adaptive context—her relationship with the boyfriend, his gift, and the abortions. Some of that, on a latent level, refers to the therapeutic relationship; some she may be working over apart from the therapeutic relationship. We want to keep that in mind. I don't think that's the area of her neurotic communications for the moment—it's too direct—but we shall see.

So, there are three main possibilities: one is that she's working over some inner turmoil of her own, involving her relationship with Frank, and the adaptive context of the references to him and his gifts will then be the significant day residue for the dream; on a manifest level, a direct quality will prevail. The second and third are that the same day residues on a latent level allude to the therapeutic relationship, either primarily in terms of her own fantasies and turmoil, or mainly in terms of inputs from the therapist, based on his sense of chaos or clinic policy—his interventions and the beginning of a new year, and her concern about whether treatment is going to continue through the coming year, or whether it's going to be interrupted. All this could be alluded to in derivative form through the abortion and the absent boyfriend. Here, in essence, the latent themes may refer to an outside relationship or to the therapeutic relationship, in terms primarily of transference or of nontransference.

Discussant: Will therapy be interrupted?

Therapist: It hasn't come up.

Langs: And you didn't tell her: Treatment will be such and such a length of time? You just saw her open-endedly and she doesn't know whether it's going to be interrupted or not?

Therapist: Yes.

Discussant: That's not such a hot idea, not to tell her whether and when the therapy is going to end.

Langs: Well, we'll go over that when we go over the ground rules. I think that any treatment that's known to have a time limit should be so specified from the very beginning, of course.

Therapist: Except for the fact that I could take her into private practice with me in July.

Langs: But the length of time in the clinic is what I'm talking about. In any case, the timing of this dream suggests to me that after having gone along with some rumination, she now comes to a vehicle through which she'd like to work over more specifically what's distrubing her in the therapeutic relationship—primarily in the realm of nontransference. So that would be my prediction. It's now in the hands of the gods.

Therapist: Can I say what I thought at the time?

Langs: You mean, what you had anticipated?

Therapist: Yes, what I had anticipated. Well, I was working over the material and made the interventions in this session, as well as the last session, with the idea that this all had to do with the abortion and her feelings about Frank.

Langs: I can only hope that her material will help you understand why that has to be appended to the therapeutic interaction to really have true meaning—that, separate from that interaction, it will just be isolated, lacking in functional meaning, and really a barrier to the truth. I know that's an hypothesis now, but I want to try to show you the difference in what happens in therapy with interventions based on these two types of hypotheses involving direct and indirect communication. It comes up all the time and I haven't crystallized it yet. I've worked it over a number of times. The key question is: in terms of the active locus of the patient's neurosis, does the outside relationship serve functionally and latently to communicate unresolved, dynamically pertinent aspects of the theraputic relationship? It is difficult to prove that that is the case via Type Two derivative validation. We'll have to see what comes up. Please continue.

Therapist: Okay. She says, I had a dream. It was very frightening. Then she smiles, but it wasn't in an appropriate sense—it really wasn't. She said it was very frightening; then she paused, then she smiled. She said, I might have to give up murder mysteries before bed.

Langs: So the dream has more affect, more anxiety, and more primitive qualities than the material we've been hearing until now.

Therapist: She said: I can't figure it out. I can't figure out if I killed the guy or just incriminated myself. I had the dream after I got the locket.

Langs: So she suggests, as the first day residue for the dream, the gift from Frank. We'll see what happens. I'm not the least bit concerned about that, because that's what she would offer as the manifest day residue. We must eventually determine its latent content, and whether it is serving as a screen for another day residue or is the main precipitant, after all. That is, whether it functions as a direct or indirect adaptive context. We'll see.

Therapist: There was a small room. And she pauses again. She says, It was like the place Frank and I stayed in, in Los Angeles. There was a closet to the left of the door. It was an old hotel room. It was empty, it was dingy, it was shabby. Now at this point I intervened and said, Did it remind you of anything? And she said...

Langs: In terms of technique: let her tell the dream, let her shape the session. See again, your intervention suggests that you're not interested in resistances, just in contents; that you're not interested in indirect communication, just direct associations. If she doesn't want to associate to the dream, you want to know about that. You don't want to set it aside.

Discussant: The first time a patient presents a dream, you might instruct them in the use of dreams.

Langs: I don't do that directly. It's implicit in the way we work. I don't offer directives.

Therapist: This was either the first or the second dream she had. Actually, she had one other dream.

Langs: Okay, go ahead.

Therapist: I had a dream. It was very frightening. Pause. Smile. I might have to give up murder mysteries before bed. I can't figure out about...

Langs: That's another day residue: she had been reading a murder mystery.

Therapist: I can't figure out if I killed the guy or just incriminated myself. It was after I got the locket. There was a small room. Pause. Like the place Frank and I stayed in in Los Angeles. There was a closet to the left of the door. It was an old hotel room. It was empty, it was dingy, it was shabby. I said,

Did it remind you of anything? Pause. She said, Yes, it was a little like Frank's apartment.

Then she goes on: I don't know how it happened. There was a woman's corpse on the floor of our room. (I guess I'm emphasizing what I thought was significant: she said *our* instead of *my*.) I dragged her into a small pantry. She kind of resembled me. She was too tall to fit into the closet. She had red hair. (The patient is tall and has red hair.) I covered her face. She was bleeding clear fluid. I propped her legs vertically against the wall of the pantry, like a yoga position. Then I realized that I was going to get into trouble. No one would believe that I didn't kill her. I started feeling very guilty. I hid the body because I was expecting someone to arrive.

At that point, I said, Who? She said, I don't know. She goes on: I remember a feeling of—a feeling that I would have to go to prison for the rest of my life. Even if I didn't kill her, I was an accessory after the fact. There was a real panicky feeling at the end of the dream. Long silence. Then she smiled, and she said, I think it's a very funny dream. Who would I kill? I have no intended victims. She goes on: I was tidying up. They never showed up. That was the end of the dream.

Langs: Now, how have we listened to this dream? (Pause.)

Therapist: I'd like to add my interpretation. I thought it was very eloquent.

Langs: We'll get to that in a moment.

Therapist: I'm sure you'll disagree.

Langs: That seems likely, since our basic thesis differs. It seems to me that all we can say for now is that the communicative properties of this field are such that a great deal remains obscure and unintelligible. She offers two day residues, both rather manifest and both readily linked to her relationship with Frank. So both the day residue and the manifest dream are linked to associations to Frank and can be readily tied to her abortions, and initially there are few bridges to the therapist or treatment. Perhaps the small room—an image that came up earlier in the session—perhaps the dingy qualities, but it's not very convincing.

Discussant: Most of these offices are small and dingy.

Langs: So we hear some manifest threads: something about murder, somebody dead, having to hide the corpse, punishment, hair like hers, a dead man and a dead woman. And we also hear something else: we hear a dream that has rather primitive, frightening qualities to it. It begins to tell you something of the very frightening stuff that she would have to deal with if the field opened up, if she opened up. And the therapist would have to deal with all of that as well.

The idea of staying in prison forever could have something to do with the theme of separation. But I must say this stuff is quite fragmented. I will not try to force meaning into it. There is a reference to the truth not being believed. Dead persons often come up in the presence of a Type C field. Still what's striking to me about the dream is that despite its morbid quality, it doesn't readily organize around what I consider a meaningful adaptive context. It's all either too evident or too disguised. We can readily see that she had two abortions after being made pregnant by her boyfriend and that she's angry with him. The murder: maybe she feels you're trying to destroy her, or she wishes to destroy you. But this whole thing could in some way refer to the experience of the abortions and all— guilt over the lost children. It's all there, but it's there in a way that doesn't generate unexpected meaning, as far as I'm concerned. There's something missing. Whether she's going to provide it in this session, I don't really know.

But I'm telling you, in terms of my listening process, something is missing. You see, to me a dynamically meaningful adaptive context is an immediate situation that brings up the past. It's not the past sitting there in isolation or coming up out of nowhere. I don't have the immediate adaptive context, and that's making it very difficult for me to organize the dream, which I listen to as I listen to all other material— though, of course, dreams are often very meaningful condensations of associations that can help you organize or reorganize the material from the patient.

So you'll notice that the dream—far more than the other material—does start to bring in morbid feelings, anxieties, affects, dread—primitive contents and qualities that were really lacking in her initial associations. So it does have a special quality in this session. All right, we've got to hear more to see if anything else crystallizes.

Therapist: Okay, she says, They never showed up. So I made an intervention, asked a question: What position would they have found the corpse in if they opened the closed door? She laughed.

Discussant: I suppose she said it was like being examined. Gynecologically.

Therapist: I thought that it was like being in stirrups and that's exactly why I asked her.

Langs: But these should be silent impressions that should be validated by the patient's spontaneous communications.

Therapist: Again, my interpretation, as I said at the beginning, was that the adaptive context was the abortions, and that the dream would refer to Frank and the abortions.

Langs: Yes, I know. What you are saying is quite true on the manifest level, and in terms of ready inferences—Type One derivatives. A gift from Frank, a discussion of the abortions. They are certainly powerful adaptive contexts and I am well aware that the dream organizes around them—especially the abortions—in terms of her perceptions and fantasies of herself and Frank as murderers who should be punished. Though in the dream, note that it is not true that she has committed the murders, and while you could see that as an effort at undoing or denial, it suggests to me the flaw in the thesis. It's all too pat; there are no surprises.

And actually, this is rather interesting to me. I had sensed this mixture of a Type A and a Type C field, and this dream has exactly those qualities. It seems filled with symbolic communication, and yet I sense that it is functioning as a

Type C barrier, a massive and impenetrable cover to truths more painful than the abortion—though I do believe that these truths are in some way connected to the abortion—and that access to the missing present painful truths would really open up the necessary access to the patient's unconscious reactions to her abortions, as well as to the earlier genetic connections to that experience.

Of course, we must continue to hear more—but without biasing the patient. We may well have to conclude that, under certain circumstances, outside traumas are so overwhelming that their links to the therapeutic relationship are for the moment entirely secondary, such as here, when you learn in response to your question that this body was in the position of a woman being gynecologically examined. On the one level this continues to allude to the abortion, but on another it is certainly a derivative of the treatment situation. It is, however, a weak derivative, so perhaps, partly because of her defensive needs and partly because of the therapist's, the material will crystallize around the abortions. The memories prompted by Frank's recent gift and the connections to the treatment situation would therefore be unavailable in any active and analyzable form. And we'll then take this, I hope, as the exception that proves the rule. Actually, it is high time—after nine sessions in which the material unfolded exactly as I had predicted—it is high time to get into some difficulty, to be reminded of the complexities of the listening process and of the therapeutic situation, and to have to understand a possible exception. Let's hear more.

Therapist: She said, It's a position I often read in—on my back with my legs up. Frank wouldn't let me do it in San Francisco; I broke one of his precious chairs once. She laughs again. He was very upset.

Then she goes on: As a teenager I had a similar dream. All my friends were getting killed off by a sniper. It was exciting. It was interesting. I woke up but went back to sleep to finish. It turns out the sniper was a boy I had known in elementary school and had a crush on. So I couldn't decide if I wanted to continue with that part of the dream, or not. She goes on, But this dream I definitely didn't want to continue. And there's a pause. I say, Why Not? She said, I didn't want to get in trouble. And another pause. I said, At the beginning of the dream, it sounded like your roommate might get in trouble instead.

Discussant: The adaptive context here might be her perception that the therapist thought she would be upset about the abortions.

Langs: Yes, that's a possibility, but I suspect something even more powerful.

Discussant: She may be getting to some aggression, some sadistic feelings that she has, that she feels are not going to be tolerable.

Langs: Yes, there is something about her feeling that the therapist won't tolerate the destructive stuff inside of her. Also, we don't know how her belief that the therapist expected her to be upset could serve as an adaptive context—whether it was more reality than fantasy, or the reverse. And I must say again that none of this seems to organize this material as a selected fact would organize it. It's not really crystallizing. There are many possible hunches, but no buildup and accumulation of meaning. This material begins to have the qualities of the Type C narrative, especially as she adds more and more dream material. On the simplest level, we sense a state of resistance—there is far too much to deal with and interpret. And while the themes of death and murder remain prominent, there are many additional fragments that generate a sense of so much meaning as to constitute nonmeaning. And all of this certainly suggests that it is unlikely that a central adaptive context, unconscious fantasy or perception, or introject, will emerge and prove interpretable.

But we wander around with this material, trying out each adaptive context, hearing the reference to the earlier boyfriend, who could be a derivative related to Frank, or to some earlier figure in her life—her father or brother—but who also could represent the therapist and her unconscious perceptions of his interventions. Nothing jells. There is no center and satellites, so to speak—no clear-cut figure and ground. It's all quite scattered, much like the therapist's interventions, even though he has already made up his mind as to where he is heading. Another fragment that flitted by in derivative form could also allude to his interventions: her viewing them as little bits of sniping at her. Still, it doesn't really fit together that well.

What's striking about this material for the moment is its fragmentation. It isn't coalescing around an adaptive context, and since the therapist's interventions are certainly maintaining that fragmentation, we're not getting a sense of depth, despite the primitive qualities, earlier memories, and all. We just know that violence and murder are in the air, and that she's becoming frightened. She tries counterphobic defenses, manic defenses, but they failed her during the dream, though in the session she may be more effectively mobilizing them—again, with the therapist's help. All right, if we hear more, we may get to the selected fact we need.

Therapist: She said: This dream I definitely didn't want to continue. And I said, Why not? She said, I didn't want to get in trouble. Pause. I said, At the beginning of the dream it sounded like your roommate might get in trouble instead. She said, Yes.

What I was referring to, even though I didn't say it, is that when she said, The woman's corpse on the floor of our room, I was thinking, if only halfway, of the fact that she said *our* room, rather than *my* room. And she made two references to her impression that it was like the room she shared with Frank, and then only halfway through the dream she started getting upset about it and started panicking. So...

Langs: The roommate you had in mind was Frank?

Therapist: Yes, and my hypothesis was that she wanted Frank to get into trouble. So I said: At the beginning of the dream, it sounded like your roommate might get in trouble instead. She paused. She said, Yes. I remember thinking that fiendishly. Then she laughs. She says, Yes, I like the idea. I finished her sentence for her: Of your roommate getting in

trouble. She said yes. I said, who was your roommate? She
pauses, and says, I don't know. Silence.

Langs: She's not following you. She's implying, Do you
mean then or now—right here in this room? You say, I mean
then, not now. Not me. Please. See, it's just playing with this,
going around, vague implications. You're leading her too
much. Go ahead.

Therapist: She pauses. I said, Whose room did it look like?

Langs: Try to get a feeling for this type of therapeutic work.
He keeps trying to lead the patient rather than stating his
silent hypothesis as an interpretation. But also, see where he's
leading: here's a man who impregnated the patient twice—it
led to two abortions—and he wants to now show the patient
that she hates him and would like to see him dead. Well, of
course that's true, and we might even wonder if it's really
neurotic. Would it be more neurotic if she didn't hate him and
didn't want him to suffer?

That's what I mean by the linear qualities of this approach.
Oh, you could say that her feelings are overly intense, that she
should have forgiven him or worked this all through long ago,
and of course there's a grain of truth in that. Perhaps. But I
want to show you that you're dealing with a development that
is self-evident, and that neurotic mechanisms—again, using
the term neurosis in its broadest sense—are more convoluted
and considerably more filled with the unexpected and surprises.

Despite the likelihood that this must all relate to her
neurosis on some level, despite the intensity of this material,
this particular line could easily turn out a blind alley, a ready
displacement from the therapeutic relationship. At the very
least, I would want to be clear as to the ties between these two
spheres of her life. Does this patient experience these
interventions as seductive and destructive? Perhaps, but in
stating that, I must acknowledge that I speak again from a
weak position. I do not have convincing Type Two derivatives
from the patient and, given the level at which this therapist is
intervening, these may not become available. Then, we'll

simply have to see whether the patient truly validates an intervention based on the hypotheses formulated by the therapist. If there is clear-cut validation, then I would accept this as an exception to the principles I have been detailing throughout this course. I am prepared to revise those hypotheses, but we'll wait and see.

Therapist: The fact that she defends against it, that she says she still loves him: to me, that seemed inappropriate.

Langs: Yes, she does make use of denial, and I guess some therapists would interpret that defense and show her the extent to which it is contradicted by this dream. But for the moment, you are really pushing things; you are leading her, rather than allowing her to put the material and intervention into you. I myself can't convincingly lead you out of the hypothesis you have developed—I can do it only with the help of the patient who will have to lead the way if I am to develop support for my own thesis.

Therapist: I said, Who was your roommate? She said, I don't know. There was a pause. I said, Whose room did it look like? And there's a very long silence. And she's a little upset and she says, Why would I want to get Frank in trouble? Then she looks at me, waiting for an answer, and I respond: He wouldn't let you lie on your back with your legs up when you were in San Francisco.
She responds immediately: That didn't bother me so much, not as much as other things. I say, As what other things? She says, You know. Pause. You know how the quality, we both know. I ask, What else do women do lying on their back with their legs up?

Langs: Now you introduce your associations, and it's interesting how you are avoiding the abortions, considering your own thesis. But the main quality is how much you are pressing her, forcing her to follow a particular line of thought. It has the qualities of an inquisition.

Therapist: I introduce my associations. There's a pause and she starts crying. Then she says, That woman in the closet was me? I answer. I say, You say that she was tall, that she had red hair, and that she resembles you. There's another long pause. She says, Why would I kill myself?

Langs: I hope somebody is getting a feeling of how intellectualized this is, despite all of the pain, and how this is a really hammering home process. I must say you're from the hammering home school of psychotherapy. I mean, each little detail—this is where the sniper image does take on some meaning. I now begin to wonder if the limitations that I have experienced in connecting these manifest dream images to the therapeutic interaction are not based on an unfamiliarity with the previous sessions: the therapist's technique, the nature of his unconscious communications, and the specific issues that he has explored with this patient. I suspect that the selected fact is contained in those areas.

For the moment, I trust that you can see the difference between this technique and letting the patient shape the material in the session. It's important to get a feeling for that and to see, too, that with each of these details, the therapist shifts about, no longer using anything that resembles an adaptive context, but reading these dreams in isolation as Type One derivatives related to her relationship with Frank, telling her one moment that she'd like to kill him and the next moment that she wants to kill herself. This becomes confusing for the patient and, in the name of meaning, generates a sense of chaos—again, not unlike that conveyed in this dream.

I see now that time is getting short, and I think it would help if I applied the listening exercise to aspects of this dream. I believe now that none of this presentation clearly contradicts the principles I have developed, and that the therapist's interventions have not been validated. It seems to me that we are dealing for the moment with a situation in which some recent events, adaptive contexts, appear to have stirred up a whole series of unconscious and conscious fantasies, memories, and introjects related to two traumatic abortions the patient experienced. This constellation to some extent overshadows, and is being used to conceal, apparent difficulties in the therapeutic relationship and within the therapist, regarding which some links are, indeed, evident, though for the moment they do not seem available to interpretation. This seems to be the case partly because of the enormity of the outside trauma, and partly because of the defensive pressures from the therapist. There are qualities of a bastion here.

In principle it might be possible to intervene in the context of the gift from the boyfriend, as it has stirred up recollections of the patient's relationship with him, and of the abortions, though, as I said earlier in the course, I would not do so without derivative responses and ties to the therapeutic interaction, which arc lacking here for the moment. Further, I would maintain an awareness of unconscious perceptions and fantasies related to the therapist, unconscious links to treatment, and I would be prepared to deal with them once they emerge through closer derivatives. I would therefore not have intervened as yet here and, had I done so, I would havc commented in a manner that hints at ties to the therapeutic relationship, rendering that aspect open to a further communication from the patient and to interpretation from the thcrapiot. In essence, I would have allowed the patient to continue to associate to the dream, and I suspect that she might then have presented a clearer bridge to the therapeutic relationship—at which point I would have intervened in regard to her reactions to the abortion and to Frank, and would probably have linked them in some way to current adaptive contexts related to the therapeutic interaction.

As for the listening process, I trust that you can see that we do, indeed, listen to a dream in a manner virtually identical to the way we listen to any material. It's just that we often expect to be able to generate meanings—contents and defenses—in the presence of a dream, while realizing that dreams may be used as resistances and diversions, and for purposes other than symbolic communication.

Now, I will not attempt to conceptualize work with dreams here; I have done some of that in *The Bipersonal Field* (1976a) and I am preparing a manuscript on that very subject. But in applying the listening process to this dream, we begin first on the cognitive level. We hear a welter of themes, an experience that can suggest both major cognitive defenses and the active presence of projective identification—the use of the dream for discharge and interactional projection, rather than for cognitive communication. In fact, this dream has qualities both of cognitive and symbolic meaning and of discharge through projective identification. There is an effort here to place into the therapist terrifying, guilt-ridden contents that are generating considerable disturbance for the patient, an attempt at getting rid of that disturbance, rather than experiencing and comprehending it—and who knows how and by whom that particular spiral was initiated?

So, the main adaptive context for the dream is the gift from the boyfriend, with its latent content of the details of their prior relationship, their present separation, the pregnancies and the abortions. There are hints in derivative form that these latent themes in some way pertain to the therapeutic relationship as well, but these are not especially developed.

Now, there are many first-order themes, but before we push for a sense of meaning we must experience the possibility that the patient is intending to confuse us, to render us helpless, and, as I suggested, to projectively identify into us—this, far more than to provide us material for interpretation. It is important to be open to the experience of nonmeaning, especially in the face of long dreams and extended narrative associations.

In the course of our listening exercise, we have identified several adaptive contexts and can now allude to a number of first-order themes. I will be selective, rather than repeat the entire dream: small room ... hotel ... resort ... woman's corpse ... hiding it ... yoga position ... not being believed ... bleeding clear fluid ... a dead man ... confusion. These are perhaps the most salient first-order themes. Next we shift to generalizations: murder ... death ... hiding ... guilt and accusation ... concealment ... again, to name a few. Next, we generate second-order themes around the adaptive context of the abortion, to isolate that component and sense the patient's guilt over the murder of the fetuses, and possibly rage toward both herself and Frank for their destructiveness.

But we are not done. We must also monitor this material around the therapeutic interaction—whether the derivatives are close and clear or remote and distant—and along the me–not-me interface in particular. Here again the themes would be the same, and I have already posed them in terms of self-representations. You can see again that the most painful and difficult task with this dream would be to see it as an introject of the therapist, and as an unconscious perception of his having done something destructive, murderous, something that he wishes to conceal. I said unconscious perception, though actually we must take this first as possibly either unconscious perception or unconscious fantasy. And then, with each of these second-order derivatives, we must relate it both to the boyfriend and the abortion and to the therapeutic interaction. Finally, we must determine reality and separate it from fantasy, veridical perception from distortion.

Once those efforts have been completed, we have to take the patient's associations—the teenage dream…friends getting killed off…the sniper who was a boy the patient had a crush on…her wishes to continue or not continue the dream—and apply the listening process to that material as well, both in terms of the day residues for the initial dream and as latent content for that dream as well.

Since the hour is late, I will not carry out that exercise, but leave it to those of you who are attempting to sort out this material. For the moment, I want to stress that the manifest dream itself contains the latent contents, which are revealed when it is organized around the adaptive context. And while the issues are complicated, I simply want to propose that every session—even those in which a dream appears—should be organized around the day residues or adaptive contexts of that session, and that all manifest associations, dreams or otherwise, should be subjected to the listening process so that they may yield their latent contents—derivatives of unconscious fantasies, memories, and perceptions. It is my belief that this is what we mean by the latent content of a dream, and it applies to the latent content of any manifest communication from the patient. It can be derived only by knowing the adaptive context and applying the listening process to all of the material.

I know that all of this is a bit rushed, but I think it's important to hear this session out and perhaps the beginning of the next hour as well. There are many hypotheses to be validated. In fact, I should state my main thesis at this point:

this dream and the rest seem designed to flood or overwhelm the therapist and to projectively identify into him a state of anxiety, guilt, and destructiveness. There is thus an attempt to deny him any opportunity to meaningfully metabolize and organize these contents, thereby ultimately destroying the meaning so contained, breaking affective linkage with the therapist, attacking his capacity to integrate, and ridding the patient of disturbing inner contents—themselves derived from a destructive relationship with her boyfriend and the therapist. For me, the main thrust is toward excessive inputs, the frustrating destruction of meaning in the face of an apparent wealth of meaning, and an attack on the therapist and her links to him. However, validating that hypothesis in this field will be quite difficult. In a sense, my own integrating capacities have been disrupted by this patient-therapist interaction. Please continue.

Therapist: She paused and said, Why would I kill myself? I say, and this is really the interpretation, To get Frank in trouble, to make him sorry that he wouldn't marry you, to make him sorry he wouldn't let you have his baby, to make him appreciate how much you loved him, to make him realize how much he loved you. And she started crying and continues for a few minutes, and it then lessens. Eventually, she smiles. She looks at her watch and says, Is our time up? I nod yes, and she says thank you. She smiles and leaves.

Langs: Unfortunately, there is little time to discuss this intervention at any length. But I think it is important to see it as a product of your own application of the listening process, and to recognize that the introduction of the theme of revenge came almost entirely from you. Much of what you said made use of elements from this manifest dream which you then shaped and even distorted according to your own personal interpretation and needs. I would not view her crying as validation, and her only verbal communication after the intervention was to ask whether time was up, whether she could leave. We will have to consider her opening communications in the next hour as her commentary on your intervention, and we will get to that in a moment.

In brief, I would have allowed this session to unfold without intervening for a long while. And I believe that would have had more derivatives that allude on some level to the therapeutic relationship than were available as this session actually developed. In general, I would have formulated that the dream seemed to be prompted by the gift from Frank, which had evoked many memories, especially those related to her abortions, and that there clearly was concern with issues related to murder, to being discovered, and the resultant need to conceal. I would have added that in some way all of this must also refer to some aspect of her relationship with the therapist, since it all takes place in a small, dingy room much like his office, and that much of it has to do with her relationship with another man. I must say that those are rather weak bridges, and I would probably not have used them. Actually, I found little silent validation and would have shifted to a thesis related to the destruction of interpersonal links and meanings. Had that been validated, I would have intervened in that area, identifying from her associations contributions from myself, as therapist, and from the patient.

Finally, and I think this is important as it relates to the listening process, the patient had in several ways emphasized that these traumatic and murderous experiences were exciting and gratifying for her. This was expressed in her continued love for Frank and in her attraction to the adolescent sniper in her earlier childhood dream. And I would have wanted in some way to point out to her, had I made any intervention, that these traumatic experiences seem to stimulate and gratify her in some way—a point that you omitted and one I think crucial to the evident masochistic gratification this patient derives from destructive relationships. In fact, it may well be that such gratifications are available to her in the therapeutic relationship as presently constituted, and that may account for her reluctance to clearly identify the misalliance between yourself and her, even in derivative form, and to go about the work of rectification. I suspect now that her powerful masochistic tendencies, in addition to the aggressive and other factors I mentioned before, have made this session quite difficult to understand and formulate. But perhaps some of this will become clearer when we hear the beginning of the next hour.

Therapist: She begins the next session by saying, I did something that you'll be pleased to hear about. I dreaded this date I had set up. My first impression was right—he always gets into arguments

Langs: Well, it seems to me that organizing this material right off around the adaptive context of the interventions that you made toward the end of the last session suggests that she is reacting to your manner of intervening, that there are unconscious fantasies and perceptions related to a datelike relationship with you, and that she is introjecting the provocative qualities of your interventions.

Therapist: She said: He has to prove he's right.

Discussant: That seems to be in keeping with many of your formulations, Dr. Langs.

Langs: Yes, I think that she's starting to work over the therapeutic interaction and to offer unconscious interpretations to the therapist. This is her way of alluding to the school of hammer-it-home psychotherapy. But let's hear more.

Oh, by the way, it seems worth mentioning that despite the evident obstacles it would appear that we did rather nicely in predicting the latent content of the dream. I mention it only because I think it's a special reward of the proper application of the listening process and we lost sight of that aspect in our discussion. We missed, I think, the extent to which the dream was designed as a projective identification and as an effort to confuse and destroy meaning. But much of that came from our lack of knowledge of the prior sessions and our ignorance of the current adaptive contents within the therapy.

As we hear these opening fragments, it occurs to me that another way of characterizing what troubled me about the previous session, and perhaps of explaining it as well, is that I am quite prepared to work with a major traumatic adaptive context outside the therapeutic relationship, but would be concerned that I was missing something if I could not identify derivative connections to the therapeutic relationship and the influence of that outside context on ongoing aspects of the therapeutic interaction itself. It is those qualities that seemed lacking in the last session, but I think that this may well have been a mistaken impression based largely, as I said, on our not having had an opportunity to hear a number of sessions from this treatment or even the details of the prior hour. Perhaps the kind of provocative questioning that we were hearing—the approach to the patient as a kind of hostile witness who is to be somewhat badgered, led toward damning evidence, etcetera—and the use of confronting and seemingly interpretive interventions through which the therapist introduces many of his own countertransference-based fantasies and needs—and which unconsciously have the qualities of an assaultive projective identification, an attack upon the patient—perhaps such efforts have characterized the work of this therapist, who is able to control his impulses only up to a point, and that this was not immediately evident to us.

But if you begin to sense these unconscious communicative qualities in his style of working, you can see that the dream actually contains many more bridges to the therapeutic interaction that I initially noted. And perhaps, unconsciously, the patient has rather nicely perceived and introjected the nature of this therapist's work, and has conveyed it in the manifest and latent content of her dreams: that he is unwittingly murderous, that he is not really committing crimes, though it seems that way; and that he is unaware of the impact of his destructiveness. Maybe the patient blames his supervisor. I don't want to get too speculative, but there seems to be an impression on her part that he tries to hide or deny the impact of his interventions on the patient, and there are fantasies, as well, that the therapist should be punished. I say all of this because I think the patient is getting more directly to it in this session, largely because the therapist's last intervention brought it to a head. And remember, this is a sadomasochistic couple in which the patient is deriving unconscious gratification, so she will accept the misalliance initially and will perhaps only reluctantly make unconscious efforts to modify it.

So this is actually quite rich material, and perhaps some of my hypotheses can be validated by hearing some more. Accept the revisions in my thinking about these sessions, first, as reflecting another level of what the patient is communicating; and, second, as a reflection of the clarity that follows upon a clearer delineation of the adaptive context. As always, my confusion was an interactional product; much of it stemmed from my ignorance of this therapeutic interaction. Please go on.

Therapist: Still speaking of her date, she said, He has no sense of humor at all, but I went through with it. I didn't enjoy it. At the end I said to him, I'll see you around. Now on the contrary, last Friday I had lunch with two male friends of mine, both of whom are married, both of whom are absolutely charming. They like to talk to me. My social isolation will be complete for next week; my parents are going to Mexico, and I'll be alone in the house. Some people are supposed to call. I'm going to go visit a friend in Boston. She starts talking about the friend in Boston: Peggy had a baby two years ago. (She had mentioned Peggy at the end of the session that had preceded the dream.) She's a good old friend; I stopped by in July. I'll go next weekend. Then she starts talking about some of the museums in Boston, and about relics. She says, I was talking to somebody, and he asked if my Medieval History professor had seduced me yet. (She's taking some graduate courses in history.) He's had affairs with lots of his graduate students. Last year my professor in Asian history was a homosexual.

Langs: Now she's working you over—she's getting tough on you. Just monitoring this material around the adaptive context of your last interventions, we have the seducer, the homosexual, the failure to maintain proper boundaries.

Therapist: She says, he hasn't given me my course assignment, and he hasn't attempted to seduce me, either.

Langs: Which is a nice example of a transversal communication: you have and you haven't. Go ahead.

Therapist: I make my first intervention. I say, You sound disappointed. (Laughter.)

Langs: He says as he unbuckles his belt. See, it's as if you're saying, No, it has nothing to do with me, with here and now. And in terms of my hypothesis, look at how your intervention sounds, the kind of unconscious communications it may well contain: You sound disappointed that I have neither done therapy with you nor seduced you. So this is an example of what can happen when you listen naively: your own unconscious fantasies and wishes are exposed, and the patient will, on some level, detect them.

Therapist: (I said as I was crawling over my desk.) She says, In a sense I am—why should I be left out? He was married twice, he's divorced, and now he owns an apartment in the building where his last wife lives, but he doesn't live there. I don't know what I would do if he did try to seduce me. He's a very urbane man so it wouldn't be clumsy. It could be refused gracefully, I suppose. I like him in many ways, but he's very strange. He doesn't meet people well, he doesn't know how to make small talk. I don't think he gets close to people, even though he's friendly.

Langs: On one level, these are all unconscious interpretations based on unconscious perceptions. Go ahead.

Therapist: He keeps a part of himself remote. He has an excellent sense of humor, he's very devoted to his work. (I have a note here that I was thinking of interpreting the resemblance to me, but I write that it's too early, so I don't say anything. I just let her talk.)

Langs: It comes to your mind at this point.

Therapist: The excellent sense of humor, devoted to his work—the similarity is so overwhelming. (Laughter.)

Langs: Yes, now that the evoked images are positive, you

are more open to recognizing the allusions to yourself on a latent level: first-order themes, generalizations, second-order themes related to the therapeutic interaction. And now we see an interesting facet of the me–not-me interface: you are prepared to see yourself when the associations are flattering—a seducer of woman, an urbane man, excellent sense of humor, all the rest—though notice also that the reference is to someone who does not maintain proper boundaries. You are now less prepared to see these as self-representations of some part of the patient. In addition, you'll note that you are far more open to monitoring the not-me part of the interface with this material than you were with the material from the last session, when the images conveyed were those of a seducer who impregnated her and participated in two abortions—a murderer, someone trying to hide corpses.

This is also an excellent opportunity to see the influence of your own self-image on your capacity to maintain a free-floating role responsiveness and openness to image evocations. And it shows how you may be prone, based on countertransference influences, to reject certain communications as alluding to yourself while actually welcoming others. Undoubtedly, the truth of the situation is that your behavior with this patient, your interventions and management of the framework, justifies both views of you. And, while this may reflect some split in the patient's self-image, we will not be able to identify it until you have rectified your own interventions to the point where these communications no longer tally with valid conscious and unconscious perceptions of yourself.

So we are beginning to develop an accumulation of evidence that the patient is working over her relationship with the therapist in derivative form. This material can be seen as reflecting coalescing Type Two derivatives based on the general nature of the ongoing therapeutic interaction and on the specific unconscious communications contained in the therapist's interventions in the previous sessions.It seems to me that this material supports my hypotheses that the dream-associational network of the prior hour did indeed allude to the therapist in ways that were not immediately clear to us—for whatever reason—and that there were undoubtedly links between the day residue that pertained to the gift from the boyfriend and day residues derived from the therapist's interventions in the hour prior to the dream. On that basis it would seem that her comment, the one regarding your having expected her to be upset while she talked about her abortions, unconsciously contained her perceptions of a series of interventions on your part. And it did indeed allude to a major day residue for the dream, namely, your specific interventions in that prior hour and the countertransference-based qualities that they contained.

Incidentally, I would take this kind of mixed image as encouraging. While we will have to sort out many actualities before determining just how destructive and how seductive you have behaved—and some of this may actually stem from the conditions of her therapy here in the clinic, and from alterations in the framework that are beyond your control— we do, in addition, have evidence that some of it derives from the manner and nature of your interventions. Still, at this stage of your training, it is encouraging that the patient sees positive potential within you, and is not overwhelmed by un-analyzed destructive trends. I know that that doesn't sound like much of a complement, but, believe me, it is. Please continue.

Therapist: She says: He's honest. He's as nice as he can be— or nice as he can be without compromising his professional-ism. He doesn't ask very much of me. I look forward to my parents' going away because they never seem to go away. Maybe they'll enjoy themselves. I don't think they enjoy life at all—especially my mother. They seem to be waiting for the undertaker. But I realize they really enjoy mundane things. My father really has no interests, no hobbies. He repairs cars occasionally, that's the only thing he does. But he repairs them badly.

Langs: Just keep monitoring this material in terms of the therapeutic interaction, as unconscious perceptions and interpretations to the therapist, including allusions to the genetic ties to the introjects generated by the therapist—that is, as nontransference first. Then we'll look for the transference-based distortions of her image of the therapist based on her experiences with her parents.

Therapist: She said: My father never reads, but my mother reads a lot of fiction. She encouraged me to read as a child, but she discouraged me once I became an adolescent, because I would stay up and read late into the night. I feel closer to my mother than to my father—both now and when I was growing up.

Langs: I find it so interesting to get the feeling that even though she is now attempting to develop some genetic aspects of her actual experiences in the therapeutic interaction—and maybe, also, some of the underlying genetic factors in her involvement with this destructive boy friend and her abortions—the material is really getting more and more boring and empty. It is beginning to take on the qualities of Type C communication. And once again, some of it undoubtedly derives from the therapist's intervention about her disappointment, and some from her own defensive needs. But there is a continued effort on her part to suppress bridges between this material and the therapeutic relationship, and, undoubtedly, such connections had not been developed and interpreted in previous sessions. As a result, much of what I have said has to be left as a set of silent hypotheses, to which the material now nicely fits, though definitive validation is lacking.

And I think that this is a fitting note on which to end a seminar on listening: at a point of interactional resistance, a moment of uncertainty—a point at which, though the material seems to coalesce around the set of silent hypotheses, the patient fails to produce the selected fact, the link that would integrate and validate these formulations and thereby permit their interpretation to the patient.

Well, I see that our time is up. I want to thank you for another forthright and stimulating presentation.

Discussant: Before we stop, would you just list the four basic components of the listening process that you identified earlier today?

Langs: Yes. One, searching for the adaptive context. Two, generating first-order specific themes—then generalizations and abstractions—leading to second-order specific themes, through which you generate Type One and Type Two derivatives. Three, monitoring the material in terms of the therapeutic interaction and around the me–not-me interface, as communications alluding to both patient and therapist, self- and object-representations. And four, sorting out the elements of fantasy and reality in each product of the listening and formulating process. These four basic steps are complemented by the validating process, and all of this is done in each of the three basic spheres: the cognitive; interactional mechanisms (projective identifications); and object relations (role and image evocations).

In closing out this part of the course, I would like to remind you again, apropos of that last question, that I have tended to stress the more formal qualities of the listening process and the means through which we formulate and validate: first, because they have been so terribly neglected, and, second, because they lend themselves, as I said earlier, to a teaching experience, while the more ineffable and unconscious aspects of the listening process can best be developed through your own maturation and therapy or analysis. They also have been studied more extensively in the psychoanalytic literature and are, of course, more difficult to conceptualize and teach in the practical clinical sense that is the hallmark of this course.

All of this leads me to suggest, as a final message regarding this segment of the course, that you now let it all settle. Consciously and unconsciously you undoubtedly have taken in a great deal, so for the moment set aside any active wish to memorize, remember, or learn. Approximate that model of entering the session without memory, desire, or understanding; allow the digestive process to occur spontaneously, and you can eventually determine how much has been meaningfully incorporated and how much remains to be done. Then, as we make use of the listening process through the other segments of this course, you can make additional efforts to fill the gaps and supplement what you have learned during these first ten weeks. And perhaps then it will even be possible for you to generate creative responses through which you add new insights—and whether they're personal or have universal application need not concern us. All of this is my way of saying that I hope this seminar will ultimately generate personal creativity in each and every one of you. On that note, I want to thank each of you for your excellent presentations and active, probing, and challenging participation. I am grateful, and can only hope that I have responded well to your needs to learn.

Appendix A

SOME COMMUNICATIVE
PROPERTIES OF
THE BIPERSONAL FIELD

When a psychoanalytic investigator is struggling to develop a new perspective on disquieting clinical observations, there is often a most constructive interplay between his ill-formed ideas, his ongoing clinical observations, and his reading of the literature. Preoccupied with clinical data that momentarily defy organization, he searches for the *selected fact* (Bion, 1962) that would synthesize and properly link together his still divergent conceptions and observations. The analyst may actively sift others' contributions in the hopes of discovering clues to the missing integrating elements. More often than not, however, such active efforts do not bear fruit; the problem lies fallow or repeatedly frustrates efforts at resolution, until either a moment of clinical insight develops or, through serendipity, reading undertaken for a quite different purpose provides catalytic insights that allow for the elusive solution.

This paper was written for *Do I Dare Disturb the Universe? A Festschrift for Wilfred Bion,* edited by James S. Grotstein. It appears also in *The International Journal of Psychoanalytic Psychotherapy,* Vol. 7, 1978.

This proved to be the case in regard to my efforts to conceptualize the communicative dimension of the patient-analyst interaction. In the course of many years of struggle, bits of insight, new uncertainties, further understanding, new dissatisfactions, further clinical observations, and minor clues from reading generated a seemingly endless cycle in which fragments of resolution alternated with additional clinical observations that raised new and pertinent questions. Along the way, it was the reading of Bion's *Learning from Experience,* and especially his discussion of alpha functions and of alpha and beta elements—supplemented by a study of his later works (see Bion, 1977)—that provided me with a critical selected fact that finally helped to organize my experiences and ideas in a somewhat stable manner. This presentation offers a broad outline of the crystallizations that followed: it describes some basic communicative properties of the psychotherapeutic and psychoanalytic bipersonal fields[1] and suggests a major means of categorizing the overall qualities of these fields. The implications of these conceptualizations for the understanding of the analytic interaction and for the technical approach of the analyst will also receive special emphasis.

THE DEVELOPMENT OF BACKGROUND CONCEPTS

In outlining the developments that have led me to a basic type-classification of communicative therapeutic fields, I will sketch historically some of the major observations that contributed to these formulations. My own training as a psychoanalyst and my recent study of the psychoanalytic literature related to the analytic experience (Langs, 1976c) have indicated that, on the whole, classical psychoanalysts assume the psychoanalytic experience to take place in a single type of communicative field. With few exceptions (see below) analysts in general—Freudians, Kleinians, the middle group who have followed the lead of Winnicott, and others who have attempted an integrated approach—have written an enormous number of clinical papers related to the psychoanalytic interaction and psychoanalytic technique with the inherent assumption that there is a single basic analytic model. As a result, little or no attention had been paid to the communicative style of the patient (and still less, to that of the analyst) except to suggest that certain patients who do not develop a so-called transference neurosis are essentially not analyzable (see Greenson, 1967). Such a suggestion implies that the patient is unable to fit into the analyst's stereotyped communicative model and is therefore unanalyzable (for another relevant example see Angel, 1971). Not all, however, of these difficult patients, generally viewed as having borderline syndromes or psychotic reactions, have been considered unsuitable for analysis, while many have been so considered, for a variety of reasons, with seemingly less severe disturbances (for a similar discussion of this trend see Giovacchini, 1975).

The type of communicative field which these analysts accepted and found workable can be characterized as one in which the patient readily and verbally free associates, conveys analyzable derivatives of his inner mental world— his unconscious fantasies, memories, introjects, self-representations, and the like—and in which the analyst in reponse interprets relevant contents, defenses, and dynamic constellations as they have a bearing on the patient's intrapsychic conflicts and psychopathology. Disturbances in this flow and analytic work generally appear in the form of interference with the communication of derivatives (primarily those related to the analyst) and as those readily identifiable behaviors which have been termed acting out, or as I prefer, either *living out* or *enactments* (see Langs, 1976c). These serve primarily as resistances, although they do simultaneously communicate, in some sense, unconscious contents and dynamics.

Inevitably every analyst experiences exceptions to this model. In fact, it is my current clinical impression, based on experiences directly with patients and in supervision, that exceptions are far more common than the rule. Quite early in my analytic work I was confronted with analysands whose associations did not appear to be readily interpretable. I was also struck by patients, both in therapy and in analysis, who seemed relatively uninterested in the acquisition of cognitive insights, but who, it eventually turned out, remained in treatment for a variety of other reasons: to gain direct support against a spouse, to spend large sums of money as a means of harming a spouse or parent, to provide a cover for directly destructive intentions toward another person, to gain in the therapist a gratifying companion in an otherwise empty life, or to find a target for unbridled expressions of aggression and sexuality. (This latter type of patient has been described in the literature on erotized and aggressive transferences; see Langs, 1976c.) Such analysands challenged for me the generally accepted image of analysis and the tenet that the role of the analyst was to create a secure analytic setting and therapeutic alliance within which the derivatives of the patient's transference constellation (his unconcious transference fantasies) could unfold and be analyzed.

Although I observed much of this well before Bird (1972), in a relatively isolated contribution, dramatically stated that at times patients attempt to harm their analysts, Searles (1965) was writing during this period of such matters as patients' efforts to drive their analysts crazy and the realistic impact that patients have on their analysts—including the much delayed discovery of the patient's therapeutic intentions and efforts toward the analyst (see especially Searles, 1959, 1975, and Langs, 1975b, 1976a, 1976b). At this time, I was painfully aware that the overidealized and unrealistic world-of-fantasy model of analysis and therapy was something of a myth, a point expressly made in the second volume of *The Technique of Psychoanalytic Psychotherapy* (1974). My understanding of the problem, however, was limited to an awareness that patients enter analysis with deviant motives and to the technical recommendation that these needs and intended or actual misuses had to be discovered, analyzed, worked through, and resolved before other analytic work would be feasible.

My perception of this aspect of the analytic situation began to change gradually as a consequence of the development of several new clinical concepts. Largely because *The Technique of Psychoanalytic Psychotherapy* (Langs, 1973, 1974) was empirically derived, I had approached the study of transference within an adaptive framework, thereby reformulating aspects of the influence of the patient's unconscious transference fantasies and stressing his exquisite, unconscious sensitivity to the therapist's errors. Having already written on the relationship between day residues and dreams (Langs, 1971), I found this model quite serviceable in considering the patient's reactions to the therapist, since it stressed the precipitants of these responses as one key to their understanding. I pointed out that transference responses do not occur ex nihilo, but are consistently prompted by life events, especially by occurrences within the therapeutic or analytic interaction. Recognizing the presence of many reactions in the patient derived primarily from the countertransference-based errors of the therapist, I described a series of iatrogenic syndromes (Langs, 1974).

This adaptive, interactional approach crystallized while I was completing the *Technique* volumes, and I embodied it in the concept of the *adaptive context* (Langs, 1972, 1973)—the internal or, more usually, the external reality stimulus for the patient's intrapsychic responses. The discovery of a reality precipitant for every intrapsychic reaction consolidated the adaptive dimension of my approach to understanding the patient and led to an extensive consideration of the nature of these adaptive stimuli, especially as they pertained to the therapist's interventions and failures to intervene. Many new perspectives followed from the principles that all of the patient's associations subsequent to an intervention bore on the analyst's communication and that the patient's responses were always a mixture, on the one hand, of valid perceptiveness and commentary and, on the other, of distorting fantasies. It was then feasible to extend these concepts to the therapist's management of the ground rules—a position that led to a number of additional discoveries.

I soon realized that the patient was, unconsciously, exquisitely sensitive to the analyst's errors and I could trace the vicissitudes of his responses. I found that the clinical data readily reaffirmed and extended Searles's concept (see 1965, 1972, 1975) that the patient not only unconsciously perceives the analyst's errors, but also unconsciously introjects dimensions of the analyst's maladaptive inner world and functioning as they are unconsciously communicated through his errors. This led to studies of the patient's unconscious curative efforts toward the therapist, an insight first described by Little (1951) and then specifically elaborated upon by Searles (1965, 1975), and was counterbalanced by investigations of the positive effects of valid interventions.

While I was developing an appreciation of the complexities of the analytic interaction and of the extent of the analyst's continuous involvement and conscious and unconscious communication with the patient—aspects of the interaction which I once again found Searles (1965, 1972, 1975) especially sensitive to—my reading and clinical work prompted me to consider more carefully the analyst's demeanor, his basic attitude or stance, toward the patient. In this respect, Balint's *The Basic Fault* (1968) was especially important in that he suggested that certain types of patients require both a different than usual mode of listening by the analyst and a distinctive manner of relating He referred to patients suffering from what he termed a *basic fault*, an ego defect or sector of inner mental damage derived from such disruptive preoedipal experiences as acute traumas and faulty mothering. These analysands required a response from the analyst that created a sense of *primary love*; the analyst essentially became the medium through which the patient could regress, discover his basic fault, mourn it, and then progress once again. He drew an analogy to the oxygen we breathe and the water through which the swimmer swims: neither the oxygen nor the water asks anything of the recipient and yet offers essential support. For Balint, this therapeutic carriage was essential with patients for whom two-person interactions were far more important than those at a three-person level.

Here was an important indication that in addition to his interpretations, the manner in which the analyst created the analytic situation and related to the analysand could have a significant influence on the analytic work and outcome. Winnicott (1958, 1965), who stressed the *holding* qualities of the analytic setting and of the analyst's stance, had suggested as early as 1956 that with certain patients the holding environment, of which the analyst is a part, would have to do all the essential therapeutic work for long periods of time. It is no coincidence that Winnicott's metaphor of the maternal-like holding functions of the analyst bears a striking resemblance to Bion's metaphor (1977) of *the container* and *the contained* which he too applied, in part, to the analyst's functions (see below, and also Langs, 1976a, 1976b, 1976c). Khan too (1963, 1964), in writing of the *maternal shield,* offered a metaphor for certain inherently protective, and yet noninterpretive, aspects of the analyst's relationship with his patient.

It had, then, become increasingly clear (a) that many patients did not confine themselves to the largely verbal communication in an analyzable form of derivatives both of unconscious fantasies and of other inner contents and defenses, and (b) that the analyst's functions extended beyond his development of a safe setting and the use of verbal interventions geared toward neutral interpretations. He had an additional responsibility to create a special setting and hold for the patient, to manage the ground rules, and to maintain his hold as long as necessary. It had also become evident that there was an ever-present interaction between the patient and the analyst, much of it on an unconscious level, with continuous pressures toward both health and regression on both sides—though hopefully in different proportions for patient and analyst(see Searles, 1965, and his concept of *therapeutic symbiosis*). Finally, with the development of the concept of the adaptive context, it was possible to study more carefully the communications from the patient and to recognize that at times his associations provided interpretable derivatives, while at other times they did not: either there were many apparent derivatives and no adaptive context in which to dynamically organize and understand them, or the adaptive context was evident, but clear-cut and meaningful derivatives were lacking (see Searles, 1973b for a related discussion). Further, the production of these derivatives was not solely a function of the intrapsychic balances, contents, and state of the analysand, but was continuously influenced by the analyst as well (Langs, 1975a, 1975b, 1975c, 1976a, 1976c).

I had begun to develop clinical material for a new book, and intending a rather comprehensive investigation of this area, I decided to review very carefully the relevant literature.

Among many, for me truly remarkable, discoveries (Langs, 1976c), I was especially drawn to a paper by the Barangers (1966) in which they discussed the development of insight in the analytic situation—the *bipersonal field,* as they termed it. While I can remember vividly my initial, utter confusion in response to their discussion of projective identification as the major mechanism within that field—my first exposure to the term—I nonetheless found their conception of the analytic relationship in terms of a bipersonal field not only extremely attractive, but soon quite productive of additional personal insights.

The field concept led me to intensify my investigations of the ground rules of analysis, since it was evident that these tenets were, in part, the delimiting determinants of the field— both as its internal and external boundaries and, as a key factor in the very nature of the transactions within its confines. The field metaphor was supported by Milner's analogy (1952) between the ground rules of analysis and the frame of a painting: each sets off the world within its confines from the rest of reality and gives that inner world its special qualities and rules. In analysis, for example, the frame makes the transference illusion possible. In these two ways, the ground rules of analysis took on three-dimensional qualities and a reexamination of their functions became vital. I soon saw that since they could be viewed as the framework of the bipersonal field, their establishment and maintenance were perhaps the major factors giving the analytic field its therapeutic qualities and communicative characteristics—a point suggested by Bleger (1967) and explicity elaborated upon by Viderman (1974).

Among the many important ideas to which the bipersonal field concept led, several are most pertinent to this presentation. The metaphor suggests that every point in the field— every communication, interaction, structure, and occurrence within and between the two members of the dyad—receives vectors from both participants, albeit in varying proportions. Thus, every communication from the patient is influenced to a greater or lesser extent by the analyst, and vice versa. Futher, every point in the field is layered and thus requires equal consideration of its realistic and fantasied components. Each content and communication, with its conscious and unconscious elements, must be scrutinized for its veridical core (primarily its nontransference layer for the patient and its noncountertransference layer for the analyst) as well as for its intrapsychically distorted aspects (primarily transference for the patient and countertransference for the analyst). In addition, both intrapsychic and interactional processes and mechanisms must consistently be considered.

One can hypothesize an interactional interface along which the communications from patient and analyst take place, and then consider the vectors that determine its position and qualities: its location vis-à-vis the respective pathologies of patient and analyst; the extent to which it is fixed or mobile, in terms of the relative contributions of the patient and analyst; the degree to which its primary qualities are related to unconscious fantasies, memories, and introjects, or to projective and introjective identifications; and the degree to which it embodies what I have termed the *me–not-me* property—the manner in which the communications from each participant allude both to the self and the not-self. (In other words), the patient's associations consistently refer to both himself and the analyst, in terms of both valid perceptions and distorted fantasies; see Langs, 1976c).

The bipersonal field concept also directs the analyst to a consideration of the nature of the communications that take place within the field: the extent to which verbal communications prevail and maintain their intended meaning; the degree to which symbolic and illusory verbal and behavioral communication is present; the openness of the interactional flow; the presence of projective identifications; and the use of language and behavior for discharge and direct gratification rather than for insight (Langs, 1976a, 1976c). The concept also encourages a study of the defenses that exist within the field, stressing the contributions of both participants, thereby supplementing the strictly intrapsychic viewpoint of both defenses and resistances. Thus, while the Barangers (1966) had described *bastions* of the bipersonal field (shared sectors of the communicative field that are split off, repressed, and denied by both participants), I delineated various sectors of *therapeutic misalliance* (Langs, 1975b, 1976a, 1976c) which involves unconscious collusion between the patient and analyst directed toward noninsightful sympton relief and other inappropriate, shared defenses and gratifications. Similarly, I delineated *interactional resistances* that were created and shared by the two participants. This line of thought led to the recognition of *interactional syndromes:* symptoms in either participant to which both patient and analyst contribute in varying proportions—a notion that provides an interactional addendum to the concept of the intrapsychically based transference and countertransference neuroses (or syndromes).

Work on the bipersonal field interdigitated with studies of the nature of the unconscious and conscious communication between the patient and analyst—the unconscious communicative interaction. For the patient, the stress was on a balanced appreciation of his valid functioning, as compared to his pathological responses, so that both unconscious preception and unconscious fantasy received attention. The former, while most often valid, could also be distorted—*unconscious misperception.* Such perceptions form the core of the patient's introjects of the analyst—realistic nuclei which may then be surrounded by pathological, intrapsychically-founded distortions. Unconscious preceptions and introjections of the therapist's countertransference-based behaviors and their underlying psychopathology may, on the one hand, be misappropriated by the patient to reinforce his own psychopathology and may, on the other, evoke both unconscious retaliation and unconscious efforts at cure (Searles, 1965, 1975, Langs, 1975b, 1976a, 1976c). Valid interventions by the analyst, however, not only generate cognitive insight and the related resolution of intrapsychic conflicts, anxieties, and distorted fantasies and introjects, but they also inherently provide the patient with positive and curative introjects based on the analyst's sound functioning.

For the analyst, his manifest interventions—interpretations and managements of the frame—were seen to extend beyond their direct contents into a wide range of unconscious communications. Erroneous interventions and mismanagements of the frame were found, since they were not in keeping with the patient's communications and needs, to convey aspects of the analyst's pathological unconscious fantasies, memories, and introjects, and to constitute the projective identification into the patient of aspects of the analyst's own pathological inner mental world. Here too Bion's unique investigations of projective identification, and his specific development of the metaphor of the container and the contained (1977), facilitated the understanding of this dimension of the unconscious interaction between the patient and analyst. While heretofore the stress had been on the patient's pathological projective identifications into the analyst and on the latter's capacity to contain, metabolize, and interpret these contents (see for example, Grinberg, 1962; Bion, 1977; Langs, 1976a, 1976b, 1976c), the bipersonal field concept prompted an equal consideration of the analyst's pathological projective identifications into the patient, and his use of the patient as a pathological or inappropriate container for these contents (Langs, 1976a, 1976c).

In this connection, I also recognized that projective identification could range from primitive omnipotent fantasies with almost no effort at interactional fulfillment to more mature, structuralized interactional efforts to placing contents into the dyadic partner. I suggested the use of the term *interactional projection* (Langs, 1976a, 1976c) to stress the actuality of the projective effort in projective identification and to contrast it with projection which I—and others—defined as an essentially intrapsychic mechanism. Finally, by making extensive use of Wangh's concept (1962), the *evocation of a proxy,* I was able to recognize uses of projective identification beyond its usually described role as a means of getting rid of bad inner contents, placing good contents into an object for safekeeping, and externalizing one's troubling inner representations in order to better manage them from without (Segal, 1967). Wangh's work implied that projective identification also serves the subject as a means of evoking adaptive responses in the object which can then be introjected by the subject.

One final clarification helped to set the stage for the main subject of this paper—the identification of major types of communicative bipersonal fields. This took the form of clarifying the types of communications from the patient and the ways in which the analyst could organize and conceptualize this material (Langs, 1978b). In essence, it was suggested that on the first level, a patient's associations could be organized around their *manifest contents*. This approach, which is essentially nonanalytic since it totally rejects all notions of unconscious process and content, confines itself to the surface of the patient's communications.

On the second level, the analyst organizes material from the patient by attending to the mainfest associations, isolating various segments of this material, and imputing to each a specific unconscious meaning; I term these inferences *Type One derivatives*. Here, the mainfest content is addressed in relative isolation, and the latent content—the unconscious communication—is determined by the recognition of obvious displacements, the use of symbols, the intuitive understanding of underlying meanings, and a knowledge of a given patient's communicative idiom. By and large, the distinction between unconscious fantasy and unconscious perception is ignored, and Type One derivatives are conceived of primarily in terms of the former.

A third level of organizing the material from the patient is feasible through the use of the *adaptive context* as the dynamic organizer of the patient's associations; this yields *Type Two derivatives*. The model here is that of the day residue and the mainfest dream, the latent content of which is fully comprehended only with the knowledge of the dream's precipitant and related associations (Langs, 1971, 1978b). Each adaptive context itself has both manifest and latent meanings. Further, most crucial adaptive contexts for the patient in analysis stem from his interaction with the analyst; as a result, a true understanding of the nature of an adaptive stimulus and of the responses it evokes (associations and behaviors) is founded on the self-knowledge of the analyst— his sensitivity to the conscious, and especially, unconscious meanings and projections conveyed in his verbal interventions, silences, and efforts to manage the frame.

Type Two derivatives, then, are always viewed dynamically and as responses to adaptive stimuli. As a rule, they imply that virtually all of the communications from the patient must, on this level, be appended or related to the analytic interaction—those representing perceptions and introjections, as well as fantasies and distortions. At this level, many seemingly divergent and relatively undecipherable associations accrue significance in the light of the recognized adaptive context.

In all, then, my investigations of the bipersonal field had, at this point, provided me with the following tools: (1) the concepts of the adaptive context and of Type Two derivatives, means through which it became feasible to determine whether the communications from the patient constituted analyzable derivatives of unconscious fantasies and perceptions, (2) an understanding of basic interactional mechanisms and of the unconscious communications and projective efforts of both patient and analyst, (3) a comprehension of the essential role played by the framework of the analytic situation in determining the communicative properties of the therapeutic field, and (4) a conception of the dimensions of the bipersonal field itself, as created and continued by both patient and analyst.

At this juncture, there was evident need for a basic conceptualization of major types of therapeutic or communicative bipersonal fields. In continued clinical observations, I experimented with a number of possibilities, but a satisfactory classification seemed to elude crystallization until a point at which a reorganization of my clinical observations coincided with a rereading of Bion's writings, especially a series of comments in his 1962 book, *Learning from Experience*. Much later, after the necessary concepts had been developed, I found independent confirmation of aspects of my ideas in an important paper by Khan (1973). At the time of writing this paper, I restudied a series of additional ideas in Bion's writings (1977) that, on the one hand, suggested an unconscious influence on the delineation of these fields that I had not previously explicity recognized and that, on the other, helped to further refine my understanding of the concepts I was attempting to define. Finally, I have just now become aware of efforts by Liberman (in press) to study styles of communication in patients.

THE THREE MAJOR BIPERSONAL FIELDS

For some time, I had developed, as I have described, considerable evidence for distinctly different types of bipersonal fields. In the course of struggling with these clinical observations, I found that Winnicott's (1965, 1971) conception of the analytic setting as a type of transitional or play space within which the capacity for illusion plays a central role seemed pregnant with meaning. I could see that, in my terms, this implied the presence of analyzable Type Two derivatives, and I was aware that certain bipersonal fields possessed this quality, while others certainly did not. This, however, seemed insufficient for a full classification; the crucial variables had not emerged. Still, I had made a number of fascinating clinical observations along the following lines: as a rule, when the analyst modified the framework of the bipersonal field, the transitional-play qualities tended to diminish or disappear. This could be seen in the flatness of a patient's subsequent communications and in the relative absence of interpretable derivatives (see Halpert 1972, for an illustration). Often, under these conditions the patient would eventually make such comments as "I can no longer write or paint," or, "My child's school does not have a playground."

These observations provided further evidence of the importance of the analyst to both the patient's communicative style and to the overall communicative qualities of the bipersonal field, and placed special stress on the role of a **secure** framework in creating a transitional-play-illusory communicative space. Still, they did not facilitate an understanding of those fields in which these qualities were more or less absent. Under the latter conditions it was evident that patients and perhaps analysts tended to overuse projective identification, denial mechanisms, and acting out on gross and far more subtle levels but these findings still lacked an organizing element.

In *Learning from Experience,* Bion (1962) postulates the presence in the mind of an *alpha function,* which operates on sense impressions and raw emotions to create *alpha elements* that are suitable for storage and dreaming—that is, for symbolic usage (see also Khan, 1973). This function is essential for memory, conscious thinking, and reasoning. It is developed in the infant through an interaction with a mother capable of *reverie,* who subjects a young child's projective identifications to her own alpha functioning and returns, into the child, detoxified projective identifications which were formerly terrifying and morbid. When alpha functioning is disturbed, either because of innate factors or by attacks based on hate and envy, the infant is left with *beta elements* which are things-in-themselves, suitable for projective identification and acting out, but not for dream thoughts; nor can these elements cohere into a *contact barrier* that will enable the mechanisms of repression, suppression, and learning to occur. Beta elements essentially are objects that can be evacuated to rid the psyche of accretions of stimuli and to eject unwanted contents.

Perhaps most crucial to the development of alpha functioning and elements is the capacity of the infant to modify, rather than evade, frustration. Thus, thinking may remain at a level modeled on muscular movement and may function as a means of unburdening the psyche, largely through projective identification; here, the infant does not attempt to actualize his omnipotent fantasies of projective identification because he has an undeveloped capacity to tolerate frustration. This type of projective identification, primarily a flight from reality, is quite different from that used excessively to have the mother or analyst experience the inner contents of the child-patient. In Bion's discussion, the mother's capacity for reverie was seen as comparable to the analyst's hold and to his receptivity to the patient's projective identifications (see also Bion, 1965, 1970, and Langs, 1976a, 1976c).

While these basic concepts are subjected to extensive elaboration by Bion, the outline presented here is sufficient for the purposes of this paper. Most relevant is his thesis that there are two types of communicative elements: *alpha* and *beta.* The former are suitable for symbolic usage and creative communication and may readily be seen as comparable to what I have termed "analyzable derivatives of unconscious fantasies, memories, and introjects"—Type Two derivatives. They are one of the major organizing elements of the Type A field that I will soon describe. In contrast, beta elements are not utilized symbolically or for the purposes of communication and cognitive understanding; they are primarily discharge products, largely projective identifications designed to lessen inner psychic tension. This concept relates to the finding that patients may free associate verbally without producing analyzable derivatives organized around meaningful adaptive contexts and without permitting valid interpretations in terms of their unconscious contents and functions. These elements are an important factor in the Type B field (see below). It seems evident that these discharge products require a particular type of analyst intervention, either in the form of appropriately holding and containing the patient and his projective identifications or of interpretations based on the *metabolism* (Langs, 1976a) and understanding of the relevant projected contents and processes. In Bion's terms, such holding and intervening may foster the development of alpha functions and elements in a patient previously blocked in this regard and are the expression of the analyst's capacity for reverie.

One additional group of interrelated concepts almost exclusively developed by Bion (1977) pertain to the static, noncommunicative Type C field that rounds out the classifications to be presented here. These brilliant and original ideas are scattered throughout Bion's (1977) four major works and may be briefly organized around four basic concepts: (1) the -K link (Bion 1962), (2) the functions of column two of the grid—the psi function (Bion, 1963, 1965), (3) the phenomenon of reversible perspective (Bion, 1963), and (4) his discussion of lies and the thinker (Bion, 1970).

In brief, Bion (1962) postulated three types of links between objects: K (knowledge), L (love), and H (hate). The K link is "commensal" in that it involves two objects (persons) who are dependent on each other for mutual benefit without harm for either. It is growth promoting and permits both particularization and abstraction. In contrast, the -K link tends to be infused with envy and to be parasitic in that it may be destructive to both objects and may interfere with growth. It is characterized by not-understanding (misunderstanding or misrepresenting) and it functions to defeat the analyst and to denude and strip of meaning all interactional elements, thus generating a worthless residue. This link destroys knowledge, has a primary quality of "withoutness," converts alpha elements into beta elements, and creates a feeling in the patient of being surrounded by the bizarre objects that represent in part his thoughts stripped of meaning and ejected.

Although Bion's (1977) development of a grid with horizontal and vertical axes designed for the classification and comprehension of the elements of psychoanalysis cannot be fully detailed here, several of its aspects are relevant. The horizontal axis provides "the definitory function of a formulation" (Bion 1963, p. 65)—that is, the use of a communication. Communications are placed into column two of this grid, the psi function, when they constitute hypotheses known to be false and maintanined as a barrier against anxiety lest any other theories take their place. These communications are utilized to inhibit thought; they constitute ideas used to deny more accurate, but more frightening, ones and serve as barriers against turbulence and psychological upheaval. At times, in the form of commonsense facts, they are used to deny expressions of fantasy; their mainfestations pertain to the patient's defenses and resistances. This language function cannot, however, be interpreted until the column-two dimension is apparent and has evolved. Bion (1965) suggests that the criterion for intervening relates to the analyst's capacity to experience resistances in the patient that would be evoked if an interpretation were given.

To explain reversible perspective, Bion (1963) draws upon the familiar line drawing which may be seen either as two profiles or as a vase. Through this metaphor he suggests that in the area of sensibility—the experience of the lines per se— there may be agreement between two individuals, while in the area of insensibility—the conception of what is seen—there

may be disagreement. Applying this to the patient and
analyst, Bion describes analytic situations in which both
appear to agree on the facts, while the patient conceals an
important level of disagreement that relates to the basic
assumptions of the analytic relationship and situation. The
patient's glib agreement is designed to conceal his lack of
conviction; even when painful emotions are evident, the
patient has a facile explanation for them. Basically, the
patient's responses, designed to disguise the real nature of his
experiences, invite interventions regarding contents that will
not be confirmed. This occurs because the patient accepts
interpretations on the surface, while secretly rejecting the
premises on which they are based. The analyst may
comprehend, but the patient does not, and views the analyst's
premises as false. The debate, however, is unspoken; it derives
from the patient's maintaining a point of view that is different
from that of the analyst. The patient's agreement, then, serves
-K and column-two functions in that it is a barrier against
pain and a defense against change. Such analytic situations
are stalemated; they lack real progress and are quite static.
Splitting is arrested, as is the evacuation of beta elements, and
action is unnecessary. The conditions are similar to those
under which the patient uses an hallucination as a substitute
for reality. There is a no engagement on the issues; rather than
agreeing or disagreeing, the patient simply reverses the
perspective and shifts his point of view. For Bion, the main
factor here is the patient's impaired capacity to tolerate pain.

In his comments on "Lies and the Thinker," Bion (1970)
extends and elaborates upon many of the earlier ideas
outlined here. He investigates the lie and demonstrates its
frequent column-two function, while noting that, at times, it
may fall into his column six—an action-oriented group of
communications—as well. In the former function, the lie
serves as a barrier against statements that would lead to
psychological upheaval, while in the latter, it may actually
generate that upheaval. The lie is also studied in terms of its -K
function, and its role in preventing catastrophic change. Bion
notes that the patient tries to induce the analyst to accept and
work with the lie in order to prevent the experience of inner

disruption. The patient in analysis will often experience a conflict between the need to know and the need to deny, and the problem is complicated by their being no absolute value to either truth or lie. Bion suggests the need to investigate column two in order to see in what respects its pains compare with those of other systems. He notes that this category involves conflicts with impressions of reality. When the conflict between needing to know and to deny becomes acute, the patient may usher in attacks on linking in order to stop the stimulation that has led to the conflict; however, with some liars, such an aim is not detectible and they do not betray a pattern of this kind. In general, the relationship between the liar and his audience is parasitic, and the lie functions as a means of denudation.

While this highly condensed résumé of Bion's ideas has undoubtedly generated some degree of confusion in the reader, I trust that the main themes are evident: (a) that certain communications may function as barriers, lies, forms of concealment, attacks on interpersonal links, and attempts to destroy rather than generate meaning, and (b) that there are many patients who attempt to maintain a static and stalemated analytic situation through extremely subtle and difficult to detect means—this, largely in the service of preventing a dreaded psychological upheaval. The relevance to the Type C field to be described below will soon become evident.

Before completing this final introductory survey, I must openly express certain misgivings in the context of the present discussion. I have been quite concerned that the concepts of beta elements and the discharge qualities of projective identifications draw upon an economic model of the mental apparatus that is open to serious theoretical and clinical questions (see the recent discussion by Wallerstein, 1977). This economic view of the mental apparatus is a throwback to Freud's earlier, topographic model, much of which is now no longer serviceable according to most writers. It may well be that such metaphors are more descriptive than theoretically meaningful, but despite repeated efforts to search for a different type of conception, I continue to find the present

delineation eminently useful for clinical conception, prediction, and interpretation. I am well aware that many analysts
will believe that these descriptions of column-two functions
(efforts at destruction of meaning) are merely restatements of
familiar concepts related to our present understanding of
defense and resistance. It is beyond the scope of this paper to
establish the important distinctions and their clinical
implications that I believe to be pertinent here, although I will
offer initial clinical observations and ideas in this respect in
my discussion of the three communicative fields. These vital
clinical and theoretical issues are all unsettled, and I would
welcome revision and refinement based on additional clinical
observations and conceptual rethinking.

In all, then, the insights provided by Bion's discussions and
my own continued clinical observations finally led me to a
tripartite classification of communicative fields. While I will
stress this point less here, these styles of communication seem
also to be descriptive of individual propensities. I will now
identify each major type of bipersonal field, and describe its
principal characteristics. Although, in actual clinical situations, one finds intermixtures, my own observations indicate
that a particular group of characteristics do indeed tend to
predominate. Each field will be described as bipersonal and
communicative, under the influence of both patient and
analyst.

The Type A field

In the Type A field of symbolic communication, analyzable
derivatives and symbolic interpretations of inner mental
contents and mechanisms predominate. The patient's associations and behaviors convey workable derivatives, and the
analyst offers valid interpretations of their functions,
contents, and meanings. This is the communicative field in
which transference as an illusion (a complex concept in itself,
see Langs, 1976c), the use of symbolic communication, and the
broader use of illusion prevail. It has been described as an
analytic play space (Winnicott, 1971) or as a transitional
space (Khan, 1973). The patient's verbal and behavioral
communications are readily organizable around significant

adaptive contexts, thereby yielding derivatives of his unconscious fantasies, memories, introjects, perceptions, and self-
representations (aspects of id, ego, and superego) expressed in
a form that lends itself to verbal interpretation. In addition,
the patient is prepared to understand the symbolic meaning of
the analyst's interventions, which are themselves conveyed in
this idiom. It is this type of field, as I indicated previously, that
is implicitly the ideal of the classical psychoanalyst, who
expects to work under these conditions and who may view
patients who are unable to comply as unanalyzable—that is,
because their associations seem uninterpretable or because
they are prone to what is viewed as intractable acting out.

In this type of bipersonal field, the communications from
the patient organize primarily around adaptive responses,
analyzable derivatives of unconscious transference fantasies
and perceptions, and the verbal and nonverbal resistances to
their expression. It is to be stressed, however, that when
resistances and defenses predominate, the unconscious
derivatives relevant to their nature and to the material being
defended against are, in general, available in the communications from the patient. It is possible to establish the adaptive
context and precipitant for these resistances. Ultimately they
are analyzable in terms of unconscious meanings and
defenses.

In the Type A field, a secure frame is an essential and silent
element, consistently maintained while the analyst interprets
the patient's communications. It therefore requires an analyst
capable of securing and managing the framework—one who,
in addition, has the capacity to think symbolically and utilize
the transitional space as a place both for understanding the
patient's derivatives and for their synthesis into valid,
sensitively timed symbolic interpretations. The patient must
be capable of symbolic communication, must have a tolerance
for the regression and anxiety invoked by a secure frame
(Langs, 1976a, 1976c), or must possess an ability to use
illusion and derivative expression, and must have a capacity
to understand and utilize the analyst's interpretations on that
level. It is my impression that Searles's description (1970,
1971, 1973a) of a workable therapeutic symbiosis refers to this
type of field.

Not all analysts are capable of synthesis and symbolic communication at this level, nor are all analysts capable of securing the framework needed for a bipersonal field characterized by these communicative qualities. As will become evident, virtually all previous so-called training analyses have taken place in a field under consistent pressure to deviate from this Type A form to either the more discharge-oriented field (Type B) or the more static, noncommunicative interaction (Type C). Such analytic experiences tend to occur within bipersonal fields whose frames are modified, often extensively so since so-called training analysts are prone to nonillusory and nonsymbolic communication toward their analysands. They may use language or mismanage the frame in order to projectively identify into their analysands their own inner disturbance, thereby fostering Type B communication, or they may make cliché-ridden, stereotyped interventions, unconsciously designed as falsifications and barriers, which promote the development of a Type C field. As a result, an analyst's own analysis has tended to reinforce his own greater or lesser need for either the discharge or the nonmeaningful modes of communication characteristic, respectively, of Types B and C interactions. Either outcome, of course, greatly influences the communicative interaction with his own patients. Often, these propensities are outside the analyst's awareness and are expressed despite his manifest intentions to secure the ground rules of each analytic situation and to create opportunities for interpreting. His actual, unconsciously determined communicative style and use of language may deviate significantly from the optimal Type A mode.

There are strong, inherent needs within both patient and analyst to shift away from a Type A communicative field toward the more direct and inappropriate gratifications that are relatively absent in the symbolic mode. It has been assumed in the classical psychoanalytic literature, so far as I can determine, that all analysts attempt to create a Type A field and that they are capable of doing so and of offering relevant interpretations within such a field. If I may be permitted a well-founded, but undocumented, thesis, I would suggest that, to the contrary, there are many classically trained analysts who are quite incapable of consistently maintaining this Type A field, and it is quite likely that this is even more the case with therapists with other backgrounds.

In brief, the analyst may be the prime mover in modifying a Type A field into Type B or C, or he may accept the latter types when patients attempt to create them. He does this through inappropriate silences, erroneous verbal interventions, and alterations in the framework of the bipersonal field that are, almost without exception, quite inappropriate. This latter is the single most overlooked vehicle both for countertransference expressions and as a means of detrimentally altering the communicative properties of the bipersonal field (see Langs, 1975c, 1976a, 1976c, 1978a). In one sense, all such technical errors tend to express failures in the analyst's holding capacity, containing functions, and use of alpha function; they therefore reflect the nonsymbolic use of language and behavior for pathological projective identification and to express beta elements and thus rid the analyst of accretions of inner tension. They may also serve as Type C barriers (see below).

Characteristically, patients will respond to such efforts in kind. They will shift away from the use of alpha elements, and away from derivative and symbolic communication if this has been their communicative style, and move either toward holding the analyst and containing his projective identifications or toward the discharge of projective identifications and beta elements on their own part. Atternately, they too shift to a Type C idiom. In addition, patients who suffer from inadequate alpha functioning and are blocked in their use of symbolic and derivative communication will tend themselves to maintain Type B and Type C fields and be refractory toward any possible shift to a Type A field. Under these conditions, verbal interventions are virtually useless. The analyst must first *rectify* the altered frame and shift to symbolic communicationg only then will his interventions have their consciously intended meanings and effects. Clearly, both self-awareness and the resoultion of the underlying countertransference problems are a vital part of such work.

In this context, it should be noted first, that I have not suggested that a Type A field is characteristic of patients at the more neurotic end of the psychopathological continuum, nor will I later suggest that Type B and Type C fields are necessarily characteristic of those with more severe psychopathology—that is, borderline, narcissistic, and schizophrenic patients. While in general, it may well be that this is the general trend, I have noted many exceptions to this rule and leave the matter open to empirical study. Secondly, implicit in these ideas is the suggestion that the analyst move the patient toward the utilization of a Type A communicative mode through his appropriate management and maintenance of the framework and his valid verbal, symbolic interpretations. These are essential for the Type A field itself; howevern I do not wish to suggest, as implied in the classical psychoanalytic literature, that the Type A field is the only viable therapeutic field. While Khan (1973) has suggested that what I term the Type A field is optimal and has indicated that it requires a high level of maturation, my own clincal observations suggest that communicative styles are genetically and intrapsychically determined and that effective analytic work will tend more to create interludes of symbolic communication in Type B and Type C patients, rather than, as a rule, to effect a shift to a fundamentally Type A mode (see below). In any case, it is evident that effective analtyic work and adaptive, insightful and structural inner change can accrue to a patient in types of fields other than the Type A. It is therefore my belief that further clinical research will be needed to identify the advantages and limitations of analytic work within each of the three types of fields described here.

One final point: while the Type A field is most efficacious for cognitive insight, it is also the field in which the patient and, to a lesser extent, the analyst most intensely experience their pathological and primitive inner mental contents and the related anxieties and temporary mental disorganization. While this is an aspect of a therapeutic (or analyzable) regression (Langs, 1976a) with great curative potential, it is a quite disturbing experience that prompts major defensive reactions. In part, then, a shift to a Type B or C field initiated by either participant has an importnat defensive function.

The Type B Field

The Type B field is an action-discharge field in which projective identification predominates. In it, either the patient or the analyst makes extensive use of projective identification designed to rid the psyche of disturbing accretions of inner stimuli, to make use of the other member of the dyad as a container for disruptive projective identifications, and to evoke positive proxy responses. Major contributions to the development of this type of communicative field may come from either the patient or the analyst, and often come from both.

There are patients of all psychopathological types who show deficient alpha functioning and impairment in the use of illusion and symbolic communication—failures in the expression of analyzable derivatives of inner contents and dynamisms. Such patients make extensive use of projective identification, largely as a means of denying reality and utilizing the analyst as a container for their disturbing inner contents, endeavoring to transform the analytic situation into a place of discharge and action.

In a Type B field either participant may also seek inappropriate, direct gratification of pathological, instinctual drive needs. In the patient, this usually takes the forms of direct demands for alterations in the frame and of subtle or gross efforts to obtain a variety of noninterpretive satisfactions. Should these be gratified, his use of this mode of communicating—and functioning—is reinforced.

Despite the relative absence of a contribution from the analyst that would shape the field along Type B lines, patients so inclined tend to adhere to this type of communication for long periods; their fundamental use of this mode is, perhaps, essentially unmodifiable. This suggests that this form of communication is a long-standing, basic personality attribute and mode of interaction. While the matter should be left open in that it may well be feasible analytically to modify the pathological aspects of Type B communication to where the patient will shift to a basic Type A mode, an equally constructive analytic goal appears to be to develop longer, more effective use of alpha functioning with more usable alpha elements and modify the pathological use of projective identification and efforts at discharge so that the Type B communicative mode is maintained in a less pathological form. Such a modification also implies the analyst's development of nonpathological defenses and capacities to manage his own inner mental world. Analytic experience supports Bion's (1977) concept that it is essential that the analyst have the capacities to hold the patient, to maintain a state of reverie, to think symbolically, and to contain and metabolize the patient's projective identifications toward symbolic understanding. In this way, he creates an interaction in which the patient is able to introjectively identify with these attributes of the analyst, to incorporate detoxified projective identifications, and to develop his own alpha functioning.

In a Type B field, there are actually few analyzable derivatives of unconscious mental contents, and interpretations of contents and defenses along usual symbolic lines are virtually never confirmed by the patient, either on the cognitive or introjective-interactional levels (Langs, 1976a, 1976c, 1978b). The analyst must work within the communicative medium of the patient, in which projective identification and the excretion of tension producing stimuli prevail. He must therefore contain these projective identifications, metabolize them toward understanding, and offer interpretations of these interactional efforts, holding the frame steady all the while. Only the maintenance of a secure frame and interpretations of the unconscious functions of the Type B communicative style will adaptively modify its pathological meanings and uses.

As for the analyst, any alteration that he makes in the frame will express his own propensity for a Type B communicative field and pressure the patient in that direction. His own use of pathological projective identification and discharge as reflected in his verbal interventions and other behaviors will have a similar influence. All of his communications to the patient, therefore, must be scrutinized in depth for such expressions. The development of a Type B communicative field calls for *rectification* of an altered frame and a resumption of symbolic-interpretive work by the analyst. It is characteristic of patients who tend to communicate along Type B lines to momentarily shift to the communication of analyzable derivatives in response to the analyst's unneeded alterations in the framework. Such associations, however, are only relevant to the impaired frame and tend to be quite fleeting; these patients will, as a rule, return to action-discharge and projective identification soon after initial efforts to convey their unconscious perceptions and introjections of the erring therapist—their unconscious efforts to cure the therapist. In general, however, it is consistent analytic work in keeping with the attributes of the Type B field, undertaken in a secured framework, that promotes the gradual shift toward a greater use of Type A communications and a lessened use by the patient of pathological projective identifications and other interactional mechanisms. Finally, it appears to me that the Type B field has many of the characteristic of the pathological symbiosis described by Searles (1971).

The Type C Field

In delineating this static, noncommunicative field I would stress at the outset that while the Type A and Type B fields reflect modes of positive communication and are designed to convey derivatives of inner mental states, contents, and mechanisms, the Type C field is designed for noncommunication, for the destruction of meaning, and for the absence of derivative expression. To the extent that such efforts do indeed destroy meaning, relevant interaction, relatedness, and positive communication, they have a negative function and meaning; in this restricted and unusual sense, then, the Type C field reflects and conveys a meaningful mode of relating and interacting.

The Type C field is characterized by the pervasive absence of interpretable derivatives of unconscious fantasies, memories, and introjects and by the presence of massive defensive barriers. As a rule, the patient's communications are on a manifest content level, and there is a remarkable sense of flatness and emptiness to behaviors and associations. When an adaptive context is evident, the patient's associations do not meaningfully organize around its conscious and unconscious implications; similarly, when the patient's associations seem filled with potential meaning, there will be no adaptive context to serve as the essential organizer. Typically, these patients ruminate emptily for long periods of time or tend to report detailed, extended narratives in a form that renders their possible unconscious meanings indecipherable—the "Type C narrator." Occasionally, there is a circumscribed sense of depth and metaphorical communication; at such times, these patients tend unconsciously to represent the static, noncommunicative, walled-off qualities of their communicative style and the bipersonal field within which it is embedded. Without interpretive efforts directed toward these massive defenses, the therapist or analyst almost never has material available for interpretation. The most common exception occurs only occasionally, when the patient responds to an erroneous interpretation or an unneeded modification in the framework with derivatives related to the unconscious perceptions and introjections of the therapist's communicated and projected pathology, and briefly works over these pathological introjects.

In a Type C field, patient behaviors and associations are essentially intrapsychic and interpersonal barriers, falsifications, and lies (in the nonmoral sense) designed to seal off meaningful mental contents and to maintain the therapeutic interaction and work in a stalemated state. These massive barriers differ in important ways from the defenses utilized by patients in the Type A and Type B communicative fields, and are, I believe, significantly different from the defenses described in the classical psychoanalytic literature.

For example, in a Type A field, defenses and resistances are communicated in both manifest and derivative forms; eventually the unconscious fantasies and memories on which they are based and the sector of unconscious, anxiety provoking material against which they defend are communicated indirectly by the patient and become available for interpretive analytic work. While there are moments of flatness and emptiness in such a field, the patient consistently and spontaneously shifts to derivative and indepth communication that permits symbolic understanding and intervention.

In contrast, in a Type C field, the patient's massive defenses are, most of the time, essentially amorphous and impervious to any possible underlying meaning and derivatives. They are impenetrable barriers whose own essential meanings tend not to be communicated by the patient. Although from time to time he will indeed represent more metaphorically the nature of these defensive walls, he reveals little of the quality of what lies beyond them. Type C patients typically speak from time to time of things being meaningless, of huge brick and concrete walls, of empty vacuums and abysses, of death and coffins and graves, of entombment in metal containers such as army tanks, and of similar representative images. Most of the time, they destroy not only the positive meaning of their words and behaviors, but the basic links between themselves and their objects, including the therapist, and between their conscious awareness and their unconscious inner mental world. Their associations are filled with clichés, the commonplace, and that which is already known, and they turn the analyst's previously meaningful interpretations and formulations into noncommunication, repeating them in endless and empty detail.

Except for the remarkable studies of Bion (1977), the systematic identification of the Type C field has tended to elude analysts. Certainly, analysts in general have been aware of major difficulties in working with certain types of patients and in generating validated interpretations to them. More specifically, it seems likely that some of the narcissistic patients described by Kohut (1971, 1977) and Kernberg (1975), patients who treat their analyst as seemingly nonexistent and who generate intense boredom in these analysts, are operating within a Type C communicative field. Still, the analyst's commitment to search for truth and meaning, plus his possible need to deny his own propensities toward Type C communication, seems to have defensively delayed the delineation of this type of communicative field. Similarly, it may well be that in addition to the patient's own inherent propensities toward this type of communication, those of the analyst play a significant role in the creation of a Type C field. In the main, the analyst mismanages the framework and intervenes on a manifest content level, or he may even use Type One derivatives (specifically, through not working with Type Two derivatives) that actually constitute psychoanalytic clichés, falsifications, and barriers, rather than meaningful interpretations.

It is, I believe, the Type C field in which reversing perspective, as described by Bion (1963), often occurs. Under these conditions, both patient and analyst are aware of the behaviors and words exchanged, and yet the analyst may attempt to ascribe meaning to communications which for the patient are meaninglessness and function as barriers. At times, of course, the reversing perspective may occur in the other direction: the patient actually communicates in derivative form while the analyst experiences defensiveness and an absence of meaning. Communications in this field often resemble the figures embedded in a field of multi-colored dots used to test individuals for color-blindness. In a Type C field, the analyst or patient may well see the numbers because he is not "colorblind," while the other is only able to see a series of meaningless dots.

Another way to conceptualize the flat and elusive quality of this field is to think of the patient's communications as reflections in a mirror. To treat such unreal images as actualities and attempt to touch them or to experience them in depth would be to fail to recognize the function of the mirror. In such a case the mirror itself is a barrier to reality, actuality, and substance. There is a significant sense of deception and invalidation when the analyst treats as actual the falsified and unreal communications of the patient. In this field the distinction between language and communication becomes evident: while language may indeed serve as a means of conveying meaning, it is evident that its main function may also be the destruction of meaning and the creation of impenetrable barriers to such meaning—that is, noncommunication.

Initial observations suggest that the Type C communicative mode constitutes a massive defensiveness against what may be variously termed a psychotic core, excessive psychic pain, inner mental catastrophe, and inner disorganization. These patients—and therapists—are often quite able to function socially and within work situations as long as they can utilize these massive defensive barriers. Often well-defended latent psychotics and depressives, they may appear to have narcissistic character disorders and to be severely depressed or paranoid-like. As a rule, there are isolated clues to the massive underlying disturbance: either in the reported history of the patient or in an occasional early session during which there is a momentary, and as a rule quite limited, breakthrough of the underlying turmoil. The extremely guarded and suspicious patients destroy the sense of meaning in any effort by the analyst to interpret unconscious contents, doing so because they dread the inner core and need to maintain their rigid, impenetrable defenses. On the other hand, because of wishes for cure and relief, they will accept and work with interpretations related to their massive defensiveness, as long as these are well timed and affectively meaningful; it is at such moments that these patients are likely to meaningfully communicate derivatives of their chaotic, pathological inner mental disturbance, thus permitting momentary periods of deeper interpretive work.

In a Type C field, the interaction is characteristically static and immobile. Very little projective identification and few analyzable derivatives are available from the patient. The field is characterized by its holding qualities. However, while the analyst's main function for long periods may well be that of securing the framework and holding the patient, these patients often show little apprecation of being held (in the analytic sense) and seem instead disconnected and detached because of the destruction of their links to the analyst on so many levels. By distinguishing these holding functions from the analyst's containing capacities, which relate to the introjection of the patient's projective identifications and other communications, we can see that there is also little for the analyst to contain and metabolize. These patients often

endure long unproductive analyses or periods of psychotherapy and often generate stalemated treatment situations.
Because of these qualities of the Type C patient, the analyst
often feels bored, empty, unrelated, and poorly held by the
patient as well It may well be that these patients fall into the
group described by Searles (1965, 1970, 1971, 1973a) as in the
autistic phase of analysis. In addition to often disregarding
the presence of the analyst, the patient will treat him as part of
the nonhuman environment.

While I have characterized the Type C Field largely in terms
of the patient's needs and characteristics, it should be stressed
that many analysts and therapists have comparable needs
and communicative propensities that contribute significantly
to the development of the Type C field. These propensities are
manifested in unneeded modifications in the frame which
function as massive barriers to meaningful communication in
derivative form, and which serve to generate interactional
defenses within the patient. Through failing to interpret and
through a variety of erroneous interventions, especially those
that fail to utilize the adaptive context and derivative
communication, these analysts express clichés and false
premises. Their ultimately nonmeaningful communications
unconsciously invite and encourage Type C relatedness in
their patients. Such analysts wish to be held inappropriately
by the patient. They fear placing destructive projective
identifications into the patient and wish instead to maintain a
static field that will reinforce their own massive barriers
against the chaotic and unresolved inner mental worlds of
both themselves and their patients. As Bion (1977) noted, the
container may fear the contained, and the contained may fear
the container: each dreading attack, denudation, and destruction. The analyst may therefore dread both containing the
patient's pathological mental contents and projecting his own
disruptive inner mental world into the patient. Immobiliza-
tion and noncommunication are rigidly maintained as the
only seemingly safe harbor.

Technically, in a Type C Field the analyst must wait
patiently for unconscious communications from the patient
that represent the massive defensive barriers and falsifica-

tions characteristic of this mode of communication. When such material appears, often accompained by some suggestion of the dreaded underlying derivatives, the analyst is in a position to help the patient understand the presence and nature of these massive barriers and to provide hints as to the nature of the underlying contents that they serve to so massively seal off. In general, such efforts are validated largely through the additional revelation of dreaded unconscious derivatives which may then be interpreted cognitively, introjected, metabolized, detoxified, and reprojected in less disruptive form. While efforts to interpret unconscious contents directly are, by and large, doomed to failure, an approach that understands the true nature of the communicative mode of these patients and concentrates on the interpretive modification of these defensive barriers will prove effective in modifying their psychopathology and the aspects of that pathology reflected in their communicative styles.

To carry out such work, however, the analyst must be capable of managing his responses to the patient's barriers and falsifications, his destruction of links, his forms of nonrelating, and his use of falsifying clichés. He must control propensities to modify the frame, to intervene erroneously based on an inappropriate need within himself to suggest meaning in its absence or to jar and stir up the rigid and stalemated Type C patient. The analyst must also be capable of full use of the validating process, lest he continue to intervene in terms of manifest content and Type One derivatives, considering the clichéd and unmeaningful responses of his patient as validation. Such interactions are characteristically filled with self- and mutual-deception, and produce no true insight or inner structural change. In addition to being capable of symbolic communication, such an analyst must be able to tolerate the anxiety and dread related to experiencing the intensely primitive and horrifying inner mental world of these patients and to the threats to his own defenses against surprisingly similar inner contents. He must also analyze and resolve his dread of containing his patient's underlying, destructive projective identifications and his fear of being driven crazy by the patient—an anxiety studied by

Searles (1958, 1959). He must master his dread of being attacked and even annihilated by the patient's noncommunication and negative projective identifications, which create a void in which his capacity to think, formulate, and organize— to function meaningfully and relatedly—are being destroyed by the patient's Type C style.

ADDITIONAL RELEVANT LITERATURE

In his quite original and creative contribution, "The Role of Illusion in the Analytic Space and Process," Khan (1973) studied the constitution of the analytic space and interaction. He did this initially in terms of the analytic framework as defined by its basic taboos—motility, sight, and touch. These taboos facilitate the patient's expression of his incestuous and parricidal wishes through the word. For Khan, these taboos— in my terms, the ground rules or framework—create an area of illusion in which language may explore and express wish systems beyond mere humiliation and remorse.

Noting the importance of the increment of affect which the area of illusion provides through transference, Khan suggests that Freud (1914), in his basic study of repetition and action as compared to remembering, had stressed the distinction between (a) action as converted into language and affective expression and (b) action that involves muscular and behavioral expression. The former requires a degree of growth and a stability of personality organization for both parties, so that they may work in the area of illusion through symbolic discourse. Acting out is therefore defined as behavior that transgresses symbolic discourse and seeks concrete expression and need fulfillment. Within this framework, Khan offered two clinical vignettes—patients either unable to develop an area of illusion or with whom it was precariously held.

With one patient, he felt that he had been eliminated from the analytic space and had become a passive witness whom the patient victimized with her excruciating pain and inexhaustible demands. He found her unable to relate to her own self-knowledge or to his interpretive interventions. In a dream, the patient observed a stained-glass ceiling of a cathedral crumbling and disintegrating, a communication that Khan saw as a warning of what she was going to do to the illusional space of the analytic situation—disrupt and destroy both the illusion and its structure.

This patient had been involved in direct physical contact with previous analysts and had actually seduced one of them. Khan felt that she was perpetually either acting into language, which he noted was not symbolic discourse, or acting upon life, which constitutes the total negation of any positive experience of relating that might take place in her analysis. Her language failed to assimilate her experiences on the intrapsychic and interpersonal levels, just as her body personalized her instincts and her affects. He soon referred this patient to another analyst. In his discussion of this patient, Khan stressed her total negation of his presence, her negation of herself as a person, and her invention of the fetishistic object of her psyche with which she provoked the analyst in order to destroy rather than be cured. These factors did not allow the space of illusion in the analytic situation to crystallize; instead, the patient seemed to live in a delusional reality that she wished to shed.

The second patient described was unable to respond to the demands of a previous analyst that she should verbalize her feelings and unconscious fantasies; instead, she had traumatized her analyst, pulling her hair, and breaking up the furniture in her consultation room. Khan was able to sympathize with her incapacity to use language as an idiom either to express herself or to relate to him. He permitted open motility and limited touching of his books, and he felt that his capacity to hold her in the analytic space gradually led her to tolerate him as a separate person, distant but related. He described the development of some distance between himself and the patient and the gradual creation of an illusional space in which the patient could begin to explore language as playing. Her incapacity and rage were valid to Khan as existential facts. Crucial in the developments described in this analysis was the fact that he had not tried to intrude upon these two areas of her experience with interpretations.

Khan discussed his findings in terms of Winnicott's paper (1951) on transitional objects and phenomena, in which the concept of illusion was first introduced to psychoanalysis. Khan stressed the importance of a period of hesitation, as related to playing and transitional phenomena, which provides the matrix for the emergence of the area of illusion. He noted that the concept of resistance in classical analysis takes for granted the capacity to operate in such an area, while his concept of a period of hesitation, borrowed from Winnicott (1951), connotes the emergence of a capacity which is as yet far from established as an ego function. Following Winnicott (1945), Khan also wrote of the importance of the maternal holding environment for the development of these ego functions, noting that moments of illusion develop as mother and child live and experience together.

In concluding, Khan suggested that his first patient had made of language and mentation a frenzied existence that had a momentum all its own; neither vehicles of self-knowledge or relating, they had functioned to negate the reality of the analytic space and the analyst, as well as that of emotionality. This was seen as a usurpation of the legitimate functions of the bodily organs; illusion breaks down and fantasy generates into mentation, while language usurps the functions that belong to organs of experience and discharge—a pathogenic distortion of the ego. Khan stressed the importance of recognizing that with certain patients who have not established this area of illusion, the analyst must technically endeavor to curtail his hypermentation to facilitate the emergence of this area of illusion in the period of hesitation.

It may be seen, then, that Khan has described here, to use the terms developed in his paper, his own recognition that not all patients are able to create a Type A communicative bipersonal field. The particular patients that he described appear to have developed Type B and Type C communicative fields respectively, possibly, however, in part because his own responses had qualities that fosterd their specific development. His clinical observations vividly define some of the qualities of these two communicative fields, and his discussion serves to clarify aspects of their genetic basis and the distinctive analytic techniques required by each.

In a separate series of studies, most of them published in Spanish, Liberman (in press) has attempted to delineate styles of psychoanalytic dialogue that he identified in terms of both the patient's ways of offering his material and the analyst's manner of receiving and interpreting it. These styles are correlated with specific ego states, anxieties, and mechanisms of defense and are classified in terms of clinical diagnostic entities, modes of communication, and linguistic styles. The latter are described as occurring in persons looking for unknowns without creating suspense, lyrical, epic, narrative, seeking unknowns and creating suspense, and dramatic with esthetic impact. Each requires a distinctive interventional response by the analyst.

It is beyond the scope of this presentation to further describe the typology developed by Liberman and to compare it with the classification offered here. Perhaps most important for the moment is the recognition that this analyst is attempting to explore a dimension of the analytic interaction that is comparable to the area under investigation in this paper, and that his particular contribution attempts to investigate the interrelatedness of clincial diagnosis, style of defense, mode of communication, linguistic usage, and interpretive response— an endeavor that points to the rich complexities and extensive clinical importance of these studies.[2]

CLINICAL VIGNETTES

Because of my unmodifiable commitment to the total confidentiality of my own therapeutic and analytic work, it will not be feasible for me to present material from this work, even though such an approach would, due to the interactional emphasis, prove especially meaningful. I will instead offer a series of highly condensed clincal segments drawn from supervisory experiences and trust that they will orient the reader sufficiently to discover and elaborate personally the basic concepts presented here. I do plan to offer far more elaborate and specific clinical vignettes in a series of future publications.

Case 1

Mr. A was in psychotherapy with Dr. Z, who had also treated his brother. The early phase of this treatment was characterized by occasional family sessions, contacts with Mr. A's parents, a wide variety of noninterpretive interventions by Dr. Z, and frequent modifications in the basic ground rules. At one point, an emergency arose and it was necessary for Dr. Z to take an extended vacation. Dr. Z explained the details of the illness in one of his parents that had necessitated the trip, and the patient had responded in a rather chaotic manner with a multiplicity of questions; he missed the last session prior to the therapist's trip and two of the three initial sessions when therapy was resumed.

In subsequent sessions, the patient was rather directly demanding and provocative of Dr. Z, who attempted to interpret these reactions as a reflection of Mr. A's anger over the unexpected interruption. There was no sense of validation of these interventions: the patient tended to deny hostile feelings regarding his therapist's trip and instead behaved quite provocatively at home—to the point of evoking urgent telephone calls from Mr. A's mother to Dr. Z. This situation remained chaotic until Dr. Z began to refuse to talk to Mr. A's parents on the telephone and interpreted directly to the patient that he seemed involved in efforts to either destroy the treatment process itself or to so disturb Dr. Z. that he would feel inordinately frustrated, angry, or disorganized. To this, the patient responded by remembering how, just prior to the session, he had fought with his mother over a petty issue, refusing to allow her to offer any possible compromise and refusing to even understand what he now recognized were her rather sensible arguments. He had virtually driven her up a wall.

As a tentative thesis, I would suggest that through a variety of noninterpretive interventions and inappropriate modifications of the framework, this therapist was utilizing his patient as an inappropriate container for his own pathological projective identifications (Langs, 1976a) and that his own propensity to create a Type B communicative field had reinforced the patient's tendencies in this direction. As a result, this bipersonal field was characterized by unconscious exchanges of projective and introjective identifications, and pathological reprojections, without insight or control in either participant. Efforts by the therapist to treat the patient's behaviors and associations as symbolic communications, based on the mistaken implicit hypothesis that a Type A field prevailed, were met with nonconfirmation and the intensification of disruptive behaviors and projective identifications by the patient. There is evidence too that while this therapist considered his interventions themselves to be symbolic communications, they actually constituted a vehicle for pathological projective identifications on his part—a means of discharging inner tension rather than offering true cognitive insight.

Under the influence of supervision, the therapist undertook extensive efforts toward self-analysis and toward rectifying the frame. Further, by limiting his interventions to the symbolic interpretation of the patient's pathological projective identifications, he found derivative, symbolic validation, as illustrated in the patient's recollection of his quarrel with his mother. In addition to offering cognitive insight, this interpretation provided the patient with an opportunity (a) to experience the therapist's capacity to metabolize and understand his potentially disruptive projective identifications and (b) to receive a reprojection that had been detoxified. Subsequent associations alluded to a teacher who was able to handle another instructor's class when it got out of control and included references to the calming effect on all concerned. This positive introject also helped the patient better manage his own inner impulses and propensities toward pathological projective identification. With additional working through, his behavior calmed down considerably both in the treatment situation and at home.

The patient began a session some months later by wondering if his mother had again called the therapist. He had been anxious in a restaurant while eating with his parents, and for the first time his mother was tolerant; Mr. A felt that this reflected the direct influence of the therapist. The patient had two oral presentations pending and wanted the therapist to tell him how to manipulate his professors so that he would not have to present in front of the classes. One of the teachers might understand, but the other would be very destructive. When the therapist remained silent, the patient kept asking what he should do and demanded an answer. The therapist then intervened and noted that the patient appeared to have assumed that he, the therapist, had spoken to his mother and had told her how to handle him, and that on this basis, Mr. A felt that he, the therapist, should advise him about the school problem as well.

The patient now alluded to past telephone conversations between the therapist and his mother and said that on the one hand, the therapist did not like to be rude, but on the other hand, he would not violate his patient's trust. The patient had spoken to a friend (a peer with whom he had an evident latent homosexual relationship) rather extensively about his own therapy and about his fantasies of collusion between his therapist and his parents. He thought of his mother and father as weak and incompetent fools.

The therapist pointed out that the patient had very intense feelings regarding the prior contacts with his parents and seemed quite infuriated by them. Mr. A then insisted on his trust of the therapist, but after some elaboration in this direction, he suddenly indicated that these conversations had indeed been a violation—something like his parents coming into his room and opening his drawers but finding nothing. He turned to the onset of his symptoms, which included intense anxiety when speaking in class and when eating, and wondered if he could now understand what had really happened.

In this hour, we can see continued efforts by the patient to create with the therapist a Type B field in which the discharge of tension and immediate gratification would prevail. When the therapist did not respond in kind, and implied as well that the frame was now secure in regard to the confidentiality of the treatment, the patient shifted to symbolic communication and the bipersonal field took on characteristics of a Type A field. In the adaptive context of the previous alteration of the framework and its present rectification, the patient offerred Type Two derivatives that implied an unconscious perception of the deviant therapist as one who was gratifying unconscious homosexual fantasies and defending himself against them as well, whatever additional homosexual gratification and defense the arrangements and qualities of the interaction had for Mr. A himself. The patient also commqnicated his unconscious perception of himself and the therapist in this context as foolish and incompetent. With the further effort at interpretation, the patient modified his massive denial regarding the therapist's violation of his confidentiality and conveyed this realization through a simile. This constituted a symbolic representation of a type previously quite unusual for this patient. Thus, there was a growing change not only in this patient's behaviors, but also in his mode of interacting and in the form of his communication. I would view the patient's return to his initial symptoms and his renewed search for understanding as a reflection of his hope for more insightful resolution of the relevant unconscious fantasies, memories, conflicts, etc.—a hope based on the growing development between himself and his therapist of a Type A communicative field.

I would make a particular point of the patient's comment that the violation in confidentiality was something like his parents' searching his drawers and finding nothing. In addition to extensively exchanging pathological projective identifications, this patient and therapist had created interactional interludes which were quite static and empty. These occurred despite the therapist's efforts at intervening. The patient's unconscious communication here seems to stress the extent to which pathological projective identification and mutual acting out, as well as clichéd interventions, are designed on one level to create voids and absence of true meaning.

Case 2

Mr. B was in psychotherapy with Dr. Y. During the initial months, his sessions were characterized by lengthy and detailed narratives with no apparent adaptive context. He would talk of both major and sometimes seemingly insignificant problems on his job, of the details of his sexual exploits, and of a variety of problems with his male peers. Efforts by the therapist, based largely on Type One derivatives, to suggest general unconscious hostility, sexual and bodily anxieties, and competitiveness with his peers, and additional attempts to relate these themes and anxieties to the therapeutic relationship, generated both responses that were flat and nonvalidating, and new lengthy tales.

Soon, the therapist became relatively silent. When the patient hinted at a possible source of anxiety, Dr. Y. suggested concerns about treatment and anxieties about becoming involved. In general, the patient rather flatly acknowledged such worries, but had little more to say. In one session during this period, the patient began his hour by describing his sense of invincibility and how readily he gets past dangers and problems: he had once been suspended from his job and had neatly manipulated his reinstatement. He had nicely evaded serving in the armed forces. After describing in some detail the relevant experiences, he alluded to an address before a meeting of the tenants in his apartment house. He was the vice president of the tenant organization, but the president, frightened because a tenant had been killed in the building, had turned the meeting over to the patient. Under these pressures, Mr. B felt weak and forced to reveal himself. Although that night he had had some kind of homosexual dream, he denied homosexual fears and went on in some detail regarding his preference for women, noting, however, that he had had many strange fantasies about them. He concluded this hour by stating that he wanted to get to know himself better, but somehow it all seemed so pointless.

In the following session the patient went on in great detail about his job, about games and roles, about not knowing what to believe and about how disturbed he was with his way of life.

His parents had never helped him discover himself and he had had to learn how to meet his own needs. Again in some detail, he described a sexual relationship with a girlfriend who seldom talked to him and who had been shocked when he revealed his own secrets, including his fears of impregnating her. Sometimes he liked women that he could dominate even when he was afraid of them. The next few hours were similarly ruminative.

In assessing this clinical situation, there was evidence that both patient and therapist had initially created a Type C field in which the patient generated extended narratives without a relevant adaptive context or meaningful bridges to the therapeutic relationship. It seems likely that his use of language in these hours was designed as a barrier and falsification with which he covered underlying homosexual fantasies and perceptions pertinent to his relationship with the therapist. Unconsciously, the therapist had attempted to give these manifest associations pertinence and meaning, without, however, alluding to the underlying homosexual problems. His interventions had proved to serve as clichés that reinforced the patient's own facade and intensified the Type C qualities of the bipersonal field. The patient felt disillusioned and even bored at times, while the therapist felt somewhat confused and distracted, finding little to grasp in the patient's long tales.

Under the influence of supervision, the therapist became relatively silent and intervened occasionally in respect to the patient's needs for defensive obstacles. While these interventions did not sufficiently utilize the various metaphorical representations of these barriers communicated by the patient, unconsciously they sufficiently conveyed the therapist's willingness to modify the Type C field into a Type A mode so that the patient responded with the main session described here.

In this particular hour, unconsciously the patient described the false sense of invincibility that one can derive from impenetrable Type C field barriers. He implied, however, that such manipulations leave one vulnerable and proceeded to talk of the tenant's meeting—a situation with a background of violence in which he was forced into the spotlight. This appeared to be, in part, the patient's experience of the therapist's recent interventions, and it conveyed the therapeutic anxiety characteristic of a Type A field. Compromising but endeavoring to communicate, the patient then referred vaguely to a homosexual dream, but immediately denied homosexual anxieties. He turned to fantasies of women and yet recognized that something was awry. He went on in some detail, indicated his wish to get to know himself better, and when the therapist failed to intervene, he became disillusioned. In the following hour, there was a static and flat quality, some indirect, Type Two derivative allusions to the therapist's failure to help the patient discover himself and to an unconscious perception of Dr. Y's dread of containing Mr. B's primitive inner mental world—a dread undoubtedly shared by Mr. B as well.

In the adaptive context of the therapist's silent listening and interventions regarding the patient's undue defensiveness, this session conveys in Type Two derivative form the patient's fear of revealing himself within the therapeutic situation and the underlying violence-related and homosexual fantasies, perceptions, and anxieties. The patient had offered a bridge to the treatment situation, and the therapist should have interpreted that Mr. B was experiencing pressures in the treatment situation to reveal himself and that he—the patent—sensed the background of violence and homosexual fears which he tried to obliterate through vagueness and a shift to thoughts about women. In this way, the therapist would have responded with a cognitive symbolic interpretation of his own to the patient's shift toward a Type A mode of communication. In the communicative realm, this would have reinforced the patient's development of a Type A field and conveyed the therapist's capacity to contain and metabolize the patient's primitive inner mental fantasies and perceptions, his valid unconscious perceptions of the therapist's anxieties, and the symbolic mode of communication. Based on what we must postulate as his own need for massive defensiveness and noncommunication, the therapist failed to intervene, and the patient responded with relatively embedded or concealed derivatives—centered for the moment on the therapist's inappropriate anxieties and failures to contain. When the therapist was unable to understand the meanings of these latter communications, the patient shifted back to the Type C mode for several sessions.

Case 3

Mrs. C was a fifty-eight-year-old woman in treatment with Dr. X. For some months therapy had been based on a so-called supportive approach, filled with such alterations in the framework as last-minute changes in the hours, self-revelations by the therapist, and extensive use of noninterpretive interventions. There had been, however, no sense of progress, and the patient's difficulties with an insensitive husband and a drug-addicted daughter continued to plague her and to generate repeated episodes of depression.

Under the influence of supervision, the therapist, over several weeks, rectified the frame and initiated efforts to intervene, primarily on an interpretive level. The patient's sessions, which had been quite disorganized and seemingly meaningless to the therapist, became filled with affect and a unique sense of meaning.

During one hour at this time, the patient tearfully spoke of her drug-addicted daughter and her need for proper limits. She had visited another daughter and for the first time had spoken meaningfully to her and experienced a sense of warmth. The patient had felt a great sense of relief, but there had been something disquieting and strange about the experience. Together with this daughter, the patient for the first time confronted her husband regarding his drug-addicted child and he became disorganized and wanted to leave. When this daughter had been ill as a child, her husband had been unavailable. During the pregnancy with this child, the patient had nearly suffered a miscarriage but her obstetrician had put her to bed and changed her medication, thereby saving the situation.

At this point in the session, the patient asked the therapist if she should take medication. He answered that the patient was now expressing feelings she had previously suppressed and which both she and her family feared, and that now, in response, she wanted to run away from them again. Mrs. C then said she had been thinking of a vacation, but was afraid of leaving her addicted daughter in the house, since she and her friends would wreck it. The patient recalled a similar discussion early in treatment and remembered the therapist as saying it would have been better for everyone if the house had caught fire when the daughter was in it. The therapist responded that the patient was becoming quite afraid of the feelings she was now experiencing in treatment and that she had a need to generate an image of him as unfeeling and destructive. The patient ended the hour by saying that she had been afraid that the therapist would give up on her and was relieved that he hadn't; she felt that she would be able to make it someday.

In the adaptive context of the rectified frame, we may sense the therapeutic regression and anxiety developing in this patient as she shifted from a Type C to a Type A communicative field. Prior to the corrective efforts of the therapist, Mrs. C and Dr. X had used language primarily for noncommunication, and the bipersonal field had a distinctly static quality. The therapist's seeming kindnesses unconsciously were designed to help cover over his patient's inner destructiveness and, in all probability, parallel problems within himself. They were part of an effort at creating falsifications that could conceal far more painful truths.

In a sense, then, it is no coincidence that the patient responded to the securing of the frame with the communication of Type Two derivatives related to her unconscious perception and introjection of the therapist's initial stance and its alteration. Her reference to her husband's fear of the truth and wish to flee, along with her request for medication, contains in derivative form both (a) her dread of her own inner mental world and a Type A communicative field, plus related efforts to shift back to the Type C field through the use of medication as an obliterating agent, and (b) the therapist's previous dread of these same inner contents and his reinforcement of the patient's massive defenses.

The patient's validating responses to the therapist's initial interventions, however lacking in specifics, demonstrates how the interface of the bipersonal field shifts significantly toward the pathology of the patient in the absence of countertransference-based inputs from the therapist. In derivative form, the patient now communicated both her dread of inner devastation and her fear of her uncontrolled destructiveness toward her addicted daughter. It is no coincidence that the patient attempted to project and projectively identify these impulses into the therapist and that, in addition, she communicated these anxieties in the form of a fabrication (however destructive the therapist's attitude had been toward both the patient and this daughter, he was certain that he had never consciously expressed a blatantly murderous wish toward either of them).

It appears that the patient wished once again to utilize the therapist in creating a misalliance and bastion through which the truth might still remain unknown. In this situation, however, it is quite evident that the patient's defenses are no longer in the form of amorphous and impenetrable barriers, but instead quite clearly reveal both the underlying nature of the defense itself and the fantasies and impulses that are being defended against. It is, as I said above, the presence of such derivatives in the face of the patient's defensiveness, and their analyzability as Type Two derivatives within a specific adaptive context, that characterizes resistances in the Type A field. Showing some appreciation for the symbolic qualities of the patient's communications, the therapist interpreted aspects of the patient's defenses and anxieties, and, despite the fact that his intervention once again fell short of the specificity and depth required in this situation, the patient responded with a sense of appreciation for the therapist's perseverance and, by implication, for their shared capacity to modify the Type C field into a more hopeful, however painful, Type A mode.

Case 4

As a final illustration, I will turn to the psychotherapy of Mr. D, who had been treated some years earlier in a clinic for what had appeared to be an ambulatory schizophrenic syndrome with multiple obsessions, phobias, and depression. He was now in twice-weekly psychotherapy with a private therapist who essentially had offered the patient a secure frame and hold, occasional general interpretations based on Type One derivatives, and a sense of tolerance for the patient's anxieties, along with some capacity to contain Mr. D's disruptive projective identifications—although these were seldom metabolized toward interpretive insights. Over many months, the patient's symptoms had gradually improved to the point where he appeared capable of confronting his dreaded phobic situations and his obsession seemed no longer horrifying, overintense, or disruptive to his functioning. It seemed evident that termination was somewhere invisibly in the air, although neither patient or therapist had as yet suggested it.

During one session at this time, the patient meticulously detailed a journey that he had taken recently by railroad in connection with his job as a salesman. He described the experience several times over and emphasized how fine he felt and how different it was from years ago when he would panic and fear being overwhelmed as the train moved along, or even worse, getting upset that it might suddenly break down and get stuck. His girlfriend of several years had been surprised that he had handled this particular trip so well, and the patient spent much of the final part of the session asking the therapist what he thought about what his patient had accomplished.

During the next hour, Mr. D described another trip in some detail. On this occasion, the train had been stuck in a tunnel, and the patient had been momentarily frightened, but then felt quite well. For a moment, he felt that it was not himself who was on that train, but this passed, as did another transient feeling that the train was not really stuck—that nothing was happening. He then ruminated at length over earlier episodes in which he had been stuck on trains and elevators, and the type of panic and anxiety that he had experienced. He stressed the extent to which this was not present now and how this characterized him in the past, not in the present. In response to continued inquiries as to the therapist's thoughts about all of this, Dr. W suggested that the patient seemed to have mastered his bodily anxieties and fears of disintegration. The patient felt quite reassured and repeated his therapist's formulation in several different versions.

During the next hour, the patient ruminated in some detail about how well he was feeling. He recalled a dream in which a young man, E, who had recently been fired at the patient's place of business, invited Mr. D to undress and get into bed with him. He suggested that they perform fellatio on each other. The dream reminded him of homosexual fantasies and anxieties that he had had some years back, although, he said, he had none of these feelings in the present. He had enjoyed working with E and would miss him. E was very good at making up stories and at hiding from the boss, and all this reminded the patient of times when he would lock himself in the bathroom at work in order not to be disturbed. After ruminating about his job, the patient asked Dr. W what he thought about the dream, and the therapist remained silent. The patient ended the hour by ruminating further about his job.

During the next session, the patient described a battle with his girlfriend and his rage at her for always changing the subject and not facing issues. He spoke in some detail again about the firing of E and his own concerns about suddenly losing his job. For him, it would be an unreal experience, and he would just disappear for a few weeks if it were to happen. On the other hand, he might want to come to his sessions; he would be afraid of losing the therapist's support. Here, the therapist intervened and suggested that the patient was concerned about the eventual termination of his treatment and that he had a need to put such a possibility at a distance and create barriers to the anger and turmoil it would create for him. The patient stated that he had had a strange thought that the therapist might want to end the treatment. He had had a fleeting image of going berserk but had then gotten himself under control and really didn't feel worried about it. Besides, it was too soon to end treatment, and he really didn't think that the therapist would just kick him out.

In the next hour, the patient reported a dream about a man who seemed to be chasing him out of his own apartment. There was some sense of a sexual threat, something like the danger of rape, but then the patient had found himself in an empty vault with the door closed and he felt safe and protected. The patient ruminated about a man at the bank that he mistrusted and about details of his job. He had had thoughts of changing his bank because he no longer felt appreciated as a customer, but he had really put the matter quite out of his mind. Often, when he felt conflicted, he could make his mind a blank and feel relief. The therapist pointed out that the patient had a tendency to seal himself off from dangers and to seek safety in voids; he suggested that this was reflected not only in his dream but in the way in which he was communicating in the session. The patient responded by recalling childhood fears of bombs and explosions, and by remembering fantasies about attacking his boss for firing E— fantasies that he had forgotten until that moment. In a rather tentative way, he wondered if all this had something to do with the possibility of his treatment's ending; he did feel much better and perhaps it was time to think about it after all.

This material illustrates the development of a Type C communicative field, largely based on the patient's intense need for unmodifiable barriers, an impenetrable container for his psychotic core. While the therapist appears initially to have contributed to the Type C field by attempting to interpret contents that had been communicated by the patient largely as a means of denying any difficulty and creating an impenetrable obstacle to the underlying anxieties and fantasies, we see in the sequence that Dr. W soon recognized that such interventions were not being confirmed and seemed to have little effect on the patient.

In the adaptive context of anxieties regarding eventual termination, this material initially served as a distracting fabrication designed to avoid this subject and its ramifications for the patient. Perhaps in part because the therapist introduced bodily anxieties which the patient introjected as Dr. W's unconscious homosexual difficulties, Mr. D did report an overtly homosexual dream. However, despite a few fragmented derivative associations—e.g., the firing of Mr. E— the material remained quite flat and was without a clear-cut adaptive context (the day residue related to Mr. E's loss of the job actually represented in derivative form and covered the more significant concern about termination which the patient essentially avoided). The subsequent associations did not generate derivative meaning. In this session, the patient represented the Type C field symbolically through the references to hiding and locking himself in the bathroom, but the therapist failed to intervene. As a result, the following hour was quite ruminative, although the patient did eventually produce rather remote and thin derivatives related to possible termination. When the therapist intervened in this regard, the patient responded with initial validation and then denial.

During the following hour, there was a shift toward Type A communication, especially after the therapist interpreted the patient's use of denial, emptiness, and barriers. The dream itself appears to represent fantasies and anxieties related to the possible termination of the treatment, as do the additional associations prior to the therapist's next intervention. Following that comment, the patient found a means of representing his dread of losing control of his explosive and primitive inner mental world; he then quickly reconstituted.

This sequence reflects, first, the type of underlying material that tends to be revealed by patients in a Type C field when their massive defensiveness and use of fabrication to generate nonmeaning are pointed out to them. Secondly, we see that in a Type C field dreams are quickly sealed off and that even when there are some derivative associations and a meaningful adaptive context, the patient remains rather constricted and fearful. Through the therapist's proper intervening, it appears that this patient was able to express aspects of his dreaded inner mental world and that he felt capable of managing these disruptive contents. Subsequent sessions suggest that this was not a return to rigid Type C barriers, but instead, that it represented a greater degree of flexibility, a softening of his defenses, and a capacity to better manage the inner contents experienced when he momentarily modified these defenses. Earlier in treatment, such breakthroughs of explosive content were followed by repeated ruminative sessions and intense efforts at noncommunication and barrier formation, including rather striking use of denial and projection. At this point in treatment, the therapist felt that these efforts had been considerably modified in a positive direction.

Earlier in treatment, this patient had repeatedly objected to the therapist's interventions on the grounds that he—the patient—made it a practice to conceal his most important communications from the therapist for several weeks at a time. As a result, since every effort at interpretation undertaken by this therapist was actually based on accepting the patient's ruminations, which served essentially as fabrications or lies designed to cover the painful underlying truths, his comments were met with ridicule and refutation. The therapist soon became aware of the significance of this mechanism, and began to interpret its function, no longer endeavoring to interpret content. In a manner that cannot be detailed here, these efforts to deal first with the patient's communicative mode significantly modified this defense to the point that the patient was able to significantly alter its use. During the period within which the patient maintained this mechanism, the therapist felt enormously frustrated: he was working with images that the patient would immediately make disappear by telling him that these were not his important associations, and he experienced himself as if he were under a vicious attack designed to destroy his integrity, his capacity to interpret, and perhaps even his own sanity. While I will not attempt to further document this therapeutic interlude, I refer to it in concluding these clinical vignettes in an effort to characterize the underlying envy and destructiveness that prevails in a Type C communicative field, the truly deceptive qualities of the patient's associations as they function to destroy meaning and relatedness rather than to generate it, the ungraspable mirror image quality of these associations, and the absurdity of attempting to interpret such contents in light of their true nature and functions.

CONCLUDING COMMENTS

It is my impression that the delineation of three major communicative styles and fields has extensive clinical and theoretical ramifications. Investigations of the communicative properties of the bipersonal field not only shed light on the intrapsychic and interactional realms, and their interplay, but also generate an additional level of conceptualization that extends beyond these two familiar spheres. I shall therefore conclude this presentation with a brief listing of some of the major implications of these concepts.

1. Basic to the conceptualization of communicative bipersonal fields is the listening process. In this respect, consistent efforts must be maintained to identify the adaptive context for the patient's associations and behaviors, and it is essential to organize this material in terms of manifest content and Type One and Type Two derivatives. In addition, one needs sensitivity to interactional mechanisms and a capacity to experience, metabolize, and understand the patient's projective identifications, validating all such experiences through the patient's verbal associations. These listening, experiencing, and organizing abilities must be applied not only to the patient's communications, but also to those of the therapist as well. In this manner, it becomes feasible to monitor fluctuations in the nature of the communicative field and to identify the main instigator for such shifts.

2. While it appears evident that the Type A communicative mode is essential for the therapist or analyst, and represents the greatest degree of maturation for both patient and therapist, insightful therapeutic work is feasible in each communicative field. Such endeavors, however, require a symbolic interpretive capacity in the therapist, without which he will be unable to interpret the patient's unconscious fantasies, memories, and introjects as they appear in a Type A field related to the patient's intrapsychic conflicts and anxieties; neither will he be able to properly metabolize and interpret projective identifications in the Type B field nor the negation of meaning and use of amorphous barriers in the

Type C field. Inherent to such an interpretive approach is the generation of positive, ego building introjective identifications that occur quite unconsciously in the course of the therapeutic interaction. Insight and positive introjection go hand and hand, and are the essential basis of adaptive structural changes (Langs, 1967a, 1976c).

3. The intrapsychic and interactional nature of defensive formations are distinctive to each communicative field. In a Type A field we find the array of defenses described in the classical psychoanalytic literature—repression, displacement, isolation, and the like. However, in addition to their intrapsychic basis, they are open to interactional influence in that both pressures toward, and models of, defensiveness and resistance may be offered to the patient by the therapist, generating what I have termed *interactional defenses and resistances* (Langs, 1976a, 1976c). In the Type A field, the patient characteristically expresses these resistances in a form that includes the communication of Type Two derivatives related both to the unconscious meaning and functions of the defense-resistance itself and the unconscious fantasies, memories, and introjects which are being defended against— most often in relation to the analyst. There is a sense of depth to the patient's resistances and they are essentially analyzable over a reasonable period of time.

In a Type B field, the major defenses will be interactional, with intrapsychic underpinnings. They will take the form of defensive utilization of projective identification as a means of disburdening the psyche of anxiety and placing intolerable fantasies and introjects into the object—here, from patient into therapist (or the reverse). However, these defensive projective identifications have in common with the resistances seen in the Type A field that they serve a positive communicative function, so that the patient's behaviors and verbal associations tend ultimately to reveal the unconscious nature, meaning, and function of the defensive projective identification and the underlying contents that the patient wishes to externalize.

In a Type C field, however, the patient's defenses and resistances have a distinct sense of flatness and emptiness and are in themselves basically designed for noncommunication, absence of understanding, falsification, and impenetrable barrier. For long periods in such therapies, there are few, if any, interpretable derivatives related to these defenses and the disturbing contents that they seal off. At best, the Type C patient will communicate occasional metaphors—usually Type One derivatives—with which they represent the nature of their communicative style. It is therefore not feasible to interpret these defense-resistances in depth or, as a rule, in terms of a specific adaptive context and Type Two derivatives.

4. The therapist's basic interventions are also distinctive for each bipersonal field. In the Type A field, his basic tools involve the maintenance of a secure framework and the use of interpretations and reconstructions derived largely from Type Two derivatives—unconscious fantasies and perceptions—related to the therapeutic interaction, in terms of both transference and nontransference. Such work will center upon the analysis of defenses and resistance on the first level, and core unconscious fantasies, memories, and introjects on the second.

In a Type B field, the basic tool is the acceptance and containment, metabolism and understanding, and interpretation of the patient's projective identifications in terms of their defensive and core meanings. In this field, the maintenance of a secure frame is also essential; the work proceeds from resistances to core contents as it does in the Type A field. However, while Type Two derivatives are the main material for interpretation in the Type A field, in the Type B field much of the analytic work is based on the patient's projective identifications. These interactional projections can, however, be organized around meaningful adaptive contexts and thus permit dynamic and genetic interpretations, much of it once again related to the therapeutic interaction in terms of both transference and nontransference.

In the Type C field, specific adaptive contexts are rare, as are Type Two derivatives. Much of the therapeutic work is based on the patient's projective identification into the therapist of meaninglessness, and his use of falsifications, noncommunication, and opaque barriers. The interpretive work must therefore utilize Type One derivatives in the form of metaphors from the patient related to these defensive barriers and the efforts at noncommunication; the effective interpretation of these resistances will also permit periods of interpretation and reconstruction of the emerging material.

5. It follows from this discussion that we can no longer maintain the unitary model of the course of a satisfactory psychoanalysis or psychotherapy, of the indications for termination, and of the definition of *cure*. To date, the classical psychoanalytic literature has delineated these factors in terms of the Type A field, correctly suggesting that with such patients the analytic work concentrates on the analysis of transference (and nontransference) in terms of resistances, core fantasies, memories, and introjects, current dynamics, and reconstructions of significant past experiences and responses to them. True structural change is defined accordingly and derives primarily from the cognitive insight accrued from these interpretive and reconstructive efforts, and secondarily from the positive introjections of the analyst that occur spontaneously and unconsciously in the course of such work. Termination is indicated at the point of symptom relief based on the working through of the relevant areas of conflict and disturbance, and on the establishment of stabilized insight and other inner adaptive changes. Such accomplishments imply a diminution in the use of pathological defenses and an improved capacity to manage one's inner mental world.

In a Type B field, much of the analytic work is done through the metabolism and interpretation of the patient's pathological projective identifications, efforts that include the interpretation of their defensive and unconscious content dimensions. In the course of a successful treatment, there is a modification in the extent to which the patient utilizes pathological projective identifications. This is accomplished in part through the interpretation of their nature and function and in part through the introjective identification by the patient of the constructively modified projective contents as they are validly reprojected by the therapist into the patient. This interactional process generatives constructive introjective

identifications based on therapist introjects, process introjects, and the reception of detoxified reprojections. Overall,
the therapeutic process may be seen as achieving a diminution in the use of pathological projective identifications and a
modification or detoxification of the contents and inner states
so projected. In addition, from time to time, there will be
opportunities for the interpretation and reconstruction of
symbolic communications and Type Two derivatives as well.

In all, then, the goal of analysis or therapy with these
patients is symptom relief based primarily on insightful and
structuralized modifications of their use of pathological
projective identifications and secondarily on alterations of
the related pathological unconscious fantasies, memories,
and introjects. With some Type B patients, it may be feasible
to shift their basic mode to Type A communication, while with
others, the outcome may take the form of more frequent use of
Type A communications along with a less pathological use of
the Type B mode. It is to be stressed that the pursuit of
cognitive insights and symbolic interpretations of the
patient's use of interactional mechanisms is a *sine qua non*; it
is fundamental to the constructive cognitive and identificatory changes that take place within this field. My initial
impression is that both definitive reconstructions and specific
interpretations of unconscious fantasies, memories, and
introjects, will be feasible somewhat less often than with Type
A patients.

In the Type C communicative field, the goal is to analyze
and work through the efforts by these patients to destroy
meaning, relatedness, and communication, and to maintain
their impervious barriers against a highly disturbed inner
core. Interpretive efforts concentrate on the metaphors of
these defenses and the patient's interactional projections of
nonmeaning. From time to time, as the patient begins to
modify the rigidity and destructiveness of these defenses, the
primitive underlying contents—unconscious fantasies, memories, and introjects—will be expressed in derivative form
and will lend themselves to interpretation and reconstruction.
However, as one would expect, such interventions are less
common with these patients than in the other two communica-

tive fields. Termination with Type C patients is based both on the gradual modification of their rigid defenses plus their needs to destroy meaning and falsify, and on the periodic interpretation and reconstruction of the underlying contents and processes. Both cognitive and identificatory factors are involved, but an initial impression suggests that most of these patients maintain this communicative mode throughout their treatment, albeit in a gradually less pathological form. Occasionally, there may be a major shift to the Type A form.

6. We may briefly consider the interaction between patient and analyst, or therapist, based on their individual preferred communicative mode. A Type A therapist will feel adequately held and stimulated by a Type A patient and should work well in developing interpretations and reconstructions of the patient's Type Two derivative symbolic communications. Potentially, such a therapist should be capable, with a Type B patient, of containing, metabolizing, and interpreting the patient's projective identifications, though there is a danger of countertransference-based defensiveness and other inappropriate reactions. At times this type of therapist may feel and be somewhat overwhelmed by these interactional pressures. A common countertransference problem in this symbolically functioning Type A therapist takes the form of a failure to consciously recognize the patient's interactional projections and a related tendency to disregard the interactional sphere.

Finally, with the Type C patient there may be a strong sense of boredom, and a possibility of failure to understand the true nature and functions of the patient's associations. A Type A therapist may have difficulty in empathizing with a Type C patient and may have problems in recognizing the need of such a patient to destroy meanings and to erect impenetrable barriers. Such therapists may be inclined to attribute and interpret meaning where none is intended, experiencing the reversing-perspective and embedded-figure types of phenomena referred to earlier in this paper. There may be countertransference-based hostility and seductiveness in Type A therapists with Type C patients, as well as efforts unconsciously designed to rupture their most frustrating defensive alignment. The implicit envy and destructiveness in the Type C form of communication may evoke countertransference-based reactions of various types within a Type A analyst. If such a therapist comes to terms with the patient's communicative mode, he can then become capable of patient and meaningful interventions when indicated.

The Type B therapist will tend to be bored by a Type A patient, will have difficulties in interpreting and reconstructing, and will tend to use language as a means of discharging his own anxieties and as a form of interactional projection into his patients. The therapist's communicative mode will exert great pressures on the Type A patient to shift toward a responsive Type B mode or a defensive Type C form. Because virtually all therapists maintain an ideal of Type A functioning, it is often difficult to recognize one's own tendencies toward Type B communication through the discharge use of language and mismanagements of the framework that are consciously intended and mistaken as validly therapeutic. In particular, the development of a Type B mode of communication in a patient should direct the therapist toward the possibility of similar propensities within himself, although in general, each therapist should undertake an extensive self-examination to determine his own communicative style and its fluctuations.

With the Type C patient, the Type B therapist is likely to feel quite bored and empty. He will tend to be prone to traumatic sexual and aggressive and other projective identifications into the Type C patient in an effort to rupture his defenses and to evoke responsive interactional projections.

A Type C therapist will be threatened by both the Type A and Type B patient. The former, with his symbolic communications and therapeutic regressive anxiety, will constitute a threat to the Type C therapist who dreads the inner mental world of both his patient and himself. These patients generate meaning and communication, and the Type C therapist will unconsciously intervene in a manner designed to destroy such meaning, to falsify, and to evoke amorphous barriers. Similarly, with a Type B patient who is generating meaningful and anxiety provoking projective identifications, the Type

C therapist will be refractory in containing such projective identifications and will unconsciously endeavor to obliterate their presence. He will be greatly threatened by such interactional pressures, in that they could rupture his massive defenses and generate meaning and relatedness in the face of his efforts to destroy such qualities. His own intensely sealed off psychotic core is under persistent pressures from the communications of both the Type A and Type B patient, and he will tend to respond countertransferentially in an effort to maintain his own relatively fragile equilibrium. In contrast, with the Type C patient he will feel comfortable and even interested, tending to share clichés and falsifications, as well as barriers, and to generate a typically stalemated therapeutic interaction.

In brief, a Type A patient will feel comfortable and work well with a Type A therapist. He will feel threatened and disorganized by a Type B therapist, and the experience of the therapist's pathological projective identifications will tend to evoke both unconscious curative efforts on his part and pathological interactional mechanisms as well. With a Type C therapist, he will experience a sense of emptiness and a lack of progress.

The Type B patient will find the Type A therapist who can interpret his projective identifications quite helpful, although he will make consistent efforts to evoke a misalliance in which pathological projective identifications are exchanged. With the Type B therapist, he may well feel a sense of comfort and become embroiled in a serious misalliance based on unconscious and repeated sequences of pathological projective identification, introjection, and reprojection. In the long run, however, such an interaction is destructive to both participants and may well lead to a rupture in the therapy. The Type B patient will feel little sense of relatedness to a Type C therapist, and will sense the extent to which he is a danger to such a therapist, and will experience an uncertain treatment course of little valid help.

The Type C patient will endeavor to break his links or relatedness to the Type A therapist, but should such a therapist respond interpretively and empathically, he will undergo a slow development of progress and adaptive inner change. With a Type B therapist, the Type C patient will feel quite threatened and often will simply interrupt the treatment. With a Type C therapist, this patient will feel quite safe and will tend to accept the falsifications and barriers offered by such a therapist. Some Type C patients, however, ultimately become dissatisfied with the stalemate and generate efforts at true communication. Should the therapist be incapable of modifying his own communicative style at such times, these patients will either become depressed and accept the stalemate or will terminate.

7. A few final comments: Dreams, symbols, and affects may appear in any of the three communicative fields. In a Type A field, all are utilized for meaningfully symbolic communication, while in a Type B field, they are in the service of discharge and projective identification rather than cognitive understanding. In a Type C field, they are designed as falsification and deceptions, and as a means of noncommunication.

Somatization seems more common in the Type B and Type C fields, especially the latter. In another vein, the genetics of communicative style, and their relationship to personality, interaction, intrapsychic structure, self, and identity—all require extensive investigation. It appears too that the classical Freudians have been investigating the Type A field and it is their belief that they themselves characteristically work within the Type A mode. On the other hand, the Kleinians seems to be working a Type B field, whatever the contribution to this communicative mode may be from both patient and analyst. Many of the narcissistic patients recently described by Kohut (1971, 1977) and Kernberg (1975) appear to function in the Type C field, and the therapeutic techniques described by Kohut have qualities of both the Type A and Type C communicative mode, while the formulations presented by Kernberg have both Type A and Type B dimensions. Finally, it appears that once a patient has been in treatment with a Type B or Type C therapist, it is extremely difficult for them to work with a Type A therapist and to tolerate the necessary therapeutic regression, symbolic communication, and anxiety required for effective analytic work in such a field.

These are but a few of the implications of the present formulations, many of which deserve extensive clinical investigation. In this context, I am reminded that there are those who feel that psychoanalysis is in a state of basic consolidation or even stalemate (see Rangell, 1975), and others who find analysis to be in a state of considerable flux and creativity (see Green, 1975). In addition to hoping that I have prompted the reader to take a fresh look at his interaction with his patients, I hope also to have demonstrated that there are many original and imaginative thinkers in psychoanalysis today—some of whom have been mentioned in the course of this presentation. Psychoanalysts should master their propensities for the Type B and Type C modes of communication, not only with their patients, but in their work at large, and should be capable of maintaining a Type A field in which they welcome new and even strange ideas and concepts, and the growth-promoting anxieties and potential reorganization so contained (see Stone, 1975). It is on this note that I conclude with the following:

Medium is message;

Medium determines message;

Medium must be analyzed before message.

NOTES

1. In this paper, I will not attempt to distinguish between the psychoanalytic and psychotherapeutic situations. Although in large part the ideas that will be developed have equal applicability to both modalities, I will allude primarily to the analytic experience, since most of the relevant literature is so focused. I wish to apologize for the personal historical approach I have adopted in developing the themes of this paper: to the extent that they represent discoveries, the ideas presented here have had a very personal development and I have found no other means of doing full justice to my subject. I do, as well, offer full acknowledgement of the contributions of others (see also Langs, 1967c).

2. After completing this paper, I found a study by Fiumara (1977) of the development of the symbolic function in infancy and in analysis. Many of her ideas overlap with and extend basic concepts discussed here. Fiumara's work indicates, as does that of Khan (1971), that the Type A field and mode of communication is, indeed, the most mature and optimal. Fiumara is sensitive as well to the roles of the

framework and interpretations in creating conditions for possible symbolic communication and alludes to the use of pseudosymbols and falsifications that are protective but inimical to growth.

REFERENCES

Angel, K. (1971). Unanalyzability and narcissistic transference disturbances. *Psychoanalytic Quarterly* 40: 264-276.

Balint, M. (1968). *The Basic Fault: Therapeutic Aspects of Regression.* London: Tavistock.

Baranger, M. and Baranger, W. (1966). Insight and the analytic situation. In *Psychoanalysis in the Americas,* ed. R. Litman, pp. 56-72. New York: International Universities Press.

Bion, W. (1962). *Learning from Experience.* In *Seven Servants.* New York: Aronson, 1977.

———(1963). *Elements of Psycho-Analysis.* In *Seven Servants.* New York: Aronson, 1977.

———(1965). *Transformations.* In *Seven Servants.* New York: Aronson, 1977.

———(1970) *Attention and Interpretation.* In *Seven Servants.* New York: Aronson, 1977.

———(1977). *Seven Servants.* New York: Aronson.

Bird, B. (1972). Notes on transference: universal phenomenon and the hardest part of analysis. *Journal of the American Psychoanalytic Association* 20: 267-301.

Bleger, J. (1967). Psycho-analysis of the psychoanalytic frame. *International Journal of Psycho-Analysis* 48: 511-519.

Fiumara, G. (1977). The symbolic function, transference and psychic reality. *International Review of Psycho-Analysis* 4: 171-180.

Freud, S. (1914). Remembering, repeating, and working-through. *Standard Edition* 12: 145-156.

Giovacchini, P. (1975). The concrete and difficult patient. In *Tactics and Techniques in Psychoanalytic Therapy,* ed. P. Giovacchini, pp. 351-363. New York: Aronson.

Green, A. (1975). The analyst, symbolization and absence in the analytic setting (on changes in analytic practice and analytic experience). *International Journal of Psycho-Analysis* 56: 1-22.

Greenson, R. (1967). *The Technique and Practice of Psychoanalysis.* Vol. 1. New York: International Universities Press.

Grinberg, L. (1962). On a specific aspect of counter-transference due to the patient's projective identification. *International Journal of Psycho-Analysis* 43: 436-440.

Halpert, E. (1972). The effect of insurance on psychoanalytic treatment. *Journal of the American Psychoanalytic Association* 20: 122-133.

Kernberg, O. (1975). *Borderline Conditions and Pathological Narcissism.* New York: Aronson.

Khan, M. (1963). The concept of cumulative trauma. *The Psychoanalytic Study of the Child* 18: 286-306.

———(1964). Ego distortion, cumulative trauma, and the role of reconstruction in the analytic situation. *International Journal of Psycho-Analysis* 45: 272-278.

———(1973). The role of illusion in the analytic space and process. In *The Privacy of the Self,* pp. 251-269. New York: International Universities Press, 1974.

Kohut, H. (1971). *The Analysis of the Self: A Systematic Approach to the Psychoanalytic Treatment of Narcissistc Personality Disorders.* New York: International Universities Press.

————(1977). *The Restoration of the Self*. New York:International Universities Press.

Langs, R. (1971). Day residues, recall residues, and dreams: reality and the psyche. *Journal of the American Psychoanalytic Association* 19: 499-523.

————(1972). A psychoanalytic study of material from patients in psychotherapy. *International Journal of Psychoanalytic Psychotherapy* 1(1): 4-45.

————(1973). *The Technique of Psychoanalytic Psychotherapy*. Vol. 1. New York: Aronson.

————(1974). *The Technique of Psychoanalytic Psychotherapy*. Vol. 2. New York: Aronson.

————(1975a). The patient's unconscious perception of the therapist's errors. In *Tactics and Techniques in Psychoanalytic Therapy, Vol 2: Countertransference*, ed. P. Giovacchini, pp. 239-250. New York: Aronson.

————(1975b). Therapeutic misalliances. *International Journal of Psychoanalytic Psychotherapy* 4: 77-105.

————(1975c). The therapeutic relationship and deviations in techique. *International Journal of Psychoanalytic Psychotherapy* 4: 106-141.

————(1976a). *The Bipersonal Field*. New York: Aronson.

————(1976b). On becoming a psychiatrist. *International Journal of Psychoanalytic Psychotherapy* 5: 255-280.

————(1976c). *The Therapeutic Interaction*, Vols. 1 and 2. New York: Aronson.

————(1978a). *Dreams in the Bipersonal Field*. New York: Aronson (in press).

————(1978b). Validation and the framework of the therapeutic situation. *Contemporary Psychoanalysis* 14: 98-124.

Liberman, D. (in press). Complementarity between the styles of the patient's material and the interpretation. *International Journal of Psychoanalytic Psychotherapy*.

Little, M. (1951). Countertransference and the patient's response to it. *International Journal of Psycho-Analysis* 32: 32-40.

Milner, M. (1952). Aspects of symbolism and comprehension of the not-self. *International Journal of Psycho-Analysis* 33: 181-195.

Racker, H. (1957). The meaning and uses of countertransference. *Psychoanalytic Quarterly* 26: 303-357.

Rangell, L. (1975). Psychoanalysis and the process of change: an essay on the past, present and future. *International Journal of Psycho-Analysis* 56: 87-98.

Searles, H. (1958). The schizophrenic's vulnerability to the therapist's unconscious process. *Journal of Nervous and Mental Disease* 127: 247-262.

————(1959). The effort to drive the other person crazy—an element in the aetiology and psychotherapy of schizophrenia. *British Journal of Medical Psychology* 32: 1-18.

————(1960). *The Nonhuman Environment*. New York: International Universities Press.

————(1965). *Collected Papers on Schizophrenia and Related Subjects*. New York: International Universities Press.

————(1970). Autism and the phase of transition to therapeutic symbiosis. *Contemporary Psychoanalysis* 7: 1-20.

————(1971). Pathological symbiosis and autism. In *The Name of Life,* ed. B. Landis and E. Tauber, pp. 69-83. New York: Holt, Rinehart and Winston.

————(1972). The functions of the patient's realistic perceptions of the analyst in delusional transference. *British Journal of Medical Psychology* 45: 1-18.

————(1973a). Concerning therapeutic symbiosis. *The Annual of Psychoanalysis* 1: 247-262.

————(1973b). Some aspects of unconscious fantasy. *International Journal of Psychoanalytic Psychotherapy* 2: 37-50.

————(1975). The patient as therapist to his analyst. In *Tactics and Techniques in Psychoanalytic Therapy, Vol. 2: Countertransference,* ed. P. Giovacchini. New York: Aronson.

Segal, H. (1967). Melanie Klein's technique. *Psychoanalytic Form* 2: 197-211.

Stone, L. (1975). Some problems and potentialities of present-day psychoanalysis. *Psychoanalytic Quarterly* 44: 331-370.

Viderman, S. (1974). Interpretation in the analytic space. *International Review of Psycho-Analysis* 1: 467-480.

Wallerstein, R. (1977). Psychic energy reconsidered: Introduction. *Journal of the American Psychoanalytic Association* 25: 529-536.

Wangh, M. (1962). The "evocation of a proxy": a psychological maneuver, its use as a defense, its purposes and genesis. *Psychoanalytic Study of the Child* 17. 451-469.

Winnicott, D. (1945). Primitive emotional development. In *Collected Papers: Through Paediatrics to Psycho-Analysis,* pp. 145-156. London: Tavistock, 1958.

————(1951). Transitional objects and transitional phenomena. In *Collected Papers: Through Paediatrics to Psycho-Analysis,* pp. 229-242. London: Tavistock, 1958.

————(1956). Primary maternal preoccupation. In *Collected Papers: Through Paediatrics to Psycho-Analysis,* pp. 300 305. London: Tavistock, 1958.

————(1958). *Collected Papers: Through Paediatrics to Psycho-Analysis.* London: Tavistock.

————(1965). *The Maturational Processes and the Facilitating Environment.* London: Hogarth.

————(1971). *Playing and Reality.* New York: Basic Books.

Appendix B

THE BASICS OF
THE LISTENING PROCESS

I. The intaking process
    A. Entering each session without desire, memory, or under-
       standing
    B. An openness to the unknown, the nonsensuous, and the
       neurotic (used in its broadest sense)
    C. The use of free-floating attention, role and image responsive-
       ness, and containing
    D. Allowing each session to unfold and be its own creation
    E. Permitting the patient to generate all formulations and
       interventions
    F. The application of each aspect of the listening process to all
       communications from both patient and therapist
    G. Additional tools
        1. Unconscious sensitivities
        2. Empathy
        3. Intuition
        4. Trial identifications and limited introjections
        5. Limited and controlled use of projections and projective
           identifications
        6. Conscious fantasies—processed toward understanding
           of latent contents

7. Physical sensations, symptoms, altered states of consciousness, etc.

II. The major interrelated realms of the listening process
A. The cognitive sphere
1. Sources: the patient's verbal associations, affects, and behaviors; the therapist's use of audition, sight, touch, affect, etc.; the behaviors and interventions of the therapist, and the patient's use of his senses
2. All verbal and nonverbal communications, processed cognitively toward the identification of unconscious fantasies, memories, and introjects—the inner state and inner mental world of the patient and, secondarily, of the therapist
B. The sphere of interactional mechanisms and processes
1. Experiences of pressure related to interactional projections and complementary introjective identifications
2. The metabolism of projective identifications toward cognitive understanding
C. The object relational sphere: role and image evocations
1. The use of signal subjective experiences and self-knowledge to identify roles and images being evoked, and the contributions to such experiences from each participant.

III. Generating formulations based on cognitive listening (organizing the material)
A. Free-floating and unbiased listening, permitting random impingements, chaos, and disorganization
B. Identifying the adaptive context—if available
1. Distinguishing neurotic from nonneurotic contexts
2. Using all interventions by the therapist as supplementary —or central—adaptive contexts
3. Monitoring the therapeutic interaction for day residues—precipitants
C. Monitoring all material from patient—and therapist—in terms of the ongoing therapeutic interaction
1. Using the me–not-me interface in considering the communications from both patient and therapist

    2. Assessing the source of each communication: how much from patient; how much from therapist

D. Three levels of organizing the material

    1. Manifest content

    2. Type One derivatives—readily available inferences from manifest contents

    3. Type Two derivatives—organized around a specific adaptive context

E. Organizing a segment of material (applicable to the communications from both patient and therapist)

    1. Identifying the adaptive context

    2. Monitoring the material for Type One derivatives

       a. Specific first-order themes

       b. General themes

       c. Specific second-order themes

       d. The additional search for embedded derivatives

    3. Monitoring the material along the me–not-me interface and in terms of the therapeutic relationship

    4. Generating Type Two derivatives based on specific second-order themes defined in terms of a definitive adaptive context

    5. Assessing the qualities of each derivative—Type One and Type Two—in terms of:

       a. Unconscious perceptions—valid and distorted

       b. Unconscious fantasies—distorted and nondistorted

       c. Introjects—distorted and nondistorted

       d. Projections—distorted and nondistorted

    6. The discovery of the coalescence of derivatives—or its absence

    7. The generation of a selected fact—the discovery of a new meaning with which to organize and understand the available material

    8. Relating the material to an available therapeutic context

IV. Generating formulations from interactional listening-intaking

A. Role evocations and generation of self-images

    1. Free-floating role and image responsiveness

    2. The use of signal reactions

       a. Controlled impulses to act or deviate inappropriately

   b. Limited experiences of an evoked self-image
   c. Openness to images and roles that are discordant
      with present self-image and idealized self-image
   d. Openness to the patient's self-images and roles, and
      those of his external objects
3. Processing subjective impulses and images toward
   cognitive understanding
   a. Organizing these subjective experiences around a
      current adaptive context
   b. Generating meaning in terms of Type Two deriva-
      tives
   c. Determining the contribution from patient and
      therapist—treating one's subjective reactions as an
      interactional product
   d. Determining the validity of the subjective experience
      and the degree of distortion
   e. Assessing additional dynamic and genetic implica-
      tions
B. Projective identifications
   . Experiences of interactional pressures or voids
   2. Processing these subjective experiences in terms of the
      prevailing adaptive contexts
   3. Metabolizing the subjective experience toward cognitive
      understanding of the contents, defenses, proxy evoca-
      tions and the like, that are being interactionally project-
      ed

V. Three types of communicative field
   A. Field A: symbolic communication
   B. Field B: projective identification and action-discharge
   C. Field C: barriers, falsifications, clichés, destruction of mean-
      ing and relatedness, etc.

VI. The validating process (applied to every subjective
    experience and formulation,
    A. The confirmatory sequence
       1. The development of a silent hypothesis
       2. Confirmation derived from the ongoing associations
          which coalesce ultimately around a specific adaptive
          context

3. Offer of an intervention: a management of the framework or an interpretation
4. Further confirmation
    a. Cognitively: new material that reorganizes known data and provides it with new meanings—the selected fact
    b. Additional cognitive validation through the appearance of previously repressed material
    c. Interactional confirmation through derivatives of positive introjective identifications
B. The nonconfirmatory sequence
    1. Silent hypothesis
    2. Noncoalescence
    3. The absence of a meaningful adaptive context
    4. An erroneous intervention
    5. Nonconfirmation
        a. Cognitively: absence of a selected fact, truly new material, or the modification of repressive barriers
        b. Interactionally: derivatives of negative introjective identifications
    6. Unconscious sectors of misalliance and bastions
    7. Patient's initial exploitation of the error, and subsequent unconscious efforts to rectify the mistake and to cure the therapist

Appendix C

GLOSSARY

Abstracting-Particularizing Process, the. That aspect of the listening process in which first-order, manifest themes are used to derive more general or abstract themes, from which second-order specific themes are generated. The latter are often monitored in terms of the therapeutic relationship and the me–not-me interface.

Adaptational-Interactional Viewpoint, the. A clinical-metapsychological approach to the patient and therapeutic interaction which takes into account both intrapsychic and interactional processes, conscious and unconscious in both spheres.

Adaptive Context, the. The specific reality stimulus that evokes an intrapsychic response. *Direct* or *nonneurotic* adaptive contexts are those stimuli which evoke linear intrapsychic reactions and nonneurotic communicative responses; in essence, they are unrelated to psycho-pathological reactions and mechanisms. *Indirect* or *neurotic* adaptive contexts are those precipitants that evoke convolut-ed, derivative intrapsychic responses that contain pathological unconscious fantasies, memories, and introjects; they are related to psychopathology and to neurosis. Often an adaptive context outside of the therapeutic relationship will have a direct context within its manifest content, and an indirect context in its latent content. The latter is, as a rule, a derivative of a significant adaptive context within the therapeutic situation itself, communicated in disguised form. On the whole, the major indirect and neurotic adaptive contexts derive from the therapeutic interaction. The term *primary adaptive task* is a synonym for adaptive context.

Bastion. A term first used by Baranger and Baranger (1966) to allude to a split-off part of the bipersonal field which is under interactional repression and denial, so that the contents involved are avoided by both patient and therapist or analyst.

Bipersonal Field, the. A term first used by Baranger and Baranger (1966) as a metaphor for the therapeutic situation. It stresses the interactional qualities of the field, and postulates that every experience and communication within the field receives vectors from both patient and therapist or analyst. The metaphor requires the concept of an *interface* along which communication occurs between the two members of the therapeutic dyad, and points to the need to conceptualize the presence, role, and function of a framework for the field.

Commentary. A term used to describe the patient's responses to an intervention from the therapist (management of the framework or verbal). These associations and behaviors contain validating and nonvalidating communications, and they are to be viewed as a mixture of fantasy and reality, accurate perceptiveness and distortion. Often, commentaries take the form of *transversal communications;* unconsciously, they convey the patient's evaluation of the intervention.

Communication, Convoluted. An image used to describe the presence of derivatives and the indirect expression of pathological unconscious fantasies, memories, introjects, and interactional contents and mechanisms. It is one of the hallmarks of neurotic communication. See *Neurotic Communication.*

Communication, Linear. A sequence evoked by an adaptive context in which the intrapsychic response is relatively logical, readily apparent or easily inferred, directly responsive, and relatively undisguised. It is a form of reaction that characterizes the direct adaptive context and nonneurotic communication. See *Nonneurotic Communication.*

Communicative Field. The amalgam from patient and therapist that characterizes the dominant mode of communicative interaction in a given bipersonal field. See *Bipersonal Field, Type A Field, Type B Field, Type C Field.*

Communicative Space. A metaphor for the interior of the bipersonal field and for the realm in which communication occurs between patient and therapist or analyst. The image suggests that there are a number of possible communicative spaces, each with a set of defining attributes. It allows, too, for the recognition that patient and therapist may be in separate communicative spaces, rather than sharing the same mode.

Communicative Style or Mode. The form of communicative expression that characterizes the interactional thrusts and form of relatedness of the patient and therapist or analyst. See *Type A Field and Mode, Type B Field and Mode, Type C Field and Mode.*

Conception. A term first used by Bion (1962, 1977) to describe the outcome when a preconception mates with appropriate sense impressions. More broadly, the term may be used to describe the saturation of a preconception through a realization that satisfies its inherent expectations.

Confirmation, Primary. A term used to describe the patient's initial response to an intervention, often in the form of direct affirmation or negation. In general, direct agreement has little bearing on the validity of the intervention, while negation often suggests nonvalidation, though, in exceptional circumstances, it will constitute a defensive response that emerges prior to secondary confirmation.

Confirmation, Secondary. The extended response to the therapist's interventions (management of the frame and verbal) which contain selected facts, uniquely original and previously unknown communications from the patient that extend the intervention, especially in the form of Type Two derivatives. Psychoanalytic confirmation of an intervention requires the presence of truly unexpected Type Two derivatives. In general, their absence constitutes nonconfirmation.

Contained, the. A metaphor first used by Bion (1962, 1977) to allude to the contents and psychic mechanisms that are projectively identified by an infant into his mother, and by a patient into his analyst. More broadly, they allude to the contents and functions of a projective identification emanating from a subject toward an object.

Container, the. A metaphor first used by Bion (1962, 1977) for the recipient of a projective identification. The container may be open to containing such projective identifications, or may be refractory. The metaphor also implies the processing or metabolizing of the introjected contents and functions. An adequate container is seen as being in a state of *reverie.*

Containing and Containing Function. A metaphor used to describe the taking in and processing of projective identifications. An adequate containing function has been described by Bion (1962, 1977) as a state of *reverie* in the mother or analyst, and may also apply to the therapist or patient. Containing function alludes to the receptiveness to projective identifications, and to an ability to metabolize and detoxify pathological *interactional projections,* returning them to the subject in appropriately modified form. For the therapist or analyst, this process implies the metabolizing of a projective identification to conscious insight, imparted to the patient through a valid interpretation and through the maintenance of a secure framework and hold.

Countertransference. A term used in this volume to allude to all inappropriate and pathological responses of the therapist to his patient. These reactions are founded on pathologicial unconscious fantasies, memories, introjects, and interactional mechanisms (see Langs, 1976b).

Day Residue. A term first used by Freud (1900) to allude to the reality stimulus for the dream. More broadly, it may be seen as the external stimulus, filled with latent and unconscious meaning, that evokes any intrapsychic reponse. In that sense, it is virtually synonymous with the *adaptive context.*

Denudation. A term used by Bion (1962, 1977) to metaphorically represent one type of effect that the contained may have on the container, and the reverse: the generation of a disruptive and destructive experience and set of affects, leading to some form of inner disturbance that often is characterized by the destruction of function and meaning.

Derivatives. Manifest communications, verbal and non-verbal, which contain in some disguised form expressions of unconscious fantasies, memories, introjects, and perceptions. These are, then, the communicative expressions of neuroses, and the basis on which they are maintained. See *Type One Derivatives, Type Two Derivatives.*

Derivatives, Embedded. A representation of an unconscious fantasy, memory, introject, or perception that is communicated as a seemingly irrelevant component of a sequence of manifest contents, in a form that seems peripheral to the main conscious intention and to the major first-order and general themes.

Detoxification. A term used to describe the metabolism of a projective identification so that its relatively primitive and destructive qualities are altered through some appropriate means, usually through cognitive understanding directed toward insight. This process is an essential quality of *reverie.*

Empathy. A form of emotional knowing and noncognitive sharing in, and comprehending, the psychological and affective state of another person. Empathy involves both affect and cognition, and is based on a relatively nonconflicted interplay of introjective and projective mechanisms, and a variety of forms of unconscious sharing. It is a temporary form of immediate engagement and understanding, which must then be processed and validated along the lines designated for any subjective experience by the therapist or analyst—or patient.

Faith. A term used by Bion (1972) to describe a form of passive listening or intuiting by the therapist or analyst that is founded upon entering each session without desire, memory, or understanding. It implies a fundamental belief that the patient will put into the therapist or analyst in derivative form all that he needs for his own cure, and all that that the latter requires for his interventions. It also implies an appreciation of the principle that each session should be its own creation, and that, unconsciously, the patient will provide the therapeutic situation with all that is necessary for his cure, except for the therapist's or analyst's interpretive interventions and management of the framework, which are themselves based on the ingredients provided by the patient.

First-Order Themes. See *Themes, First-Order*.

Frame. A metaphor for the implicit and explicit ground rules of psychotherapy or psychoanalysis. The image implies that the ground rules create a basic hold for the therapeutic interaction, and for both patient and therapist, and that they create a distinctive set of conditions within the frame that differentiate it in actuality and functionally from the conditions outside the frame. The metaphor requires, however, an appreciation of the human qualities of the frame and should not be used to develop an inanimate or overly rigid conception.

Framework. A term used synonymously with *frame*,

usually as a means of referring to the ground rules of the bipersonal field.

Framework Cures. The maladaptive alleviation of symptoms through an inappropriate modification in the frame.

Functional Meaning. Synonymous with *Functional Capacity.* A term used to indicate that associations never exist as isolated mental products, and that among their most essential dynamic implications are the unconscious communications contained within the material as they pertain to the therapeutic relationship and interaction. In essence, it is a concept that stresses that all associations have some dynamic relevance to the therapeutic interaction.

Ground Rules. The implicit and explicit components of the analytic or therapeutic situation which establish the conditions for treatment and the means through which it shall be undertaken (for details, see Langs, 1975b, 1976a,b).

Holding. A term used to describe the therapist's or analyst's establishment and maintenance of a secure and safe therapeutic situation. The result is a holding environment that is created through the implicit and explicit delineation of the ground rules, explicated through their maintenance, and significantly elaborated through valid interpretive efforts. The holding capacity of the therapist or analyst may be likened to his containing capacity, although the former is a more general concept, while the latter specifically refers to the taking in of interactional projections.

Identification. An intrapsychic process through which the self-representations and other aspects of the subject's internal mental world and defenses are unconsciously modified in keeping with a model derived from an external object.

Interactional Defenses. Intrapsychic protective mechanisms which are formed through vectors from both patient and therapist. This type of defense may exist in either participant to the therapeutic dyad, and has both intrapsychic and interactional (external) sources.

Interactional Projection. A synonym for projective identification (Langs, 1976a).

Interactional Resistances. Any impediment to the progress of therapy that receives vectors, usually on an unconscious level, from both patient and therapist.

Interactional Symptoms. An emotional disturbance in either participant to the therapeutic dyad with significant sources from both participants (Langs, 1976b).

Interactional Syndrome. Clusters of interactional symptoms (Langs, 1976b).

Interface, Me-Not-Me. See *Me-Not-Me Interface.*

Interface of the Bipersonal Field. A metaphor used to describe a hypothetical line along which the communications between patient and therapist take place within the bipersonal field. It implies that vectors which determine this interface are derived from both patient and therapist, and that these may be contained in relatively fixed intermixtures or may vary considerably. Among the determinants of the qualities and location of the interface, pathological inputs from both patient and therapist are especially significant.

Introject. An intrapsychic precipitate which stems from the process of introjective identification. Among its qualities is the extent to which it is transient or becomes structuralized, the degree to which it is incorporated into the self-image and self-representations or maintained as separate from them, the extent to which it is pathological or nonpathological, and the degree to which it is constructive or benign rather than destructive or malignant. In addition, these internal representations of conscious and unconscious traits and interactions have a variety of specific qualities in keeping with the nature of the object, the subject, their relationship, and the qualities of their separate and shared experiences. See *Unconscious Introject*.

Introjective Identification. The interactional process through which introjects are formed. As a rule, it is invoked by a projective identification from the object, although it may also entail active incorporative efforts by the subject. The process is influenced both by the nature of the object, the contents and processes that are being taken in, and the inner state of the subject.

Intuition. An immediate form of knowing, understanding, or learning developed without the conscious use of reasoning and knowledge.

Latent Content. The hidden dimension of the patient's associations contained in disguised form within the surface of that material. The term is usually used to refer to readily available inferences from the manifest content—disguised specific unconscious fantasies, memories, introjects, and perceptions.

Listening Process, The. A term used in the broadest possible psychoanalytic sense to refer to all conscious and unconscious intaking and organizing processes within both patient and therapist. For the therapist, the term includes all available cognitive and interactional sources of information about the patient, verbal and nonverbal, and his own use of sensory and nonsensory, conscious and unconscious, sensitivities. Included too are efforts at synthesizing and formulating cognitive material, the experience of role pressures and image evocations, and the metabolism of projective identifications. The process culminates in conscious understanding or insight, in proper holding and containing, and in the formulation of a valid intervention. Similar processes take place within the patient, although, as a rule, much of it on an unconscious level.

Manifest Content. The surface of the patient's associations and the therapist's interventions. The term refers to the direct and explicit meanings so contained.

Me-Not-Me Interface, the. An imaginary interface of the patient's communications so designed that every aspect refers on one level to the patient himself, while on another level to the therapist or analyst. The me–not–me is stated from the patient's vantage point and indicates that every communication contains allusions to both himself and the therapist or analyst.

Metabolism, or the Metabolism of Projective Identifications. A term first used by R. Fliess (1942) to describe the processing by the analyst of temporary trial identifications with the patient. The concept is used more broadly to refer to all efforts to work over sensory and nonsensory inputs from the patient, and in another specific sense to refer to the introjective identification and containing of a projective identification from the patient, ultimately processed toward cognitive understanding and insight. This last sense of the term may also be applied to the patient's efforts to introjectively identify and contain projective identifications from the therapist, so long as efforts are made toward understanding.

Misalliance. A quality of the basic relationship between patient and therapist, or of a sector of that relationship, which is consciously or unconsciously designed to bypass adaptive insight in favor of either some other maladaptive form of symptom alleviation or the destruction of effective therapeutic work (see Langs, 1975c).

Neuroses. A term used in a special sense to allude to all forms of psychopathology, ranging from symptomatic disturbances to character disorders, from neurotic disturbances to borderline syndromes and narcissistic disorders to psychoses, and from psychosomatic disorders to addictions, perversions, and other emotionally founded syndromes. In essence, then, the term refers to all types of syndromes based on intrapsychic and interactional emotional disturbances and dysfunctions.

Negative Projective Identification. A term used to describe an empty or voidlike interactional projection designed to destroy meanings within the bipersonal field and to disrupt the mental capacities of the object or recipient of the interactional projection.

Neurotic Communication. That form of behaving and conveying meanings that is related to the neuroses, and which is characterized by the use of derivative and convoluted sequences, related ultimately to pathological unconscious fantasies, memories, introjects, and perceptions.

Nonconfirmation. See *Nonvalidation.*

Noncountertransference. The essentially nonconflicted sphere of the therapist's or analyst's functioning expressed in his appropriate capacity to relate to the patient, listen, intervene, manage the framework, and the like.

Nonneurotic Communication. A means of conveying conscious and unconscious meaning that is essentially unrelated to neuroses. It is characterized by manifest messages, readily available inferences, and linear causal sequences.

Nontransference. The essentially nonconflicted areas of the patient's valid functioning within the therapeutic relationship. It is exemplified by validatable conscious and unconscious perceptions and reactions to the therapist, and by other spheres of adequate functioning and interacting.

Nonvalidation. A response to an intervention by the therapist or analyst (management of the framework or verbal) that is flat, lacking in unique contents or a selected fact, repetitious, linear, and without surprise. It is an indication that the intervention has been erroneous, and is largely in the sphere of secondary confirmation—here constituting secondary nonconfirmation.

Preconception. A term first used by Bion (1962, 1977) to represent a state of expectation and more broadly a state of need, a quality in need of fulfillment or closure, an unsaturated state, which, once saturated, would generate a *conception.*

Precipitant or Reality Precipitant. A synonym for *day residue,* and a term synonymous with *adaptive context* when used to refer to the evocation of an intrapsychic response.

Predictive Clinical Methodology. A mode of psychoanalytically oriented therapy founded on the validating process, and especially on efforts at prediction so designed that validation takes the form of Type Two derivatives.

Primary Adaptive Task. A synonym for *adaptive context* (Langs, 1973a).

Projective Counteridentification. A term coined by Grinberg (1962) to allude to all countertransference-based responses within the analyst to the patient's projective identifications. The term implies a failure to metabolize the relevant interactional projections and the reprojection into the patient of nondetoxified contents and mechanisms.

Projective Identification. An interactional effort by a subject to place into the object aspects of his own inner mental state, inner contents, and unconscious defenses. The term *identification* is used here in the sense of remaining identified with the externalized contents and wishing to evoke in the object an identification with the subject.

Proxy, Evocation of a. A form of projective identification described by Wangh (1962) which stresses an interactional effort to place into the object areas of malfunctioning and disturbance, largely as a means of evoking adequate responses which can then be introjected.

Psychoanalytically Oriented Psychotherapy, or Insight Psychotherapy. A form of psychotherapy which takes place within a well-defined bipersonal field and which is designed to provide the patient symptom relief based on cognitive insights and the inevitable positive introjective identifications that derive from the therapist's capacity to hold the patient, contain and metabolize his projective identifications, establish and manage the framework, and interpret the neurotic communications and expressions from the patient.

Psychoanalytic Cliché. An intervention based on psychoanalytic theory and on the material from the patient at a point at which it is communicated in a nonneurotic form. It is a statement of apparent psychoanalytic meaning or truth which is essentially and functionally false in light of the prevailing sources of inner anxiety and turmoil, conflict and disturbance within the patient and/or the therapist. It is therefore unconsciously designed to serve as a barrier to the underlying catastrophic truths and as a means of disrupting the meaningful relationship links between patient and therapist.

Regression, Nontherapeutic. A shift toward more primitive communication and expression of derivatives of unconscious fantasies, memories, introjects, and perceptions that takes place under conditions of unneeded modifications in the framework and in response to other errors in technique by the therapist or analyst. The impairments in the framework render such regressions difficult to analyze and resolve, and the restoration of the frame is essential to a shift from a nontherapeutic to a *therapeutic regression.*

Regression, Therapeutic. An adaptive form of re-regression that takes place within a secure bipersonal field and is a means of describing the constructive emergence of unconscious fantasies, memories, introjects, and perceptions related to the patient's neurosis as mobilized by the therapeutic interaction and based on earlier genetic experiences and traumas. This emergence of relatively primitive material occurs in a form and under conditions that render the neurotic components analyzable and modifiable through insight (Langs, 1976a).

Resistance. A term used to describe any impediment within the patient to the work of therapy or analysis. It is a conception that is based on a subjective evaluation by the therapist or analyst. In its narrow clinical sense, these obstacles are founded on defenses against intrapsychic conflicts and anxieties, as they are expressed within the therapeutic relationship. See *Interactional Resistances*.

Reverie. A term used by Bion (1962, 1977) to describe the state of the mother, therapist, or analyst who is capable of receiving the projective identifications from the infant or patient, appropriately metabolizing them, and returning them to the subject in a relatively detoxified form. In a psychotherapeutic situation, this implies a correct interpretation and appropriate management of the framework.

Second-Order Themes. See *Themes, Second-Order*.

Selected Fact, the. A term used by Bion (1962), borrowed from Poincaré, to describe a newly discovered formulation, finding, or fact that introduces order and new meaning into, and unites into a whole, previously disparate elements. It is the realization, then, that links together elements not previously seen to be connected.

Silent Hypothesis. A formulation derived from the various avenues of the intaking aspect of the listening process, developed, as a rule, around a specific adaptive context. Its development relies too on the abstracting-particularizing process, monitoring material around the therapeutic interaction, and utilizing the me–not-me interface, as well as all other means available to the therapist or analyst for generating dynamic, adaptive conceptions of the most pertinent unconscious meanings of the patient's material. In its most complete form, it will entail the identification of the most active unconscious fantasies, memories, introjects, and perceptions within the patient, and will relate these to the present therapeutic interaction, to important genetic experiences for the patient, and to his psychopathology. While these hypotheses may be developed at any point in a session, they are especially common in the opening segments of each hour, and are maintained by the therapist without intervening. In principle, they should be subjected to *silent validation* before the therapist or analyst intervenes, doing so most often at a point when there is a relevant bridge between the silent hypothesis itself and the communications from the patient.

Silent Question. An issue that arises within the mind of the therapist as he listens to the patient, leading him to raise it subjectively while not directing it to the patient. When pertinent, such queries will, as a rule, be answered in some derivative form by the patient's ongoing associations. In principle, silent questions are to be preferred to direct queries of the patient, which tend to serve a variety of defensive and countertransference needs within the therapist or analyst, and to impair the patient's use of indirect, derivative communication.

Silent Validation. An aspect of the evaluation of the material from the patient that follows the development of a silent hypothesis. When subsequent material further coalesces with the initial hypothesis, and supports it through the communication of Type Two derivatives, the silent hypothesis is seen as confirmed. See also *Validation.*

Themes, First-Order. The general contents and specific subject matter that can be derived from an examination of the manifest content of the patient's material.

Themes, Second-Order. Derivative contents developed through the use of the abstracting-particularizing process. First-order manifest themes are identified and general thematic trends are then formulated; inference derived on that basis are considered second-order themes. As a rule, such themes are developed in terms of the ongoing therapeutic relationship and interaction, and take on specific form and meaning when related to pertinent adaptive contexts within that relationship.

Therapeutic Context. Any communication from the patient that suggests a need for understanding and resolution. As an indication for interventions, the therapeutic context is an important organizer of the patient's material. This material is first organized around the prevailing adaptive contexts; it is then reorganized around the therapeutic context in order to reveal the unconscious meanings and functions of the adaptive context. Among the more common therapeutic contexts are resistances, symptoms, living out, and other indications of emotional disturbance within the patient, and on the part of the therapist, contertransference-based errors in intervening, both in the interpretive sphere and in his establishment and management of the framework.

Therapeutic Interaction. A term used to describe the conscious and unconscious communicative interplay between the patient and therapist or analyst.

Therapeutic Misalliance. An attempt to achieve symptom alleviation through some means other than insight and the related positive introjective identifications with the therapist. See *Misalliance,* an essentially synonymous term.

Therapeutic Relationship. A term that embraces all components, conscious and unconscious, pathological and nonpathological, of the interaction between patient and therapist. For the patient, the therapeutic relationship involves both transference and nontransference components, while for the therapist it involves countertransference and noncountertransference elements. The term is strongly preferred to "transference" when describing the patient's relationship with the therapist, and equally preferred to "countertransference" when describing the therapist's or analyst's relationship to the patient. See *Transference,*

Nontransference, Countertransference, and *Noncounter-transference.*

Transference. The pathological component of the patient's relationship to the therapist. Based on pathological unconscious fantasies, memories, and introjects, transference includes all distorted and inappropriate responses and perceptions of the therapist derived from these disruptive inner mental contents and the related mechanisms and defenses. These distortions may be based on displacements from past genetic figures, as well as on pathological interactional mechanisms. Unconscious transference fantasies and mechanisms are always communicated in some derivative form, while the manifest communication may allude to either the therapeutic relationship itself (disguised, however, in regard to the latent content) or to outside relationships. Transference responses are always maladaptive and can only be understood in terms of specific, indirect adaptive contexts (see Langs, 1976b).

Transversal Communication. Associations from the patient that bridge, and therefore simultaneously express, both fantasy and reality, transference and nontransference, unconscious perception and distortion, truth and falsehood, self and object. Such communications are, on one level, entirely valid, while on another level, essentially distorted.

Transversal Intervention. A particular type of communication from the therapist or analyst to the patient which is shaped in keeping with the presence of a transversal communication. In essence, such interventions, usually in the form of interpretations, although sometimes developed through the playback of derivatives related to an unidentified adaptive context, take into account the dual qualities of transversal communications, and are stated in a manner that is open to the contradictory elements contained in the patient's associations.

Trial Identification. An aspect of the listening process especially developed by Fliess (1942) as an important means of empathizing with and cognitively understanding the communications from the patient. It entails a temporary merger with, or incorporation of, the patient and his material in the presence of distinct self-object boundaries in most other respects. It is a temporary form of being and feeling with the patient, and the cognitive-affective yield from such experiences must then be processed toward insightful understanding and subjected to the validating process.

Type A Field, the, and Type A Communicative Mode, the. A bipersonal field and communicative style in which symbolism and illusion play a central role. Such a field is characterized by the development of a play space or transitional space within which the patient communicates analyzable derivatives of his unconscious fantasies, memories, introjects, and perceptions, ultimately in the form of Type Two derivatives. Such a field requires a secure framework, and a therapist or analyst who is capable of processing the material from the patient toward cognitive insights which are then imparted through valid interpretations. Such endeavors represent the therapist's capacity for symbolic communication. The Type A communicative mode is essentially symbolic, transitional, illusory, and geared toward insight.

Type B Field, the, and Type B Communicative Mode, the. A bipersonal field characterized by major efforts at projective identification and action-discharge. The field is not essentially designed for insight, but instead facilitates the riddance of accretions of disturbing internal stimuli. The Type B communicative mode is one in which efforts at projective identification and action-discharge prevail.

Type C Field, the, and Type C Communicative Mode, the. A field in which the essential links between patient and therapist are broken and ruptured, and in which verbalization and apparent efforts at communication are actually designed to destroy meaning, generate falsifications, and to create impenetrable barriers to underlying catastrophic truths. The Type C communicative mode is designed for falsification, the destruction of links between subject and object, and for the erection of barriers designed to seal off inner and interactional chaos.

Type C Narrator, the. A patient who utilizes the Type C communicative mode through the report of extensive dream material or the detailed description of events and experiences within his life or in regard to the therapeutic interaction. Such material is characterized by the absence of a meaningful adaptive context, the lack of analyzable derivatives, and the use of these communications essentially for the generation of nonmeaning and the breaking of relationship links. It is not uncommon for the Type C narrator to interact with a therapist or analyst who makes extensive use of psychoanalytic clichés, generating a therapeutic interaction falsely identified as viable analytic work, while its primary dynamic function falls within the Type C communicative mode.

Type One Derivatives. Readily available inferences derived from the manifest content of the patient's associations, without the use of an adaptive context. These inferences constitute one level of the latent content, arrived at in isolation and without reference to the dynamic state of the therapeutic interaction and to the adaptive-dynamic function of the material at hand.

Type Two Derivatives. Inferences from the manifest content of the patient's material that are arrived at through the abstracting-particularizing process when it is organized around a specific adaptive context. These disguised contents accrue specific dynamic-adaptive meaning when so organized, and are the main medium for the therapist's or analyst's interpretations, primarily in terms of the therapeutic interaction.

Unconscious Fantasy. The working over in displaced form of a particular adaptive context. The relevant contents are outside the patient's awareness and are expressed in derivative form in the manifest content of his associations. This is a type of daydreaming without direct awareness of the essential theme, and may be either pathological or nonpathological. The derivatives of unconscious fantasies are an essential medium of interpretive work and have important genetic antecedents. Among the most crucial unconscious fantasies are those related to the therapist, and when they are distorted they fall into the realm of transference, while those that are nondistorted belong to nontransference. These daydreams include representations from the id, ego, superego, self, and from every aspect of the patient's inner mental world, life, and psychic mechanisms.

Unconscious Interpretation. A communication from the patient to the therapist, expressed in disguised and derivative form, and unconsciously designed to help the therapist understand the underlying basis for a countertransference-based intervention. These interpretations can be recognized by taking the therapist's intervention as the adaptive context for the material from the patient that follows; hypothesizing the nature of the therapist's errors; and accepting the patient's material as reflecting an introjection of the error, and an effort to heal the disturbing aspects of that introject. Put in other terms, the patient's responses are viewed as a commentary on the therapist's intervention, and are found to contain unconscious efforts to assist the therapist in gaining insight in regard to the sources of his errors.

Unconscious Introject. A network of intrapsychic precipitants derived from interactions between the subject and object, in the past and present. They are derived from the process of introjective identification, and depend on the nature of the contents and mechanisms involved, as well as qualities within both subject and object. Introjects may be short-lived or relatively stable, pathological and non-pathological, incorporated into the self-image and self-representations or isolated from them, and may involve any of the structures of the mind, id, ego, and superego. In psychotherapy, an especially important form of introjection occurs in response to the therapist's projective identifications, either helpful or traumatic, nonpathological or pathological, which generate alterations in the inner mental world of the patient. Such a process is continuous with the therapeutic interaction and may, in addition, occur within the therapist as a result of projective identifications from the patient. See also *Introjects.*

Unconscious Memory. Derivative precipitates of past experiences—mixtures of actuality and distortion—expressed through indirect communication and inner representations of which the subject is unaware. Such reminiscences without awareness may be pathological or nonpathological, and the former are an important aspect of the genetic basis of the patient's psychopathology.

Unconscious Perception. A term used to describe evidence of valid perceptiveness of another person's (an object's) communications and cues of which the subject is unaware. These may be identified through a correct appraisal of the nature of an adaptive context, including an accurate understanding of the object's unconscious communications. While outside the subject's awareness, his derivative communications demonstrate an essentially veridical perception in terms of the prevailing underlying realities. When the adaptive context is known, unconscious perceptions are reflected in Type Two derivatives. They are the basis for nondistorted introjects.

Validated Hypothesis. A silent hypothesis that has been confirmed via Type Two derivatives, and especially an interpretation or management of the frame that has been communicated to the patient and which is affirmed through the development of Type Two derivatives and the appearance of a selected fact.

Validation, Indirect. See *Validation via Type Two Derivatives,* with which it is essentially synonymous.

Validation via Type Two Derivatives. A form of confirmation that is synonymous with the development of a selected fact, and with the modification of repressive barriers. This type of indirect, derivative validation is the essential proof of the truth of a psychoanalytic clinical formulation and intervention. Every clinical psychoanalytic hypothesis can be accepted as a general truth only if it has been subjected to this type of validation.

Validating Process, the.   A term used to describe conscious and unconscious efforts within either patient or therapist to affirm, support, and substantiate conscious or unconscious formulations and hypotheses. It is a crucial component of the listening process, receives its ultimate test in the patient's responses to the therapist's interpretations and management of the framework, and must take the form of confirmation via Type Two derivatives and the development of a selected fact (see Langs, 1976b, 1978a).

REFERENCES

Works marked with an asterisk are especially pertinent to the listening process.

*Arlow, J. (1969b). Fantasy, memory, and reality testing. *Psychoanalytic Quarterly* 38:28-51.
*Arlow, J. (1969a). Unconscious fantasy and disturbances of conscious experience. *Psychoanalytic Quarterly* 38:1-27.
Arlow, J. (1969b). Fantasy, memory, and reality testing. *Psychoanalytic Quarterly* 38:28 51.
Baranger, M., and Baranger, W. (1966). Insight in the analytic situation. In *Psychoanalysis in the Americas,* ed. R. Litman, pp. 56-72. New York: International Universities Press.
*Bellak, L. (1961). Free association: conceptual and clinical aspects. *International Journal of Psycho-Analysis* 42:9 20.
*Beres, D. (1962). The unconscious fantasy. *Psychoanalytic Quarterly* 31:309-328.
*Beres, D., and Arlow, J. (1974). Fantasy and identification in empathy. *Psychoanalytic Quarterly* 43:26-50.
Bibring, E. (1954). Psychoanalysis and the dynamic psychotherapies. *Journal of the American Psychoanalytic Association* 2:745-770.
Bion, W. (1959). *Experiences In Groups.* London: Tavistock

Bion, W. (1962). Learning from experience. In *Seven Servants*. New York: Jason Aronson, 1977.

Bion, W. (1967). *Second Thoughts: Selected Papers on Psycho-Analysis*. New York: Jason Aronson.

*Bion, W. (1970). Attention and interpretation. In *Seven Servants*. New York: Jason Aronson, 1977.

*Bion, W. (1977). *Seven Servants,* New York: Jason Aronson.

Brenner, C. (1976). *Psychoanalytic Technique and Psychic Conflict*. New York: International Universities Press.

Chertok, L. (1968). The discovery of the transference: toward an epistemological interpretation. *International Journal of Psycho-Analysis* 49:560–576.

*Deutsch, H. (1926). Occult processes during psychoanalysis. In *Psychoanalysis and the Occult,* ed. G. Devereux. New York: International Universities Press, 1953, 1970.

*Fenichel, O. (1941). *Problems of Psychoanalytic Technique. Trans. D. Brunswick. New York: Psychoanalytic Quarterly*.

*Ferenczi, S. (1919). The technique of psycho-analysis. In S. Ferenczi, *Further Considerations to the Technique of Psycho-Analysis,* pp. 177–188. London: Hogarth Press, 1950.

*Ferreiara, A. (1961). Empathy and the bridge function of the ego. *Journal of the American Psychoanalytic Association* 9:91–105.

Fiumara, G. (1977). The symbolic function, transference and psychic reality. *International Review of Psycho-Analysis* 4:171–180.

*Fliess, R. (1942). The metapsychology of the analyst. *Psychoanalytic Quarterly* 11:211–227.

Freud, S. (1900). The interpretation of dreams. *Standard Edition* 4 and 5.

Freud, S. (1905). Fragment of an analysis of a case of hysteria. *Standard Edition* 7:3–122.

Freud, S. (1908). Hysterical fantasies and their relation to bisexuality. *Standard Edition* 9:155–166.

Freud, S. (1912a). The dynamics of transference. *Standard Edition* 12:97–108.

Freud, S. (1912b). Recommendations to physicians practicing psychoanalysis. *Standard Edition* 12:111–120.

Freud, S. (1912c). Types of onset of neurosis. *Standard Edition* 12:227–238.

*Freud, S. (1913). On beginning the treatment (further recommendations on the technique of psycho-analysis, I). *Standard Edition* 12:121–144.

Freud, S. (1914). Remembering, repeating, and working through (further recommendations on the technique of psycho-analysis, II). *Standard Edition* 12:145–156.

Freud, S. (1915a). Observations on transference-love (further recommendations on the technique of psycho-analysis, III). *Standard Edition* 12:157–171.

Freud, S. (1915b). The unconscious. *Standard Edition* 14:159–216.

Freud, S. (1918). From the history of an infantile neurosis. *Standard Edition* 17:3–122.

Freud, S. (1919). Lines of advance in psychoanalytic therapy. *Standard Edition* 17: 159–168.

Freud, S. (1920). Beyond the pleasure principle. *Standard Edition* 18:3–64.

Freud, S. (1925). An autobiographical study. *Standard Edition* 20:3–76.

Freud, S. (1937). Analysis terminable and interminable. *Standard Edition* 23:209–253.

Gill, M. (1963). Topography and systems in psychoanalytic theory. *Psychological Issues,* Vol. III, No. 2, Monograph 10. New York: International Universities Press.

Greenacre, P. (1954). The role of transference.*Journal of the American Psychoanalytic Association* 2:671 684.

Greenacre, P. (1957). The childhood of the artist. *Psychoanalytic Study of the Child* 12:47 72.

Greenacre, P. (1959). Certain technical problems in the transference relationship. *Journal of the American Psychoanalytic Association* 7:484–502.

*Greenson, R. (1960). Empathy and its vicissitudes. *International Journal of Psychoanalysis* 41:418–424.

Greenson, R. (1965). The working alliance and the transference neurosis. *Psychoanalytic Quarterly* 34:155–181.

Greenson, R. (1966). That "impossible" profession. *Journal of the American Psychoanalytic Association* 14:9–27.

Greenson, R. (1967). *The Technique and Practice of Psychoanalysis* Vol. I. New York: International Universities Press.

Greenson, R. (1969). The origin and fate of new ideas in psychoanalysis. *International Journal of Psycho-Analysis* 50:503–515.

Grinberg, L. (1962). On a specific aspect of counter-transference due to the patient's projective identification. *International Journal of Psycho-Analysis* 43:436–440.

Haley, J. (1963). *Strategies of Psychotherapy.* New York:Grune and Stratton.

Horowitz, M. (1976). *Stress Response Syndromes*. New York:Jason Aronson.

Isakower, O. (1963) Minutes of faculty meeting, New York Psychoanalytic Institute, Nov. 20, 1963.

*Jacobs, T. (1973). Posture, gesture, and movement in the analyst: cues to interpretation and countertransference. *Journal of the American Psychoanalytic Association* 21:77–92.

Kanzer, M. (1952). The transference neurosis of the Rat Man. *Psychoanalytic Quarterly* 21:181–189.

*Kanzer, M. (1958). Image formation during free association. *Psychoanalytic Quarterly* 27:465–484.

*Kanzer, M. (1961). Verbal and nonverbal aspects of free association. *Psychoanalytic Quarterly* 30:327–350.

*Kanzer, M. (1972). Superego aspects of free association and the fundamental rule. *Journal of the American Psychoanalytic Association* 20:246–266.

Kanzer, M. (1975) The therapeutic and working alliances: an assessment. *International Journal of Psychoanalytic Psychotherapy* 40:48–68.

Kernberg, O. (1975). *Borderline Conditions and Pathological Narcissism* New York: Jason Aronson.

*Khan, M. (1973). The role of illusion in the analytic space and process. *The Annual of Psychoanalysis* 1:231–246.

*Kohut, H. (1959). Introspection, empathy and psychoanalysis. *Journal of the American Psychoanalytic Association* 7:459–483.

Kohut, H. (1971). *The Analysis of the Self*. New York: International Universities Press.

Kohut, H. (1977). *The Restoration of the Self*. New York: International Universities Press.

Langs, R. (1971). Day residues, recall residues, and dreams: reality and the psyche. *Journal of the American Psychoanalytic Association* 19:499–523.

*Langs, R. (1972). A psychoanalytic study of material from patients in psychotherapy. *International Journal of Psychoanalytic Psychotherapy* 1(No. 1):4–45.

*Langs, R. (1973a). *The Technique of Psychoanalytic Psychotherapy*, Vol. I. New York: Jason Aronson.

Langs, R. (1973b). The patient's view of the therapist: reality or fantasy? *International Journal of Psychoanalytic Psychotherapy* 2:411–431.

Langs, R. (1974). *The Technique of Psychoanalytic Psychotherapy*. Vol. II. New York: Jason Aronson.

Langs, R. (1975a). The patient's unconscious perception of the therapist's errors. In *Tactics and Techniques in Psychoanalytic Therapy, Vol. II: Countertransference,* ed. P. Giovacchini, pp. 239-250. New York: Jason Aronson.

Langs, R. (1975b). The therapeutic relationship and deviations in technique. *International Journal of Psychoanalytic Psychotherapy* 4:106-141.

Langs, R. (1975c). Therapeutic misalliances. *International Journal of Psychoanalytic Psychotherapy* 4:77-105.

*Langs, R. (1976a). *The Bipersonal Field.* New York: Jason Aronson.

*Langs, R. (1976b). *The Therapeutic Interaction.* 2 vols. New York: Jason Aronson.

*Langs, R. (1976c). On becoming a psychiatrist. *International Journal of Psychoanalytic Psychotherapy* 5:255-280.

*Langs, R. (1978a). Validation and the framework of the therapeutic situation. *Contemporary Psychoanalysis* 14:98-124.

*Langs, R. (1978b). Some communicative properties of the bipersonal field. *International Journal of Psychoanalytic Psychotherapy,* in press.

Langs, R. (1978c). Responses to creativity in psychoanalysts. *International Journal of Psychoanalytic Psychotherapy,* in press.

Langs, R. (In press a). The misalliance dimension in Freud's case histories, II: The Rat Man. In *Freud and His Patients,* ed. M. Kanzer and J. Glenn. New York: Jason Aronson.

Langs, R. (In press b). The misalliance dimension in Freud's case histories, III: The Wolf Man. In *Freud and His Patients,* ed. M. Kanzer and J. Glenn. New York: Jason Aronson.

Langs, R.; Klauber, J.; Milner, M.; Sandler, J.; and Segal, H. (In press). *Psychoanalytic Dialogues, IV: British Views on Psychoanalytic Technique.* New York: Jason Aronson.

Little, M. (1951). Countertransference and the patient's response to it. *International Journal of Psycho-Analysis* 32:32-40.

Malin, A., Grotstein, J. (1966). Projective identification in the therapeutic process. *International Journal of Psycho-Analysis* 33:181-185.

*McLaughlin, J. (1975). The sleepy analyst: some observations on states of consciousness and the analyst at work. *Journal of the American Psychoanalytic Association* 23:363-382.

Milner, M. (1952). Aspects of symbolism and comprehension of the not-self. *International Journal of Psycho-Analysis* 33:181-185.

*Olinick, S. (1969). On empathy, and regression in the service of the other. *British Journal of Medical Psychology* 42:41-49.

Olinick, S.; Poland, W.; Grigg, K.; and Granatir, W. (1973). The psychoanalytic work ego: process and interpretation. *International Journal of Psycho-Analysis* 54:143-151.

Peterfreund, E. (1975). How does the analyst listen? On models and strategies in the psychoanalytic process.*Psychoanalysis and*

*Racker, H. (1957). The meaning and uses of countertransference. *Psychoanalytic Quarterly* 26:303-357
26:303 357.

*de Racker, G. (1961). On the formulation of the interpretation. *International Journal of Psycho-Analysis* 42:49-54.

*Reich, A. (1966). Empathy and countertransference. In A. Reich, *Psychoanalytic Contributions,* pp. 344-360. New York: International Universities Press, 1973.

*Reik, T. (1948). *Listening with the Third Ear.* New York: Farrar, Straus.

*Rosner, S. (1973). On the nature of free association. *Journal of the American Psychoanalytic Association* 21: 558-575.

*Sandler, J. (1976). Countertransference and role-responsibleness. *International Review of Psycho-Analysis* 3:43-47.

*Schafer, R. (1959). Generative empathy in the treatment situation. *Psychoanalytic Quarterly* 28: 342-373.

Searles, H. (1955). The informational value of the supervisor's emotional experiences. *Psychiatry* 18:135-146.

Searles, H. (1959). The effort to drive the other person crazy—an element in the aetiology and psychotherapy of schizophrenia. *British Journal of Medical Psychology* 32:1-18.

Searles, H. (1965). *Collected Papers on Schizophrenia and Related Subjects.* New York: International Universities Press.

Searles, H. (1970). Autism and the phase of transition to therapeutic symbiosis. *Contemporary Psychoanalysis* 7:1-20.

Searles, H. (1971). Pathological symbiosis and autism. In *In the Name of Life,* ed. B. Landis and E. Tauber, pp. 69-83. New York: Holt, Rinehart, and Winston.

Searles, H. (1973). Concerning therapeutic symbiosis. *The Annual of Psychoanalysis* 1:247-262.

Searles, H. (1975). The patient as therapist to his analyst. In *Tactics and Techniques in Psychoanalytic Therapy, Vol. II: Counter-transference,* ed. P. Giovacchini, pp. 95-151. New York: Jason Aronson.

Segal, H. (1967). Melanie Klein's technique. *Psychoanalytic Forum* 2:197-211.

Segal, H. (1977). Countertransference. *International Journal of Psychoanalytic Psychotherapy* 6:31-38.

*Shapiro, T. (1974). The development and distortions of empathy. *Psychoanalytic Quarterly* 43:4-25.

Slap, J. (1977). The eroding concept of intrapsychic conflict. *International Journal of Psychoanalytic Psychotherapy* 6:469-478.

*Spiegel, L. (1975). The functions of free association in psychoanalysis: their relation to technique and theory. *International Review of Psycho-Analysis* 2:379-388.

Szasz, T. (1963). The concepts of transference. *International Journal of Psycho-Analysis* 44:432-443.

Tarachow, S. (1962). Interpretation and reality in psycho-therapy. *International Journal of Psycho-Analysis* 43:377-387.

Viderman, S. (1974). Interpretation in the analytic space. *International Review of Psycho-Analysis* 1:467-480.

Wangh, M. (1962). The "evocation of a proxy": a psychological maneuver, its use as a defense, its purpose and genesis. *Psychoanalytic Study of the Child* 17:451-469.

Winnicott, D. (1935). The manic defense. In D. Winnicott, *Collected Papers: Through Paediatrics to Psycho-Analysis*, pp. 129-144. London: Tavistock, 1958.

Winnicott, D. (1951). Transitional objects and transitional phenomena. in *Collected Papers: Through Paediatrics to Psycho-Analysis*, pp. 229-242. London: Tavistock, 1958.

Winnicott, D. (1969). The use of an object. *International Journal of Psycho-Analysis* 50:711-716.

INDEX